# DR. AXELROD'S
# ATLAS
## OF
## FRESHWATER
## AQUARIUM FISHES
### SECOND EDITION

## BY
## DR. HERBERT R. AXELROD
## DR. WARREN E. BURGESS, NEAL PRONEK AND JERRY G. WALLS

Title page photo of *Pterophyllum scalare* by K. Paysan.

ISBN 0-86622-139-5

Distributed in the UNITED STATES by T.F.H. Publications, Inc., 211 West Sylvania Avenue, Neptune City, NJ 07753; in CANADA to the Pet Trade by H & L Pet Supplies Inc., 27 Kingston Crescent, Kitchener, Ontario N2B 2T6; Rolf C. Hagen Ltd., 3225 Sartelon Street, Montreal 382 Quebec; in CANADA to the Book Trade by Macmillan of Canada (A Division of Canada Publishing Corporation), 164 Commander Boulevard, Agincourt, Ontario M1S 3C7; in ENGLAND by T.F.H. Publications Limited, 4 Kier Park, Ascot, Berkshire SL5 7DS; in AUSTRALIA AND THE SOUTH PACIFIC by T.F.H. (Australia) Pty. Ltd., Box 149, Brookvale 2100 N.S.W., Australia; in NEW ZEALAND by Ross Haines & Son, Ltd., 18 Monmouth Street, Grey Lynn, Auckland 2 New Zealand; in SINGAPORE AND MALAYSIA by MPH Distributors (S) Pte., Ltd., 601 Sims Drive, #03/07/21, Singapore 1438; in the PHILIPPINES by Bio-Research, 5 Lippay Street, San Lorenzo Village, Makati Rizal; in SOUTH AFRICA by Multipet Pty. Ltd., 30 Turners Avenue, Durban 4001. Published by T.F.H. Publications Inc. Manufactured in the United States of America by T.F.H. Publications, Inc.

# Contents

# PREFACE TO THE SECOND EDITION

I was amazed that the huge first printing, the first edition, of this book sold out in a matter of 45 days. Big, expensive books just are not expected to behave this way, but these are golden problems!

Naturally, when I had finished the editorial work on the first edition, I immediately began searching for ways to improve it. This basically was a search for photographs of fishes that were better than those in the first edition or fishes that were not represented in the first edition. My preliminary search yielded about 600 new photos. These new plates have been marked with letters A,B,C,D, etc., since they fall between plates that have already been numbered. Many fish importers used the first edition and the plate numbers for identification purposes. To facilitate their computers, we did not want to change these plate numbers.

We hope to sell another 50,000 copies of this book quickly and increase the next edition by new plates of new fishes . . . but this second edition probably has every fish that the ordinary pet shop or hobbyist might ever come across.

Dr. Herbert R. Axelrod
*March 15, 1986*
*Neptune, N.J.*

# THE PURPOSE OF THIS BOOK

This book was created with the express purpose of making the identification of fishes easier for the scientist, pet dealer and hobbyist. It attempts to standardize, as much as possible, the common names applied to fishes in the English-speaking world, especially as this applies to those fishes that are so similar in size, shape and form that they cannot even be distinguished readily by an ichthyologist. These difficult fishes include the popular tank-raised varieties of swordtails, platies, mollies, guppies, angelfish and discus. As aquarists develop more skills in fish breeding, especially with the ever-increasing use of hormone injections to stimulate ripe fishes to spawn, more and more color varieties will be developed . . . and more and more books of fish standards will be needed, books that will clearly identify a fish by its color photograph.

For many years the science of ichthyology has recognized the value of a color illustration of a fish, and often a scientific name is accepted if its description is enhanced with a suitable color illustration even though there may be fatal flaws in the technical description of the fish.

But there is a great distinction between color illustrations of a fish whose body was preserved for further study after the photograph or drawing was made and one that merely happened to be photographed in someone's aquarium . . . and that's where this book fits in so well.

Throughout more than 35 years of intensive fish collecting in all the major aquarium fish areas of the world, Dr. Axelrod has specialized in collecting aquarium fishes and photographing them on the spot just where they were found. He then preserved their bodies and had them scientifically verified as to nomenclature. Thus, while many of his photographs lack the artistic beauty of an aquarium scene, they are authentic color photos of a fish whose identity is as certain as can be determined by a trained fish scientist or ichthyologist. This is especially helpful, for example, with discus for without his photographs we wouldn't know what the original species and subspecies looked like. He is the only one who has collected and photographed every species and subspecies of that popular group of fishes, the discus, known scientificially as the genus *Symphysodon*. Hundreds of his photographs have been used to describe the types of new species and many are the first and only color photographs of those fishes . . . even today!

Thus this book is unique and authentic . . . and there can never be another book like it because there can never be another color photograph made of a type in living colors since, by definition, a type is THE SINGLE FISH selected to represent the species. Of course you may photograph a fish and then identify it as being the same species as the type, but many times the characters upon which the identification is made change and that second picture loses its value while the original photograph of the type stands forever!

## HOW FISHES ARE IDENTIFIED

Fishes are not identified by photographs alone, nor can anyone make an absolutely positive identification of a fish photograph without the fish's body at hand.

There are about 25,000-40,000 different kinds of fishes in the world. This includes species and subspecies, but not color varieties developed by man. There are as many species of fishes as there are combined species of the other vertebrates (amphibians, reptiles, birds and mammals) in the world. That's a lot of fishes, and unless a strict system of identification had been set up there would be lots of confusion. Even with the system there is lots of confusion, and as you go through this book you will often find remarks to the effect that much more study is needed in a certain group to make identifications certain. This can be clearly understood when you consider, for example, the author's (W.E.B.) famous work on angelfishes of the genus *Pterophyllum*. Over the years there were many species of angelfish scientifically described, such as *Zeus scalaris, Pterophyllum eimekei, P. altum, Plataxoides dumerilii,* and *Plataxoides leopoldi.* These fishes were found widely scattered from Guyana to the Rio Negro and the Rio Madeira, distances of thousands of kilometers. As additional collections of angelfishes were made between the points of original discovery, the differences between "species" became smaller and smaller as these newly discovered angelfishes had to be accommodated among the previously discovered forms. This led to the grouping of all these names into just two species. This is only one tiny example of Dr. Burgess's experiences in naming fishes, but it serves to show the complexities of fish identification.

In 1758 the famous botanist Linnaeus of Sweden proposed the binomial system for naming living things. The process of "How Fishes Get Their Scientific Names" was best described by the world's greatest living ichthyologist, Dr. Leonard P. Schultz, in *The Handbook of Tropical Aquarium Fishes* (Axelrod and Schultz). With their permission, the following section is reprinted from that book.

"This binomial system provides a generic and a specific name, usually based on Latin or Greek words, such as *Gambusia affinis* (Baird and Girard). The scientific names are followed by the name of the author who first described the species and named it according to the International Rules of Zoological Nomenclature. When the author's name is enclosed in parentheses, that means that the species was described in another genus and that recent authors have transferred it to the present genus, in this case *Gambusia,* since Baird and Girard in their original description named this species *Heterandria affinis.* It is not necessary for scientific names of animals to have a specific or significant meaning, although many do.

"Both generic and specific names may be chosen in honor of the collector, a friend, or a colleague, as well as for a geographical locality, a ship, or almost anything. Species names must be latinized, however; and when named after a man they must end in *i,* for example, *hollandi,* or after a woman, in *ae,* for example, *aliceae.* Although the International Commission of Zoological Nomenclature has established many pages of rules governing the naming of animals, the basic theory of the system is that of priority—the oldest name established for genus, species, or subspecies is the valid one, going back to the year 1758, the tenth edition of *Systema naturae* by Linnaeus.

"Whenever an ichthyologist thinks he has a new species, he must search the ichthyological literature all the way back to 1758 to be certain that it is not already named. This is a difficult and time-consuming process, requiring the facilities of extensive libraries such as the Library of Congress at Washington and those in the largest universities which have specialized in ichthyological literature. Bibliographical indices are used, such as the three-volume work by Bashford Dean, *Bibliography of Fishes* (1916-1923), along with the Pisces section of the *Zoological Record,* to find papers on the group being studied. The *Zoological Record,* published in London since 1864, classifies natural history literature on an annual basis. Although these tools are useful, the experience of the ichthyologist is important, too. The more expert ichthyologists do not name new species of fish on hunches; instead they review all other species in the genus to which they assign their new one, and if they are able to construct a key that separates the new one from all other species in that genus, they then feel that much reliance may be placed on their claim that the species is actually new.

"The expert ichthyologists of today are continually confronted with the inadequate descriptions and figures of fishes printed during the past 200 years. So many authors have named fishes that were already named that on the average each species has one or two synonyms, and some may have as many as a dozen or more. This troublesome affliction of systematic ichthyology could be greatly improved if novices in the field submitted their new species to ichthyologists in the larger museums of the world for expert opinion. These museums, with a million or more specimens distributed among 10,000 to 20,000 species, are in a fine position to make careful comparisons.

"The International Rules of Zoological Nomenclature require that whenever a new species is described and named a specimen must be designated as the *holotype*, the specimen on which the species is based. Other specimens used in describing the new species become *paratypes*, and data from them are included in the description. It is the custom for ichthyologists to give the type specimens to museums for permanent preservation, such as the United States National Museum in Washington, which makes its research collections available for study to all qualified students and professional ichthyologists.

"To illustrate how complicated the process of naming a species may become before the matter is finally settled, let us refer to one of our commonest aquarium fishes, the molly or sailfin.

"The first author to publish a description and give a scientific name for the molly was the early American ichthyologist, LeSueur. In the year 1821, in volume 2, page 3, of the *Journal of the Academy of Natural Sciences of Philadelphia*, there appeared as a boldface center head the name *Mollinesia latipinna*. This generic and specific name as first published would be the valid scientific name under ordinary circumstances, but further study of the original article indicates that the generic name was intended to honor Monsieur Mollien. However, there was a great amount of carelessness in those days, and on the plate in this first printing the name is spelled *Molienisia Latipinua*, whereas in the reference to the plate on page 409 it is spelled *Molinesia Latipinna*. Thus the molly had its generic name spelled three ways and the specific name two ways when first published. For more than 100 years the generic name of the molly has been spelled in at least three ways. To settle this and similar controversies in nomenclature, rules were established more than half a century ago to pass on such matters. The commission that considers nomenclatorial problems acts as a sort of international "supreme court" and the rule of priority, or the rule of long established use, is followed.

"Two recent papers have given the history of the name. Fowler in 1945 and Bailey and Miller in 1950 chose to emend the name to *Mollienesia*, which follows closely the name of the man LeSueur intended to honor, and they use the ending *-esia*, which appears twice in the article. Thus the best conclusion that can be reached, according to usage and rules, is that the common molly should carry the name *Mollienesia latipinna* LeSueur.

"This is only one of many complicated cases that occur in the naming of fishes; in general, about 95 per cent are named with sufficient care and accuracy so that no controversies are involved.

"By 1900 the number of fish species became so numerous that the trend was to revise or review fishes on the basis of genera or of families. During the past 25 years statistical methods of analysis have been applied to what were previously considered species. Carefully made counts and measurements now reveal that many of these early species can actually be differentiated into subspecies or into two or more species.

"To make these statistical studies large series of specimens are needed from numerous localities. This trend has caused a change in the policies of research museums. Whereas in the early days a species was represented by a single specimen, now that species should be represented by 25 or more specimens per lot, and each lot from as many localities within the range of the species as is practical. Such large collections in museums open the way for the solution of innumerable problems in ichthyology and in racial investigations in the field of fisheries biology. These methods apply to fresh-water fishes as well as marine. Many fresh-water species differ from stream system to stream system, whereas in marine fishes the differences appear from island group to island group, or according to latitude.

"At times the layman naturalist will argue about 'lumpers' and 'splitters'. Lumpers have a tendency to throw doubtful species together as a single form, whereas splitters differentiate a species into its component populations and give these populations a subspecific scientific name.

"Isaac Ginsburg has proposed a principle to guide him as to when it is mathematically sound to give a population a scientific name and when it is not. This 'law' or yardstick proposes that two subspecies are distinct biological units in nature when the character showing the greatest divergence overlaps approximately 10 to 20 percent. A full species may overlap in one character by not more than 10 per cent. The percentage is calculated on the total number of observations for both supposed species or subspecies combined.

"In the recognition of species and subspecies there remain certain characters that cannot be measured or counted, for example, the basic color pattern. This may be defined as those colors which occur regularly on specific areas of the fish. The basic color pattern may not include quality, tone, or shade of colors.

"Experience has demonstrated that in both fresh-water and marine fishes the importance of basic color patterns cannot be overemphasized. Once the variability has been determined for a series of specimens, it is of the utmost importance as a factor in the recognition of species and subspecies. This has been demonstrated in studies of the reef-inhabiting species of the Phoenix, Marshall, and Philippine Islands by the constancy with which basic color patterns of browns, blackish shades, and light areas, in the form of spots, bars, and streaks, occur in preserved specimens of certain species and subspecies. These patterns were observed first in live specimens and were recorded by means of color photographs and colored drawings. Their persistence after a few years of alcoholic preservation was later confirmed by comparison of the photographs and drawings with the preserved specimens. Thus as a result of careful observation the older idea of lumping species or combining species into one catch-all species was not the true picture in nature. Authors who disregard such details as the basic color pattern are guilty of lumping species and subspecies incorrectly.

"The recognition of genera has never been placed on so definite a mathematical basis. Therefore, the splitters and lumpers have had a freer hand and sometimes the splitters actually have set up new generic and subgeneric units for nearly every species in a particular group. This has been especially noticeable in the poeciliid fishes.

"The concept of a genus should be to group closely related species together so that these species represent a small natural phyletic line. These phyletic lines are not all of the same value or definiteness in any family of fishes; they represent to a considerable extent the personal opinion of the ichthyological researcher.

"The characters by which genera are recognized are variable. In general, dentition and small constant differences in the bones, their shape and relationship to each other, are excellent guides. Fleshy characters such as barbels or their absence, development of glandular scales, specializations of the digestive tract, presence or absence of luminous glands or scales, specialized development of lips, fins, arrangement and size of scales are most useful in recognition of fish genera.

"No particular character or set of characters can be named in advance to cover the recognition of genera because fishes are so variable in structure from one order to another and from one family to another that the ichthyologist must test the characters he uses for each family. Those that reveal constancy for large series of specimens among few to several species may be used as generic characters."

# CONTINENTAL DRIFT AND FISH DISTRIBUTION

The last few decades have seen a gradual accumulation of data to prove the once-maligned theory of continental drift. The basic idea of this theory is that the existing continents have not always been where they are now but have gradually drifted to their present positions over millions of years, the cooler and more solid rocks of the Earth's crust floating on the semi-liquid magma under the crust.

During the period when life was becoming well established on earth and even as late as the first terrestrial experiments by invertebrates and vertebrates, all the major land masses were connected to form a single ancient continent, Pangaea. Sometime about 170 to 200 million years ago, during the Jurassic period, Pangaea began to break up because of internal stresses and the fragments slowly drifted apart.

For convenience of terminology and also because of the way certain groups of plants and animals are distributed in the fossil record, two "supercontinents" are said to have come into being, the northern Laurasia (comprising the present North America, Europe, Asia, and Greenland) and the southern Gondwana (made up of Africa, South America, Antarctica, Australia, Madagascar, and India). Antarctica until recently was tropical and had a large fauna and flora. Over the last 100 million years or so the continents have continued to separate and collide seemingly at random until they reached their present positions. India broke totally away from Gondwana and drifted north to collide with Asia, forming the Himalayas.

With them the continents carried their floras and faunas, allowing the evolution of some groups of plants and animals to be traced along with the movements of the continents. For instance, certain early terrestrial amphibians are known only as fossils from Antarctica, Australia, South Africa, and India, a distribution well in keeping with the former close connection of these now widely separated areas. Similarly, a small freshwater fossil reptile is known from the same sediments of eastern South America and western Africa. These animals were not capable of crossing the oceans from one present continent to the other, but were carried as the continents separated.

There is increasing evidence that the history of many groups of living fishes is a long one, as most of the living major families of freshwater fishes were recognizable by at least the Cretaceous period, about 140 to 65 million years ago. Thus at least some freshwater fishes have had their current distributions influenced or controlled by the drifting continents. The varous tetras, for instance, are almost strictly African and South American in distribution, the expansion into Central America being of geologically recent origin. A look at a map will show that Africa and South America were once connected and would have certainly shared the same fauna to some extent. In fact, it is not impossible that the predecessors of some of the existing rivers of Brazil once flowed together with the ancestral Congo of Africa. The osteoglossid fishes are also found in South America and Africa (plus a genus in southern Asia and Australia), and of course the cichlids are typically South American—African fishes. It would seem likely that these groups of fishes originated at least in part in Pangaea in the area that was to later become Gondwana and then even later South America and Africa.

Other fish families that may trace their distribution to continental drift are the Cyprinidae and Galaxiidae. The typical cyprinids are northern in distribution, with fossils in North America and Eurasia. The great abundance of cyprinids in tropical Asia is perhaps a recent event, with cold-oriented fishes moving into an area with little competition and speciating rapidly and abundantly. The odd little galaxiids of Australia are not alone in the world—they also occur in New Zealand (readily explainable) and southwestern South America (not so readily understandable).

By the way, the continents are still moving. Recent satellite measurements plus other data indicate that North America and Europe are moving 2 cm farther apart each year, a seemingly insignificant figure that mounts up over millions of years.

# THE ANCIENT CONTINENTS

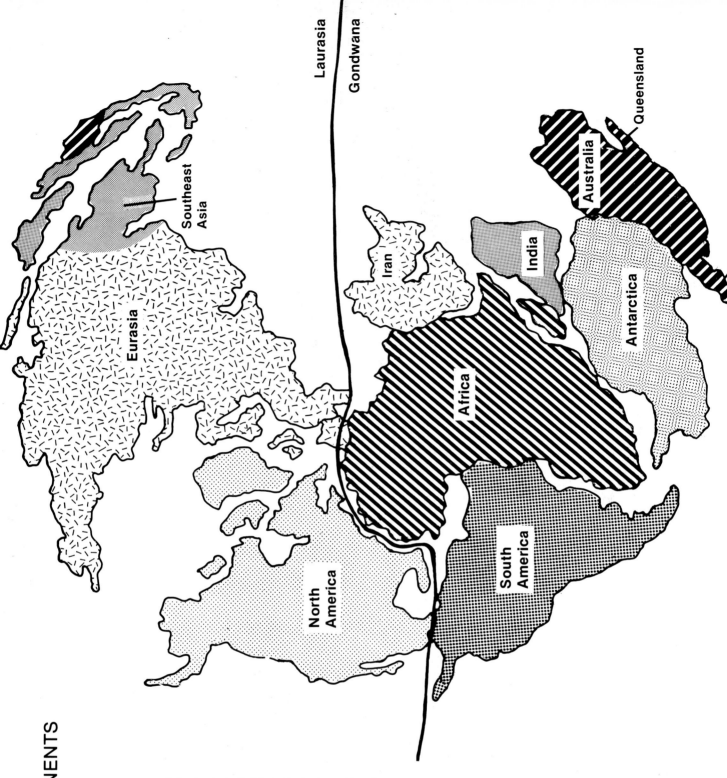

Movement of the continents. Shown at right is Pangaea after its breakup into the predecessors of the modern continents. The area above the line constitutes Laurasia, that below the line Gondwana. The shading corresponds to the current continental limits as used in this book. Notice especially that India, originally part of the southern continent, is now part of a northern continents, Southeast Asia of Eurasia. This helps explain the unusual fauna of modern India, which retains many relicts of the old southern fauna. North and South America have undergone a complicated history of connection and disconnection across the Central American area, resulting in faunas that are remarkably different for such closely linked areas. When using these maps, remember that the map of the modern continents is on a flat plane projection to allow all the areas to be seen in one surface, while the map of the ancient continents is on more of a polar projection, so distances are distorted. Smaller islands are shown on neither map unless important zoogeographically.

THE MODERN CONTINENTS

North
America

South
America

Eurasia

India

Southeast
Asia

Africa

Australia

Antarctica

# ABOUT THE AUTHORS

Dr. Herbert R. Axelrod (HRA), Dr. Warren E. Burgess (WEB), Neal Pronek and Jerry G. Walls are all full-time employees of T.F.H. Publications in Neptune, New Jersey. ("T.F.H.," by the way, refers to the initials of *Tropical Fish Hobbyist* magazine, a monthly publication.) They are in daily contact with the aquarium world, the ichthyological world, and the world of publishing. This unique combination has used its talents to produce this book.

T.F.H. owns and operates its own engraving, typesetting, art, printing, and binding facilities in what is considered to be the most modern publishing plant in the book-publishing world. Very few book publishers do their own manufacturing. T.F.H. found it necessary to produce its own books so the ichthyologists working on the premises could "OK" proofs on press, etc. T.F.H. is also the world's largest publisher of fish books, and its magazine (*Tropical Fish Hobbyist*) has the widest paid circulation of any aquarium magazine in any language. Thus this book is one produced by people who are specialists in producing books like this. . .and we are very proud of this book, which took more effort than any book we've published in our 35 years of existence under the continuous management of our founders.

# HOW TO USE THIS BOOK

There are many ways to lay out a book of fishes: alphabetically; anatomically (systematically by families, genera and species); haphazardly (say, for example, classifying fishes by their color or color pattern); or zoogeographically. Some books are even organized according to a fish's spawning habits such as egglayers, livebearers, etc. But each of these methods has its shortcoming.

The problem with an ALPHABETICAL listing of fishes is that name changes are difficult to accommodate in future editions, and every book on fishes is obsolete by the time the printing, editing and binding processes are completed.

The problem with a rigid evolutionary ANATOMICAL listing is that most people in the fish hobby and business don't know to which group most of the fishes belong and thus would be unable to easily locate a fish they have before them without thumbing through the whole book.

The problem with a HAPHAZARD color cataloging of fishes is that colors change and color varieties (just think about guppies, platies and swordtails!) would of necessity be listed in different sections of the book. Sexual dimorphism also would split species into different sections. Turmoil!

The problem with a ZOOGEOGRAPHICAL listing is that you would have to know the continent on which a certain fish is found. For some reason, aquarium fishes from within a certain zoogeographical area have a "familiar" look, and many hobbyists and dealers can fairly accurately identify the continent from which a fish comes just by looking at it, even if they have never seen it before. The main advantage of this system is that dealers who export fishes can use this as the basis of a price list and dealers who import fishes can more easily identify the fishes they get from a certain area even if the exporter doesn't clearly identify them. Many rarities slip in unidentified and mixed in with more usual, familiar species. These often grow up in a dealer's tank and must be identified. The final value of this kind of book design is that new species or new identifications can readily be dealt with without the very expensive alternative of moving color plates from one part of the book to the other.

This book is laid out zoogeographically. It took many, many years to produce this book since the accumulation of identified and verified photographs took so long. Simply buying photographs without having the fish's body available for verification was the worst case; having photographs of the holotype was the best case. This book is rich in that regard, bringing together many of the original illustrations used in the descriptions of many of these new species.

# Photography

In addition to the photos taken by Dr. Axelrod, this book also contains many photographs by other photographers of fishes and aquarium subjects. The book is indebted to all of the people listed here . . . and to anyone else whose name might have been inadvertently omitted from the list.

Hiromitsu Akiyama
Dr. Gerald R. Allen
K. Attwood
Glen Axelrod
Dr. Hiroshi Azuma
Heiko Bleher
Pierre Brichard
Dr. Martin Brittan
Dr. Warren E. Burgess
Dr. Brooks Burr
Vojtech Elek
Dr. Augustin Fernandez-Yepez
Walter Foersch
Dr. Stanislav Frank
H. J. Franke
Dan Fromm
Dr. Jacques Gery
Dr. Robert J. Goldstein
Dr. Myron Gordon
Dr. Harry Grier
K. Jeno
Rodney Jonklaas
Burkhard Kahl
S. Kochetov
R. Lawrence
Ken Lucas, Steinhart Aquarium
Gerhard Marcuse
Dr. Richard L. Mayden
Hans Mayland
Manfred Meyer
Marine Planning (Aqua Life, Japan)

Midori Shobo (Fish Magazine, Japan)
New York Zoological Society
Leo G. Nico
Aaron Norman
Dr. Joanne Norton
Y. W. Ong
Dr. Lawrence M. Page
Klaus Paysan
Kurt Quitschau
Hans-Joachim Richter
Mervin F. Roberts
Erhard Roloff
Andre Roth
Jorgen Scheel
Gunter Schmida
Harald Schultz
Dr. Wolfgang Staeck
Rainier Stawikowski
Glenn Y. Takeshita
Donald C. Taphorn
Edward C. Taylor
Dr. D. Terver, Nancy Aquarium
Gerald J. M. Timmerman
Dr. Bruce J. Turner
Arend van den Nieuwenhuizen
Braz Walker
Wardley Products Co.
Franz Werner
Uwe Werner
Gene Wolfsheimer
Ruda Zukal

# North American Region

## *Ichthyomyzon bdellium* (Jordan) • Ohio Lamprey

RANGE: The U.S.A. in lakes, rivers, and streams of the Ohio River Valley.

HABITS: A parasitic fish that occurs in rivers and lakes. May be kept in an aquarium and fed normal fish foods, but should be isolated from other fishes.

WATER CONDITIONS: Lives in unheated aquarium waters that are from fresh to very slightly brackish.

SIZE: Small lampreys are interesting aquarium inhabitants, but this species grows to 37.5 cm.

FOOD REQUIREMENTS: Depending upon the size and age, this fish will usually take chunks of spinach and chopped beef heart. Smaller specimens eat algae.

## *Aphredoderus sayanus* (Gilliams) • Pirate Perch

RANGE: Atlantic coast of the U.S. from New York to Texas; Mississippi Basin to Michigan.

HABITS: Nocturnal predator. Will hunt for food at night and will eat any smaller fishes in the aquarium.

WATER CONDITIONS: Not critical.

SIZE: Attains a length of about 12.5 cm.

FOOD REQUIREMENTS: Usually spurns anything but live foods, with minnows its favorites.

## *Polyodon spathula* (Walbaum) • Paddlefish

RANGE: The Mississippi River drainage and its larger tributaries in the U.S.A.

HABITS: An interesting inhabitant of the large aquarium. It must have lots of room as it grows quickly, reaching about 100 kg. (The Chinese paddlefish, *Psephurus gladius,* is reputed to reach 20 feet (610 cm) in length!)

WATER CONDITIONS: Fresh, clean, filtered water. pH as close to 7.0 as possible. Not fussy once it acclimates.

SIZE: A large fish perhaps reaching 225 pounds (100 kg).

FOOD REQUIREMENTS: It swims constantly with its mouth open, eating tiny cladoceran and copepod crustaceans. Swarms of daphnia living in its tank would probably suffice.

## *Lepisosteus oculatus* (Winchell) • Spotted Gar

RANGE: From the Great Lakes of North America south to the Gulf of Mexico.

HABITS: A slow-moving fish often staying stationary in the water until a meal swims by, at which time it moves with great speed. Not meant for the home aquarium, though successful in large tanks. Beware: The eggs of this fish may be poisonous. The same is true of all gars.

WATER CONDITIONS: A freshwater fish that tolerates most aquarium conditions.

SIZE: Grows to about 2½ meters and more than 140 kg.

FOOD REQUIREMENTS: Thrives on small living fishes that it preys upon, but it can be acclimated to dead fish.

## *Scaphirhynchus platorynchus* (Rafinesque) • Shovelnose Sturgeon

RANGE: Mississippi Valley south to Texas in the U.S.A.

HABITS: These make very interesting aquarium inhabitants when they are small. They swim in top-to-bottom upside-down circles at times and are very active when live foods are placed into their tanks. Their eggs make caviar, and their flesh is a smoked delicacy.

WATER CONDITIONS: Unheated freshwater aquaria with heavy filtration and aeration.

SIZE: They get very large in nature, but the record for an aquarium specimen is growing a 20 cm fish to 50 cm.

FOOD REQUIREMENTS: Will take small worms and insect larvae from the bottom.

## *Acipenser transmontanus* Richardson • White Sturgeon

RANGE: Pacific shores of North America from the Aleutian Islands to Monterey, California.

HABITS: In nature this anadromous fish spends most of its time in the Pacific Ocean, returning to freshwater to spawn several times during its long life. Aquarium specimens thrive on chironomids.

WATER CONDITIONS: Large unheated aquarium with filtration. Not fussy about pH, salinity, hardness, or clarity.

SIZE: Probably the largest freshwater fish now available. Grows to 20 feet (610 cm) and well over 1,000 pounds.

FOOD REQUIREMENTS: Heavy, constant feeding of chironomids or any similar small insect larvae and worms. They gradually accept everything including dried food.

## *Lepisosteus spatula* Lacepede • Alligator Gar

RANGE: Southeastern United States in both freshwater and saline waters of varying densities, including the Gulf of Mexico.

HABITS: This is a predatory fish that rarely accepts anything but live foods in the form of smaller fishes. It is only suitable for very large public aquaria.

WATER CONDITIONS: Tolerates almost any kind of water from fresh to salt with temperatures between 10° and 23°C.

SIZE: A very large fish reaching 3 meters in length and 150 kg.

FOOD REQUIREMENTS: A heavy eater of smaller living fishes. It grows fast if properly fed, otherwise it quickly perishes.

## *Lepisosteus osseus* (Linnaeus) • Longnose Gar

RANGE: North America; Gulf states, Mississippi Basin northward to Great Lakes, eastern seaboard.

HABITS: Highly predatory and not to be trusted with fishes small enough to swallow; rather slow-moving most times, but capable of great bursts of speed.

WATER CONDITIONS: Not at all critical; often found surviving where other fishes have succumbed. Tolerates a wide temperature range.

SIZE: To 2 meter in nature, much less in aquaria; size can be reasonably controlled.

FOOD REQUIREMENTS: Live fishes preferred; acclimated fish can often be converted to strips of beef heart or other substitutes.

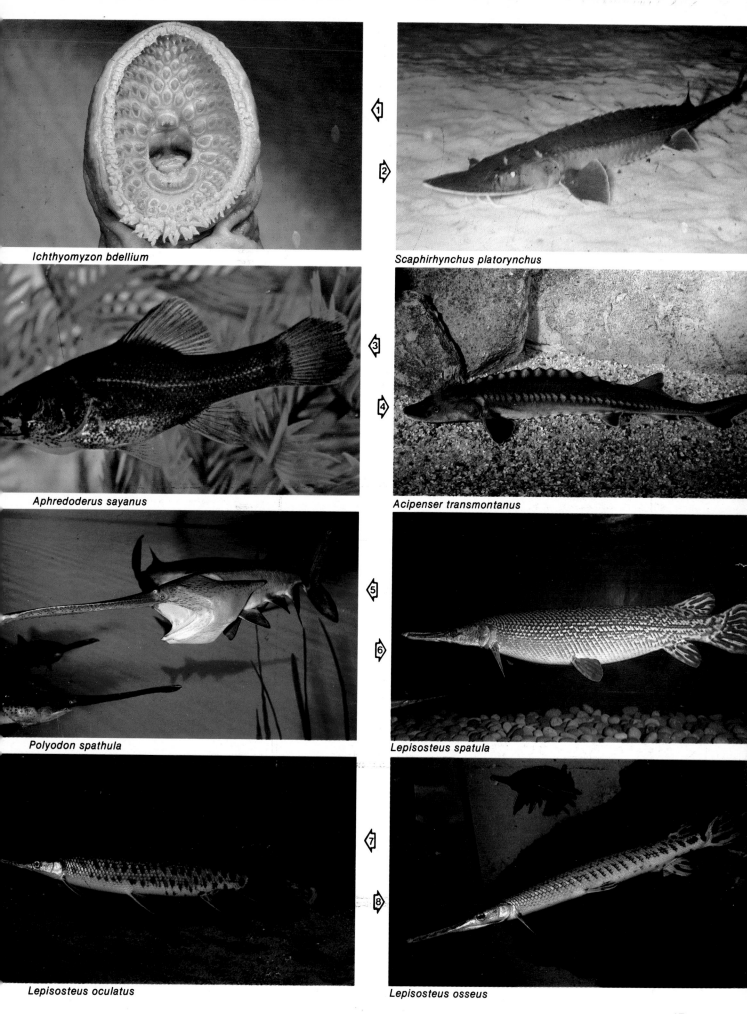

Ichthyomyzon bdellium

Scaphirhynchus platorynchus

Aphredoderus sayanus

Acipenser transmontanus

Polyodon spathula

Lepisosteus spatula

Lepisosteus oculatus

Lepisosteus osseus

1
2
3
4
5
6
7
8

*Lepisosteus platostomus*

*Lepisosteus oculatus*

*Salmo gairdneri* (top); *Salvelinus fontinalis* (bottom)

*Salmo trutta*

*Umbra limi*

*Umbra limi*

*Culaea inconstans*

*Gasterosteus aculeatus*

Plate #1A

Amia calva (adult)

Amia calva (juvenile)

Oncorhynchus kisutch

Megalops atlanticus

Salmo trutta

Salvelinus fontinalis

Salvelinus fontinalis

Salvelinus namaycush

*Plate #2*

19

## Esox americanus (Gmelin) • Redfin Pickerel

RANGE: Throughout eastern North America.
HABITS: Though a very streamlined fish, this predator prefers still waters in lakes or ponds, especially those heavily vegetated.
WATER CONDITIONS: Large aquarium necessary. Unheated, clean water. Thrives in unheated tanks but can tolerate temperatures in the 15-22°C. range.
SIZE: A small pickerel that hardly ever gets larger than 375 mm.
FOOD REQUIREMENTS: They prefer live fishes smaller than themselves, but they can be acclimated to chunks of fish, shrimp or beef.

## Esox lucius Linnaeus • Northern Pike

RANGE: Circumpolar distribution in the Northern Hemisphere. In the U.S.A., from Alaska to Missouri; also in the British Isles and most of Europe, through the USSR to Lake Baikal. Very widely distributed.
HABITS: Its wide distribution attests to its ability to acclimate to all types and temperatures of water including brackish (it is found in brackish waters in the Baltic Sea). Spawns in the spring.
WATER CONDITIONS: Cold, clear waters. Must be kept in refrigerated aquarium waters.
SIZE: Up to about 75 cm; exceptional specimens are larger.
FOOD REQUIREMENTS: It eats living fishes but is easily tempted by both dried and fresh dead fishes.

## Gila robusta Baird & Girard • Roundtail Chub

RANGE: Colorado River drainage, western U.S.A.
HABITS: Spawning individuals with breeding tubercles were taken in shallow pools and eddies over rubble or boulder substrates covered with silt. Spawning generally occurred in June or July when temperatures rose to about 18°C.
WATER CONDITIONS: Clear, well-oxygenated water required. This is a coldwater species, so refrigerated tanks may be necessary.
SIZE: Attains a length of about 14 to 15 inches (35-40 cm).
FOOD REQUIREMENTS: Adults will eat small fishes and insects as well as plant debris and algae in nature. Juveniles ate only insects.

## Notemigonus crysoleucas (Mitchill) • Golden Shiner

RANGE: Over most of the eastern half of North America from the Maritime Provinces south to Florida and west to the Dakotas and Texas.
HABITS: It spawns in the spring and early summer, attaching sticky eggs onto bushy plants or protruding fine root systems.
WATER CONDITIONS: Clear, heavily vegetated non-flowing waters are preferred. Can easily be kept in unheated (or heated) aquaria.
SIZE: Records of over 26 cm are known, but the usual size is 6 cm.
FOOD REQUIREMENTS: Eats anything in the way of aquarium foods, both flake and freeze-dried.

## Umbra pygmaea (DeKay) • The Eastern Mudminnow

RANGE: Eastern United States from New York to Florida.
HABITS: A small mudminnow that is found in swamps and very slow moving streams.
WATER CONDITIONS: They do well in unheated aquariums where their tankmates are not too active. The water must be well aged or they develop skin problems manifested by fungus growth.
SIZE: About 150 mm is the maximum size but most aquarium specimens are much smaller.
FOOD REQUIREMENTS: They prefer live foods (as do most fishes) but they quickly adapt to a typical aquarium diet.

## Esox niger Lesueur • Chain Pickerel

RANGE: Eastern and south-central North America.
HABITS: A spring spawner that makes an interesting aquarium pet when small. The smaller fish (shown here) does not have the chain pattern of coloration that only develops in specimens over 150-200 mm.
WATER CONDITIONS: Freshwater with a high pH, though it tolerates most waters which are fresh, clear, and cool. A solitary fish that hides motionless in vegetation awaiting its next meal.
SIZE: As large as 80 cm.
FOOD REQUIREMENTS: Live fishes are preferred, though pickerel are usually easily acclimated to other foods when young.

## Exoglossum maxillingua (Lesueur) • Cutlips Minnow

RANGE: Northeastern North America.
HABITS: A rather sluggish, slow-moving fish. It stays on the bottom picking on the gravel and hiding under larger stones, plants, etc. It eagerly takes tubifex worms and daphnia that are near the bottom of the tank. Available from bait dealers. A good substitute for catfish as scavengers.
WATER CONDITIONS: Not fussy, but the water should be cool. Does well in the unheated aquarium.
SIZE: Males: 140 mm. Females: smaller, about 130 mm maximum.
FOOD REQUIREMENTS: They eat most of the ordinary fish foods, both living and prepared.

Esox americanus

Umbra pygmaea

Esox lucius

Esox lucius

Gila robusta

Esox niger

Notemigonus crysoleucas

Exoglossum maxillingua

21

*Notropis welaka* Evermann & Kendall • Bluenose Shiner

RANGE: Restricted to the area from eastern Florida (St. Johns River) to the Pearl River which forms part of the boundary between Louisiana and Mississippi.
HABITS: Peaceful. Can be kept with other fishes of similar size and temperament.
WATER CONDITIONS: Not critical. Tolerates a wide range of pH and hardness, but for best results should be kept in soft, slightly acid water. Temperature range from about 6° to 26°C, but prefers it cool.
SIZE: Reaches a maximum length of about 65 mm (average 50 mm).
FOOD REQUIREMENTS: Will accept a wide range of aquarium foods.

*Notropis cornutus* (Mitchill) • Common Shiner

RANGE: Central North America from the Mississippi valley to Nova Scotia and south to Virginia's James River system.
HABITS: Spawns in the spring when water temperatures reach 16°C. Spawns over gravel beds excavated in a half-hearted manner.
WATER CONDITIONS: They prefer clear, cool water, but they can take heated or unheated aquaria.
SIZE: Males grow large, to 200 mm, while females rarely exceed 160 mm.
FOOD REQUIREMENTS: These are basically bottom feeders, searching for small worms and crustaceans in nature. They also take dried foods in aquaria.

*Notropis atherinoides* Rafinesque •Emerald Shiner

RANGE: Large lakes and rivers in Canada and throughout the north central states along the Mississippi River valley.
HABITS: The emerald shiner is an open water, pelagic species. It requires larger tanks to really thrive and it schools when enough fish are in one tank. Not really a home aquarium fish. Lives about three years.
WATER CONDITIONS: Cool, still water. Very easy to acclimate to life in a very large aquarium (over 500 liters). Best kept in an unheated aquarium.
SIZE: Males reach 85 mm.
FOOD REQUIREMENTS: Prefers live foods like daphnia, but quickly learns to accept typical dried aquarium fare.

*Ptychocheilus lucius* Girard • Colorado Squawfish

RANGE: Colorado basin.
HABITS: Voracious pike-like predators that put up a respectable fight when caught on hook and line and are good to eat.
WATER CONDITIONS: Need cold, clear water. A large refrigerated tank in public aquariums would be the most likely place to see one in captivity.
SIZE: Said to attain a length of over 1½ meters and a weight of 35 kilos in past years but now even 1 to 1⅓ meters long specimens are generally rare.
FOOD REQUIREMENTS: Voracious feeders on other fishes, commonly young trout and salmon in the wild. Will accept other available fishes, such as feeder goldfish.

*Notropis hypselopterus* (Guenther) • Sailfin Shiner

RANGE: South Carolina, Georgia, Florida and Alabama.
HABITS: A peaceful, active fish which will not molest its tankmates.
WATER CONDITIONS: Clean, soft, slightly acid water and a good-sized, well-planted tank are preferred.
SIZE: 8 cm.
FOOD REQUIREMENTS: Will take dried as well as live or frozen foods.

*Notropsis lutrensis* (Baird and Girard) • Red Shiner

RANGE: Wyoming to Minnesota, Iowa, Illinois, south to Mexico, and west to Colorado and California.
HABITS: The breeding males have bright orange ventral fins and very dark vertical bars on the sides. The males are covered almost completely with fine tubercles, giving them the nickname "Sandpaper Shiners."
WATER CONDITIONS: Prefers unheated tanks that are very cool in the winter and not more than 23°C in the summer.
SIZE: This very popular bait minnow reaches a maximum of 76 mm with the male usually larger than the female.
FOOD REQUIREMENTS: Prefers live foods as do most fishes, but gets along quite well on dried and frozen aquarium diets.

*Phoxinus erythrogaster* Rafinesque • Southern Redbelly Dace

RANGE: Restricted to the tributaries of the Mississippi, from the Cannon River to the Missouri drainage
HABITS: This is one of the most colorful of all American fishes. Unfortunately the photo is of a female. In breeding males the ventral fins, flanks, and belly are blood red, bright and obvious.
WATER CONDITIONS: Unheated or heated aquariums suit them equally well.
SIZE: About 80 mm. Males are larger and have longer fins.
FOOD REQUIREMENTS: Dried aquarium foods are accepted but they need daphnia or live brine shrimp to achieve spawning condition.

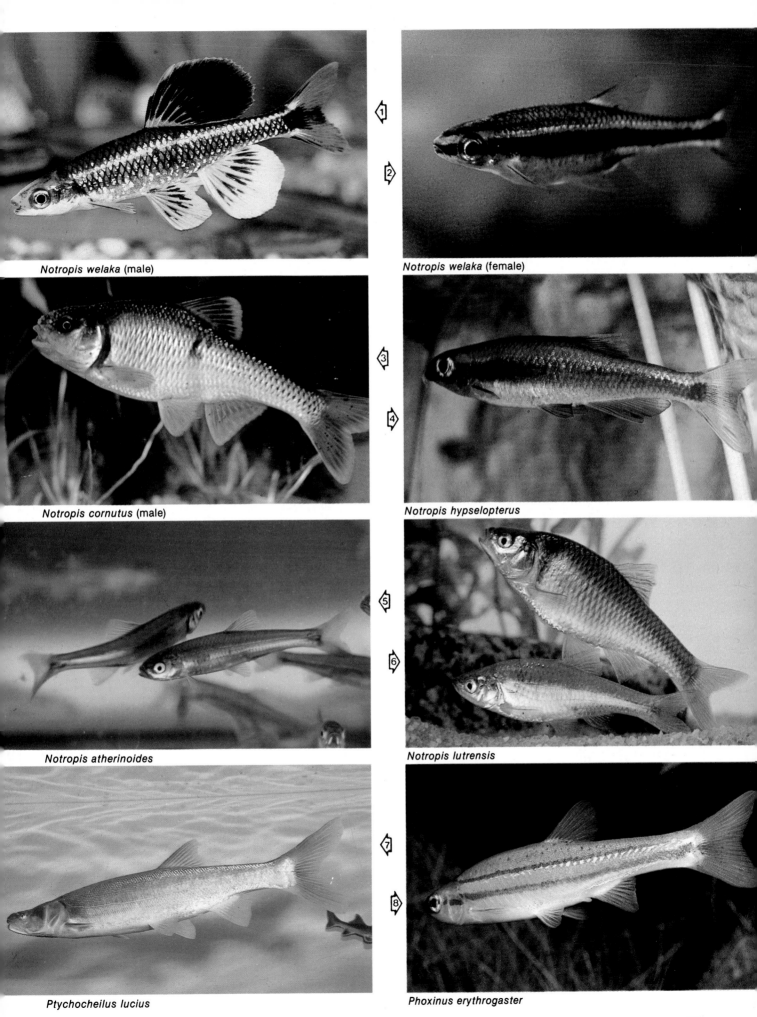

Notropis welaka (male)

Notropis welaka (female)

Notropis cornutus (male)

Notropis hypselopterus

Notropis atherinoides

Notropis lutrensis

Ptychocheilus lucius

Phoxinus erythrogaster

23

## Rhinichthys atratulus (Hermann) • Blacknose Dace

RANGE: Manitoba and Nova Scotia in Canada to North Dakota, North Carolina, and Nebraska.

HABITS: Spawns in riffles over gravel and debris in very shallow water (sometimes only two inches deep). Eggs are laid in a nest of stones, but the eggs are not cared for.

WATER CONDITIONS: Clear, aerated water. Unheated tanks are necessary and if the water gets over 23°C it should be cooled down.

SIZE: Rarely exceed 100 mm. Breeding males have a dark red lateral band; males have longer fins.

FOOD REQUIREMENTS: In nature it feeds on small algae, small insects, and small worms. In the aquarium it readily accepts live brine shrimp, tubifex, and daphnia plus the usual dry food fare.

## Catostomus catostomus (Forster) • Longnose Sucker

RANGE: North America, from Maryland to Minnesota, to the Arctic and northern Asia.

HABITS: Spawns in the spring in streams or any other place when the water thaws to 5°C. They prefer to spawn in moving water during daylight hours. White, sticky eggs fall to the bottom as several fish spawn together.

WATER CONDITIONS: Prefers colder water. Cannot live for long under heated aquarium conditions.

SIZE: Various populations grow to different lengths. Individuals from the Great Slave Lake, Canada, population reach 642 mm, while the Saskatchewan fish rarely get over 439 mm.

## Xyrauchen texanus (Abbott) • Razorback Sucker

RANGE: Lower parts of the Colorado River. Rare and on the endangered species list.

HABITS: Lives in swift-flowing waters where the unusual shape of its back is said to act like an inverted keel causing the flowing water to push them down against the bottom

WATER CONDITIONS: Lives in cold, highly oxygenated water that at the same time may also be silt-laden.

SIZE: Attains a length of up to 60 cm.

FOOD REQUIREMENTS: Apparently feeds primarily by taste like many other suckers. This is a bottom-grubbing species feeding on material living on or attached to the substrate.

## Noturus miurus Jordan • Brindled Madtom

RANGE: From Iowa and Minnesota to Lake Erie and its tributaries to New York and south to Mississippi, Louisiana, Arkansas, and northeastern Oklahoma.

HABITS: Lives in riffles to quiet areas on sand/clay bottoms; does not like mud bottoms. May bury themselves in the bottom during the day and forage at night. Their dorsal and pectoral fin spines are mildly poisonous.

WATER CONDITIONS: They do best in clear, clean, well-oxygenated water. A gravel bottom and hiding places are recommended. Breed at 25-30°C.

SIZE: Less than 12 cm.

FOOD REQUIREMENTS: Brine shrimp, raw liver, flake food, and tubifex worms are favorites.

## Semotilus atromaculatus (Mitchill) • Creek Chub

RANGE: From Montana to the Gaspe Peninsula in Canada, south to the Gulf states. Several subspecies are recognized.

HABITS: In nature the fish is a creek fish rather than a lake fish. It spawns in fast-moving water riffles over gravel about 1 cm in diameter. The breeding males are beautiful, with large tubercles on their heads and sides which are orange, blue and purple.

WATER CONDITIONS: Depends upon the source of the fish. Southern fishes do well under normal aquarium conditions. Northern fishes require unheated tanks.

SIZE: May reach 30 cm in 7 years.

FOOD REQUIREMENTS: They eat everything and are often caught on a hook by fly fishermen or trout fishermen.

## Erimyzon sucetta (Lacepede) • Lake Chubsucker

RANGE: Eastern North America to midwest, from southern New York to Florida, west to Texas, and north to Minnesota, Michigan and Wisconsin.

HABITS: A specialty fish that should be kept in cool water aquaria.

WATER CONDITIONS: Variable except that temperatures higher than 21°C usually cause problems.

SIZE: Reaches a length of about 25 cm.

FOOD REQUIREMENTS: Will usually take daphnia, brine shrimp, chironomids, copepods.

## Ictalurus catus (Linnaeus) • White Catfish

RANGE: Eastern United States from New England to Florida. Widely introduced elsewhere in the U.S.

HABITS: Typical catfish, grubbing on the bottom with their barbels for food. Spawned eggs of some bullheads (Ictalurus) have been known to stick to wading birds' legs and thereby become distributed into other areas.

WATER CONDITIONS: Not critical. These catfish can survive in water with a very low oxygen content due to their accessory breathing apparatus.

SIZE: To 7 kilos, but average closer to 1½ kilos.

FOOD REQUIREMENTS: Will eat almost anything and have very good appetites. Normally take food from the bottom like other catfishes.

## Ictalurus punctatus (Rafinesque) • Channel Catfish

RANGE: U.S.A., Great Lakes to Florida and Texas.

HABITS: Small ones are excellent scavengers and peaceful.

WATER CONDITIONS: Not critical as long as the water is clean and not too warm. Temperature about 18°C.

SIZE: Only babies are recommended for the aquarium; reaches 90 cm in length.

FOOD REQUIREMENTS: Tubifex worms and frozen brine shrimp are eaten with gusto by juveniles, but adults have large mouths and large appetites.

Rhinichthys atratulus

Semotilus atromaculatus

Catostomus catostomus

Erimyzon sucetta

Xyrauchen texanus

Ictalurus catus

Noturus miurus

Ictalurus punctatus (albino)

*Fundulus chrysotus* (Guenther) • Golden Ear, Golden Topminnow

RANGE: South Carolina, Georgia, Florida; found in standing water near the coastline.
HABITS: Peaceful when kept with fishes its own size.
WATER CONDITIONS: It is advisable to add one teaspoon of salt to every 20 liters of aquarium water. Temperature 23 to 25°C.
SIZE: To 7 cm.
FOOD REQUIREMENTS: Will eat most aquarium fish foods, including dried flake food, freeze-dried food and live food.

*Cyprinodon macularius* Baird & Girard • Desert Pupfish

RANGE: Salton Sea, Colorado delta, and Rio Sonoyata, southwestern United States.
HABITS: Usually peaceful, but best kept by themselves because of their water requirements and spawning type.
WATER CONDITIONS: Hard, alkaline water with temperatures from 24 to 32°C. Some salt may be added to the water.
SIZE: Up to about 6 to 8 cm.
FOOD REQUIREMENTS: Prefers live foods like tubifex and brine shrimp but can be coaxed onto frozen, flake or other types of foods.

*Fundulus heteroclitus* (Linnaeus) • Zebra Killie, Mummichog

RANGE: Atlantic Coast from Canada to Florida.
HABITS: Fairly peaceful, but may pick on smaller fishes.
WATER CONDITIONS: Water should be alkaline and hard (about 20 DH), with some salt added, at least a teaspoonful to every 4 liters; will take full salt water. Should be kept at room temperature.
SIZE: To 20 cm.
FOOD REQUIREMENTS: All kinds of live foods, also dried foods which have a vegetable content, such as the so-called "Molly food."

*Fundulus cingulatus* Cuvier & Valenciennes • Banded Topminnow

RANGE: South Carolina, Georgia, Florida; found in standing water near the coastline.
HABITS: Peaceful when kept with fishes its own size.
WATER CONDITIONS: It is advisable to add one teaspoon of salt to every 20 liters of aquarium water. Temperature 23 to 25°C.
SIZE: To 7 cm.
FOOD REQUIREMENTS: Will eat most aquarium fish foods, including dried flake food, freeze-dried food and live food.

*Lucania goodei* Jordan • Bluefin Killifish

RANGE: Southern Florida.
HABITS: An active species which will sometimes pursue other fishes, but seldom attacks.
WATER CONDITIONS: Should be kept in roomy aquaria, well planted and cool (15°C).
SIZE: 5 cm.
FOOD REQUIREMENTS: Small live foods only; dried foods are accepted only if the fish are starving.

*Jordanella floridae* Goode & Bean • American Flagfish

RANGE: Florida, especially in the southern portion.
HABITS: Males are apt to be very quarrelsome, especially at spawning time; it is best to give pairs their own aquarium.
WATER CONDITIONS: Prefers a sunny aquarium with slightly alkaline water. Temperature should be around 21°C, slightly higher for spawning.
SIZE: About 5 cm.
FOOD REQUIREMENTS: Will eat dried as well as live foods, but should get a good deal of vegetable matter in its diet.

*Heterandria formosa* Agassiz • Least Killifish

RANGE: U.S., North Carolina to eastern Texas, coastal.
HABITS: Peaceful; males are small enough to be eaten by bigger fish, and this species is best kept by itself.
WATER CONDITIONS: Not critical, as long as the water is not too far from neutral. Temperature about 24°C.
SIZE: Males about 2 cm; females almost 3.5 cm.
FOOD REQUIREMENTS: All small live foods, also frozen. Prepared foods also taken.

*Leptolucania ommata* (Jordan) • Swamp Killie, Pygmy Killifish

RANGE: Southern Georgia to Florida, in swamps.
HABITS: Peaceful, but should not be kept with larger fishes.
WATER CONDITIONS: Neutral to slightly acid water; tank should be well planted. Temperature 21 to 24°C.
SIZE: To about 4 cm.
FOOD REQUIREMENTS: Small living foods are preferred, but dried foods are accepted.

Fundulus chrysotus

Cyprinodon macularius

Fundulus heteroclitus

Fundulus cingulatus

Lucania goodei

Jordanella floridae

Heterandria formosa

Leptolucania ommata

27

Spawning the American Flagfish, *Jordanella floridae*
Goode & Bean

There are two patterns of spawning in this fish. In habitats with a muddy, mulm bottom, the fish hang their eggs among floating plants. When the bottom is clean and gravelly, they spawn like many cichlids. The male usually searches out a site (on # 1 photo facing page). When he finds it he indicates his acceptance by taking a position over the site. The female then comes to inspect the site (# 2) and the male tries to inspire her acceptance by dancing about her with extended fins (# 3). He then sidles up to her (#4) and tries to press her into a mass of fine roots (#5). If she cooperates, he will drape his large dorsal fin over her back (# 6, 7 and 8), pressing her as he quivers. He fertilizes the eggs as they are expelled. The male then guards the eggs. The female should be left in the aquarium since she often comes back every day for a week to add more eggs to the nest. Hatching of the first eggs takes about a week. The male also cares for the young.

Spawning the American Flagfish, *Jordanella floridae*

*Cyprinodon nevadensis*

*Cyprinodon nevadensis*

*Cyprinodon variegatus*

*Priapella intermedia*

*Centrarchus macropterus*

*Ictalurus melas*

*Pomoxis nigromaculatus*

Plate #7A

*Lepomis gibbosus*

*Gasterosteus aculeatus*

*Micropterus salmoides*

*Centrarchus macropterus*

*Archoplites interruptus*

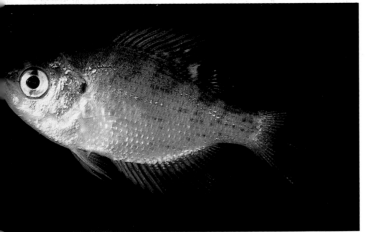

*Elassoma evergladei*

*Enneacanthus chaetodon*

*Enneacanthus gloriosus*

*Enneacanthus obesus*

Plate #8

31

## *Lepomis megalotis* (Rafinesque) • Longeared Sunfish

RANGE: Eastern United States, Canada to Mexican border.
HABITS: Best kept by themselves.
WATER CONDITIONS: Not critical, but water should be clean and well aerated.
SIZE: Wild specimens 20 cm; in the aquarium seldom over 13 cm.
FOOD REQUIREMENTS: Hearty eaters whose live food diet can be supplemented with chopped beef heart, liver, etc.

## *Pomoxis nigromaculatus* (LeSueur) • Black Crappie

RANGE: Common in lakes and large streams from southern Manitoba to Quebec and south along the eastern United States to Florida and Texas.
HABITS: Very prolific, spawning up to 140,000 eggs at a time. May spawn in their first or second year in the late spring. Nests for spawning are constructed in water a meter or two deep.
WATER CONDITIONS: Not critical. A cool water species that can live in an unheated aquarium.
SIZE: Seldom more than 30 cm.
FOOD REQUIREMENTS: Feed on a wide variety of foods such as aquatic insects, small crustaceans, and small fishes.

## *Lepomis gibbosus* (Linnaeus) • Sunfish, Pumpkinseed

RANGE: Maine to Florida west to the Mississippi.
HABITS: Should be kept by themselves or with others of the same genus.
WATER CONDITIONS: Tank should be roomy and the water clean. Room temperatures suffice without any additional heat.
SIZE: Seldom larger than 15 cm.
FOOD REQUIREMENTS: Hearty eaters which require frequent feeding with large live foods such as chopped earthworms or frozen foods like beef heart.

## *Lepomis macrochirus* Rafinesque • Bluegill

RANGE: United States from Minnesota to Texas (and south to northern Mexico) and eastward to the East Coast from New York to Florida. Introduced into areas as far west as California.
HABITS: Generally aggressive. Diggers and plant uprooters.
WATER CONDITIONS: Not critical. A cool-water species but can tolerate temperatures from 2-30°C.
SIZE: Reaches maturity at about 9 cm, but a record Bluegill of 380 cm has been recorded.
FOOD REQUIREMENTS: Easily fed on a variety of foods including earthworms, small live fishes, beef heart, etc.

## *Lepomis gulosus* (Cuvier) • Warmouth

RANGE: Widely distributed in the United States with the exception of the extreme northeastern section.
HABITS: Spawns in depressions constructed in the bottom like other species of *Lepomis.*
WATER CONDITIONS: Water chemistry not critical. An unheated tank with clean, clear, well-aerated water is recommended.
SIZE: Attains a length of up to 25 cm.
FOOD REQUIREMENTS: Feeds on small fishes and aquatic invertebrates. Food should be living when offered.

## *Lepomis humilis* (Girard) • Orangespotted Sunfish

RANGE: From the Dakotas to Ohio and south to Texas and northern Alabama.
HABITS: Spawns like other *Lepomis* species and in the same areas, sometimes leading to hybridization.
WATER CONDITIONS: Water chemistry not critical. Clean, clear water at room temperatures will suffice.
SIZE: A small species of usually 5 to 8 cm but occasionally to 10 cm.
FOOD REQUIREMENTS: Feeds on small crustaceans and aquatic insects.

## *Micropterus punctulatus* (Rafinesque) • Spotted Bass

RANGE: From Ohio River system in Indiana, Illinois, and Ohio to the Gulf states.
HABITS: Usually found in deep pools of moderate or large streams. Behaves much like other species of *Micropterus.*
WATER CONDITIONS: Requires a large tank. Water should be clean, cool, and well aerated. Likes slightly higher temperatures than other species of *Micropterus.*
SIZE: Attains lengths of up to 50 cm.
FOOD REQUIREMENTS: Adults thrive on live fishes; smaller individuals take smaller live fishes and live crustaceans (brine shrimp, etc.).

## *Micropterus dolomieui* Lacepede • Smallmouth Bass

RANGE: From Lake of the Woods region to Quebec and south to eastern Oklahoma and northern Alabama. Has also been introduced elsewhere.
HABITS: Prefers clear, moderately cool, swift-flowing streams or clear gravel-bottomed lakes. Spawns over clean gravel and sand bottoms in a current. Nests are hollow depressions. Normally blackish fry spread out over the spawning bed shortly after darkness and turn a light gray color; at sunrise next day they return to their natural dark color.
WATER CONDITIONS: Need a large, clean, well-aerated tank, preferably with some current. Unheated tanks are preferred (they spawn at 18°C).
SIZE: Attains a length of over 31 cm.
FOOD REQUIREMENTS: Small individuals will take live crustaceans; larger ones take larger crustaceans and small live fishes. Dead food is usually ignored.

Lepomis megalotus

Pomoxis nigromaculatus

Lepomis gibbosus

Lepomis macrochirus

Lepomis gulosus

Lepomis humilis

Micropterus punctulatus

Micropterus dolomieui

33

# The Darters

Darters are strictly North American in distribution, with species to be found in suitable habitats in most of the drainages of the Mississippi and Ohio Rivers, the Great Lakes, the Gulf of Mexico, Hudson Bay in Canada, and on the Atlantic coastal plain. Many species are found in the eastern mountain ranges, the Appalachians, Ozarks, and their outliers. All together there are about 150 species contained in three genera that constitute the tribe Etheostomatini of the family Percidae. All darters have two dorsal fins, with spines present only in the first dorsal. The three genera are *Percina*, *Ammocrypta*, and *Etheostoma*. It is often difficult to differentiate between the genera by observing them in an aquarium since they are told apart primarily by such things as possessing translucent bodies, specialized scales in males, and form of the lateral line system on the head. There are numerous subgenera as well.

For the aquarist, the darters present a rare challenge, for here are fishes that almost always require running water habitats (like some of the rainbowfishes of Australia and New Guinea) and range in size from the tiny *E. fonticola* (to about 4 cm long) to the giant *P. lenticula*, which reaches the length of about 16 cm. They are often colorful and will eat most live foods and many dried foods. Darters are hardy, easy to sex and breed, and usually don't require heaters, pumps, or filters if you know how to properly maintain an aquarium and don't overfeed your fishes!

Almost every creek and stream within their range contains one darter species or another, and they often occur in great numbers where found. As a matter of fact, in studies made of darter population densities, a rare density would be a mere one fish per square yard; some studies collected 33 to the square yard! In drought-affected areas in New Jersey, the author (H.R.A.) found *E. olmstedi* in a small stream with a sandy bottom in numbers of 80 individuals to the square yard; this was likely an unnatural concentration due to the lack of rain in the area over an extended period of time.

To effectively collect darters, get yourself a minnow seine about 6 feet long and, with some help, wedge the seine in sand or rocks on the bottom of a stream where darters have been observed. Set the seine up in such a way that once the darters have been driven into the seine they become trapped. Then merely wade toward the seine trap from a distance of about 20 yards upstream, shuffling your feet so as to drive the fleeing darters in front of you. Take only as many fish as you need—perhaps five males and five females—and release the rest.

Be sure to check with your local conservation authorities as to the laws governing fishing with a seine in your area. Local regulations vary, and some conservation officers may look the other way where a dozen darters are concerned—but

check first! Many darters are on state and/or federal endangered species lists and cannot be taken at all under normal circumstances.

Once collected, set the fish up in a small tank with a sandy bottom. Most darters can be found by determining and locating their preferred habitat. Most like open, fast-running water flowing over sand, gravel and rocks. Young fish are often found in quieter waters, however. Try to collect some smooth stones from the same area in which you found the fish.

Most darters reach maturity in a year. A few species occurring in Canada's colder northern areas may take two years to reach adulthood, but for aquarists, if you catch them in more open waters, they are probably already mature. While most darters spawn only in the spring, they often breed year-round in captivity if provided with a diet of live daphnia and tubifex worms. The spawning cycle is similar to that of the African annuals—eggs are laid continually. A six-month breeding period can normally be expected, but the heightened color of the male and the abdominal bulge of the female will be the best indications that spawning is imminent . . . don't worry about the calendar. Females usually spawn an average of once a week during their spawning cycle, but the author has kept individuals that spawned every two or three days!

Darter eggs are strongly adhesive, heavier than water, translucent, and contain a few oil droplets. Egg sizes vary from 0.7 to 2.7 mm, with the smaller species, of course, producing the smallest eggs. To induce the fish to spawn, give good feedings of live daphnia or brine shrimp for a week. Then a gradual increase in water temperature should guarantee spawning. In at least one species studied, the length of the day or intensity of the light doesn't affect their spawning cycle; rather, it is determined by temperature and the condition of the fish.

Darters have two modes of reproduction. Perhaps after aquarists have studied the species in the genus *Ammocrypta*, additional modes may be described, for up to now no *Ammocrypta* species have been spawned in an aquarium.

The basic reproductive mode is the attachment of the sticky eggs to a rock or leaf, while some species bury their eggs. All species of *Percina* so far studied bury their eggs, and a few species of *Etheostoma* do so as well. As a rule, though, *Etheostoma* species usually attach their eggs to natural objects in the habitat. The following chart, taken from Dr. Page's book, *Handbook of Darters*, identifies the spawning habits of the various species for which this information is known.

With species as similar in appearance and behavior as these, hybridization would not be an unlikely occurrence in captivity. Some hybrids have even been found in nature.

**Species in Each of Three Categories of Spawning Behavior in Darters and, in Parentheses After the Name, Mean Diameters of Eggs in mm.**

| | Attached to rocks, plants, *etc.* | |
|---|---|---|
| Buriers (Eggs buried in substrate) | Attachers (Eggs attached and abandoned) | Clusterers (Eggs clustered on underside of stone and guarded by male) |
| P. (Alvordius) maculata (2.0) | E. (Etheostoma) blennioides (1.9) | E. (Boleosoma) nigrum (1.5) |
| P. (Alvordius) peltata | E. (Nanostoma) zonale | E. (Boleosoma) olmstedi |
| P. (Alvordius) notogramma (1.2) | E. (Nanostoma) atripinne | E. (Boleosoma) perlongum |
| P. (Hypohomus) aurantiaca (2.1) | E. (Nanostoma) sp. (Barren R.) | E. (Nothonotus) maculatum (2.0) |
| P. (Cottogaster) copelandi (1.4) | E. (Nanostoma) sp. (Green R.) | E. (Catonotus) olivaceum (2.0) |
| P. (Percina) caprodes (1.1-1.3) | E. (Ioa) vitreum | E. (Catonotus) squamiceps (1.8) |
| E. (Litocara) nianguae | E. (Vaillantia) chlorosomum | E. (Catonotus) neopterum |
| E. (Etheostoma) tetrazonum | E. (Belophlox) okaloosae | E. (Catonotus) kennicotti (2.1) |
| E. (Etheostoma) variatum | E. (Villora) edwini | E. (Catonotus) flabellare (2.2-2.7) |
| E. (Doration) stigmaeum (1.7) | E. (Ozarka) boschungi | E. (Catonotus) virgatum |
| E. (Nothonotus) rufilineatum | E. (Ozarka) trisella | E. (Catonotus) smithi (2.2) |
| E. (Nothonotus) camurum | E. (Oligocephalus) lepidum (1.3) | E. (Catonotus) striatulum (2.0) |
| E. (Nothonotus) tippecanoe | E. (Oligocephalus) grahami | |
| E. (Oligocephalus) spectabile (1.2-1.5) | E. (Oligocephalus) ditrema (1.1-1.2) | |
| E. (Oligocephalus) caeruleum (1.6-1.9) | E. (Boleichthys) fusiforme | |
| E. (Oligocephalus) radiosum (1.2-1.5) | E. (Boleichthys) exile (1.1) | |
| | E. (Boleichthys) gracile (1.0) | |
| | E. (Boleichthys) proeliare (0.7) | |
| | E. (Boleichthys) fonticola (1.1) | |
| | E. (Boleichthys) microperca (0.9-1.1) | |

*Percina sciera*. 63 mm SL male, Embarras River, Cumberland Co., IL, 5 Nov. 1978.

*Percina aurolineata*. 62 mm SL male, Little Cahaba River, Bibb Co., AL, 18 Feb. 1978.

*Percina sciera*. 73 mm SL female, Middle Fork, Vermilion Co., IL, 7 June 1977.

*Percina aurolineata*. 56 mm SL female, Little Cahaba River, Bibb Co., AL, 2 July 1978.

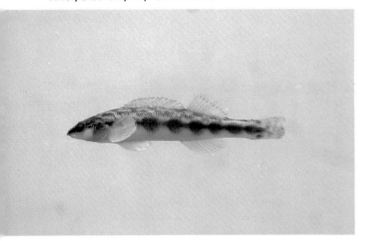

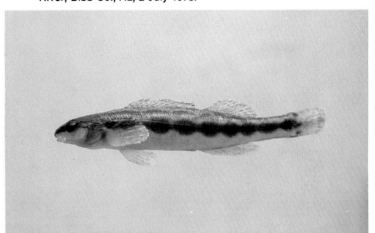

# North American Fishes • *Plate #10* • *Darters*

*Percina nigrofasciata*. 85 mm SL male, Murphy Creek, Blount Co., AL, 19 Apr. 1977.

*Percina squamata*. Male, Watauga River, Johnson Co., TN, 17 June 1973 (photo by D.A. Etnier).

*Percina nigrofasciata*. 62 mm SL female, Tangipahoa River, Pike Co., MS, 12 Apr. 1977.

*Percina squamata*. Female, Nolichucky River, Hamblen Co., TN, 13 Aug. 1978 (photo by D.A. Etnier).

Percina lenticula. 79 mm SL male, Schultz Creek, Bibb Co., AL, 18 Feb. 1978.

Percina oxyrhyncha. 78 mm SL male, Elk River, Braxton Co., WV, 28 Apr. 1979.

Percina nasuta. 66 mm SL male, Ouachita River, Polk Co., AR, 26 May 1978.

Percina nasuta. 69 mm SL female, Ouachita River, Montgomery Co., AR, 25 May 1978.

# North American Fishes • Plate #11 • Darters

Percina phoxocephala. 58 mm SL male, Embarras River, Cumberland Co., IL, 22 July 1980.

Percina phoxocephala. 54 mm SL female, Embarras River, Cumberland Co., IL, 22 July 1980.

Percina macrocephala. 73 mm SL male, Elk River, Braxton Co., WV, 28 Apr. 1979.

Percina pantherina. 62 mm SL male, Cossatot River, Howard Co., AR, 17 March 1978 (alcohol-stored spec.).

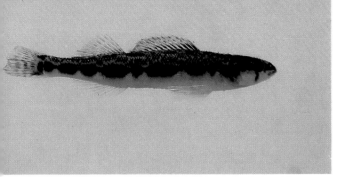

*Percina maculata.* 52 mm SL male, Kankakee River, Kankakee Co., IL, 12 Oct. 1979.

*Percina notogramma.* 43 mm SL male, Craig Creek, Craig Co., VA, 25 May 1980.

*Percina maculata.* 56 mm SL female, Kankakee River, Kankakee Co., IL, 12 Oct. 1979.

*Percina notogramma.* 43 mm SL female, Craig Creek, Craig Co., VA, 25 May 1980.

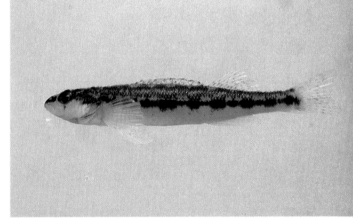

# North American Fishes • Plate #12 • Darters

*Percina gymnocephala.* 50 mm SL male, Little River, Alleghany Co., NC, 5 May 1979.

*Percina crassa.* 67 mm SL male, Little Alamance Creek, Guilford Co., NC, 26 June 1977.

*Percina peltata.* 56 mm SL female, Little River, Durham Co., NC, 1 May 1979.

*Percina crassa.* 66 mm SL female, Little Alamance Creek, Guilford Co., NC, 26 June 1977.

*Percina roanoka*. 57 mm SL male, Roanoke River, Roanoke Co., VA, 30 Apr. 1979.

*Percina palmaris*. 81 mm SL male, Conasauga River, Bradley Co., TN, 24 Feb. 1978.

*Percina roanoka*. 54 mm SL female, Blackwater River, Franklin Co., VA, 26 June 1977.

*Percina palmaris*. 64 mm SL female, Conasauga River, Bradley Co., TN, 24 Feb. 1978.

# North American Fishes • Plate #13 • Darters

*Percina evides*. 53 mm SL male, Cane River, Yancey Co., NC, 4 May 1979.

*Percina evides*. 64 mm SL male, St. Francis River, Wayne Co., MO, 18 May 1977.

*Percina evides*. 46 mm SL female, Cane River, Yancey Co., NC, 4 May 1979.

*Percina evides*. 58 mm SL female, St. Francis River, Wayne Co., MO, 18 May 1977.

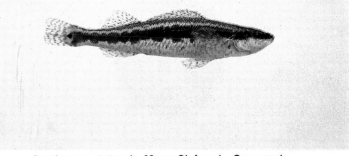

Percina cymatotaenia. 64 mm SL male, Gasconade R., LaClede Co., MO, 11 Oct. 1970 (alcohol-stored spec.).

Percina (Odontopholis) species. 62 mm SL male, Red Bird Creek, Clay Co., KY, 22 Mar. 1978.

Percina cymatotaenia. 68 mm SL female, Gasconade River, Pulaski Co., MO, 21 May 1977.

Percina tanasi. 45 mm SL male, Little Tennessee River, Loudon Co., TN, 6 June 1975 (alcohol-stored spec.).

## North American Fishes • Plate #14 • Darters

Percina aurantiaca. 103 mm SL male, Middle Prong Pigeon R., Sevier Co., TN, 22 June 1973 (D.A. Etnier photo).

Percina copelandi. 50 mm SL male, Blue River, Johnston Co., OK, 26 May 1978.

Percina aurantiaca. 93 mm SL female, Little River, Blount Co., TN, 9 Apr. 1980.

Percina copelandi. 43 mm SL female, Ouachita River, Polk Co., AR, 26 May 1978.

Percina shumardi. 50 mm SL male, Ditch No. 1, New Madrid Co., MO, 31 Oct. 1980.

Percina shumardi. 45 mm SL female, Ditch No. 1, New Madrid Co., MO, 31 Oct. 1980.

Percina uranidea. 52 mm SL male, Current River, Randolph Co., AR, 17 Aug. 1979.

Percina uranidea. 58 mm SL female, Current River, Randolph Co., AR, 17 Aug. 1979.

## North American Fishes • Plate #15 • Darters

Percina ouachitae. 50 mm SL male, Mud River, Muhlenberg Co., KY, 30 Oct. 1980.

Percina ouachitae. 48 mm SL female, Mud River, Muhlenberg Co., KY, 30 Oct. 1980.

Percina antesella. 70 mm SL male, Conasauga River, Bradley Co., TN, 20 Sept. 1977 (photo by D.A. Etnier).

Percina antesella. 57 mm SL female, Conasauga River, Bradley Co., TN, 24 Apr. 1979.

*Percina burtoni.* 90 mm SL male, Copper Creek, Scott Co., VA, 21 Apr. 1979.

*Percina burtoni.* 74 mm SL female, Little River, Blount Co., TN, 10 Aug. 1979.

*Percina carbonaria.* 98 mm SL male, Guadalupe River, Kerr Co., TX, 27 May 1978.

*Percina carbonaria.* 85 mm SL female, Guadalupe River, Kerr Co., TX, 27 May 1978.

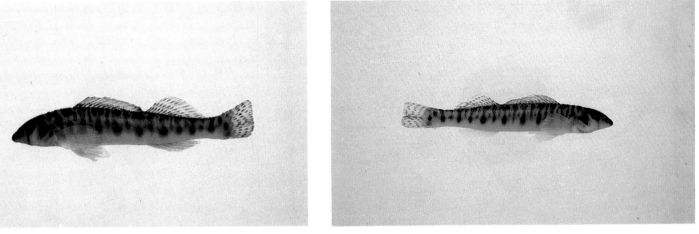

## North American Fishes • Plate #16 • Darters

*Percina caprodes fulvitaenia.* 132 mm SL male, Big Piney River, Texas Co., MO, 25 Apr. 1978.

*Percina c. caprodes?* 86 mm SL male, Ouachita River, Polk Co., AR, 26 May 1978.

*Percina c. caprodes.* 120 mm SL female, Embarras River, Cumberland Co., IL, 22 July 1980.

*Percina c. caprodes.* 79 mm SL female, Big Sycamore Creek, Claiborne Co., TN, 21 Mar. 1978.

# North American Fishes • Plate #17 • Darters

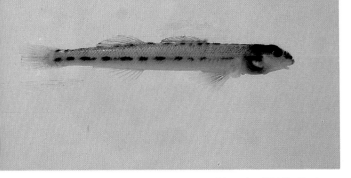

Ammocrypta pellucida. 53 mm SL male, Middle Fork Vermilion River, Vermilion Co., IL, 11 July 1978.

Ammocrypta beani. 46 mm SL male, Big Black River, Marion Co., MS, 21 June 1980.

Ammocrypta clara. 43 mm SL male, Mississippi R., Pike Co., MO, 26 June 1963 (alcohol-specimen).

Ammocrypta beani. 43 mm SL female, Big Black River, Marion Co., MS, 21 June 1980.

## North American Fishes • Plate #18 • Darters

Ammocrypta bifascia. 50 mm SL male, Escambia Creek, Escambia Co., AL, 24 June 1980.

Etheostoma tuscumbia. 31 mm SL male, Buffler Spring, Lauderdale Co., AL, 14 Aug. 1978.

Ammocrypta bifascia. 44 mm SL female, Escambia Creek, Escambia Co., AL, 24 June 1980.

Etheostoma tuscumbia. 34 mm SL female, Buffler Spring, Lauderdale Co., AL, 14 Aug. 1978.

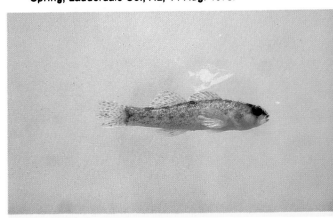

*Etheostoma nianguae.* Male, Big Tavern Creek, Miller Co., MO, 6 Apr. 1972 (photo by W.L. Pflieger).

*Etheostoma nianguae.* 79 mm male, Brush Creek, St. Clair Co., MO, 14 Aug. 1979.

*Etheostoma sagitta.* 64 mm SL male, Youngs Creek, Whitley Co., KY, 19 Mar. 1978.

*Etheostoma sagitta.* 56 mm SL female, Little Clear Creek, Bell Co., KY, 14 Mar. 1977.

# North American Fishes • Plate #19 • Darters

*Etheostoma euzonum euzonum.* 92 mm SL male, Beaver Creek, Taney Co., MO, 25 Apr. 1978.

*Etheostoma e. euzonum.* 81 mm SL female, Beaver Creek, Taney Co., MO, 25 Apr. 1978.

*Etheostoma euzonum.* 57 mm SL male, Fourche Creek, Randolph Co., AR, 15 Aug. 1979.

*Etheostoma euzonum.* 60 mm SL female, Fourche Creek, Randolph Co., AR, 15 Aug. 1979.

*Etheostoma cinereum*. Male, Little River, Blount Co., TN, 11 Feb. 1978 (photo by B.H. Bauer).

*Etheostoma cinereum*. 58 mm SL female, Buffalo River, Lewis Co., TN, 14 Apr. 1978.

*Etheostoma tetrazonum*. 55 mm SL male, Mill Creek, LaClede Co., MO, 24 Apr. 1978.

*Etheostoma tetrazonum*. 48 mm SL female, Mill Creek, LaClede Co., MO, 24 Apr. 1978.

# North American Fishes • Plate #20 • Darters

*Etheostoma variatum*. 77 mm SL male, Red Bird Creek, Clay Co., KY, 22 Mar. 1978.

*Etheostoma variatum*. 60 mm SL female, Red Bird Creek, Clay Co., KY, 22 Mar. 1978.

*Etheostoma kanawhae*. 60 mm SL male, Little River, Floyd Co., VA, 27 Apr. 1979.

*Etheostoma kanawhae*. 58 mm SL female, Little River, Floyd Co., VA, 27 Apr. 1979.

*Etheostoma osburni.* 69 mm SL male, Greenbrier
River, Pocahontas Co., WV, 28 Apr. 1979.

*Etheostoma thalassinum.* 50 mm SL male, South
Saluda River, Pickens Co., SC, 25 June 1977.

*Etheostoma osburni.* 60 mm SL female, Greenbrier
River, Pocahontas Co., WV, 28 Apr. 1979.

*Etheostoma thalassinum.* 52 mm SL female, Mid-
Saluda River, Greenville Co., SC, 25 June 1977.

## North American Fishes • Plate #21 • Darters

*Etheostoma inscriptum.* 51 mm SL male, Eastatoe
Creek, Pickens Co., SC, 25 June 1977.

*Etheostoma swannanoa.* 85 mm SL male, Little
Pigeon River, Sevier Co., TN, 20 Mar. 1978.

*Etheostoma inscriptum.* 53 mm SL female, Eastatoe
Creek, Pickens Co., SC, 25 June 1977.

*Etheostoma swannanoa.* 69 mm SL female, Little
Pigeon River, Sevier Co., TN, 20 Mar. 1978.

Etheostoma blennius blennius. 60 mm SL male, Thompson Creek, Bedford Co., TN, 20 Apr. 1977.

Etheostoma b. blennius. 60 mm SL female, Thompson Creek, Bedford Co., TN, 20 Apr. 1977.

Etheostoma b. sequatchiense. 60 mm SL male, Sequatchie River, Bledsoe Co., TN, 10 Aug. 1977.

Etheostoma b. sequatchiense. 47 mm SL female, Sequatchie River, Bledsoe Co., TN, 10 Aug. 1977.

## North American Fishes • *Plate #22* • *Darters*

Etheostoma blennioides pholidotum. 76 mm SL male, Jordan Creek, Vermilion Co., IL, 17 May 1979.

Etheostoma b. newmani. 119 mm SL male, Jacks Fork, Shannon Co., MO, 30 Mar. 1980.

Etheostoma b. newmani. 82 mm SL male, Little Pigeon River, Sevier Co., TN, 21 Mar. 1978.

Etheostoma b. gutselli. 68 mm SL female, Tuckasegee River, Swain Co., NC, 22 May 1980.

Etheostoma rupestre. 54 mm SL male, Cahaba
River, Bibb Co., AL, 26 Feb. 1978.

Etheostoma rupestre. 48 mm SL female, Opintoloco
Creek, Macon Co., AL, 26 Feb. 1978.

Etheostoma histrio. 50 mm SL male, Bayou Pierre,
Copiah Co., MS, 16 Feb. 1979.

Etheostoma histrio. 42 mm SL female, Bayou
Pierre, Copiah Co., MS, 16 Feb. 1979.

# North American Fishes • Plate #23 • Darters

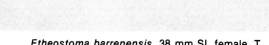

Etheostoma barrenensis. 44 mm SL male, Trammel
Fork, Allen Co., KY, 13 Apr. 1978.

Etheostoma barrenensis. 38 mm SL female, T
mel Fork, Allen Co., KY, 13 Apr. 1978.

Etheostoma rafinesquei. 41 mm SL male, Nolin
River, LaRue Co., KY, 19 May 1980.

Etheostoma rafinesquei. 49 mm SL female, C
Fork, Green Co., KY, 19 May 1980.

Lowland snubnose darter. 46 mm SL male, Pickens Creek, Tishomingo Co., MS, 20 Apr. 1977.

Lowland snubnose darter. 48 mm SL female, Pickens Creek, Tishomingo Co., MS, 20 Apr. 1977.

Red snubnose darter. 54 mm SL male, Terrapin Creek, Henry Co., TN, 29 May 1981.

Red snubnose darter, 44 mm SL female, Terrapin Creek, Henry Co., TN, 29 May 1981.

## North American Fishes • Plate #24 • Darters

*Etheostoma baileyi.* 45 mm SL male, Sexton Creek, Clay Co., KY, 22 Mar. 1978.

*Etheostoma baileyi.* 44 mm SL female, Little Sexton Creek, Clay Co., KY, 20 May 1980.

Golden snubnose darter. 55 mm SL male, Jones Creek, Dickson Co., TN, 15 Apr. 1978.

*Etheostoma simoterum.* 46 mm SL female, Wartrace Creek, Bedford Co., TN, 2 Mar. 1977.

*Etheostoma sellare*. 58 mm SL male, Deer Creek, Harford Co., MD, 10 Nov. 1965 (alcohol-stored spec.).

Warrior darter. 50 mm SL male, Murphy Creek, Blount Co., AL, 19 Apr. 1977.

*Etheostoma sellare*. 55 mm SL female, Deer Creek, Harford Co., MD, 10 Nov. 1965 (alcohol-stored spec.).

Warrior darter. 38 mm SL female, Murphy Creek, Blount Co., AL, 19 Apr. 1977.

## North American Fishes • Plate #25 • Darters

Tallapoosa darter, 58 mm SL male, Crooked Creek, Clay Co., AL, 25 Feb. 1978.

Coastal Plain darter. 52 mm SL male, trib., Minter Creek, Greene Co., AL, 17 Apr. 1977.

Tallapoosa darter. 52 mm SL female, Crooked Creek, Clay Co., AL, 25 Feb. 1978.

Coastal Plain darter. 42 mm SL female, trib., Minter Creek, Greene Co., AL, 17 Apr. 1977.

*Etheostoma zonale zonale.* 57 mm SL male, Trammel Fork, Allen Co., KY, 18 Oct. 1977.

*Etheostoma z. lynceum.* 41 mm SL male, Leaf River, Jones Co., MS, 16 Apr. 1977.

*Etheostoma z. zonale.* 45 mm SL female, Gasconade River, LaClede Co., MO, 21 May 1977.

*Etheostoma z. lynceum.* 40 mm SL female, Terrapin Creek, Graves Co., KY, 1 Oct. 1978.

# North American Fishes • Plate #26 • Darters

*Etheostoma atripinne.* 52 mm SL male, Brush Creek, Smith Co., TN, 16 Apr. 1978.

*Etheostoma simoterum.* 53 mm SL male, Copper Creek, Scott Co., VA, 21 Apr. 1979.

*Etheostoma atripinne.* 51 mm SL female, Brush Creek, Smith Co., TN, 16 Apr. 1978.

*Etheostoma simoterum.* 54 mm SL female, Little River, Blount Co., TN, 20 Mar. 1978.

Etheostoma duryi. 53 mm SL male, Walker Creek, Madison Co., AL, 29 Apr. 1978.

Etheostoma etnieri. 64 mm SL male, Charles Creek, Warren Co., TN, 20 Apr. 1977.

Etheostoma duryi. 44 mm SL female, Walker Creek, Madison Co., AL, 29 Apr. 1978.

Etheostoma etnieri. 43 mm SL female, trib., Calf-killer River, White Co., TN, 25 July 1978.

# North American Fishes • Plate #27 • Darters

Etheostoma coosae. 49 mm SL male, Salacoa Creek, Gordon Co., GA, 9 June 1976.

Etheostoma jessiae. 66 mm SL male, Little Pigeon River, Sevier Co., TN, 21 Mar. 1978.

Etheostoma coosae. 45 mm SL female, Salacoa Creek, Gordon Co., GA, 9 June 1976.

Etheostoma jessiae. 57 mm SL female, Little Pigeon River, Sevier Co., TN, 21 Mar. 1978.

*Etheostoma stigmaeum.* 45 mm SL male, Opintoloco Creek, Macon Co., AL, 26 Feb. 1978.

*Etheostoma nigrum.* 44 mm SL male, North Branch Otter Creek, Winnebago Co., IL, 7 May 1980.

*Etheostoma stigmaeum.* 43 mm SL female, West Fork Drakes Creek, Sumner Co., TN, 31 Jan. 1979.

*Etheostoma nigrum.* 56 mm SL female, North Branch Otter Creek, Winnebago Co., IL, 7 June 1979.

# North American Fishes • Plate #28 • Darters

*Etheostoma olmstedi.* 57 mm SL male, trib., Potomac River, Morgan Co., MD, 5 June 1975.

*Etheostoma perlongum.* 70 mm SL male, Lake Waccamaw, Columbus Co., NC, 2 May 1979.

*Etheostoma olmstedi.* 38 mm SL female, trib., Potomac River, Morgan Co., MD, 5 June 1975.

*Etheostoma perlongum.* 51 mm SL female, Lake Waccamaw, Columbus Co., NC, 2 May 1979.

*Etheostoma longimanum.* 62 mm SL male, Dunlap Creek, Alleghany Co., VA, 29 Apr. 1979.

*Etheostoma podostemone.* 59 mm SL male, Roanoke River, Montgomery Co., VA, 30 Apr. 1979.

*Etheostoma longimanum.* 45 mm SL female, Dunlap Creek, Alleghany Co., VA, 29 Apr. 1979.

*Etheostoma podostemone.* 51 mm SL female, Blackwater River, Franklin Co., VA, 26 June 1977.

# North American Fishes • Plate #29 • Darters

*Etheostoma vitreum.* 59 mm SL male, Blackwater River, Franklin Co., VA, 26 June 1977.

*Etheostoma chlorosomum.* 45 mm SL male, Copiah Creek, Copiah Co., MS, 12 Apr. 1977.

*Etheostoma vitreum.* 44 mm SL female, Blackwater River, Franklin Co., VA, 26 June 1977.

*Etheostoma chlorosomum.* 40 mm SL female, Lees Creek, Washington Co., MS, 16 Apr. 1977.

*Etheostoma davisoni.* 46 mm SL male, East Pitman
Creek, Holmes Co., FL, 27 Feb. 1978.

*Etheostoma davisoni.* 42 mm SL female, Five Runs
Creek, Covington Co., AL, 27 Feb. 1978.

*Etheostoma juliae.* 55 mm SL male, Beaver Creek,
Taney Co., MO, 25 Apr. 1978.

*Etheostoma juliae.* 50 mm SL female, Beaver Creek,
Taney Co., MO, 25 Apr. 1978.

## North American Fishes • Plate #30 • Darters

*Etheostoma microlepidum.* 49 mm SL male, East
Fork Stones River, Rutherford Co., TN, 6 May 1981.

*Etheostoma microlepidum.* 40 mm SL female, East
Fork Stones River, Rutherford Co., TN, 6 May 1981.

*Etheostoma aquali.* 57 mm SL male, Buffalo River,
Lewis Co., TN, 14 Apr. 1978.

*Etheostoma aquali.* 52 mm SL female, Buffalo River,
Lewis Co., TN, 14 Apr. 1978.

Etheostoma maculatum sanguifluum. 57 mm SL male, Big South Fork, Scott Co., TN, 23 Oct. 1976.

Etheostoma m. vulneratum. 43 mm SL male, Little River, Blount Co., TN, 10 Aug. 1979.

Etheostoma m. maculatum. 55 mm SL male, French Creek, Crawford Co., PA, 27 July 1980.

Etheostoma m. maculatum. 60 mm SL female, French Creek, Crawford Co., PA, 27 July 1980.

# North American Fishes • Plate #31 • Darters

Etheostoma rufilineatum. 52 mm SL male, Copper Creek, Scott Co., VA, 6 May 1979.

Etheostoma rufilineatum. 56 mm SL female, Little River, Blount Co., TN, 20 Mar. 1978.

Etheostoma acuticeps. 60 mm SL male, Nolichucky River, Hamblen Co., TN, 17 June 1976.

Etheostoma acuticeps. 51 mm SL female, Nolichucky River, Hamblen Co., TN, 17 June 1976.

*Etheostoma rubrum*. 48 mm SL male, Bayou Pierre, Copiah Co., MS, 16 Feb. 1979.

*Etheostoma rubrum*. 46 mm SL female, Bayou Pierre, Copiah Co., MS, 21 May 1976.

*Etheostoma moorei*. 51 mm SL male, South Fork Red River, Van Buren Co., AR, 25 May 1978.

*Etheostoma moorei*. 40 mm SL female, South Fork Red River, Van Buren Co., AR, 25 May 1978.

# North American Fishes • Plate #32 • Darters

*Etheostoma chlorobranchium*. 73 mm SL male, Little Pigeon River, Sevier Co., TN, 20 Mar. 1978.

*Etheostoma chlorobranchium*. 60 mm SL female, Tuckasegee River, Swain Co., NC, 22 May 1980.

*Etheostoma camurum*. 60 mm SL male, Middle Fork Vermilion River, Vermilion Co., IL, 13 Aug. 1970.

*Etheostoma camurum*. 48 mm SL female, Middle Fork Vermilion River, Vermilion Co., IL, 7 June 1977.

Etheostoma bellum. 51 mm SL male, Trammel Fork, Allen Co., KY, 18 Oct. 1977.

Etheostoma jordani. 46 mm SL male, Stamp Creek, Bartow Co., GA, 9 June 1976.

Etheostoma bellum. 54 mm SL female, Trammel Fork, Allen Co., KY, 18 Oct. 1977.

Etheostoma jordani. 50 mm SL female, Stamp Creek, Bartow Co., GA, 9 June 1976.

# North American Fishes • Plate #33 • Darters

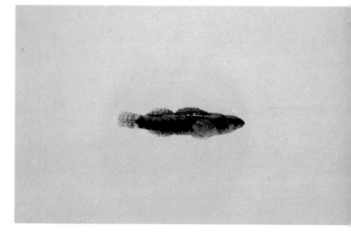

Etheostoma tippecanoe. 29 mm SL male, Big South Fork, Scott Co., TN, 23 Oct. 1976.

Etheostoma parvipinne. 41 mm SL male, trib., Powell Creek, Weakley Co., TN, 16 July 1980.

Etheostoma tippecanoe. 26 mm SL female, Big South Fork, Scott Co., TN, 23 Oct. 1976.

Etheostoma parvipinne. 38 mm SL female, trib., Powell Creek, Weakley Co., TN, 16 July 1980.

*Etheostoma fricksium.* 47 mm SL male, Little Selkehatchee River, Bamberg Co., SC, 24 June 1977.

*Etheostoma fricksium.* 43 mm SL female, Little Selkehatchee River, Bamberg Co., SC, 24 June 1977.

*Etheostoma mariae.* 54 mm SL male, trib., Lumber River, Hoke Co., NC, 13 June 1976.

*Etheostoma mariae.* 46 mm SL female, trib., Lumber River, Hoke Co., NC, 13 June 1976.

## North American Fishes • Plate #34 • Darters

*Etheostoma okaloosae.* 29 mm SL male, Toms Creek, Okaloosa Co., FL, 18 Aug. 1978.

*Etheostoma okaloosae.* 35 mm SL female, Toms Creek, Okaloosa Co., FL, 18 Aug. 1978.

*Etheostoma edwini.* 39 mm SL male, Rocky Creek, Walton Co., FL, Apr. 1977 (photo by M.F. Mettee).

*Etheostoma edwini.* 28 mm SL female, Swift Creek, Okaloosa Co., FL, 18 Aug. 1978.

*Etheostoma trisella*. 28 mm SL male, trib., Mill Cr.,
Bradley Co., TN, 10 Mar. 1979 (B.H. Bauer photo).

*Etheostoma trisella*. 38 mm SL female, Conasauga
River, Bradley Co., TN, 24 Feb. 1978.

*Etheostoma punctulatum*. 68 mm SL male, Massie
Creek, Warren Co., MO, 13 Apr. 1980 (T.M. Keevin photo).

*Etheostoma punctulatum*. 52 mm SL female, trib.,
Spring River, Lawrence Co., MO, 2 Sept. 1976.

## North American Fishes • Plate #35 • Darters

*Etheostoma boschungi*. 60 mm SL male, Shoal
Creek, Lawrence Co., TN, 16 May 1978.

*Etheostoma boschungi*. 67 mm SL female, Shoal
Creek, Lawrence Co., TN, 16 May 1978.

*Etheostoma cragini*. 41 mm SL male, trib., Spring
River, Lawrence Co., MO, 2 Sept. 1976.

*Etheostoma cragini*. 43 mm SL female, trib., Spring
River, Lawrence Co., MO, 2 Sept. 1976.

*Etheostoma pallididorsum*. 43 mm SL male, Caddo River, Montgomery Co., AR, 26 May 1978.

*Etheostoma pallididorsum*. 41 mm SL female, Caddo River, Montgomery Co., AR, 26 May 1978.

*Etheostoma whipplei*. 57 mm SL male, Heard Branch, Crawford Co., AR, 31 Mar. 1980.

*Etheostoma whipplei*. 52 mm SL female, Heard Branch, Crawford Co., AR, 31 Mar. 1980.

## North American Fishes • Plate #36 • *Darters*

*Etheostoma radiosum*. 44 mm SL male, Caddo River, Montgomery Co., AR, 26 May 1978.

*Etheostoma radiosum*. 43 mm SL female, Caddo River, Montgomery Co., AR, 26 May 1978.

*Etheostoma ditrema*. 42 mm SL male, pond (Conasauga drainage), Murray Co., GA, 24 Feb. 1978.

*Etheostoma ditrema*. 33 mm SL female, pond (Conasauga drainage), Murray Co., GA, 24 Feb. 1978.

*Etheostoma nuchale.* 34 mm SL male, Roebuck Spring, Jefferson Co., AL, 17 Aug. 1978.

*Etheostoma swaini.* 46 mm SL male, Sandy Hook Creek, Marion Co., MS, 3 Mar. 1978.

*Etheostoma nuchale.* 32 mm SL female, Roebuck Spring, Jefferson Co., AL, 17 Aug. 1978.

*Etheostoma swaini.* 48 mm SL female, Sandy Hook Creek, Marion Co., MS, 3 Mar. 1978.

## North American Fishes • Plate #37 • *Darters*

*Etheostoma collettei.* 57 mm SL male, Little Corney Bayou, Union Pa., LA, 18 Feb. 1977.

*Etheostoma asprigene.* 54 mm SL male, trib., Cache River, 1 mi. S Unity, Alexander Co., IL, 27 Oct. 1979.

*Etheostoma collettei.* 50 mm SL female, Little Corney Bayou, Union Pa., LA, 18 Feb. 1977.

*Etheostoma asprigene.* 45 mm SL female, trib., Cache R., 1 mi. S Unity, Alexander Co., IL, 27 Oct. 1979.

*Etheostoma caeruleum caeruleum.* 46 mm SL male, South Fork Little Red R., Van Buren Co., AR, 25 May 1978.

*Etheostoma c. caeruleum.* 47 mm SL female, Bledsoe Creek, Sumner Co., TN, 18 Oct. 1977.

*Etheostoma c. caeruleum.* 50 mm SL male, Jordan Creek, Vermilion Co., IL, 2 May 1980.

*Etheostoma c. subspecies.* 51 mm SL male, Beaver Creek, Taney Co., MO, 25 Apr. 1978.

# North American Fishes • Plate #38 • Darters

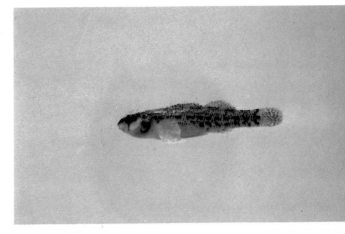

*Etheostoma luteovinctum.* 50 mm SL male, Wartrace Creek, Bedford Co., TN, 2 Mar. 1977.

*Etheostoma luteovinctum.* 36 mm SL female, Wartrace Creek, Bedford Co., TN, 2 Mar. 1977.

*Etheostoma lepidum.* 45 mm SL male, Comal Creek, Comal Co., TX, 16 Feb. 1977.

*Etheostoma lepidum.* 35 mm SL female, Comal Creek, Comal Co., TX, 16 Feb. 1977.

Etheostoma spectabile uniporum. 40 mm SL male, Myatt Creek, Fulton Co., AR, 30 Mar. 1980.

Etheostoma s. fragi. 48 mm SL male, Piney Fork, Izard Co., AR, 30 Mar. 1980.

Etheostoma s. pulchellum. 45 mm SL male, Little Frog Bayou, Crawford Co., AR, 31 Mar. 1980.

Etheostoma s. squamosum. 45 mm SL male, Spring River, Lawrence Co., MO, 25 Apr. 1978.

## North American Fishes • Plate #39 • Darters

Etheostoma s. spectabile. 42 mm SL male, Osage Fork, Webster Co., MO, 18 March 1977.

Etheostoma s. spectabile. 47 mm SL male, trib., Goose Creek, Russell Co., KY, 18 Mar. 1978.

Etheostoma s. spectabile. 56 mm SL male, Buffalo River, Lawrence Co., TN, 14 Apr. 1978.

Etheostoma s. spectabile. 46 mm SL female, Jordan Creek, Vermilion Co., IL, 2 May 1980.

*Etheostoma hopkinsi.* 45 mm SL male, Log Creek, Edgefield Co., SC, 24 June 1977.

*Etheostoma hopkinsi.* 40 mm SL female, Log Creek, Edgefield Co., SC, 24 June 1977.

*Etheostoma australe.* 47 mm SL male, Rio Santa Isabel, Chihuahua, 24 Feb. 1979.

*Etheostoma australe.* 41 mm SL female, Rio Santa Isabel, Chihuahua, 24 Feb. 1979.

# North American Fishes • *Plate #40* • *Darters*

*Etheostoma grahami.* 35 mm SL male, Devils River, Val Verde Co., TX, 29 May 1978.

*Etheostoma grahami.* 32 mm SL female, Devils River, Val Verde Co., TX, 29 May 1978.

*Etheostoma pottsi.* 41 mm SL male, Rio Atotonilco, Zacatecas, 14 July 1975.

*Etheostoma pottsi.* 36 mm SL female, Rio Atotonilco, Zacatecas, 14 July 1975.

*Etheostoma olivaceum.* 56 mm SL male, Brush
Creek, Smith Co., TN, 16 Apr. 1978.

*Etheostoma squamiceps.* 63 mm SL male, Ferguson
Cr., Livingston Co., KY, 26 Apr. 1975 (alcohol-spec.).

*Etheostoma olivaceum.* 47 mm SL female, Brush
Creek, Smith Co., TN, 16 Apr. 1978.

*Etheostoma squamiceps.* 58 mm SL male, Wartrace
Creek, Bedford Co., TN, 20 Apr. 1977.

# North American Fishes • Plate #41 • Darters

*Etheostoma squamiceps.* 61 mm SL male, Buffler
Spring, Lauderdale Co., AL, 14 Aug. 1978.

*Etheostoma neopterum.* 48 mm SL male, Beaver-
dam Cr., Benton Co., TN, 12 May 1973 (alcohol-spec.).

*Etheostoma squamiceps.* 42 mm SL female, Rich-
land Creek, Davidson Co., TN, 1 Mar. 1977.

*Etheostoma neopterum.* 47 mm SL female, Jona-
than Creek, Calloway Co., KY, 15 July 1980.

Etheostoma flabellare. 51 mm SL male, North Branch Kishwaukee River, McHenry Co., IL, 7 May 1980.

Etheostoma flabellare. 53 mm SL male, Catawba River, McDowell Co., NC, 12 June 1976.

Etheostoma flabellare. 46 mm SL male, Little Alamance Creek, Guilford Co., NC, 26 June 1977.

Etheostoma flabellare. 53 mm SL female, Roanoke River, Roanoke Co., VA, 30 Apr. 1979.

# North American Fishes • Plate #42 • *Darters*

Etheostoma kennicotti. 36 mm SL female, Big Creek, Hardin Co., IL, 10 Apr. 1979.

Etheostoma kennicotti. 49 mm SL male, Big Creek, Hardin Co., IL, 10 Apr. 1979.

Etheostoma virgatum. 56 mm SL male, trib., Indian Creek, Jackson Co., KY, 20 May 1980.

Etheostoma virgatum. 47 mm SL female, trib., Indian Creek, Jackson Co., KY, 20 May 1980.

Etheostoma obeyense. 64 mm SL male, Smith
Creek, Clinton Co., KY, 21 May 1980.

Etheostoma obeyense. 47 mm SL female, Smith
Creek, Clinton Co., KY, 21 May 1980.

Etheostoma smithi. 40 mm SL male, Bradley Creek,
Rutherford Co., TN, 14 Apr. 1978.

Etheostoma smithi. 31 mm SL female, Ferguson
Creek, Livingston Co., KY, 10 Apr. 1979.

# North American Fishes • Plate #43 • Darters

Etheostoma striatulum. 38 mm SL male, Wartrace
Creek, Bedford Co., TN, 20 Apr. 1977.

Etheostoma striatulum. 36 mm SL female, Wartrace
Creek, Bedford Co., TN, 2 Mar. 1977.

Etheostoma barbouri. 46 mm SL male, trib., Trace
Creek, Casey Co., KY, 20 May 1980.

Etheostoma barbouri. 40 mm SL female, trib., Trace
Creek, Casey Co., KY, 20 May 1980.

*Etheostoma exile.* 51 mm SL male, Wolf Lake, Cook Co., IL, 8 May 1980.

*Etheostoma serriferum.* 38 mm SL male, South River, Bladen Co., NC, 1 May 1979.

*Etheostoma exile.* 43 mm SL female, Wolf Lake, Cook Co., IL, 8 May 1980.

*Etheostoma serriferum.* 34 mm SL female, South River, Bladen Co., NC, 1 May 1979.

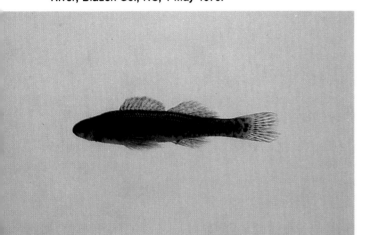

## North American Fishes • Plate #44 • Darters

*Etheostoma gracile.* 44 mm SL male, Wades Creek, Calloway Co., KY, 11 Apr. 1979.

*Etheostoma zoniferum.* 36 mm SL male, Chilatchee Creek, Dallas Co., AL, 23 July 1980.

*Etheostoma gracile.* 39 mm SL female, Max Creek, Johnson Co., IL, 10 Apr. 1979.

*Etheostoma zoniferum.* 24 mm SL female, Chilatchee Creek, Dallas Co., AL, 23 July 1980.

Etheostoma fusiforme. 39 mm SL male, Chenerie
Lake, Ouachita Pa., LA, 21 June 1980.

Etheostoma fusiforme. 43 mm SL female, Chenerie
Lake, Ouachita Pa., LA, 21 June 1980.

Etheostoma saludae. 40 mm SL male, trib., Little
Saluda River, Saluda Co., SC, 3 May 1979.

Etheostoma saludae. 40 mm SL female, trib., Little
Saluda River, Saluda Co., SC, 3 May 1979.

# North American Fishes • Plate #45 • Darters

Etheostoma collis. 50 mm SL male, North Fork
Crooked Creek, Union Co., NC, 2 May 1979.

Etheostoma collis. 42 mm SL female, North Fork
Crooked Creek, Union Co., NC, 2 May 1979.

Etheostoma proeliare. 28 mm SL male, Max Creek,
Johnson Co., IL, 10 Apr. 1979.

Etheostoma proeliare. 30 mm SL female, Max
Creek, Johnson Co., IL, 26 Feb. 1976.

*Etheostoma microperca*. 31 mm SL male, trib., Iroquois River, Iroquois Co., IL, 8 May 1980.

*Etheostoma microperca*. 29 mm SL female, trib., Iroquois River, Iroquois Co., IL, 8 May 1980.

*Etheostoma fonticola*. 32 mm SL male, San Marcos River, Hays Co., TX, 16 Feb. 1977.

*Etheostoma proeliare* spawning in an aquarium. Eggs are being attached to the leaf.

*Etheostoma atripinne* spawning in an aquarium. Eggs are being deposited on the rock.

*Etheostoma squamiceps* spawning in an aquarium. Eggs are being attached to the underside of the stone.

Big South Fork Cumberland River, Scott Co., TN, 30 Sept. 1978. Swift rocky riffles contain *Percina squamata*, *P. caprodes*, *Etheostoma camurum*, *E. caeruleum*, *E. maculatum*, *E. tippecanoe*, *E. blennioides*, and *E. zonale*; adjacent pools contain *P. copelandi*, *E. cinereum*, and *E. stigmaeum*.

Gasconade River, LaClede Co., MO, 21 May 1977. Swift rocky riffle is habitat of *Percina evides* and *Etheostoma tetrazonum*.

Gasconade River, LaClede Co., MO, 21 May 1977. Vegetated backwater pool is habitat of *Percina cymatotaenia*.

Tributary of Calfkiller River, Putnam Co., TN, 19 Oct. 1977. Pool is habitat of *Etheostoma etnieri*.

Max Creek, Johnson Co., IL, 4 May 1977. Sluggish mud-bottomed pool is habitat of *Etheostoma chlorosomum*, *E. proeliare*, and *E. gracile*.

Toms Creek, Okaloosa Co., FL, 18 Aug. 1978. Habitat of *Etheostoma okaloosae*.

Buffler Spring, Lauderdale Co., AL, 14 Aug. 1978. Habitat of *Etheostoma tuscumbia*.

*Etheostoma neopterum* male and his nest of eggs on the underside of a stone removed from a stream on 15 April 1978. The male was guarding the eggs prior to their removal from the stream (Page & Mayden, 1979).

Caddo River headwaters, Montgomery Co., AR, 26 May 1978 (photo by R.L. Mayden). Habitat for *Etheostoma pallididorsum*.

*Ammocrypta pellucida* buried in sand in an aquarium. The habit of burying in sand with only the eyes and top of the head exposed is probably typical behavior of all sand darters.

## *Stizostedion vitreum* (Mitchill) • Walleye

RANGE: Northwest Territories in Canada into northern Labrador, then south along the Atlantic Coast to North Carolina, west to Arkansas.
HABITS: A very voracious fish whose greed makes it a year-round game fish within its range. It is a favorite ice-fishing target and has been transplanted into hundreds of lakes throughout its range, with stocking by the millions being the norm.
WATER CONDITIONS: The fish likes still water lakes that run deep and don't freeze solid. Suitable for unheated tanks. Feeds both day and night.
SIZE: A prized food fish and game fish. Reaches 15 pounds but most are caught at less than half that weight.
FOOD REQUIREMENTS: Eats everything small enough to swallow in terms of live foods; easy to acclimate to chunky pieces of beef, fish, shrimp, and large pellets.

## *Agonostomus monticola* (Bancroft) • Mountain Mullet

RANGE: Fresh waters surrounding the Caribbean Sea and Gulf of Mexico.
HABITS: A freshwater and brackish water fish that apparently spawns in the sea since fry were found in the sea but not in fresh water.
WATER CONDITIONS: Not fussy about water chemistry, but does best in clean, clear water between 15 and 25°C. Water should be aerated and filtered.
SIZE: Attains a length of 25 to 30 cm.
FOOD REQUIREMENTS: Basically a plankton feeder. Thrives on brine shrimp, clouds of daphnia, and other small crustaceans. Can be trained to a prepared aquarium diet.

## *Dormitator maculatus* (Bloch) • Spotted Sleeper

RANGE: Atlantic coastal waters from the Carolinas to Brazil.
HABITS: Inactive and predatory; should not be kept with small fishes.
WATER CONDITIONS: Water should have a salt content, about a quarter teaspoonful per liter. Temperatuare 21 to 24°C
SIZE: To 25 cm.
FOOD REQUIREMENTS: Eats anything and everything; bits of raw fish are especially relished.

## *Cottus bairdi* Girard • Mottled Sculpin

RANGE: Widely dispersed from Georgia and Alabama north through Labrador and west to the entire Great Lakes system. . .skipping over to the Pacific northwest.
HABITS: There are dozens of color varieties and this fish is known by many names in various parts of North America. Spawns in early summer, May, and early June. Likes sandy bottom lakes and streams.
WATER CONDITIONS: Prefers cool, clean water at 16°C. Best kept in unheated aquaria. Water chemistry not important as long as the water is clean.
SIZE: Averages about 76 mm.
FOOD REQUIREMENTS: Eats everything small enough to ingest. Especially fond of other fishes' eggs. Thrives on brine shrimp, both live and frozen.

## *Perca flavescens* (Mitchill) • Yellow Perch

RANGE: Ranges around the world in the northern hemisphere since the Yellow Perch of North America is considered by many to be identical to the Eurasian perch *P. fluviatilis*.
HABITS: This is a major commercial and sport fish. It spawns in the spring from mid-April to mid-May, except far north where it spawns later. Spawning habits are not precisely known but it has never spawned in captivity.
WATER CONDITIONS: Unheated, very large aquaria with clean, clear water. Does best with water temperatures between 8-15°C.
SIZE: A large size yellow perch is 260 mm.
FOOD REQUIREMENTS: Eats everything living and small enough to ingest from fishes to insects. Can be trained to the more usual aquarium diet.

## *Cichlasoma cyanoguttatum* (Baird & Girard) • Texas Cichlid

RANGE: Southern Texas and northern Mexico.
HABITS: All the bad cichlid habits: digs a great deal and uproots plants; usually quarrelsome if kept with other fishes.
WATER CONDITIONS: Not critical; not sensitive to temperature drops. Best breeding temperature about 24°C.
SIZE: In native waters up to 30 cm. In captivity seldom exceeds 15 cm.
FOOD REQUIREMENTS: Larger specimens require chunks of food, such as cut-up earthworms or pieces of beef heart or other lean meat.

## *Mugil cephalus* Linnaeus • Striped Mullet

RANGE: Throughout the southern United States in fresh water, brackish water, and pure ocean water.
HABITS: This fish is found in a very wide range of habitats from the Gulf of Mexico in very deep waters, to shallow ponds, streams, and bayous.
WATER CONDITIONS: Warmer waters and lots of room. Does well in large tropical aquariums with either fresh, brackish or salt water. Thrives at temperatures over 20°C.
SIZE: May reach 60 cm, but usually found at half that size.
FOOD REQUIREMENTS: A plankton feeder. Eats brine shrimp when small.

## *Gobioides broussonetti* Lacepede • Violet Goby

RANGE: Most common in brackish water marshes of the Gulf of Mexico; rarely found in deep waters.
HABITS: A shallow water species that attacks any size fish to defend its eggs. A very beautiful fish.
WATER CONDITIONS: Brackish water is preferred; but adapts to fresh and marine environments; temperatures above 18°C.
SIZE: Maximum about 50 cm; small aquarium sizes (under 10 cm) are difficult to find.
FOOD REQUIREMENTS: Eats small crustaceans. Thrives on live brine shrimp and tubifex worms.

Stizostedion vitreum

Perca flavescens

Agonostomus monticola

Cichlasoma cyanoguttatum

Dormitator maculatus

Mugil cephalus

Cottus bairdi

Gobioides broussonetti

# Eurasian Region

## *Huso huso* (Linnaeus) • Beluga Sturgeon

RANGE: Caspian and Black Seas, Volga River.
HABITS: The largest sturgeon and a major source of caviar since a female could have as many as 5 million eggs. Small fish are released into the aquarium trade (from Hungary where they are cultivated). They are interesting aquarium fish, constantly swimming about the tank.
WATER CONDITIONS: A coldwater fish that requires lots of room and copious amounts of food because of its rapid growth rate. May be stunted in a small aquarium. Requires aerated, clean water.
SIZE: Probably lives as long as the average man and grows to 9 m (almost 30 feet) and may weigh almost 1½ tons.
FOOD REQUIREMENTS: In the aquarium they do well on a diet of chopped fish. They take a long time to find the food so keep them in a dedicated aquarium without competitive fishes.

## *Umbra krameri* Walbaum • European Mudminnow

RANGE: Danube and Baltic River systems.
HABITS: Stays around the muddy bottoms of lakes and streams.
WATER CONDITIONS: Colder waters. Does best in unheated aquaria. Not sensitive to most unpolluted water chemistries.
SIZE: Females may reach 115 mm; males smaller.
FOOD REQUIREMENTS: Thrive on small crustaceans but may be acclimated to other foods.

## *Alburnoides bipunctatus* (Bloch) • Tailorfish

RANGE: Central, temperate Europe to the U.S.S.R.
HABITS: Resembles the bleak but prefers fast-moving waters. In an aquarium it must have cold, highly aerated water.
WATER CONDITIONS: Cold water fish that can take temperatures as low as freezing but not higher than 22°C for very long. Water should be clean.
SIZE: 15 cm is the maximum size.
FOOD REQUIREMENTS: Eats live brine shrimp and daphnia; can be acclimated to the usual aquarium fare.

## *Cyprinus carpio* Linnaeus • Carp

RANGE: Throughout Europe; introduced to every temperate area of the world, more or less.
HABITS: Cultivated in China, Japan, Israel, and eastern Europe. A staple food fish in eastern Europe. Fished for in Pennsylvania and New Jersey. This is the parent stock from which Japanese koi was derived.
WATER CONDITIONS: Thrives in almost any freshwater environment where the water doesn't move too fast. Lakes are its usual habitat. Insensitive to most water chemistry as long as the water is moderately clean. Lives where most other fishes perish.
SIZE: Averages about 3 kg at 50 cm but may grow to 20 kg.
FOOD REQUIREMENTS: Eats everything from plant matter to small living fishes and crustaceans.

## *Acipenser ruthenus* Linnaeus • Sterlet Sturgeon

RANGE: The rivers that drain into the Black, Azov, and Caspian Seas.
HABITS: There are about 15 species of sturgeons in central Europe and about 9 species in North America. They all have the same habits of poking over the bottom with their whiskers. Their eyes are small and they have poor vision.
WATER CONDITIONS: Clean, clear fresh water; unheated aquaria.
SIZE: This is a small species, growing to a maximum length of 125 cm and a weight of 16 kilograms.
FOOD REQUIREMENTS: Chopped fishes is an adequate aquarium diet.

## *Pseudoscaphirhynchus kaufmani* (Bogdanov) • Whiptail Sturgeonfish

RANGE: Amudarja River.
HABITS: Occurs in channels or river beds with sand bottom. Reaches sexual maturity at 25 cm and between 6 and 7 years (females) or 7 or 8 years (males). Spawns in April, releasing 1,000-2,000 eggs (a larger female may release as many as 3,700 eggs). Juveniles descend to the lower parts of the river.
WATER CONDITIONS: Requires clean, clear, unheated water.
SIZE: Attains a length of 60 cm standard length and a weight of about a kilogram.
FOOD REQUIREMENTS: Feeds on aquatic insects as well as the eggs and fry of other fishes.

## *Abramis brama* (Linnaeus) • Bronze Bream

RANGE: British Isles through central Europe to the Caspian Sea basin.
HABITS: Likes warmer waters and is a highly prized game fish in its range. Its usual habitat of lowland waters makes it available inside city limits of many European cities built along rivers.
WATER CONDITIONS: Not sensitive to any particular water conditions providing the water is fresh, unpolluted, and aerated.
SIZE: Reaches to 30 cm.
FOOD REQUIREMENTS: Small fish eat small crustaceans such as brine shrimp, daphnia, and cyclops; larger fish eat larger crustaceans as well as algae, weeds, and organic debris.

## *Alburnus alburnus* (Linnaeus) • Bleak

RANGE: Northern Europe, parts of Scandinavia.
HABITS: A gregarious species that prefers settled waters in lakes and very slow moving streams. Spawns from April to June depending upon the water temperature.
WATER CONDITIONS: Prefers cold water from 5 to 15°C. Does well in large, unheated aquaria.
SIZE: Reaches about 20 cm.
FOOD REQUIREMENTS: This pelagic fish thrives on live brine shrimp and most other living things that are very small, even small schooling fishes. Easily acclimated to aquarium foods.

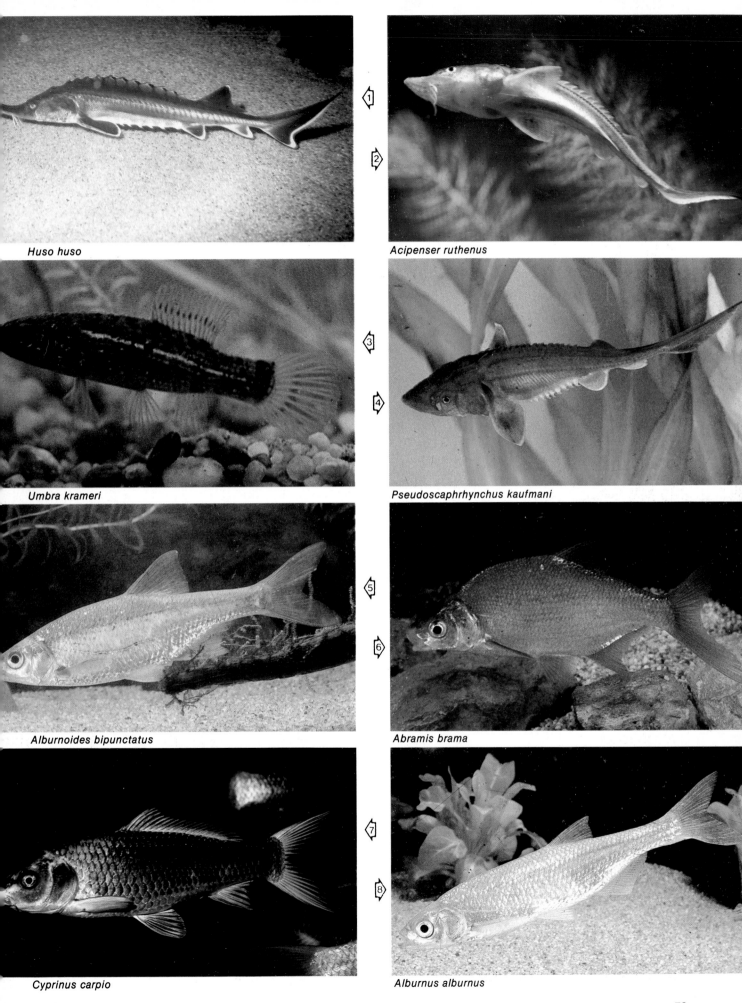

Huso huso

Acipenser ruthenus

Umbra krameri

Pseudoscaphrhynchus kaufmani

Alburnoides bipunctatus

Abramis brama

Cyprinus carpio

Alburnus alburnus

79

## Koi, Japanese Colored Carp

Koi are highly developed forms of the common Carp in a similar way that fancy-tail Guppies are highly developed forms of the common Guppy. The Koi is particularly well suited to keep in a garden pool, where its touch of brilliant colors would add a great deal of decorative effect. The Koi was produced by Japanese breeders. The results came in a great variety of color variations, and selective breeding did the rest. At the present time there are many recognized basic varieties, with the possibility of many more to come.

## Koi Varieties

Because of their size, Koi are basically pool fish and do best in an outdoor environment. They are able to withstand a wide temperature range and are undemanding as to water composition, provided that their water is richly supplied with oxygen. In an outdoor pool, suitable filtration and aeration can easily be provided through the use of the pool filters designed specifically for use with garden ponds. Feeding Koi presents no great problems, as they are heavy eaters and accept a wide variety of foods. Worms, shrimp, insects and insect larvae form the major portion of the Koi diet, but vegetable materials in the form of chopped terrestrial and aquatic plants must be included as regular portions. Although Koi are heavy eaters, they will not eat food that is left to stagnate in their pool, so all uneaten food should be removed immediately. After they become accustomed to their surroundings Koi are quite willing to accept food right from their owner's fingers.

Koi breed substantially the same as goldfish, scattering their eggs into the fine leaves or root systems of plants (water lettuce and water hyacinths are ideal) after a vigorous chase by the males of the females. Normally, more than one male per female is used. Sex differences among mature Koi are easily distinguishable; viewed from directly above, females will be seen to be much stockier from behind the head to just behind the dorsal fin.

Maruten-Kohaku (Gin-Goke)

Sandan-Kohaku (Gin-Goke)

Hana-Shusui

Taisho-Sanke

Taisho-Sanke

Tancho-Sanke

Doitsu Taisho-Sanke

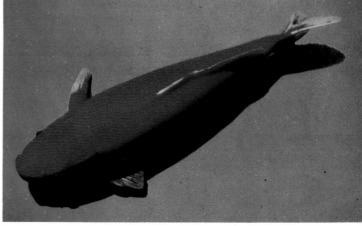
Aka-Muji

81

Doitsu Kuyaku

Hikari-Moyo-Mono

Showa Sanke

Kawari-Mono

Shiro-Utsuri

Hikari Shiro-Utsuri

Shiro-Bekko Ginlin

Doitsu Ogon

*Plate #52 • Koi*

82

Asagi

Asagi

Yamabuki Ogon or Ogon (Gold)

Harewake-Ogon or Ogon (Platinum)

Matsuba-Ogon or Ogon (Orange)

Kin Ki-Utsuri

Sakura Kanoko Ogon

Kohaku-Ginrin

*Plate #53 • Koi*

## Goldfish (*Carassius auratus*)

The hobby of fish-keeping owes its popularity more than anything else to the Goldfish. Goldfish are mentioned as early as 970 A.D. by the Chinese, and in the sixteenth century their care and breeding, which were at first playthings of the nobility, became commonplace and a number of fancy breeds were developed. Because of their innate love for beauty and living things, the Chinese and Japanese have remained the world leaders in the development and production of the many fancy breeds of Goldfish available today. We see such freakish fish as the Lionhead, Pompon, Telescope, Celestial, Eggfish and many others too numerous for this small space. There are fish with short single fins and others with long flowing fins. Some breeds have double fins; some have large, sail-like dorsal fins; and others have no dorsal fin at all. Some are pure white; others are midnight black. Still others vary from light yellow to deep red, and some are peppered with red, white, black, yellow and even blue. Goldfish have a wide temperature tolerance, and fish which have been kept outdoors can live under a layer of ice for quite a time. They are also kept successfully in the tropics.

## Fancy Goldfish Varieties

It seems that the lessened popularity of the common Goldfish has come about as result of the recognition on the part of hobby newcomers of the advantages the true tropical fishes have over Goldfish. However, warm-water fish tanks within the home have not greatly affected the interest in fancy Goldfish varieties. Really good Goldfish of the hard-to-get varieties are eagerly sought after and command high prices. Unfortunately, not enough hobbyists ever get a chance to see some of the fancier varieties; the excellent Goldfish photos shown here will help to make these products of patient and skillful breeding programs more familiar to everyone.

Common

Comet

Pearl Scale

Pearl Scale

Calico Fantail

Red Curly-Tail Fantail

Japanese Fantail (Ryukin)

Veiltail

Lionhead

Lionhead

Oranda (Immature)

Redcap, Tancho or Hon Tou

Young Bubble-Eye

Bubble-Eye

Bubble-Eye

Bubble-Eye

*Plate #55 • Goldfishes*

Chinese Oranda (Hi-Cap)

Chinese Oranda (Hi-Cap)

Oranda

Chinese Oranda (Hi-Cap)

Telescope Calico

Albino Oranda

Telescope Black Moor

Telescope Black Moor

*Plate #56* • *Goldfishes*

87

Gobio gobio

Barbus barbus

Tinca tinca

Tinca tinca

Blicca bjoerkna

Carassius carassius

Alburnoides bipunctatus

Alburnoides bipunctatus

Plate #57

*Leuciscus idus (var.)*

*Leuciscus idus*

*Gnathopogon chankaensis*

*Leuciscus cephalus*

*Ctenopharyngodon idella*

*Gobio gobio*

*Carassius carassius*

*Chondrostomas nasus*

Plate #57A

89

## *Phoxinus phoxinus* (Linnaeus) • Eurasian Dace

RANGE: Throughout Europe and the U.S.S.R.
HABITS: Inhabits every type of clean, clear water, even high up in the Alps (to 2000 m). Must be kept in a large, unheated aquarium with lots of room. This is the bait fish and food fodder fish for most of central Europe. It occurs in large schools in some lakes.
WATER CONDITIONS: Cold, clean, clear water that is aerated and filtered.
SIZE: Rare specimens get to 12 cm; most are found at 8 cm.
FOOD REQUIREMENTS: Eats small crustaceans, diatoms, algae, and higher plants.

## *Scardineus erythrophthalmus* (Linnaeus) • Rudd

RANGE: Throughout central Europe, Scandinavia, and England.
HABITS: Widespread in still and slowly moving waters but not necessarily present in contiguous bodies of water where predators eat them as soon as they appear. A food fish in eastern Europe but not eaten by people of higher economic means.
WATER CONDITIONS: Thrives in many lakes, rivers, and streams. Not fussy about water conditions as long as their aquarium is clean, well filtered, and aerated. This is a coldwater species.
SIZE: Exceptional specimens reach 30 cm. Usually found at 20 cm.
FOOD REQUIREMENTS: Prefers live or frozen foods, but accepts prepared foods when hungry.

## *Vimba vimba* (Linnaeus) • Vimba

RANGE: Isolated areas in Sweden and Germany and along the brackish marshes of the Baltic Sea.
HABITS: Found in the lower reaches of lakes and rivers. Netted in Sweden, where large quantities used to be consumed. The fish usually stays on the bottom of rivers and lakes, but it migrates during the breeding season (as do many fishes), and that's when it is trapped.
WATER CONDITIONS: Clean, clear, aerated water. Does better in slightly brackish water with a specific gravity of about 1.005.
SIZE: Rarely reaches its maximum growth of about 50 cm.
FOOD REQUIREMENTS: Mostly a mollusc and worm eater, but it feeds on several other categories of living foods when its special foods are not available. Can be weaned to chopped fish in the aquarium.

## *Acanthorhodeus asmussi* (Dybowski) • Russian Bitterling, Gorchak

RANGE: Occurs in the middle and lower Amur River basin.
HABITS: Reaches sexual maturity in its third year (at 7+ cm). Spawns from the end of May to July, releasing an average of 300 to 600 eggs (up to 1100). A black spot on the juvenile disappears with growth.
WATER CONDITIONS: Acclimates to aquarium life relatively easily. An unheated tank with scattered rocks and cleaned mussel shells is recommended.
SIZE: Attains a length of 16 cm on the average.
FOOD REQUIREMENTS: Feeds on aquatic plants.

## *Rhodeus sericeus* (Pallas) • Bitterling

RANGE: Throughout central Europe.
HABITS: A unique fish whose relatives join it in laying their eggs inside mussels belonging to the genera *Anodonta*, *Pseudanodonta*, and *Unio*. In return the Bitterling is the host of the parasitic early stages of the mussels.
WATER CONDITIONS: A very popular aquarium fish that is very difficult to spawn. Aquarists introduced it into English waters (Lancashire and Cheshire) in the 1920's but it has since become expensive and probably has been seined out of existence in England.
SIZE: A small fish that rarely reaches its maximum size of 10 cm.
FOOD REQUIREMENTS: Eats most aquarium diets but prefers mosquito larvae and small crustaceans.

## *Tinca tinca* (Linnaeus) • Tench

RANGE: Throughout central Europe including the British Isles.
HABITS: A stillwater fish occurring mostly in lakes. They have a great ability to survive in marginal water situations and can be raised side-by-side with carp in many fish farms.
WATER CONDITIONS: They thrive in unaerated, unfiltered water where most other fishes perish, but they do best in clean, cool, aerated water providing they do not have aggressive tankmates.
SIZE: Reaches a maximum of about 63 cm but usually are caught at half that size.
FOOD REQUIREMENTS: Young fish eat algae; older fish eat everything found on the bottom of a lake including snails and water fleas of all types. In the aquarium it eats the usual aquarium diet for coldwater fishes.

## *Chilogobio czerskii* Berg • Rainbow gudgeon, Peskar

RANGE: Amur River basin.
HABITS: Reaches sexual maturity in third year (about 6 cm). It has a short spawning season (June-July) when it deposits its large yellowish eggs. Juveniles have a dark longitudinal stripe and will school with fishes similarly patterned.
WATER CONDITIONS: Requires an unheated aquarium with relatively clean water.
SIZE: Attains a length of 11 cm.
FOOD REQUIREMENTS: Will accept many of the live foods available to aquarists.

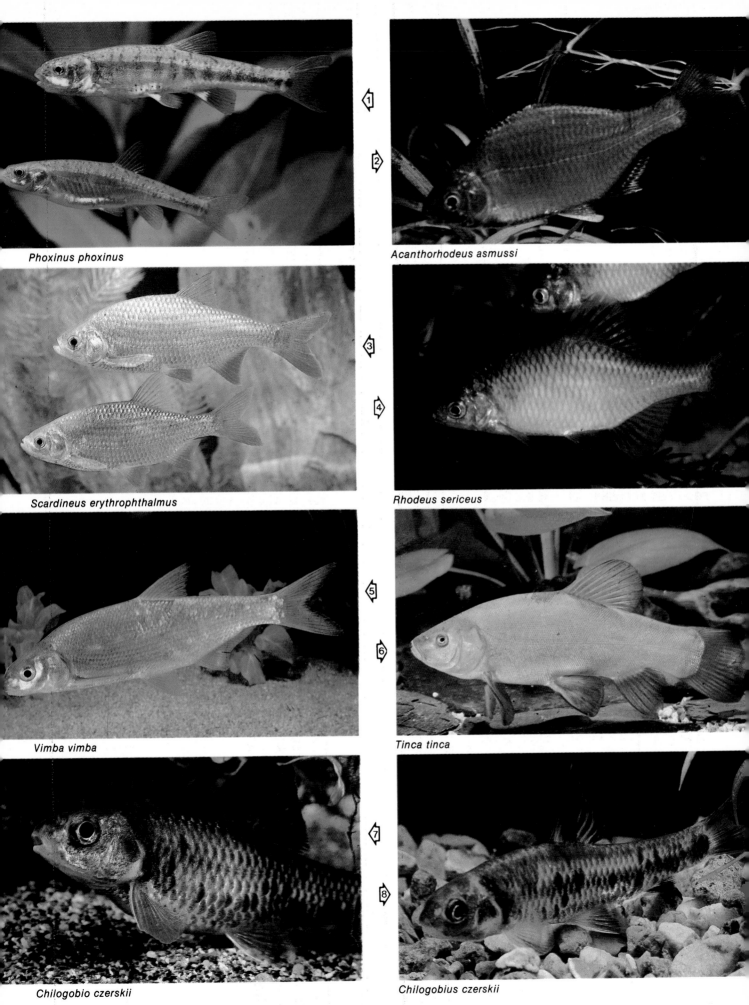

*Phoxinus phoxinus*

*Acanthorhodeus asmussi*

*Scardineus erythrophthalmus*

*Rhodeus sericeus*

*Vimba vimba*

*Tinca tinca*

*Chilogobio czerskii*

*Chilogobius czerskii*

91

*Leucaspius delineatus*

*Phoxinus phoxinus*

*Scardineus erythrophthalmus*

*Rhodeus sericeus*

*Rutilus rutilus*

*Chondrostoma nasus*

*Ctenopharyngodon idella*

*Leuciscus idus*

Plate #58A

*Cobitis taenia*

*Leptobotia mantchurica*

*Lefua costata* (female)

*Lefua costata*

*Nemacheilus kessleri*

*Nemacheilus barbatulus*

*Misgurnus fossilis* (var.)

*Misgurnus fossilis*

*Plate #59*

93

A loach of the genus *Niwaela*

*Misgurnus anguillicaudatus*

Golden form of *Misgurnus anguillicaudatus*

Above and below: *Leptobotia curta*

*Nemacheilus barbatulus toni*

*Cobitis taenia*

*Cobitis biwae*

*Cobitis taenia taenia*

*Cobitis taenia taenia*

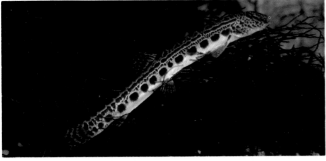

Left and right above: The same loach shown over different substrates

*Cobitis taenia striata*

*Cobitis taenia striata (spotted form)*

*Cobitis takatsuenis*

*Cobitis takatsuensis*

Nemacheilus barbatulus

Sarcochilichthys sinensis lacustris

Perca fluviatilis

Anguilla anguilla

Pungitius pungitius

Stizostedion lucioperca

Aphanius iberus

Cottus gobio

Plate #61A

*Pseudobagrus fulvidraco*

*Pelteobagrus brashnikowi*

*Siniperca chuatsi*

*Silurus glanis*

*Perca fluviatilis*

*Stizostedion lucioperca*

*Perccottus glehni*

*Proterorhinus marmoratus*

Plate #62

97

Spawning Bitterlings

Bitterlings are small freshwater fishes that are found throughout the entire temperate zone of Europe, eastward through Russia and China, and into Korea and Japan. As far as is known, they spawn by laying their eggs in living mussels. They may be the only group of fishes that do this, though many small cichlids in Africa and South America lay their eggs inside dead, vacated snail shells.

Depending upon the species, the bitterling searches for a suitable mussel in early spring, summer, or fall. The male is the one that does the hunting. When he finds a suitable mussel he has a way of teasing the mussel to make it open its shell. Once it has been able to do this, the male then searches for a suitable female with a clearly projecting ovipositor (egg tube). During this time the male protects the mussel from other fishes, especially other male bitterlings.

When a female is encountered, she is wooed onto the spawning mussel and deposits her eggs in the inlet siphon of the mussel. She may lay from one to six eggs at a time. Then the male takes a position over the inlet siphon and releases sperm. This continues for an hour or two until the female is depleted. Both fish then leave the scene and the eggs become attached to the areas between the mussel's gills. They remain there for up to a month before they hatch.

The fry of most species are between 6 and 8 mm in length when they have absorbed their yolk sacs. They do not parasitize the mussel but rely upon the food stored in their egg sacs. The mussel seems to be annoyed by these wriggling fry and "exhales" them with its waste breathing water. During their stay within the mussel, many of the fry become parasitized by mussel larvae, and when the fry are liberated they have a cargo of mussel larvae attached to them. The mussel larvae feed on the juices of the developing fish, but there are never enough larvae to seriously hurt the developing bitterling. This then ensures the distribution of the mussel, as the mussel larvae fall off after a few weeks.

The aquarist would find it almost impossible to obtain the exact kind of freshwater mussel to which a particular species of bitterling is attracted in nature, but many bitterlings will accept almost any healthy mussel as a host for their eggs. Some species will spawn readily in a well-aerated clean tank kept at room temperature and stocked with several types of local mussels.

After spawning, the breeders should be placed in a separate tank and the mussel be allowed to roam about the sandy bottom of the tank. No filtration should be used, as the mussel gets its food by filtering microorganisms from the water. Use only enough aeration to keep the surface of the water broken. The bitterling fry require freshly hatched brine shrimp when they appear and soon graduate to powdery fine foods.

*Tanakia tanago*

*Acheilognathus cyanostigma*

*Acheilognathus lanceolata*

*Acheilognathus tabira tabira*

*Acheilognathus tabira*

*Acheilognathus moriokae*

*Acheilognathus limbata*

*Acheilognathus rhombea*

Rhodeus ocellatus ocellatus

Rhodeus ocellatus

Above and below: *Rhodeus ocellatus* spawning

Rhodeus suigensis

*Plate #64 • Bitterlings*

Rhodeus ocellatus

100

*Acheilognathus longipinnis*

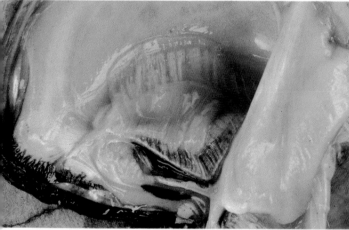

*Barbodes sinensis*

*Rhodeus sericeus*

Above and below: Eggs and fry of *Rhodeus ocellatus* in the gills of mussels.

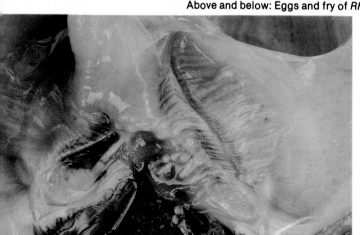

Plate #65 • Bitterlings

# Neotropical Region

## Freshwater Stingrays

The stingrays shown on the facing page were all collected by the author (HRA) in Brazil. These are small rays that are typical of those exported in the aquarium trade. Most are juveniles and have lots of growing to do. Most South American freshwater stingrays grow to a diameter of about one meter, but some are a bit larger. Stingrays are not recommended for the home aquarium because the stings are venomous and dangerous. The fish also spend most of their time half buried in the sand and are difficult to feed unless some shellfish are available for them.

In Brazil, these rays are found lying semi-hidden in the sand close to shore. They burrow through the top layer of the sand in search of small clams, mussels, and invertebrates living in the sand. The natives who live where stingrays are found are very wary of stepping on them and usually patrol the beach areas with a raised harpoon ready to lance the familiar sandy outline of the hidden stingray.

The Brazilian stingrays have very powerful teeth that easily crush the shells of the most dense-shelled animals. Clams are their preferred diet, though freshwater mussels are equally acceptable. In the aquarium they may be trained to take a clam or mussel from your hand . . . but be careful, for many of these stingrays can swing their tails forward as well as sideward. I once saw a Brazilian Indian so crazy with the pain of a sting that he tried to commit suicide by running headfirst into a tree! Children in the jungle have sometimes been painfully killed by diving into shallow water, landing on a buried stingray, and getting lanced in the abdomen. Death may occur within a day of the infliction of an abdominal wound.

Wounds in the hands or feet are never fatal of themselves, but infections following the wound may be fatal if not treated immediately. The wound should be flushed with water either from a hose or from a bucket. Then the wound should be searched for remnants of the spine. All areas should be carefully cut open to probe for tiny hidden pieces of broken spine teeth. This is done carefully with a fine probe to feel for something hard buried in the flesh. The injured part should then be soaked for an hour in the hottest water possible. If it is high on the arm or leg, the wound should be wrapped in heavy towelling and hot water poured on it as often as necessary. The hotter the water the better, but don't scald the patient. After an hour of hot soaks the search for spine fragments should continue. When cleaned, the wound may be sutured and bandaged, and a regimen of antibiotic and anti-tetanus agents should be administered. Professional medical care should be sought as quickly as possible. Of course these treatments should only be emergency first aid treatments; if a doctor or hospital is available, rush the victim there as quickly as possible.

All stingrays are livebearers, giving birth to living young.

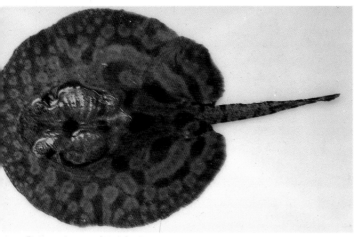

*Potamotrygon hystrix*

*Potamotrygon hystrix*

*Potamotrygon motoro*

*Potamotrygon motoro*

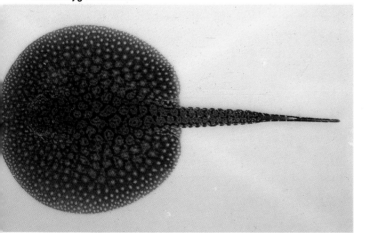

*Potamotrygon reticulatus*

*Pomatotrygon reticulatus*

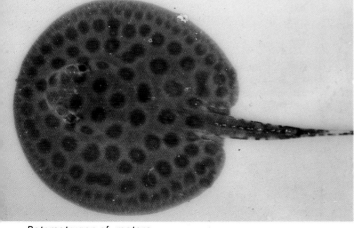

*Potamotrygon cf. motoro*

*Potamotrygon hystrix*

### Osteoglossum ferreirai Kanazawa • Black Arowana

RANGE: Rio Banco tributary of the Rio Negro in Brazil.
HABITS: Large specimens won't hesitate to swallow anything they can cram in their very spacious mouths, but neither adults nor young specimens are quarrelsome with fishes not regarded as food; rather unpredictable in temperament, frequently showing disturbance when there is no visible cause for alarm.
WATER CONDITIONS: Soft, slightly acid water desirable. Temperature 25 to 28°C.
SIZE: Wild adult specimens run up to about 40 cm; juveniles of about 8 cm most often seen.
FOOD REQUIREMENTS: Variable from individual to individual; some will take prepared aquarium foods, while others refuse all except small live fishes.

### Osteoglossum bicirrhosum Vandelli • Arowana

RANGE: Guianas and most parts of the Amazon.
HABITS: Only small ones may be kept together; big ones are best kept alone.
WATER CONDITIONS: Should be moved as little as possible. Temperature 24 to 26°C.
SIZE: To about 60 cm, but usually much smaller.
FOOD REQUIREMENTS: Greatly prefers fishes which can be swallowed whole, but can be trained to take pieces of raw fish, shrimp, etc., from the fingers.

### Lepidosiren parodoxus Fitzinger • South American Lungfish

RANGE: Amazon Basin, South America.
HABITS: This ancient fish is not for the home aquarium. They are very hardy and easy to keep alive, but they hardly ever move and are of little interest other than as a curiosity. They eat almost everything and have a very well-studied history since they are truly "living fossils."
WATER CONDITIONS: These very hardy fish can live under almost any conditions. Even if the water dries out, the fish can make a mud cocoon and last out the drought. Typical aquarium conditions are acceptable.
SIZE: They may grow to 120 cm.
FOOD REQUIREMENTS: These fish are very difficult to feed but may take chunks of fish. Every curator has his own "secret" for keeping lungfishes alive.

### Arapaima gigas (Cuvier) • Arapaima, Pirarucu

RANGE: Entire tropical South American region, usually in the deeper, larger streams.
HABITS: Because of their size, any more than one to a large tank would be unthinkable.
WATER CONDITIONS: Water conditions are not particularly important with this species. Temperature 24 to 27°C.
SIZE: To about 4.5 m in the open; captive specimens seldom over 60 cm.
FOOD REQUIREMENTS: In captivity they will eat nothing but small living fishes.

Osteoglossum ferreirai (juv.)

Osteoglossum ferreirai (young)

Osteoglossum ferreirai (subadult)

Osteoglossum ferreirai (adult)

Osteoglossum bicirrhosum (newly born)

Osteoglossum bicirrhosum (juv.)

Lepidosiren paradoxus

Arapaima gigas

Boulengerella maculata

Hoplerythrinus unitaeniatus

Crenuchus spilurus

Crenuchus spilurus

Characidium fasciatum

Characidium "Dusky"

Characidium cf. fasciatum

Plate #67A

Characidium "Gery"

*Characidium brevirostre*

*Characidium catenatum*

*Poecilocharax weitzmani*

*Crenuchus spilurus*

*Ctenolucius hujeta*

*Boulengerella maculata*

*Hoplerythrinus unitaeniatus*

*Hoplias malabaricus*

Plate #68

109

## *Characidium fasciatum* Reinhardt • Banded Characidium

RANGE: South America, Orinoco region in the north to La Plata region in the south.
HABITS: Comes from streams where there is some current; therefore requires fresh, clean water in an uncrowded aquarium.
WATER CONDITIONS: Clean, well-oxygenated water, about neutral. Temperature should not exceed 24°C.
SIZE: 6 cm.
FOOD REQUIREMENTS: Not a fussy eater, but prefers living foods.

## *Elachocharax junki* Gery • Junk's Darter Tetra

RANGE: Discovered by the author (HRA) in the Rio Madeira, Brazil.
HABITS: A bottom-dwelling fish that scoots about in short jerks from which its name darter tetra derives. Named to honor Dr. Junk of INPA in Manaus, Brazil. Junk is charged with protecting the Amazonian fishes.
WATER CONDITIONS: Clear water, shady situations. Temperature as close to 25°C as possible. Neutral to slightly acid water.
SIZE: A small, chunky fish. The specimens collected average 3.1 cm.
FOOD REQUIREMENTS: Ate small living foods; prefer newly hatched brine shrimp but accepts dry food as well.

## *Characidium* "Gery" • Gery's Characidium

RANGE: Discovered in Brazil by the author (HRA). This undescribed species is known in the trade as *Characidium* "Gery," but this is not to be taken as its scientific name; it has never been scientifically described.
HABITS: Typical habits of South American darter tetras, moving about in a jerky, darting pattern.
WATER CONDITIONS: Slightly acid, still water was used for the first fish imported; they thrived, but they were collected in fast-moving streams.
SIZE: To 5.3 cm.
FOOD REQUIREMENTS: Tubifex worms and other small live foods, but they also accept dried foods small enough to ingest whole.

## *Nannostomus espei* (Meinken) • Barred Pencilfish

RANGE: Guyana.
HABITS: Peaceful and active; a skilled jumper whose tank should be covered.
WATER CONDITIONS: Soft water, neutral to slightly acid. Temperature 24 to 27°C.
SIZE: To 5 cm.
FOOD REQUIREMENTS: Not choosy as to foods, but very partial to live daphnia.

## *Lebiasina panamensis* (Gill) • Panama Pencil

RANGE: Panama, Central America.
HABITS: A devourer of mosquito larvae. This fish is always seen with a full, rotund belly if there are enough mosquito larvae in its habitat. It has been successfully transplanted for mosquito control.
WATER CONDITIONS: Thrives under most non-toxic aquarium conditions. Likes warm water between 25-30°C.
SIZE: Reaches a maximum length of 8.2 cm.
FOOD REQUIREMENTS: Seems to prefer live mosquito larvae, but accepts almost all aquarium foods.

## *Nannostomus beckfordi* Guenther • Beckford's Pencilfish

RANGE: Guianas, Parana, Rio Negro, middle and lower Amazon.
HABITS: Peaceful toward other fishes and plants; should be kept in a group of their own kind or other related species.
WATER CONDITIONS: Prefers soft, slightly acid water but is not intolerant to other types. Temperature 24 to 27°C.
SIZE: To 5 cm.
FOOD REQUIREMENTS: Prefers the smaller living foods, but can be accustomed to taking frozen or dried foods when the others are not available.

## *Nannostomus harrisoni* Eigenmann • Harrison's Pencilfish

RANGE: Guyana and the upper Amazon.
HABITS: Peaceful, a good community tank fish.
WATER CONDITIONS: Aged water that is slightly acid, hardness less than 10 DH and a temperature of 24-27°C. are recommended.
SIZE: Attains a length of about 5-6.5 cm.
FOOD REQUIREMENTS: Small live foods preferred but will eventually accept flake foods.

Characidium fasciatum

Characidium fasciatum

Elachocharax junki

Characidium "Gery"

Nannostomus espei

Lebiasina panamensis

Nannostomus beckfordi

Nannostomus harrisoni

111

*Lebiasina multimaculata*

*Characidium "Diamond"*

*Elachocharax georgiae*

*Elachocharax georgiae*

*Nannostomus digrammus*

*Nannostomus espei*

*Nannostomus unifasciatus*

Plate #69A

*Nannostomus harrisoni*

Pyrrhulina brevis "Aguaro"

Pyrrhulina brevis "Aguaro"

Pyrrhulina brevis "Boa Vista"

Nannostomus eques

Nannostomus unifasciatus

Nannostomus trifasciatus

Nannostomus marginatus

Nannostomus bifasciatus

Plate #70

113

Copella nigrofasciata

Copella nigrofasciata

Pyrrhulina aff. brevis

Copella arnoldi

Copeina guttata

Pyrrhulina brevis (melanistic)

Pyrrhulina cf. rachowiana

Plate #70A

Pyrrhulina laeta

Copella arnoldi

Copella arnoldi

Copella metae

Copeina guttata

Copella metae juvenile

Copella nattereri

Pyrrhulina spilota

Pyrrhulina laeta

*Plate #71*

115

### SPAWNING IN *COPEINA* AND *COPELLA*

Most fishes in a single genus spawn in approximately the same fashion. If one lays adhesive eggs on leaves, so do most of the others. Yet in the single genus *Copella* and its close relative *Copeina* are found three very different spawning methods, one of which is extremely unusual to say the least.

The large, spotted *Copeina guttata* is somewhat unusual among tetras in that it clears a small depression in the substrate (fine silt or sand) and, after a rather brief spawning ritual, lays its eggs in the depression and fertilizes them. In some ways the spawning behavior is similar to that of cichlids although obviously not as "advanced" as in that family.

Most *Copella* species lay their eggs on the substrate, especially large heavy leaves. *Copella metae* is fairly representative of this type of spawning behavior, as shown in the photos.

*Copella arnoldi* and perhaps one or two other species are the "splash tetras" of aquarium legend. They are among the very few fishes known to spawn *totally out of the water*. The spawning pair goes through a short pre-spawning ritual just below the surface of the water and under a large leaf or similar object overhanging the water at the distance of 20-50 mm. At the peak of the "dancing" the male leaps from the water followed by the smaller female. The surface tension of the water on their bodies allows them to adhere to the surface of the leaf for a few seconds, long enough to lay and fertilize the eggs. After the clutch is completed the male stays below the leaf, occasionally splashing the eggs with sprays of water from his tail to keep them moist. The eggs develop rapidly, the fry soon leaving the eggs and dropping into the water below, where they then go through a normal "fishy" life. In the aquarium *Copella arnoldi* has been known to lay its eggs on the sides of the tank above the waterline and on the glass cover. The advantage of laying eggs out of water would seem to be that they are less subject to predators in their niche in the air but still near the water.

The male *Copeina guttata* (farther from camera in both photos above) approaches the female from the side and slightly to the rear as she enters the depression in the gravel to deposit her eggs.

A *Copella metae* pair (male is above female in photo at left, behind female in photo at right) station themselves above the leaf they've selected to receive the eggs.

At left the pair of *Copella arnoldi* (male above) are shown leaving the water; at right they are shown actually adhering to the leaf to which the eggs are being attached.

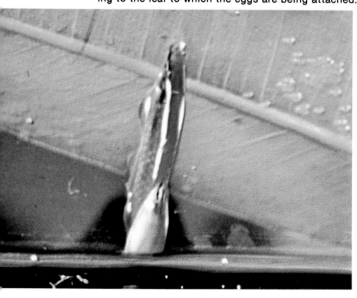

Pyrrhulina aff. brevis

Pyrrhulina laeta

Pyrrhulina cf. rachowiana

Pyrrhulina laeta

Leporellus vittatus

Pyrrhulina aff. brevis

Leporinus arcus

Leporinus arcus

Plate #72A

*Leporinus agassizi*

*Leporinus melanopleura*

*Leporinus nigrotaeniatus*

*Schizodon fasciatum*

*Copella callolepis*

*Copella compta*

*Copella nattereri*

*Copella "Bleher"*

Plate #73

119

## Leporinus jamesi Garman • James's Leporinus

RANGE: This fish came from the Rio Negro, where it was collected by the author (HRA). It probably represents a new subgenus of *Leporinus*.

HABITS: Not much is known about the fish since only few specimens have been found to date. It probably needs acid, warm water since it came from the Rio Negro in Brazil.

WATER CONDITIONS: Slightly acid to neutral.

SIZE: To at least 12.5 cm in length.

FOOD REQUIREMENTS: The stomach contents contained small insects.

## Leporinus pellegrini Steindachner • Striped Leporinus

RANGE: Upper Amazon, Peru and Colombia.

HABITS: This species stays small. At least no large ones have been found, though it it possible that they look different when larger than the specimen shown here.

WATER CONDITIONS: Warm, clear water with a pH of 6.0-7.2; temperature 22-28°C.

SIZE: About 10 cm.

FOOD REQUIREMENTS: Prefers small insects but gets along well on a typical aquarium diet.

## Leporinus octofasciatus Steindachner • Eight-banded Leporinus

RANGE: Southeastern Brazil in larger streams and rivers.

HABITS: In cool, clear, running water. It has never been spawned in the aquarium. It belongs to a group of transverse-banded *Leporinus*, all of which probably are closely related.

WATER CONDITIONS: Water 20-26°C, clear and well aerated.

SIZE: To 15.6 cm.

FOOD REQUIREMENTS: Enjoys live daphnia but quickly adapts to an aquarium diet of prepared foods.

## Leporinus striatus Kner • Striped Leporinus

RANGE: Amazon River south to the Parana in Uruguay.

HABITS: Peaceful and very active; tank should be kept well covered.

WATER CONDITIONS: Neutral to slightly alkaline. Temperature 23 to 26°C.

SIZE: About 30 cm in nature; in captivity about half that.

FOOD REQUIREMENTS: Omnivorous; likes to nibble on plants, so should be given an occasional lettuce or spinach leaf.

## Leporinus pearsoni Fowler • Pearson's Leporinus

RANGE: Colombia.

HABITS: Never spawned in the aquarium. Feeds from the bottom. A jumper that should be maintained in a covered aquarium.

WATER CONDITIONS: Slightly acid to neutral water; 23-28°C.

SIZE: Aquarium specimens are about 15 cm long; in nature they reach 30 cm.

FOOD REQUIREMENTS: While they prefer daphnia, they do well on most aquarium diets.

## Leporinus fasciatus (Bloch) • Banded Leporinus

RANGE: Widely distributed in South America from the Guianas to the La Plata.

HABITS: Active and peaceful toward other fishes, but inclined to be destructive to plants; keep their tank covered because they jump.

WATER CONDITIONS: Neutral to slightly alkaline water. Being active, they require a good-sized tank. Temperature 23 to 26°C.

SIZE: In their home waters to 33 cm; in captivity, seldom over 15 cm.

FOOD REQUIREMENTS: Omnivorous, with a preference for vegetable matter; crushed lettuce leaves or spinach leaves should be frequently provided.

## Leporinus multifasciatus Cuvier • Many-banded Leporinus

RANGE: Rio Branco, Brazil, probably going as far north as Guyana.

HABITS: There are many look-alikes in the *Leporinus fasciatus* complex; their appearance changes as they get larger and their bands either split like the one shown here or disappear as in *L. pellegrini*. They are probably all closely related.

WATER CONDITIONS: Warm, clear water, pH 5.8-7.4. Temperature 23-30°C.

SIZE: This specimen was caught on hook and line and measured about 30 cm.

FOOD REQUIREMENTS: Insects are preferred in nature, but in the aquarium they thrive on a typical aquarium diet.

## Leporinus arcus Eigenmann • Lipstick Leporinus

RANGE: Venezuela, the Guianas and parts of Brazil.

HABITS: Peaceful; likely to jump out of an uncovered tank.

WATER CONDITIONS: Neutral to slightly acid. Temperature 23 to 26°C.

SIZE: Reaches 40 cm, but only 5-10 cm when imported.

FOOD REQUIREMENTS: Live and frozen foods preferred; should have an occasional lettuce leaf to nibble on.

Leporinus jamesi

Leporinus pearsoni

Leporinus pellegrini

Leporinus fasciatus

Leporinus octofasciatus

Leporinus multifasciatus

Leporinus striatus

Leporinus arcus

Leporinus desmotes

Leporinus desmotes

Abramites hypselonotus

Leporinus aff. megalepis

Abramites hypselonotus

Anostomus ternetzi

Anostomus trimaculatus

Plate #74A

Schizodon cf. fasciatum

*Rhytiodus microlepis*

*Rhytiodus argenteofuscus*

Abramites hypselonotus

Leporinus megalepis

Leporinus maculatus

Leporinus granti

Leporinus melanostictus

Leporinus melanopleura

Plate #75

## Anostomus anostomus (Linnaeus) • Striped Headstander

RANGE: Guyana; Amazon River above Manaus.
HABITS: Mostly peaceful; prefers large aquaria which are well-planted. Likes to nibble algae.
WATER CONDITIONS: Fairly soft water is preferable, neutral to slightly acid. Temperature 24-25.5°C.
SIZE: 18 cm; usually collected and sold at 8 to 10 cm.
FOOD REQUIREMENTS: All living foods are preferred, but dried or frozen foods are also taken. Diet should be supplemented with green foods.

## Anostomus trimaculatus (Kner) • Three-spotted Headstander

RANGE: Amazon Basin, the Guianas and Surinam
HABITS: Moderately peaceful; may be kept safely with fairly large fishes.
WATER CONDITIONS: Soft and slightly acid water. Temperature 25 to 26°C.
SIZE: 20 cm; specimens are usually sold at about 10 cm.
FOOD REQUIREMENTS: Live foods and dried foods, with the addition of occasional feedings of green foods such as chopped spinach.

## Anostomus gracilis (Kner) • Four-spot Anostomus

RANGE: There are similar specimens to be found throughout Amazonia from the Rio Guapore, Rio Purus, and Rio Madeira all the way north to the Rio Negro and Rio Orinoco. They are always found in slow-moving streams.
HABITS: These are mid-water fish found in shallow streams about 2 meters deep at the most. They are very beautiful but have never been spawned in an aquarium.
WATER CONDITIONS: Clear water with a pH range from 5.8-7.2. Warm water is appreciated, average 28°C.
SIZE: Averages about 17.5 cm. Small specimens under 10 cm have never been found; they probably have been identified as something else.
FOOD REQUIREMENTS: Small live foods like newly hatched brine shrimp or daphnia are sought eagerly; dried aquarium diets are tolerated.

## Anostomus garmani Borodin • Gray-lined Anostomid

RANGE: Rio Araguaia to most rivers in Para, Brazil.
HABITS: Found in shallow streams under 2 m deep. Only large specimens were collected by the author (HRA) in these areas. They eat insects in their natural habitat. The species has never been spawned in an aquarium.
WATER CONDITIONS: Prefer warm, clear water with a pH of 6.6-7.2, which is like the waters from which they were collected.
SIZE: To 15 cm, but probably larger.
FOOD REQUIREMENTS: Small insects, mosquito larvae, brine shrimp, and daphnia. Will probably take aquarium foods, too.

## Anostomus taeniatus (Kner) • Lisa

RANGE: The Amazon from Brazil to the upper Amazon in Colombia and Peru.
HABITS: Jumps at the slightest provocation. Its tiny mouth indicates it must have small particled food.
SIZE: To 12.5 cm.
WATER CONDITIONS: Prefers warm, soft, slightly acid water. Temperature 25°C.
FOOD REQUIREMENTS: Small particles of dry food and tiny worms are accepted. Frozen brine shrimp is a favorite food.

## Leporinus badueli Puyo • Golden Leporinus

RANGE: Upper Rio Branco to Guyana.
HABITS: A delicate fish that has never been kept for more than a few months in the aquarium. This is probably the juvenile of a fish that grows much larger.
WATER CONDITIONS: Warm, clear water with heavy aeration and lots of room; pH 6.0-7.2; temperature 23-30°C.
SIZE: The small fish shown in the photo is 8.4 cm long, with a lovely golden color. It has the larger, darker spots when it gets larger. Probably reaches 30 cm.
FOOD REQUIREMENTS: Prefers living foods such as daphnia and brine shrimp, but will quickly acclimate to a typical aquarium diet supplemented with freeze-dried or frozen live foods.

## Anostomus proximus Garman • Banded Anostomid

RANGE: Amazon and Rio Negro in Brazil.
HABITS: Found in shallow streams and rivers; sometimes jumps for insects, but only when hungry. Prefers small, quiet environments but needs a large aquarium of 200+ liters in capacity.
WATER CONDITIONS: Water must be warm and clear with lots of aeration. Temperature between 25-30°C with pH 6.0-7.0.
SIZE: The known specimens were under 25 cm.
FOOD REQUIREMENTS: Brine shrimp and daphnia are preferred, but they take dried food when hungry.

## Anostomus plicatus Eigenmann • Black Anostomus

RANGE: Northern Amazon to the Guianas.
HABITS: Never spawned in an aquarium, though this male is in obvious breeding colors. A fast-moving fish that readily jumps from an uncovered aquarium.
WATER CONDITIONS: Warm, clear water, heavily aerated. pH 6.0-7.0; temperature 23-30°C.
SIZE: To 26.5 cm.
FOOD REQUIREMENTS: Its small upturned mouth means it digs around for small living creatures like daphnia, tubifex, and the like. Difficult to acclimate to non-living foods.

Anostomus anostomus

Anostomus taeniatus

Anostomus trimaculatus

Leporinus badueli

Anostomus gracilis

Anostomus proximus

Anostomus garmani

Anostomus plicatus

125

Hemiodopsis aff. microlepis

Hemiodopsis gracilis

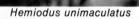

Hemiodus unimaculatus

Hemiodopsis aff. goeldi

Bivibranchia protractila

Hemiodopsis sterni

Parodon suborbitale

Plate #76A

Parodon cf. affinis

*Synaptolaemus cingulatus*

*Sartor respectus*

*Hemiodopsis sterni*

*Hemiodopsis immaculatus*

*Hemiodopsis gracilis*

*Hemiodopsis gracilis*

*Hemiodopsis* of the *microlepis* group

*Hemiodus unimaculatus*

Plate #77

## *Parodon piracicabae* Eigenmann • Brazilian Darter Tetra

RANGE: Tiete-Parana River basins in southeastern Brazil.
HABITS: Darts along the bottom in jerky movements. It has never been spawned, but would make a wonderful scavenger for the aquarium in which dried food is used.
WATER CONDITIONS: They thrive under almost all aquarium conditions even in unheated aquaria that stay about room temperature.
SIZE: Up to 7.5 cm.
FOOD REQUIREMENTS: Scavengers on the bottom of aquaria, picking up everything including live foods.

## *Parodon caliensis* Boulenger • Barred Darter Tetra

RANGE: Found in the Andes Mountains in Colombia in cold water at up to 1 km in altitude.
HABITS: In fast-moving streams the fish scouts the bottom over sand and stone searching for anything edible.
WATER CONDITIONS: Prefers colder waters in an unheated tank, though it lives in warmer waters typical of tropical aquaria. The water must be highly aerated.
SIZE: To 5 cm.
FOOD REQUIREMENTS: Eats just about everything small enough to ingest.

## *Bivibranchia* "Gery" • Spotted Sandsucker

RANGE: Surinam. An undescribed species of a poorly known genus.
HABITS: Digs its snout into the sand, where it forages for small crustaceans. It has special skeletal adaptations that enable it to sift the sand and filter it for food organisms.
WATER CONDITIONS: Likes sandy bottoms to poke around in. Tolerates most aquarium water conditions.
SIZE: To 10 cm.
FOOD REQUIREMENTS: Seems to eat everything small enough to ingest. A bottom-feeder.

## *Hemiodopsis goeldii* (Steindachner) • Goeldi's Hemiodus

RANGE: Guianas and the Rio Xingu, Brazil.
HABITS: Peaceful and highly active; likely to jump out if the tank is not covered.
WATER CONDITIONS: Neutral to slightly alkaline. Temperature 24 to 27°C.
SIZE: To about 15 cm.
FOOD REQUIREMENTS: Prepared foods accepted, but likes to nibble on plants occasionally. Lettuce or spinach leaf should be provided for this reason.

## *Parodon pongoense* (Allen) • Pongo Pongo

RANGE: Peruvian Amazon, Ecuador and Colombia.
HABITS: Peaceful; prefer to school.
WATER CONDITIONS: Soft acid water is preferred. Temperature from 23 to 30°C.
SIZE: About 5 cm.
FOOD REQUIREMENTS: Prefers live foods but can readily take frozen brine shrimp and prepared dry foods.

## *Parodon affinis* Steindachner • Paraguay Darter Tetra

RANGE: La Plata, Parana, and Rio Paraguay basins. Very common in its range. Often still called *P. paraguayensis*.
HABITS: Stays on the bottom moving about in a jerky, darter-like fashion. Makes a good scavenger. The six bands on the back are hardly visible in this photo. Has never been spawned.
WATER CONDITIONS: Likes highly aerated waters and cool temperatures. Thrives in unheated tanks at room temperatures.
SIZE: To 6.5 cm.
FOOD REQUIREMENTS: Eats everything small enough to ingest. An active feeder.

## *Hemiodopsis parnaguae* (Eigenmann & Henn) • One-spot Hemiodus

RANGE: Found in the Rio Parnagua. There are many fish that look like this found throughout northern South American waters connected to the Amazon.
HABITS: A small-mouthed fish that jumps, so keep the aquarium covered. Has never been spawned in the aquarium.
WATER CONDITIONS: Prefers warm, clear water with a pH of 6.0-7.0 and temperature of 24-30°C.
SIZE: To 20 cm.
FOOD REQUIREMENTS: Prefers small live foods but easily acclimates to any aquarium diet.

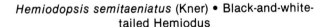

## *Hemiodopsis semitaeniatus* (Kner) • Black-and-white-tailed Hemiodus

RANGE: Rio Guapore and Rio Madeira, Brazil.
HABITS: A middle-water fish that stays on the bottom when young (the fish in the photo is a juvenile). They are great jumpers, so keep their aquarium covered.
WATER CONDITIONS: Slightly acid waters with a pH 6.5-7.4. Temperature 23-30°C.
SIZE: Probably reaches 20 cm.
FOOD REQUIREMENTS: Prefers live foods but quickly acclimates to an aquarium diet.

Parodon piracicabae

Parodon pongoense

Parodon caliensis

Parodon affinis

Bivibranchia "Gery"

Hemiodopsis parnaguae

Hemiodopsis goeldii

Hemiodopsis semitaeniatus

Chilodus punctatus

Chilodus punctatus

Curimata spilura

Curimata spilura

Curimata aff. vittata

Curimata rhomboides

Curimata (Semitapicis) altamazonica

Curimata (Semitapicis) altamazonica

Plate #78A

*Semaprochilodus taeniurus* (juvenile)

*Semaprochilodus taeniurus*

*Semaprochilodus theraponura*

Chilodus "Black-band"

*Chilodus punctatus*

*Caenotropus labyrinthicus*

*Caenotropus maculosus*

*Parodon suborbitale*

*Plate #79*

### *Semaprochilodus squamilentus* Fowler • Sailfinned Prochilodus

RANGE: Upper Rio Negro into Colombia and Peru; north-eastern Brazil.
HABITS: A high-jumping fish that travels in schools and seems to migrate past such natural barricades as small cataracts and falls.
WATER CONDITIONS: Not fussy about water chemistry, but likes warm water. Very difficult to keep in an aquarium when they are large.
SIZE: Grows to 25 cm or larger.
FOOD REQUIREMENTS: They seem to eat anything in small quantities, but they are at starvation level in most cases under aquarium conditions.

### *Prochilodus ortonianus* Cope • Gray Prochilodus

RANGE: Brazilian Amazon; a similar fish is found in Guyana.
HABITS: The fish shown was discovered by the author (HRA) in the Rio Urubu along with several other prochilodid fishes. It thrived for several years in a large (400-liter) aquarium that was heavily vegetated.
WATER CONDITIONS: Typical aquarium conditions. pH 6.2-7.2; temperature 23-30°C.
SIZE: To 25 cm, perhaps larger. The fish shown here is a juvenile.
FOOD REQUIREMENTS: Eats the usual aquarium diet.

### *Curimata lineopunctata* Boulenger • Line-spotted Curimata

RANGE: Found in the Rio Calima, Colombia, by the author (HRA).
HABITS: A well-defined species that does well in the aquarium as long as it retains its juvenile teeth. A bit aggressive and a good jumper.
WATER CONDITIONS: Cool, clear water with a pH 6.0-7.0 and a temperature of 23-30°C.
SIZE: It is not known how large they grow, but the juveniles reached 10-12 cm before they lost their teeth.
FOOD REQUIREMENTS: The teeth of the juveniles enable them to accept most foods, but the toothless adults soon die because aquarists have not figured out how to feed them.

### *Prochilodus nigricans* Agassiz • Black Prochilodus

RANGE: Wide-ranging throughout western Brazil in Amazonia.
HABITS: This is a common food fish with very firm flesh that is difficult to pierce with a harpoon and requires a very sharp knife. The meat is delicious and chewy and is a favorite of the Indians.
WATER CONDITIONS: Highly aerated, moving water. Does not thrive under aquarium conditions.
SIZE: Over 30 cm.
FOOD REQUIREMENTS: They have never been kept long in an aquarium, and nothing is known of their feeding habits.

### *Curimata ciliata* (Mueller & Troschel) • Hairy Curimata

RANGE: Northern South America, primarily imported from Guyana by the pet trade.
HABITS: When young this species has sharp teeth and they require different handling than the adult form. Youngsters may bite and attack each other over food and territorial jealousies.
WATER CONDITIONS: Cool, clear water with a temperature of 23-29°C and a pH 6.2-7.0.
SIZE: Probably reaches 20 cm but small specimens are brought in for the aquarium trade.
FOOD REQUIREMENTS: Young fish eat a normal aquarium diet and do very well on almost everything; as they get older you must watch what they eat carefully and only offer them that diet or they will slowly starve.

### *Curimata isognatha* Eigenmann & Eigenmann • Chunky Curimata

RANGE: The Amazon basin south to the Pantanal in Brazil.
HABITS: A large fish that is easily confused with many other curimata species because it has no significant markings and is just plain silvery. It is longer and shallower in form than most species.
WATER CONDITIONS: Very tolerable of many poor aquarium situations and thrives in waters from 22-30°C with a pH of 6.0-7.4.
SIZE: Reaches 26 cm.
FOOD REQUIREMENTS: As a juvenile it has teeth and chases live foods, including small fishes; as an adult it eats a normal aquarium diet, but they never live very long in captivity.

### *Curimata elegans* Steindachner • Spotted Curimata

RANGE: The Amazon basin south to Rio de Janeiro area.
HABITS: This fish was collected by the author (HRA) from the same area and at the same time he collected *C. isognata*. They are similar in appearance until you notice the body proportions and the spot in the dorsal. All *Curimata* with a spot in the dorsal are said to be in the "elegans" group.
WATER CONDITIONS: Takes many different aquarium conditions. Temperature 22-30°C and pH 6.0-7.4.
SIZE: Reaches 25 cm.
FOOD REQUIREMENTS: Juveniles have sharp teeth and use them for feeding. Adults present a problem in feeding and don't last more than a few months in captivity.

*Semaprochilodus squamilentus*

*Prochilodus nigricans*

*Prochilodus ortonianus*

*Curimata ciliata*

*Curimata ciliata (juvenile)*

*Curimata isognatha*

*Curimata lineopunctata*

*Curimata elegans*

133

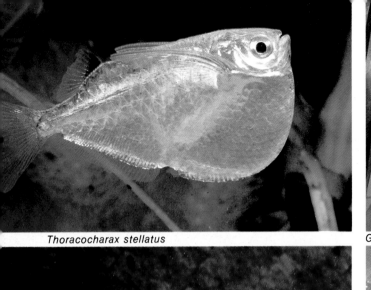

Thoracocharax stellatus

Gasteropelecus sternicla

Carnegiella aff. marthae

Carnegiella strigata strigata

Mylossoma aureum

Mylossoma duriventre

Metynnis lippincottianus

Metynnis hypsauchen

Plate #80A

*Curimatopsis evelynae*

*Curimatopsis macrolepis*

*Curimatella alburna*

*Curimata elegans*

*Curimata vittata*

*Curimata latior*

*Curimata gilberti*

*Curimata rhomboides*

*Plate #81*

135

### *Curimatopsis macrolepis* Steindachner • Shiny-scaled Curimata

RANGE: From the Amazon basin north to the Guianas.
HABITS: These are two males in good color. They thrived in the author's (HRA) tank for more than one year. They might have spawned, for the female kept with them lost her girth about the time they lost their color.
WATER CONDITIONS: The usual aquarium conditions of pH 6.8 and water at 25°C.
SIZE: The males reached 15 cm and the female reached 17 cm, but they were probably stunted from growing up in an aquarium.
FOOD REQUIREMENTS: They did well on a normal aquarium diet of mostly flake foods.

### *Thoracocharax securis* (Filippi) • Pectorosus Hatchetfish

RANGE: Upper Amazon in shallow sidestreams.
HABITS: Stays on top of the water, leaping for insects. Their aquarium must be covered. They cannot tolerate cold water.
WATER CONDITIONS: Warm, aerated water. Keep the surface film broken by an airstream.
SIZE: About 7.5 cm. A population with a much larger maximum size has been reported but never seen by any of the authors.
FOOD REQUIREMENTS: Floating vestigial-winged *Drosophila* is their best food, along with mosquito larvae and some floating dried foods.

### *Gasteropelecus sternicla* (Linnaeus) • Silver Hatchetfish

RANGE: Peruvian Amazon, Guianas and the Orinoco Basin in Venezuela.
HABITS: A top-feeder which spends most of its time waiting quietly for a passing insect.
WATER CONDITIONS: Prefers warm, soft water with a pH of about 6.4. Temperature 24 to 26°C.
SIZE: About 6 cm maximum.
FOOD REQUIREMENTS: Floating foods, wingless *Drosophila* flies and floating bits of frozen brine shrimp.

### *Carnegiella strigata strigata* (Guenther) • Marbled Hatchetfish

RANGE: Guyana, middle and upper Amazon region, especially in jungle streams.
HABITS: Occurs in schools near the surface. In the aquarium they are peaceful, but are likely to jump if a cover is not provided.
WATER CONDITIONS: Soft, slightly acid water. Temperature about 26°C.
SIZE: About 8 cm.
FOOD REQUIREMENTS: Will readily accept dried foods which float on the surface, but anything which falls to the bottom cannot be picked up.

### *Curimata spilura* Guenther • Diamond-spot Curimata

RANGE: Amazon basin to Guyana; probably more widespread.
HABITS: This is a relatively small species that might do well in the aquarium under the proper circumstances. It likes to peck on wood upon which algae are growing.
WATER CONDITIONS: Typical aquarium conditions of 25°C and pH 6.8 are satisfactory.
SIZE: Under 12.5 cm.
FOOD REQUIREMENTS: Seems to do well in a heavily planted tank with a normal aquarium diet consisting mainly of flake foods and daphnia.

### *Thoracocharax stellatus* (Kner) • Silver Hatchetfish

RANGE: Amazon, Paraguay, Orinoco basin to Venezuela.
HABITS: An extremely peaceful surface fish; a good jumper, so its tanks should be covered.
WATER CONDITIONS: Soft, slightly acid water a necessity; this fish dies easily if maintained in hard, alkaline water. Temperature 23 to 26°C.
SIZE: 8 cm.
FOOD REQUIREMENTS: Floating foods of all kinds taken, provided they can be swallowed.

### *Carnegiella myersi* Fernandez-Yepez • Myers's Hatchetfish; Pygmy Hatchet

RANGE: Peru and Bolivia on the eastern side of the Andes.
HABITS: A top-swimming fish that is very difficult to maintain in the aquarium without small floating live foods such as *Drosophila* and mosquito larvae.
WATER CONDITIONS: Warm water with a neutral pH and a temperature about 26°C. The surface of their water must be kept clean by a constant stream of bubbles.
SIZE: A small fish about 4 cm long.
FOOD REQUIREMENTS: Must have small floating foods, preferably insects.

### *Carnegiella strigata fasciata* (Garman) • Marbled Hatchetfish

RANGE: Guyana.
HABITS: Found in shaded pools where it leaps from the water for insects flying very close to the surface.
WATER CONDITIONS: Very sensitive to temperature and water changes. Prefers very soft, slightly acid water. Temperature 23 to 26°C.
SIZE: Under 8 cm.
FOOD REQUIREMENTS: This species must have small live food. Dropping wingless *Drosophila* flies onto the surface is an ideal way to feed this species. They also take small amounts of floating foods containing brine shrimp.

Curimatopsis macrolepis (male)

Curimata spilura

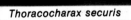

Thoracocharax securis

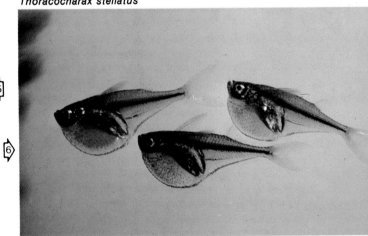

Thoracocharax stellatus

Gasteropelecus sternicla

Carnegiella myersi

Carnegiella strigata strigata

Carnegiella strigata fasciata

①
②
③
④
⑤
⑥
⑦
⑧

Metynnis "Red Eye"

Myleus rubripinnis

Myleus cf. rubripinnis

Myleus rubripinnis

Serrasalmus nattereri

Serrasalmus nattereri

Catoprion "Bleher"

Serrasalmus hollandi

Plate #82A

*Carnegiella marthae*

*Colossoma brachypomum*

*Colossoma macropomum*

*Colossoma brachypomum*

*Mylossoma paraguayensis*

*Mylossoma duriventre*

*Mylossoma aureum*

*Mylossoma* cf. *aureum*

*Plate #83*

139

## *Myleus pacu* (Schomburgk) • Brown Metynnis

RANGE: Guianas and Amazon Basin.

HABITS: Depending upon its age, it has different colors, needs, and habits. The young fish are brown-colored as shown in the photo on the facing page, but as adults they become silver except during spawning time when the male may be flushed with red or have red splotches.

WATER CONDITIONS: Only acquire small, brown specimens, the larger ones are too difficult to maintain. The small ones are vegetarians that acclimate to a flake food diet. Normal aquarium conditions suit them fine when small: pH 6.8, temperature 25-28°C.

SIZE: Probably exceeds 200 mm.

FOOD REQUIREMENTS: Youngsters eat flake foods while adults are basically vegetarians. They like small fishes, too.

## *Myleus rubripinnis* (Mueller & Troschel) • Redhook Metynnis

RANGE: Guyana and Surinam to Brazil.

HABITS: Peaceful and shy if kept by itself, but less so if kept in small groups; cannot be safely kept with vegetation because of their plant-eating tendencies.

WATER CONDITIONS: Clean, soft and highly oxygenated water is necessary. Temperature (at least for breeding) should be about 25 to 27°C.

SIZE: Matures at about 9 to 12 cm; maximum size not known.

FOOD REQUIREMENTS: Takes a variety of foods, but their diet must contain vegetable matter.

## *Myelus ternetzi* (Norman) • Paramyloplus

RANGE: Northern South America; the Guianas.

HABITS: Their actions are typical. A very active fish. They have never been spawned. They require lots of swimming space in a large tank.

WATER CONDITIONS: Clear, aerated water with a pH of 6.8 and a water temperature of 26°C. These conditions can vary quite a bit because the fish are very hardy.

SIZE: They grow to over 200 mm and are eaten by the local people in the jungle.

FOOD REQUIREMENTS: They eat flake foods in the aquarium, especially the youngsters. Adults like small live foods, too.

## *Metynnis argenteus* Ahl • Silver Metynnis

RANGE: Very common throughout northern South America. This specimen is from the Rio Aguaro, Venezuela.

HABITS: *Metynnis* comprise another group of species that are poorly known because of their wide range and their color changes as they mature. Almost all look alike when fully grown and not in breeding condition.

WATER CONDITIONS: Deep water is preferred when they are large. The water should be clear and aerated and with a pH of 6.2-7.0 and a temperature between 24-30°C.

SIZE: Exceeds 120 mm.

FOOD REQUIREMENTS: Flake foods are accepted by the youngsters but the adult needs more substantial dietary supplements in the form of small living fishes like baby guppies.

## *Myleus micans* (Reinhardt) • Golden Dollar; Sheephead Metynnis

RANGE: Sao Francisco River, Brazil.

HABITS: *M. pacu* and *M. micans* are often confused with each other. Both have a characteristic "sheep look." Both are brown when small but *micans* has more anal and dorsal fin rays. Both are plain in adulthood (like the photo on the facing page) and males of both species are red splotched during breeding season.

WATER CONDITIONS: Normal aquarium water is fine, with a pH about 6.8 and a water temperature near 25°C.

SIZE: About 200 mm.

FOOD REQUIREMENTS: The small ones eat normal flake foods, as do the larger specimens, but the larger specimens need little fishes too.

## *Myleus rubripinnis* (Mueller & Troschel) • Red Hook Metynnis

This is the female of the species; compare it to the male in photograph # 3. The spots and blotches on the males are only evident during the spawning season which usually occurs around Christmas time depending upon the flood conditions in their particular habitat. The identification of almost all species of *Myleus, Metynni*, etc. is a mess since they change color and finnage as they grow and mature. Almost all have red blotches during spawning time. But that doesn't matter since their care, feeding, and breeding are almost identical.

## *Myleus schomburgki* (Jardine) • Black-barred Metynnis

RANGE: Throughout the rivers that run south of the Amazon. Varieties exist in the Xingu, Araguaia, and Madeira Rivers of Brazil.

HABITS: Easily recognizable by the broad vertical band on its side. There is more than one species with this characteristic but the fishes of this genus are very poorly known because they change so radically as they mature. One other species with the black band has black fins.

WATER CONDITIONS: They prefer large aquaria with heavily aerated water with a pH between 6.2 and 6.8 and a water temperature ranging from 23-30°C.

SIZE: May reach 225 mm.

FOOD REQUIREMENTS: Young fish eagerly take flake food but the adults require some live foods and lots of soft vegetation in their diets.

## *Metynnis luna* Cope • Moon Metynnis

RANGE: Very common in northern South America.

HABITS: The red spot shown on the specimen here is the remnant of a lot of red spots characteristic of a breeding male. Normally all the fish are silver and only the roundness of their bodies is diagnostic of the species for aquarists.

WATER CONDITIONS: They require lots of aquarium space with a slightly acid to neutral water (pH 6.4-7.0) at a temperature of about 26°C.

SIZE: To 200 mm.

FOOD REQUIREMENTS: The small mouth and numerous gill rakers (60-62) indicate it feeds on small items. Appreciates vegetable matter in with its regular food. This is usually provided with certain flake foods offered by major manufacturers.

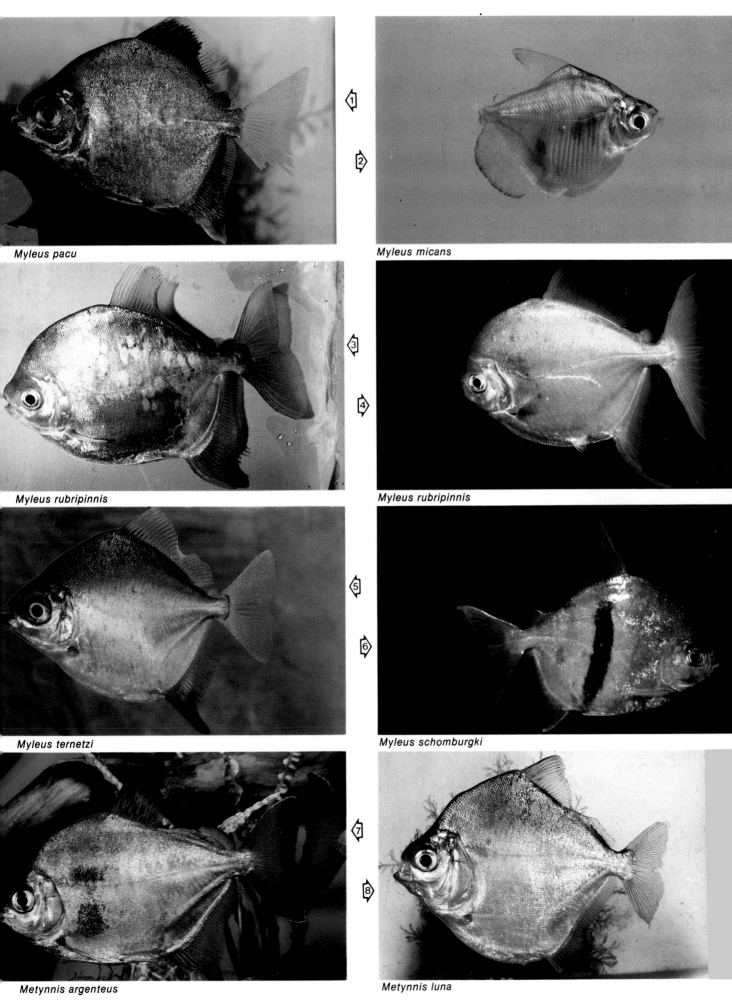

*Myleus pacu*

*Myleus micans*

*Myleus rubripinnis*

*Myleus rubripinnis*

*Myleus ternetzi*

*Myleus schomburgki*

*Metynnis argenteus*

*Metynnis luna*

1

2

3

4

5

6

7

8

*Serrasalmus eigenmanni*

*Serrasalmus eigenmanni*

*Serrasalmus (Pygocentrus) notatus*

*Serrasalmus eigenmanni*

*Serrasalmus (Pygocentrus) notatus*

*Serrasalmus (Pristobrycon) "Iridescent"*

*Serrasalmus (Pristobrycon) striolatus*

*Serrasalmus elongatus*

Plate #84A

*Metynnis maculatus*

*Metynnis hypsauchen*

*Serrasalmus gibbus*

*Serrasalmus sanchezi*

*Serrasalmus spilopleura*

*Serrasalmus antoni*

*Serrasalmus denticulatus*

*Serrasalmus striolatus*

*Plate #85*

## PIRANHAS, FAMILY SERRASALMIDAE

Every aquarist knows the piranhas, the often large and always heavily toothed characoids that have inspired so much fascination and unnecessary fear. The piranhas form the subfamily Serrasalminae of the family Serrasalmidae (which also contains the pacus and silver dollars) in the classification of the characoids proposed by Gery. The true piranhas comprise only about 20 or so very similar species of the single genus *Serrasalmus* with at least five subgenera. Unlike any other tetras, the true piranhas have the large jaw teeth closely spaced and interlocked into a continuous saw; if one tooth has to be replaced, the entire set on that side has to be replaced.

For several years I (HRA) served as chairman of the Exotic Fishes Committee of the American Fisheries Society, and while in that post I had the responsibility for making recommendations to the Congress about the best means of protecting American waters from such menaces as piranhas from South America, walking catfish from Southeast Asia and tilapia from Africa. The fear with which American conservationists viewed the piranhas is amazing, and even though I argued that prohibiting the importation of piranhas would not stop their availability since they are so easy to breed, they still proposed laws that made importation illegal except under certain very special circumstances.

I'm frequently asked why piranhas are so feared if I go swimming with them in every river of Brazil, without the slightest hesitation. I'm not that brave. . .but I'm not stupid either. After spending so much time with Brazilian Indians, I've learned to do what they do. They know that piranhas never attack humans in rivers or lakes in which the fish have enough food. They are dangerous only when they are starving, such as in artificial situations (new reservoirs, aquaria) or in pools that are drying out and have been isolated from the main body of water (intermittent ponds).

In 25 years of travel and fishing in almost every river system in South America, nearly all of which had schools of piranha, I NEVER was bitten, nor did I ever meet anyone who was bitten . . .nor did I ever meet anyone who even *knew* anyone who was bitten by a piranha. . .and these are mostly Indians who live on the river and swim in it every day. But this does not mean that you can't be bitten if you stick your hand in your aquarium or grab one in a net! So be careful, but not frightened.

Serrasalmus elongatus

Serrasalmus hollandi

Serrasalmus nattereri

Serrasalmus nattereri

Serrasalmus manueli

Serrasalmus piraya

Serrasalmus rhombeus

Serrasalmus serrulatus

*Plate #86*

145

*Serrasalmus elongatus* Kner • Elongate Piranha

RANGE: Rio Madeira; very common in lakes around
    Humaita, Brazil, where the specimen shown in the photo
    on page 145 was caught.
HABITS: This is basically a lake-dwelling species that is very
    fast moving. It does not school in the usual sense, but
    large dying animals attract a lot of them. They are not to
    be trusted in the aquarium as they eat other fishes and
    may bite an aquarist's hand.
WATER CONDITIONS: Warm water between 25-32°C and a
    pH of 6.4-7.2
SIZE: Over 300 mm.
FOOD REQUIREMENTS: Live goldfish suits them fine, but
    they also take chunks of meat and fish. They do not thrive
    on a typical aquarium diet.

*Serrasalmus nattereri* (Kner) • Natterer's Piranha;
Red-bellied Piranha

RANGE: Widely distributed throughout the Amazon and
    Orinoco basins.
HABITS: Vicious; must be kept alone in the average tank.
WATER CONDITIONS: Soft, slightly acid water. Temperature
    24 to 27°C.
SIZE: Up to 30 cm in natural waters; shipped specimens
    usually much smaller.
FOOD REQUIREMENTS: Smaller living fishes or strips of
    raw fish or beef heart.
COLOR VARIATIONS: Back steel gray with many tiny shining
    scales; large black spots on sides; throat, belly and anal
    fin bright red.

*Serrasalmus manueli* Fernandez-Yepez • Manuel's
Piranha

RANGE: Venezuela; collected by the author (HRA) in Rio
    Aguaro. Has never since been imported.
HABITS: Not known. Specimens were caught on hook and line,
    but none were collected with poison! In the aquarium
    they are very nasty, killing everything else in the tank.
WATER CONDITIONS: A pH of 6.4-7.0; water temperature
    of 24-30°C.
SIZE: To 200 mm, probably larger.
FOOD REQUIREMENTS: Live goldfish or chunks of meat and
    fish. Does not accept normal aquarium foods.

*Serrasalmus rhombeus* (Linnaeus) • White Piranha;
Spotted Piranha

RANGE: Amazon river system and northeastern South
    America.
HABITS: Dangerous to most other fishes; perhaps smaller
    ones can be kept with larger fishes in a community tank.
WATER CONDITIONS: Soft, slightly acid water best. Temper-
    ature 24 to 27°C.
SIZE: To about 32 cm.
FOOD REQUIREMENTS: Does well on fishes and raw meat.

*Serrasalmus hollandi* (Eigenmann) • Holland's Piranha

RANGE: South of Amazon basin.
HABITS: Vicious; cannot even be kept with another of its own
    kind.
WATER CONDITIONS: Soft, slightly acid water. Temperature
    24 to 27°C.
SIZE: About 13 cm.
FOOD REQUIREMENTS: Smaller living fishes preferred; can
    be trained to take strips of raw fish.

*Serrasalmus piraya* Cuvier • Man-eating Piranha

RANGE: Rio Sao Francisco basin.
HABITS: "Piraya" is the general word for "piranha." This
    is a greatly feared fish because it occurs in small
    streams that break down into a series of drying-out pools.
    The piraya in these pools eat everything, then begin
    starving. If a person walks into such a pool they are
    usually attacked.
WATER CONDITIONS: Tolerates extremes of temperature
    from 20-35°C.; the pH is not important, either, as long as
    it's between 6.0 and 7.4.
SIZE: To 320 mm.
FOOD REQUIREMENTS: Must have living fishes or chunks of
    fresh meat and fish.

*Serrasalmus serrulatus* (Valenciennes) • Serrated
Piranha

RANGE: Guyana and northern South America.
HABITS: This is often shipped in as a *Metynnis* because of
    its deep body. It is a peaceful piranha and can be kept in
    the community aquarium if it is well fed. It has never
    been spawned but probably this will not be too difficult.
WATER CONDITIONS: Water should be warm, 24-30°C , with
    a pH between 6.0 and 7.0.
SIZE: Grows to only 165 mm, though larger specimens
    might be found.
FOOD REQUIREMENTS: Live foods or chunks of meat and
    fishes.

## Hydrolycus scomberoides (Cuvier) • Tiger Characin

RANGE: Guianas and Amazon, Orinoco, and Paraguay basins.

HABITS: It is frightening just to look at their teeth but they only eat very small fishes.    For some reason the Indians don't eat them and don't like them either. They have never been kept alive in an aquarium.

WATER CONDITIONS: They inhabit rivers. Nothing is known about their aquarium needs but it would have to be a large, well aerated tank. A good start would be a 2000 l aquarium with a pH of 6.8 and a temperature around 26°C.

SIZE: They grow large to almost 400 mm.

FOOD REQUIREMENTS: Small live fishes.

## Charax gibbosus (Linnaeus) • Glass Headstander

RANGE: Guianas, lower and middle Amazon region and Rio Paraguay.

HABITS: Perfectly peaceful and harmless.

WATER CONDITIONS: Not critical. Temperature should average about 24°C.

SIZE: 15 cm; aquarium specimens are usually much smaller.

FOOD REQUIREMENTS: Prefers live foods, but dried foods may be fed when others are not available.

## Asiphonichthys condei Gery • Glass Tetras

RANGE: Throughout the Amazon basin.

HABITS: Found in quiet, small pools, in shallow waters. They are very delicate and hard to "bring back alive." Nothing is known about their breeding or sex differences but this probably could be easily managed once they became available.

WATER CONDITIONS: Slow moving water with lots of hiding places. A pH of 6.8-7.0 is recommended with a temperature between 26-30°C.

SIZE: Under 100 mm.

FOOD REQUIREMENTS: Does well on a normal aquarium diet but should be started with live brine shrimp or daphnia.

## Gnathocharax steindachneri Fowler • Biting Tetra

RANGE: Northern South America from the Amazon and Rio Negro to the Upper Orinoco and Guyana.

HABITS: A nasty fish with nasty teeth. It usually jumps for insects, especially at night, in its natural habitat, but when it gets hungry it tears up its tankmates, especially at night.

WATER CONDITIONS: A pH of 6.2-7.0; temperature 27°C. The populations of these fish in the Rio Negro are darker and tolerate acid water down to pH 5.8.

SIZE: About 80-90 mm.

FOOD REQUIREMENTS: Prefers live insects floating on the surface but quickly acclimate to adult live brine shrimp and other live foods.

## Catoprion mento (Cuvier) • Wimple Piranha; Flag Piranha

RANGE: Rare in nature but usually found in rivers north and south of the Amazon, especially the Guapore and Rio Negro.

HABITS: There are probably two species in the genus, one with short fins (the one shown on the next page) and one with long fins with anal and dorsal filaments extending far beyond the tail. Their piranha-like look is misleading. They have been imported by Heiko Bleher of Frankfurt, Germany.

WATER CONDITIONS: They thrive under normal aquarium conditions. They like clear, running water but aeration is good enough. A pH of 6.4-7.0 with a water temperature of 25-30°C is sufficient for their needs.

SIZE: Probably reaches 200 mm.

FOOD REQUIREMENTS: Supposedly eats scales of other fishes but the author (HRA) has never witnessed this action even among starving fish. They do take normal aquarium foods.

## Rhaphiodon vulpinus Agassiz • Skinny Tiger Characin

RANGE: Amazon and Paraguay-Parana basins.

HABITS: Not known to aquarists. The author (HRA) has never been able to bring them back alive because they seem to require more water than is available for transporting the fish. They are feared by the Indians but no one knows why.

WATER CONDITIONS: Not known, but probably a pH of 6.8 and a temperature of about 26°C would serve as this is the kind of water they were found in.

SIZE: Probably reach 500 mm.

FOOD REQUIREMENTS: Probably small living fishes.

## Gilbertolus alatus Eigenmann • Dwarf Biting Tetra

RANGE: Extreme northern South America.

HABITS: Same habits as Gnathocharax. Both fishes, by the way, are the sole members of their genera. Since Gilbertolus is about half the size of Gnathocharax and both look so much alike, Gilbertolus is usually sold as the juvenile of Gnathocharax.

WATER CONDITIONS: pH 6.2-7.0 with a water temperature of about 27°C.

SIZE: 45 mm, perhaps a bit larger.

FOOD REQUIREMENTS: They are jumpers and like to take insects from the surface of their tanks.

Hydrolycus scomberoides

Catoprion mento

Charax gibbosus

Rhaphiodon vulpinus

Asiphonichthys condei

Asiphonichthys condei

Gnathocharax steindachneri

Gilbertolus alatus

*Plate #87*

148

Heterocharax macrolepis

Roeboides descalvadensis

Roeboides caucae

Exodon paradoxus

Oligosarcus argenteus

Acestrorhynchus falcatus

Acestrorhynchus heterolepis

Acestrorhynchus falcirostris

*Plate #88*

149

**Heterocharax macrolepis** Eigenmann • Blue-lined Glass
Tetra

RANGE: Guyana, the Rio Negro and other dark waters of the
Amazon basin.
HABITS: Shallow streams with dark water. Nothing is known
about this fish in the aquarium world except for the sole
importation by the author (HRA).
WATER CONDITIONS: It was kept with cardinal tetras in pH
5.8; water temperature 27°C. Never spawned.
SIZE: About 10 cm.
FOOD REQUIREMENTS: Prefers live foods but quickly adapts
to dried aquarium foods.

**Roeboides caucae** Eigenmann • Cauca Humpback

RANGE: Colombia.
HABITS: Probably a scale-eater; the mouth and lips are full
of sharp teeth that are very pointed. They are not safe for
the home aquarium, and they seem to be especially aggressive at night.
WATER CONDITIONS: Water temperature between 26-30°C;
pH 6.2-7.0.
SIZE: About 14 cm.
FOOD REQUIREMENTS: It is difficult to feed this fish. Because it is a scale-eater, you'll have to supply goldfish for
it to chew on. Often it takes regular aquarium foods, but
it never lives long in an aquarium.

**Oligosarcus argenteus** Guenther • Silver Fish-killer

RANGE: These are cool-water fish found throughout southern
South America. They are nasty predaceous fish.
HABITS: There are now twelve species of *Oligosarcus*, all of
which cannot be trusted in the home aquarium unless the
aquarium is dedicated to this genus only. They eat fishes
almost half their size in one gulp and are powerful
swimmers.
WATER CONDITIONS: Clear, cool water. Do best in unheated
tanks that are maintained between 15-23°C, with a pH of
6.4-6.8.
SIZE: Probably reach 10 cm.
FOOD REQUIREMENTS: Only can be kept alive on small
living fishes even though they take chunks of meat and
fish.

**Acestrorhynchus heterolepis** (Cope) • Amazonian
Cachorro

RANGE: Amazon River basin, Brazil.
HABITS: A predatory fish that is often found in small streams,
where it preys upon any fish that swims by. It prowls in
open waters looking for food. Not safe for a community
aquarium unless kept with fishes much larger than itself.
WATER CONDITIONS: A large aquarium is needed, with neutral water with a temperature between 26-30°C.
SIZE: May reach 30 cm.
FOOD REQUIREMENTS: Only living fishes, though some
specimens learn to eat bits of fish and meat in between
the live fishes they crave.

**Roeboides descalvadensis** Fowler • Humpbacked
Characin

RANGE: Mato Grosso, Brazil, where it is very common.
HABITS: Found in shallow, slow-moving streams with clear
water. The fish is very translucent, and specimens of all
sizes had the humeral spot and the caudal peduncle
mark. The fins always have a rosy hue.
WATER CONDITIONS: pH 6.0-7.2; temperature 24-30°C.
SIZE: Up to 15 cm.
FOOD REQUIREMENTS: Prefers living foods, especially
brine shrimp and daphnia, but these can be bolstered
with freeze-dried or flake foods. However, the fish only
thrives on live foods.

**Exodon paradoxus** Mueller & Troschel • Bucktoothed
Tetra

RANGE: Guyana and Brazil.
HABITS: Small specimens are mostly peaceful toward other
fishes; bigger ones are likely to fight among themselves.
WATER CONDITIONS: Should have a large, sunny tank with
plenty of vegetation. Rather high temperatures are required, not under 25°C.
SIZE: Attains a size of about 15 cm, but specimens in the
aquarium seldom exceed 10 cm.
FOOD REQUIREMENTS: Should get mostly live foods, but will
also take frozen foods and pieces of fish, shrimp, etc.

**Acestrorhynchus falcatus** (Bloch) • Spotted Cachorro

RANGE: Northern South America. As many as five different
fishes are grouped under the *falcatus* name, and the
group needs revision.
HABITS: A nasty, predatory fish. In Brazilian Portuguese
the name "cachorro" means "dog," and this is a nasty
dog of a fish that bites other fishes, often just for the sport
of it. They are very pike-like and have teeth like a bar-
racuda.
WATER CONDITIONS: They cannot live for long in the aquarium unless they have lots of room and heavily aerated
water with a pH close to 7.0 and a water temperature that
is warm, between 27 and 30°C.
SIZE: Range to 30 cm, probably larger.
FOOD REQUIREMENTS: They only thrive on living fishes,
though they can be coaxed into taking bits of meat and
fish.

**Acestrorhynchus falcirostris** (Cuvier) • Giant Cachorro

RANGE: Throughout northern South America.
HABITS: A predatory pike-like fish that is a good game fish
but is rarely eaten by the people who catch it. In Guyana
it is often caught by fly fishermen as well as by spoons
being trawled behind slow-moving boats.
WATER CONDITIONS: A neutral pH between 6.8 and 7.2 with
a water temperature between 25-30°C.
SIZE: The largest of the almost 20 fishes in this genus. It
may reach 38 cm in standard length.
FOOD REQUIREMENTS: Live fishes small enough to ingest
whole.

## *Acestrorhynchus isalinae* Menezes & Gery • Isaline's Cachorro

RANGE: Known only from specimens collected by the author (HRA) and colleagues near Humaita, Brazil.
HABITS: Like the other species of the genus, it is a vicious predator.
WATER CONDITIONS: Warm (26-30°C) water with a neutral pH.
SIZE: Probably reaches at least 25 cm.
FOOD REQUIREMENTS: Should do well on a diet of small live fishes.

## *Brycon melanopterus* (Cope) • Common Brycon

RANGE: Throughout the Amazon; very common.
HABITS: This is the most unusual of the South American trout tetras imported. It is distinct because of the black marking that runs from the ventral fins to the upper lobe of the caudal. This fish has never been spawned in aquaria.
WATER CONDITIONS: Requires a large aquarium with lots of room. Prefers a pH of 6.2-6.8 with a water temperature of 24-30°C.
SIZE: About 27.5 cm; some reports have them larger.
FOOD REQUIREMENTS: Live fishes or chunks of fish and beef.

## *Chalceus erythrurus* (Cope) • Yellow-finned Chalceus

RANGE: The Amazon basin south to the Mato Grosso.
HABITS: A jumper and live fish eater. It has never been spawned, and not much is known about their aquarium habits since they are so rare in the hobby, the reason being that they are difficult to ship.
WATER CONDITIONS: Require very large aquaria with a pH of 6.2-6.8 and a water temperature between 25-30°C.
SIZE: Grows to about 30 cm.
FOOD REQUIREMENTS: Live fishes or chunks of meat and fish.

## *Brycon brevicauda* Guenther • Short-tailed Trout Tetra

RANGE: The Amazon and its southern tributaries.
HABITS: There are almost 50 species of *Brycon*, the South American trout tetras, as they are called. The species are generally very poorly described so the species have been broken down into groups. Those brycons with a black V in the tail base are in the *falcatus* group, of which this species is part.
WATER CONDITIONS: Deep water and a large tank with a pH about 6.8 and a water temperature about 27°C. They do not do well in a home aquarium.
SIZE: To 25 cm.
FOOD REQUIREMENTS: Prefers live foods, but they can be acclimated to bits of meat or fish depending upon their size.

## *Brycon orbignyanus* (Valenciennes) • Striped Brycon

RANGE: This species, which has between 27 and 31 anal fin rays, ranges over almost all of South America from the Guianas to the La Plata basin; it is even found in Central America!
HABITS: This fish takes on many faces depending upon where it is found. It has many scientific names, too, depending upon the country and the scientist who described it. It does not do well in a small tank.
WATER CONDITIONS: The preferred water temperature varies with the origin of the specimen. If that is unknown, ascertain the water chemistry from the last person to keep it alive. Probably about 25°C with a neutral pH of 7.0 will do for most specimens.
SIZE: Specimens vary up to 32 cm.
FOOD REQUIREMENTS: Live fishes; also takes chunks of fish or meat.

## *Chalceus* "Jacques Gery" • Gery's Chalceus

RANGE: Amazon basin.
HABITS: *Chalceus* was thought to be composed of only two species, one with red fins (*macrolepidotus*) and one with yellow fins (*erythrurus*). Then the author (HRA) found the fish shown here and Dr. Jacques Gery, expert on characoids, found the same variety somewhere else. He has not officially named it yet, but it carries his name in the trade and is very expensive because it is so beautiful when small and can be kept alive in the aquarium.
WATER CONDITIONS: Water about pH 6.8 and 27°C.
SIZE: Probably reaches 30 cm, but the maximum size is not known for sure.
FOOD REQUIREMENTS: Live foods or chunks of meat or fish.

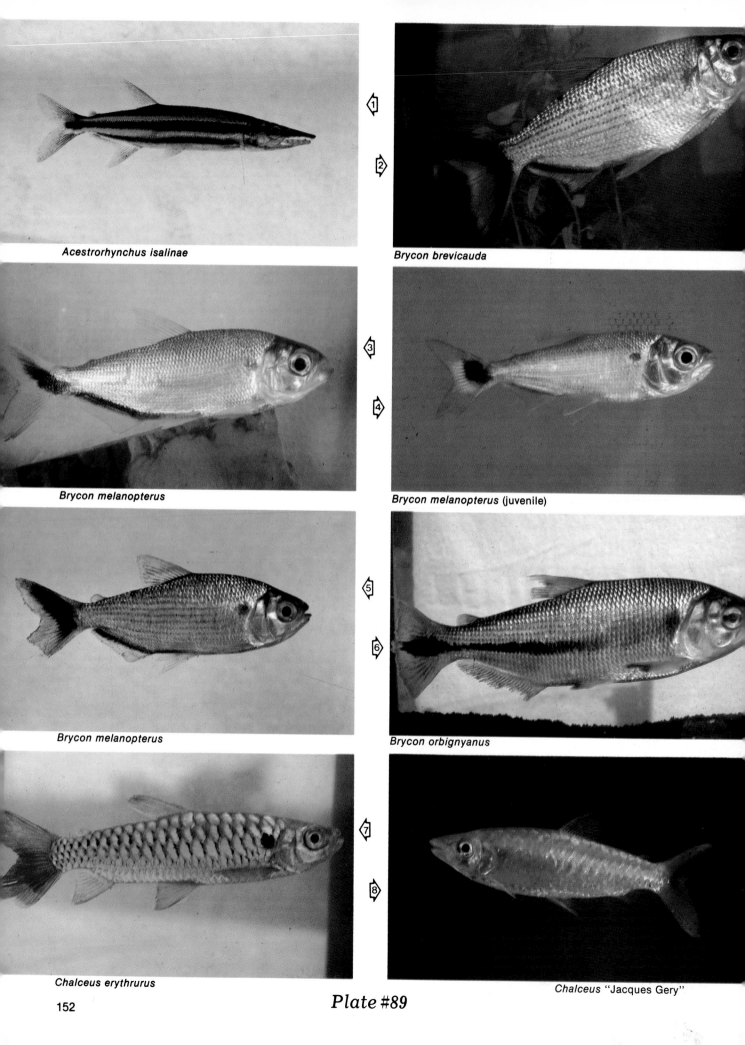

*Acestrorhynchus isalinae*

*Brycon brevicauda*

*Brycon melanopterus*

*Brycon melanopterus* (juvenile)

*Brycon melanopterus*

*Brycon orbignyanus*

*Chalceus erythrurus*

*Chalceus "Jacques Gery"*

152

*Plate #89*

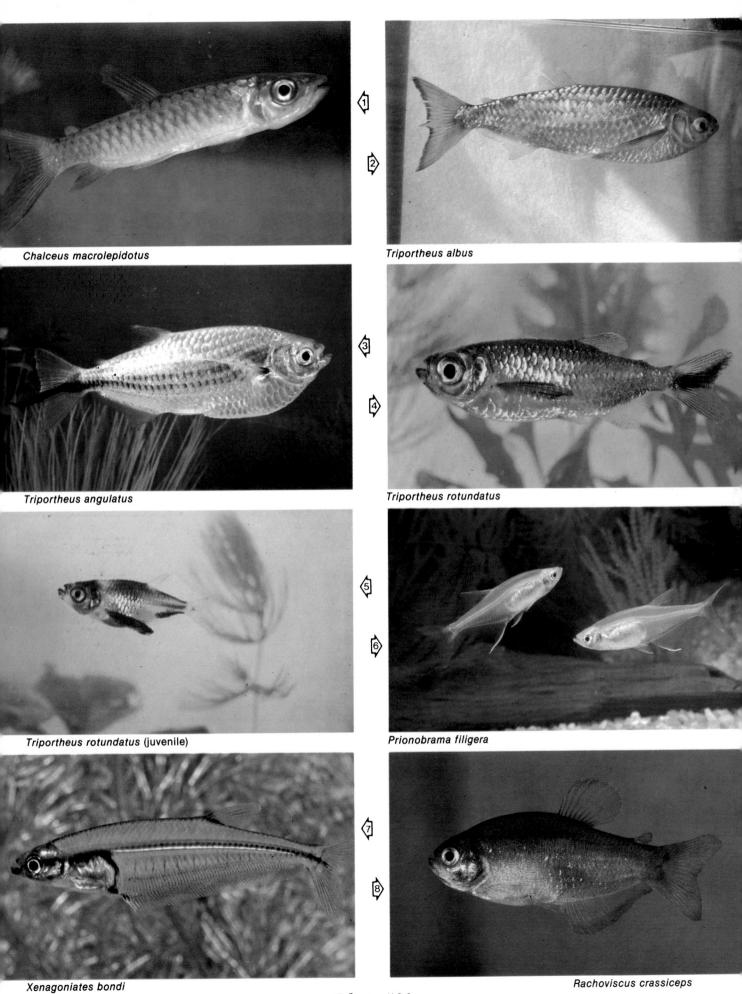

Chalceus macrolepidotus

Triportheus albus

Triportheus angulatus

Triportheus rotundatus

Triportheus rotundatus (juvenile)

Prionobrama filigera

Xenagoniates bondi

Rachoviscus crassiceps

*Plate #90*

*Chalceus macrolepidotus* Cuvier • Pink-tailed Chalceus

RANGE: Guyana, Surinam and French Guiana.
HABITS: Peaceful if kept in a school with no small fishes in the same tank.
WATER CONDITIONS: Not critical; best temperature about 25°C. Once they have become established, they should be moved as little as possible.
SIZE: To 25 cm.
FOOD REQUIREMENTS: Generous feedings are necessary, using earthworms, tubifex worms or chopped beef heart.

*Triportheus angulatus* (Spix) • Narrow Hatchetfish

RANGE: Middle and Lower Amazon, Rio Madeira, Rio Negro, Orinoco and the Guianas.
HABITS: Active and peaceful with other fishes of its own size.
WATER CONDITIONS: Not critical; tank should be in a sunny location and permit ample swimming space. Temperature about 25°C.
SIZE: Wild specimens attain a size of about 20 cm.
FOOD REQUIREMENTS: Not very fond of dried foods, so should be richly fed with living foods such as daphnia or adult brine shrimp.

*Xenagoniates bondi* Myers • Long-finned Glass Tetra

RANGE: Venezuela and Colombia.
HABITS: This elongated, translucent fish in many ways resembles an Asian glass catfish. Although not especially colorful, the odd shape and delicate pattern make it an interesting addition to the aquarium. It can be separated from the similar barred glass tetra by the longer body and presence of black at the base of the dorsal fin and front of the anal fin.
WATER CONDITIONS: Neutral to slightly acid pH and warm water temperatures are preferred.
SIZE: To about 10 cm.
FOOD REQUIREMENTS: Will take most small live foods and some prepared foods.

*Triportheus albus* Cope • Pretty Chalcinus

RANGE: Throughout the Amazon basin.
HABITS: This species is the type of the genus. It is very common but is rarely imported because it is "just another silver fish." These fish are jumpers, and their aquarium must be covered.
WATER CONDITIONS: pH 6.2-7.0
SIZE: May reach 24 cm.
FOOD REQUIREMENTS: Live foods are preferred, but they become acclimated to an ordinary aquarium diet without too much difficulty.

*Triportheus rotundatus* (Schomburgk) • Black-winged Triportheus

RANGE: From northern South America; usually imported from Guyana.
HABITS: The young of this fish are completely different from their elders. The fully mature fish may show a broad band from its ventral fins through the upper lobe of the caudal, mimicking in some respects *Brycon melanopterus*, to which it is closely related (except for the size of the scales).
WATER CONDITIONS: A jumper that likes to spend time close to the surface of the water, thus the water should be aerated to keep the temperature at the surface uniform with the rest of the tank. pH 6.8 at 27°C.
SIZE: About 16.5 cm.
FOOD REQUIREMENTS: A lover of live foods (as are most fishes), but it soon learns to accept the usual aquarium fare.

*Prionobrama filigera* (Cope) • Glass Bloodfin

RANGE: Tributaries of the Rio Madeira.
HABITS: Peaceful, very active fish which prefer to be in groups.
WATER CONDITIONS: Soft, slightly acid water is best; the tank should afford a good amount of swimming room. Temperature 23 to 26°C.
SIZE: To 6 cm.
FOOD REQUIREMENTS: Prepared foods accepted, but live foods should be given at least several times a week.

*Rachoviscus crassiceps* Myers • Golden Tetra

RANGE: Coastal blackwater streams of southeastern Brazil, from Parana perhaps to Rio de Janeiro.
HABITS: Relatively peaceful community tank species.
WATER CONDITIONS: Not critical; widely adaptable to various kinds of water, but for breeding may require a pH of about 5.0 to 5.5 and a DH of 2 to 3. Temperature 18 to 28°C; courtship occurs at the middle to upper range of these temperatures.
SIZE: Attains a length of about 4.5 cm.
FOOD REQUIREMENTS: Will accept a variety of aquarium foods, including flake food. Live foods are recommended for breeding.

## *Paragoniates alburnus* Steindachner • Pasca

RANGE: Northern South America from the Amazon basin to Venezuela.
HABITS: A nice aquarium fish, one of only two members of the genus *Paragoniates*. This rare fish has only been imported once or twice, and there are conflicting reports about it, but generally they are peaceful, attractive members of same subfamily as *Aphyocharax*. Their bodies are much more translucent than the accompanying photograph indicates.
WATER CONDITIONS: pH 6.2-7.0; temperature 24-30°C.
SIZE: Up to about 9.5 cm.
FOOD REQUIREMENTS: Live foods are preferred, especially brine shrimp, but they are easily acclimated to flake foods and, especially, freeze-dried foods.

## *Aphyocharax anisitsi* Eigenmann & Kennedy • Argentinian Bloodfin

RANGE: Argentina to Paraguay.
HABITS: A peaceful, colorful aquarium fish that has been around a long time under the scientific name of *Aphyocharax rubripinnis*, a synonym. It is commercially bred, but the tank-raised specimens hardly have the color of the wild ones shown in the accompanying photograph.
WATER CONDITIONS: Likes cooler water between 22-25°C, with a neutral pH.
SIZE: May reach 7.5 cm.
FOOD REQUIREMENTS: Likes live foods, especially live brine shrimp, but takes the usual flake foods fed to a community tank.

## *Aphyocharax rathbuni* Eigenmann • Rathbun's Bloodfin

RANGE: Paraguay basin, South America.
HABITS: Peaceful and attractive. Does well in a community tank.
WATER CONDITIONS: Not critical. Temperature 24 to 27°C.
SIZE: Attains a length of about 4.5 cm.
FOOD REQUIREMENTS: Not fussy. Prepared foods accepted, but living food should be provided whenever possible.

## *Gephyrocharax caucanus* Eigenmann • Arrowhead Tetra

RANGE: Rio Cauca, Colombia.
HABITS: In constant motion; active to the point of always having to do something, including bothering its tankmates.
WATER CONDITIONS: Temperature should range between 24 to 26°C. They prefer water that is somewhat soft and a pH that is slightly on the acid side.
SIZE: Up to 6 cm.
FOOD REQUIREMENTS: Live foods best, but will accept freeze-dried feedings; dry foods will be accepted if very hungry.

## *Phanagoniates macrolepis* (Meek & Hildebrand) • Barred Glass Tetra

RANGE: Extreme northern South America; usually exported from Venezuela and Colombia.
HABITS: This is a very beautiful translucent fish that contains specimens (perhaps males in breeding color) that have red glowspots on their caudal peduncles. They have a set of sharp teeth but are peaceful with fishes that are as large as they themselves.
WATER CONDITIONS: pH 6.2-7.0; temperature 22-27°C, but tolerates warmer conditions.
SIZE: About 10 cm.
FOOD REQUIREMENTS: Live foods that are small enough to ingest whole, as this fish has a small mouth. Aquarium foods are generally accepted.

## *Aphyocharax erythrurus* Eigenmann • Flame-tail Tetra

RANGE: Guyana.
HABITS: Peaceful, very active and likes to jump. Must be kept covered.
WATER CONDITIONS: Clean, well-aerated water. pH and hardness not important unless they affect spawning. Temperature 22 to 26°C.
SIZE: To 6 cm; males a little smaller.
FOOD REQUIREMENTS: Prepared foods accepted but frozen or live foods should be given occasionally.

## *Aphyocharax* "Bleher" • Bleher's Bloodfin

RANGE: Mato Grosso, Brazil.
HABITS: A typical bloodfin, probably undescribed. The specimens collected by Heiko Bleher and photographed by the author all had very bright red markings more vivid than its sister species. Gery is working on a scientific description.
WATER CONDITIONS: Most aquarium conditions are acceptable between pH 6.2-6.9, with a temperature between 24-30°C.
SIZE: Up to 6.3 cm.
FOOD REQUIREMENTS: Live foods small enough to eat whole but quickly; learns to take the usual dried foods.

## *Gephyrocharax valenciae* Eigenmann • Mountain Minnow Tetra

RANGE: A whole genus of *Gephyrocharax* ranges north from Bolivia along the Andes mountains at about 1,000 m; some species extend up to Costa Rica.
HABITS: In each area of their range the fish changes a bit in color, and in all populations their colors are very delicate. The fish are active swimmers and investigate every ecological niche, which makes them a nuisance in an aquarium but well dispersed in nature.
WATER CONDITIONS: pH 6.2-6.8, with water at 24-26°C. They probably can tolerate much colder water.
SIZE: To 6 cm.
FOOD REQUIREMENTS: Mosquito larvae and pupae are their principal food in nature, but they take small live foods and the usual aquarium diet as well.

Paragoniates alburnus

Phanagoniates macrolepis

Aphyocharax anisitsi

Aphyocharax erythrurus

Aphyocharax rathbuni

Aphyocharax "Bleher"

Gephyrocharax caucanus

Gephyrocharax valenciae

*Plate #91*

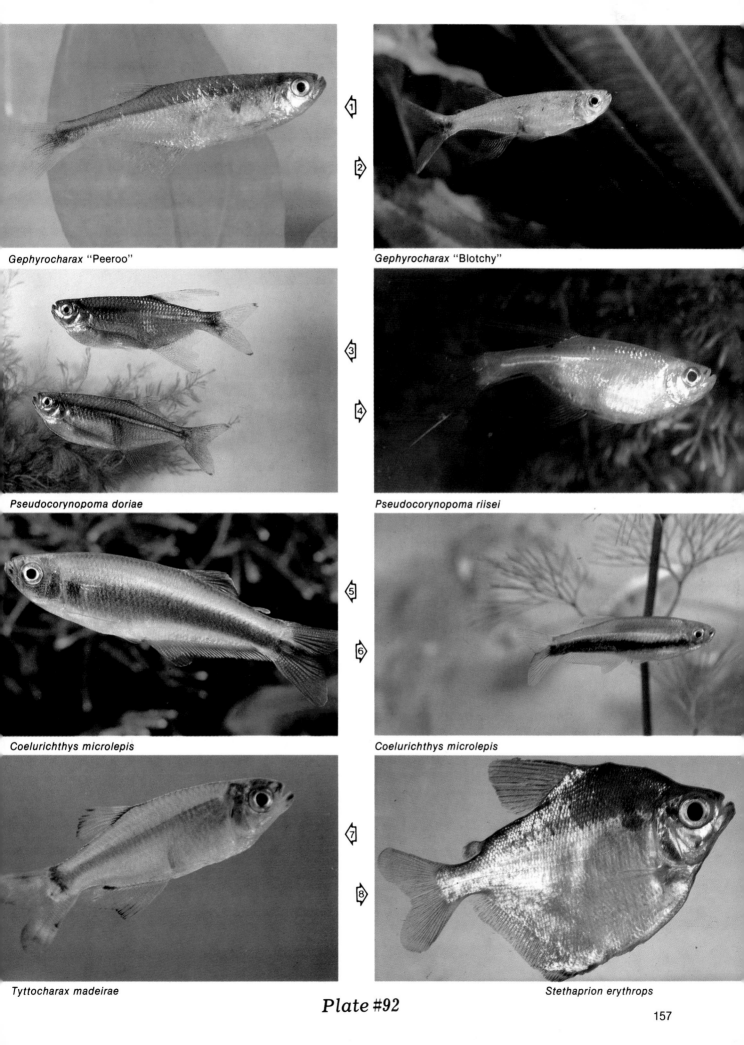

Gephyrocharax "Peeroo"

Gephyrocharax "Blotchy"

Pseudocorynopoma doriae

Pseudocorynopoma riisei

Coelurichthys microlepis

Coelurichthys microlepis

Tyttocharax madeirae

Stethaprion erythrops

*Plate #92*

157

## *Gephyrocharax* "Peeroo" • Peruvian Gephyrocharax

RANGE: Peruvian Andes about 1,000 m high.
HABITS: Only once did this seemingly undescribed fish come into the U.S., and that was with a shipment of neon tetras. They were small fish and were grown up by the author (HRA). The results were not exciting, and this commonly colored fish was never again imported.
WATER CONDITIONS: Slightly acid conditions, colder water. pH 6.2-6.8, with a water temperature in the 20-26°C range.
SIZE: Barely reaches 10 cm under ideal aquarium conditions.
FOOD REQUIREMENTS: They were constantly fed live foods and dried flake foods daily, but they can subsist on either.

## *Gephyrocharax* "Blotchy" • Blotchy Gephyrocharax

RANGE: Central America.
HABITS: A typical (and probably undescribed) *Gephyrocharax* that swims about constantly and quickly and is usually very disturbing to the peace and tranquility of a community aquarium. It has never been bred, and no one knows the sexual differences of this genus as yet.
WATER CONDITIONS: Cooler water between 22-26°C at a pH of 6.8.
SIZE: Probably reaches 7.5 cm.
FOOD REQUIREMENTS: Prefers live foods but takes dried food as well, especially if in the company of fishes that are eating the dried food.

## *Pseudocorynopoma doriae* Perugia • Dragonfin Tetra

RANGE: Southern Brazil and the La Plata region.
HABITS: Will not annoy other fishes or chew plants.
WATER CONDITIONS: Soft, slightly acid water. Temperature 21 to 25°C.
SIZE: To 8 cm.
FOOD REQUIREMENTS: Will take any foods, but live foods are of course preferred.

## *Pseudocorynopoma riisei* Gill • Swordtailed Characin

RANGE: Trinidad, Colombia and Venezuela.
HABITS: Peaceful and hardy; a good community fish.
WATER CONDITIONS: Not critical. Temperature between 22 to 28°C. A sunny, well-planted tank and clear water show it at its best.
SIZE: Males 6 cm; females 5 cm.
FOOD REQUIREMENTS: Will take prepared foods. Best foods are daphnia, tubifex worms and especially white worms, of which they are very fond.

## *Coelurichthys microlepis* (Steindachner) • Croaking Tetra

RANGE: Southeastern Brazil, Rio Grande do Sul.
HABITS: Peaceful and active; does not disturb plants.
WATER CONDITIONS: Should be kept in a roomy aquarium at a temperature slightly lower than most tropical species, 21 to 24°C.
SIZE: Males about 5.5 cm; females about 4.5 cm.
FOOD REQUIREMENTS: Not a fussy eater; besides live foods, will also eat dried foods.

## *Tyttocharax madeirae* Fowler • Bristly-mouthed Tetra

RANGE: Middle and upper Amazon basin.
HABITS: Peaceful, but because of their small size they should have a tank of their own; prefer to swim in schools.
WATER CONDITIONS: Soft, slightly acid water. Temperature 24 to 27°C.
SIZE: Up to 2 cm.
FOOD REQUIREMENTS: Smallest live foods.

## *Stethaprion erythrops* Cope • Bumpy-back Silver Dollar

RANGE: Amazon basin, probably extending north and south from there as very similar specimens come in periodically.
HABITS: The fish of this group that come from the northern part of South America, specifically Guyana, have a dorsal spot and some very sharp but fine teeth. They dart quickly through the water and eagerly take insects from the surface.
WATER CONDITIONS: Warm water at 25-30°C with a pH of 6.4-6.8.
SIZE: To about 8 cm.
FOOD REQUIREMENTS: Prefers live foods but quickly adapts to flake foods.

*Poptella orbicularis* Valenciennes • Silver Dollar Tetra

RANGE: Found throughout South America from Guyana to
  Paraguay.
HABITS: A popular aquarium fish that flutters about the
  aquarium. They are the silver equivalent to the black
  tetra, *Gymnocorymbus ternetzi*, and are often confused
  with *Gymnocorymbus thayeri*. The color of the anal fin
  varies with the particular strain.
WATER CONDITIONS: Colder water between 22-26°C, with a
  pH of 6.2-7.2.
SIZE: Up to 12 cm.
FOOD REQUIREMENTS: Prefers live foods but gets along
  perfectly well on a good flake food.

*Iguanodectes* • Slender Tetras

  This genus of smelt-like tetras is found throughout South
America and is now thought to be closely related to the
typical tetras. They are not popular aquarium fishes for they
are difficult to maintain and they don't take readily to flake
foods, preferring small living foods such as mosquito larvae
and daphnia. The identifications of these fishes are very
confused, but most seem to belong to *I. spilurus* or a very
similar species. All look virtually identical, with a pale
lateral band and black caudal blotch. They do well at first
under normal aquarium conditions but they gradually fade
away from dietary deficiencies.

*Hemibrycon polydon* (Guenther) • Racer Tetra

RANGE: Peru and Ecuador in fast-moving mountain streams.
HABITS: These fish are found swimming in a single spot
  by racing against the fast-moving mountain stream
  waters. The group is very poorly known, and
  ichthyologists sometimes identify them by assigning a
  name to each geographical type. They are extremely
  common in their range once you find their habitat.
WATER CONDITIONS: Cold, highly aerated water. pH 6.6-
  7.4, with temperatures from 18-26°C.
SIZE: They reach 10 cm in length.
FOOD REQUIREMENTS: These are insect eaters that will
  quickly take foods that are moving, even dried foods
  caught in a stream of air bubbles.

*Boehlkea fredcochui* Gery • Cochu's Blue Tetra

RANGE: Peruvian Amazon region, near Leticia, Colombia.
HABITS: Peaceful but very sensitive; best kept with other
  fishes with similar characteristics.
WATER CONDITIONS: Soft, slightly acid water is highly important with this species. The addition of acid peat moss
  in the filter is beneficial. Temperature 23 to 26°C.
SIZE: Up to 5 cm.
FOOD REQUIREMENTS: Live or frozen foods; dried foods only
  when there is nothing else at hand.

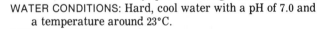

*Piabucus dentatus* (Kohlreuter) • Keel-bellied Slender
Tetra

RANGE: Guyanas through the Amazon basin and the southern Amazon tributaries. This fish is one of the few
  Brazilian species noted as far back as the 1600's in European literature.
WATER CONDITIONS: Not choosy, but prefers somewhat acid
  water and temperatures above 24°C.
SIZE: Reaches at least 17.5 cm in length.
FOOD REQUIREMENTS: Prefers small living foods such as
  mosquito larvae, brine shrimp, and small crustaceans;
  often feeds near the surface.

*Carlastyanax aurocaudatus* (Eigenmann) • Red-finned
Tetra

RANGE: Rio Cauca, Colombia.
HABITS: A peaceful aquarium fish that is imported in large
  numbers from time to time though it has never been
  spawned. This fish is quite different from its closest
  relatives and is the only species in the genus known so far.
WATER CONDITIONS: Hard, cool water with a pH of 7.0 and
  a temperature around 23°C.
SIZE: About 5.5 cm.
FOOD REQUIREMENTS: Prefers live foods but quickly acclimates to dried foods in an aquarium situation.

*Nematobrycon lacortei* Weitzman & Fink •
Rainbow Tetra

RANGE: San Juan basin, Colombia.
HABITS: Peaceful; inclined to be a bit shy.
WATER CONDITIONS: Soft, slightly acid water is best. Tem-
  perature 24 to 27°C.
SIZE: To 5 cm.
FOOD REQUIREMENTS: Live foods are best, but the fish
  can be trained to accept frozen and dried foods.

159

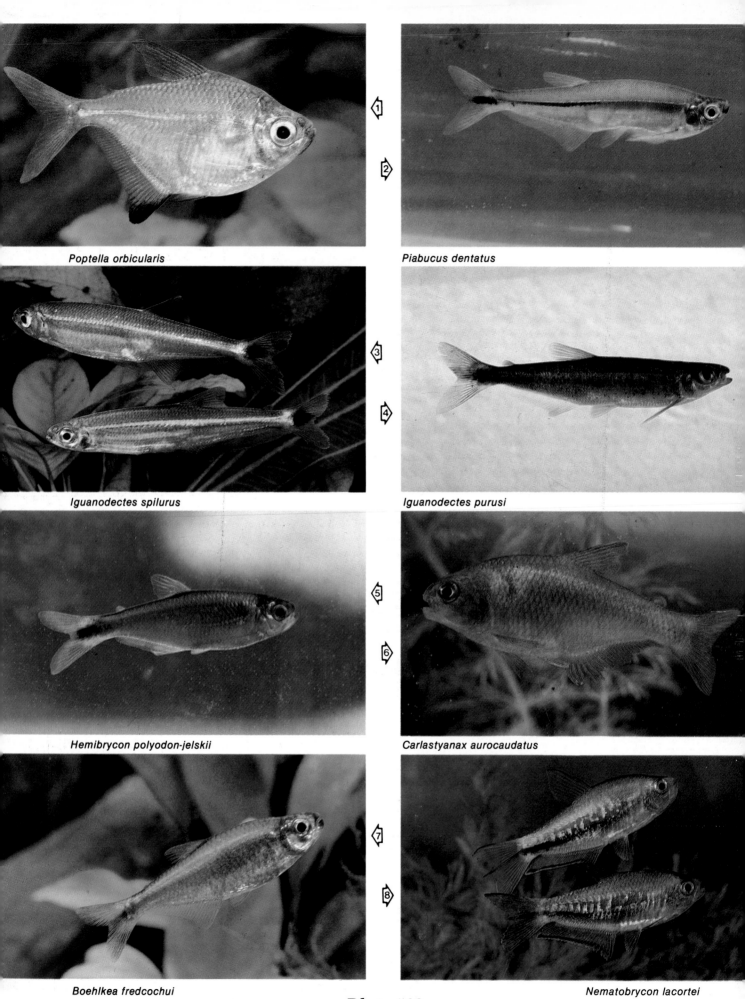

Poptella orbicularis

Piabucus dentatus

Iguanodectes spilurus

Iguanodectes purusi

Hemibrycon polyodon-jelskii

Carlastyanax aurocaudatus

Boehlkea fredcochui

Nematobrycon lacortei

*Plate #93*

160

Nematobrycon "Gery"

Nematobrycon palmeri

Inpaichthys kerri

Bryconamericus loisae

Creagrutus cochui

Knodus breviceps

Creagrutus beni

Pseudochalceus kyburzi

*Plate #94*

161

## Nematobrycon "Gery" • Gery's Emperor Tetra

RANGE: Colombia in side streams of the Rios San Juan and Atrato.

HABITS: The author (HRA) has collected all three "species" of *Nematobrycon* in various pockets of the Atrato and San Juan Rivers during the dry season when the rivers are merely dried out bottoms with intermittent pools and feeder streams. The "species" seem to freely interbreed and their fin ray and tooth counts fall into a narrow range of variation. At best they are subspecies, because each time the author found them he discovered minor variations in fin ray counts and teeth. It is usual for many fishes to show these variations within species when the waters in which they live assume different temperatures and when the fishes have different foods available, especially when they are juvenile. Care of *N.* "Gery" is the same as for the other "species."

## Inpaichthys kerri Gery & Junk • Blue Emperor

RANGE: Upper Rio Aripuana, Mata Grosso, Brazil.

HABITS: Similar to the Emperor Tetra, but perhaps more timid.

WATER CONDITIONS: Water should be soft to medium hard with a pH around neutral. Temperature about 26 to 28°C.

SIZE: Reaches a length of at least 5 cm.

FOOD REQUIREMENTS: Will accept frozen or dried foods but prefers live foods.

## Creagrutus cochui Gery • Fred Cochu's Tetra

RANGE: Discovered in the upper Amazon by the author (HRA).

HABITS: There are more than 20 species of *Creagrutus*, and they are very difficult to tell apart. Only an expert like Dr. Jacques Gery can be depended upon to describe a new species in this group until they are totally reworked. The only logical characters for identification are the size, shape and location of the humeral spot and the lateral band.

WATER CONDITIONS: Most of the *Creagrutus* take the same normal pH between 6.4 and 7.2 and a water temperature between 24-30°C. Even the coldwater species of *Creagrutus* thrive at this range.

SIZE: Rarely exceeds 10 cm.

FOOD REQUIREMENTS: Accepts life in the aquarium with its usual flake foods, but likes an occasional feeding of live food.

## Creagrutus beni Eigenmann • Benny Tetra

RANGE: The fish illustrated is from the Rio Meta in Colombia, but the species was named from a fish found in the Rio Beni, Bolivia. So many of these fish look alike that this must also be called *C. beni*, however.

WATER CONDITIONS: pH 6.4-7.2; water temperatures between 24-30°C.

SIZE: Up to 5.2 cm.

FOOD REQUIREMENTS: Thrives under usual aquarium conditions.

## Nematobrycon palmeri Eigenmann • Emperor Tetra

RANGE: San Juan basin and Atrato Rivers, Colombia.

HABITS: Peaceful and a bit shy; inclined to remain singly or in pairs rather than forming a school.

WATER CONDITIONS: Clean, soft, slightly acid water is best. Temperature 23 to 25°C.

SIZE: To 5 cm.

FOOD REQUIREMENTS: Excellent appetite; will accept dried or frozen foods, but of course live foods are preferred.

## Bryconamericus loisae Gery • Pico Peixe

RANGE: Rio Meta, Colombia.

HABITS: There are about 40 *Bryconamericus* species, almost all of which have very few interesting colors and are thus rarely imported even though they are hardy, relatively peaceful and common in their ranges. This fish is typical of the genus. It has never been spawned.

WATER CONDITIONS: Harder than normal water, slightly cool, with a pH around neutral (6.8-7.2) at a temperature of 24°C.

SIZE: About 5 cm.

FOOD REQUIREMENTS: Eats normal aquarium foods but, like almost all aquarium fishes, does better on feedings of live foods every few days.

## Knodus breviceps (Eigenmann) • Soap Eater

RANGE: Throughout the Amazon there are species of *Knodus*, perhaps as many as 50 different species, very few of which have been described, and those that have been described are uncertain in many cases.

HABITS: This fish got its common name from the author (HRA), who was washing himself while sitting in a small, clear-water creek. As he lathered his body and laid down for the water to rinse off the soap, he was "attacked" by thousands of *Knodus breviceps* as they pecked off the soap. He described the sensation of these tiny "bites" as "uncomfortable but not painful and they didn't draw blood."

WATER CONDITIONS: The fish thrive under most aquarium conditions.

SIZE: Probably reaches a size of 5 cm.

FOOD REQUIREMENTS: Will tackle anything small enough to chew.

## Pseudochalceus kyburzi Schultz • Kyburz Tetra

RANGE: Colombia.

HABITS: Active and aggressive, even with their own kind.

WATER CONDITIONS: Soft, slightly acid water. Temperature 24 to 26°C.

SIZE: To 8 cm.

FOOD REQUIREMENTS: Various live foods including insects.

## Astyanax daguae Eigenmann • Plain-tailed Astyanax

RANGE: Colombia.
HABITS: Should not be kept with smaller fishes which it may attack.
WATER CONDITIONS: Soft, slightly acid water. Temperature 24 to 26°C.
SIZE: About 8 cm.
FOOD REQUIREMENTS: Will accept most foods.

## Astyanax kennedyi Gery • Kennedy's Astyanax

RANGE: Upper Amazon near Iquitos. The fish probably has a much wider distribution, but this has never been verified.
HABITS: A typical tetra with a nice glowing line on the caudal peduncle and a black spot in the tail that make it an attractive but not beautiful species. Therefore it is rarely imported except accidentally with other species from Iquitos, one of the capitals of the aquarium fish world.
WATER CONDITIONS: pH 6.2-6.9 at a water temperature of 25-30°C.
SIZE: Barely reaches 5 cm.
FOOD REQUIREMENTS: Prefers live foods but quickly acclimates to dried foods.

## Astyanax abramis (Jenyns) • Confusing Astyanax

RANGE: Throughout most of temperate and tropical South America.
HABITS: Indistinguishable under aquarium conditions from *A. kennedyi* and *A. zonatus* except for the amount of black in the tail.
WATER CONDITIONS: pH 6.2-6.9 at a temperature of 25-30°C.
SIZE: To about 5 cm.
FOOD REQUIREMENTS: Prefers live foods but gets along on a typical aquarium diet.

## Astyanax fasciatus (Cuvier) • Silvery Tetra

RANGE: Texas to Argentina.
HABITS: Will get along with other fishes of its size; very likely to eat plants.
WATER CONDITIONS: Not at all critical, but slightly alkaline water is best. Temperature 21 to 24°C.
SIZE: To 9 cm.
FOOD REQUIREMENTS: All foods accepted, but there should be some vegetable substances included, such as lettuce or spinach leaves.

## Astyanax fasciatus mexicanus (de Philippi) • Blind Cave Tetra

RANGE: The blind form of this fish (known formerly as *Anoptichthys jordani*) occurs in caves in a restricted area in Mexico, especially La Cueva Chica.
HABITS: This is a blind fish that has been the subject of many interesting investigations, and it poses interesting problems for the scientist. Previously it was placed in the genus *Anoptichthys*, then it was discovered that it freely interbred with *Astyanax* even in nature and on this basis it was reclassified as a "form" of the fish with which it breeds in nature. If interbreeding is a test for species integrity, then many species of *Nematobrycon*, *Pterophyllum*, *Symphysodon*, platies, mollies and swordtails plus most of the small lake cichlids of central Africa would be lost and the basis of scientific classification would be in shambles.
SIZE: Barely reaches 7 cm.
FOOD REQUIREMENTS: Eats everything from flake foods to live foods, which it finds with extraordinary ease.

## Astyanax zonatus Eigenmann • False Kennedy Tetra

RANGE: Very common in the upper Amazon in Brazil and Peru. This fish is almost identical to *A. kennedyi* except for the intensity of the humeral spot.
HABITS: A typical tetra that swims about peacefully, schooling with its own species (including *A. kennedyi*), occupies mid-water, and doesn't attack fishes that are smaller than itself but too large to eat in one gulp.
WATER CONDITIONS: pH 6.2-6.9 with a temperature of 25-30°C.
SIZE: About 5 cm.
FOOD REQUIREMENTS: Prefers live foods but takes flake foods, too.

## Astyanax gymnogenys Eigenmann • One-spot Astyanax

RANGE: In Brazil south of the Amazon system.
HABITS: A very nice aquarium fish. Very peaceful, with a small mouth. It has never been spawned and has rarely been imported. It is usually sold as a *Ctenobrycon*, which it resembles in a very general way in many respects.
WATER CONDITIONS: pH 6.2-7.2 with a temperature between 22-28°C.
SIZE: To 12.5 cm.
FOOD REQUIREMENTS: Prefers live foods small enough to ingest like brine shrimp, but quickly adapts to a normal aquarium diet.

Astyanax daguae

Astyanax fasciatus

Astyanax fasciatus (albino)

Astyanax f. mexicanus, formerly Anoptichthys

Astyanax kennedyi

Astyanax zonatus

Astyanax abramis

Astyanax gymnogenys

164

*Plate #95*

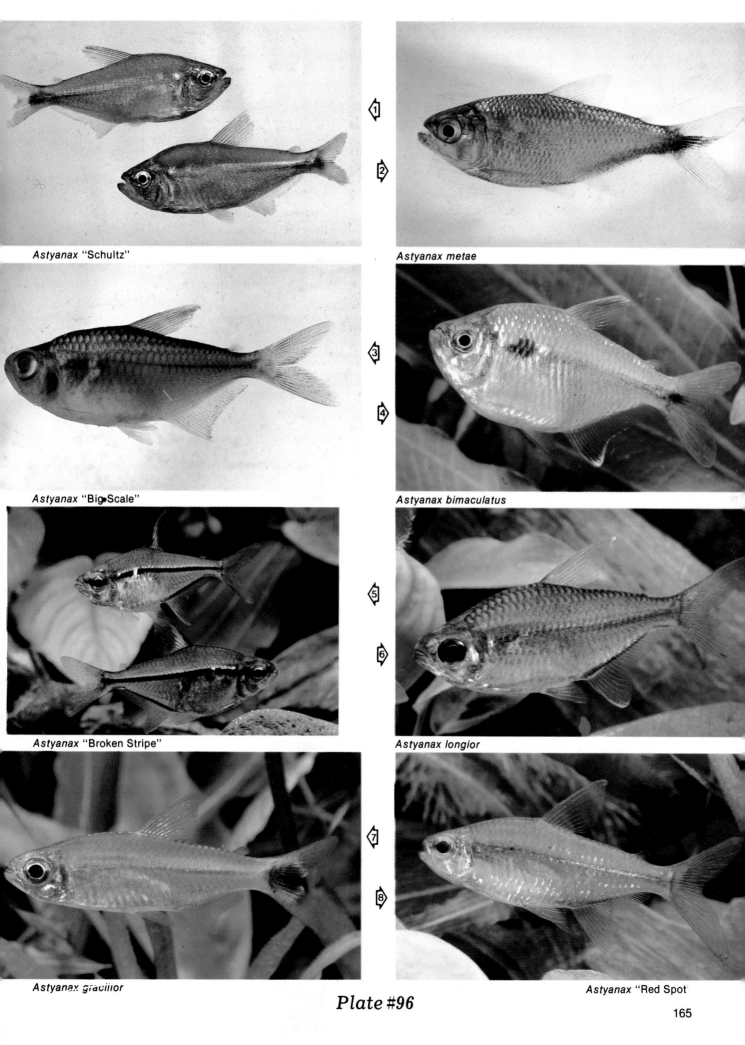

Astyanax "Schultz"

Astyanax metae

Astyanax "Big Scale"

Astyanax bimaculatus

Astyanax "Broken Stripe"

Astyanax longior

Astyanax gracilior

Astyanax "Red Spot"

*Plate #96*

## ASTYANAX TETRAS

If you are collecting in Central or South America and find a deep-bodied 50-100 mm silvery tetra with indistinct black markings on the shoulder and along the midsides, you probably have a species of *Astyanax*. With over 100 described species and subspecies in the genus, it is almost impossible to obtain a realistic identification of a specimen unless it belongs to one of the handful of well-marked species with odd patterns. Even the experts such as Dr. Jacques Gery, author of *Characoids of the World,* are often stumped. Not only are the old names hard to place, but there are dozens of undescribed species as well, some of which reach the petshops in America and Europe.

The author (HRA) has collected dozens of species of the genus but I've never found them especially interesting. They are usually just some of the "silvery tetras" that come up in the seine when looking for more colorful or worthwhile fishes. In the aquarium they are active and, when properly fed, usually iridescent fishes,but they tend to be fin-nippers and can drive more sedentary species crazy with their unwanted attentions. Since most of the species are cheap, hardy and adapt to many different water and temperature conditions, they can make good beginner fishes. Like other tetras, they will spawn in the aquarium if conditions are to their liking and the breeders are properly conditioned on live foods.

The most famous species of *Astyanax* is certainly the blind cave tetra of Mexico, *Anoptichthys jordani.* Yes, *Anoptichthys* is actually an *Astyanax.* Although the blind cave tetra shows modifications associated with other types of cave-dwellers, especially the absence of eyes and pigment and the strong development of sensory line organs to help it orient itself and find food, in the 1960's scientists found that the distinctive *Anoptichthys* interbred totally with *Astyanax fasciatus mexicanus* in surface streams that flowed into its caves. For this reason *Anoptichthys jordani* and the several other described species of the "genus" are now placed as synonyms of *Astyanax fasciatus mexicanus,* a non-descript silvery tetra that ranges north into the Rio Grande basin of Texas. (*Astyanax f. mexicanus* is the only tetra to be found naturally in the United States. It is often sold as fish bait in Texas!) This is one situation in which the usual rules of binomial nomenclature are hard to apply —if you call the blind cave tetra by the same name as the silvery surface fish you do nothing but confuse aquarists. Yet *Anoptichthys* just is not a real genus, so that name cannot be used in a technical sense. For convenience we are calling it by the boring and cumbersome term "*Astyanax fasciatus mexicanus,* formerly *Anoptichthys,*" but there must be a better way. Any suggestions?

## *Ctenobrycon spilurus* (Cuvier & Valenciennes) • Silver Tetra

RANGE: Northern South America from Surinam to Venezuela.

HABITS: Peaceful with fishes of its own size or larger, but likely to pick on smaller ones.

WATER CONDITIONS: They prefer clean water, and their tank should be large. Temperature may range from 20 to 25°C.

SIZE: About 8 cm.

FOOD REQUIREMENTS: Greedy eaters, they may extend their appetites to some of the plants. Will also take all kinds of dried foods.

## *Bryconops affinis* (Guenther) • Red-topped Tetra

RANGE: Found along with *B. melanurus* except for Colombia. This species is not as common as *melanurus*.

HABITS: This fish is more colorful in many respects than *B. melanurus,* a fish with which it is often confused for some reason. They sometimes school together, therefore are collected and shipped together.

WATER CONDITIONS: Thrives under normal aquarium conditions, pH 6.0-7.2 and a temperature from 24-30°C.

SIZE: Up to 65 mm.

FOOD REQUIREMENTS: Prefers small live foods but gets along well on a good dried aquarium diet.

## *Moenkhausia collettii* (Steindachner) • Collett's Tetra

RANGE: Widely ranging throughout northern South America in large numbers.

HABITS: Found in quantity in shallow, slowly moving waters that are clear and slightly cool. They have never been spawned. The juveniles lack any color whatsoever.

WATER CONDITIONS: Slightly acid, cool waters about pH 6.5 and 23°C.

SIZE: To about 55 mm.

FOOD REQUIREMENTS: Does well on dried foods, but some live food makes them more active.

## *Moenkhausia gracilima* (Eigenmann) • Graceful Moenkhausia

RANGE: Widely scattered over northern South America. There are several fishes that look alike, once again making identification difficult. This specimen was discovered by the author (HRA) in Tefe, Brazil.

HABITS: At times, when the fish is in breeding dress, the colors are intense and striking. These colors usually are good indications of species since the normal colors of many *Moenkhausia* are so similar. A very peaceful fish that makes a nice addition to a large tank if schools of them are available.

WATER CONDITIONS: A pH of 6.2-7.0 at a temperature of 25-30°C is recommended.

SIZE: About 60 mm.

FOOD REQUIREMENTS: Prefers live foods, especially brine shrimp and daphnia, which enhances their color.

## *Bryconops melanurus* (Bloch) • Tail-light Tetra

RANGE: Middle through northern South America. Very common.

HABITS: This fish is so common it has played an important role in three taxa in which it has been assigned. It was the type species for the genus *Creatochanes* and has been placed in both the genus *Bryconops* and the subgenus *Brycochandus*. There are many fishes that look almost exactly like this one; even scientists find them difficult to distinguish.

WATER CONDITIONS: It thrives under most aquarium conditions.

SIZE: 63 mm is a large size for this fish.

FOOD REQUIREMENTS: Prefers live foods but gets along very well on a good flake food.

## *Moenkhausia agnesae* Gery • Agnes' Tetra

RANGE: Igarape Preto (Black Stream), Brazil.

HABITS: This fish has only been imported once when the author (HRA), with Harald Schultz, brought back a dozen or so specimens for their aquariums. The fish lost the immensely outstanding colors they had in nature. They were never spawned or they would have been popular.

WATER CONDITIONS: They did well in acid water, pH 5.6-6.6, at 27°C.

SIZE: They reached about 100 mm.

FOOD REQUIREMENTS: They did well on small crustaceans and dried foods.

## *Moenkhausia georgiae* Gery • Georgi Gery's Tetra

RANGE: Widely distributed but rare in most areas. Specimens have been found from Guyana to Mato Grosso, Brazil.

HABITS: A very pretty fish with a deep body, sparkling scales and an apparent black eye. This fish was especially suitable for naming after his wife for Jacques Gery thought this fish was beautiful, too. His wife is a stunningly beautiful blonde.

WATER CONDITIONS: Thrives in water with a pH 6.0-6.8 and at a water temperature between 25-30°C.

SIZE: About 65 mm.

FOOD REQUIREMENTS: Prefers live foods but gets along well on normal flake foods.

## *Moenkhausia intermedia* (Eigenmann) • False Spot-tailed Tetra

RANGE: Throughout northern South America. Very common throughout its range.

HABITS: This fish and several species that look very much alike (such as *M. dichroura*) are difficult to distinguish since they are differentiated solely by the bones of their jaws.

WATER CONDITIONS: All species that have the central parts of their caudal lobes pigmented in black have the same needs: pH 6.2-6.6; temperature 25-30°C.

SIZE: Reaches about 75 mm.

FOOD REQUIREMENTS: Prefers live foods but accepts flake foods readily.

Ctenobrycon spilurus

Bryconops melanurus

Bryconops affinis

Moenkhausia agnesae

Moenkhausia collettii

Moenkhausia georgiae

Moenkhausia gracilima

Moenkhausia intermedia

Plate #97

Moenkhausia

Moenkhausia lepidura

Moenkhausia oligolepis

Moenkhausia sanctaefilomenae

Moenkhausia lepidura icae

Moenkhausia pittieri

Moenkhausia robertsi

Moenkhausia takasei

*Plate #98*

*Moenkhausia ?* • Moenkhausia Question Mark

RANGE: *Moenkhausia* ranges over northern South America but this species is nowhere abundant.
HABITS: *Moenkhausia* Question Mark isn't as funny as it sounds! It looks a lot like *Moenkhausia comma* from the Amazon Basin and may be one of the prettiest species of *Moenkhausia* with its specially marked humeral spot ringed in gold and a golden line running into the blood red tail. The author (HRA) discovered this fish and brought back some specimens that were necessarily carried in the unheated hold of the plane where they all died.
WATER CONDITIONS: They thrive in slightly acid water that's a bit cool; pH 6.4 at 25°C.
SIZE: Up to 100 mm; perhaps larger.
FOOD REQUIREMENTS: In nature they have insects as their main diet but they probably will accept any small live foods.

*Moenkhausia oligolepis* (Guenther) • Glass Tetra

RANGE: Guyana and the upper Amazon regions.
HABITS: Quite peaceful, but must not be kept with smaller fishes.
WATER CONDITIONS: Soft, slightly acid water and a large tank are required. Temperature 22 to 25°C.
SIZE: 11 cm, usually smaller.
FOOD REQUIREMENTS: Must be fed generously with mostly live or frozen foods; if hungry they may nip plants.

*Moenkhausia lepidura icae* Eigenmann
The description of *Moenkhausia lepidura* applies to this subspecies from Rio Ica as well.

*Moenkhausia robertsi* Gery • Iquitos Moenkhausia

RANGE: Upper Amazon. The fish shown here was discovered by the author (HRA) near Iquitos, Peru.
HABITS: A very active and hardy fish for the aquarium. It has never been spawned but it doesn't appear to be a fish that would give the serious breeder a problem.
WATER CONDITIONS: Slightly acid, about pH 6.6-7.0, at a temperature ranging from 25 to 30°C.
SIZE: About 60 mm.
FOOD REQUIREMENTS: Prefers live foods but easily acclimates to an aquarium diet.

*Moenkhausia lepidura* (Kner) • Half-mast Flag Tetra

RANGE: Throughout the Amazon basin north to the Guianas. Very abundant and with slightly different coloration in some forms (see *Bryconops affinis*).
HABITS: The *Lepidura*-group of *Moenkhausia* have all their color concentrated in the unpaired fins especially along the dorsal edges, including only the upper lobe of the caudal (tail) fin. Compare this coloration to *Bryconops* sp. *cf. affinis*, *B. melanurus*, and *M. l. icae*. Note that all have the same color pattern even though they do not have the same colors.
WATER CONDITIONS: They thrive in acid water, pH 6.0-6.4, at 27°C but they get along in a widely variable environment.
SIZE: To 56 mm.
FOOD REQUIREMENTS: They enjoy live food and attack it voraciously, but they can easily be trained to accept flake foods, too.

*Moenkhausia sanctaefilomenae* (Steindachner) •
Yellow-banded Moenkhausia

RANGE: Paraguay Basin.
HABITS: Peaceful toward other fishes and very active.
WATER CONDITIONS: Not critical, but slightly acid, soft water is preferred. Temperature 24 to 26°C.
SIZE: To 7 cm.
FOOD REQUIREMENTS: Omnivorous, with a good appetite; if fed with a good amount of vegetable substances, it will not nibble plants to any great extent.

*Moenkhausia pittieri* Eigenmann • Diamond Tetra

RANGE: Environs of Lake Valencia, Venezuela.
HABITS: Peaceful and very active.
WATER CONDITIONS: Large, well-planted tanks are best. Temperature 24 to 27°C.
SIZE: To 6 cm.
FOOD REQUIREMENTS: A good eater which will take practically any kind of food but should have a supplement of vegetable matter, like lettuce leaves.
COLOR VARIATIONS: Body color yellowish, darker above; upper half of body gleams golden, the lower part iridescent; unpaired fins milky violet.

*Moenkhausia takasei* Gery • Takase's Moenkhausia

RANGE: This species was discovered and collected by Mr. Takase and Harald Schultz in the Mato Grosso region of Brazil and other areas south of the Amazon.
HABITS: Takase was a Japanese fish collector and breeder who settled in Sao Paulo, Brazil and became friends with the author (HRA) and Harald Schultz. The author frequently sent him fishes from the jungle to be held for months until it was time to return to New Jersey. Specimens were sent to Dr. Gery with the request to name it in honor of Takase. All specimens living were given to Takase but they all perished before he was able to breed them and nothing is known about their aquarium habits.
SIZE: To about 45 mm.
FOOD REQUIREMENTS: They ate flake foods in the jungle when we kept them in net traps; Takase fed them live foods.

*Moenkhausia* sp. • Undescribed Moenkhausia species

Throughout Brazil where the author (HRA) has spent almost 40 years collecting both fishes and fish fossils, he has discovered some 26 different *Moenkhausia*. Many (most) of them have never been described because of the complexity of the task or the lack of interest by scientists who by their very nature work slowly and carefully. Through this book you will find fishes that are simply called "species" because they have not been identified. Hopefully, in future editions of this book there will be additional information or the fishes will be described so that we can give a name to these "species." They have never been imported alive and nothing is known about their aquarium needs.

*Tetragonopterus argenteus* Cuvier • Silver Tetra

RANGE: Amazon and La Plata Basins.
HABITS: Generally peaceful, but larger individuals may become unsociable.
WATER CONDITIONS: Prefers mature, slightly acid water with a hardness about 10°DH. Temperature should be about 24° to 27°C.
SIZE: About 115 mm.
FOOD REQUIREMENTS: Will accept a wide variety of foods including brine shrimp, daphnia, tubifex, mosquito larvae, chironomid larvae, and flake foods.

*Schultzites axelrodi* Gery • Axelrod's Moenkhausia

RANGE: Discovered by the author (HRA) in the Rio Meta, Colombia.
HABITS: It closely resembles the two fishes *Moenkhausia dichroura* and *M. intermedia* but it has twice as many teeth as they do which is obvious as soon as you see them. They behave well in an aquarium but they probably are scale eaters who mimic the *Moenkhausia*.
WATER CONDITIONS: Cooler water with a pH 6.4-7.0 at 24°C.
SIZE: Reaches about 100 mm but most of the specimens are half that size.
FOOD REQUIREMENTS: They seem to accept flake foods as well as live foods. They never eat scales in the aquarium but the stomach contents of two fish collected by the author had scales in them.

*Gymnocorymbus ternetzi* (Boulenger) • Black Tetra

RANGE: Paraguay and Rio Guapore Basins in southern Brazil, Argentina and Bolivia.
HABITS: A fast moving fish which is responsible for some fin nipping, but it cannot do real damage to fishes larger than itself.
WATER CONDITIONS: This is not a warm water fish as so many people think. It does best in temperatures in the low 20's (°C).
SIZE: In nature specimens as large as 8 cm are found; tank-raised specimens rarely grow larger than 4 cm.
FOOD REQUIREMENTS: To be at its best this fish requires live food, but it can live for years with nothing but pelletized dry food and a bit of frozen brine shrimp now and then.

*Tetragonopterus chalceus* Agassiz • False Silver Tetra

RANGE: Throughout South America east of the Andes, but mostly from the Guianas and Rio Sao Francisco.
HABITS: An easily collected fish as it favors small, open slow-moving streams making netting it easy. The genus *Tetragonopterus* was once the catchall genus for some 130+ species of "tetras."
WATER CONDITIONS: Slightly acid and cool water with a pH 6.5 and a water temperature between 23-25°C.
SIZE: Reaches about 100 mm.
FOOD REQUIREMENTS: Eats everything that is normal for aquarium fishes including flake foods and live foods.

*Bario steindachneri* (Eigenmann) • Blotch-tailed Bario

RANGE: Peruvian Amazon.
HABITS: Peaceful toward fishes of comparable size.
WATER CONDITIONS: Prefers slightly acid, clean, soft water. Temperature 24 to 27°C.
SIZE: Specimens of 10 cm have been known.
FOOD REQUIREMENTS: Eats all kinds of foods, but is especially fond of frozen brine shrimp. Live foods should be offered once a week.

*Gymnocorymbus socolofi* Gery • Rio Meta Black Tetra

RANGE: Upper Rio Meta, Colombia.
HABITS: This species was discovered by the author (HRA) in the 1960's. It became quite popular when it was imported in large numbers because it was found with other valuable fish and the success of the collecting ventures depended upon filling an airplane full of fishes. Once the economic pressure disappeared the fish fell into disfavor because of its tendency to bite other fishes and it was no longer worth collecting for itself.
WATER CONDITIONS: Acid water with the pH about 6.0 and with a temperature between 25-27°C.
SIZE: Reaches over 100 mm.
FOOD REQUIREMENTS: Unless it is fed live foods it loses its red color. Insects especially (drosophila) are needed to keep this fish in color.

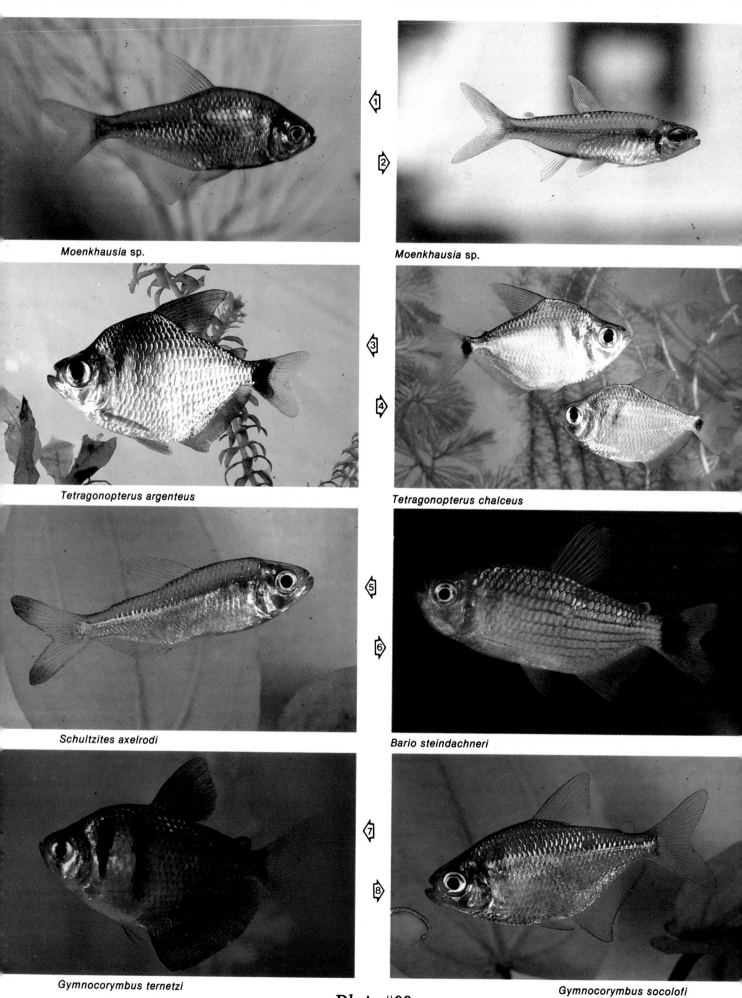

Moenkhausia sp.

Moenkhausia sp.

Tetragonopterus argenteus

Tetragonopterus chalceus

Schultzites axelrodi

Bario steindachneri

Gymnocorymbus ternetzi

Gymnocorymbus socolofi

*Plate #99*

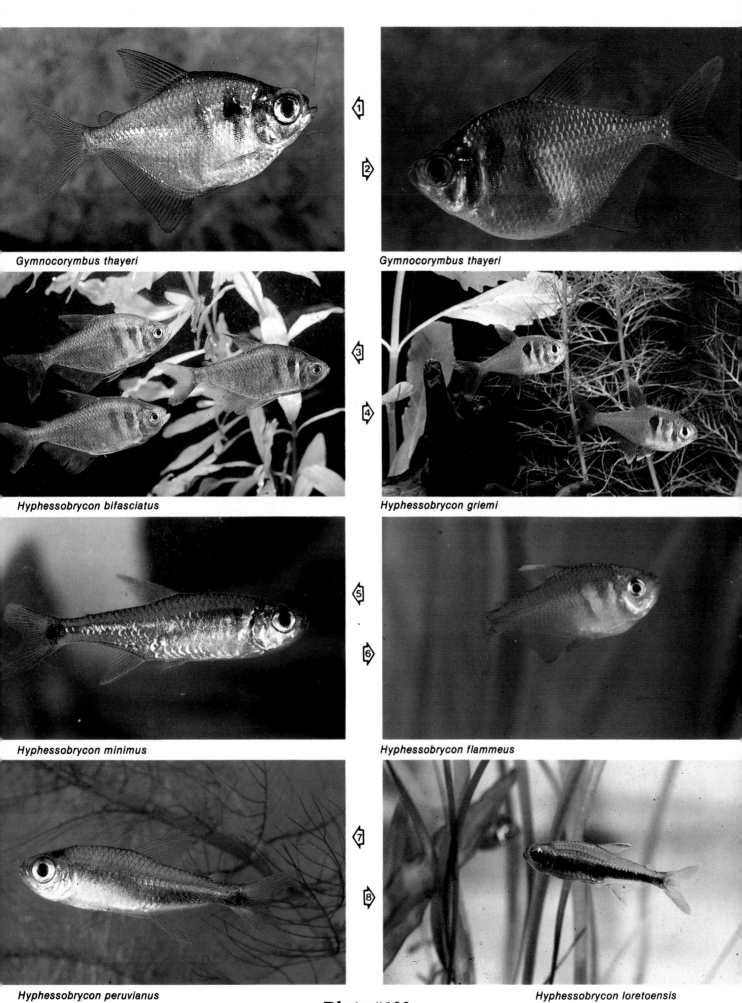

Gymnocorymbus thayeri

Gymnocorymbus thayeri

Hyphessobrycon bifasciatus

Hyphessobrycon griemi

Hyphessobrycon minimus

Hyphessobrycon flammeus

Hyphessobrycon peruvianus

Hyphessobrycon loretoensis

*Plate #100*

173

**Gymnocorymbus thayeri** Eigenmann • Straight-finned
Black Tetra

RANGE: Upper Amazon, Bolivia and Colombia in warmer
waters.
HABITS: A fast swimming fish which should be well fed at
all times if kept in a community aquarium.
WATER CONDITIONS: Prefers warmer, softer and more acid
waters than its much blacker cousin, *G. ternetzi*.
Temperature 24 to 26°C.
SIZE: Not larger than 5 cm.
FOOD REQUIREMENTS: Prefers copious feedings of live
foods, but does equally well if fed frozen brine shrimp
and a varied diet of prepared foods. Some live food
should be offered weekly.

**Hyphessobrycon bifasciatus** Ellis • Yellow Tetra

RANGE: Southeastern Brazil, near the coast.
HABITS: Very peaceful; will not attack other fishes or plants.
WATER CONDITIONS: Neutral to slightly acid. Temperature
22 to 24°C.
SIZE: Up to 5 cm.
FOOD REQUIREMENTS: All foods gratefully eaten, prepared
as well as live or frozen.

**Hyphessobrycon griemi** Hoedeman • Griem's Tetra

RANGE: Brazil, in the vicinity of Goyaz.
HABITS: Perfectly peaceful; like the other small members
of the family, they also prefer to be kept in groups of at
least six.
WATER CONDITIONS: Soft, slightly acid water is best but not
necessarily essential. Temperature 24 to 26°C.
SIZE: About 4 cm.
FOOD REQUIREMENTS: Prepared foods are accepted, but
live or frozen foods are preferable.

**Hyphessobrycon minimus** Durbin • False Gold Tetra

RANGE: Guyana.
HABITS: A peaceful little characin that often came in mixed
with similar looking fishes from Guyana. It was never
pretty enough to be spawned commercially as cheap imports were always available.
WATER CONDITIONS: Water with a pH of 6.4-7.2 and a temperature between 25-30°C.
SIZE: Up to about 65 mm.
FOOD REQUIREMENTS: Likes all kinds of typical aquarium
diets.

**Hyphessobrycon flammeus** Myers • Flame Tetra, Red
Tetra, Tetra from Rio

RANGE: Region near Rio de Janeiro.
HABITS: Peaceful; best kept with other small fishes and in
a school of at least six.
WATER CONDITIONS: Not critical; water is best if slightly
acid and soft, but this is not absolutely essential.
Temperature of 24 to 26°C.
SIZE: To 4 cm.
FOOD REQUIREMENTS: Prepared foods accepted, but live or
frozen foods are preferred.

**Hyphessobrycon peruvianus** Ladiges • Loreto Tetra

RANGE: Peruvian Amazon.
HABITS: Peaceful and a bit shy; should not be kept with large
or aggressive fishes.
WATER CONDITIONS: Soft, slightly acid water is best but
is not absolutely essential. Temperature 24 to 28°C.
SIZE: 5 cm; most specimens smaller.
FOOD REQUIREMENTS: Live foods preferred, but frozen or
prepared foods are accepted without any trouble.

**Hyphessobrycon loretoensis** Ladiges • Tetra Loreto

RANGE: Peruvian Amazon.
HABITS: A very peaceful fish that previously was imported
in huge quantities but gradually fell into disfavor. It is
rarely seen any more as tank-bred specimens lose much
of their purple color.
WATER CONDITIONS: Do best in acid water at a pH of 6.0-6.6
and a temperature between 26-30°C.
SIZE: A small tetra about 40 mm.
FOOD REQUIREMENTS: Likes newly hatched brine shrimp as
do most fishes, but it accepts fine flake foods as well.

## *Hyphessobrycon saizi* Gery • Saiz' Tetra

RANGE: Colombia, where it was discovered by the author (HRA) and named after an employee of TFH, Capt. Emilio Saiz.
HABITS: This is probably just a diseased form of *H. metae*, but it doesn't matter since the fish has disappeared. This strange disappearance adds strength to the conclusion that the fish is *H. metae* with the gold disease.
WATER CONDITIONS: Slightly acid water (pH 6.5) at a temperature of 25°C.
SIZE: Almost 53 mm.
FOOD REQUIREMENTS: Eats a normal aquarium diet.

## *Hyphessobrycon herbertaxelrodi* Gery • Black Neon Tetra

RANGE: Rio Taquary, Brazil.
HABITS: Peaceful toward other fishes; prefers to be kept in a group of at least six.
WATER CONDITIONS: Soft, slightly acid water preferred but not essential. Temperature 25°C.
SIZE: About 3 cm.
FOOD REQUIREMENTS: Hearty eaters; prepared foods as well as live or frozen foods are eaten with equal gusto.

## *Hyphessobrycon vilmae* Gery • Vilma's Tetra

RANGE: Northern and central Brazil.
HABITS: A lively nature yet not aggressive, but can be a fin-nipper.
WATER CONDITIONS: Somewhat on the acid size; a small fluctuation of DH will be tolerated. Temperature 24°C.
SIZE: To 4 cm.
FOOD REQUIREMENTS: Will accept freeze-dried foods and also dry foods; live foods are naturally relished.

## *Hyphessobrycon agulha* Fowler • Red-tailed Flag Tetra

RANGE: Upper Amazon region.
HABITS: Peaceful; likes to swim in schools.
WATER CONDITIONS: Soft, slightly acid water. Temperature 24 to 26°C.
SIZE: About 5 cm.
FOOD REQUIREMENTS: Will accept dried foods, but live or frozen foods should be given frequently.

## *Hyphessobrycon scholzei* Ahl • Black-lined Tetra

RANGE: Vicinity of Para, Brazil.
HABITS: Peaceful; will not harm other fishes or plants.
WATER CONDITIONS: Soft and slightly acid water is preferable but not essential. Temperature 23 to 26°C.
SIZE: To 5 cm.
FOOD REQUIREMENTS: Prepared foods accepted readily, but they should be supplemented with frozen and live foods.

## *Hyphessobrycon heterorhabdus* (Ulrey) • Flag Tetra, False Ulreyi

RANGE: Lower and middle Amazon region.
HABITS: Peaceful and very active.
WATER CONDITIONS: A little sensitive if not given soft, slightly acid water. Temperature should be kept around 25°C.
SIZE: About 5 cm.
FOOD REQUIREMENTS: Will take dried foods readily, but should also get frequent feedings of live or frozen foods.

## *Hyphessobrycon georgettae* Gery • Georgette's Tetra

RANGE: Surinam.
HABITS: A pretty little tetra that Dr. Jacques Gery thought was pretty enough to be named after his wife, Georgette. The fish is nicely colored when wild and the translucent flesh is rose colored, but after being bred once the fish is not very attractive unless fed heavily on brine shrimp.
WATER CONDITIONS: Acid water, about pH 6.3, and a temperature of 25-30°C.
SIZE: About 50 mm.
FOOD REQUIREMENTS: Needs live brine shrimp but subsists on the normal aquarium diet.

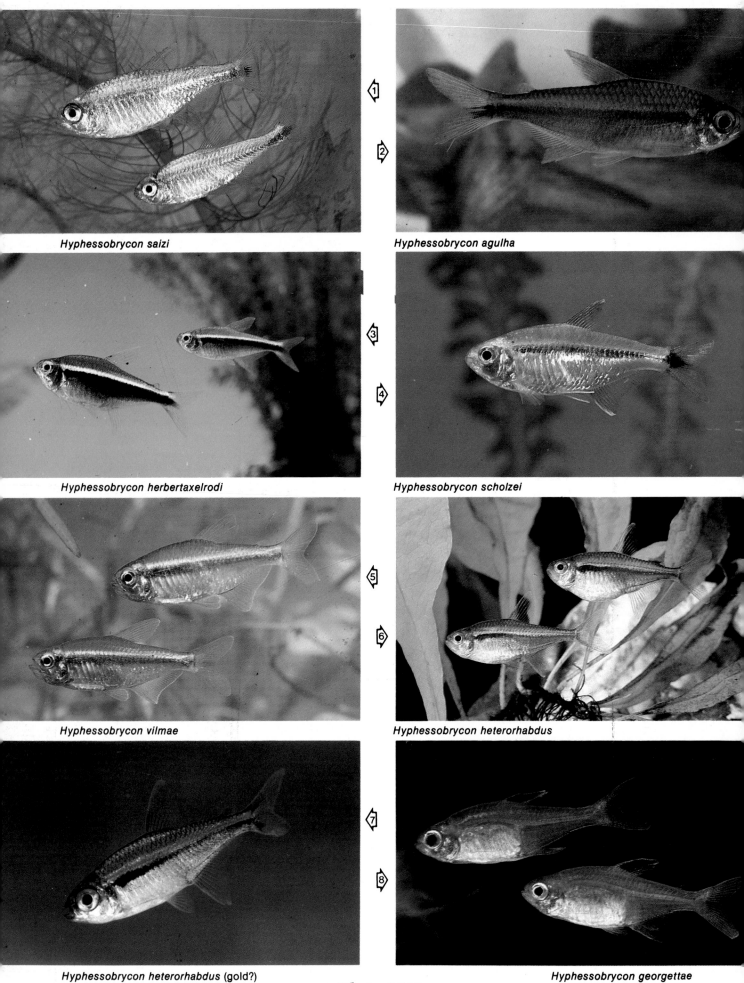

Hyphessobrycon saizi

Hyphessobrycon agulha

Hyphessobrycon herbertaxelrodi

Hyphessobrycon scholzei

Hyphessobrycon vilmae

Hyphessobrycon heterorhabdus

Hyphessobrycon heterorhabdus (gold?)

Hyphessobrycon georgettae

*Plate #101*

Above: Beginning the spawning ritual, the male (lower fish in both photos) pursues the female and drives her through the tank. Below: At left, the male displays before the female near the plant thicket; at right, the fish have entered the plant thicket and are shown just before the actual moment of spawning.

Plate #102

## SPAWNING THE SERPAE TETRA, *HYPHESSOBRYCON SERPAE*

The serpae tetra does best in schooling groups. One should, therefore, keep 8 to 12 of them in a roomy tank. At a minimum temperature of 20°C, they feel happiest in a medium to large tank with good illumination. The water should be clear, soft (but not too soft) and slightly acid.

The sexual differences among *H. serpae* individuals are not always easy to make out. Male and female look very much alike, and their coloration is the same. The adult male is more slender, however, and—as can be seen against the light—the male's air bladder is more pointed at its rear. For breeding, it is best to select a courting male from the school. Put the male in the spawning tank one day earlier than the female. The fish spawn very readily and are content with an all-glass tank containing 10 to 15 liters of water that is not too hard. The temperature should be raised to 24-26°C. The fish use fine-leaved plants for spawning. The male starts to court by fluttering about in front of the female; he later swims around the female on the way to the spawning site, though mostly he stays in front of her, luring her on and not getting alongside until immediately before the act of spawning. Sometimes, not always, the male puts his caudal fin underneath the female's body. With a sudden jerk, the sexual products are discharged, the fish separate, and the eggs fall down. All this happens within a fraction of a second. The act of spawning is repeated about 20 times within 2 to 4 hours, and several hundred eggs are laid. A good pair often produces 300 fry.

Immediately after the spawning has ended the parents should be removed from the spawning tank. No harm is done by darkening the spawning tank. As soon as the fry have resorbed their yolk sacs they should be given the finest live food, being graduated to larger fare as soon as they can eat it.

*Hyphessobrycon copelandi* Durbin • Callistus Tetra

RANGE: Upper and middle Amazon basin.
HABITS: This is one of the many tetras that have the same general shape and color pattern and that are found in non-overlapping ranges. Most of them are simply called *Hyphessobrycon "callistus"* in the aquarium trade.
WATER CONDITIONS: Slightly acid water with a pH of 6.4-6.8 and a water temperature between 25-30°C.
SIZE: About 48 mm.
FOOD REQUIREMENTS: Prefers live foods but gets along well on small aquarium foods.

*Hyphessobrycon socolofi* Weitzman • Lesser Bleeding Heart

RANGE: Upper Amazon basin.
HABITS: A pale, sickly looking fish when compared to the rest of the *Hyphessobrycon* on this page. It is far from an aquarium favorite and it probably has no future. It has never been bred and it is doubtful that it ever will. No fish with a deep red humeral spot in the family Characidae has ever been spawned. It is distinguished from the bleeding heart tetra by the uniform width of the white anal fin band.
WATER CONDITIONS: Survives under all normal aquarium conditions. No special requirements.
SIZE: Reach 60 mm.
FOOD REQUIREMENTS: Eats a normal aquarium diet.

*Hyphessobrycon takasei* Gery • Coffee Bean Tetra

RANGE: Amapa Territory in northern Brazil.
HABITS: Very peaceful; will not harm plants or other fishes.
WATER CONDITIONS: Soft, acid water is optimal. Temperature 24 to 26°C.
SIZE: About 3 cm.
FOOD REQUIREMENTS: Prefers live foods, but will accept frozen, freeze-dried or dried foods as well.

*Hyphessobrycon serpae* Durbin • Serpae Tetra

RANGE: Amazon River (Madeira and Guapore regions) and upper Paraguay.
HABITS: Mostly peaceful, but will sometimes take a dislike to a fish and nip fins.
WATER CONDITIONS: Soft, slightly acid water.

SIZE: Up to 4 cm; usually smaller.
FOOD REQUIREMENTS: Does very well on dried foods, but of course should get occasional feedings with live or frozen foods.

*Hyphessobrycon erythrostigma* (Fowler) • Bleeding Heart Tetra, Tetra Perez

RANGE: Upper Amazon.
HABITS: Peaceful if kept with fishes of its own size.
WATER CONDITIONS: Slightly acid, soft water. Temperature 23 to 26°C.
SIZE: To 8 cm.
FOOD REQUIREMENTS: Live or frozen foods preferred; prepared foods taken if hungry.

*Hyphessobrycon bentosi* Durbin • Rosy Tetra

RANGE: Amazon Basin and Guianas.
HABITS: Peaceful; should be kept in groups of at least six.
WATER CONDITIONS: Soft, slightly acid water is best. Temperature 24 to 27°C.
SIZE: To 5 cm.
FOOD REQUIREMENTS: Prepared foods accepted, but live and frozen foods preferred.

*Hyphessobrycon species* • Tetra Robertsi

RANGE: There are "robertsi" found in Peru, Colombia, and Brazil.
HABITS: There are many fish, mostly of a difficult scientific group, which are sold as "callistus", "robertsi", "Perez", etc. These are all what once were called "flag-fin" tetras. If you look at photos 7 and 8 you can see the most colorful (known as "robertsi") and most plain (known as "callistus").
WATER CONDITIONS: They prefer warm, slightly acid waters at a pH of 6.4-6.8 and a water temperature between 26-30°C.
SIZE: Up to 65 mm.
FOOD REQUIREMENTS: They prefer live foods but they take to a normal flake food diet without any difficulty.

Hyphessobrycon copelandi

Hyphessobrycon serpae

Hyphessobrycon socolofi

Hyphessobrycon erythrostigma

Hyphessobrycon takasei

Hyphessobrycon bentosi

Hyphessobrycon sp. (callistus group)

*Plate #103*

Hyphessobrycon sp. (tetra Robertsi)

Parapristella georgiae

Hemigrammus stictus

Hemigrammus erythrozonus

Hemigrammus bellottii

Hemigrammus levis

Hemigrammus hyanuary

Hemigrammus ocellifer

*Plate #104*

Hemigrammus marginatus

181

*Parapristella georgiae* Gery • Plain Jane

RANGE: Upper Rio Meta.
HABITS: A simple little tetra is probably a species of *Hemigrammus*. There are two species in this genus, the other being *P. aubynei* from Guyana which is probably a *Pristella*.
WATER CONDITIONS: Warm, slightly acid water with a pH of 6.5-6.8 and a temperature of 25-30°C.
SIZE: Barely reaches 76 mm.
FOOD REQUIREMENTS: Eats a normal aquarium diet but its strong, numerous teeth indicate it is a live food eater, too.

*Hemigrammus erythrozonus* (Durbin) • Glowlight Tetra

RANGE: The Guianas and adjacent regions of the Amazon.
HABITS: One of the most peaceful of all tetras.
WATER CONDITIONS: Should have a clean aquarium at all times, with slightly acid, soft water. Temperature 23 to 26°C.
FOOD REQUIREMENTS: Will eat dry food, but this should often be augmented with live and frozen foods.
COLOR VARIATIONS: Body greenish and very transparent, with a brilliant, glowing red or purple line running from the upper edge of the eye to the caudal base.

*Hemigrammus levis* Durbin • Golden Neon

RANGE: The middle Amazon basin.
HABITS: Found in small, dark streams, this lovely fish doesn't look well in this photo but the body glistens with a metallic golden sheen that includes the dorsal, adipose, and upper caudal lobe, the lateral line, and the upper part of the eye and operculum. Add to this a peaceful hardy fish and you have the golden neon.
WATER CONDITIONS: Prefers acid water, pH 6.0-6.8, at a temperature of 26-30°C.
SIZE: A small tetra never reaching 50 mm.
FOOD REQUIREMENTS: Small live foods like brine shrimp should be given between normal feedings of flake foods.

*Hemigrammus ocellifer* (Steindachner) • Head and Tail Light

RANGE: Widely distributed throughout the Amazon region, especially in the southern part.
HABITS: Mostly peaceful, if kept with fishes their own size.
WATER CONDITIONS: Not critical, but warm temperatures are preferred. Temperature 25 to 26°C.
SIZE: About 4 cm.
FOOD REQUIREMENTS: Will get along very well on dry foods.

*Hemigrammus stictus* (Durbin)

RANGE: Throughout the Amazon basin north to the Guianas and the Rio Meta.
HABITS: A very peaceful fish which, in some habitats, is also very beautiful with a magnificent red blotch covering the caudal peduncle and the central parts of the caudal fin. The redness envelops the rear of the body including the adipose fin.
WATER CONDITIONS: Very acid water is preferred, from pH 5.8-6.4 at a temperature of 26-30°C. It loses the red when the water is not acid enough.
SIZE: To about 55 mm.
FOOD REQUIREMENTS: Prefers live foods, but this peaceful species gets along on the usual aquarium diet, too.

*Hemigrammus bellottii* (Steindachner) • Dash-Dot Tetra

RANGE: Upper Amazon tributaries.
HABITS: Peaceful and active; prefer to swim in a group of their own kind.
WATER CONDITIONS: Soft, acid water preferred. Temperature 24 to 27°C.
SIZE: To 2.5 cm.
FOOD REQUIREMENTS: Because of their small size, small foods of all kinds are recommended.

*Hemigrammus hyanuary* (Durbin) • January Tetra

RANGE: Amazon tributaries near Leticia, Colombia.
HABITS: Very peaceful; prefers to be in a school with others of its own kind.
WATER CONDITIONS: Not critical; best is water which is neutral to slightly acid in character. Temperature 23 to 26°C.
SIZE: About 4 cm.
FOOD REQUIREMENTS: Live or frozen foods are of course preferred, but dried foods are also accepted eagerly.

*Hemigrammus marginatus* Ellis • Bassam Tetra

RANGE: Venezuela to Argentina.
HABITS: Peaceful.
WATER CONDITIONS: Fairly soft and slightly acid. Temperature 24 to 26°C.
SIZE: To 7 cm.
FOOD REQUIREMENTS: Live or frozen foods preferred; will also accept prepared foods.

*Hemigrammus rodwayi* Durbin • Gold Tetra

RANGE: Guianas and the Upper Amazon.
HABITS: Peaceful; prefers to be kept in a school.
WATER CONDITIONS: Not critical, but water should be
 somewhere near neutral.
SIZE: About 5 cm.
FOOD REQUIREMENTS: Live foods preferred, but frozen and
 prepared foods are also readily accepted.

*Hemigrammus pulcher* Ladiges • Garnet Tetra

RANGE: Peruvian Amazon, Loreto region.
HABITS: Peaceful; will not bother plants or other fishes.
WATER CONDITIONS: Prefers a roomy, well-planted tank.
 Most important requirement is warmth, 26 to 27°C.
SIZE: About 5 cm.
FOOD REQUIREMENTS: Will not refuse dried foods, but
 should be given frequent changes to live or frozen foods.
COLOR VARIATIONS: Greenish body with a small shoulder
 spot and indistinct horizontal line. Upper half of caudal
 base deep red, with black area below.

*Hemigrammus unilineatus* (Gill) • Featherfin Tetra

RANGE: Trinidad and northern South America from Venezuela
 to Brazil.
HABITS: Peaceful; a heavy eater which should have plenty
 of swimming room.
WATER CONDITIONS: Should have a sunny aquarium with
 fairly high temperatures, 26 to 27°C.
SIZE: Attains a length of 5 cm; most specimens smaller.
FOOD REQUIREMENTS: Like all active fish, a heavy eater.
 If possible, should be fed several times daily. Will take
 dried foods, but live foods should also be fed.
COLOR VARIATIONS: Body silvery with a gold horizontal
 stripe. First rays of the dorsal and anal fins white, with a
 black streak behind. Brazilian variety has red fins.

*Hemigrammus mattei* Eigenmann • Slender head
and tail light

RANGE: Paraguay, Argentina; probably more dispersed.
HABITS: A peaceful fish which during the period from 1920-
 1958 was very popular. It is now confused with every fish
 that has a shining spot over the eye and in the tail. The
 identification of this fish is tentative and it may well be a
 new species.
WATER CONDITIONS: Should be kept at   pH 6.4-7.2 and a
 temperature of 23-28°C.
SIZE: Up to 45 mm.
FOOD REQUIREMENTS: Prefers small living foods but also
 accepts a normal aquarium diet.

*Hemigrammus boesemani* (Gery) • Boeseman's Tetra

RANGE: Guianas and upper Amazon.
HABITS: A non descript fish that is only imported accidentally with other fishes. It has few redeeming features colorwise, but it is peaceful and when in superb condition does
 show a few metallic markings at the base of the upper
 caudal lobe and along the lateral line. It was formerly
 considered a subspecies of *H. micropterus*.
WATER CONDITIONS: pH 6.4-6.9 at a temperature of 25-30°C.
SIZE: To 52 mm.
FOOD REQUIREMENTS: Eats a normal aquarium diet.

*Hemigrammus barrigone* Eigenmann • Henn Meta Pink

RANGE: Rio Meta, Colombia.
HABITS: A robust and delightful fish for the aquarium. It
 changes colors dramatically but always in subtle shades
 of pink, gray, and white. The females (illustrated here)
 are very fat and full and have huge spawns of over 1,000
 eggs.
WATER CONDITIONS: A pH of 6.2-6.8 and a temperature of
 25-30°C.
SIZE: Barely reaches 50 mm.
FOOD REQUIREMENTS: Prefers live foods but takes flake
 foods readily.

Hemigrammus rodwayi (armstrongi var.)

Hemigrammus rodwayi

Hemigrammus pulcher pulcher

Hemigrammus pulcher haraldi

Hemigrammus unilineatus

Hemigrammus mattei

Hemigrammus boesemani

Hemigrammus barrigone

*Plate #105*

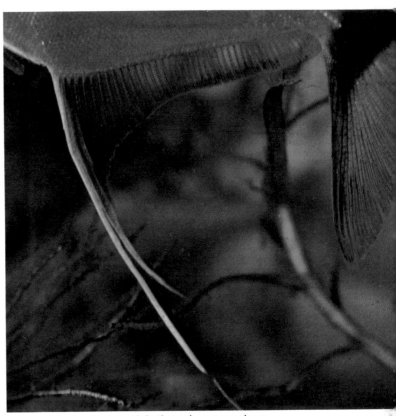

The false wimple piranha can be distinguished from the true wimple piranha mainly through a comparison of the length of the anterior rays of the dorsal and anal fins. In the photos on this page, (note especially the close up of the ventral area above right) which are of the false wimple piranha, the anterior dorsal and anal rays are seen to extend beyond the tips of the caudal lobes. Additionally, the red spot present on the cheek of many true wimple piranhas is not present on any of the false wimple piranhas.

*Plate #106*

## THE FALSE WIMPLE PIRANHA, *CATOPRION* "BLEHER"

The Mato Grosso of Brazil is a huge piece of real estate—this single Brazilian state has an area the size of Texas, Utah, Nebraska and Colorado combined. In its western corner along the Bolivian border is a virtually unexplored system of rivers, streams, and swamps that are part of the Rio Guapore drainage. Few collectors—or even scientists—have ventured into this country, but it was here that Heiko Bleher, German fish collector and dealer *extraordinaire,* collected the regal false wimple piranha. Seemingly an undescribed species, its graceful finnage puts it in a class with only the angelfish among freshwater fishes when it comes to length of fins. Heiko was able to collect only 17 specimens after days of intensive diving in the dense caiman-infested aquatic gardens of the Guapore, also making this one of the rarest and most desirable of recent aquarium imports.

Even the true wimple piranha, *Catoprion mento,* is far from being a common fish in the aquarium hobby, and there are few specimens in museum collections. The oddly undershot lower jaw of the wimples is a specialization for scale-eating, although this unusual habit was only confirmed a bit over 30 years ago. In the aquarium the wimples take most normal aquarium foods as well as small fishes and seldom bother their neighbors for a bite of scales.

The most obvious difference between the true wimple piranha and the undescribed false wimple is of course the length of the anterior rays of the dorsal and anal fins. In fully developed specimens of the new species these rays extend beyond the tips of the caudal lobes. The red spot on the cheek that is so prominent in at least many true wimples seems to be lacking in *Catoprion* "Bleher," and there are probably consistent small differences in structural characters. Dr. Jacques Gery, eminent authority on the taxonomy of the characoid fishes, is studying the status of the false wimple and will eventually clarify the situation.

Heiko Bleher reported in full on his trip to the Mato Grosso in the June, 1983, issue of *Tropical Fish Hobbyist* magazine, an article well worth reading.

## *Hemigrammus schmardae* (Steindachner) • Schmard Tetra

RANGE: Upper Rio Negro River, Brazil.
HABITS: Very peaceful.
WATER CONDITIONS: Soft, acid water preferred, but not essential. Temperature 24 to 27°C.
SIZE: Up to 5 cm.
FOOD REQUIREMENTS: Dried as well as live foods.

## *Hemigrammus rhodostomus* Ahl • Rummy-nose Tetra

RANGE: Lower Amazon region, around Aripiranga and Para.
HABITS: Peaceful; is most at home with lively fishes of about its own size.
WATER CONDITIONS: Best kept in a well planted, well established, well heated tank. Temperature about 26°C.
SIZE: 4 to 5 cm.
FOOD REQUIREMENTS: Will get along fairly well on dried food, but should get an occasional meal of live or frozen food.

## *Hemigrammus caudovittatus* Ahl • Buenos Aires Tetra

RANGE: Region around Buenos Aires.
HABITS: Fairly peaceful with fishes about its size; should not be kept with thread-finned fishes, whose fins it nips.
WATER CONDITIONS: Neutral to slightly acid. Can withstand temperatures around 21°C for a time; should be kept about 25° normally.
SIZE: About 10 cm.
FOOD REQUIREMENTS: Seems to like dried foods as well as live foods; has a good appetite and should be fed generously.

## *Axelrodia lindeae* Gery • Lindy Tetra

RANGE: Amazon basin near Obidos and Porto Velho.
HABITS: An extremely peaceful fish, as are all fishes of the genus. *Axelrodia* was named in honor of the author (HRA) by Dr. Jacques Gery. Only a few specimens of this species were brought out alive by the author, and they did not survive to be bred.
WATER CONDITIONS: Normal water at a pH of 6.4-7.2; temperature 25-30°C.
SIZE: Mostly less than 4 cm.
FOOD REQUIREMENTS: Does best on brine shrimp but accepts any aquarium diet small enough for it to ingest.

## *Hemigrammus coeruleus* Durbin • Coerulean Tetra

RANGE: Manacapuru, Brazil.
HABITS: Peaceful when kept with fishes of its own size.
WATER CONDITIONS: Neutral to slightly acid. Temperature 23 to 26°C.
SIZE: To about 7.5 cm.
FOOD REQUIREMENTS: Will accept prepared foods, but should also get live and frozen foods.

## *Hasemania nana* (Reinhardt) • Silver-tipped Tetra

RANGE: Rio S. Francisco basin, southeastern Brazil.
HABITS: Very peaceful; should be kept in a school of not less than six.
WATER CONDITIONS: Slightly acid and soft water. Temperature 24 to 26°C.
SIZE: To 5 cm.
FOOD REQUIREMENTS: Prepared foods accepted, but live or frozen foods are preferred.

## *Hemigrammus* "Goldi" • Red-finned Hemigrammus

RANGE: Amazon basin; extends north and south but very rare in all ranges.
HABITS: This is, unfortunately, a poor picture of a great fish discovered by the author (HRA). All fins except the caudal and pectorals are red with red spots at their bases. There is a large humeral spot, the tail is dark, and the centers of the scales are pigmented and dark.
WATER CONDITIONS: This specimen was gill-netted and lost many scales. It is found in very small streams with slightly acid, clear water with a pH of 6.2-6.8 at 23-28°C.
SIZE: Reaches over 5.5 cm.

Hemigrammus schmardae

Hemigrammus rhodostomus

Hemigrammus caudovittatus

Hemigrammus caudovittatus

Axelrodia lindeae

Hemigrammus coeruleus

Hasemania nana

Hemigrammus "Goldi"

Plate #107

188

Thayeria obliqua

Thayeria boehlkei

1

2

Phenacogaster pectinatus

Vesicatrus tegatus

3

4

Hyphessobrycon bifasciatus var.

Phenacogaster pectinatus

5

6

Petitella georgiae

*Plate #108*

Stichonodon insignis

189

## *Thayeria obliqua* Eigenmann • Short-striped Penguin

RANGE: Middle Amazon region.
HABITS: Active swimmers and peaceful; may be kept in the community aquarium.
WATER CONDITIONS: Water should be soft and slightly acid. Best temperature 24 to 26°C.
SIZE: 8 cm.
FOOD REQUIREMENTS: Will take dried foods, but these should be alternated frequently with live foods.

## *Thayeria boehlkei* Weitzman • Boehlke's Penguin

RANGE: Amazon region of Brazil (especially near Obidos).
HABITS: Peaceful, active fish that do well in a small group or school.
WATER CONDITIONS: Not critical but do better in neutral to slightly acid water; lights should not be too bright. Temperature 22 to 24°C.
SIZE: Maximum size is about 8 cm.
FOOD REQUIREMENTS: Not critical; will eat most of the usual foods.

## *Phenacogaster pectinatus* (Cope) • Pectinatus

RANGE: Middle and upper Amazon basin.
HABITS: Generally peaceful at all times.
WATER CONDITIONS: Soft, slightly acid water. Temperature 22 to 27°C.
SIZE: About 5 cm.
FOOD REQUIREMENTS: This species is omnivorous and should be given a mixed diet of plant and animal matter; it will accept prepared flake food but prefers small live or frozen foods.

## *Vesicatrus tegatus* Eigenmann • Tegatus

RANGE: Upper Paraguay basin.
HABITS: This is a single-species genus. The fish looks and acts like most of the small tetras of the genus *Hemigrammus*. The only ones brought in were imported by the author (HRA), who kept them for more than a year but was unable to spawn them. They are from colder waters and do well in an unheated aquarium.
WATER CONDITIONS: Water between pH 6.4-7.2 at 20-25°C.
SIZE: Reaches about 5 cm.
FOOD REQUIREMENTS: Prefers live foods but does well on a normal aquarium diet.

## *Hyphessobrycon bifasciatus* Ellis • Copper Bifasciatus

RANGE: Southeastern Brazil.
HABITS: This is one of the copper tetras that have been identified as parasitized forms of *H. bifasciatus*, but this is doubtful since the two black humeral bands of *H. bifasciatus* are missing. This is probably another new species.
WATER CONDITIONS: Prefers warm, acid water with a pH of 6.0-6.6 at a temperature of 26-30°C.
SIZE: Reaches 5.2 cm.
FOOD REQUIREMENTS: Survives on a normal aquarium diet.

## *Petitella georgiae* Gery and Boutiere • False Rummy-nose

RANGE: Upper Amazon basin.
HABITS: Peaceful; best kept in schools.
WATER CONDITIONS: Soft, acidic water is preferred but is not crucial. Best temperature is 23 to 25°C.
SIZE: To 8 cm.
FOOD REQUIREMENTS: Accepts all standard aquarium foods and especially relishes live freshwater crustaceans like daphnia.

## *Stichonodon insignis* Steindachner • Tefe Gymnocorymbus

RANGE: The author (HRA) collected this specimen at Tefe, Brazil, but they are reported throughout the Amazon.
HABITS: The rounded body that resembles the black tetra in form is responsible for its popular name. There is only one species in the genus, and it was only imported once by the author. It has never been spawned.
WATER CONDITIONS: Acid, warm water with a pH of 6.0-6.8 at about 28°C.
SIZE: Reaches to at least 8 cm.
FOOD REQUIREMENTS: A voracious eater that likes falling foods.

## *Brittanichthys axelrodi* Gery • Blood-red Tetra

RANGE: Found in Rio Negro streams near Manaus by Dr. Martin Brittan, one of the world's greatest experts on *Rasbora*. It has never been brought in alive. Dr. Brittan's description of the living fish is the only basis for reports about this legendary fish. This is the only photo known, too. Dr. Brittan says the fish is blood-red. . . "It looks like it's really bleeding!" The fish shown here had been dead for a day or so.

WATER CONDITIONS: Prefers acid water, as the stream in which it was found had a pH of 6.0 at 28°C.

SIZE: Probably reaches about 6 cm.

FOOD REQUIREMENTS: Not known exactly, but probably eats a normal diet.

## *Megalamphodus* "Rubra" • Red Megalamphodus

RANGE: Throughout Peru and Colombia in very small pockets; nowhere abundant. Several importations were made by the author (HRA), but they were never spawned.

HABITS: A very beautiful species occupying the ecological niche of *M. sweglesi* where *sweglesi* doesn't exist. Much prettier than *sweglesi*. There are two vertical humeral bars not quite evident in this photo.

WATER CONDITIONS: Warm acid waters at a pH of 6.0-6.4, with the water at a temperature of about 28°C.

SIZE: Barely reaches 4.5 cm.

FOOD REQUIREMENTS: Likes live foods, as do most tetras, but gets along on a normal aquarium diet. Loses color if not fed brine shrimp or daphnia once in a while.

## *Megalamphodus sweglesi* Gery • Swegles' Tetra

RANGE: Amazon region near Leticia, Colombia.

HABITS: Peaceful; like the other tetras, they prefer to be in schools.

WATER CONDITIONS: Soft, slightly acid water is preferred. Temperature 24 to 26°C.

SIZE: About 4 cm.

FOOD REQUIREMENTS: Easily fed; prefers live foods, but frozen and prepared foods also accepted.

COLOR VARIATIONS: Body reddish brown with a large lateral spot of black. Male's dorsal fin is high and pointed, the female's smaller and round.

## *Megalamphodus megalopterus* Eigenmann • Black Phantom Tetra

RANGE: Brazil.

HABITS: Peaceful and active.

WATER CONDITIONS: Soft, acid water is best, especially for breeding. Temperature 23 to 26°C.

SIZE: 4 cm.

FOOD REQUIREMENTS: Accepts live, frozen and dried foods.

## *Megalamphodus axelrodi* (Travassos) • Calypso Tetra, Red Pristella

RANGE: Trinidad.

HABITS: Peaceful; likes to swim in schools.

WATER CONDITIONS: Soft, slightly acid water. Temperature 24 to 27°C.

SIZE: About 3 cm.

FOOD REQUIREMENTS: Takes all foods eagerly, including dried flakes, but should have an occasional meal of live or frozen food.

## *Pristella maxillaris* (Ulrey) • Pristella

RANGE: Northern South America.

HABITS: Peaceful and active; swims in schools.

WATER CONDITIONS: Soft, slightly acid water. Temperature 24 to 26°C.

SIZE: To 5 cm.

FOOD REQUIREMENTS: Not at all choosy; live foods should be offered as often as available.

COLOR VARIATIONS: Sides silvery to yellowish; dorsal and anal fins each have a large black spot on a white background; tail reddish to bright red.

## *Cheirodon insignis* Steindachner • Insignificant Tetra

RANGE: Venezuela and Colombia.

HABITS: Discovered by the author (HRA) and imported, but it never became a hit. It was never spawned and was never imported again.

WATER CONDITIONS: Gets along in clear streams with a pH between 6.8-7.4 at a temperature of about 28°C.

SIZE: The specimens collected by the author barely reached 50 mm.

FOOD REQUIREMENTS: They eat everything usually offered to aquarium fishes and small enough to ingest.

Brittanichthys axelrodi

Megalamphodus "Rubra"

Megalamphodus sweglesi

Megalamphodus sweglesi

Megalamphodus megalopterus

Megalamphodus axelrodi

Pristella maxillaris

Cheirodon insignis

Plate #109

192

The eager-to-spawn male positions himself across the path of the heavily egg-laden female.

Having coaxed the female into the plant thicket, the male approaches her from the side.

Actively entwining their bodies, the spawning pair hover quiveringly above the plants.

Momentarily stupefied by their spawning ecstasy, the dazed spawning partners begin to separate; note the eggs in the water.

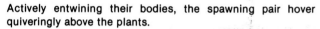

*Plate #110*

193

## SPAWNING THE NEON TETRA
### *PARACHEIRODON INNESI*

Neon tetras have long been one of the best known and most popular of all tropical fishes. They inhabit the streams of the Peruvian Amazon near Iquitos and the Yarapa River, where they travel about in schools sometimes reaching into the hundreds of thousands. Neons come from water that are nearly void of minerals, being derived to a large extent from rain water. Their colors are brought out to the fullest in water that is soft, clear and slightly acid, with a temperature between 22° and 25°C. They reach a maximum length of 37 mm, but the majority are 25 mm or less.

When attempting to breed this species, choose an attractively colored pair that is over nine months old. (Females will be filled with eggs.) Condition on ample helpings of live and freeze-dried foods. A 20-liter all-glass breeding tank that is dimly lit should be provided with several bunches of rinsed plants.

Water conditions are particularly important at this time. The water should be very soft, no more than 3 DH, acid (pH 6.5), with a temperature ranging about 23-24°C with the addition of half a teaspoon of salt to each liter. The tank must be kept clean, and there should be light aeration.

When the female has become swollen with roe, place the pair into the breeding tank. If there aren't any spawning activities within two days, remove and condition them a few more days on more generous feedings of live foods. Spawning consists of an active chase through the plant thickets. About 60 to 130 non-adhesive eggs are scattered throughout the tank.

Remove the breeders when spawning is completed and cover the tank until the eggs hatch, since they are very sensitive to light. They hatch in about a day. Keep the fry covered until the fifth day, when they are free-swimming, then increase the light gradually. Feed them the yolk of hard-boiled eggs squeezed through a porous cloth.

## *Paracheirodon axelrodi* Schultz • Cardinal Tetra

RANGE: Upper Rio Negro and Colombian waterways.
HABITS: Perfectly peaceful and active. Likes to swim in schools, and therefore it is best to keep at least 6 of them together.
WATER CONDITIONS: Water should be soft, clean and on the acid side, about pH 6.5 or lower, in order to show the fish in its brightest colors. Temperature 21 to 24°C.
SIZE: 5 cm.
FOOD REQUIREMENTS: All foods, either live or prepared, should be given with their small size in mind. Not a fussy eater.
COLOR VARIATIONS: Back is brown on top. Horizontal stripe a brilliant blue-green. Lower part of body bright red, belly white.

## *Paracheirodon simulans* Gery • False Neon

RANGE: Rio Negro, Brazil.
HABITS: Peaceful; likes to travel in schools.
WATER CONDITIONS: Water should be acid and very soft. Temperature 24 to 26°C.
SIZE: About 2.5 cm.
FOOD REQUIREMENTS: Small living foods preferred; probably would accept prepared or frozen foods readily.
COLOR VARIATIONS: Bright blue iridescent streak from opercle to caudal base, with an area of red above the anal fin.

## *Catoprion mento* (Cuvier) • Wimple Piranha

RANGE: Nowhere is it abundant, but many are to be found in the Mato Grosso streams.
HABITS: Small specimens are found in shallow waters. This is a specimen that grew very long dorsal and anal fins and may be a species different from *mento*.
WATER CONDITIONS: Young fish like a pH of 6.2-7.0 and water at 28-29°C, but they get along well in the usual aquarium environment.
SIZE: They reach 200 mm.
FOOD REQUIREMENTS: They are reputed to eat scales by scraping them from other fishes, but they also eat tubificid worms and normal aquarium fare when they are small. The fish shown here is 52 mm long.

## *Curimata lineopunctata* Boulenger • Spotted Curimata

RANGE: The author (HRA) collected this specimen in the Rio Calima, Colombia.
HABITS: This is a very rare species and only a few were caught. They might well be identified by the small black dot in the center of most of their scales.
WATER CONDITIONS: A pH of 6.2-6.8 at 27-29°C.
SIZE: Reach about 100 mm but only rarely; perhaps larger specimens are found in the rivers; this one was caught in a shallow stream.
FOOD REQUIREMENTS: Does well on a normal aquarium diet of flake foods.

## *Paracheirodon innesi* (Myers) • Neon Tetra

RANGE: Upper course of the Rio Solimoes ( = Amazon) and Rio Purus.
HABITS: Very peaceful; should be kept only with small fishes or in a tank of their own.
WATER CONDITIONS: Soft, clear, slightly acid water is preferred and brings out their best colors. Best temperature about 24°C.
SIZE: Maximum 4 cm; most specimens seen are about 2.5 cm or less.
FOOD REQUIREMENTS: Medium or finely ground dried foods, with occasional feedings of small live foods.

## *Bryconops* "Gold" • Golden Bryconops

RANGE: Amazon Basin north to Venezuela.
HABITS: Prefers a shallow, slowly moving stream with aerated water. Only a few specimens were brought back by the author (HRA). The fish shown here had a huge parasite on its back that wasn't apparent at the time of collection.
WATER CONDITIONS: Normal aquarium water, pH 6.4-7.2 at temperature 23-30°C.
SIZE: Reaches almost 100 mm.
FOOD REQUIREMENTS: Ate a normal aquarium fare, including live foods.

## *Bryconops* "Rose" • Rosy Bryconops

RANGE: The Amazon basin yields this fish, which is found mostly in shallow, heavily weeded shorelines and more open waters where the fish occur in large schools. They are a fast-moving species.
HABITS: This is another fish discovered by the author (HRA) that has not as yet been described. It does very well under normal aquarium conditions and always has a heavy rosy glow.
WATER CONDITIONS: Slightly acid water about 6.4 pH at a temperature of about 28°C.
SIZE: May reach 80 mm.
FOOD REQUIREMENTS: Eats a normal aquarium diet but much prefers living, moving foods.

## *Moenkhausia* "Dusky" • Dusky Moenkhausia

RANGE: Individual specimens were caught in many areas in the northern Amazon basin, including Colombia and Venezuela.
HABITS: This fish is a very small *Moenkhausia*; perhaps it is the juvenile of a larger fish, but it has adult coloration and ripe gonads at 50 mm. Note the orange markings in the unpaired fins and the black edge on each scale that gives it the dusky appearance.
SIZE: Up to about 70 mm. Larger specimens were never found in the creek habitat in which these fish were found.
FOOD REQUIREMENTS: They thrived on a normal aquarium diet.

Paracheirodon axelrodi

Paracheirodon innesi

Paracheirodon simulans

Bryconops "Goldi"

Catoprion mento (juv.)

Bryconops "Rosy"

Curimata lineopunctata

Moenkhausia "Dusky"

*Plate #111*

196

? Deuterodon

? Boehlkea

?

?

?

? Axelrodia stigmatias

Phoxinopsis typicus

Vesicatrus tegatus

Plate #112

## TETRA CONFUSION

No matter how hard you try, no matter how much material is available, and no matter how familiar you are with the literature, there will always be some tetras that defy identification. If series of adult specimens are available they must be placed in subfamilies and genera based on often weak and variable characters of the teeth (how many, how many rows, how many lobes, etc.) and scalation (extent of lateral line, number of scales on caudal peduncle, scaling of the lobes of the caudal fin, etc.). Some of the most common and largest genera are almost impossible to define, so several hundred species and synonyms—many known only from one or two small, poorly preserved specimens—cannot even be adequately grouped into distinctive genera. For instance, the differences between *Hemigrammus* and *Hyphessobrycon* are extremely minor (mostly scalation of the caudal area) and there are problems with the generic status of the type species.

All this is presented as a reason for the lack of identifications of most of the small tetras on this plate. All share a similar color pattern of a distinctive dark blotch, bar, diamond, etc., on the caudal peduncle, but they differ greatly in head and fin characters and may not be at all closely related. The two species we can be fairly sure of, *Phoxinopsis typicus* (from the Rio de Janeiro area) and *Vesicatrus tegatus* (from the Upper Paraguay system), have been present in the hobby since the 1930's, though they have never been truly popular. The fish tentatively identified as *Axelrodia stigmatias* is occasionally imported, as is the blue tetra seemingly related to *Boehlkea*. One very distinctive species may belong to the confusing genus *Deuterodon*. The others, although each distinctive in their own way, have not been identified with any certainty. Although the possibility exists that they are new species, they could equally well be members of obscure taxa that are seldom seen in the hobby and that have never been illustrated in a manner to show the color patterns.

New and unidentified fishes are constantly being imported for the tropical fish hobby, just one more of the reasons to visit your petshop frequently.

## THE GYMNOTID EELS

The aquarium trade, especially public aquaria, have been fascinated by the gymnotids since Georg Marcgraf described the first "carapo" discovered in Brazil. "Carapo" is a Brazilian Indian name for these fishes. *Gymnotus*, meaning naked back, is the scientific name for one of the larger genera; Gymnotidae is the family. The scientific name refers to the missing dorsal fin in the group, though some species have a single dorsal spine or filament. All the gymnotids have slippery, elongated, eel-like bodies. Some have small scales. They have no ventral fins and very degenerate pectorals, but they all have huge anal fins. The ray count within each species varies considerably. Some species have teeth. The electric eel, which the author has seen well over 2.1 meters in length, is a member of a closely related family, and it is the only gymnotoid species with strong electrical discharge capabilities. All the other gymnotoids have very weak electrical discharges that take sophisticated electronic equipment to detect. These weak discharges are used to sense their surroundings like radar. Only the electric eel is dangerous to handle, though it has never been known to kill anyone.

In the aquarium they are a nuisance. Unless you supply them with something to hide in, such as half a coconut shell inverted to form a cave, they will dig into the sand, uprooting plants and stirring up the mulm on the bottom. They all require small live foods, which are hunted at night. During the day they hide.

While they have fantastic powers of regeneration, often being able to regenerate substantial portions of their bodies, they also chew each other up unmercifully. In dealers' tanks it is not uncommon to see 100 gymnotids of about 12-20 cm all trying to hide under the same shell. The next morning they will each have a chunk bitten out of their tail! Antibiotic treatment will hinder the infection, but the fish will have to be separated.

Most gymnotids also have wonderful powers to change color. While many of them have translucent flesh through which their viscera are plainly visible, their skin does contain tiny chromatophores that give them the ability to change to a stark black or gray at times. Their muscles sometimes show a lot of blood, and this colors the fish pink or red.

Most of the gymnotids grow large, at least averaging 200 mm in length. They are therefore merely curiosities and are not to be considered for the community tank.

Not much is known about their external sexual differences or their breeding habits.

199

*Gymnotus anguillaris*

*Gymnotus anguillaris*

*Gymnotus sp. nov.*

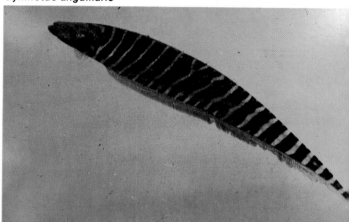

*Gymnotus carapo*

Sternarchus hasemani

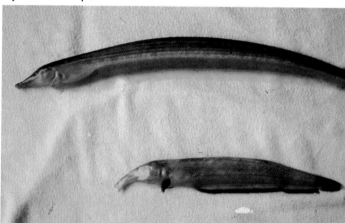

Sternarchorhamphus muelleri/Sternarchorhynchus oxyraynchus

*Rhamphichthys rostratus*

*Rhamphichthys rostratus*

*Plate #113*

Steatogenys elegans

Steatogenys elegans

Steatogenys elegans (juv.)

Eigenmannia virescens

Sternopygus macrurus

Rhabdolichops troscheli

Distocyclus conirostris

Hypopomus artedi

*Plate #114*

201

### *Steatogenys elegans* (Steindachner) • Mottled Knife Fish

RANGE: Northeastern South America, Barra do Rio Negro, Guyana, lower Amazon River and northern tributaries of the middle Amazon.
HABITS: Nocturnal; rarely seen during the daytime.
WATER CONDITIONS: Not critical; neutral, slightly soft water with a temperature between 24° and 29°C is good.
SIZE: Grows to a length of 18 to 20 cm.
FOOD REQUIREMENTS: Readily accepts live brine shrimp as well as other live foods; will also eat prepared foods, chopped fish and shrimp, etc. with a little coaxing.

### *Eigenmannia virescens* (Valenciennes) • Green Knife Fish

RANGE: Widely distributed all over northern South America.
HABITS: Mostly nocturnal; very greedy eaters which are best kept by themselves.
WATER CONDITIONS: Water should be well aged and clean. Temperature 24 to 27°C. This fish is very sensitive to fresh water.
SIZE: To 45 cm.
FOOD REQUIREMENTS: Almost any food is taken greedily; preferred of course are the larger live foods, but they also eat chunks of beef heart and oatmeal.

### *Sternopygus macrurus* (Bloch & Schneider) • Variable Ghost Knife Fish

RANGE: Much of South America from Colombia to the Guianas, south through the Amazon basin to Patagonia.
HABITS: A common, secretive fish that is used for food by the natives. Very variable in color from almost transparent to solid blue-black. Peaceful, but its large size could cause trouble in the aquarium.
WATER CONDITIONS: Not choosy, although prefers acid water. Must have cover to retreat from the light.
SIZE: Reaches at least 500 mm in length.
FOOD REQUIREMENTS: Will take any small live foods, including shrimp and fishes. Can be weaned onto prepared meaty foods.

### *Rhabdolichops troscheli* (Kaup) • Short-headed Knife Fish

RANGE: Found throughout the Amazon system.
HABITS: Shy, nocturnal. Its small size and tendency to hide make it hard to maintain in the aquarium.
WATER CONDITIONS: Warm, acid water. Must have plants or pots in which to hide.
SIZE: Usually only 100 mm in length, but reaches at least 180 mm.
FOOD REQUIREMENTS: Small live foods are preferred.

### *Distocyclus conirostris* (Eigenmann & Allen) •Yellow Knife Fish

RANGE: Iquitos, Peru, and vicinity; probably throughout the Amazon system.
HABITS: Like other small gymnotids, it is seen only at night, spending the day hiding. Peaceful, but may form weak territories.
WATER CONDITIONS: Likes densely planted, warm, acid waters.
SIZE: Only about 200 mm in length.
FOOD REQUIREMENTS: Although it may adapt to prepared foods such as beefheart, it fares best on appropriate sizes of live foods such as small crustaceans and fishes.

### *Hypopomus artedi* (Kaup) • Spotted Knife Fish

RANGE: Brazil and the Guianas.
HABITS: Peaceful toward other fishes which are not small enough to be swallowed; likely to be belligerent toward their own kind.
WATER CONDITIONS: Not critical, but the fish is sensitive to fresh water. The tank should be well planted and offer a number of places to hide. Temperature about 24°C.
SIZE: To 43 cm.
FOOD REQUIREMENTS: Prefers large live foods or chopped lean beef.
COLOR VARIATIONS: Yellowish to brownish with darker spots.

## *Gymnorhamphichthys rondoni* Miranda-Ribeiro • Mousetail Knife Fish

RANGE: River systems of Venezuela.
HABITS: Peaceful and shy; should not, however, be put with very small fishes.
WATER CONDITIONS: Soft, slightly acid water. Temperature 24 to 27°C.
SIZE: Up to 15 cm; usually 10 cm.
FOOD REQUIREMENTS: Small live or frozen foods.

## *Apteronotus leptorhynchus* Ellie in Eigenmann • Long-nosed Black Ghost

RANGE: Northern South America from Iquitos, Peru, to the Guyanas.
HABITS: A shy, peaceful, nocturnal fish that must have a hiding spot.
WATER CONDITIONS: Warm, clean, slightly acid to neutral water is best, but the fish is not too choosy.
SIZE: 100-260 mm or more.
FOOD REQUIREMENTS: Will take most live foods that reach the bottom and will also adapt to some prepared foods.

## *Polycentrus schomburgki* Mueller & Troschel • Schomburgk's Leaf Fish

RANGE: Northeastern South America and Trinidad.
HABITS: Aggressive and capable of swallowing fishes almost as large as themselves; should not be kept in a community tank.
WATER CONDITIONS: Neutral to slightly acid and soft. Temperature 24 to 26°C.
SIZE: To 10 cm.
FOOD REQUIREMENTS: Smaller fishes and pieces of earthworm preferred, but can be trained to take pieces of beef heart or other lean meat, shrimp or fish.

## *Monocirrhus polyacanthus* Heckel • Leaf Fish

RANGE: Tropical South America; Amazon, Rio Negro, Guianas.
HABITS: Occurs in sluggish streams, where it feeds on smaller fishes and aquatic insects; peaceful in the aquarium toward anything it cannot swallow.
WATER CONDITIONS: Soft, slightly acid water. Temperature about 26°C.
SIZE: Up to 10 cm.
FOOD REQUIREMENTS: Small ones may be fed with the usual live foods; larger ones must get living smaller fishes.

## *Electrophorus electricus* (Linnaeus) • Electric Eel

RANGE: Middle and lower Amazon basin.
HABITS: Because of this species's electric properties it is not suitable as a community tank fish. More than one specimen can sometimes be kept in a tank, but this is risky.
WATER CONDITIONS: Soft, slightly acid water is optimal, but not important.
SIZE: Up to 1.8 meters; aquarium specimens much smaller.
FOOD REQUIREMENTS: Live fishes are preferred; small specimens will take worms and may be taught to accept liver and similar foods.
COLOR VARIATIONS: Young specimens olive-brown with yellowish markings. Adults olive-brown with orange throat. Eyes emerald green.

## *Apteronotus albifrons* (Linnaeus) • Black Ghost

RANGE: Amazon River and Surinam.
HABITS: A peaceful, friendly fish.
WATER CONDITIONS: Soft, slightly acid water best, but this is not too important, as variations in water composition are taken in stride.
SIZE: Up to 47 cm.
FOOD REQUIREMENTS: Not a fussy eater; will take dry, frozen and live foods. Tubifex eagerly accepted.

Gymnorhamphichthys rondoni

Electrophorus electricus

Apteronotus leptorhynchus

Apteronotus albifrons

Polycentrus schomburgki (juv.)

Polycentrus schomburgki (adult male)

Monocirrhus polyacanthus

Monociirhus polyacanthus

*Plate #115*

204

Platystacus cotylephorus

Aspredo aspredo

Platystacus cotylephorus

Bunocephalus amaurus

Bunocephalus kneri

Agmus lyriformis

Bunocephalus coracoideus

Bunocephalus coracoideus

*Plate #116*

## FAMILY ASPREDINIDAE,
### The Rough-Skinned or Banjo Catfishes

In the central Amazon basin, in almost every stream and creek feeding the Amazon or its many tributaries, are very weird-looking catfishes that look as if their heads had been flattened with a hammer and their bodies stretched on a rack! They are so well camouflaged that their eyes are even difficult to find at times, and the various armies of the world might have used their skin coloration as patterns for combat uniforms.

The family has two rather distinct subfamilies, the brackish water, long anal fin species of Aspredininae, and the more familiar freshwater, short anal fin species of Bunocephalinae. The banjo cats or bunocephalids are commonly sold in petshops, but only recently have aspredinids been imported.

In Brazil, the origin of most of these species, the bunocephalids can be found lying among fallen leaves that have blown into the shallow creeks. You simply dig into a mass of leaves with your net and look for things that move (you find snakes this way, too). More than likely it will be a bunocephalid.

There are about 10 genera and over 31 species in this family, but undoubtedly there are many more, as they are very difficult to collect unless you keep searching for them specifically. Nothing is known about their sexual differences or about how they breed. But since they are often found buried in the sand of their aquarium, it is not impossible that they may even bury their eggs—but this is pure conjecture.

These are small catfishes, hardly ever reaching 200 mm in total length. Their skin is covered with a rough coating of tubercles; the coating almost looks like ich. The fishes are very hardy and thrive under most aquarium conditions, providing their minimum needs of pH 6.4-7.2, temperature 22-30°C, and well aged water are provided. They are not to be trusted with fishes that are small enough for them to swallow. They are strictly nocturnal, as their tiny, beady eyes demonstrate, and at night they easily can surprise a fish that would be impossible for them to catch during the day.

They require a large, well planted tank with a mulmy bottom and soft sand into which they can burrow. Catfishes like this are a problem in the aquarium, for should they bury themselves and then die they might really foul up a tank and necessitate a complete tear-down of the system.

## FAMILY DORADIDAE, the Spiny Catfishes

Aquarists are seeing more and more of this very interesting family, and it is only a matter of time before successful spawning is reported. The doradids are like medieval warriors. Their heads are protected above with a thick bony shield, and their bodies are protected with thorny spines, at least one row on each side of the body. These spines are dangerous to man and fishes. . . and crocodiles, many of which have died after swallowing a catfish that locked its dorsal and pectoral spines in an open position. These fin spines are also armed with serrations that are similar to the thorny spines on the sides.

This is a family of fishes that needs a lot of study. Our late, dear colleague Dr. Agustin Fernandez-Yepez, with whom the author (HRA) made many doradid collecting trips to Venezuela, wrote a monograph describing four new genera and many new species of doradids from the collections made in Venezuela. This only confused things more (for aquarists), for many of his genera were rediscovered by the author in Colombia and Brazil. When everything is considered, this narrows the differences between the known fishes of Amazon South America and the fauna of Venezuela, and it becomes likely that doradids described from Venezuela may have been described earlier from the Amazon. The species called *Pseudodoras holdeni* is one of Fernandez-Yepez' species. In Spanish it is called "sierra cachimba." It is very close to *Pseudodoras niger* except for the coloration. *P. holdeni* is gray with black fins, while *P. niger* is all black. The accompanying photos show that clearly.

In the aquarium all doradids are equal. They are generally peaceful, though nocturnal. They only eat small things, including fishes small enough to ingest whole, but they prefer scavenging at the bottom for daphnia and other small crustaceans.

They have never been spawned, but the author (HRA) has observed spiny catfishes (probably doradids) that built bubblenests under large floating leaves, assumedly to deposit their eggs like *Callichthys*, another South American catfish. But this discussion must await a more suitable arena (books on breeding aquarium fishes), for this book is large enough just dealing basically with identification of fishes and how to keep them alive.

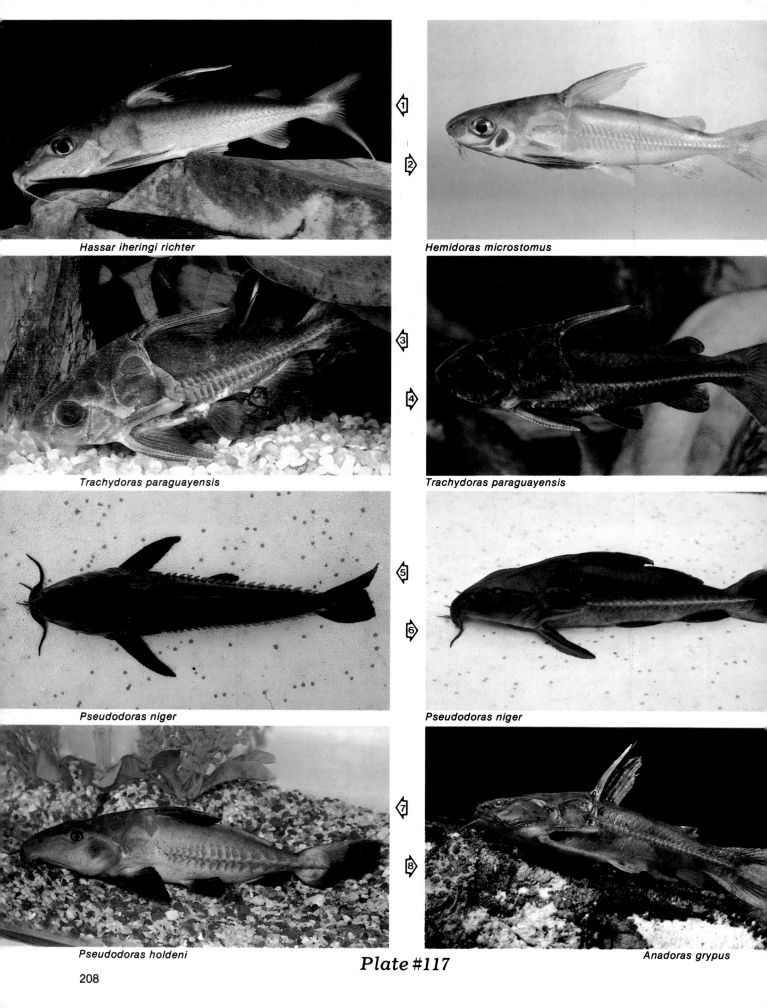

Hassar iheringi richter

Hemidoras microstomus

Trachydoras paraguayensis

Trachydoras paraguayensis

Pseudodoras niger

Pseudodoras niger

Pseudodoras holdeni

Anadoras grypus

*Plate #117*

Doras eigenmanni

Doras eigenmanni

Amblydoras hancocki

Amblydoras hancocki

Autanadoras milesi

Amblydoras hancocki

Agamyxis pectinifrons

Agamyxis pectinifrons

*Plate #118*

Platydoras armatulus

Platydoras armatulus

Platydoras costatus

Platydoras costatus

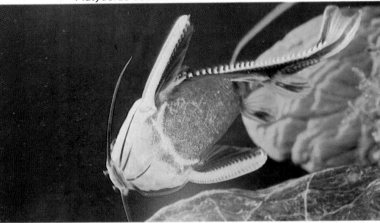

Platydoras costatus

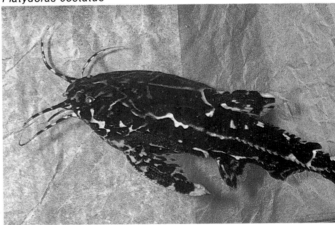

Acanthodoras cataphractus

Acanthodoras cataphractus

Acanthodoras spinosissimus

*Plate #119*

## FAMILY DORADIDAE: SUBFAMILY AUCHENIPTERINAE
## AND FAMILY AGENEIOSIDAE

The members of the family Doradidae are called the spiny or thorny catfishes, yet some have neither spines nor thorns and at first sight might be placed with the naked catfishes. These naked doradids are the auchenipterids, which form a distinct subfamily of the Doradidae. In fact, many of the more recent works on catfishes give them full family rank as the Auchenipteridae. For the moment we will follow a more conservative course and just recognize a subfamily Auchenipterinae. These fishes, basically of the genera *Tatia, Pseudepapterus, Trachelyopterichthys, Trachycorystes, Liosomadoras, Centromochlus, Pseudauchenipterus,* and *Auchenipterichthys*, are often imported as aquarium oddities. These are closely related to the fishes of the family Ageneiosidae, which are also scaleless.

There are about 135 species of known doradids, if we include the auchenipterids, but there are only 27 ageneiosids, all of which are naked-skinned.

For some reason, these naked-skinned catfishes do not really thrive in an aquarium environment. They do not live long but gradually die off. Perhaps it is because we do not truly understand their needs, as many of the more streamlined species of *Centromochlus, Pseudauchenipterus,* and *Ageneiosus* have relatively large eyes and good swimming ability, indicating that they might chase their food rather than scrounge it from the bottom.

Most aquarists treat all catfishes like scavengers and pay hardly any attention to their particular needs. Much more work needs to be done with all catfishes, except the armored catfishes of the family Callichthyidae, which adorn the tanks of just about every aquarist with a community aquarium.

*Parauchenipterus*

*Parauchenipterus*

*Entomocorus benjamini*

*Auchenipterichthys thoracatus*

*Auchenipterichthys thoracatus*

*Parauchenipterus galeatus*

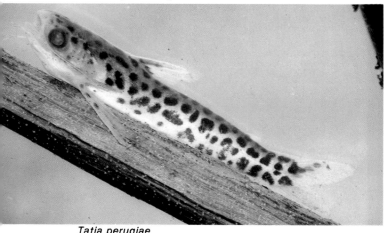

*Tatia perugiae*

*Tetranematichthys quadrifilis*

212

*Plate #120*

*Tatia creutzbergi*

*Tatia aulopygia*

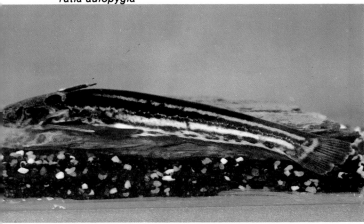

*Tatia aulopygia*

*Pseudepapterus hasemani*

*Trachelyopterichthys taeniatus*

*Trachelyopterichthys taeniatus*

*Auchenipterus demerarae*

*Auchenipterus demerarae*

*Plate #121*

213

*Liosomadoras oncinus*

*Liosomadoras oncinus*

*Liosomadoras oncinus*

*Liosomadoras oncinus*

*Centromochlus heckeli*

*Pseudauchenipterus nodosus*

*Ageneiosus caucanus*

*Ageneiosus caucanus*

*Plate #122*

## FAMILY PIMELODIDAE, the Naked Catfishes

Everywhere in tropical America and much of subtropical America as well, there are catfishes with long, thin barbels that look like whiskers (thus the name "cat" in the "catfishes"); they have neither scales nor bony armor. They almost always have three pairs of long barbels and have the dorsal fin protected by a very sharp, strong spine; this dorsal fin is usually placed very far forward. In these catfishes the tail fin is almost always forked.

For the most part these catfish are not well known, and many have still not been kept in an aquarium. TFH, as a matter of fact, sent an investigating team to the cataracts near Porto Velho, Brazil (Cachoeira Teotonio, Rondonia), to investigate reports of a large new catfish that has stripes like a tiger. This was a huge fish that was described only as recently as 1981 (by Dr. Heraldo Britski). Small specimens might well make wonderful aquarium inhabitants.

None of the pimelodids have been spawned in the home aquarium, though it shouldn't be too difficult once the special hormones are available to assist ripe fishes in spawning in their unnatural surroundings.

The author (HRA) has studied hundreds, perhaps even thousands, of these pimelodids in Brazil and Venezuela trying to ascertain sexual differences and trying to find breeding habitats, without any success at all. Many of these catfishes grow very large, upwards of one meter in some cases, but only small ones have a chance in the home aquarium—thus chances of breeding successes with these are low.

In all cases, naked catfishes are nocturnal and, in most cases, very hardy if given the basic requirements. Their water needs are simple. A pH of 6.2-7.2 at 22-30°C is suitable. Their water must be aged well, as they do very poorly in fresh (new) water. Even though they have no scales to protect their bodies and skin, they fall prey to precious few external parasites like ich.

Their aquarium should be large and extremely well planted with lots of mulm on the bottom and places to hide. Small artificial caves suit them well; halves of coconut shells are successfully used in many aquaria. Feeding them is no problem, as they are scavengers and eat just about any aquarium diet including your tank inhabitants if they are not fed well. Pimelodids have teeth, but their teeth are not too highly developed. Their food of preference is tubifex worms, which they eat from the bottom of the tank, but they also do well on flake foods that fall to the floor of the tank.

*Pinirampus pirinampu*

*Pinirampus pirinampu*

*Callophysus macropterus*

*Callophysus macropterus*

*Pimelodella gracilis*

*Pimelodella gracilis*

*Pimelodella linami*

*Pimelodella laticeps*

216

*Plate #123*

*Pimelodella parnahybae*

*Pimelodella dorseyi*

*Pimelodella metae*

*Pimelodella hartwelli*

*Duopalatinus goeldii*

*Duopalatinus barbatus*

*Gouldiella eques*

*Heptapterus mustelinus*

*Plate #124*

Pimelodus clarias

Pimelodus albofasciatus

Pimelodus maculatus (juv.)

Pimelodus sp. (clarias?)

Pimelodus maculatus

Pimelodus pictus

Duopalatinus peruanus

Pimelodus pictus

*Plate #125*

218

*Sorubim lima*

*Sorubim lima*

*Sorubim lima*

*Platystomatichthys sturio*

*Sciades pictus*

*Sciades pictus*

*Pimelodus ornatus*

*Sciades marmoratus*

**Plate #126**

219

*Phractocephalus hemiliopterus*

*Phractocephalus hemiliopterus*

*Microglanis poecilus*

*Microglanis poecilus*

*Pseudopimelodus albomarginatus*

*Pseudoplatystoma fasciatum*

*Pseudopimelodus nigricauda*

*Pseudoplatystoma fasciatum*

220

*Plate #127*

## *MERODONTOTUS TIGRINUS,* THE TIGER-STRIPED CATFISH

New fishes are being discovered all the time in South America, but admittedly most are small tetras or cichlids. Thus it was most unusual for a new species of meter-long catfish belonging to a new genus to be described in 1981. Not only was this new fish, *Merodontotus tigrinus* Britski, large, but it was strikingly patterned with oblique black stripes. When described, the fish was known from a single specimen.

In late 1984, T.F.H. was able to organize an expedition to the Teotonio Cataract on the Madeira River near Porto Velho in Rondonia, western Brazil, where the original specimen was taken. By questioning the native fishermen and following them on their trips to the cataract, several specimens of this striking catfish were found and photographed. You can see for yourself the incredible color pattern of the tiger-striped catfish and imagine how it would look in an aquarium. Because of the large size of even the smallest specimens known, *Merodontotus tigrinus* is obviously a candidate only for the largest private aquaria and for public aquaria, but there is still hope that the species will eventually be imported alive at sizes small enough to allow it to enter the aquarium hobby.

The Teotonio Cataract is a steep drop-off in the Madeira River where the river falls about 30 meters in a distance of 90 meters. Many species of large catfishes and characoids ascend the torrents of the cataract to spawn in the quieter upstream sections of the river, much as salmon ascend rivers in the Northern Hemisphere. Unfortunately the area is now being exploited for gold dredging, leading to an increased human population and its associated pollution. Perhaps even meter-long catfishes will not be able to survive for much longer in this region of Brazil unless more concern is given to stabilizing the environment. Who knows what other curious and sensational fishes exist in the area and may never even be seen by scientists before they become extinct?

Left: *Merodontotus tigrinus* with head removed; this fish had been captured by commercial fishermen.
Right: freshly caught *M. tigrinus* individual.
Below: Views of the Teotonio Cataract, at which the tiger-striped catfish was caught. The Teotonio Cataract is situated about 20 miles from Porto Velho in the Brazilian state of Rondonia.

*Plate #128*

Above and immediately below: Views of tiger-striped catfish, with unstriped belly of fish visible in photo at lower left. The big question is: are all of these individuals of the same species?

Below: Members of the 1984 T.F.H. Expedition display their finds. Left to right: Adolpho Schwartz, Heiko Bleher, and Dr. Howard Groder; Dr. Groder holds the first specimen found.

*Plate #129*

## THE ARMORED CATFISHES:
## FAMILIES CALLICHTHYIDAE AND LORICARIIDAE

The fishes of these two families are very easily distinguished from most other aquarium fishes by their being protected by a double or multiple series of "armor" plates. These dermal plates meet along the middle of the sides. Many of the armored catfishes belonging to the Callichthyidae and Loricariidae are popular aquarium fishes because they are so peaceful in the aquarium and are quite hardy if given some basic considerations. They are also very easy to spawn for the people who know their "secret": these fishes all seem to spawn after a heavy rainfall. Imitate a rainfall in your aquarium by spraying the surface with water, using an overflow device, until about 30% of the water has been changed.

### FAMILY CALLICHTHYIDAE
The family Callichthyidae is composed of three main genera, *Callichthys, Hoplosternum,* and *Corydoras,* plus three or four minor genera.

### KEY TO THE GENERA (after Gosline, 1940)
1a. Snout depressed, the interorbital width greater than or equal to the depth of the head at the forward margin of the orbit.
2a. Eye more or less superiorly situated, i.e., not equally visible from above and below, its diameter contained two or more times in its distance from the lower end of the bony opercle.
3a. Foremost plates of the upper lateral series, i.e., nuchal plates, fused across the midline between the supraoccipital and the dorsal.
4a. Abdomen between the pectoral fins completely covered with flesh; suborbital covered with flesh . . . . . . . . . . . . . . . . . . . . . . . .1. *Callichthys.*
4b. Coracoids expanded on the surface of the abdomen between the bases of the pectorals; suborbital bones not covered with flesh . . . . . . . . . . . . .
. . . . . . . . . . . . . . . . . . . . . . . . . . . . . . . . . . . . . . . . . . . . . . . . . . .2. *Hoplosternum.*
3b. Nuchal plates not meeting along the mid-dorsal line; coracoids expanded on the surface of the abdomen between the pectoral bases; eye contained 3.8 in the interorbital . . . . . . . . . . . . . . . . . .3. *Cascadura.**
2b. Eye laterally situated, i.e., equally visible from above and below, its diameter contained 1.3 times or less in its distance from lower end of bony opercle.
5a. Foremost plates of upper lateral series, i.e., nuchal plates, fused across the midline between the occipital and the dorsal . .4. *Dianema.*
5b. Nuchal plates not meeting along the mid-dorsal line . . . . . . . . . . . . . . . .
. . . . . . . . . . . . . . . . . . . . . . . . . . . . . . . . . . . . . . . . . . .5. *Cataphractops.**
1b. Snout compressed or rounded, the interorbital width considerably less than the depth of head at the forward rim of orbit; barbels at either end of the mouth, i.e., rictal barbels, not reaching much beyond gill opening; lower lips reverted to form a single pair of short barbels.

*3. *Cascadura* is now known to be based on a juvenile *Hoplosternum.*

*5. A doubtful genus known from one or two poor specimens.

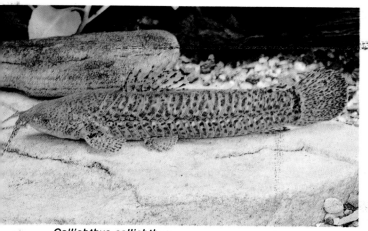
*Callichthys callichthys*

*Hoplosternum thoracatum*

*Hoplosternum pectorale*

*Hoplosternum thoracatum* (var.)

*Dianema longibarbis*

*Dianema longibarbis*

*Dianema urostriata*

*Dianema urostriata*

*Plate #130*

225

6a. Foremost plates of upper lateral series, i.e., nuchal plates, meeting along the midline between occipital and dorsal; abdomen between pectoral bases entirely covered with flesh; fontanel small, roundish . . . . . . . . . . . . . . . . . . . . . . . . . . . . . . . . . . . . . . . . . . . . . . . . . . . 6. *Aspidoras.**

6b. Nuchal plates not meeting along the mid-dorsal line; coracoids usually more or less expanded on the abdomen between pectoral bases; fontanel elongate.

7a. Dorsal fin with a spine and seven or eight, possibly nine, rays . . . . . . . . . . . . . . . . . . . . . . . . . . . . . . . . . . . . . . . . . . . . . . . . . . . . . . . . . . 7. *Corydoras.*

7b. Dorsal fin with a spine and ten to twelve rays . . . . . . . . . . . . 8. *Brochis.**

*6. Very close to *Corydoras*; the key characters may not provide a full separation of the genera.

*8. *Brochis* species with up to 17 dorsal rays are now known.

The spawning habits of *Callichthys* and *Hoplosternum* are interesting. As soon as fresh water is introduced into their aquarium in sufficient quantities to imitate a heavy rainfall and the beginning of the rainy season, these fishes build what amounts to a bubblenest. In Nature they select a strong leaf or a floating, but anchored, joint of a branch as a nest substrate. They amass bits of small vegetation that they cause to adhere to each other by slightly sticky mucus that they spit into the nest until it is quite large, perhaps as much as 200 mm in diameter. Then the eggs are put into the nest, which may rise as high as 50 mm out of the water.

The author (HRA) has had considerable experience in spawning both *Hoplosternum* and *Callichthys*. For commercial purposes a male and two bulging females are placed into a large, relatively deep (500 mm) aquarium of about 200 liters capacity. The fish are heavily fed on white worms and flake food and then a piece of *Elodea* or *Cabomba* is introduced. Only slightly browned dying plants are used. Shortly after their introduction the male begins to "sniff" them and soon begins tearing leaves from them with his pectoral fins. Using his movable barbels, he begins to accumulate the leaves in one corner of the aquarium. At this stage a floating piece of styrofoam, which has been hollowed out to resemble a soup plate, is introduced quietly onto the surface of the tank *and the water temperature is lowered*. The temperature at which the fish were prepared for spawning was between 25 and 30°C. Now the temperature is lowered to between 20 and 23°C. Soon the male begins to accumulate bubbles and bits of vegetation under the floating styrofoam. When the nest is fairly massive, about 200 mm in diameter, the female(s) begin to take interest in the male's actions, but their interest is merely sightseeing, nothing more.

The male keeps up his work until the nest actually lifts the styrofoam almost out of the water, then he begins a rather informal mating dance by nudging the female continually until she begins to spawn. She does this without the male; she merely expels a few eggs (2-6), which she manages to hold in a pocket formed by her pelvic fins just for the purpose of carrying eggs. Normally the pelvic fins are separated, but she can move them to hold the eggs. Then she swims under the bubblenest, turns on her back, and releases them into the nest. This goes on for many hours until hundreds of eggs are deposited in the nest. After each egg deposit by the female, the male follows her and showers the eggs with bubbles to ensure that they stay floating. It is not certain at which stage fertilization takes place. The author has tested the eggs and found them not to be fertile if taken from the female before she deposits them in the nest; eggs taken from the nest were always fertile even if removed before the male had showered them with bubbles. Perhaps they are fertilized by sperm already on the bubbles. No one as yet knows for sure even though what has been described above has largely been known since Hancock (the original describer of *Hoplosternum littorale*) described the nest building in an article in the *Zoological Journal*, Volume IV, page 244, in 1828.

The male cares for the nest and developing young. The female can be left with the male, but the non-breeding female(s) should be removed and the pair kept together as they are peculiarly monogamous! The nest stays together for a long time, usually about a month, and the fry keep growing without visible efforts to eat. Perhaps they eat the slime in the bubbles like baby *Symphysodon* eat the body slime from their parents, but after a month the fry emerge from the nest. . .all at once. . .at about 20 mm in length. At this stage they eat frozen baby brine shrimp and microworms, but they soon learn to scrounge other uneaten particles from the bottom of the tank.

The same mysteries surround the *Corydoras*. The female carries the eggs in her pelvic "pouch" and glues them to a spot that previously had been cleaned by the male. Each batch of eggs is attached to a different spot. Just where fertilization takes place is not exactly known.

### CARING FOR THE CALLICHTHYIDAE

The aquarium care for all of these catfishes is the same. They are peaceful and almost never bother other aquarium fishes. They scrounge along the bottom for food, but if they are hungry and only floating foods are available, they assume a belly-up position and take food from the surface. This is an unnatural position for them and they only assume it for eating and spawning purposes. The generalizations above are true for all Callichthyidae.

### HABITAT

The author (HRA) has collected more than 72 different species of Callichthyidae in South America. These armored catfishes are to be found from Trinidad through to Paraguay and Uruguay; they even live under the ice in the winter at the southern edge of their range. They all are air-breathers and can tolerate very heavy population densities. In Brazil, on many occasions the author (HRA) has found hundreds of thousands of *Corydoras* in intermittent pools, trapped by receding waters. Near

*Aspidoras pauciradiatus*

*Aspidoras pauciradiatus*

*Aspidoras lakoi*

*Aspidoras fuscoguttatus*

*Brochis splendens (juv.)*

*Brochis splendens*

*Corydoras acutus*

*Corydoras osteocarus*

**Plate #131**

228

*Corydoras aeneus*

*Corydoras aeneus*

*Corydoras aeneus*

*Corydoras aeneus*

*Corydoras aeneus*

*Corydoras aeneus*

*Corydoras latus*

*Corydoras aeneus*

**Plate #132**

229

Humaita, Brazil, the author found almost 100,000 *Dianema urostriata* in a pool barely 50 meters across and 1 to 2 meters deep. With them, by the way, were only *Pterophyllum* (angelfish).

In the aquarium all callichthyids do well in water between 20 and 30°C. The more room the better, and the more mulm on the bottom the better they appreciate it.

## MASS PRODUCTION

*Corydoras* and other callichthyids are mass produced in outdoor dirt ponds in Florida and probably in areas in Southeast Asia. The small ponds measuring roughly 30 meters in diameter and barely one meter deep have their edges decorated with pieces of flat wood or slate barely sticking out of the water. After each rain the plates are inspected for egg deposits. The spawning mass of fish in such a pond may be 2,000 fish, and not necessarily of the same species, either. The eggs are removed and artificially hatched.

## MANY SPECIES

There are over 100 species of callichthyids, mostly *Corydoras*. The author has collected many new species of *Corydoras* (more than 25), and their habitat is not always the same. In general, *Corydoras* can be found in very shallow streams that are neither very slow nor very fast-moving. The usual water depth may be only 15 cm. The author collects them at night using a square net measuring about 50 cm wide by 25 cm high and 50 cm deep. When the fish are hit by the beam of a flashlight they seem to be stunned by the light and don't move. The author then places the net in back of them, about 15 cm from their tails, and with his foot chases them into the net. They are caught the same way in the daylight, too, but at night you never miss one once you learn the technique.

The author has also collected them deep in large rivers while seining for other fishes, and of course they are also found in quiet, still pools. In pools they are usually found in huge quantities, tens of thousands at a time, while in streams they are spaced out about one per square meter of bottom.

Many years ago, when ichthyologists were often restricted in their vision of fish classifications to political boundaries rather than zoogeographical boundaries, the relationships between fishes were often obscured and many families, subfamilies, tribes, genera, species, and subspecies were constructed on an artifical basis. As more and more "holes" are filled in the evolutionary charts, the differences between these groups narrow and the groups themselves lose significance. This is especially true of the small fishes that are kept in the aquarium, fishes of the family Callichthyidae included.

One grouping that probably will persist is the separation of the almost identical looking fishes of the genus *Dianema* (tribe Dianemini) from the genera *Hoplosternum* and *Callichthys*. The tribe Dianemini contains only two genera, *Dianema* and *Cataphractops*. These fishes all look alike and are difficult to distinguish for most aquarists, but since there are only two known species of *Dianema* at present and only three or so species of *Hoplosternum*, plus one species of *Callichthys,* a few differences in color and fin position are sufficient to keep this group straight.

## CATFISH HEALTH

An experienced aquarist can tell at a glance how well a fish is in terms of health. His experienced eye quickly checks drooping fins, bloody spots, parasites, and the fish's swimming action. This is especially true of the Callichthyidae. Most normal Callichthyidae are bottom-dwellers and are constantly on the move. Even when a batch of *Corydoras* is sitting on the naked glass bottoms of a wholesaler's tanks, they immediately move into action when food is put into the tank. If you see a tankful of *Corydoras, Callichthys* or *Hoplosternum* swimming in mid-tank, you know the fish are not acting normally and disaster is imminent. Not so with *Dianema*. For some reason this catfish spends a lot of time swimming in mid-water, and this can be interpreted as their normal action.

## SEX DIFFERENCES

Several authors have suggested differences between the sexes that can ''easily'' be recognized. They point out that males of most *Hoplosternum* can be differentiated by their being more pointed than females. In a general sense this is true. If a scientist were to lay out 100 *Hoplosternum* and sort them out by the width of their mouths or noses, the widest specimens probably would all be females. The problem is that live catfish don't lie on their backs, and making a comparison is difficult since viewing the fish from the top doesn't always make it easier. So for all practical purposes there isn't any way to tell young, unripe catfishes of the family Callichthyidae apart sexually.

With ripe fishes in spawning condition there is a difference. When viewed from above, the bulging sides of the female are very noticeable, allowing females to be distinguished from males.

Both *Hoplosternum* and *Callichthys* have been spawned often, but *Dianema* has not. Most of the known species of *Corydoras* have not been spawned either, but this is only a matter of time for the species spawned so far all spawn in the same manner.

## THE TRIBE CORYDORADINI

Almost every aquarist knows a *Corydoras* when he sees one. . .or does he? There are some fishes belonging to the genus *Brochis* that look very much like *Corydoras* except they have longer dorsal fins and are deeper

*Corydoras garbei*

*Corydoras treitlii*

*Corydoras semiaquilus ?*

*Corydoras semiaquilus*

*Corydoras melanotaenia*

*Corydoras melanotaenia (juv.)*

*Corydoras zygatus*

*Corydoras sp. eques ?*

*Plate #133*

*Corydoras barbatus*

*Corydoras barbatus* (male)

*Corydoras macropterus* (female)

*Corydoras macropterus* (male)

*Corydoras nanus*

*Corydoras elegans*

*Corydoras pygmaeus*

*Corydoras hastatus*

Plate #134

233

bodied. The dorsal fin in *Brochis* has 10 or more rays, while *Corydoras* normally has fewer than 10, usually 7 to 9. Except for these small differences, the two genera are virtually identical and what has been said about *Corydoras* applies equally to *Brochis*. One species, *Brochis splendens*, looks very much like *Corydoras aeneus*, especially in the olive-green metallic flanks, except it appears like a misformed giant. Another group of similar looking fishes is *Aspidoras*. Only scientists can really tell them apart, for the opening in their parietal bone is round while *Brochis* and *Corydoras* have oval-shaped apertures.

## FAMILY LORICARIIDAE, THE SUCKER-MOUTHED CATFISHES

The major groups of fishes in the family Loricariidae can be differentiated by the following key, which was constructed by Eigenmann for *The Fishes of British Guiana* in 1912. While there have been many changes since, the key is still valid for tropical fish hobbyist purposes.

## KEY TO THE GUIANA GENERA OF LORICARIIDAE

*a.* Tail short; caudal peduncle compressed, cylindrical, or moderately depressed; haemal spines all simple; lower and fourth upper pharyngeals not toothed; belly naked, or with minute granular plates; intestinal canal very long. (*Plecostominae.*)
  *b.* Premaxillaries and dentaries nearly equal in length.
    *c.* Opercle and interopercle little and not independently movable; snout granular to its margin.
      *d.* Adipose fin present.
        *e.* Sides and back covered with plates; dorsal with seven rays ... . . . . . . . . . . . . . . . . . . . . . . . . . . . . . . . . . . . . . . . . . . . .*Plecostomus.**
        *ee.* Sides and back covered with plates; dorsal with thirteen rays . . . . . . . . . . . . . . . . . . . . . . . . . . . . . . . . . . . . . .*Pterygoplichthys.*
        *eee.* Sides and back mostly naked, with a few minute plates near the tail . . . . . . . . . . . . . . . . . . . . . . . . . . . . . . .*Lithogenes.*
      *dd.* No adipose fin; a low crest between the dorsal and caudal; margin of snout and head granular . . . . . . . . . . . . . . .*Corymbophanes.*
    *cc.* Interopercle movable, usually with spines or bristles.
      *f.* Snout granular to its margin, or with bristles; D. I, 6 or 7.
        *g.* Sides of the head without bristles . . . . . . . . . . . .*Hemiancistrus.*
        *gg.* Sides of the head with bristles, short in the female, much longer in the male . . . . . . . . . . . . . . . . . . . : . . . . . . . . . .*Pseudancistrus.*
      *ff.* Snout naked.
        *h.* No tentacles . . . . . . . . . . . . . . . . . . . . . . . . . . . . . . . .*Xenocara.**
        *hh.* Snout with tentacles . . . . . . . . . . . . . . . . . . . . . . . . .*Ancistrus.*

*\*e. Plecostomus* is now *Hypostomus.*

*\*h. Xenocara* is now considered a synonym of *Ancistrus.*

234

*bb*. Premaxillaries much shorter than the dentaries and with fewer teeth, not united. Much depressed, of small size . . . . . . . . . . *Lithoxus*.

*aa*. Tail long, depressed, with a single series of plates on the sides; intestinal canal usually not much longer than the body. Haemal spines of the vertebrae above the anal bifid; lower and fourth upper pharyngeals toothed. (*Loricariinae*.)

  *i*. Teeth in the jaws in small or moderate number, not setiform; a more or less distinct orbital notch.

    *j*. Snout rounded or pointed, not much produced.

      *k*. Lips with numerous cirri and marginal fringes; no distinct anal plate . . . . . . . . . . . . . . . . . . . . . . . . . . . . . . . . . . . . . . . . . *Loricaria*.

      *kk*. Lips papillose; a distinct anal plate . . . . . . . . . . *Loricariichthys*.

    *jj*. Snout produced, with a long rostrum.

      *l*. Snout expanded at the tip, with recurved hooks . . . . . . . . . . . . . . . . .
. . . . . . . . . . . . . . . . . . . . . . . . . . . . . . . . . . . . . *Hemiodontichthys*.

      *ll*. Snout not expanded . . . . . . . . . . . . . . . . . . . . . . . . . . . . . *Reganella*.

  *ii*. Teeth numerous, setiform; orbit circular, without a distinct notch.

    *m*. Dorsal opposite the ventrals.

      *n*. Snout rounded, not produced as a rostrum . . . . . . . . . . . . . *Harttia*.

      *nn*. Snout produced into a rostrum. Sides of the head in the male margined with bristles . . . . . . . . . . . . . . . . . . . . . . . . *Sturisoma*.

    *mm*. Dorsal opposite the anal. Very slender . . . . . . . . . . . . *Farlowella*.

The major change of concern to aquarists is that the genus *Plecostomus* as used by aquarists will now be referred to as the genus *Hypostomus* based upon Dr. M. Boeseman's paper published in 1968 entitled "The genus *Hypostomus* Lacepede, 1803, and its Surinam representatives," published by the Royal Museum of Leiden, Holland.

For many aquarists, this is the most interesting family of fishes in the whole kingdom. The loricariids contain something for everyone. To begin with, they have beautiful eyes. Not only are their eyes very attractive, but they are interesting scientifically, for they are among the very few fish eyes that possess an iris flap. Like a diaphragm, it controls the amount of light that enters the eye. Thus, if you look carefully at the accompanying photographs of the various fishes in this family, especially the *Hypostomus*, you'll be able to recognize the various "settings" at which the iris is open. Irises that are fully open mean that the photo was taken while the fish was in a darkened environment; if the iris is almost closed, then the fish was taken in full daylight or its equivalent. For the aquarist, loricariids do best in a medium light situation, where the irises of the fishes are partially closed.

But loricariids have many other interesting characteristics. These fishes are found throughout most of South America, from Panama to Argentina; from sea level or below to up to 3,000 meters high in the mountains; from pure freshwater streams to brackish tidal pools; and from

*Corydoras axelrodi*

*Corydoras axelrodi*

*Corydoras habrosus*

*Corydoras gracilis*

*Corydoras loxozonus*

*Corydoras pastazensis orcesi*

*Corydoras (cf aeneus)*

*Corydoras septentrionalis*

*Plate #135*

236

*Corydoras elegans*

*Corydoras rabauti*

*Corydoras simulatus*

*Corydoras adolfoi (imitator)*

*Corydoras adolfoi*

*Corydoras adolfoi*

*Corydoras narcissus*

*Corydoras robustus*

**Plate #136**

still ponds to rushing torrents. They can live well in torrential mountain streams that are devoid of most other fishes because they can eat and breathe where most other fishes cannot. Their sucker mouths are, in reality, vacuum cups by which the fishes can adhere to almost anything found in nature that is solid. In the aquarium they attach themselves to the aquarium glass, to large leaves, or to sticks and stones. As they adhere to this medium they sometimes assume weird positions. . .sideways, upside down, head down, tail up, etc. So fast is their adherence that they frequently cannot be removed by pulling them off without tearing their mouthparts. But how can they breathe with such an airtight mouth? Simple. Their gills operate in both directions. If you count the gill movements of a fish that is not using its mouth for attachment purposes you will find it moves between 100 to 150 times a minute. The oxygen-containing water is usually brought in through the mouth and passed over the gills, which take the oxygen out of the water and give up the carbon dioxide waste gas at the same time. These sucker-mouthed catfishes cannot bring in water through their mouths, so their gills work as an inhalant device, bringing water in and then exhaling it, thus having twice the opportunity of extracting oxygen and giving up carbon dioxide. But the mystery is why do their gills move twice as fast, from 200-300 times a minute? In theory their gills should only move half as fast. The movements clocked, by the way, were gill openings and closings, assuming that the gills work automatically as the water passes over them.

Their mouths are armed with strong, hooked teeth. These teeth, which are only found on the jaws and not the palate of the mouth, require assistance from the fish's movement to function. As the fish scoots or slides over the aquarium glass, for example, it scrapes off the algae growing on the glass and eats it. Their very long intestine that is rolled into many coils fills their soft, sometimes unprotected undersides. The skin on their bellies is very often translucent, and if the fish has been eating algae, the green can often be seen through the skin.

### BODY SCUTES

Inasmuch as the fish has its mouth under its head, thus making it difficult to defend itself with its mouth, and has a soft belly that is very vulnerable to attack, almost its sole protection is the skin covering the other parts of its body. Since it almost always assumes an attached position with its belly tight against something solid, its back, head, and exposed body parts are covered with "armor." The word "lorica" means armor, and this name refers to the very hard bony scutes that cover the exposed body parts. The scutes are so well constructed and put together, like the chain mail that covered the knights of old, that the fish is barely hampered in its wriggling and swimming movements. Ingenious slits in the armor allow for the insertion of the adipose and ventral fins. Each fish has four or five rows of these bony scutes (Callichthyidae has two rows). The head is also protected with a hard covering, and it is the construction of these head bones that in part separates the loricariids one from the other.

The body scutes are usually further protected with small denticles (tooth-like projections that aren't really teeth). All in all, the fishes in the family Loricariidae are rarely eaten by other fishes, but they are a favorite food for members of the crocodile family and turtles; and many mammals eat them, too, because they are easy to catch.

The author (HRA) had a routine on jungle collecting trips. Fish from morning until the sun was high enough in the sky to light the photo tank over his shoulder. This was usually 2 p.m. Then two hours of photography, a two-hour siesta, and then dinner in the twilight. Another two hour siesta, then two hours of night fishing. During the last siesta a large animal approached us fearlessly. We didn't take guns to the jungle for this frightened the Indians with whom we worked, so we had almost no protection from large animals and snakes except long knives (machetes). Fortunately the animal was a large dog, and it became our pet because we fed him. What did we feed him? *Hypostomus.*

One of the greatest delicacies of the world is caviar. The author (HRA) is very familiar with all types of Russian, Iranian, and American caviars since he visits Russia twice annually, but the best of all caviar is *Hypostomus* caviar. You get it by tearing off the heads of the *Hypostomus.* The ripe fish will have huge red eggs like the Russian salmon caviar. You drop the eggs into some salt water for a few minutes and then eat them. When washed down with cachaca (ka-sha-sa), the Brazilian firewater, it is unbelievably delicious. The Indians taught the author that one. But the bodies of the *Hypostomus* were unceremoniously tossed aside and they laid dried up and covered with flies all around us. The lost dog made a meal of them. . .spines, scutes, and all!

There are many other characteristics that make this family so interesting. They are endowed with a very peaceful disposition and are never the attackers. They are not territorial, and about the only problem an aquarist might have with them is when they try to attach themselves to the side of a larger fish. But this is a harmless bit of fun.

What really makes them interesting is their ability to grow different parts of their bodies at different rates during different times of their lives. The *Hypostomus* and their close relatives in the subfamily Hypostominae have offspring whose dorsal fin is larger (in proportion) than in the adults. Thus very young fish would have a sailfin; but as the fish grow larger their dorsal fins stay the same size and thus, proportionately, their fins lose size. In the subfamily Loricariinae, in many members, especially *Pterygoplichthys*, the opposite occurs and the dorsal fin outgrows the body of the fish and appears tremendous in a very old fish. In all loricariids, the pectoral fins keep growing, even after the body growth almost ceases.

As if this weren't enough to make for an interesting body, many of these fishes have heads and mouths covered with bristles and/or tentacles. In all cases where this is a species characteristic, the males have longer ones or more complex ones than do the females. Other sexual characteristics of some loricariids include the more pointed head and the broader lip flap on the underside of the mouth (lower lip) to be found in males of some genera of whip-tails, such as *Loricariichthys*. This lip adaptation enables the male to carry the eggs from one place to another.

## HOW LORICARIIDS SPAWN

There are basically two different kinds of spawning habits. *Otocinclus* and some of its close relatives lay eggs exactly the way cichlids lay them. The pair may or may not prepare a spot upon which the adhesive eggs will be attached. The female then places her eggs in the area, making a dozen or more trips to the site to deposit all her eggs there. The male visits the spot after every visit by the female and fertilizes the eggs at that time. Then the pair leave the eggs on their own. They only lay about 50 eggs. The eggs are clear when laid and oval. The only way this differs from a cichlid's spawning habits is that the female tries to lay her eggs in exactly the same spot each time. This results in a huge sticky mass of eggs, one atop the other. The eggs hatch in two to four days, with the youngest eggs hatching first. If the oldest eggs hatched first they would be trapped under the egg mass. The young grow quickly if suitable food is available to them. They do well on dead freshly hatched brine shrimp, thus frozen nauplii are usually used for feeding these fry.

The larger loricariids such as *Loricariichthys, Loricaria, Hypostomus,* and the like have a very strong cichlid-like brood care ritual. They usually dig a hole or find a cave in which to hide their eggs. The male usually moves the eggs from the spawning site to the cave where he actually sits on them like a chicken, protecting them until they hatch. Sometimes the catfish lay their eggs on a leaf or stone and the male guards them in the open tank. Most of the fishes that "sit" on their eggs and guard them have colored eggs. The color may range from light brown to bright red. The fry need lots of soft algae. This problem has been solved by Dr. P. A. Lewis, who reported (*Tropical Fish Hobbyist* magazine, February, 1983) that he successfully spawned and raised *Sturisoma panamense* fry by feeding them green bean induced infusoria, followed by mashed green peas, followed by mashed cooked green beans.

Many back issues of *Tropical Fish Hobbyist* magazine contain illustrated articles about the spawnings of these highly interesting fishes.

*Corydoras nattereri*

*Corydoras nattereri*

*Corydoras xinguensis*

*Corydoras polystictus*

*Corydoras sanchesi*

*Corydoras polystictus*

*Corydoras atropersonatus*

*Corydoras osteocarus*

**Plate #137**

241

Corydoras guapore

Corydoras caudamaculatus

Corydoras panda

Corydoras melini

Corydoras metae

Corydoras metae

Corydoras sp. (arcuatus/evelynae)

Corydoras arcuatus

*Plate #138*

242

Corydoras n. sp.

Corydoras nanus

Corydoras undulatus

Corydoras nanus

Corydoras paleatus

Corydoras paleatus

Corydoras ehrhardti

Corydoras paleatus? (albino)

**Plate #139**

Corydoras robineae

Corydoras pulcher?

Corydoras blochi blochi

Corydoras osteocarus

Corydoras bondi

Corydoras bondi

Corydoras nanus

Corydoras nanus

**Plate #140**

244

*Corydoras agassizi*

*Corydoras ornatus*

*Corydoras agassizi*

*Corydoras sp.*

*Corydoras sp.*

*Corydoras trilineatus*

*Corydoras julii*

*Corydoras trilineatus*

**Plate #141**

245

*Corydoras acutus*

*Corydoras sychri*

*Corydoras melanistius melanistius*

*Corydoras melanistius brevirostris*

*Corydoras delphax?*

*Corydoras orphnopterus?*

*Corydoras reticulatus*

*Corydoras reticulatus*

**Plate #142**

246

*Corydoras ornatus*

*Corydoras schwartzi*

*Corydoras evelynae*

*Corydoras leucomelas*

*Corydoras haraldschultzi*

*Corydoras sterbai*

*Corydoras reticulatus*

*Corydoras reticulatus*

**Plate #143**

## SPAWNING *CORYDORAS AENEUS*

Of the about 100 species of corydoras catfishes, probably the most regularly spawned is *Corydoras aeneus*. As far as known, all *Corydoras* species spawn similarly, the female mouthing the male's vent, placing her eggs in a pouch formed by the ventral fins, cleaning the substrate with her mouth, and then pressing the eggs into position on the substrate. As usual with this family, it is not certain when fertilization occurs.

## SPAWNING *HOPLOSTERNUM THORACATUM*

The species of *Hoplosternum* spawn very much like the species of *Corydoras* except that the male blows a bubblenest into which the female places the eggs. The bubblenest is often a massive structure much larger than the spawning pair.

## SPAWNING *"LORICARIA"*

Most loricariids spawn in hidden nests (in caves, hollow plant stems, under debris, or under large leaves). The eggs are large and often bright orange or even red in color. Usually one or both parents guard the nest and young. "*Loricaria*" of the hobby includes very similar-appearing species of *Dasyloricaria*, *Rineloricaria*, and probably other genera.

## SPAWNING *ANCISTRUS*

The large, often colorful eggs are guarded by the parents, as are the fry. In most *Ancistrus* the males have larger and more numerous bristles or tentacles on the snout than do the females.

## MOUTHS AND EYES

The sucking mouths of loricariids vary greatly and are important in identification. The fine teeth and very broad lips of the *Ancistrus* contrast with the narrower lips and very large teeth of the *Panaque*. Both fishes have the typical loricariid filament or lappet over the eye that serves as a sun screen to protect the iris, expanding and contracting with light intensity.

The male (upper fish in this photo) of this spawning pair of *Corydoras aeneus* is only slightly smaller than the female; most spawning males are a good deal smaller than the females.

The female has placed herself into the typical "T" position athwart the genital region of the male.

With eggs clasped within her ventral fins, the female slides along the glass side of the tank near the bottom; she has already stuck a number of eggs onto the glass.

Rising to near the water surface, the female continues to attach eggs to the side of the tank. The eggs of *Corydoras* catfishes are comparatively large and hard-shelled.

*Plate #144*

249

The spawning pair of *Hoplosternum thoracatum* maneuver under the bubblenest that has been constructed by the male.

The female *H. thoracatum* has begun to take up the position in which her mouth will be close to the vent of the male, with their bodies forming a "T" shape.

The male has rolled onto his side, and the female is approaching his vent with her mouth.

The female is now upside down beneath the nest, and the eggs have started to emerge from the pocket formed by the female's ventral fins.

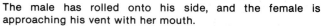

*Plate #145*

Here the male *Rineloricaria filamentosa* has taken up a position outside the bamboo shaft and shares guard duty with the female.

The eggs of this pair of spawning *Rineloricaria filamentosa* were laid within a section of bamboo that had been hollowed out to form a "cave."

Male *Ancistrus* guards large yellowish eggs at mouth of plastic cylinder.

Baby *Ancistrus* huddle with one of their parents within the hollowed-out tube used as a spawning and rearing chamber by the parent fish.

*Plate #146*

Close-up of the head of *Panaque suttoni,* the "blue-eyed plecostomus."

The *Ancistrus* species shown in this close-up exhibits the typical "omega-shaped" pupil to the eye. The number of bristles on the head is not necessarily a reliable indicator of sex; the number can vary from fish to fish regardless of sex.

Left: The relatively large teeth are visible in this view of the underside of *Panaque nigrolineatus;* they contrast with the smaller teeth of the *Ancistrus* species at right.

*Plate #147*

*Hypostomus* sp.

*Hypostomus* sp.

*Hypostomus* sp.

*Hypostomus* sp.

*Hypostomus* sp.

*Hypostomus* sp.

*Hypostomus* sp.

*Hypostomus* sp.

*Plate #148*

253

*Hypostomus* sp.

*Hypostomus* sp.

*Hypostomus* sp. (color sport)

*Hypostomus* sp. (color sport)

*Hypostomus* sp. (albino)

*Hypostomus* sp.

*Hypostomus* sp.

*Hypostomus* sp.

**Plate #149**

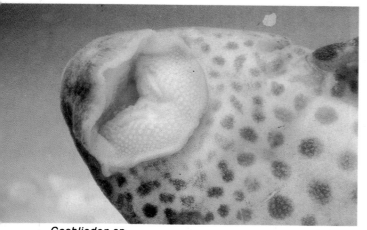

*Cochliodon* sp.

*Cochliodon* sp.

*Cochliodon* juvenile

*Pterygoplichthys* cf. *gibbiceps*

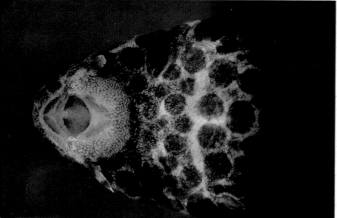

*Pterygoplichthys* cf. *gibbiceps*

*Pterygoplichthys* cf. *gibbiceps*

*Monistiancistrus* sp.

*Monistiancistrus* sp.

*Plate #150*

255

*Peckoltia* sp.

*Peckoltia* sp.

*Peckoltia* sp.

*Peckoltia* sp.

*Peckoltia* sp.

*Peckoltia* sp.

*Peckoltia* sp.

*Peckoltia* sp.

**Plate #151**

256

*Ancistrus* sp.

*Ancistrus* sp.

*Peckoltia* sp.

*Ancistrus* sp.

*Ancistrus* sp.

*Pseudacanthicus leopardus*

*Hypostomus* sp.

*Pterygoplichthys* sp.

*Plate #152*

257

*Ancistrus* sp.

*Ancistrus* sp.

*Ancistrus* sp.

*Ancistrus* sp.

*Ancistrus* sp.

*Ancistrus* sp.

*Ancistrus* sp.

*Ancistrus* sp.

*Plate #153*

258

*Ancistrus* sp.

*Ancistrus* sp.

*Ancistrus* sp.

*Ancistrus* sp.

*Panaque nigrolineatus*

*Panaque nigrolineatus*

*Panaque suttoni*

*Panaque suttoni*

*Plate #154*

259

Panaque nigrolineatus

Panaque suttoni

Otocinclus affinis

Parotocinclus maculicauda

Farlowella acus

Pterygoplichthys aff. multiradiatus

**Plate #155**

*Otocinclus* sp.

*Otocinclus* sp.

*Otocinclus* sp.

*Otocinclus* sp.

*Otocinclus* sp.

*Otocinclus* sp.

*Otocinclus* sp.

*Otocinclus* sp.

*Plate #156*

261

*Hypoptopoma* sp.

*Hypoptopoma* sp.

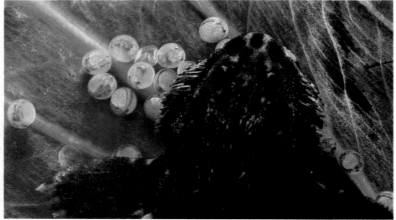

*Rineloricaria castroi*

*Rineloricaria*

*Rineloricaria* cf. *hasemani*

*Rineloricaria* cf. *hasemani*

*Cteniloricaria* sp.

*Rineloricaria fallax*

*Plate #157*

*Rineloricaria castroi*

*Rineloricaria* sp.

*Rineloricaria* sp.

*Rineloricaria lanceolata*

*Rineloricaria lanceolata*

*Rineloricaria lanceolata*

*Plate #158*

263

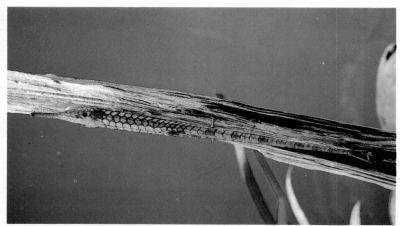

*Farlowella* sp.

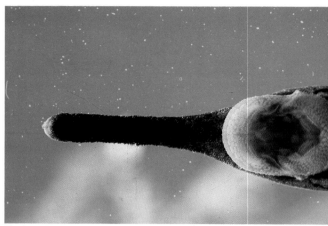

*Farlowella* sp.

*Farlowella* sp.

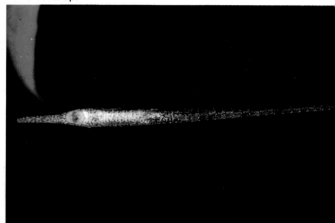

*Farlowella* sp.

*Hemiodontichthys acipenserinus*

*Hemiodontichthys acipenserinus*

*Sturisoma* sp.

*Sturisoma* sp.

*Plate #159*

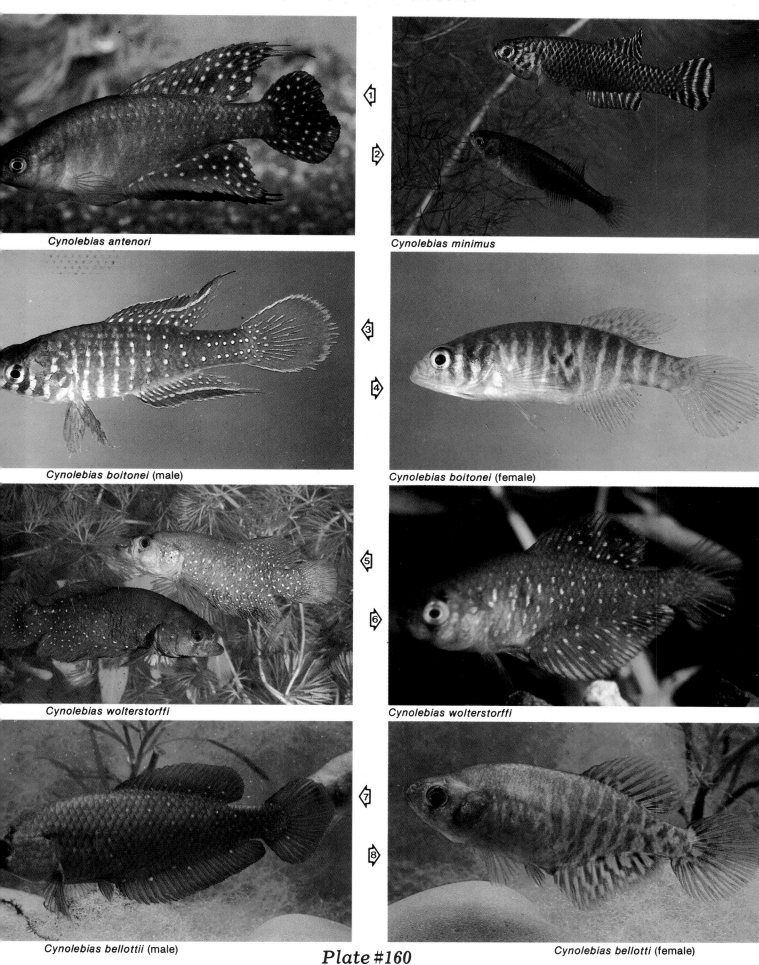

Cynolebias antenori

Cynolebias minimus

Cynolebias boitonei (male)

Cynolebias boitonei (female)

Cynolebias wolterstorffi

Cynolebias wolterstorffi

Cynolebias bellottii (male)

Cynolebias bellotti (female)

*Plate #160*

265

## Cynolebias antenori Tulipano • Red-Finned Pearl Fish

RANGE: Ceara, Rio Grande do Norte, Brazil.
HABITS: Peaceful toward other fishes, but best kept by themselves.
WATER CONDITIONS: Soft, slightly acid water. Temperature about 72-76°F. best.
SIZE: Reaches a length of about 2-2½ inches.
FOOD REQUIREMENTS: Prefers live foods. Will take frozen foods also but will only take dried food if very hungry.
COLOR VARIATIONS: Grayish blue anteriorly, more purplish posteriorly, the body spotted with white. White spots in vertical fins and reddish to orange stripe in anal fin fading posteriorly; anal fin also with black border.

## Cynolebias boitonei (Carvalho) • Brazilian Lyrefin

RANGE: Near Brasilia, Brazil at altitudes of 1000 m.
HABITS: A typical "annual" species which prefers muddy water holes that may dry out during the dry season. A good jumper so keep the tank covered.
WATER CONDITIONS: The temperature of the water in its native habitat ranges from 5 to 37°C. It is found only in rain water with a pH of about 5.8 to 7.2.
SIZE: Very small; not much larger than 2.5 cm; males larger than females.
FOOD REQUIREMENTS: Prefers mosquito larvae, freeze-dried worms and brine shrimp.

## Cynolebias wolterstorffi Ahl • Wolterstorff's Pearl Fish

RANGE: Southeastern Brazil.
HABITS: Aggressive and pugnacious. Not adaptable for community tanks. Should be given their own well planted tank.
WATER CONDITIONS: Neutral to slightly acid. Temperature 24 to 26°C.
SIZE: Males to 10 cm; females slightly smaller.
FOOD REQUIREMENTS: Frequent feedings with live or freeze-dried foods.

## Cynolebias bellotti Steindachner • Argentine Pearl Fish

RANGE: La Plata region.
HABITS: Should have a good-sized aquarium to themselves.
WATER CONDITIONS: Not critical; tank should stand in a sunny spot. A wide variety of temperatures is tolerated, but 22 to 24°C is best.
SIZE: 7 cm; female a little smaller.
FOOD REQUIREMENTS: A heavy eater; should be generously fed with live foods whenever possible, but will also accept dried foods occasionally.

## Cynolebias minimus Myers • Myers's Gaucho

RANGE: Northwest of Rio de Janeiro in pools which dry out seasonally.
HABITS: Must be kept by themselves.
WATER CONDITIONS: Soft, slightly acid. Temperature 24 to 26°C.
SIZE: To 4 cm.
FOOD REQUIREMENTS: Small live foods.
COLOR VARIATIONS: Body green with bright red bars which extend into the vertical fins. Eyes are a beautiful green. Females plain greenish brown.

Cynolebias adloffi (pair)

Cynolebias adloffi (old male)

Cynolebias alexandri

Cynolebias alexandri (male)

Cynolebias nigripinnis (female)

Cynolebias nigripinnis (male)

Cynolebias viarius

Cynolebias nigripinnis

*Plate #161*

267

*Cynolebias adloffi* Ahl • Banded Pearl Fish

RANGE: Southeastern Brazil.
HABITS: Should be kept by themselves. Males become scrappy.
WATER CONDITIONS: Tank should have a layer of about an
    inch of peat moss on the bottom. Temperature 22 to 25°C.
SIZE: Males to 5 cm; females a little smaller.
FOOD REQUIREMENTS: Live foods of all kinds which are
    small enough for easy swallowing.

*Cynolebias alexandri* Castello and Lopez • Entre Rios
Pearl Fish

RANGE: State of Entre Rios, Argentina.
HABITS: Pugnacious with members of its own species;
    generally peaceful with other fishes.
WATER CONDITIONS: Not critical.
SIZE: To about 5 cm.
FOOD REQUIREMENTS: Accepts most meaty foods.

*Cynolebias nigripinnis* Regan • Black-finned Pearl Fish

RANGE: Parana River in Argentina, above Rosario.
HABITS: Peaceful toward other fishes, but does best when
    kept with only their own kind. Annual.
WATER CONDITIONS: Soft, slightly acid water. Temperature
    22-25°C.
SIZE: Adult males to 4 cm; females smaller.
FOOD REQUIREMENTS: Small live foods are best. Frozen
    foods are accepted, but only as a second choice.

*Cynolebias viarius* Vaz-Ferreira, Sierra, & Pauletter •
Blue Pearl Fish

RANGE: Vicinity of Rocha, Uruguay, near the Brazilian
    border.
HABITS: Found in temporary pools and ditches like most
    pearl fishes. Eggs hatch in 3 to 4 months. Annual.
WATER CONDITIONS: Not overly choosy about conditions,
    but seems to prefer slightly acid water of about 20-24°C.
    Subject to shock from sudden water changes.
SIZE: 3 to 4.5 cm long; females seldom over 3.5 cm.
FOOD REQUIREMENTS: Prefers small live foods such as
    brine shrimp and mosquito larvae and pupae.

Cynolebias whitei

Cynolebias whitei

Cynolebias whitei (albino)

Cynolebias whitei (variety)

Cynolebias dolichopterus

Cynolebias dolichopterus

Cynolebias melanotaenia

*Plate #162*

Cynolebias brucei

*Cynolebias whitei* Myers • White's Pearl Fish

RANGE: Savannah ponds of the Mato Grosso region, Brazil.
HABITS: Peaceful toward other fishes, but best if kept to
    themselves.
WATER CONDITIONS: Soft, slightly acid water. Temperature
    22 to 24°C.
SIZE: To 8 cm; females slightly smaller.
FOOD REQUIREMENTS: Live or frozen foods. Dried foods
    accepted only when very hungry.

*Cynolebias dolichopterus* (Weitzman & Wourms) •
Sicklefin Killie, Saberfin

RANGE: Venezuela.
HABITS: Timid, easily spooked.
WATER CONDITIONS: Soft, acid water best for breeding,
    but neutral to slightly alkaline water suitable.
    Temperature 20 to 23°C.
FOOD REQUIREMENTS: Live foods preferred.
SIZE: 4-6 cm.
COLOR VARIATIONS: Females much less spotted than males,
    especially on fins. Bluish sheen that overlies belly area
    (and sometimes fins) of male entirely lacking in female.

*Cynolebias melanotaenia* (Regan) • Fighting Gaucho

RANGE: Southeastern Brazil.
HABITS: Do not put two males in the same tank or they will
    fight until one or both are badly mutilated or dead.
WATER CONDITIONS: Occurs in ditches and water holes,
    some of which dry out in the hot season; can adapt to
    almost any water.
SIZE: Males about 5 cm; females slightly smaller.
FOOD REQUIREMENTS: Should be given live foods of all
    kinds. Dried foods are accepted, but not willingly.

*Cynolebias brucei* (Vaz-Ferreira & Sierra) • Turner's
Gaucho

RANGE: Parana, southeastern Brazil.
HABITS: A sluggish annual fish found in ditches and pools;
    rare. The anterior anal fin rays of the male are set slight-
    ly apart from the other rays and serve as a primitive
    gonopodium. Should be kept alone.
WATER CONDITIONS: Not choosy. Some populations are
    found close to the sea, but it probably prefers acid water.
    Sex determination may be pH-dependent, as aquarium
    strains tend to throw only one sex.
SIZE: Small, seldom over 3 cm.
FOOD REQUIREMENTS: Small insect larvae such as blood-
    worms and mosquito larvae, plus brine shrimp.

## *Rivulus ornatus* Garman • Red-flecked Rivulus

RANGE: Amazon basin, Brazil, to Iquitos, Peru.
HABITS: Typical of other *Rivulus,* preferring backwaters.
WATER CONDITIONS: Warm, acid water is preferred.
SIZE: 3-4 cm.
FOOD REQUIREMENTS: Mosquito larvae and small crustaceans are readily eaten.

## *Rivulus atratus* Garman • Butterfly Rivulus

RANGE: Amazon of Peru and Brazil.
HABITS: The strongly countershaded color pattern (the belly is darker than the back) shows this to be a surface-dweller. In fact, the caudal fin and general appearance greatly remind one of the African freshwater butterfly fish, *Pantodon.*
WATER CONDITIONS: Should have clean, clear, acid water.
SIZE: 2.5- 4 cm.
FOOD REQUIREMENTS: Perhaps more selective than most *Rivulus,* so try feeding floating foods and insect larvae that stay on the surface.

## *Rivulus beniensis* Myers • Reticulated Rivulus

RANGE: Rio Beni, south at least to the Tingo Maria area of northern Peru. Occurs as several different color patterns, some of which have been given separate names. The status of these populations is very uncertain.
HABITS: Typical of most other small *Rivulus.*
WATER CONDITIONS: Vegetated backwaters with slightly to strongly acid conditions.
SIZE: 3-5 cm.
FOOD REQUIREMENTS: Like other *Rivulus,* prefers live insects and crustaceans but can often be adapted to prepared foods.

## *Rivulus limoncochae* Hoedeman • Rio Napo Rivulus

RANGE: Rio Napo system of Ecuador, perhaps ranging into Peru.
HABITS: A colorful species from lakes and streams. Very similar to *R. rubrolineatus.*
WATER CONDITIONS: May need a little cleaner, more aerated water than most *Rivulus,* but otherwise typical of the genus.
SIZE: 4-6 cm.
FOOD REQUIREMENTS: Live foods are taken readily, but it will eventually take flakes.

## *Rivulus agilae* Hoedeman • Agila Rivulus

RANGE: The Guianas of northern South America.
HABITS: A peaceful little aquarium fish that adapts readily to the aquarium. Often found in cooler, flowing water in nature. Some specimens develop a pattern very like *R. strigatus.*
WATER CONDITIONS: Not too choosy; perhaps will take a bit cooler water than most species of *Rivulus.*
SIZE: 4-5 cm.
FOOD REQUIREMENTS: Mosquito larvae, other insects, brine shrimp, and other live foods are taken readily.

## *Rivulus amphoreus* Huber • Guianas Rivulus

RANGE: The Guianas of northern South America.
HABITS: Reported to be very easy to keep in the aquarium, requiring very little maintenance. Prefers a planted tank, like most other *Rivulus.* Spawns readily, only the dominant male fertilizing the eggs. The eggs hatch in two weeks and the young mature in four months.
WATER CONDITIONS: Warm (22-25°C), somewhat acid water is preferred.
SIZE: 5-7 cm. perhaps larger.
FOOD REQUIREMENTS: Adapts to aquarium diets readily but still prefers live foods.

Rivulus ornatus (male)

Rivulus ornatus (female)

Rivulus atratus

Rivulus beniensis

Rivulus limoncochae

Rivulus agilae (male)

Rivulus amphoreus

Rivulus agilae (female)

*Plate #163*

272

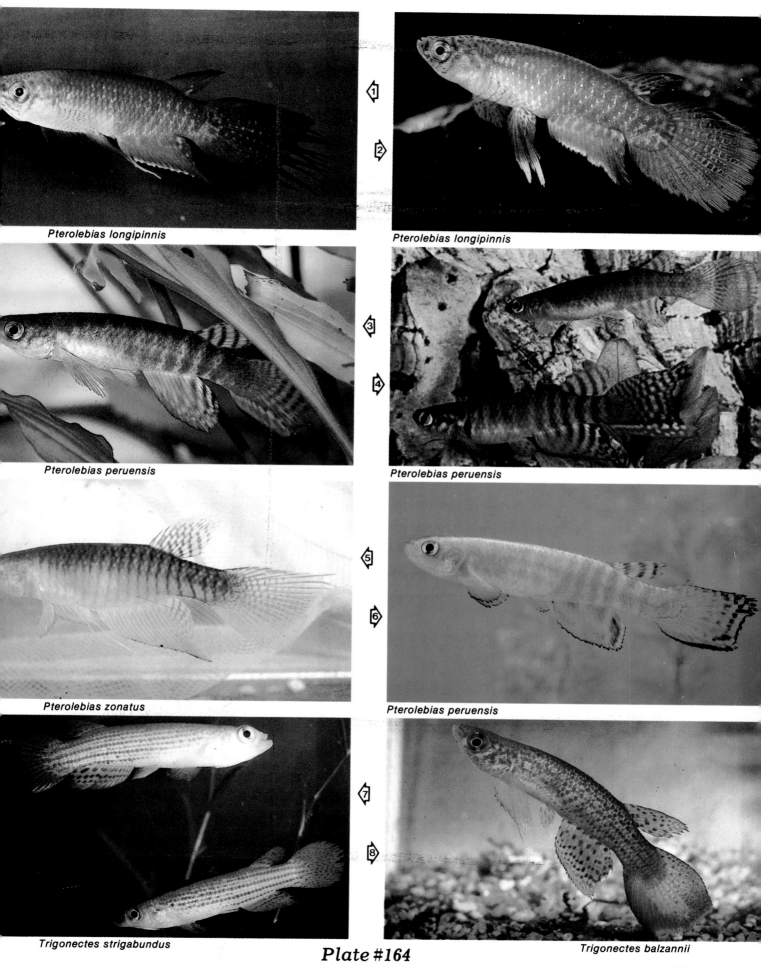

Pterolebias longipinnis

Pterolebias longipinnis

Pterolebias peruensis

Pterolebias peruensis

Pterolebias zonatus

Pterolebias peruensis

Trigonectes strigabundus

Trigonectes balzannii

**Plate #164**

*Pterolebias longipinnis* Garman • Common Longfin

RANGE: Northern Argentina northward into southeastern Brazil.
HABITS: Peaceful with other species, but males fight among themselves.
WATER CONDITIONS: Acidity and hardness factors of the water are not very important, provided the water is clean. Temperature 17 to 22°C; higher temperatures to be avoided.
SIZE: Males about 8 cm; females 6 cm.
FOOD REQUIREMENTS: Does best on live foods; will accept meaty prepared foods but will quickly go off feed if maintained on monotonous diet of dry foods.

*Pterolebias peruensis* Myers • Peruvian Longfin

RANGE: Upper Amazon region.
HABITS: Usually peaceful, but should be kept by themselves.
WATER CONDITIONS: Soft, considerably acid water; for spawning, a layer about 2 cm deep of peat moss should be provided on the bottom. Temperature 18 to 23°C.
SIZE: About 7 cm for males; females about 5 cm.
FOOD REQUIREMENTS: Live foods of all kinds.

*Pterolebias zonatus* Myers • Lace-finned Killie, Banded Longfin

RANGE: Venezuelan drainage of the Orinoco River.
HABITS: Males not overly aggressive, but in close quarters they may nip at each other's fin ray extensions.
WATER CONDITIONS: Does well in soft acid water but will readily adapt to neutral or slightly alkaline water. Best maintained between 20 and 24°C.
SIZE: Males grow to 15 cm in the wild and females reach half that size; aquarium-raised fish are not quite this long.
FOOD REQUIREMENTS: Feeds heavily on mosquito larvae and other surface-dwelling insects, but will adapt well to frozen or prepared foods.

*Trigonectes strigabundus* Myers • Brazilian False Panchax

RANGE: Rio Tocantins, Brazil.
HABITS: Peaceful with fishes it cannot swallow.
WATER CONDITIONS: Soft, slightly acid water. Temperature 24 to 26°C.
SIZE: To 6 cm.
FOOD REQUIREMENTS: Live foods of all kinds; can be trained to take frozen foods.

*Trigonectes balzanii* (Perugia) • Rivulichthys

RANGE: Paraguay drainage, Matto Grosso, Brazil.
HABITS: Generally peaceful, but will attack smaller fishes. Rather delicate.
WATER CONDITIONS: Soft, acid water is preferred; temperature 22-24°C.
SIZE: 5 to 7 cm.
FOOD REQUIREMENTS: Eats any small invertebrates or fish fry it can find.

### *Rachovia brevis* (Regan) • Magdalena Spot-finned Killie

RANGE: Rio Magdalena basin of Colombia to the Maracaibo basin of Venezuela.
HABITS: Rather sluggish but generally peaceful. Annual. Males aggressive when spawning.
WATER CONDITIONS: Soft, very warm (25-32°C) water. Prefers neutral to slightly acid conditions, but not too choosy.
SIZE: Males reach 7.5 cm, females about 6.5 cm.
FOOD REQUIREMENTS: Omnivorous predator feeding on anything small enough and sluggish enough to grab.

### *Rachovia hummelincki* DeBeaufort • Coastal Spot-finned Killie

RANGE: Coastal deserts and plains of northern Colombia and Venezuela.
HABITS: Found in stagnant temporary ponds, even cow tracks. Sluggish. An annual fish. Males may be aggressive.
WATER CONDITIONS: Not choosy. Will tolerate very warm (to 32°C), soft, acid water best. Tolerant of pollution.
SIZE: Females to about 6.5 cm, but males a cm larger.
FOOD REQUIREMENTS: Prefers live foods of appropriate size, but will take some prepared foods. Remember that this tends to be a sluggish fish.

### *Rachovia maculipinnis* (Radda) • Venezuelan Spot-finned Killie

RANGE: Venezuela.
HABITS: Peaceful, but like other killifishes should be kept in a tank by themselves.
WATER CONDITIONS: Not critical, but does best in soft, slightly acid water that is clear and clean. The best temperature range is 18-24°C.
SIZE: Attains a length of up to 10 cm in their natural habitat but only about 7.5 cm in captivity.
FOOD REQUIREMENTS: Live foods are preferred, but it will accept frozen foods. Will not accept dried foods.

### *Rachovia pyropunctata* Taphorn & Thomerson • Red-spotted Spot-finned Killie

RANGE: Eastern Maracaibo basin, Venezuela.
HABITS: Inhabits temporary ponds and ditches that are often badly polluted. Annual.
WATER CONDITIONS: Soft, acid water is preferred. Like the other species of this genus and *Austrofundulus*, it can tolerate a good deal of pollution and high water temperatures.
SIZE: Males about 7 cm long, females smaller.
FOOD REQUIREMENTS: Small insect larvae, worms, beefheart. Not choosy.

### *Austrofundulus limnaeus* Schultz • Schultz's Spot-finned Killie

RANGE: Northern Colombia to Guyana, including Venezuela.
HABITS: Found in stagnant temporary ponds and ditches. An annual fish. Males often aggressive.
WATER CONDITIONS: Very flexible in its requirements, as long as the water is somewhat soft, acid, and warm.
SIZE: 4 to 6 cm in length, the males longer.
FOOD REQUIREMENTS: Like most annual killies, it will take almost any small invertebrates and many prepared foods.

Rachovia brevis (male)

Rachovia hummelincki

Rachovia brevis

Rachovia maculipinnis

Rachovia brevis

Rachovia pyropunctata

Austrofundulus limnaeus

Austrofundulus limnaeus

**Plate #165**

276

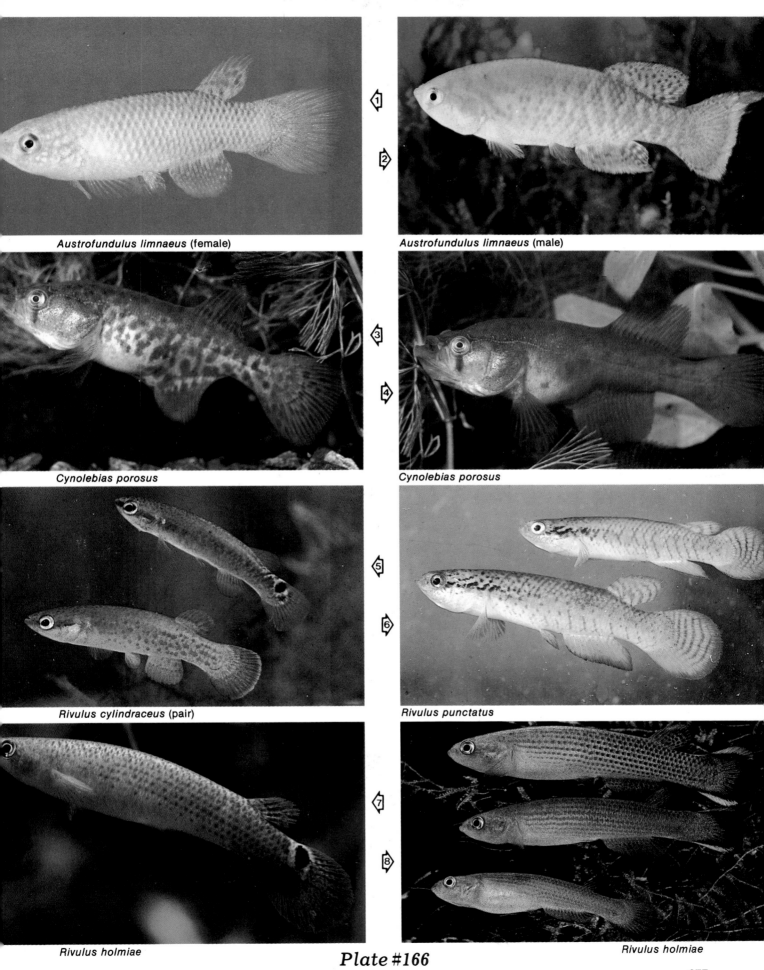

Austrofundulus limnaeus (female)

Austrofundulus limnaeus (male)

Cynolebias porosus

Cynolebias porosus

Rivulus cylindraceus (pair)

Rivulus punctatus

Rivulus holmiae

Rivulus holmiae

*Plate #166*

*(See Plate #165)*

*Cynolebias porosus* Steindachner • Big-lip Pearl Fish

RANGE: Coastal Brazil. The identification of this fish is very uncertain, as the larger, fine-scaled species of *Cynolebias* are poorly studied.
HABITS: Large for a killifish and can be a serious threat to smaller fishes.
WATER CONDITIONS: Not choosy. Will tolerate almost any combination of warm, moderately soft, acid to neutral water. Tolerant of pollution.
SIZE: Males to at least 15 cm, females smaller. One of the larger species of American killifishes.
FOOD REQUIREMENTS: Will eat almost anything small enough to swallow, including insects, worms, brine shrimp, fish fry, and prepared foods.

*Rivulus cylindraceus* Poey • Cuban Rivulus

RANGE: Cuba.
HABITS: Fairly peaceful in the community aquarium.
WATER CONDITIONS: Soft, slightly acid water preferred. Temperature 24 to 26°C.
SIZE: Males slightly under 5 cm; females slightly larger.
FOOD REQUIREMENTS: Should get live foods only, but will accept dried foods if hungry.

*Rivulus punctatus* (Boulenger) • Spotted Rivulus

RANGE: Paraguay, Bolivia and western Brazil.
HABITS: Generally peaceful, but shy with other fishes.
WATER CONDITIONS: Soft, slightly acid water. Temperature 24 to 27°C.
SIZE: To 8 cm.
FOOD REQUIREMENTS: All sorts of live foods; dry foods taken only when very hungry.

*Rivulus holmiae* Eigenmann • Golden-tailed Rivulus

RANGE: Guyana.
HABITS: Adept at jumping through the smallest opening; peaceful, but will eat small fishes.
WATER CONDITIONS: Soft, slightly acid water optimal, but not necessary. Temperature 22 to 25°C.
SIZE: About 10 cm.
FOOD REQUIREMENTS: Will accept living, frozen or freeze-dried foods.

## Rivulus magdalenae Eigenmann & Henn • Bar-tailed Rivulus

RANGE: Colombia. Usually called *R. milesi* in the hobby, but this name is now considered a synonym by most workers.

HABITS: Relatively shy and sluggish. Typical of slow-water fishes in its behavior. Spawns readily in the aquarium.

WATER CONDITIONS: Likes the usual soft, slightly acid water, but quite tolerant of most aquarium conditions.

SIZE: About 6-8 cm.

FOOD REQUIREMENTS: Prefers live foods, but takes many of the common prepared aquarium foods.

*(See Plate #166)*

*(See Plate #166)*

## Rivulus xiphidius Huber • Band-tailed Rivulus

RANGE: Oyapok drainage, French Guiana. The most distinctively patterned *Rivulus*.

HABITS: A shy, delicate species found in backwaters and stagnant pools.

WATER CONDITIONS: In nature takes very acid water, down to a pH of 5. Temperature 23°C.

SIZE: A dwarf species, seldom exceeding 3 cm.

FOOD REQUIREMENTS: Small live foods such as brine shrimp and daphnia are preferred, but will eventually take fine flake foods.

## Rivulus strigatus Regan • Chevron Rivulus

RANGE: Found in various forms and color varieties over much of the Amazon area.

HABITS: Rather sluggish but nippy. Found in small backwaters and temporary forest pools.

WATER CONDITIONS: Warm, slightly acid water, pH 6-7, temperature 22-25°C.

SIZE: 5-6 cm.

FOOD REQUIREMENTS: Likes live foods, but will adjust to many aquarium diets.

## Rivulus peruanus (Regan) • Perimparoo Rivulus

RANGE: Northeastern Peru. One of several very similar species from this area.

HABITS: Like most other species of *Rivulus*, this is a species of sluggish drainages and forest pools.

WATER CONDITIONS: Typically 22-25°C, pH 6-7.

SIZE: 6-7 cm.

FOOD REQUIREMENTS: Small crustaceans such as the daphnids and copepods form much of the natural food, along with mosquito larvae and other insects.

## Rivulus urophthalmus Guenther • Golden Rivulus

RANGE: Guianas to the lower Amazon region.

HABITS: Prefer to be kept by themselves, but a large tank is not essential; they like to hide in plant thickets and are very active jumpers.

WATER CONDITIONS: Soft, slightly acid water is best. A temperature around 24°C is best, but it is not sensitive to gradual drops.

SIZE: 6 cm.

FOOD REQUIREMENTS: Live foods are essential, preferably those which remain near the surface, like mosquito larvae.

Rivulus magdalenae

Rivulus cylindraceus

Rivulus punctatus

Rivulus punctatus

Rivulus xiphidius

Rivulus strigatus

Rivulus peruanus

Rivulus urophthalmus

*Plate #167*

280

Blue snakeskin delta flagtail (Variegated snakeskin delta)

Blue snakeskin delta flagtail (Variegated snakeskin veil)

Blue snakeskin delta flagtail (Solid snakeskin veil)

Blue snakeskin delta flagtail (Variegated snakeskin delta)

Blue snakeskin fantail (Variegated snakeskin delta)

Yellow snakeskin fantail (Variegated snakeskin delta)

Yellow snakeskin delta flagtail (Variegated snakeskin veil)

White snakeskin fantail (Variegated snakeskin delta)

*Plate #168*

281

I doubt that there is any other fish besides the guppy that almost EVERY aquarist has kept at one time or another, for one reason or another. Many keep guppies merely as foods for other fishes, while some keep ONLY guppies. For whatever reason, guppies are the best-selling of all aquarium fishes. They come in many varieties, including different colors and finnage shapes. Some strains are larger than others. In some strains females are more colorful than in others, but in no strain is the female more colorful than the male.

One of the reasons that guppies are so popular is that they are easy to keep and, with a minimum of care, thrive in most aquarium situations regardless of the pH, DH, food, or water temperature. Of course the limits of these generalizations must be within reason. Even so, winter "freezes" in Florida, where many tropical fishes are raised, hardly ever kill the guppies that are kept outside in pools.

In 1859, a scientist by the name of Wilhelm Peters described a fish from the Rio Guaire in Caracas, Venezuela, as *Poecilia reticulata*. Peters was a German and published his findings in a Berlin scientific publication. Because of the very variable colors in which the guppy is normally found, other scientists also described this abundant fish, and in short order four or five descriptions of this same fish appeared under as many different names. The name "guppy" became attached to the fish when an English botanist, Robert John Lechmere Guppy, brought some preserved specimens back from Trinidad, an island lying off Venezuela. The British Museum's able ichthyologist, Dr. Albert Guenther, mistakenly identified the fish as a new species and gave it the name *Girardinus guppyi,* in honor of Robert Guppy. It was under this name that the fish became a popular pet, being so hardy, so easy to breed, and so relatively inexpensive for the wild varieties.

Because the guppy male is such a variable individual, its genetic structure has been the study of several dedicated scientists, especially Dr. O. Winge of Denmark. As Dr. Winge's results became available and more and more laboratories stocked guppies as experimental animals, it wasn't long before the aquarium pioneers began keeping guppies for their very own pleasure and profit. Most well-known of all "fathers of the guppy" is Paul Hahnel, a German cabinet-maker who emigrated to the United States in the late 1930's. He first kept wild type guppies, but instead of just keeping them alive, he treated them with the most dedicated care. You must remember that during the 1930's aquarium-keeping was hardly at its zenith. Heaters and pumps were practically unknown, and aside from goldfish and a few other hardy fishes, tropicals were kept mostly by Germans who seemed to have a knack for attention to details and difficult projects.

Hahnel, instead of feeding and keeping his guppies the way other people kept goldfish, treated his guppies to living foods and as varied a diet as he could find. He carefully aged water and changed 20% of the water in the guppy tanks each week. Soon his plain wild guppies began to grow larger...and larger. In a few years, after Hahnel kept selecting the larger and more colorful male guppies to cross with the largest and most colorful female guppies, he developed the "Hahnel guppy," one of the first strains of fancy guppy.

Beautiful guppies just don't happen...they are cultivated. In Paul's own words, "I don't care what guppy you start with; give me any guppies. Just feed them good live foods and dried foods when you pass them from the left, and siphon off 10% of their water when you pass them from the right. Replace the water with aged good water. Throw away the bad males and just keep the good males. In a few years you'll have beautiful guppies." (Good aged water is pH 6.8 and very soft.)

The original Hahnel fancy guppies had long tails, were usually intensely colored, and swam with strong strokes as their long tails waved in undulating motions as the males danced before their enchanted mates. Hahnel's fish had mostly blues and reds predominant in them, but every strain of fancy guppy has some "blood" that came from Hahnel's tanks...because Paul Hahnel invented beautiful guppies!

If Hahnel could do it, so can you. There is no great problem involved if you are willing to give it the time and effort...and have patience. You don't need a great knowledge of genetics. You just need good eyes.

Find a pet dealer having a nice variety of tropical fishes. Tell him your needs. His should be the shop from which you bought your original equipment, for when you bought it you could have ordered a few pairs of good guppies. There are many, many kinds of fancy guppies available today. Select the guppies that appeal to your own taste. Buy at least two pairs; four pairs would be even better.

Through error or otherwise, fancy males have been sold with common females as their "mates." The young that you will get from these females will be nothing like the beautiful males that came with the pairs. This is why you should buy your fish from a knowledgeable source.

Once you have acquired good stock, take them home and float them in your aquarium in the container in which they came. Allow a little time until the temperature of the water in the container is the same as the water in the 10-gallon aquarium. Check the pH of the two waters and be sure that they are within .2 of each other. Now add the fish to the 10-gallon aquarium. Allow your guppies a day or so to become accustomed to their new surroundings before you feed them or the food will go uneaten and decay.

Daily or more frequently, you should check your guppies to look for babies hiding among the plants. Immediately start to hatch brine shrimp eggs and feed the baby guppies newly hatched brine shrimp for the first few weeks of their lives. Supplement this with fine dry food. Keep the babies on this diet for one month, feeding brine shrimp every day, supplemented with other foods. By the end of the month you can begin to feel safe enough to isolate some of the fish.

Into another 10-gallon aquarium that has no filter and no gravel, put four small (one-gallon) bowls. Add water to the aquarium so that each bowl is submerged up to 1'' below the neck of the bowl. Place small bowl filters in all the bowls, attaching them to the airline by means of four 3-way valves and plastic tubing. Also attach an airstone to a piece of plastic tubing and a 2-way valve at the end of the airline, and place the airstone into the 10-gallon aquarium containing the four bowls. Attach the heater, but do not plug it in until fish are about to be added. The idea of this setup is to use one heater to heat the four bowls; the airstone will circulate the water around the bowls so the heating will be uniform. In the summertime the bowls can be removed from the 10-gallon aquarium and it can be used for extra fish. Aquarium dividers are available at your petshop to separate the guppies from each other if you want to keep males and females apart.

Take the four largest fish from among the month-old babies and put one each into the jars in the other 10-gallon aquarium. Keep your eye on these fish, for your purpose here is to eventually end up with some virgin females. If you look closely at their anal fins as they grow, you'll find that fish that are males will begin to have thickened anal fins that develop into an intromittent organ called a "gonopodium." Females have "normal" anal fins that are fan-shaped and look like fins. Males, of course, can be kept together, and females can be kept together, too. But try as much as possible to keep your babies sorted out according to sex.

After a few months, as your fish become larger and more colorful, begin sorting them out. Give away your smaller males and females to others interested in the hobby (or feed them to larger fishes). Only keep the best one or two males and females from each brood. In six months you'll have about a dozen fish, each being the very best that your breeders have to offer. Some of the females can go back in with their parents, to breed with their father or uncle. Others can be crossed with their brothers in their own small jars. From this point on, luck and chance take over. If the odds were on your side and you picked the right fish, you might have a superior strain of guppies on their way to development. Regardless, keep inbreeding your fish for a few generations; this is the way new varieties spring up. Breed those fish which you like the best with virgin females. But check the virgins first with the following hormone test.

Female guppies are normally uncolored, though certain strains have some hint of coloration. Even in the most highly colored females, there is never any strength of coloration as can be found in males of the same strain. In order to check the coloration that the females might pass on to their male offspring I have found the following hormone test to work very well. This test brings out the full colors of the female, colors she should never have normally. If you ever find highly colored females offered for sale, you should consider the possibility that they have been treated with a hormone. Look at their anal fin carefully for indications of thickening. A female with a thickened anal fin is useless for breeding purposes.

Have your druggist dissolve 0.1 gram of methyl testosterone in 100cc of 70% methyl or ethyl alcohol. To this solution add 900cc of distilled water. This will make 1000cc or about one quart. This is your stock solution. To test a female guppy she must be put into one of the one-gallon jars. You can test more than one female at a time, of course. To the jars add two drops of the stock solution. Every other day add another two drops. Once the females begin to show color (from two to six weeks after you have started the test), stop adding hormone. As soon as you have ascertained which females have the most desirable color, remove them and place them in another container with fresh water. Now carefully wash the one gallon jar so that no traces of the hormone are left, or it might sterilize future females placed in the water. In a few weeks or a month, the color will leave the females and they will look normal again. Don't place them with the males until all abnormal coloration has faded.

As soon as you have set up your aquaria with guppies, you should regulate yourself into a routine. Set up a few gallons of water in some empty bottles that have been cleaned thoroughly with water and not soap or detergent. Set the bottles where they will be at room temperature and away from strong sunlight. This you will need in

Red lyretail

Red fantail (Multicolored delta)

Red delta flagtail (Half-black red delta)

Red common roundtail

Wild fantail (Red delta)

Wild delta flagtail (AOC delta)

Wild square flagtail (Multicolored delta)

*Plate #169*

Wild delta flagtail (Red bicolor delta)

Black square flagtail (Half-black red)

Black delta flagtail (Half-black blue veiltail)

Black round flagtail (Purple delta)

Black fantail (Delta)

Black snakeskin flagtail (Solid delta)

Black fantail (Delta)

Black flagtail (Purple veiltail)

*Plate #170*

Black fantail (Half-black AOC delta)

285

order to change about 10% of the water in the aquaria every week. The more strictly you adhere to this, the better off will be your guppies.

The guppy urinates. The urine collects in the water and in time builds up a poisonous environment for the guppy. These poisons must be constantly diluted with fresh water or the guppies will be stunted.

Your feeding routine should be as follows:

Early A.M.: Newly hatched brine shrimp for the babies and adults.

Noon: Dry food for babies and adults.

Early evening: Newly hatched shrimp for babies; adult frozen brine shrimp for breeders.

Late evening: Newly hatched brine shrimp for both.

Of course you don't *have* to feed your fish four times a day. It is ideal to do so, but they will get along very well on two or three meals a day. The people who raise champion fish are those who devote a great deal of time to their stock.

Guppies are very hardy aquarium fish. As a matter of fact, they are about the strongest of all tropical fishes, and if they get sick then you are doing something very wrong! Aside from some very rare ailments, your guppies are most likely to fall prey to the following diseases.

## ICH

Ich (pronounced variously as "itch" and "ick") is an abbreviation of the scientific name of a parasitic protozoan known as *Ichthyophthirius*. These are microscopic organisms that bore through the slime covering of the guppy and build themselves a little home in the guppy's flesh. The parasite causes white spots to form all over the guppy's body. Usually the first spots appear on the fins, especially the tail. At the first sign of the disease, increase the temperature of the water to 85° F. This speeds up the life cycle of the parasite and the white spots will hatch out into larvae. Get some ich remedy from your petshop. Ich remedies kill the larvae, not the adults. The main ingredient of a good ich cure is malachite green, so be sure that the label says the remedy contains malachite green. The white spots should disappear in a few days and the guppies will be cured without ill effect. Follow label instructions. It may be necessary to continue treatments for two weeks or more to be sure all the parasites are killed. You can expect ich if your room temperature dropped suddenly and the aquarium heater was unable to cope with the drop in temperature. Ich also may appear any other time your fish are stressed.

## WHITE MOUTH DISEASE

White mouth disease is a bacterial infection that usually begins by eating away the mouth of the fish. This bacterial infection can be cured with any of the broad-spectrum antibiotics like tetracycline, Terramycin or Aureomycin. Use 500mg per gallon of water. Change the water after the cure. This disease is brought on by bad water conditions, a chilling, or by adding unaged water to the aquarium.

## FIN AND TAIL ROT

This disease is manifested by the fins of the guppy beginning to fray and disintegrate. It should be treated the same as white mouth disease.

For a much more detailed description of diseases of fishes, ask your petshop to refer you to a good disease book.

## KINDS OF GUPPIES

Lots of books and articles have been written about guppies. Their care comes down to the best general care for all fishes: change the water as often as possible using the drip-siphon method. A change of 10% of the water per day with good, aged water is best. Feedings of live foods (brine shrimp is best) twice a day supplemented with a good dry food are highly recommended. Actually, guppies like to feed continuously, as they do in nature. The more often you can feed them, the better they will grow...but never feed them more than they will eat in one minute if you feed them more than once a day. Also, if you only feed them once a day (and that is not at all recommended), feed them mainly live foods one day with dry foods the next day. Never feed more than they can clean up in three minutes.

All guppies require about the same basic care: water quality as close to pH 7.0 (neutral) as possible; water temperatures about 75° F.; and good strong light at least 12 hours a day (more light makes them grow faster).

There are basically two kinds of guppies: *wild guppies,* which have little color compared to the fancy varieties (males, while looking similar, are almost never colored exactly alike and females all look the same); and *fancy guppies,* of which there are many strains. Fancy guppies are what this listing is all about.

While there are many aquarium clubs and guppy clubs, few have had the commanding authority to establish a name for each strain of guppy. There is really no need to name each strain except for commercial purposes and as an editorial convenience. But people who read about a "swordtail" guppy should have some idea of what a swordtail guppy looks like, so I (HRA) am therefore presenting a list of guppy strains, proposing names for them. These names are mostly derived from the literature. Each one has been illustrated with a photograph of a live fish. Fish will be categorized first by their being "wild" or fancy," and then on their finnage and their coloration.*

## FINNAGE OF GUPPIES
There are the following kinds of tail shapes: round, veil, and pointed. Each of these shapes has subdivisions as follows:

### ROUNDTAILS
1. Common roundtail.
2. Spadetail, sometimes called coffertail.

### VEILTAILS
1. Flagtial: A variety where the long tail is narrower than it is long.
2. Fantail: A variety where the long tail is wider at the end than its length.
3. Bannertail: A variety where the long tail is equal in length and breadth.

### POINTEDTAILS:
1. Speartail: A single spike coming from the center of a basically round tail.
2. Lyretail: A tail with a top spike and a bottom spike. This is also called a "double" swordtail at times.
3. Upper swordtail: A tail with a single spike growing out of the top rays of the tail.
4. Lower swordtail: A tail with a single spike growing from the bottom rays of the tail.
5. Crowntail: A tail with three spikes evenly disposed.
6. Fake swordtail: A fish whose tail rays are not extended but the top or bottom rays are colored, thus giving the fish the appearance of being a swordtail when in fact it is a veiltail.

## DORSAL FIN SHAPES
The dorsal fin shape should be related to the tail fin, and in most cases they naturally occur that way. A fish with a long, flowing tail should have a long, flowing dorsal fin. The colors, too, of the dorsal fin should match the colors of the tail. It is almost impossible to have a fish of one color with its tail and dorsal different colors. This linked characteristic depends upon the closeness of the genes for dorsal fin and tail fin coloration. As soon as the genetic engineers get their hands on guppies, we can expect some remarkable achievements.

## COLORS OF GUPPIES
Almost every color of the rainbow is to be found in guppies. It might be safe to say that the colors to be found in guppies are more varied than the colors to be found in any other single species of living thing, including plants and butterflies. For the sake of clarity, I am proposing the following color categories. I have not listed the combinations of, say, yellow and red where almost equal amounts of each are to be found in a single fish. In all cases, the basic color of the majority of the body and fin is what determines the color variety under which a fish can be classified.
1. Black
2. White
3. Yellow
4. Blue
5. Red
6. Green
7. Wild

## PATTERNS
Guppies in many colors are found to have uniform patterns. Thus far the only patterns to be readily recognized are the snakeskins, though there are many popular patterns such as fishes with red tails and almost blue-black bodies. Albino guppies have never been favorites, and their appearance on the aquarium market is spotty and causes little excitement. Many new patterns might soon be developed as breeders concentrate on serious inbreeding.

The ideal for which most guppy breeders strive is color enhanced with finnage. This is due to the fact that "color sells," so petshops want colorful fish regardless of how beautiful their fins are. The ideal, then, is a fish with uniformly bright color throughout its body...with a thousand fish that look exactly the same in the same tank from the same breeder from the same strain. That's the ideal. It is certainly possible.

*Note: On the accompanying pages of guppy photos, two names have been applied to most of the fish shown. In all cases the first name is the commercial name derived from the literature, and the second name is the official description of the fish according to the International Fancy Guppy Association, the world's leading guppy society. Where only one name is given, the name derived from commercial literature and the IFGA classification are the same.

Red common roundtail (Common)

Red spadetail (Common)

Red delta flagtail (AOC bicolor delta)

Red delta flagtail (Red bicolor delta)

Red delta flagtail (Half-black red delta)

Red delta flagtail (Red veiltail)

Red fantail (Red bicolor delta)

*Plate #171*

Red fantail (Green delta)

288

Black fantail (Half-black AOC delta)

Black delta flagtail (Half-black blue delta)

Black fantail (Half-black AOC delta)

Black delta flagtails (Half-black red deltas)

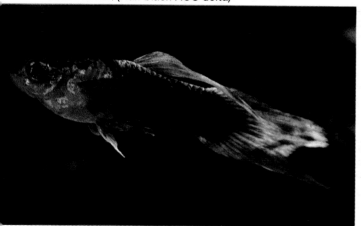

Black lower swordtail

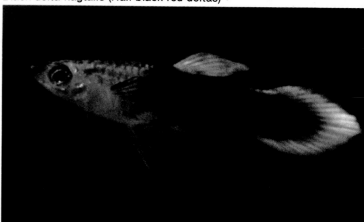

Black spadetail

Black square flagtail (Red bicolor veiltail)

Black fantail (Blue delta)

*Plate #172*

289

Yellow fantail (AOC bicolor delta)

Yellow fantail (Red delta)

Yellow common roundtail (Common)

Yellow delta flagtail (Half-black pastel delta)

Wild and yellow lyretails

Yellow delta flagtail (Red delta)

Yellow snakeskin fantail (Variegated snakeskin delta)

Yellow bannertail

*Plate #173*

Yellow lyretail

Yellow spadetail and upper swordtail (Bronze common)

Wild lower swordtail (Single swordtail)

Wild lower swordtail (Single swordtail)

Black lower swordtail

Red lower swordtail (Veil with poor tail shape)

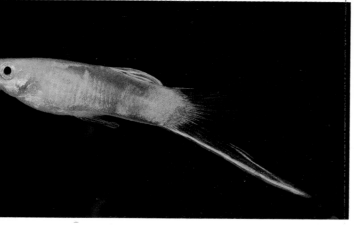

Blue lower swordtail (Single swordtail)

*Plate #174*

Wild lower swordtail (Single swordtail)

Wild upper swordtails (Single swordtail)

Wild lyretail (Double swordtail)

Wild lyretail (Double swordtail)

Wild lyretail (Double swordtail)

Yellow lyretail

Yellow lyretail

Blue spadetail

Blue crowntail

*Plate #175*

Blue fantail (Red delta)

White square flagtails (Bronze veiltails)

Blue common roundtail (Common)

Blue fantail (Red bicolor delta)

Wild common roundtail (Common)

Blue fantail (Delta).

Wild delta flagtail (AOC bicolor delta)

Wild delta flagtail (Red bicolor delta)

*Plate #176*

293

Yellow upper swordtail female (Bluegreen female)

Black delta flagtail female (Half-black AOC female)

Yellow round flagtail female giving birth (Gold)

Black male lyretail (Common)

Yellow delta flagtail female (Blue/green female)

Female yellow common roundtails

Black delta flagtail female (Half-black AOC female)

Female yellow round flagtail (Bronze female)

*Plate #177*

294

Red common roundtail female (Red female)

Female black bannertail (Black female)

Yellow fantail female (AOC)

Wild common roundtail females and males (Common)

Red common roundtail female (Red female)

Red snakeskin delta flagtails (AOC female)

Female yellow flagtail (AOC female)

Yellow female roundtail above, red snakeskin lyretail male below (AOC female above)

*Plate #178*

## PLATIES

For some reason the platies have always lagged behind the swordtail and guppy in popularity, although they are certainly among the top five or six species of popular livebearers. There are now at least 7 species of platies known from Mexico (*Xiphophorus maculatus* ranges south as far as Guatemala and Honduras), but only *X. maculatus,* the common platy, and *X. variatus,* the sunset platy or platy variatus, are currently found in the aquarium. The other   species are restricted to minor drainage basins in Mexico and are certainly not very colorful in their wild form.

Both the platies in the hobby have been widely hybridized with each other and with the swordtails, resulting in a total mess as far as telling which species is which. In fact, some authorities flatly state that there are no pure strains of swordtails or platies being bred commercially at this time. Even the distinction between platies as a group and swordtails as a separate group is now hazardous. Platies were once in the genus *Platypoecilus* and were told from *Xiphophorus* by lacking the sword, having a different body shape, and by details of the gonopodium of the male. With the discovery of the sword-platy, *X. xiphidium,* in 1932, these distinctions began to break down, for this fish is obviously a platy by body shape and color pattern, but its males have a distinct sword. Later obvious swordtails lacking the swords were discovered, and eventually the genus *Platypoecilus* was dropped. For convenience, today platies are *Xiphophorus* without any swords, while any *Xiphophorus* with even a small sword is best called a swordtail.

The genetics of the platies was studied by Dr. Myron Gordon and his students, and the variation and systematics of these fishes (especially the two species in the hobby) are perhaps better known than for any other fishes. Many of the color and finnage varieties popular today are the direct and indirect results of careful breeding by Myron Gordon between the 1930's and the 1950's. Although wild platies are rather colorless, plainly spotted fishes, their genetic background includes the ability to develop and pass on traits for brilliant red, blue, and yellow colors, as well as distinctive patterns on the caudal peduncle and caudal fin. Additionally, they have the ability to pass these traits on to their hybrids with swordtails if carefully bred, with the major disadvantage being the shortening of the sword of the offspring. The platy variatus also has a strong tendency toward a greatly enlarged and brightly colored dorsal fin, making some of its varieties among the most colorful of all aquarium fishes.

Platies are very easy to keep and breed, and they are usually regarded as beginner fishes. Yet their extreme variability, much of it carefully documented many years ago, combined with their bright colors make them worthy of the respect of all hobbyists, beginner and specialist alike. Without them aquaria would be much less brilliant.

Gold variegated "Mickey Mouse" platy

Gold platy female

Gold tuxedo platy female

Gold salt and pepper platy male

Gold salt and pepper platy

Red salt and pepper platies

Milk and ink or leopard platy

*Plate #179*

Gold salt and pepper platies

Gold comet platies, male below

Gold comet platy male

Gold platy female

Gold hifin platy female

Gold platy male

Gold platy

Gold "Mickey Mouse" platies

Gold "Mickey Mouse" hifin platy

*Plate #180*

Red comet or twinbar platy

Blue hifin platy female

Sunset hifin platy male

Black variatus platy male

Red tuxedo hifin platy male

Black hifin variatus platy male

Red salt and pepper platy male

Blue platies, male above

*Plate #181*

299

Gold wagtail platies, males

Red varigated platies

Bleeding heart platy male

Gold "Mickey Mouse" hifin platy male

Gold variatus platy

Gold platies, male right

Gold "Mickey Mouse" platy male

Gold "Mickey Mouse" platy female

*Plate #182*

Red wagtail platies

Red wagtail platy female

Red hifin wagtail platy male

Red tuxedo wagtail platy female

Red platy female

Gold wagtail platies

Red tuxedo comet platy

*Plate #183*

Sunset variatus platy male

Sunset variatus platy male

Sunset variatus var. male

Marigold variatus

Blue variatus platy male

Red-tailed gold variatus platy male

Albino variatus platy

Gold platies

*Plate #184*

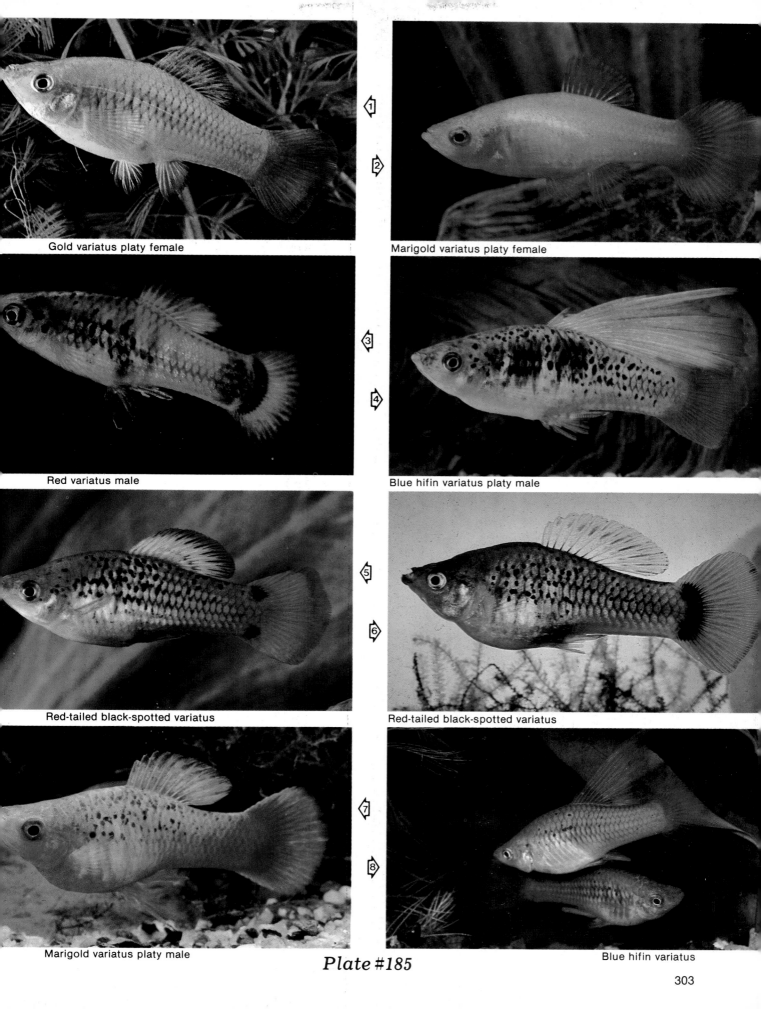

Gold variatus platy female

Marigold variatus platy female

Red variatus male

Blue hifin variatus platy male

Red-tailed black-spotted variatus

Red-tailed black-spotted variatus

Marigold variatus platy male

Blue hifin variatus

*Plate #185*

303

Blue hifin variatus platy male

Red variatus hifin platy male

Sunburst platies, male right

Black variatus platies, male below

Red hifin variatus platy male

Red variatus platy male

Gold hifin variatus platy male

Marigold variatus platy male

*Plate #186*

304

## SWORDTAILS (*XIPHOPHORUS* SPECIES)

Since their introduction as aquarium fishes in 1909, swordtails have been consistent favorites in the hobby. All the known species occur in the Atlantic coastal waters from Mexico to Honduras. The various species are often not easy to obtain in pure form since nearly every swordtail available in a petshop is the product of a cross with a platy. Pure strains from the original wild stock (*Xiphophorus helleri*) just do not exist in the commercial aquarium trade.

The roster of swordtail and platy species, now numbering 18 nominal species, includes: *Xiphophorus alvarezi, X. andersi, X. clemenciae, X. cortezi, X. couchianus, X. evelynae, X. gordoni, X. helleri, X. kosszanderi, X. maculatus, X. milleri, X. montezumae, X. nigrensis, X. pygmaeus, X. roseni, X. signum, X. variatus,* and *X. xiphidium*. Of these 18, 7 are usually called platies: *X. couchianus, X. gordoni, X. variatus, X. evelynae, X. milleri, X. roseni,* and *X. maculatus*. The other 11 are swordtails, though several look more like platies with short swords than like typical aquarium swordtails.

### How the Swordtail Got its Name

In the early 1840's, the government of the old Austro-Hungarian Empire dispatched Karl Heller to Mexico to collect plants for the City of Vienna's Botanical Gardens. In his travels through the state of Veracruz, Heller reached Mount Orizaba, Mexico's mightiest peak, one that rises 18,696 feet above the sea. In the vicinity of the village of Orizaba, at an elevation of about 4,000 feet, Heller stood amid an amazing natural display of tropical plants. With just a glance above, he could see, in the far distance, the gleaming snow-white contours of the glacial mountain peak. An abundance of moisture, both from torrential mountain brooks and from the mist-laden clouds that hover about the icy peak, in combination with the rich volcanic soil, has made the Orizaba region a natural botanic garden.

Karl Heller gathered not only plants but many small terrestrial and aquatic animals characteristic of the country. In a stream near Orizaba, Heller discovered one of the most unusual fishes in Mexico. When Herr Doktor Jacob Heckel, the famous European ichthyologist, saw the fish that Heller brought to him for identification—dead and pickled in preserving fluid though it was—he exclaimed enthusiastically that it "was so indescribably beautiful that it must appear as something extraordinary even to the layman." Heckel said, in 1848, "This species I name in honor of Karl Heller, its discoverer: *Xiphophorus hellerii*." Nothing could have been more appropriate, for the scientific name means "Heller's swordbearer."

Blood red swordtail female.

Gold tuxedo swordtails.

Brick red wag swordtail.

Brick red swordtail

Red Mexican swordtails.

Velvet red swordtail.

Black Berlin swordtails.

Red tuxedo swordtail platy hybrid.

306

*Plate #187*

*Xiphophorus montezumae.*

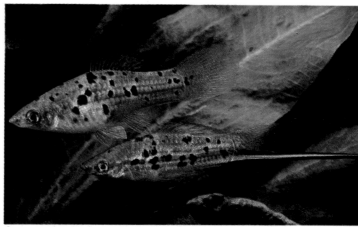

Green variegated swordtails, *X. helleri.*

Green swordtails.

Green swordtail male.

Green swordtail variation, male.

Green swordtail mickey mouse hybrid male.

Green swordtail male.

Golden swordtail male.

*Plate #188*

Brick red jet hifin swordtail male.

Brick red hifin wagtail swordtail female.

Brick red hifin wagtail swordtails.

Gold tuxedo hifin swordtail female.

Blood red wagtail lyretail swordtails.

Brick red swordtail male.

Blood red tuxedo hifin swordtails.

Albino hifin swordtail male.

*Plate #189*

308

Albino swordtail male.

Piebald swordtail male.

Marigold swordtail hybrids.

Red variegated swordtail female.

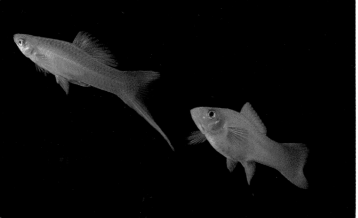

Marigold swordtails.

Red variegated swordtails, cancerous strain.

Gold variegated swordtails.

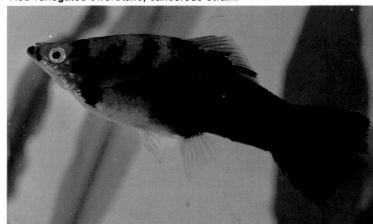

Red jet swordtail female, cancerous strain.

*Plate #190*

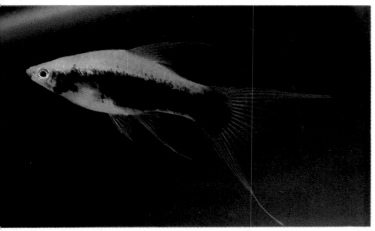
Gold tuxedo lyretail swordtail female.

Brick red lyretail swordtail Siamese female.

Albino swordtail male.

Albino lyretail swordtail male.

Brick red lyretail swordtails, male on right.

Green hifin lyretail swordtail male.

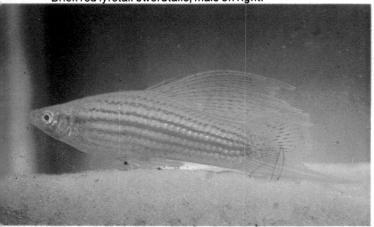
Albino golden hifin swordtail male.

Blood red hifin swordtail female.

*Plate #191*

Blood red hifin or "highfin" wagtail swordtail females.

Velvet red hifin wagtail swordtail female.

Brick red hifin wag-pintails.

Blood red hifin comet swordtails, male below.

*Plate #192*

Blood red lyretail swordtail male.

Brick red hifin swordtail male.

Blood red Berlin lyretail swordtail male.

Blood red hifin swordtail pair.

Brick red tuxedo swordtail male.

Brick red lyretail swordtail female.

*Xiphophorus cortezi* male

Red hifin swordtail male.

*Plate #193*

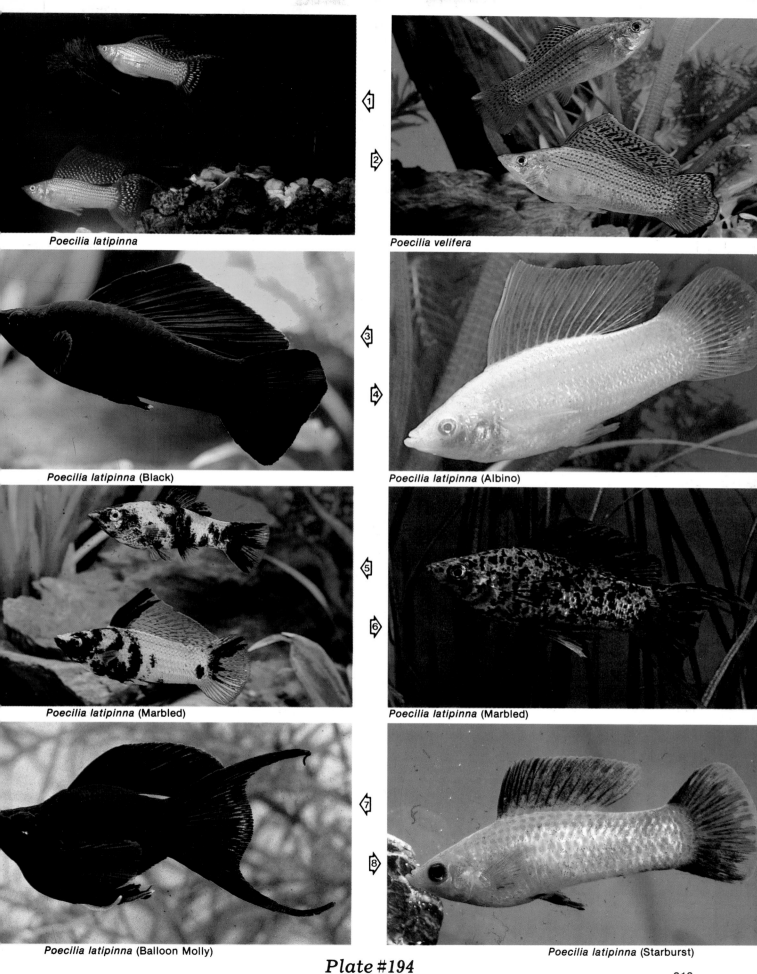

Poecilia latipinna

Poecilia velifera

Poecilia latipinna (Black)

Poecilia latipinna (Albino)

Poecilia latipinna (Marbled)

Poecilia latipinna (Marbled)

Poecilia latipinna (Balloon Molly)

Poecilia latipinna (Starburst)

*Plate #194*

313

Red pineapple swordtail male

Pineapple swordtails

Red tuxedo swordtails

Red pineapple swordtails

Black lyretail hi-fin swordtail

*Poecilia reticulata* (Common guppies)

*Belonesox belizanus*

*Belonesox belizanus*

*Plate #194A*

*Xiphophorus clemencae*

*Xiphophorus cortezi*

*Poeciliopsis monacha*

*Xiphophorus signum*

*Gambusia atrora*

*Heterophallus rachowi*

Plate #194B

Poecilia caucana

Poecilia latipunctata

Carlhubbsia stuarti

Poecilia melanogaster

Poecilia nigrofasciata

Poecilia nigrofasciata

Poecilia sphenops

Quintana atrizona

316

*Plate #195*

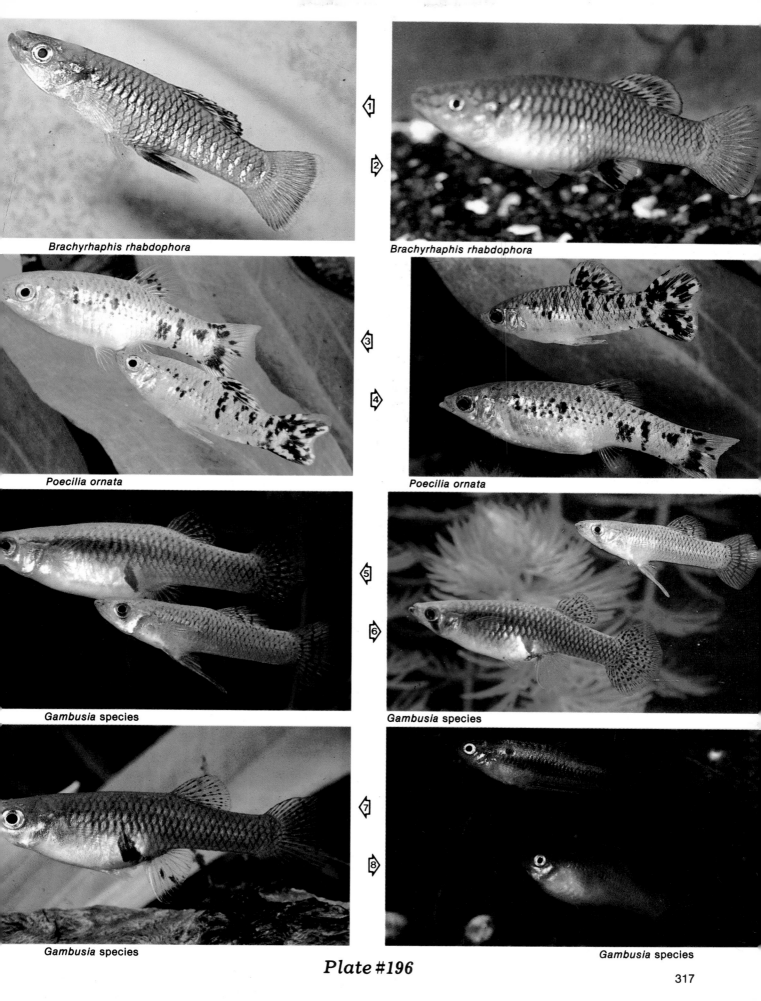

Brachyrhaphis rhabdophora

Brachyrhaphis rhabdophora

Poecilia ornata

Poecilia ornata

Gambusia species

Gambusia species

Gambusia species

Gambusia species

*Plate #196*

317

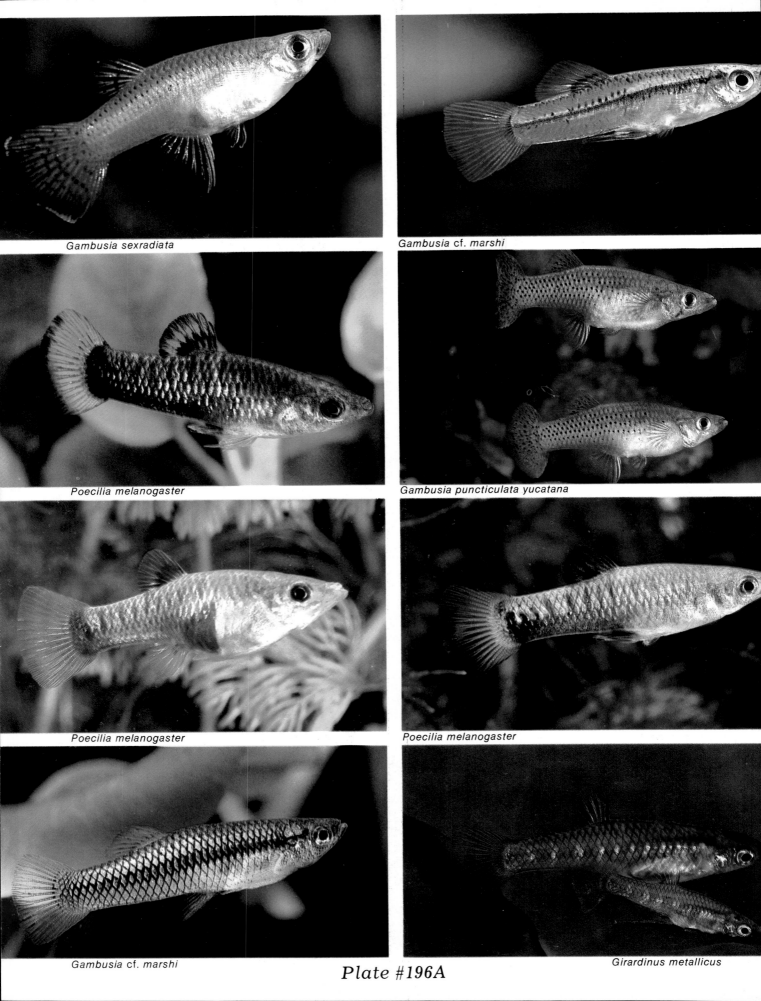

Gambusia sexradiata

Gambusia cf. marshi

Poecilia melanogaster

Gambusia puncticulata yucatana

Poecilia melanogaster

Poecilia melanogaster

Gambusia cf. marshi

*Plate #196A*

Girardinus metallicus

*Brachyrhaphis episcopi*

*Priapella compressa*

*Poecilia dominicensis*

*Poecilia dominicensis*

*Poecilia sphenops*

*Poecilia latipinna* (Chocolate)

*Poecilia latipinna* (Black)

*Poecilia velifera*

Plate #196B

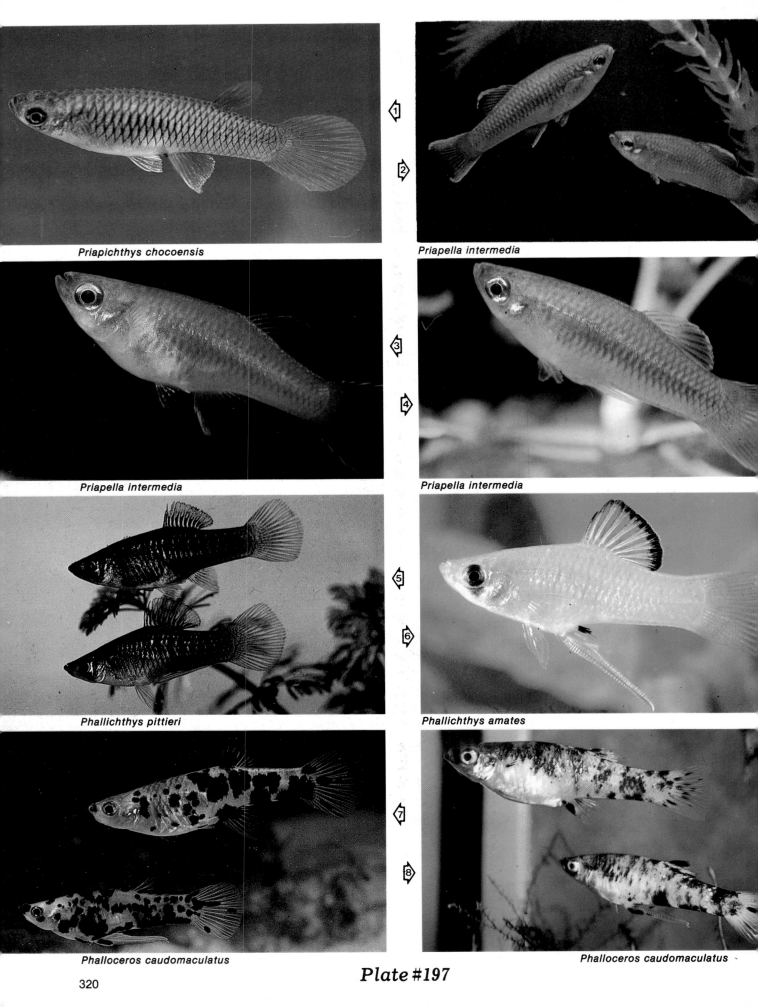

Priapichthys chocoensis

Priapella intermedia

Priapella intermedia

Priapella intermedia

Phallichthys pittieri

Phallichthys amates

Phalloceros caudomaculatus

Phalloceros caudomaculatus

**Plate #197**

*Jenynsia lineata*

*Alfaro cultratus*

*Belonesox belizanus*

*Belonesox belizanus*

*Girardinus metallicus*

*Girardinus metallicus*

*Heterandria bimaculata*

*Heterandria bimaculata*

*Plate #198*

321

Blue "Mickey Mouse" platies

Gold trident comet platy male

Tomato platy female

Sunburst platies

Red wagtail platies

Orange platies

Red tuxedo platies

Red platies

Plate #1084

*Ameca splendens*

*Xenoophorus captivus*

*Ilyodon cf. furcidens*

*Xenotoca melanosoma*

*Allodontichthys tamazulae*

*Xenotoca eiseni*

*Alfaro cultratus*

*Anableps anableps*

Plate #198B

*Ameca splendens*

*Ilyodon* "Black Band" (male)

*Xenoophorus captivus*

*Xenotoca eiseni*

*Xenotoca eiseni*

*Xenotoca eiseni*

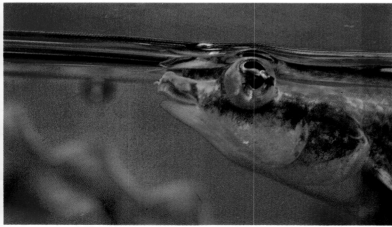

Anableps anableps

Anableps anableps

*Plate #199*

*Cichla ocellaris*

*Cichla ocellaris*

*Cichla temensis*

*Cichla temensis*

*Uaru amphiacanthoides (juv.)*

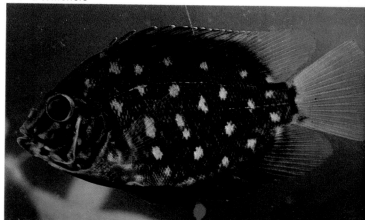

*Uaru amphiacanthoides (juv.)*

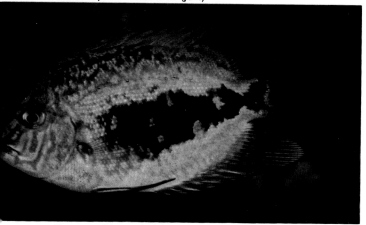

*Uaru amphiacanthoides*

*Uaru amphiacanthoides*

**Plate #200**

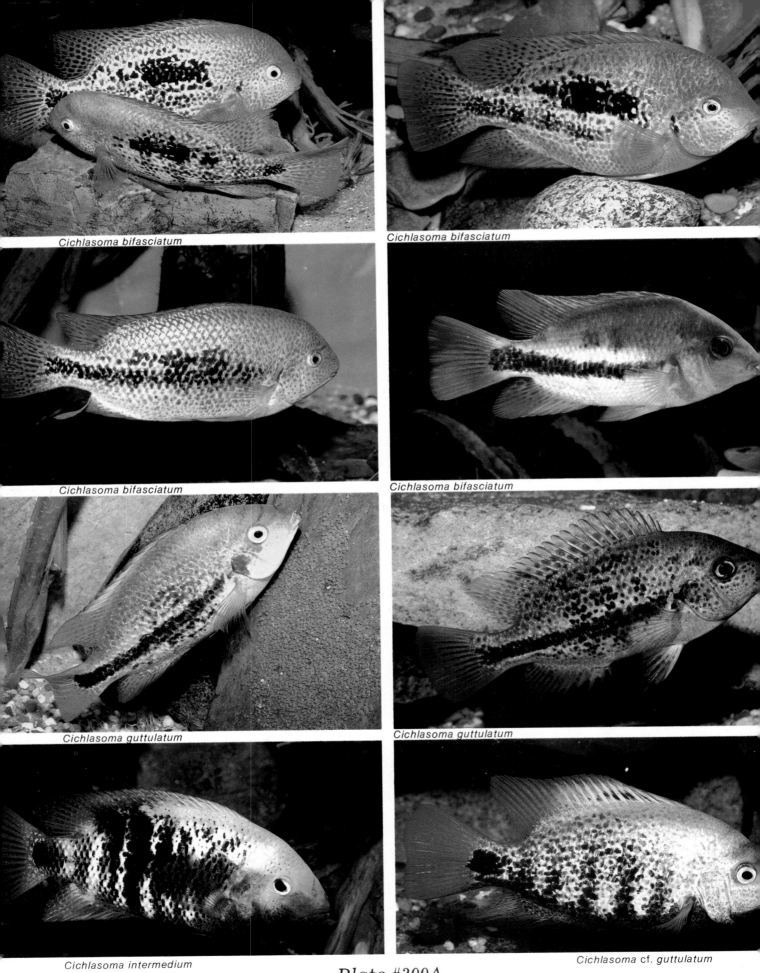

*Cichlasoma bifasciatum*

*Cichlasoma bifasciatum*

*Cichlasoma bifasciatum*

*Cichlasoma bifasciatum*

*Cichlasoma guttulatum*

*Cichlasoma guttulatum*

*Cichlasoma intermedium*

*Cichlasoma cf. guttulatum*

Plate #200A

*Cichlasoma carpintis*

*Cichlasoma cyanoguttatum*

*Cichlasoma carpintis*

*Cichlasoma carpintis*

*Cichlasoma minkleyi*

*Cichlasoma minkleyi*

*Cichlasoma octofasciatum*

*Cichlasoma octofasciatum*

Plate #200B

*Cichlasoma synspilum*

*Cichlasom synspilum*

*Cichlasoma maculicauda*

*Cichlasoma nicaraguense* (juv.)

*Cichlasoma nicaraguense*

*Cichlasoma nicaraguense*

*Cichlasoma spilurum*

*Cichlasoma spilurum*

**Plate #201**

*Cichlasoma salvinii*

*Cichlasoma motaguense* (juv.)

*Cichlasoma motaguense*

*Cichlasoma friedrichsthali*

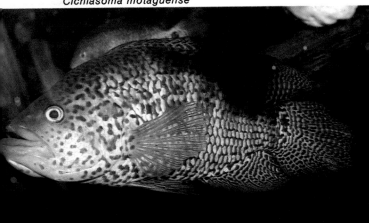
*Cichlasoma managuense*

*Cichlasoma managuense*

*Cichlasoma dovii*

*Cichlasoma dovii*

**Plate #202**

*Cichlasoma macracanthus*

*Cichlasoma macracanthus*

*Cichlasoma altifrons*

*Cichlasoma robertsoni*

*Cichlasoma alfari*

*Cichlasoma alfari*

*Cichlasoma aff. labiatum*

*Cichlasoma cf. alfari*

Plate #202A

*Cichlasoma coryphaenoides*

*Cichlasoma temporale*

*Cichlasoma temporale*

*Cichlasoma temporale*

*Cichlasoma festae*

*Cichlasoma festae*

*Cichlasoma umbriferum*

*Cichlasoma umbriferum*

Plate #202B

*Cichlasoma sajica*

*Cichlasoma sajica*

*Cichlasoma hellebruni*

*Cichlasoma hellebruni*

*Cichlasoma hellebruni*

*Cichlasoma festae ?*

*Cichlasoma coryphaenoides*

*Cichlasoma axelrodi*

**Plate #203**

*Cichlasoma popenoi*

*Cichlasoma citrinellum*

*Cichlasoma labiatum*

*Cichlasoma labiatum*

*Cichlasoma alfari*

*Cichlasoma urophtalmum*

*Cichlasoma trimaculatum*

*Cichlasoma festae*

Plate #204

333

*Cichlasoma sajica*

*Cichlasoma psittacus*

*Cichlasoma septemfasciatum*

*Cichlasoma septemfasciatum*

*Cichlasoma spilurum*

*Cichlasoma septemfasciatum var.*

*Cichlasoma spilurum*

*Cichlasoma spilurum*

Plate #204A

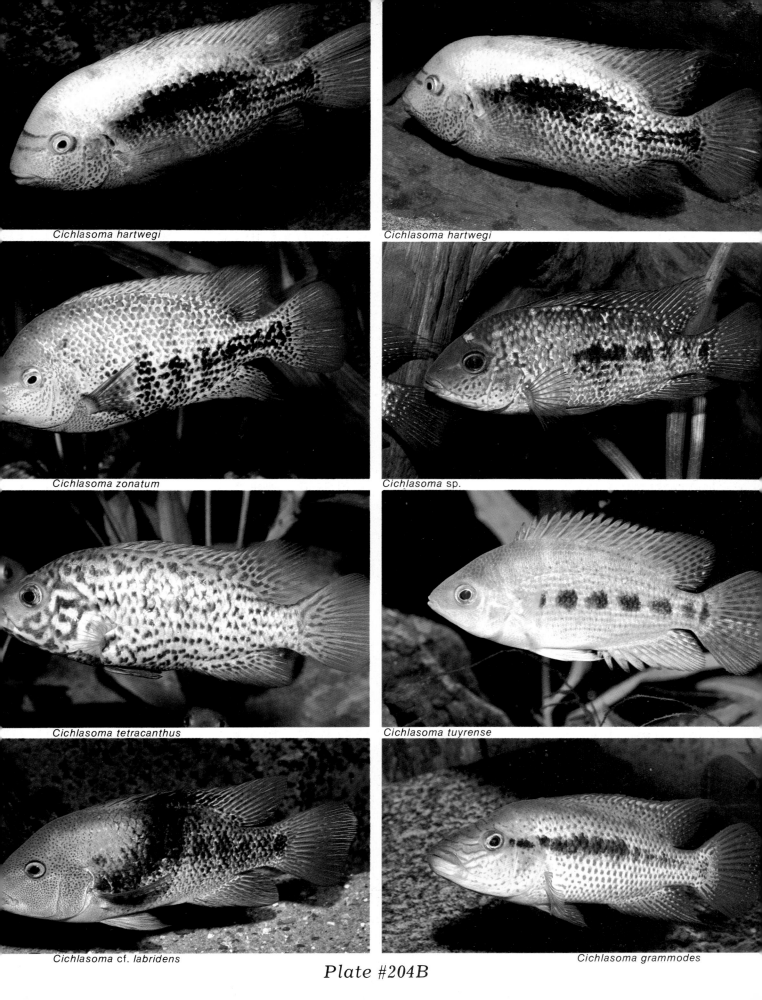

Cichlasoma hartwegi

Cichlasoma hartwegi

Cichlasoma zonatum

Cichlasoma sp.

Cichlasoma tetracanthus

Cichlasoma tuyrense

Cichlasoma cf. labridens

Cichlasoma grammodes

Plate #204B

*Cichlasoma nigrofasciatum*

*Cichlasoma nigrofasciatum* (var.)

*Cichlasoma nigrofasciatum* (var.)

*Cichlasoma centrarchus*

*Cichlasoma octofasciatum*

*Cichlasoma octofasciatum*

*Cichlasoma longimanus*

*Cichlasoma longimanus*

336

**Plate #205**

Cichlasoma bimaculatum

Cichlasoma bimaculatum

Cichlasoma severum

Cichlasoma severum

Cichlasoma severum

Cichlasoma severum (Gold)

Cichlasoma severum (juveniles)

Cichlasoma festivum

**Plate #206**

*Cichlasoma festae*

*Cichlasoma tetracanthum*

*Cichlasoma carpintis*

*Cichlasoma carpintis*

*Cichlasoma cyanoguttatum*

*Cichlasoma atromaculatum*

*Cichlasoma atromaculatum*

*Cichlasoma atromaculatum*

**Plate #207**

*Cichlasoma meeki*

*Cichlasoma meeki*

*Cichlasoma aureum*

*Cichlasoma aureum*

*Cichlasoma bartoni*

*Cichlasoma bartoni*

*Cichlasoma psittacum*

*Cichlasoma psittacum*

*Plate #208*

339

*Petenia splendida*

*Petenia kraussi*

*Petenia splendida*

*Cichlasoma umbriferum*

*Neetroplus nematopus*

*Herotilapia multispinosa*

*Herotilapia multispinosa*

*Herotilapia multispinosa*

**Plate #209**

*Aquidens curviceps*

*Aquidens curviceps*

*Aquidens dorsigerus*

*Aquidens dorsigerus*

*Aequidens portalegrensis*

*Aequidens portalegrensis*

*Aequidens portalegrensis*

*Aequidens portalegrensis*

**Plate #210**

341

*Aequidens pulcher*

*Aequidens pulcher*

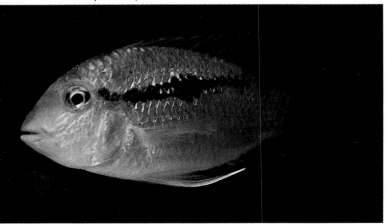

*Aequidens itanyi*

*Aequidens caeruleopunctatus*

*Aequidens rivulatus*

*Aequidens rivulatus*

*Aequidens "gold saum"*

*Aequidens "gold saum"*

*Plate #211*

*Aequidens* species

*Aequidens* species

**Aequidens**

**Aequidens dorsigerus**

**Aequidens maroni**

**Aequidens awani**

**Aequidens thayeri**

**Aequidens itanyi**

*Plate #212*

Aequidens vittata

Aequidens tetramerus

Aequidens duopunctatus

Aequidens tetramerus

Aequidens sapayensis?

Aequidens

Aequidens mariae

Aequidens awani

**Plate #213**

*Crenicichla strigata*

*Crenicichla lenticulata*

*Crenicichla lepidota*

*Crenicichla saxatilis*

*Crenicichla* species

*Batrachops* species

*Acaronia nassa*

*Acaronia nassa*

**Plate #214**

345

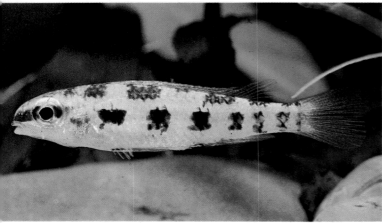

*Crenicara filamentosa* (female)

*Crenicara filamentosa* (male)

*Crenicara punctulata*

*Crenicara maculata* (female)?

*Crenicichla sp.*

*Crenicichla wallacei*

*Crenicichla geayi*

*Crenicichla johanna*

*Plate #215*

*Chaetobranchus bitaeniatus*

*Chaetobranchus bitaeniatus*

*Chaetobranchus flavescens*

*Nannacara anomala* (male)

*Nannacara anomala* (female w/young)

*Nannacara anomala* (female w/eggs)

*Apistogrammoides pucallpaensis* (male)

*Apistogrammoides pucallpaensis* (female)

**Plate #216**

347

*Taeniacara candidi*

*Apistogramma agassizi* (var.)

*Apistogramma agassizi* (var.)

*Apistogramma agassizi* (var.)

*Apistogramma agassizi* (var.)

*Apistogramma agassizi* (var.)

*Apistogramma agassizi* (female)

*Apistogramma agassizi* (pair)

**Plate #217**

*Apistogramma agassizi* (wild male)

*Apistogramma agassizi* (domestic male)

*Apistogramma borelli?* (var.)

*Apistogramma borelli* (female)

*Apistogramma bitaeniata*

*Apistogramma bitaeniata* (var.-yellow)

*Apistogramma bitaeniata* (female)

*Apistogramma bitaeniata* (pair)

*Plate #218*

Apistogramma gossei (male)

Apistogramma caetei (male)

Apistogramma eunotus?

Apistogramma caetei (female)

Apistogramma macmasteri (male)

Apistogramma macmasteri (female)

Apistogramma luelingi

Apistogramma sp. cf. macmasteri

**Plate #219**

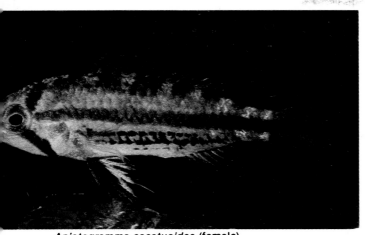

Apistogramma cacatuoides (female)

Apistogramma cacatuoides (male)

Apistogramma cacatuoides? (male)

Apistogramma cacatuoides (male)

Apistogramma gibbiceps

Apistogramma sp.

Apistogramma pertensis (male)

Apistogramma sp.

**Plate #220**

*Apistogramma steindachneri*

*Apistogramma steindachneri (male)*

*Apistogramma steindachneri (female)*

*Apistogramma steindachneri (female)*

*Apistogramma hippolytae*

*Apistogramma inconspicua*

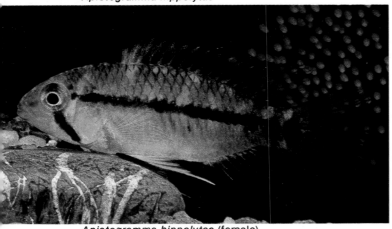

*Apistogramma hippolytae (female)*

*Apistogramma inconspicua (female)*

*Plate #221*

Apistogramma trifasciatum

Apistogramma trifasciatum

Apistogramma trifasciatum (female)

Apistogramma trifasciatum

Apistogramma trifasciatum heraldi

Apistogramma sp.

Apistogramma gossei

Apistogramma gephyra

Plate #222

*Microgeophagus ramirezi* (blond)

*Microgeophagus ramirezi* (normal)

*Biotodoma cupido*

*Acarichthys heckelii*

*Geophagus gymnogenys*

*Geophagus australis*

*Geophagus rhabdotus*

*Acarichthys geayi*

**Plate #223**

*Geophagus steindachneri*

*Geophagus steindachneri*

*Geophagus balzanii* (male)

*Geophagus balzanii* (female)

*Geophagus surinamensis*

*Geophagus surinamensis*

*Geophagus surinamensis*

*Geophagus surinamensis*

Plate #224

355

Geophagus surinamensis (var.)

Geophagus surinamensis (var.)

Geophagus brasiliensis

Geophagus brasiliensis

Geophagus acuticeps

Geophagus jurupari

Geophagus daemon

Geophagus sp. cf. daemon

356

**Plate #225**

*Astronotus ocellatus*

Astronotus ocellatus (red)

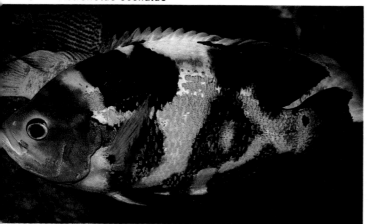

*Astronotus ocellatus* (tiger)

Astronotus ocellatus (w/ocelli)

*Astronotus ocellatus* (normal)

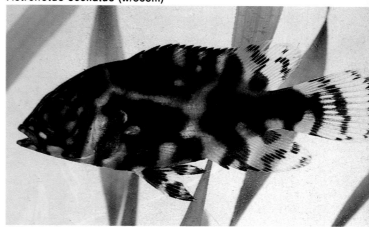

Astronotus ocellatus (juvenile)

Biotoecus opercularis

Biotoecus opercularis

**Plate #226**

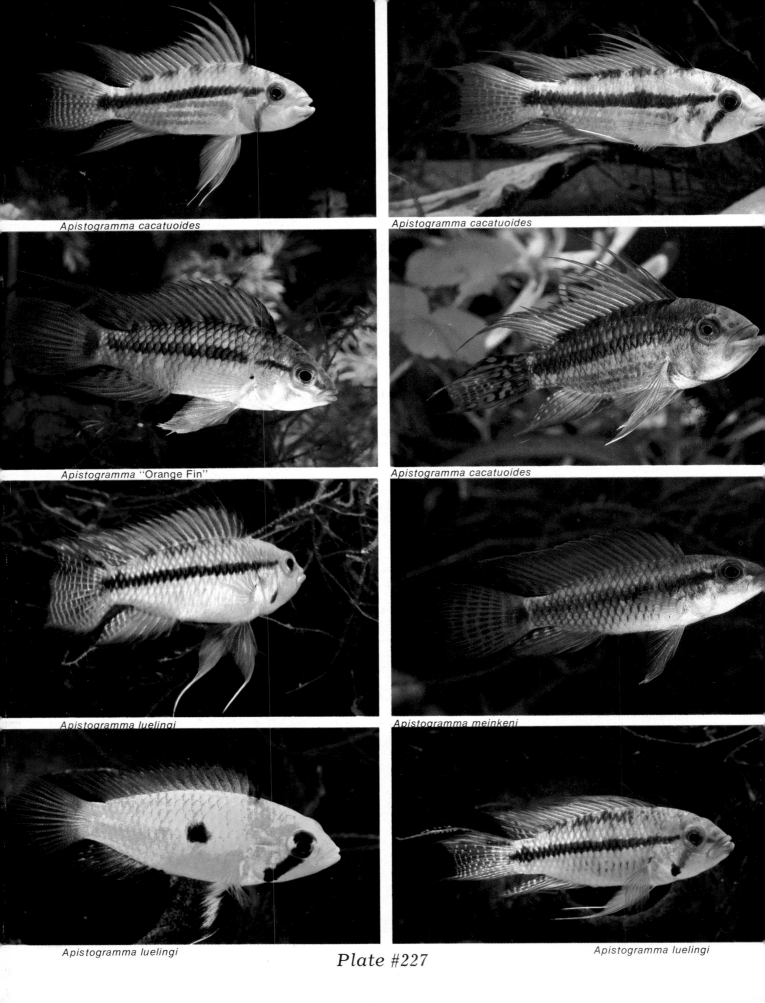

*Apistogramma cacatuoides*

*Apistogramma cacatuoides*

*Apistogramma "Orange Fin"*

*Apistogramma cacatuoides*

*Apistogramma luelingi*

*Apistogramma meinkeni*

*Apistogramma luelingi*

*Apistogramma luelingi*

Plate #227

Acarichthys geayi

Geophagus rhabdotus

Geophagus daemon

Acarichthys heckelii

Nannacara aureocephalus    male

Nannacara aureocephalus    male

Nannacara aureocephalus    female

Nannacara anomala

Plate #227A

Apistogramma viejita

Apistogramma viejita

Apistogramma viejita

Apistogramma viejita

Apistogramma macmasteri

Apistogramma viejita

Apistogramma macmasteri

Apistogramma macmasteri

Plate #227B

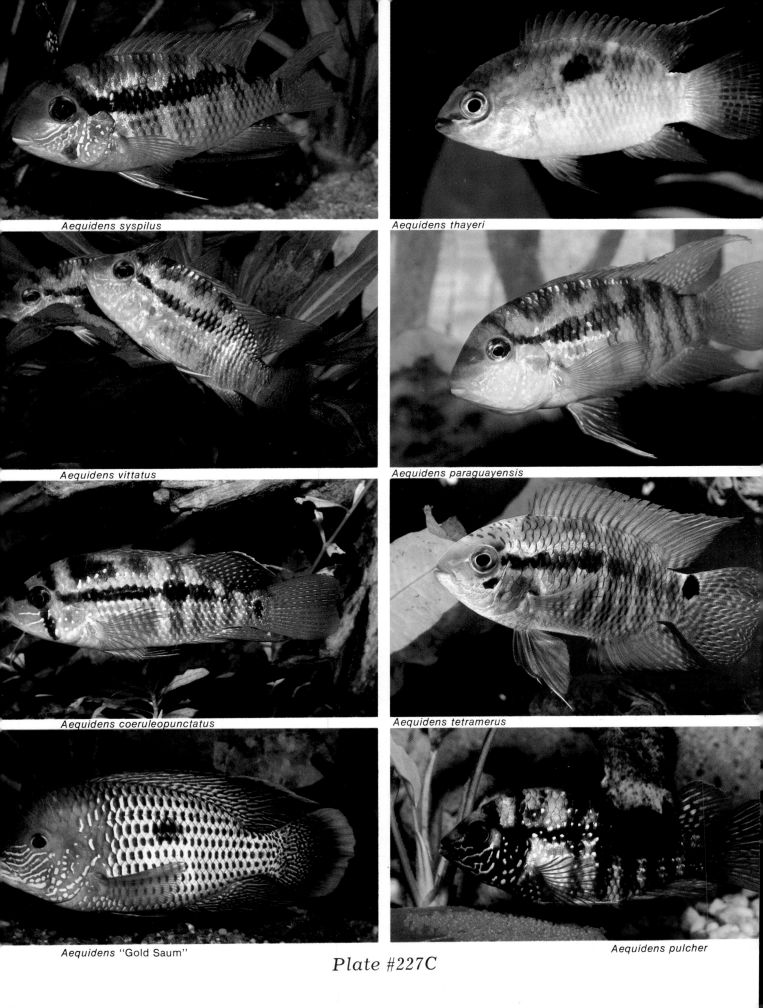

Aequidens syspilus

Aequidens thayeri

Aequidens vittatus

Aequidens paraguayensis

Aequidens coeruleopunctatus

Aequidens tetramerus

Aequidens "Gold Saum"

Aequidens pulcher

Plate #227C

Aequidens dorsigerus

Aequidens dorsigerus

Aequidens aff. dorsigerus

Aequidens cf. tetramerus

Aequidens itanyi

Aequidens aff. dorsigerus

Aequidens aff. metae

Aequidens paraguayensis

Plate #227D

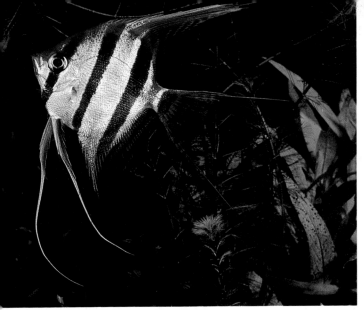

Wild *Pterophyllum scalare altum.*

*P. scalare altum*, showing long dorsal and anal fins.

The long-nosed angelfish, *P. dumerili.*

*P. dumerili*

The angelfish, *P. scalare scalare.*

*P. s. scalare*

*Plate #228*

363

Silver veiltail angelfish.

Silver veiltail angelfish.

Black veiltail angelfish.

Black angelfish.

Silver angelfish.

Blushing, or gray angelfish.

Zebra angelfish

Zebra lace angelfish

*Plate #229*

Marble angelfish.

Half-black angel var.

Marble veiltail angelfish.

Half-black angel veiltail var.

*Plate #230*

365

Juvenile gold angelfish

Juvenile gold angelfish

White or "ghost" angelfish.

Gold or Lutino angelfish.

Blushing or gray veiltail angelfish.

Blushing angelfish

White or ghost-type angelfish.

Half-black angelfish.

Variety of the spotted angelfish.

Half-striped angelfish

Partial half-black veiltail angelfish.

Blushing or gray angelfish.

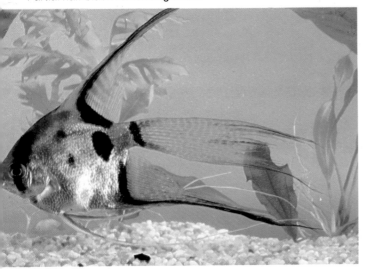

*Plate #232*

367

## DISCUS: KING OF THE AQUARIUM FISHES

Although the cichlids may comprise a thousand or more species, there is no doubt that one cichlid—and one cichlid only—is *the* most respected and desirable of all the aquarium fishes. The discus (actually two species), *Symphysodon*, has been treated with near reverence since it was first brought to the attention of aquarists in the early 1930's. Even after over 50 years in the hobby, the discus is still an expensive fish, and breeding it is considered to be the acme of successful aquarium keeping.

Both species of discus (the Common discus is *Symphysodon aequifasciata,* and the Heckel or Red discus is *Symphysodon discus)* are virtually restricted to the Amazon River and its primary tributaries. Discus can be found in all types of waters from the very acid black waters of the Rio Negro to the silty whitish waters of some of the major tributaries and from streams to lakes; few discus are taken from the Amazon itself except perhaps in the far upstream areas. The round bodies of discus are associated with their habit of staying mostly in protected areas that are heavily vegetated or have an abundance of exposed tree roots, the round bodies allowing them to slip between the plants with ease. They are also very shy and are active mainly at night, facts that do not make their collection any easier.

The two species of discus are divided into a total of five subspecies that are useful at least in a general way when discussing variation within the species. Thus *S. aequifasciata* (distinguished by having 9 equally dark bands on the body) has three recognized subspecies: *S. aequifasciata aequifasciata* Pellegrin—the Green discus from the central Amazon; *S. a. axelrodi* Schultz—the Brown discus from the lower Amazon; and *S. a. haraldi* Schultz—the Blue discus from the upper Amazon. *S. discus* (which has only 3 distinct dark bands on the body) has two recognized subspecies: *S. discus discus* (Heckel)—the Heckel or Red discus, known in modern times only from the Rio Negro and Rio Trombetas, north of the Amazon; and *S. discus willischwartzi* Burgess—the Pineapple discus, known so far only from the Rio Abacaxis (Portuguese for pineapple) south of the Amazon. There are numerous local color varieties and sports, plus a multitude of aquarium-produced stable color varieties, some of which probably originated by hybridizing the natural subspecies and species. It is virtually impossible to put a meaningful scientific name on aquarium specimens of discus, so it is perhaps most accurate to call them all just discus, *Symphysodon.*

Discussions about keeping and spawning discus usually result in heated arguments, as there are probably as many different methods to successfully keep and breed discus as there are successful discus keepers and breeders. There are many articles and books on discus, many controversial, but the subject is covered very well in two books from T.F.H.: *All About Discus,* by Dr. Herbert R. Axelrod, and Jack Wattley's *Handbook of Discus.* Both are required reading for anyone even contemplating purchasing a discus.

Color varieties of discus being bred now have little resemblance to the wild fishes found in South America. The Turquoise discus shown above also features a very high body while the Turquoise discus shown below shows a moderately high body with a deeper green. Photos by Mitsuyoshi Tatematsu courtesy of Midori Shobo Magazine.

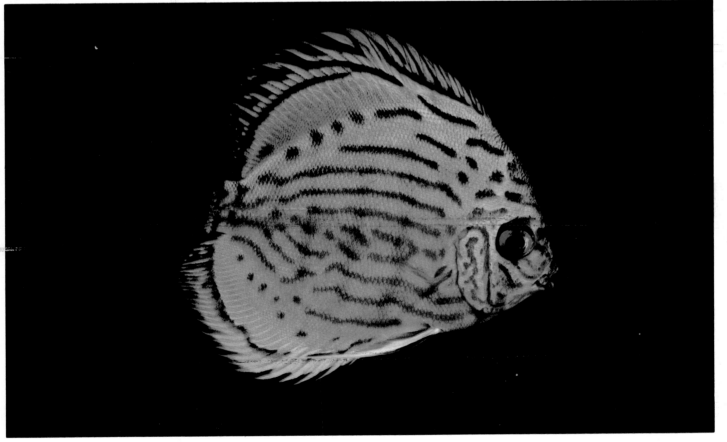

*Plate #233*

369

1

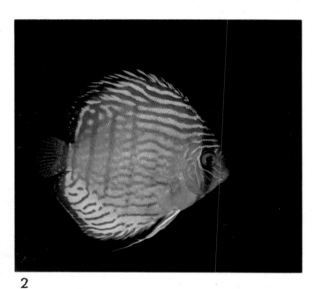

4

The Japanese people are very fond of discus. They started with *Symphysodon aequifasciata haraldi* (1) which they crossed with the Tefe discus, *Symphysodon aequifasciata aequifasciata* (2). This cross resulted in a highly colorful "Royal Blue" strain (3). "Royal Blue" has been a term applied to many strains. Then inbreeding of the *Symphysodon discus discus* resulted in this pale discus (4). The ultimate discus is the Turquoise fish shown below (5) which is being worked to produce a fish of solid turquoise, without body markings. Photos courtesy of Midori Shobo, Tokyo, Japan.

2

3

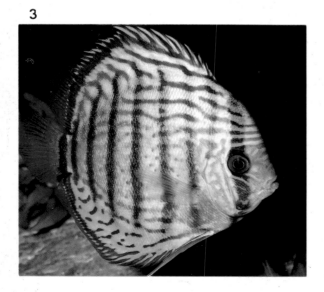

5

This is a new Japanese strain of Electric Blue discus which was derived from fishes found in the western extremes of the discus range.

The common Brown discus, *Symphysodon aequifasciata axelrodi* is being enhanced colorwise with brighter reds, yellows and greens. Photo courtesy of Midori Shobo.

The Lutino discus derived from *Symphysodon discus discus.* It is not a popular strain but is being used for the basis of many breeding experiments. Photo courtesy of Midori Shobo.

Dr. Eduard Schmidt-Focke produced this strain of almost perfect "Tomato-red-eyed Turquoise" with just a few light body markings. Photo by Heiko Bleher.

*Plate #235*

The original Green discus collected by the author in Lago Jurity.

*Symphysodon d. discus* found in Trombetas by the author (HRA).

*Symphysodon d. discus* collected by the author (HRA) in the Rio Trombetas.

*Symphysodon a. haraldi* collected by the author (HRA) in the Rio Ipixuna (near Humaita).

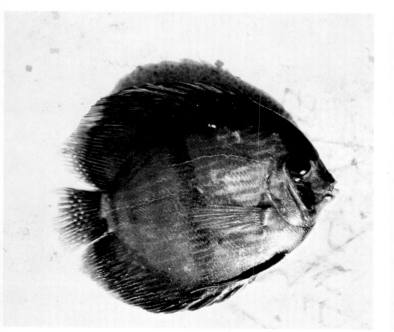

Plate #236

1

2

3

(1) A new discus color variety of *S. a. aequifasciata* discovered by HRA at Tefe. (2) A Pineapple discus, *S. d. willischwartzi* discovered by the author (HRA) at Rio Abacaxis. This is the holotype. (3) Another new color variety discovered by the author (HRA) in Tefe. (4) A typical Tefe Blue discus, *S. a. aequifasciata* (5) Another Tefe discus found by the author (HRA).

5

4

*Plate #237*

*S. a. haraldi* discovered by the author (HRA) in Rio Purus.

*S. a. aequifasciata* collected by the author in Tefe.

Constant inbreeding selectively of the *S. a. aequifasciata* from Tefe resulted in this magnificent fish. Photo courtesy of Midori Shobo.

Young Turquoise discus.
Brown discus, *S. a. axelrodi.*

*S. a. haraldi,* the Blue discus.
Hybrid Red discus derived from Tefe discus.

*Plate #239*

375

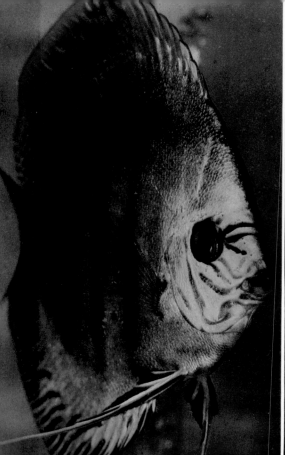

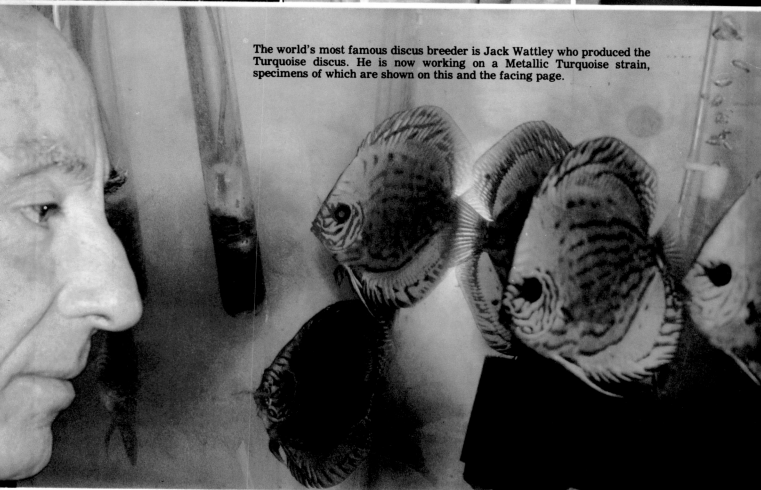

The world's most famous discus breeder is Jack Wattley who produced the Turquoise discus. He is now working on a Metallic Turquoise strain, specimens of which are shown on this and the facing page.

*Plate #240*

Plate #241

377

In this sequence of photographs, the spawning pair can be seen approaching the spawning surface; the female is above. In the top left photo, the eggs are clearly visible as the attending male completes fertilization.

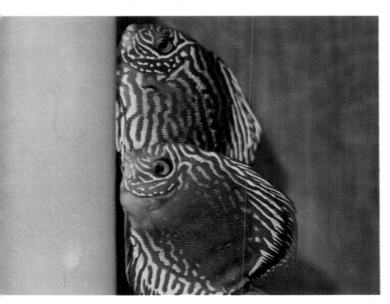

*Plate #242*

**Top, left and right:** In the two upper photos, the spawning pair approaches the spawning surface. Discus are shy and sensitive fishes at all times and especially so during spawning. Breeders should be given as much privacy as possible.
**Lower four photos:** A pair of royal blue discus depositing and fertilizing their eggs. In the bottom right photo, one of the parent fish can be seen carefully removing the whitish, fungused eggs from the spawning site.

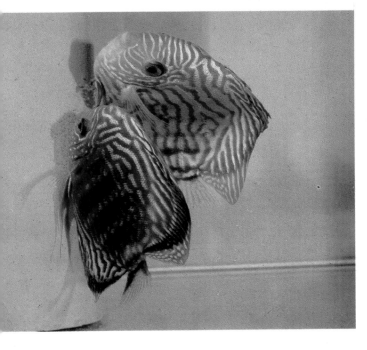

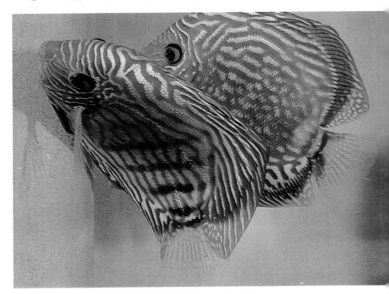

*Plate #243*

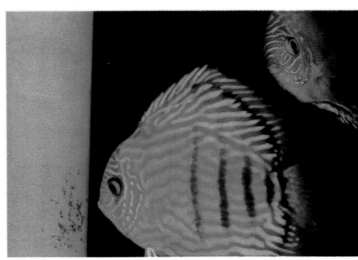

**Top, left and right:** As hatching nears, both parents hover in close attendance of the eggs. **Center, left and right:** The newly-hatched fry appear as minute specks on the PVC pipe. The adults are especially sensitive to disturbance at this point and may eat their fry if distracted. **Bottom, left and right:** The growing fry have left the hatching site and taken up positions on the parents' bodies. Here they receive both protection and nourishment, feeding on the mucus secreted by the adult fish.

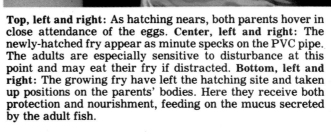

**Top, left and right:** The discus method of child-rearing is surely one of the more unique in the animal kingdom. Here the still-small young cling closely to the parent fish. **Center, left and right:** As the fry grow progressively larger, the parents alternate babysitting duties with greater frequency. In the photo to the right, the parents can be seen literally shifting responsibility from one to the other. **Bottom, left:** The same pair during the course of the exchange of the fry. **Bottom, right:** The fry cling so closely to the parent as to virtually disappear from sight.

*Plate #245*

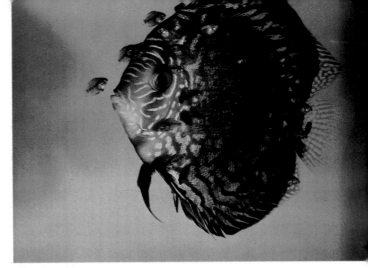

Top, left: This patient discus parent, almost hidden from view by a swarm of oversized youngsters, appears to show definite signs of tiring of its parenting duties. Top, right: This fish is shepherding a relatively small brood; discus may produce as many as 300 fry in a single spawn, but the average is between 100 and 150. Lower three photos: Although discus fry feed off the mucus secretions of the adults for only a week or ten days, growth is extremely rapid. In the photo to the extreme lower right, the fry are now on their own and measure about half an inch in length.

Plate #246

Europe's most famous discus breeder is Dr. Eduard Schmidt-Focke shown above. The fishes shown on this page are some of his many discus varieties.

*Plate #247*

## *Colomesus asellus* (Mueller & Troschel) • Brazilian Freshwater Puffer

RANGE: Throughout tropical South America, mainly in fresh water but occasionally in brackish waters.

HABITS: This is a river fish that is sometimes found in creeks or streams but always found when seining directly in the Amazon River itself. Young fish are golden when taken in the muddy waters of the Amazon. The older fish are camouflaged for life in streams. The familiar name *C. psittacus* is now applied to a much larger species found in marine to brackish waters.

WATER CONDITIONS: They thrive in most neutral to slightly alkaline waters with a pH of 6.9-7.9 at 20-30°C.

SIZE: Reaches a maximum length of 150 mm; usually smaller.

FOOD REQUIREMENTS: They eat everything but prefer live snails and small fishes.

## *Potamorrhaphis guianensis* (Schomburgk) • Freshwater Needlefish

RANGE: Guianas to Paraguay.

HABITS: Must be kept away from other fishes; likely to become very nasty.

WATER CONDITIONS: Soft, slightly alkaline water. Temperature 23 to 26°C.

SIZE: Said to attain a length of 80 cm in native waters.

FOOD REQUIREMENTS: Must be fed small living fishes.

## *Achirus lineatus* (Linnaeus) • Freshwater Flounder, Lined Sole

RANGE: Throughout much of Brazil and northern South America, with the same or a very similar species north to the eastern United States.

HABITS: These little flounders stay in fresh water and most do not migrate to the sea. Flounders all over the Americas are normally freshwater to brackish water to sea water depending upon their growth. These small flounders, being found thousands of miles from the sea, probably don't migrate.

WATER CONDITIONS: They survive in any aquarium conditions, but they thrive in brackish water. Their pH range is 6.8-7.8; temperature 23-28°C.

SIZE: They hardly reach 125 mm; mostly smaller.

FOOD REQUIREMENTS: They are bottom feeders but they lunge at small fishes that pass by them as they lie on the bottom; they learn to eat small chunks of food that fall to the bottom, but most of them starve to death in the hands of inexperienced aquarists. They are not recommended for most aquarium situations.

## *Pristigaster cayana* Cuvier • Amazonian Hatchet Herring

RANGE: Throughout the coasts of northern South America, including Brazil. Very common in the Amazon River itself.

HABITS: A freshwater herring that cannot live in captivity.

WATER CONDITIONS: Large open waters where it can feed upon plankton. Survives under brackish to freshwater conditions. In the Amazon the waters in which it was found by the author (HRA) were pH 6.5 at 25°C.

SIZE: Reaches over 140 mm.

FOOD REQUIREMENTS: Plankton.

## *Arius jordani* (Eigenmann & Eigenmann) • Jordan's Catfish

RANGE: Panama Bay to Peru, eastern Pacific Ocean.

HABITS: A peaceful bottom-feeder that normally will not bother other fishes.

WATER CONDITIONS: Not critical. Can be kept in both fresh or salt water. The temperature range should be 20 to 25°C.

SIZE: Attains a length of at least 33 cm.

FOOD REQUIREMENTS: Eats a wide variety of foods.

## *Synbranchus marmoratus* Bloch • Marbled Eel

RANGE: From Mexico to Brazil.

HABITS: This is a nasty fish that will eat anything small enough to ingest. They are also very hardy. There is a story going around that some climbed out of a holding tank at Willi Schwartz' holding facility in Brazil, snaked their way across 300 m of lawn and ended up in the swimming pool, scaring everyone because they look like snakes.

WATER CONDITIONS: These eels thrive under most aquarium conditions at temperatures of from 23-30°C with a pH of 6.0-7.6.

SIZE: They grow large, easily reaching 1500 mm (1½ m). Only the large ones are nicely mottled; small ones are uncolored.

FOOD REQUIREMENTS: They like live worms and small fishes. Sometimes they can be acclimated to chunks of fish or meat.

## *Pellona castelneana* Cuvier & Valenciennes • Golden Herring

RANGE: Probably throughout South American rivers and the coast. This specimen was collected by the author (HRA) in the Amazon.

HABITS: A typical herring. Not really suitable for the home aquarium. Lives a very short time (only minutes) when captured.

WATER CONDITIONS: This specimen was collected by the author in the Amazon River where the water had a pH of 6.5 at 25°C.

SIZE: The typical size is 29 cm, but it does grow larger.

FOOD REQUIREMENTS: A plankton-feeder that cannot be properly maintained in a home aquarium.

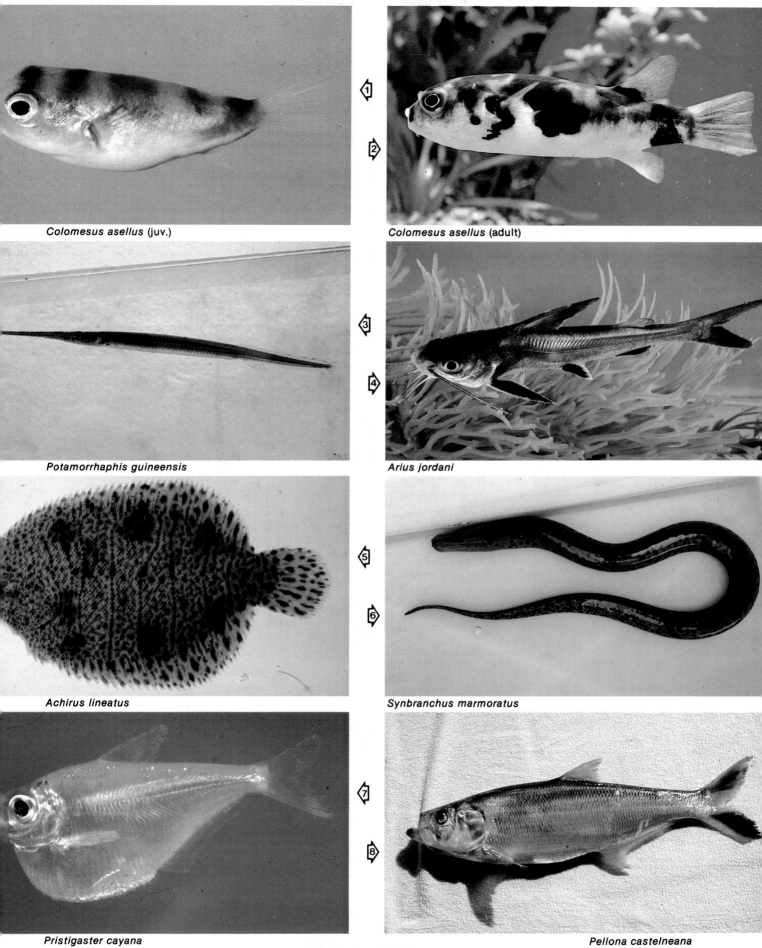

Colomesus asellus (juv.)

Colomesus asellus (adult)

Potamorrhaphis guineensis

Arius jordani

Achirus lineatus

Synbranchus marmoratus

Pristigaster cayana

Pellona castelneana

*Plate #248*

385

# African Region

## *Protopterus dolloi* Boulenger • Spotted African Lungfish

RANGE: Congo and Gabon.
HABITS: A large swamp fish that is sold in its cocoon in native fish markets and is considered a delicacy. Dangerous with small fishes.
WATER CONDITIONS: Thrives under most aquarium conditions but prefers soft water with a neutral to alkaline pH between 6.8-8.8 at warm temperatures between 26-30°C.
SIZE: A large aquarium fish reaching 830 mm.
FOOD REQUIREMENTS: Prefers live fishes but soon takes chunks of meat and fish.

## *Protopterus aethiopicus* Heckel • Speckle-bellied Lungfish

RANGE: Eastern Sudan to the borders of Lake Tanganyika.
HABITS: A very ancient fish, one of Africa's oldest forms. Small specimens are interesting when kept alone in a large aquarium. Not very mobile.
WATER CONDITIONS: Does well under most aquarium conditions.
SIZE: Reaches a size of over 1400 mm.
FOOD REQUIREMENTS: Does not eat much for its size since it moves so rarely, but it takes live fishes that swim by. Can be trained to take chunks of meat and fish. A favorite public aquarium fish.

## *Erpetoichthys calabricus*     Smith • Rope Fish

RANGE: Niger Delta, Cameroon.
HABITS: Largely nocturnal; spends most of its time on the bottom. Best kept only with its own kind.
WATER CONDITIONS: Not critical; is not dependent upon the oxygen content of the water for breathing.
SIZE: Up to 40 cm; tank-raised specimens do not attain this size.
FOOD REQUIREMENTS: All living foods which are not too large to be swallowed are accepted; also strips of lean beef, beef heart or earthworms.

## *Polypterus congicus* Poll • Tanganyikan Fossilfish

RANGE: Congo and Lake Tanganyika.
HABITS: This specimen was collected by the author (HRA) in Lake Tanganyika near Burundi. It was brought back alive under the worst of conditions but lived even after the plastic bag in which it was transported leaked almost all of the water. The fish lived for two days by only being kept damp.
WATER CONDITIONS: pH 9.0 at 25°C.
SIZE: Over 700 mm.
FOOD REQUIREMENTS: Eats smaller fishes but can be trained to take chunks of fish and meat.

## *Protopterus annectens* Owen • African Lungfish

RANGE: Widespread from central to southeastern Africa, mostly in low-lying swampy areas.
HABITS: Strictly a predator; will ignore small fast-moving fishes but will eat anything slow enough to be caught.
WATER CONDITIONS: Not critical.
SIZE: To well over 60 cm.
FOOD REQUIREMENTS: Younger specimens will accept most standard aquarium foods.

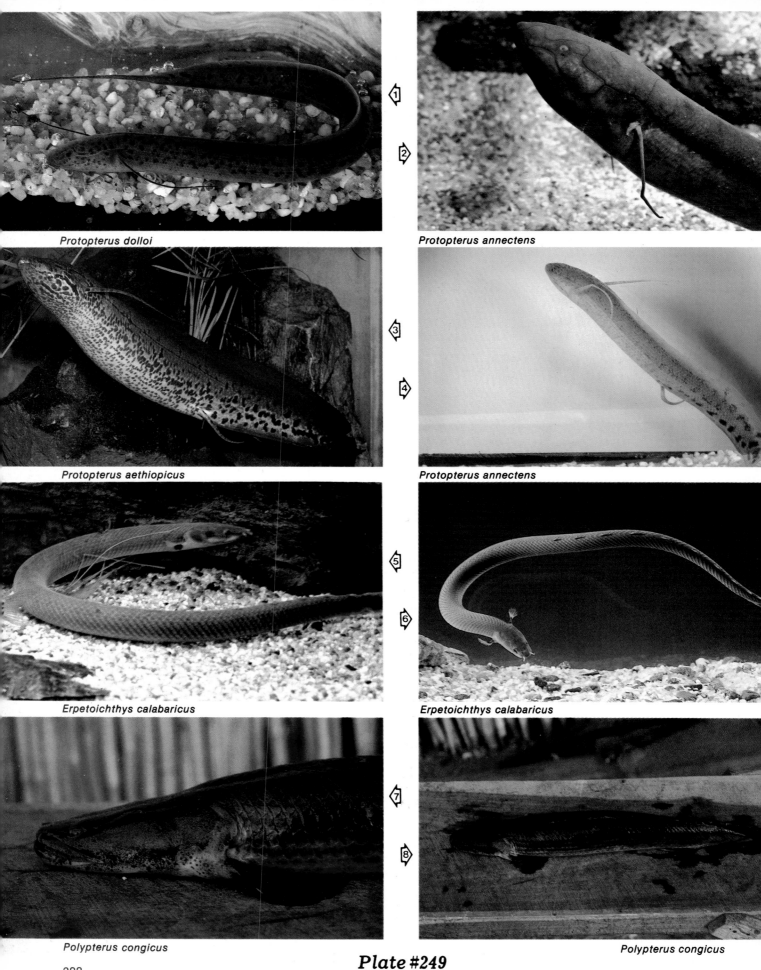

Protopterus dolloi

Protopterus annectens

Protopterus aethiopicus

Protopterus annectens

Erpetoichthys calabaricus

Erpetoichthys calabaricus

Polypterus congicus

Polypterus congicus

**Plate #249**

388

*Polypterus ornatipinnis*

*Polypterus senegalus*

*Polypterus palmas*

*Polypterus palmas*

*Polypterus congicus*

*Polypterus congicus*

*Polypterus palmas*

*Polypterus delhezi*

**Plate #250**

## THE GENUS *POLYPTERUS*

The fishes of the genera *Polypterus* and *Erpetoichthys* have been around for a very long time. Their ancestry has been traced back almost 200 million years based upon a scale found in Egypt, and skeletal fossils are known since the Triassic period.

The scales of these fishes are rather unique. They are diamond-shaped and protected with a glazed coating. They also have very fine tooth-like projections. The fishes of the genus *Polypterus* have ventral fins, while the single species of *Erpetoichthys* has none.

Polypterids are superficially similar, though probably not closely related, to the lungfishes of the genus *Protopterus* and are able to take air into their swim bladders and use it for breathing. They can remain alive for days out of water since their scales are not porous. They also have a very characteristic spiral end to their intestine that is not exhibited by other modern fishes.

There have been several reports of preserved fishes having contained developing eggs, which would indicate that internal fertilization takes place. This type of reproduction is not unknown among similarly primitive fishes, so it might not be long before a "spawning" of one of these fishes takes place since more and more polypterids are being imported. Unfortunately for aquarists, most of these polypterids grow rather large. The best known species are:

*P. bichir* Geoffrey, which is found in the Nile, Lake Rudolf and the Chad basin. It grows to 720 mm;

*P. lapradii* Steindachner, which ranges in Senegal, Gambia and Niger waters and reaches 740 mm in length;

*P. congicus* Boulenger, from the Congo and Lake Tanganyika. This fish reaches a total length of over 700 mm;

*P. endlicheri* Heckel, which is found in the White Nile, Bahr-el-Gebel, Lake Chad and the Niger River. It reaches 630 mm;

*P. weeksii* Boulenger is found in the upper Congo and Katanga. It is one of the smaller species, growing to 380 mm;

*P. ornatipinnis* Boulenger, from the Monsembe and Kassai Rivers in the upper Congo, reaches 370 mm in length;

*P. delhezi* Boulenger, from the upper Congo, reaches 340 mm;

*P. senegalus* Cuvier is a very widespread species found in Lakes Albert, Chad, and Rudolf as well as in Senegal, Gambia and Niger. It reaches 420 mm in length;

*P. palmas* Ayres is found in Sierra Leone, Liberia and the Congo and reaches 320 mm in length;

*P. retropinnis* Vaillant may very well be the smallest species, reaching only 230 mm. It has a restricted range in the Alima River, upper Congo.

All species are very hardy and thrive under most aquarium conditions. They prefer small fishes as their diet, but they learn to take chunks of fish and meat. Because of their ability to live under abnormally poor aquarium conditions, aquarists rarely see them in full color.

*Xenomystus nigri* Guenther • African Knife Fish

RANGE: Broad east-to-west range in tropical Africa.
WATER CONDITIONS: Soft, acid water is best. Temperature
    range 24 to 28°C.
HABITS: A nocturnal prowler; should be provided with good
    cover within the tank. Young, small fish are peaceful, but
    older fish are quarrelsome among themselves and
    definitely predatory upon small tankmates.
SIZE: Up to 20 cm; usually seen much smaller.
FOOD REQUIREMENTS: Accepts all standard aquarium
    foods, but especially prefers live foods and frozen foods;
    floating dry foods are usually not accepted.

*Papyrocranus afer* Guenther • African Featherfin

RANGE: Widely distributed from Gambia to the Congos.
HABITS: Swims with a wave-like movement that enables it to
    move forward and backward. The anal fin joins the
    caudal fin and the dorsal fin is rather small. Sometimes
    called the "African knifefish."
WATER CONDITIONS: Found in stagnant, heavily vegetated
    waters. Prefers warmth from 25-30°C with a pH from
    4.8-7.8.
SIZE: May reach 600 mm, but only small specimens are
    imported.
FOOD REQUIREMENTS: Usually only takes live foods such as
    small fishes, worms, daphnia, brine shrimp and the like.
    Eats mostly under very subdued light.

*Phractolaemus ansorgei* Boulenger • African Mudfish

RANGE: Mouth of the Ethiope river, Niger Delta and the
    Upper Congo.
HABITS: Apparently not very aggressive. Can be kept with
    smaller fishes.
WATER CONDITIONS: Soft, slightly acid water best, with a
    temperature about 24 to 26°C.
SIZE: Attains a length of about 16 cm.
FOOD REQUIREMENTS: Bottom-feeder with a preference for
    worms.

*Pantodon buchholzi* Peters • Butterfly Fish

RANGE: Tropical West Africa.
HABITS: Harmless to other fishes, but better kept by them-
    selves to prevent damage to their filamentous ventral fin
    extensions.
WATER CONDITIONS: Soft, slightly acid water is preferable.
    The tank should not be too heavily planted; it must have
    a large surface and be covered. Temperature 23 to 27°C.
SIZE: To 10 cm.
FOOD REQUIREMENTS: Prefers live insects but it can be
    trained to take bits of shrimp.

*Petrocephalus catostoma* Guenther • African Whale

RANGE: Rovuma River and Lake Malawi.
HABITS: Prefers dimly lit aquarium conditions where it can
    hide. This small fish is an aquarium favorite, but it
    doesn't live very long in captivity. Nothing is known
    about its spawning habits.
WATER CONDITIONS: Warm waters with high alkalinity,
    about pH 8.8 at 28-30°C.
 SIZE: Barely reaches 60 mm; usually imported at about
    45 mm.
FOOD REQUIREMENTS: Small worms and live daphnia and
    brine shrimp.

Xenomystus nigri

Xenomystus nigri

Papyrocranus afer

Phractolaemus ansorgii

Pantodon buchholzi

Pantodon buchholzi

Pantodon buchholzi

Petrocephalus catostoma

*Plate #251*

Petrocephalus simus

Petrocephalus simus

Pollimyrus nigripinnis

Pollimyrus castelnaui

Marcusenius angolensis

Campylomormyrus cassaicus

Gnathonemus elephas

Gnathonemus petersii

Plate #252

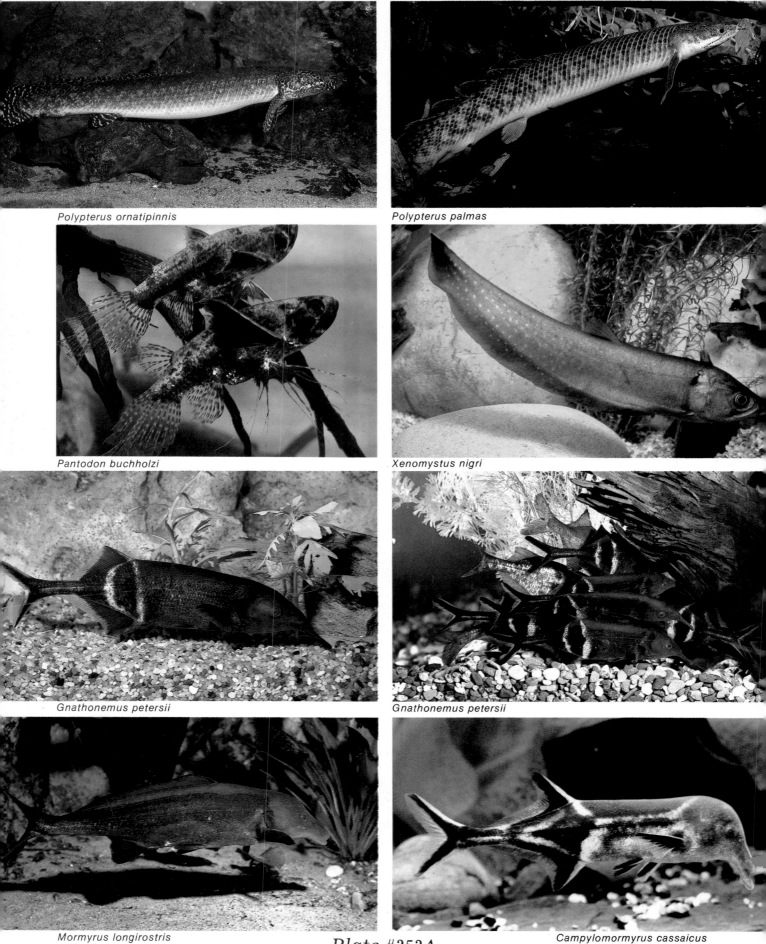

*Polypterus ornatipinnis*

*Polypterus palmas*

*Pantodon buchholzi*

*Xenomystus nigri*

*Gnathonemus petersii*

*Gnathonemus petersii*

*Mormyrus longirostris*

Plate #252A

*Campylomormyrus cassaicus*

*Distichodus affinis*

*Distichodus affinis*

*Distichodus noboli*

*Distichodus lusosso*

*Distichodus sexfasciatus*

*Distichodus decemmaculatus*

Neolebias ansorgei

Phago cf. boulengeri

Plate #252B

*Campylomormyrus rhynchophorus*

*Mormyrus longirostris*

*Mormyrops engystoma*

*Brienomyrus brachistius*

*Mormyrops boulengeri*

*Gymnarchus niloticus*

*Gymnarchus niloticus*

*Gymnarchus niloticus* (albino)

**Plate #253**

396

*Hepsetus odoe*

*Bryconaethiops microstoma*

*Bryconaethiops boulengeri*

*Brycinus macrolepidotus*

*Brycinus taeniurus*

*Brycinus lateralis*

*Brycinus nurse*

*Brycinus brevis*

**Plate #254**

397

Phenacogrammus interruptus

Hemigrammopetersius caudalis

Arnoldichthys spilopterus

Arnoldichthys spilopterus

Nannocharax "Narrow Band"

Nannocharax "Broad Band"

Hemigrammopetersius intermedius

Ladigesia roloffi

Plate #254A

Hepsetus odoe

Hepsetus odoe

Brycinus aff. imberi

Brycinus longipinnis

Brycinus longipinnis

Micralestes stormsi

Phenacogrammus "Diamond"

Phenacogrammus "Diamond"

Plate #254B

*Brycinus longipinnis*

*Brycinus chaperi*

*Micralestes acutidens*

*Micralestes stormsi (female)*

*Micralestes stormsi (male)*

*Phenacogrammus interruptus*

*Phenacogrammus huloti*

*Phenacogrammus urotaenia*

**Plate #255**

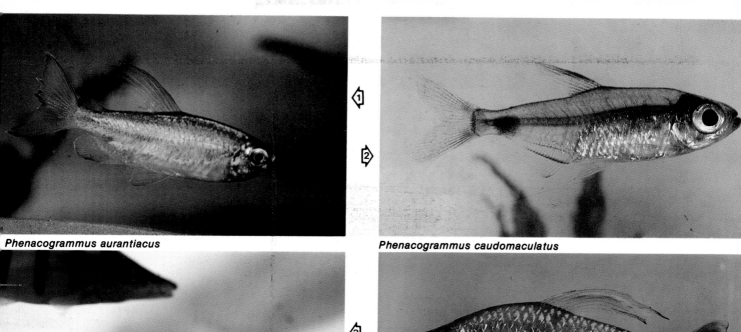

*Phenacogrammus aurantiacus*

*Phenacogrammus caudomaculatus*

*Phenacogrammus deheyni*

*Hemigrammopetersius caudalis*

*Hemigrammopetersius intermedius*

*Hemigrammopetersius rhodesiensis*

*Arnoldichthys spilopterus*

*Ladigesia roloffi*

**Plate #256**

*Phenacogrammus aurantiacus* (Pellegrin) •
Gold Congo Tetra

RANGE: Congo Basin.
HABITS: A wonderful aquarium fish that has many of the
  characteristics associated with Congo tetras, namely
  sexual dimorphism in which the male has longer fins
  with extended dorsal and caudal filaments, very shiny
  scales, and a peaceful aquarium disposition.
WATER CONDITIONS: pH 6.2-6.8 at a temperature of 25-30°C.
SIZE: Up to 100 mm.
FOOD REQUIREMENTS: Prefers live, swimming foods but
  adapts to flake foods and freeze-dried foods.

*Phenacogrammus caudomaculatus* (Pellegrin) • African
Moon Tetra

RANGE: Congo River region.
HABITS: A shoaling fish which is happiest among its own
  kind; generally peaceful toward fishes of a comparable
  size.
WATER CONDITIONS: Soft, slightly acid water. Temperature 22 to 25°C.
SIZE: Males to 8 cm; females to 6 cm.
FOOD REQUIREMENTS: Its diet should consist primarily of
  live or frozen foods, but can be supplemented with flake
  foods.

*Phenacogrammus deheyni* Poll • Deheyni's Congo Tetra

RANGE: Congo Basin.
HABITS: The dark band along the lateral line, which is only
  hinted at in the accompanying photo, is stark in many
  cases (especially when the fish is preserved). This is a
  typical Congo tetra with large shining scales and good
  aquarium deportment.
WATER CONDITIONS: pH 6.2-6.8 at a temperature of 25-30°C.
SIZE: About 100 mm.
FOOD REQUIREMENTS: Prefers live foods but takes a normal
  aquarium diet.

*Hemigrammopetersius caudalis* (Boulenger) • Yellow-
tailed Congo Tetra

RANGE: Congo Basin.
HABITS: One of the "super" Congo tetras with very shining,
  iridescent scales and extremely sexually dimorphic with
  the males sporting extended fins ray elements on almost
  all fins. They are wonderful aquarium inhabitants.
WATER CONDITIONS: pH 6.2-6.8 at a temperature of 25-30°C.
SIZE: Up to 100 mm.
FOOD REQUIREMENTS: Prefers live foods but takes a normal
  aquarium diet.

*Hemigrammopetersius intermedius* (Blache & Miton) •
Short-finned Congo Tetra

RANGE: Amazon Basin.
HABITS: A large-scaled iridescent fish similar in behavior
  and general appearance to most of the other Congo tetras.
  Very similar to *H. barnardi* of East Africa. Males are
  smaller and more colorful than females. The photo shows
  a pair with the female being larger and more rotund.
WATER CONDITIONS: pH 6.2-6.8 at a temperature of 25-30°C.
SIZE: Up to 95 mm.
FOOD REQUIREMENTS: Prefers live foods but takes a normal
  aquarium diet.

*Hemigrammopetersius rhodesiensis* (Ricardo-Bertram)
• Rhodesian Tetra

RANGE: Rhodesia (now called Zimbabwe).
HABITS: A small but typical "Congo" tetra that is very rarely
  imported because Zimbabwe is short on aquarium
  species. These do make nice aquarium fish when kept
  in a school.
WATER CONDITIONS: pH 6.2-6.8 at a temperature of 25-30°C.
SIZE: Up to 60 mm.
FOOD REQUIREMENTS: Prefers live foods but takes a normal
  aquarium diet.

*Arnoldichthys spilopterus* (Boulenger) • Arnold's
Characin, Red-eyed Characin

RANGE: Tropical West Africa, especially the Lagos region
  and the Niger Delta.
HABITS: A peaceful species which is usually out in front.
WATER CONDITIONS: Soft, neutral to slightly acid water.
  Temperature 26 to 28°C.
SIZE: Seldom exceeds 6 cm.
FOOD REQUIREMENTS: Has a good appetite and will eat
  dried food as well as live foods; some live foods should be
  provided, however.

*Ladigesia roloffi* Gery • Jelly Bean Tetra

RANGE: Sierra Leone, West Africa.
HABITS: Initially very shy; it will attempt to jump out of
  tank, so a covered tank is a definite necessity;
  reasonably hardy and peaceful.
WATER CONDITIONS: Temperature should be from 24 to 26°C,
  and the pH should be on the acid side, 6.7.
SIZE: To 4 cm.
FOOD REQUIREMENTS: Will accept dry foods after a certain
  amount of training; freeze-dried foods are accepted will-
  ingly and live foods are never refused.

## *Neolebias ansorgi* Boulenger • Ansorge's Neolebias

RANGE: Cameroon to lower Congo basin.
HABITS: Peaceful and very shy in a community tank; should be kept by themselves.
WATER CONDITIONS: Sensitive to hard, alkaline water; water must be well-aged and should never undergo great changes. Temperature 24 to 28°C.
SIZE: To 4 cm.
FOOD REQUIREMENTS: Small live foods only.

## *Neolebias trewavasae* Poll & Gosse • Trewavas's Neolebias

RANGE: Nile to lower Congo River.
HABITS: Peaceful and very shy in a community tank; should be kept by themselves.
WATER CONDITIONS: Sensitive to hard, alkaline water; water must be well aged and the aquarium should never undergo large percentage water changes. Temperature 22 to 28°C.
SIZE: To 5 cm.
FOOD REQUIREMENTS: Small live foods only, of a size comparable to newly hatched brine shrimp.

## ...*dus affinis* Guenther • Silver Distichodus

...ower Congo region.
...Peaceful; can be trusted with other fishes, but re-quires a large aquarium.
...CONDITIONS: Soft, slightly acid water. Temperature ...27°C.
...o 13 cm.
...REQUIREMENTS: Large amounts of live or frozen ...ods, with an addition of vegetable matter like lettuce or ...pinach leaves.

## *Citharinus citharus* (Geoffroy) • Lined Citharinid

RANGE: Widespread from the Nile to Senegal.
HABITS: Unfortunately the very large body and the disproportionately small head are not clearly visible in this dark photo. The fish is rarely imported because there are very few collectors in its range.
WATER CONDITIONS: Almost neutral water between 6.8-7.2 pH at a temperature of 28-31°C.
SIZE: Probably grows larger than the 72 mm of the specimens with which the author (HRA) has experience.
FOOD REQUIREMENTS: Pokes about in every niche in the aquarium searching for small crustaceans and bits of vegetable matter. An excellent scavenger until it becomes acclimated to normal aquarium fare.

## *Neolebias unifasciatus* Steindachner • One-lined African Tetra

RANGE: From Portuguese Guinea to Gabon.
HABITS: Very common in its range. A wonderful aquarium fish but not very colorful. Has never been bred. Like most African characins, it is difficult or impossible to spawn in the aquarium. Best kept alone in a small tank.
WATER CONDITIONS: Slightly acid warm water with a pH of 6.4-6.8 at 30°C.
SIZE: A midget barely reaching 40 mm.
FOOD REQUIREMENTS: Likes newly hatched brine shrimp but will eat a normal aquarium diet once it becomes acclimated.

## *Neolebias trilineatus* Boulenger • Three-lined Neolebias

RANGE: Congo basin.
HABITS: Peaceful and shy.
WATER CONDITIONS: Not very critical, but the best is slightly acid and soft water. Temperature 23 to 26°C.
SIZE: To 4 cm.
FOOD REQUIREMENTS: Live and frozen foods greatly preferred, but when not available dry foods can be given for a time.
COLOR VARIATIONS: Back brown, sides silvery with three dark horizontal stripes; fins are reddish.

## *Nannaethiops unitaeniatus* Guenther • One-lined African Tetra

RANGE: Equatorial Africa.
HABITS: Peaceful; a good community fish which does not bother plants.
WATER CONDITIONS: Soft and slightly acid. Requires some warmth, about 24 to 26°C.
SIZE: Males 5 to 6 cm; females slightly larger.
FOOD REQUIREMENTS: Live food preferred, but will take dry foods otherwise.

Neolebias ansorgii

Citharinus citharus

Neolebias trewavasae

Neolebias unifasciatus

Nannaethiops unitaeniatus

Neolebias trilineatus

Distichodus affinis

Nannaethiops unitaeniatus

**Plate #257**

Distichodus lusosso

Distichodus sexfasciatus

Distichodus notospilus

Distichodus noboli

Nannocharax fasciatus

Hemistichodus vaillanti

Hemigrammocharax multifasciatus

Phago maculatus

*Plate #258*

405

## *Distichodus lusosso* Schilthuis • Long-nosed Distichodus

RANGE: Upper and middle Congo River including Stanley Pool; Angola.
HABITS: A docile fish, but tends to nibble plants.
WATER CONDITIONS: Neutral to slightly acid water of moderate hardness. Temperature 24 to 26°C.
SIZE: To 40 cm in nature, but smaller in the aquarium.
FOOD REQUIREMENTS: In nature it feeds on worms and other bottom-dwelling invertebrates as well as on soft vegetation. It will adapt to most aquarium fare, but should be given small amounts of soft lettuce or spinach as a dietary supplement.

## *Distichodus notospilus* Guenther • Red-finned Distichodus

RANGE: From the southern Cameroons to Angola.
HABITS: Feeds on small crustaceans and bits of algae and vegetation. In the aquarium it has quite a problem adjusting to the normal fare, and small tubificids and live daphnia must be offered to supplement the diet.
WATER CONDITIONS: Cooler waters from 23-26°C at about a neutral pH from 6.8-7.2. They do best in large, well-planted tanks.
SIZE: They probably get a lot larger than the 100 mm specimens the author (HRA) collected in the Cameroons.

## *Nannocharax fasciatus* Guenther • African Characidium

RANGE: Found widely dispersed across central Africa from east to west. Museums have specimens from Liberia, Guinea, Niger and Gabon.
HABITS: Found in shallow, moving creeks where it scoots about on sandy bottoms, usually those bottoms with small stones, searching for tiny micro-life. In the aquarium it makes a good scavenger. Almost indistinguishable superficially from the South American characins of the genus *Characidium*.
WATER CONDITIONS: They thrive under most aquarium conditions.
SIZE: Reaches about 80 mm.
FOOD REQUIREMENTS: Tiny live foods such as brine shrimp nauplii and daphnia suit them well, but they take dried foods, too.

## *Hemigrammocharax multifasciatus* (Fowler) • Checkerboard African Darter Tetra

RANGE: Zambezi River.
HABITS: A bottom-dwelling fish that darts about in short hops searching for food on the interspaces between rocks. Requires an open bottom with sandy patches.
WATER CONDITIONS: pH 6.2-7.2, temperature between 25-30°C. Very well adapted to a scavenger's life in the aquarium and very well camouflaged against sandy bottoms.
SIZE: Reaches about 110 mm.
FOOD REQUIREMENTS: Eats just about everything small enough to ingest, but it does appreciate some live foods from time to time.

## *Distichodus sexfasciatus* Boulenger • Six-barred Distichodus

RANGE: Lower Congo region.
HABITS: Peaceful toward other fishes, but will nibble plants.
WATER CONDITIONS: Neutral to slightly acid. Temperature 24 to 27°C.
SIZE: To 25 cm.
FOOD REQUIREMENTS: Large amounts of live or frozen foods, supplemented with green foods like lettuce or spinach leaves.
COLOR VARIATIONS: Body pinkish to white with six dark bands. Fins are brilliant deep red.

## *Distichodus noboli* Boulenger • Nobol Distichodus

RANGE: Lower Congo River System.
HABITS: Peaceful; a good community tank fish, but requires a large aquarium. Nibbles plants.
WATER CONDITIONS: Soft, slightly acid water. Temperature 24 to 26°C.
SIZE: To 10 cm.
FOOD REQUIREMENTS: Large amounts of live or frozen foods, with an addition of vegetable matter like lettuce or spinach leaves. Will occasionally accept flake food.

## *Hemistichodus vaillanti* Pellegrin • Black-finned Fin-eater

RANGE: Gabon, but probably more dispersed.
HABITS: This fish has a bad reputation for chewing on the fins of its tankmates. Many of its relatives of the subfamily Ichthyborinae are guilty of this intolerable behavior.
WATER CONDITIONS: They thrive under most aquarium conditions, with a pH of 6.3-7.2 at 25-28°C.
SIZE: They may grow larger than the 100 mm known to the authors.
FOOD REQUIREMENTS: It likes to chew on other fishes' fins, but it quickly adjusts to small live foods and bits of fish and meat. Not a good community fish at all.

## *Phago maculatus* Ahl • African Pike Characin

RANGE: West Africa, in the Niger River.
HABITS: A decidedly nasty fish which will kill for the sheer pleasure of killing.
WATER CONDITIONS: Neutral, medium-soft water best. Temperature 23 to 24°C.
SIZE: Up to 20 cm, but usually seen much smaller.
FOOD REQUIREMENTS: Wants plenty of meaty foods, preferably live fishes, although it will also accept dead ones.

## *Clarias angolensis* Steindachner • Black Walking Catfish, Spotted Walking Catfish

RANGE: Widely dispersed over Nigeria, the Congo, Gabon, the Cameroons and Angola.
HABITS: This species is so widely dispersed and so poorly described that the name has been applied to many species. This group needs much more study. The fish shown here has also been called the normally pigmented *Clarias batrachus*. The pattern of small white spots is characteristic of the species.
WATER CONDITIONS: A wide variety of warm waters house this fish at a pH of 6.4-9.0 and temperatures from 22-30°C.
SIZE: Reaches 350 mm.
FOOD REQUIREMENTS: Prefers small fishes but takes almost anything, especially chunks of fish and meat.

## *Channallabes apus* (Guenther) • Eel Catfish

RANGE: Zaire and Angola regions.
HABITS: Mostly nocturnal. Young specimens will not bother the other fishes, but it is best to keep larger ones by themselves.
WATER CONDITIONS: Not critical. Temperature 21 to 24°C.
SIZE: Up to 30 cm.
FOOD REQUIREMENTS: Greedy eaters which will consume great amounts of tubifex worms. Other foods may be substituted, such as beef heart or pieces of fish.

## *Gymnallabes heterocercalis* Loennberg • Fatheaded Eel Catfish #2

RANGE: Cameroons.
HABITS: This fish is identical to *G. typus* in all respects except for its tail, which is turned up giving it the appearance of being heterocercal. All *Gymnallabes* have no bones on the sides of their heads. The dorsal and anal are united with the caudal fin.
SIZE: Reaches over 400 mm.
FOOD REQUIREMENTS: Prefers small living fishes but learns to take other aquarium diets. Not much is known as only a few specimens were collected and imported by the author (HRA).

## *Gymnallabes typus* Guenther • Fatheaded Eel Catfish

RANGE: Lower Niger and Old Calabar coast area, western Africa.
HABITS: An eel-like fish that stays on the bottom and hides during the day, sometimes even buried in the sand. A very active feeder at night, eating any fish small enough to ingest, but it usually pokes about on the bottom, especially in debris.
WATER CONDITIONS: Typical aquarium conditions suit this hardy fish. It was collected in pH 7.1 at 27°C.
SIZE: Reaches 250 mm.
FOOD REQUIREMENTS: Prefers worms and small bottom-dwelling living things, but gradually takes small bits of meat and fish.

## *Clarias mossambicus* Peters • Tanganyikan Clarias

RANGE: Very widespread from East Africa, Ethiopia and Lakes Victoria and Tanganyika to the Zambesi.
HABITS: This is another walking catfish; it can be more or less recognized by the dark bands on the sides of the head. The specimen shown here was collected by the author (HRA) in Lake Tanganyika near Burundi.
WATER CONDITIONS: pH high, about 9.0 at 25°C.
SIZE: Grows very large, to about 650 mm.
FOOD REQUIREMENTS: Eats everything but prefers small fishes or chunks of fish or meat.

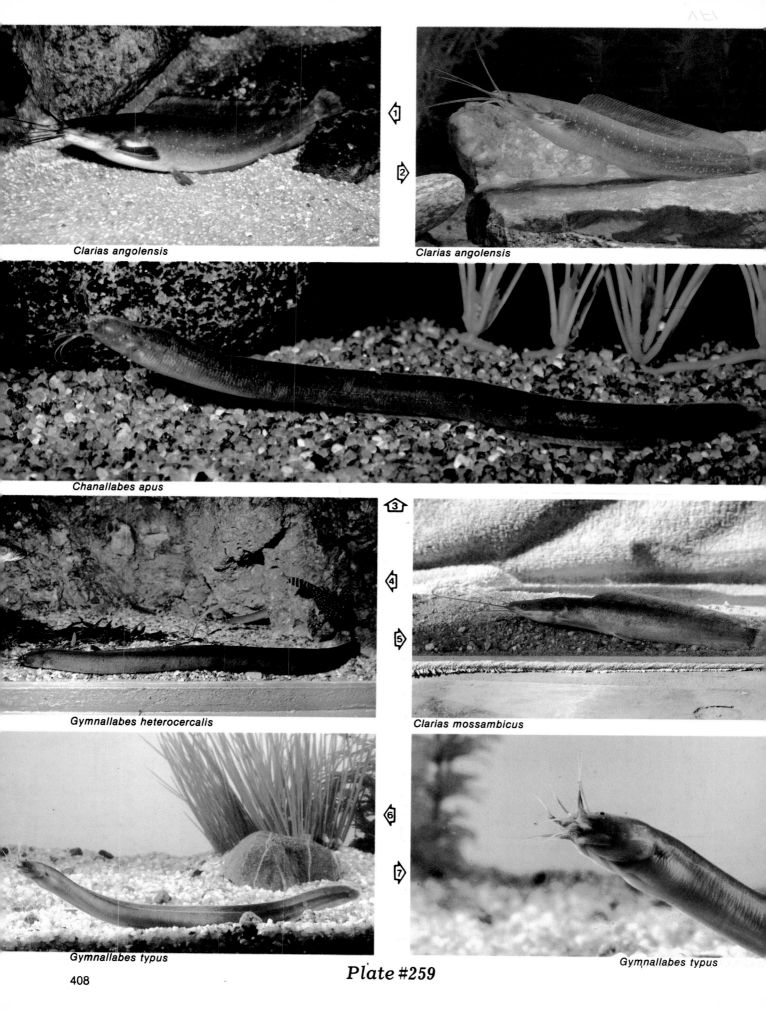

Clarias angolensis

Clarias angolensis

Chanallabes apus

Gymnallabes heterocercalis

Clarias mossambicus

Gymnallabes typus

Gymnallabes typus

408

*Plate #259*

Schilbe marmoratus

Schilbe uranoscopus

Eutropiellus debauwi

Eutropiellus debauwi

Parailia longifilis

Schilbe mystus (juvenile)

Physailia villiersi

Physailia pellucida

*Plate #260*

409

*Schilbe marmoratus* Boulenger • African Shoulder-spot Catfish

RANGE: Congo River and its tributaries.
HABITS: Peaceful; inclined to be shy, so hiding places should be provided.
WATER CONDITIONS: Soft, neutral to slightly acid water. Temperature 24 to 27°C.
SIZE: To 16 cm.
FOOD REQUIREMENTS: Prefers live foods, but may possibly be trained to accept frozen foods.

*Eutropiellus debauwi* (Boulenger) • Three-striped Glass Catfish

RANGE: Stanley Pool region of the Congo River.
HABITS: Very active and peaceful; should be kept in groups rather than singly.
WATER CONDITIONS: Soft, slightly acid water is preferable. Temperature 24 to 26°C.
SIZE: Maximum a little over 7.5 cm.
FOOD REQUIREMENTS: Live foods such as daphnia, tubifex worms and white worms.

*Parailia longifilis* Boulenger • Speckled African Glass Catfish

RANGE: Upper Congo.
HABITS: The very large eye in the very small head is characteristic of this fish. It is not hardy but does well if given its own aquarium without stress from aggressive fishes.
WATER CONDITIONS: pH 6.4-7.4 at 25-28°C.
SIZE: Reaches 100 mm, but smaller specimens are imported.
FOOD REQUIREMENTS: Live brine shrimp and daphnia are preferred by this and most other aquarium fishes, but they soon learn to eat prepared foods.

*Physailia villiersi* Boulenger • Dusky African Glass Catfish

RANGE: Chiloango and Lucola Rivers near Cabinda (northern Angola).
HABITS: Hovers in mid-water, preferably in small schools.
WATER CONDITIONS: Clean, neutral to alkaline water over 24°C.
SIZE: 60-70 mm.
FOOD REQUIREMENTS: Likes small crustaceans that stay suspended in the water; prefers not to feed from the bottom.

*Schilbe uranoscopus* Rueppel • Silver Schilbe Catfish

RANGE: Very widespread from the Lower Nile through East Africa.
HABITS: Never spawned, and nothing is known about their sex differences, if any. They are not nocturnal, as they move about both day and night. Not to be trusted with small fishes.
WATER CONDITIONS: pH 6.0-7.8 at 23-28°C.
SIZE: Reaches 300 mm.
FOOD REQUIREMENTS: Small live foods, especially worms and daphnia. They also take small fishes.

*Schilbe mystus* Linnaeus • Striped Schilbe Catfish

RANGE: Very widespread through every jungle river in Africa plus the Nile.
HABITS: An active catfish that is very hardy. *Schilbe* is very similar to the genus *Eutropius* except for lacking an adipose fin.
WATER CONDITIONS: Very tolerant of aquarium conditions from pH 5.4-9.0 at 22-30°C.
SIZE: Reaches 340 mm.
FOOD REQUIREMENTS: Eats small fishes and tubifex worms, but probably eats almost anything that once was a living aquatic animal.

*Physailia pellucida* Boulenger • African Glass Catfish

RANGE: The upper Nile.
HABITS: Stays motionless in mid-water most of the time, waiting for bits of food to drift or swim by. Never spawned, and nothing is known about sex differences.
WATER CONDITIONS: Prefers clean, clear water that is well aerated, with a pH of 6.2-8.6 at 23-30°C.
SIZE: Reaches at least 93 mm.
FOOD REQUIREMENTS: Prefers daphnia and brine shrimp (living) but quickly learns to accept a normal aquarium diet of dried foods.

*Malapterurus electricus* (Gemlin) • Electric Catfish

RANGE: Tropical Africa, except for some lake and river systems.
HABITS: Decidedly predatory, so not safe with other species.

WATER CONDITIONS: Neutral water in the medium-soft range is best. Temperature 23 to 28°C.
SIZE: Over 60 cm in nature, but rarely seen at this size when offered for sale.

FOOD REQUIREMENTS: Wants small live fishes which are usually swallowed whole; will also eat plants.

*Amphilius platychir* Guenther • African Kuhli

RANGE: Tropical Africa including the Great Lakes Tanganyika and Malawi. One of the few Great Lakes fishes not endemic to these lakes.
HABITS: A typical naked catfish that grubs about mostly on the bottom and almost always at night. Its tiny eyes are barely visible on the fish. It is a good scavenger, but you never see them in the aquarium since they hide most of the time the tank is lighted.

WATER CONDITIONS: Slightly hard, alkaline water, pH 6.8-7.8 at 26°C.
SIZE: To 88 mm.
FOOD REQUIREMENTS: They scavenge what they can from the bottom. They like frozen newly hatched brine shrimp that falls to the bottom, where they actively gorge themselves.

*Amphilius atesuensis* Boulenger • Golden African Kuhli

RANGE: Western tropical Africa, especially Ghana.
HABITS: Spends most of its time hiding from the light. Has never been spawned, and no one seems to know their sexual difference or their reproductive behavior.

WATER CONDITIONS: Water with a pH of 6.8-8.0 at 26°C.
SIZE: To 60 mm.
FOOD REQUIREMENTS: Scrounges small things from the bottom. Seems to enjoy freshly hatched, but frozen, brine shrimp, which it picks off as it falls onto the bottom.

*Phractura ansorgei* Boulenger • African Whiptail Catfish

RANGE: The lower Niger basin; very common.
HABITS: A widely dispersed catfish that has a very small mouth and is often mistaken for a South American loricariid catfish because of its longitudinal imbricate scutes that are expanded vertebral processes. This is an aquarium favorite and has been spawned on occasion.
WATER CONDITIONS: They enjoy normal aquarium conditions with a pH of 6.2-7.4 at 23-28°C.
SIZE: They are very small, barely reaching 50 mm. The one shown in the illustrations was 49 mm long.
FOOD REQUIREMENTS: Picks small animalcules up from wherever it can find them, but probably eats bits of algae, too.

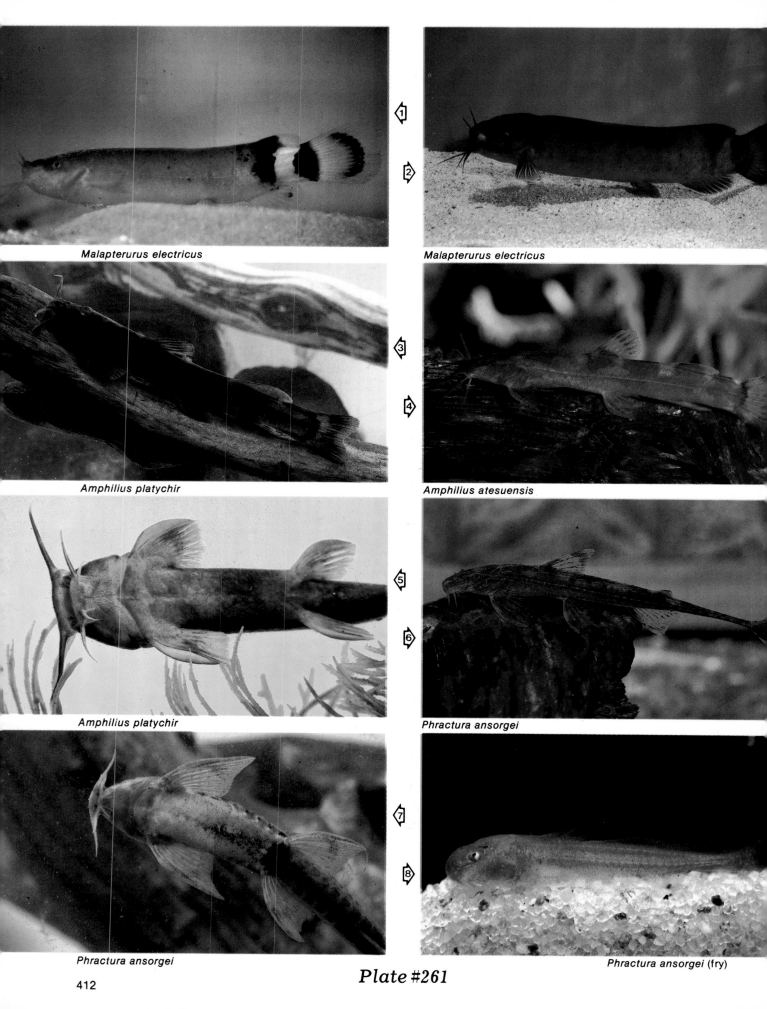

Malapterurus electricus

Malapterurus electricus

Amphilius platychir

Amphilius atesuensis

Amphilius platychir

Phractura ansorgei

Phractura ansorgei

Phractura ansorgei (fry)

*Plate #261*

412

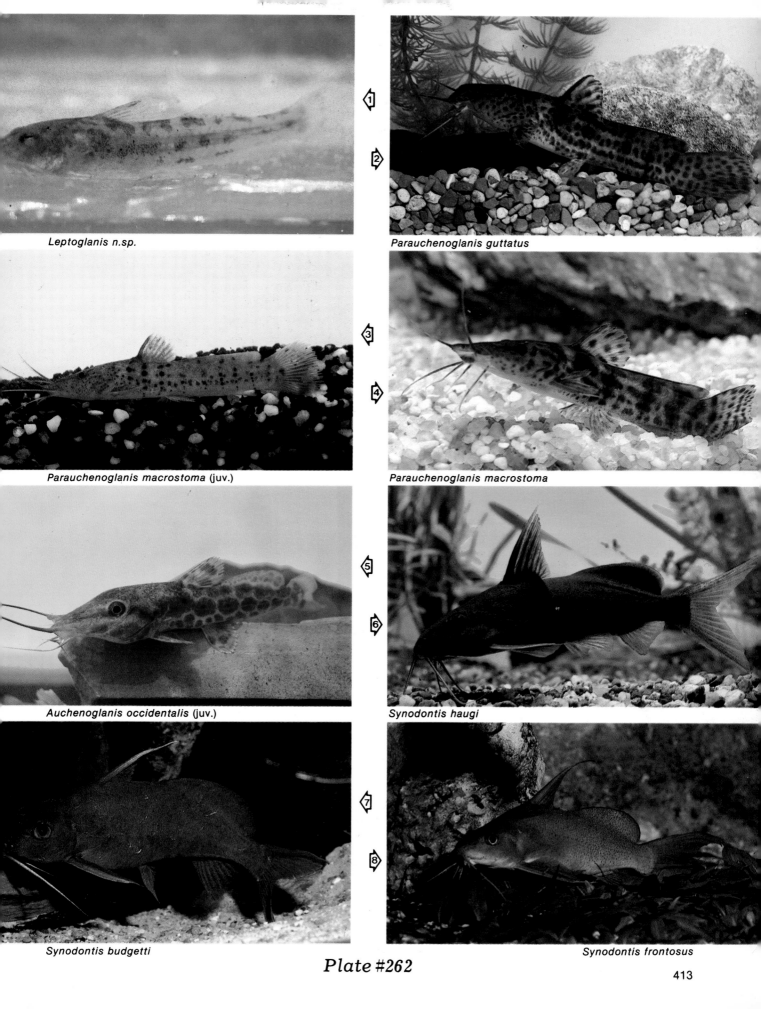

Leptoglanis n.sp.

Parauchenoglanis guttatus

Parauchenoglanis macrostoma (juv.)

Parauchenoglanis macrostoma

Auchenoglanis occidentalis (juv.)

Synodontis haugi

Synodontis budgetti

Synodontis frontosus

*Plate #262*

413

### *Leptoglanis* sp. • Spotted Mountain Catfish

RANGE: Lake Malawi. This species, which is yet to be named, was discovered hiding in an otherwise empty shell by Dr. Warren E. Burgess.

HABITS: Small enough to take refuge in empty shells, hide under stones and in vegetation, this fish is almost never seen in the aquarium because they are so shy. Their eyes seem to look up giving them a celestial appearance.

WATER CONDITIONS: pH 6.4-7.0 at a temperature of 20-26°C.

SIZE: Up to 45 mm.

FOOD REQUIREMENTS: They are bottom, detritus feeders.

### *Parauchenoglanis macrostoma* (Pellegrin) • African Spotted Catfish

RANGE: Tropical West Africa (Gabon).

HABITS: Peaceful; usually remains hidden in daylight and comes out at night.

WATER CONDITIONS: Soft, neutral to slightly acid water. Temperature 24 to 27°C.

SIZE: To 25 cm in natural waters; much smaller in the aquarium.

FOOD REQUIREMENTS: All sorts of live or frozen foods.

### *Auchenoglanis occidentalis* (Cuvier & Valenciennes) • Giraffe-nosed Catfish

RANGE: Widespread throughout the central part of Africa from the Niger River to the Congo River and Blue Nile, as well as Lakes Chad, Bangwelu, Mweru, and Tanganyika.

HABITS: A voracious predator which cannot be kept with smaller fishes.

WATER CONDITIONS: Not critical as long as extremes are avoided. Optimum temperatures are about 24 to 28°C.

SIZE: Attains a length of just over 50 cm.

FOOD REQUIREMENTS: Live foods of all kinds preferred. Voracious feeders, so plenty of food must be available.

### *Parauchenoglanis guttatus* (Loennberg) • African Flathead Catfish

RANGE: Cameroon; Congo basin.

HABITS: Nocturnal, and shy and retiring, so should be provided with rocks, caves, etc; predatory, so do not keep with fishes that might be swallowed.

WATER CONDITIONS: Not critical; tolerates most local water types quite well, but, as with other fishes, extremes of pH or hardness should be avoided. A temperature range of 21 to 27°C.

SIZE: Up to 30 cm.

FOOD REQUIREMENTS: Prefers earthworms and other live foods but also relishes ground beef heart, chopped fish and other meat- or fish-based foods; some individuals will accept cooked oatmeal (rolled oats).

*Synodontis sorex* GUNTHER, 506mm

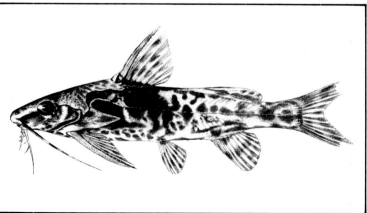

*Synodontis afro-fischeri* HILGENDORF, holotype, 134mm, Victoria Nyanza

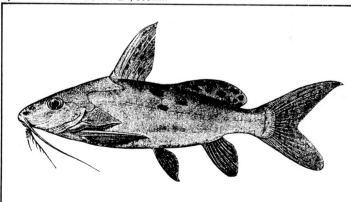

*Synodontis robbianus* SMITH, holotype, 138mm

## The genus SYNODONTIS

*Synodontis* is a catfish genus of about 100 species that are found throughout Africa except for the Sahara and the waters north of it. The fish are naked, without scales, and are found in most contiguous bodies of water, never being found in intermittent pools. They have dorsal and pectoral spines that are very strong and serrated. These spines make them very easy prey for the fisherman with a net since they become enmeshed in the netting and cannot escape. Of course, the fisherman has his work cut out for him when he tries to remove the fish from its entrapment. The author (HRA) remembers well the first night fishing in the Stanley Pool looking for *Synodontis angelicus* and *S. nigriventris*. A 20-meter by 3-meter seine was pulled through the water at midnight. We collected about 1,200 *Synodontis* in the first haul then spent the rest of the night removing them from the net, finally resorting to cutting pliers to free the fishes by cutting off the three serrated spines (one dorsal and two pectorals). The majority of the fishes lived, even after being out of the water (but in a wet seine) for hours, and then having their spines cut off about halfway down!

The *Synodontis* met by the author in their native habitats have all been nocturnal, and most swim in schools upside down. *S. angelicus*, on the other hand, never schooled but could be found hiding at night inside old tires attached to the docks as bumpers for docking boats. We were able to get a few specimens every night at the yacht club in old Leopoldville (now Kinshasa).

In the aquarium the *Synodontis* species are all peaceful and good scavengers. They are forever on the prowl, searching for food, and they eat everything from flake foods to live foods. They never seem to attack other fishes, but they do caress them from time to time with their three pairs of barbels, making them a pest to other fishes. There have been no concerted spawnings, but random successes have been achieved using hormonal injections of ripe fish.

Dr. Max Poll revised the genus *Synodontis* in 1971, and the authors have relied upon his illustrated descriptions for the identification of the plates. We have also used his black and white drawings to illustrate those fishes for which no color photos were available.

*Synodontis eupterus*

*Synodontis robertsi*

*Synodontis longirostris*

*Synodontis longirostris*

*Synodontis longirostris*

*Synodontis nigromaculatus*

*Synodontis nyassae*

*Synodontis nigromaculatus*

**Plate #263**

Synodontis multipunctatus

Synodontis multipunctatus

Synodontis petricola

Synodontis eurystomus

Synodontis acanthomias

Synodontis nigromaculatus

Synodontis nigromaculatus

Synodontis robbianus

Plate #264

417

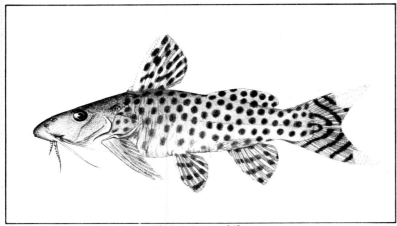

*Synodontis katangae* POLL, holotype, 240mm

*Synodontis velifer* NORMAN, holotype, 214mm

*Synodontis centralis* POLL, holotype, 116mm

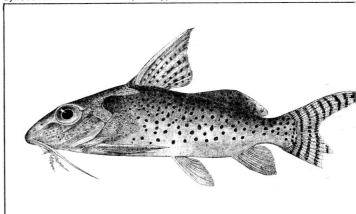

*Synodontis ornatus* BOULENGER, holotype, 152mm

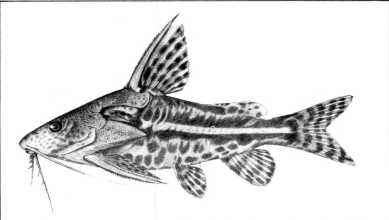

*Synodontis albolineatus* PELLEGRIN, holotype, 118mm

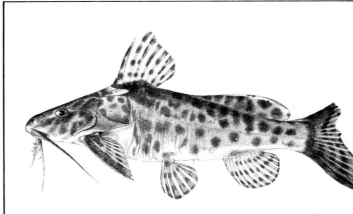

*Synodontis dorsomaculatus* POLL, holotype, 137mm

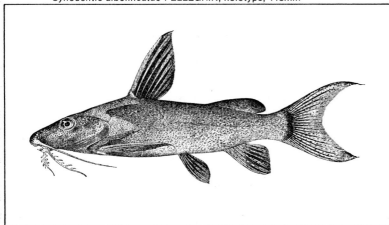

*Synodontis steindachneri* BOULENGER, holotype, 172mm, Akonolinga

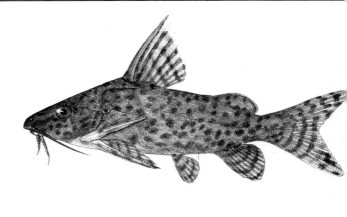

*Synodontis nigrita* CUVIER et VALENCIENNES, holotype, 149mm, fleuve Sen

**Plate #265**

418

*Synodontis caudovittatus* BOULENGER, lectotype, 258mm

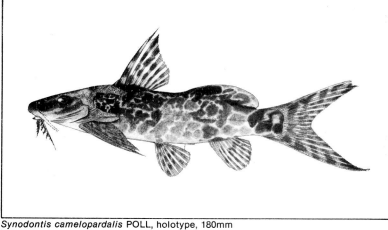

*Synodontis camelopardalis* POLL, holotype, 180mm

*Brachysynodontis batensoda* (RUPPELL), 220mm

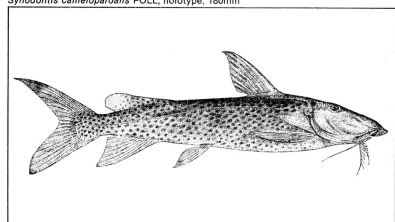

*Synodontis guttatus* GUNTHER, holotype, 700mm

*Synodontis filamentosus* BOULENGER, holotype, 220mm

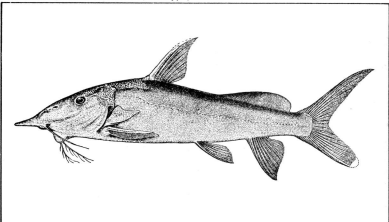

*Synodontis xiphias* GUNTHER, holotype, 670mm

*Synodontis koensis* PELLEGRIN, holotype, 140mm

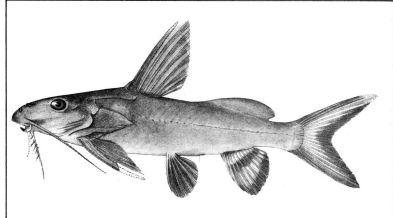

*Synodontis tessmanni* PAPPENHEIM, lectotype, 168mm

*Plate #266*

419

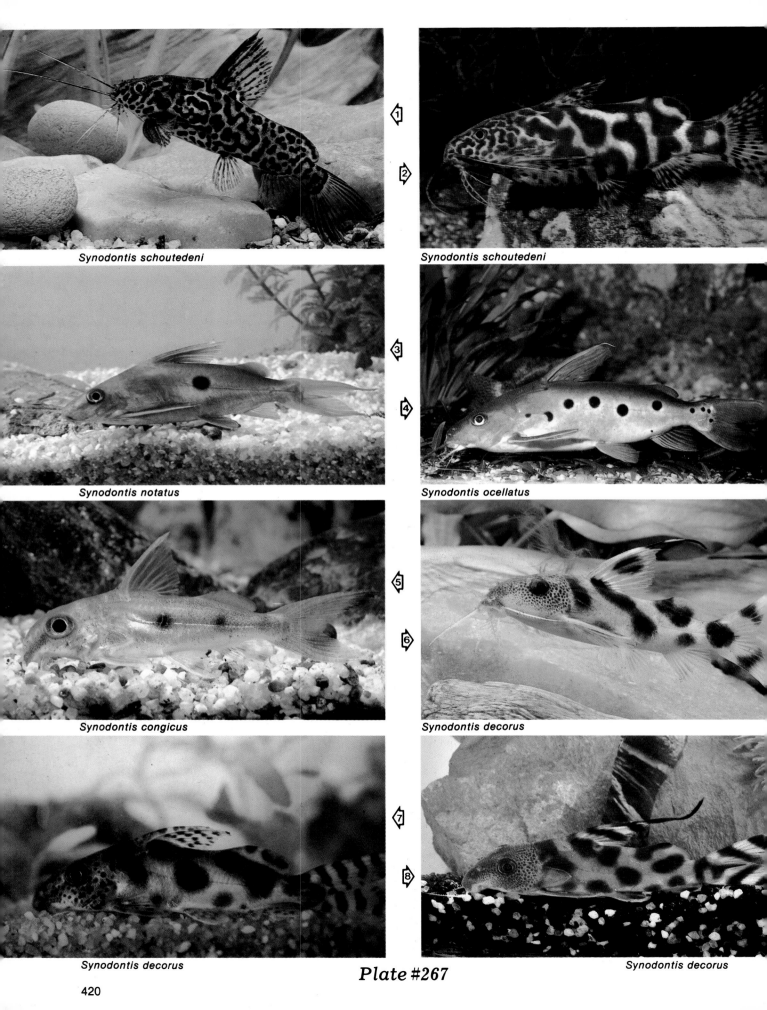

Synodontis schoutedeni

Synodontis schoutedeni

Synodontis notatus

Synodontis ocellatus

Synodontis congicus

Synodontis decorus

Synodontis decorus

Synodontis decorus

*Plate #267*

420

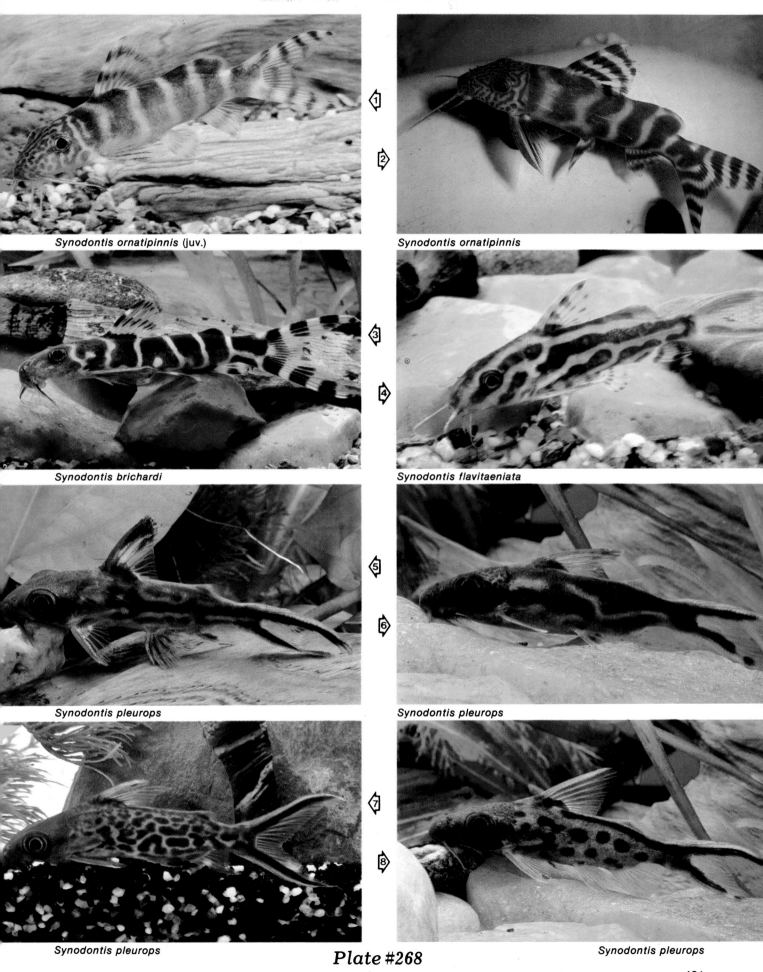

Synodontis ornatipinnis (juv.)

Synodontis ornatipinnis

Synodontis brichardi

Synodontis flavitaeniata

Synodontis pleurops

Synodontis pleurops

Synodontis pleurops

Synodontis pleurops

*Plate #268*

421

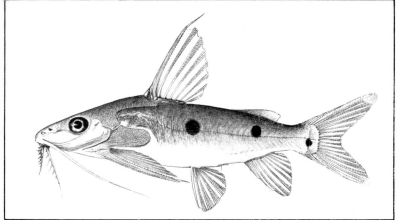

Synodontis notatus VAILLANT, lectotype, 207mm

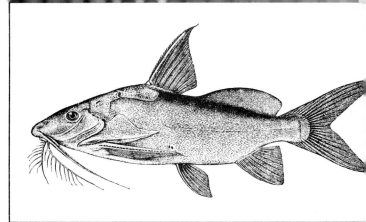

Synodontis geledensis GUNTHER, holotype, 307mm

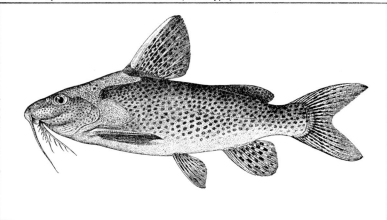

Synodontis woosnami BOULENGER, holotype, 164mm

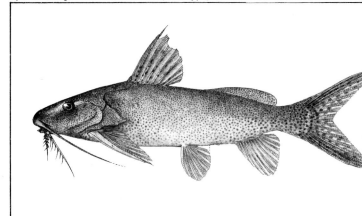

Synodontis punctulatus GUNTHER, lectotype, 222mm

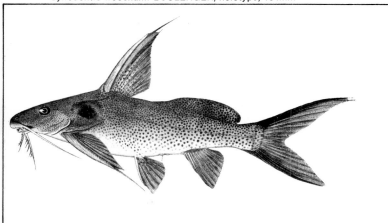

Synodontis eburneensis DAGET, holotype, 281mm

Synodontis khartoumensis ABU GIDEIRI, paratype, 150mm

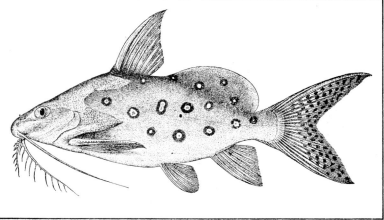

Synodontis ocellifer BOULENGER, lectotype, 225mm

Synodontis pulcher POLL, holotype, 150mm

*Plate #269*

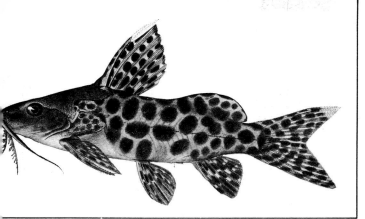

*Synodontis polystigma* BOULENGER, lectotype, 198mm

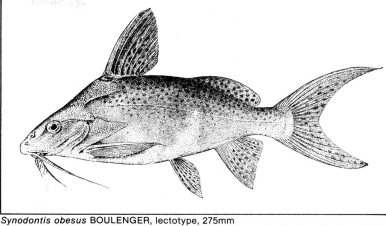

*Synodontis obesus* BOULENGER, lectotype, 275mm

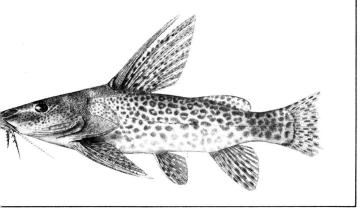

*Synodontis leopardinus* PELLEGRIN, holotype, 137mm

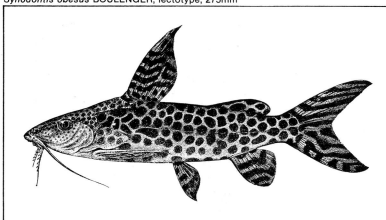

*Synodontis pardalis* BOULENGER, lectotype, 229mm

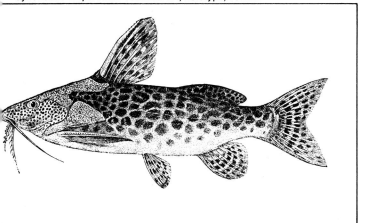

*Synodontis macrostigma* BOULENGER, lectotype, 171mm

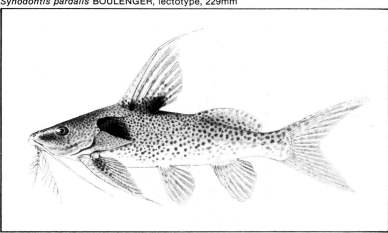

*Synodontis punctifer* DAGET, holotype, 190mm

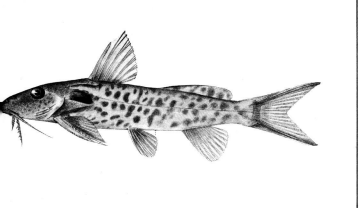

*Synodontis bastiani* DAGET, holotype, 84mm

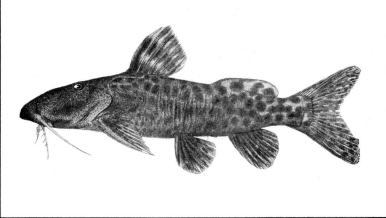

*Synodontis gobroni* DAGET, paratype Markala, riv. Niger

*Plate #270*

423

Synodontis contractus

Synodontis greshoffi

Synodontis nigriventris

Synodontis nigriventris

Synodontis angelicus

Syndontis angelicus

Synodontis alberti

Synodontis alberti

*Plate #271*

424

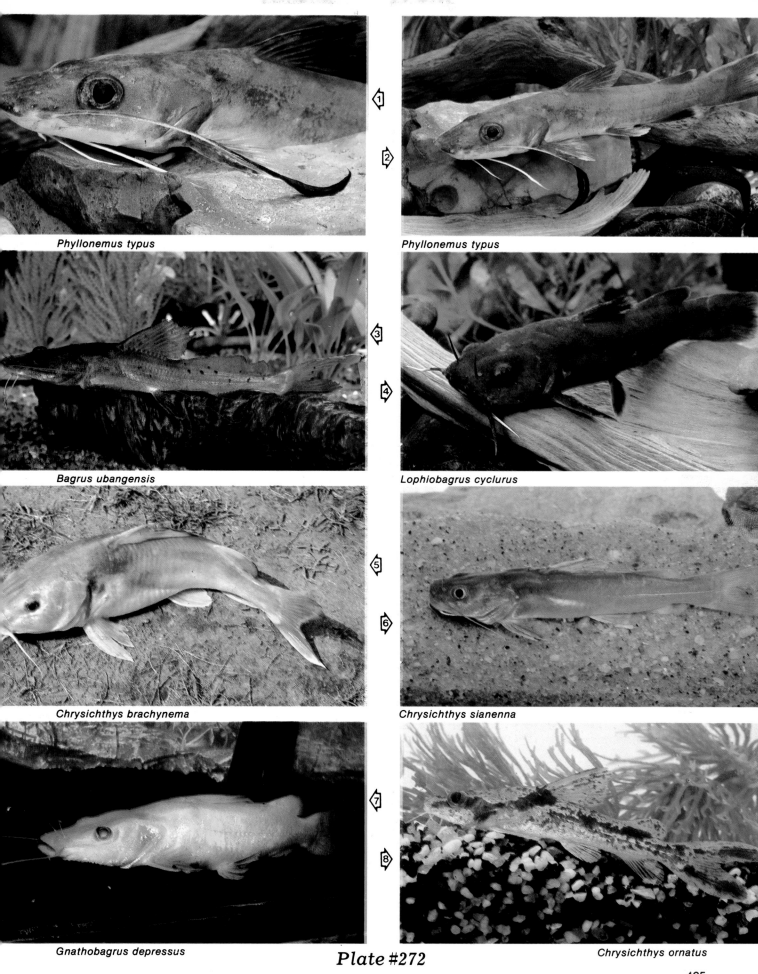

Phyllonemus typus

Phyllonemus typus

Bagrus ubangensis

Lophiobagrus cyclurus

Chrysichthys brachynema

Chrysichthys sianenna

Gnathobagrus depressus

Plate #272

Chrysichthys ornatus

425

*Phyllonemus typus* Boulenger • Spatula-barbeled
Catfish

RANGE: Lake Tanganyika.
HABITS: This genus only contains one species. The fish is
easily recognized by the spatulate or leaf-like membrane
on the distal part of the maxillary barbels. There are no
nasal barbels.
WATER CONDITIONS: pH 6.8-7.6 at 25°C.
SIZE: A small catfish that barely reaches 75 mm.
FOOD REQUIREMENTS: A scavenger, as are most catfishes.
Thrives on every normal aquarium diet but prefers to
catch it from the bottom of the tank.

*Bagrus ubangensis* Boulenger • Ubangi Shovelnose
Catfish

RANGE: Congo.
HABITS: This fish grows very large for the small aquarium
and must be given plenty of room. It swallows tankmates
small enough to ingest in one gulp. This only takes place
at night, in the dark. Normally the fish is much darker
than the small silver specimen shown in the photo.
WATER CONDITIONS: pH 6.2-6.8 at 27°C.
SIZE: Reaches over 300 mm.
FOOD REQUIREMENTS: Small fishes or flake food, which it
learns to gobble.

*Chrysichthys brachynema* Boulenger • Salmon Catfish

RANGE: Lake Tanganyika.
HABITS: This is a catfish too large for the home aquarium. Its
red meat has been used to make substitute smoked
salmon for homesick Europeans living on Lake
Tanganyika. The author (HRA) tasted it and it wasn't
bad, especially if you've been on the lake for any length
of time.
WATER CONDITIONS: Alkaline water, pH 9.0 at 25°C.
SIZE: Over 400 mm.
FOOD REQUIREMENTS: Eats smaller fishes but can be
trained to take chunks of fish and meat.

*Gnathobagrus depressus* Nichols & Griscom • Long-
jawed Catfish

RANGE: Congo basin.
HABITS: A bottom-dwelling catfish found in low-light areas.
Very similar to *Chrysichthys* except for the long lower
jaw.
SIZE: Reaches at least 200 mm.
FOOD REQUIREMENTS: Probably eats small fishes and
invertebrates found while scavenging at night.

*Lophiobagrus cyclurus* Worthington & Ricardo • African
Bullhead

RANGE: Found only in Lake Tanganyika.
HABITS: Not much is known about this species except that it
is difficult to collect and was misidentified as *L. lestradei*
by Poll himself! Recently it has been imported in fair
numbers and has been spawned (accidentally). Reports
that its slime is poisonous to other fishes have not been
confirmed.
WATER CONDITIONS: pH 9.0 at about 25°C.
SIZE: The largest specimen ever collected was 92 mm long.
FOOD REQUIREMENTS: Partially digested small fishes,
shrimps and insects were found in its stomach, so it probably feeds on any small living foods of appropriate size.

*Chrysichthys sianenna* Boulenger • Olive-silver Catfish

RANGE: Lake Tanganyika.
HABITS: A nocturnal fish that performs poorly as a scavenger in the home aquarium. Hides most of the time among
dense vegetation.
WATER CONDITIONS: Prefers very alkaline environment
with a pH of 9.0 and a hardness of about DH 10°.
SIZE: Reaches over 220 mm, but smaller specimens are
usually imported for the aquarium trade.
FOOD REQUIREMENTS: Prefers worms and other bottom-
dwelling morsels, but also takes pelleted aquarium
foods.

*Chrysichthys ornatus* Boulenger • Mottled Catfish

RANGE: Upper Congo and Ubangi Rivers.
HABITS: A nocturnal scavenger. Well marked but of limited
interest for aquarists.
WATER CONDITIONS: Tolerates a wide range of conditions
from pH 6.8-9.0 at 25-28°C.
SIZE: Reaches 200 mm.
FOOD REQUIREMENTS: A typical scavenger that feeds from
the bottom. Prefers small worms but takes pelleted
aquarium diets.

## AFRICAN BARBS AND OTHER CYPRINIDS

The cyprinids are one of the dominant groups of freshwater fishes, with literally hundreds of species in North America, Asia, Europe, and Africa. There are over 300 species of barbs in Africa alone. Although Asian barbs are a staple of the aquarium hobby, the African species have never become especially popular, although several species have had a short vogue. The butterfly barb, *Capoeta hulstaerti*, for instance, was imported in numbers from the Congo in the 1960's, but it soon faded from sight. The major problem with the African barbs (and the other African cyprinids, for that matter) is that few of them are especially colorful or hardy. Like the cool-water minnows of North America, the males may be colorful when spawning, but this lasts for only a few weeks or months and the rest of the year they are similar to the silvery to tan females. Also, most African barbs that have been imported so far have been like the type usually called *Barbodes vivipara*—silvery with a black lateral band, a few black scale edgings, and a bit of color in the fins. They are seldom imported in numbers, and because they virtually never breed in the aquarium they soon disappear from the hobby until the next importation.

This is not to say that the African barbs are poor aquarium fishes. In fact, in a small tank with clean, slightly acid water and a fairly warm temperature, a small school of barbs can be quite a sight. There is no reason that they cannot be spawned on a regular basis if the aquarist is willing to take the time to do so, as many spawn in much the same manner as do the Asian barbs and American minnows, laying large numbers of eggs that settle into the substrate or plants. The fry are often very small and may require infusoria, but that is seldom held against a popular species. The small mountain stream species from the southern African area are perhaps most colorful, but their colors are best only when spawning; they would tolerate cooler water than the Congo River species that are sometimes imported.

African barbs can be split into two rather vague groups on the basis of adult size. At one extreme are the large species such as *Barbodes capensis* from South Africa. These fishes are usually rather coarse and have more scales in the lateral row than do the smaller species, in this respect resembling the large Eurasian *Barbus* species. Reaching a weight of 10 kilograms or more, the large species are often popular food and sporting fishes. They are predatory on other fishes, frogs, crabs, and just about anything else they can find. When they live in larger, rapid rivers they are good game fishes, taking many types of artificial lures and fighting well. Juveniles of such species would probably outgrow their tanks in a few months and do poorly.

The small species of African barbs (under 150 mm) are found nearly everywhere, from jungle ponds to rapid mountain streams. We at T.F.H. place them in the genera *Barbodes*, *Capoeta*, and *Puntius*, as is correct in most American aquarium literature, but the advanced hobbyist should be aware that, as in so many groups of fishes, there is considerable

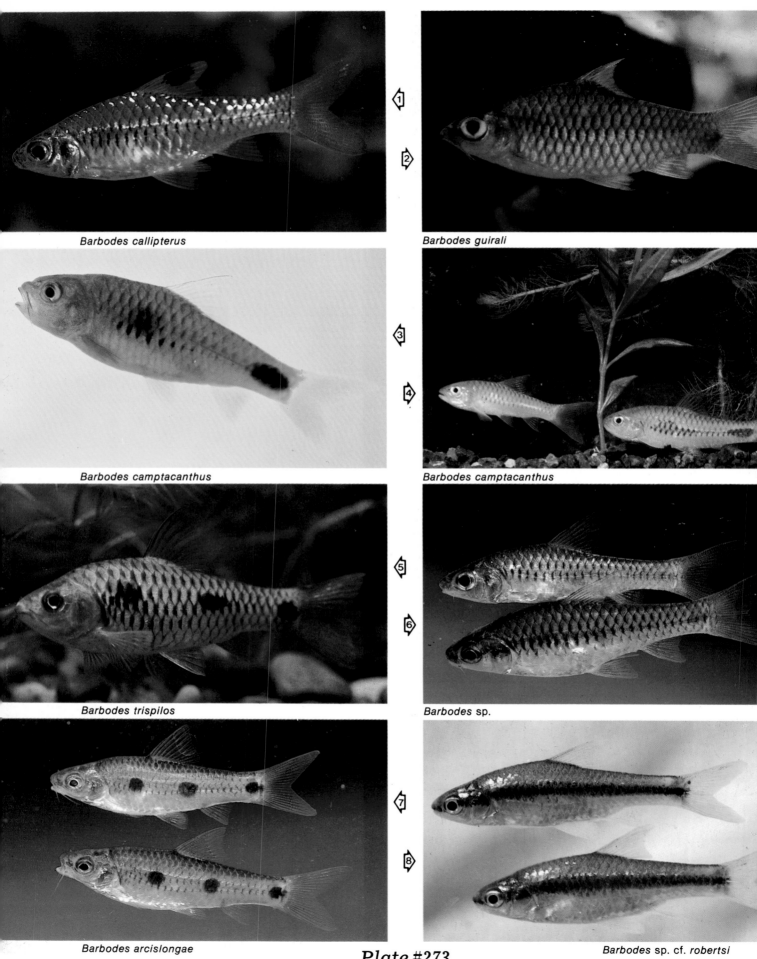

Barbodes callipterus

Barbodes guirali

Barbodes camptacanthus

Barbodes camptacanthus

Barbodes trispilos

Barbodes sp.

Barbodes arcislongae

Barbodes sp. cf. robertsi

*Plate #273*

428

Barbodes fasciolatus

Puntius jae

Barbodes brookingi

Barbodes eutenia

Barbodes macrops

Barbodes nicholsi

Barbodes kerstenii

Barbodes prionocanthus

*Plate #274*

debate about the correct names for our common fishes. Thus the European literature tends to use the name *Barbus* for virtually all the barbs, large and small, while we restrict that name to the large, fine-scaled species of Eurasia. Probably neither system of names is actually correct, as several other generic names, especially *Beirabarbus*, are currently being applied by African ichthyologists. So for the moment we'll stick at least provisionally to *Puntius* for species with no barbels, *Capoeta* with two barbels, and *Barbodes* with four barbels. These differences are purely pedantic, however, as members of all three genera look much alike and are found in the same types of habitats, as well as spawning in a similar manner.

The mountains of south-central Africa have numerous small, colorful species that at first glance would be very difficult to distinguish from the colorful shiners of the southeastern United States. When in spawning colors, the males tend to have bright red and yellow in the fins along with areas of milky white as a contrast. Males of many small barbs develop large breeding tubercles on the head and fins, as in the goldfish and minnows in general. Females and males out of spawning season may have touches of color in the fins and on the body, but they are generally tannish with black lateral bands, like the normal run of African barbs. In southern Africa these small species are kept as native fishes and fare well in aquaria, but they are seldom imported.

Most imported African barbs come from the Great Lakes area or from the western coast, where they are often used as "bag stuffers" by exporters. When an exporter pays for cargo space on an airplane, he may as well put in as many fish bags as he can find, whether they contain premium fishes or not. So after he has packed all his desirable cichlids, catfishes, and oddballs, a few barbs may be added to the shipment to make the best use of the space and maybe make a few extra dollars at the retail end. (Now that most airlines charge by weight, not volume, this practice is ending.) These barbs are seldom very colorful, and rarely is anything really known about their life history or even how to sex them. When the butterfly barb, *C. hulstaerti,* was first imported from the Congo, the colorful specimens were sexed by many "experts," but the fish proved impossible to spawn. Only after many shipments had been imported was it discovered that the first shipments were all males and real females were easily sexed by differences in fin colors. Even today it is doubtful if anyone really knows much about such species as *Barbodes camptacanthus* from the Cameroons and Gabon, although it is imported fairly regularly and has a distinctive color pattern. The species that appear in the hobby only once a decade or so never seem to become established and soon fade from memory.

Although there are over 20 genera of cyprinids (family Cyprinidae) on the most recent checklist of African fishes, only two or three genera other than the barbs are ever imported for the aquarium hobby. Of these *Labeo* is the most familiar, though certainly not common. Like the barbs, African *Labeo* can be divided into large species of 10 kilograms or more that are of most interest as food and game fishes, and small species under 300 mm long that are somewhat suitable for keeping in large aquaria. Of the small species that enter the trade, only *Labeo cylindricus* (southeastern

Africa), *L. forskalii* (Nile drainage), and *L. variegatus* (Congo) are fairly often seen. Of the three, only *L. variegatus* is really small enough (less than 100 mm) for most aquaria, the others often exceeding 300 mm. *Labeo* species feed much like carp, using their ventral mouths and thick lips to extract organic matter, live and dead, plant and animal, from the substrate. Africa has several true dwarf *Labeo* species (under 75 mm long), but they are virtually unknown to ichthyologists, let alone aquarium hobbyists.

Two unusual genera of fishes are rarely imported, *Garra* and *Barilius*. *Garra* is certainly nothing beautiful to look at, the brownish body having nearly parallel surfaces so it looks like a small branch. However, it does make an efficient algae-eater, using the ventral mouth as a scraper. Curiously, this genus is found in both Africa and southern Asia, a distribution pattern shared with *Labeo* and the genera of barbs but found in few other fishes. *Discognathus*, sometimes seen in the aquarium literature, is a synonym of *Garra*.

The species of *Barilius* are streamlined fishes that at first glance look more like South American tetras or marine herring than cyprinids. The silvery bodies are long and slender, and the head is usually pointed and has a large mouth. These fishes are active, schooling species that are predators on small prey and often live in fast waters, though many species are also found in lakes. Some species have recently begun to be imported regularly because they occur in the Great Lakes and are sent as fillers in cichlid shipments. Although most species are not especially colorful (unless you are partial to silvery fishes), the males of a few species, such as *Barilius ubangensis*, are attractively banded and have colored fins. *Barilius* is also an Afro-Asian genus, but recently it was split into two separate genera, *Barilius* proper being restricted to Asian species and *Opsaridium* being used for African species. Regardless of name, remember that these fishes are jumpers in the worst sense of the word and need a covered tank.

Barbodes vivipara

Capoeta hulstaerti

Puntius puellus

Puntius sylvaticus

Barbodes vivipara

Barbodes radiatus aurianticus

Puntius woehlerti

*Plate #275*

Barbodes sp. cf. greenwoodi

432

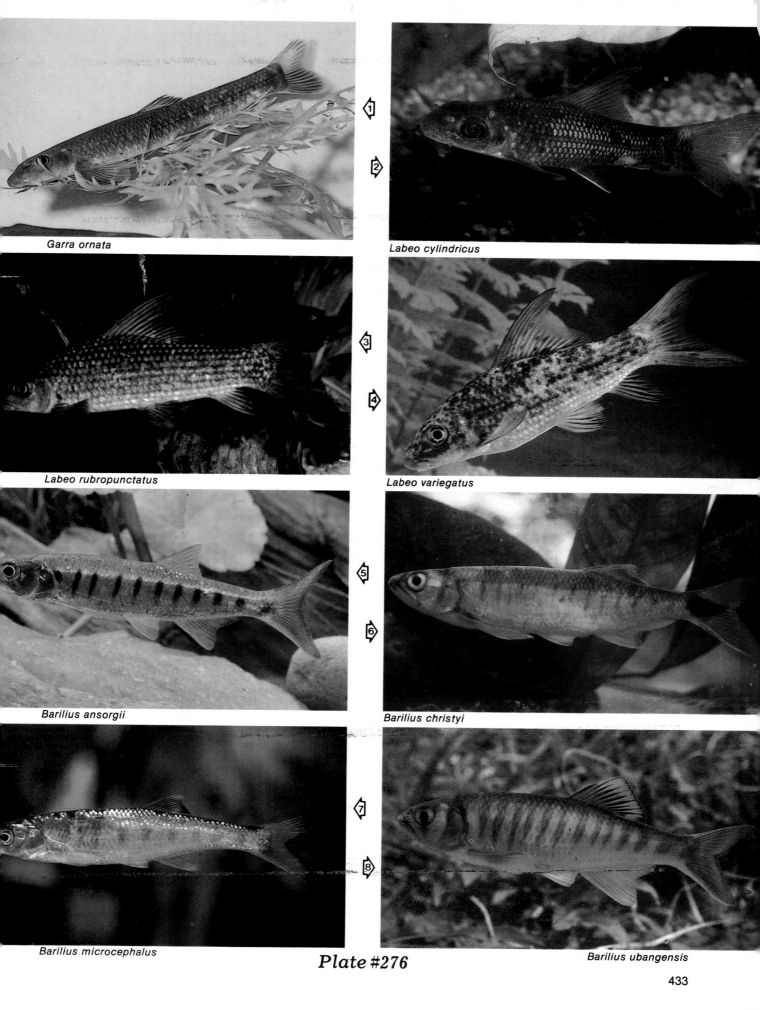

Garra ornata

Labeo cylindricus

Labeo rubropunctatus

Labeo variegatus

Barilius ansorgii

Barilius christyi

Barilius microcephalus

Barilius ubangensis

**Plate #276**

433

## AFRICAN KILLIFISHES

The Germans may call them "eierlegende Zahnkarpfen" (egg-laying toothcarps), but to American and British hobbyists the small, often brightly colored fishes of the Cyprinodontidae are the killifishes. Of the several hundred species, the majority are found in Africa south of the Sahara and have become one of the most sought-after groups of fishes in the entire aquarium hobby. Admittedly, you will seldom see an African killifish for sale in a general petshop (for various reasons they are considered hard to profitably merchandise), but there is a gigantic group of killie specialists who purchase and trade fishes through the international and national mails. Many books on their identification and care have been written (of which one of the most comprehensive on African species is the monumental *Rivulins of the Old World* by Jorgen Scheel), but new species are still being described each year and more unusual species enter the hobbyist market all the time.

African killifishes—particularly the genera *Aphyosemion* (commonly called lyretails although many species lack distinctive tail streamers), *Nothobranchius* (the nothos or fire killies), *Epiplatys* (the panchax, the most plainly marked of the common genera), and *Aplocheilichthys, Procatopus,* and *Lamprichthys* (collectively called lampeyes and ranging in size from under 25 mm to over 125 mm)—are noted for their unusual and often brilliant color patterns in the males (females are usually plain) and especially for their odd spawning habits. Species of *Nothobranchius* (probably all) and *Aphyosemion* (just a few) are annual fishes like the South American *Cynolebias*, the fry developing rapidly into usually brilliantly colored adults that spawn special eggs capable of resting (entering diapause) in the mud bottom of the drying pond for several months before hatching with the next rains. After laying their eggs and fertilizing them, the adults of the first generation die, usually at the age of 8 to 10 months, certainly less than a year. In the aquarium these annual fishes are very popular because the development time of the eggs can be controlled to allow hatching just when the young are wanted. The eggs are also easy to ship as they can be maintained in an almost dry condition for months or perhaps even years.

Lyretails show a great amount of variation in spawning habits, the various species laying their eggs anywhere from the surface to the top layer of the substrate. Although most are probably happiest using spawning mops in midwater, some species will lay their eggs almost anywhere that is available, adapting their behavior to the circumstances within the tank. Most killifishes are best bred in trios, the single aggressive male being allowed to vent his energy on two or even three females (males of many killifishes can and will kill lone females when spawning).

The lampeyes are not seen too often in the aquarium although there are many common species, some of them extremely attractive. Most of the species are small and more iridescent than beautiful, although when kept in schools they look fine in a small tank. The larger types, such as *Proca-*

*topus* and *Lamprichthys*, are colorful and will spawn in the aquarium, but they tend to be short-lived and not very hardy. Many or perhaps most lampeyes place their eggs in crevices such as floating pieces of natural cork or behind airline tubing in the darkest corner of the tank. Identification of lampeyes is almost impossible even from specimens, and they are poorly covered in available aquarium literature.

On a final and more scientific note, it must be mentioned that the placement of the killifishes in a single family has been in question since a controversial revision by Parenti in 1981. Instead of just the family Cyprinodontidae with several subfamilies, another classification recognizing up to 10 families has begun to establish itself. In this system the lyretails, fire killies, and panchax would be in family Aplocheilidae, the lampeyes in Aplocheilichthyidae, and the American killies would belong to several non-African families, especially Rivulidae (*Cynolebias, Rivulus*, etc.), Fundulidae (*Fundulus, Lucania*, etc.), and Cyprinodontidae (*Cyprinodon, Aphanius, Jordanella*, etc.). Also, there is a recent (and probably justified) trend to consider the African genus *Epiplatys* a synonym of the Asian genus *Aplocheilus*—certainly the two groups of species are superficially and behaviorially very similar and distinguished mainly by geography.

Killifish hobbyists may be among the most satisfied of aquarists because there is so much material available to them at all times. Thanks to a tradition of trading among individuals and groups, literally dozens of African (and American) species are readily available to the specialist and dozens more are available on an occasional basis. No two killies look exactly the same, and their colorful males make even 4-liter tanks bright.

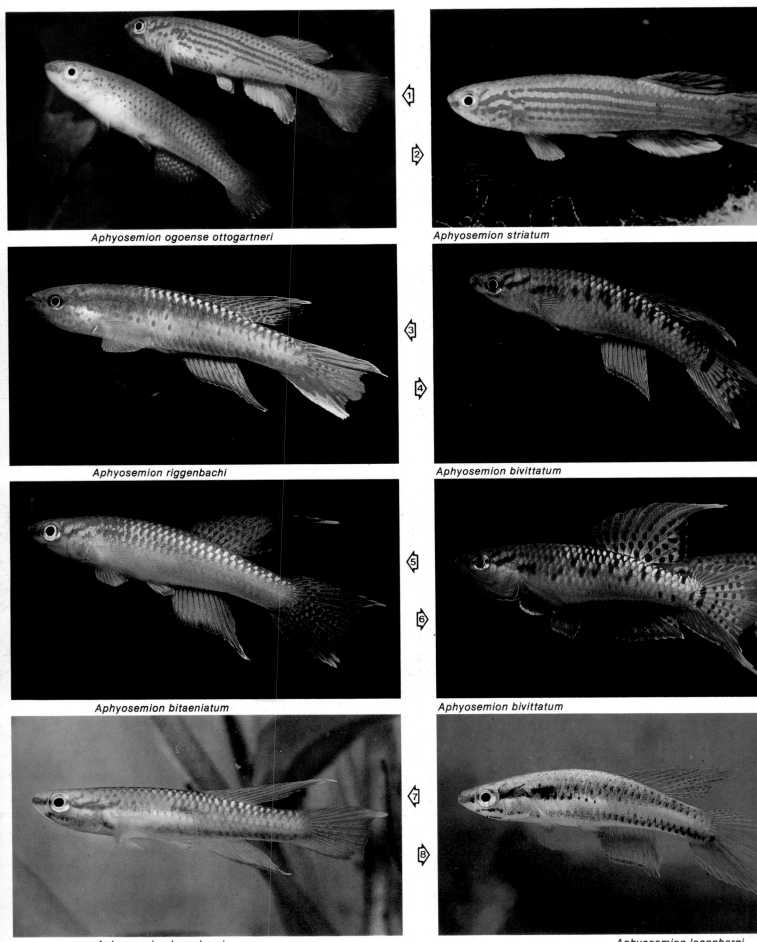

Aphyosemion ogoense ottogartneri

Aphyosemion striatum

Aphyosemion riggenbachi

Aphyosemion bivittatum

Aphyosemion bitaeniatum

Aphyosemion bivittatum

Aphyosemion loennbergi

Aphyosemion loennbergi

**Plate #277**

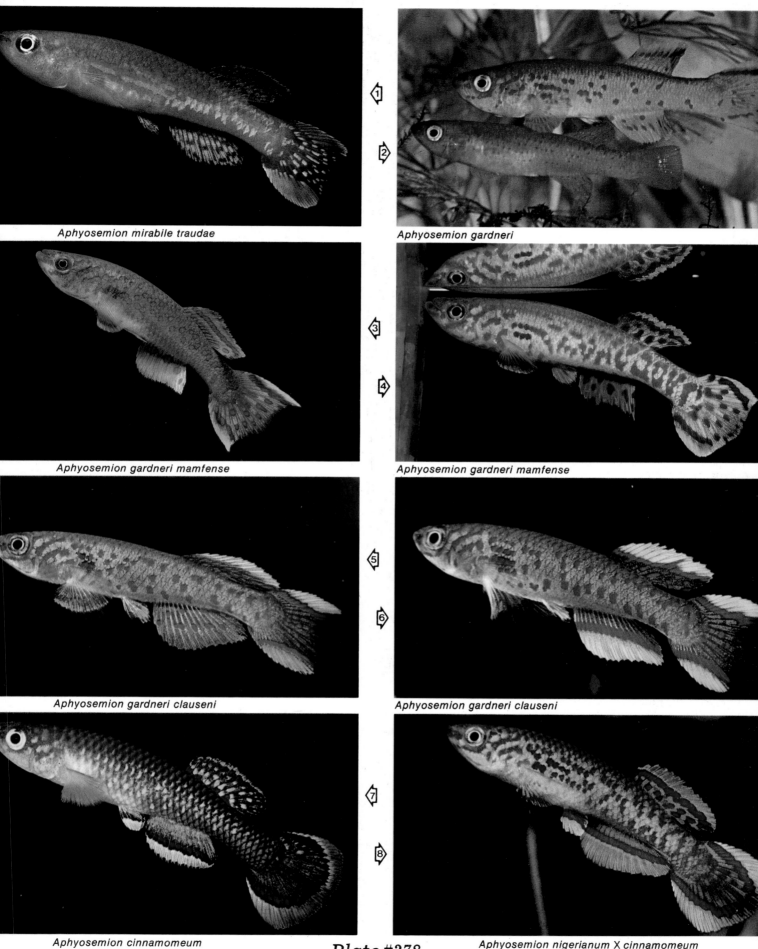

Aphyosemion mirabile traudae

Aphyosemion gardneri

Aphyosemion gardneri mamfense

Aphyosemion gardneri mamfense

Aphyosemion gardneri clauseni

Aphyosemion gardneri clauseni

Aphyosemion cinnamomeum

Aphyosemion nigerianum X cinnamomeum

*Plate #278*

437

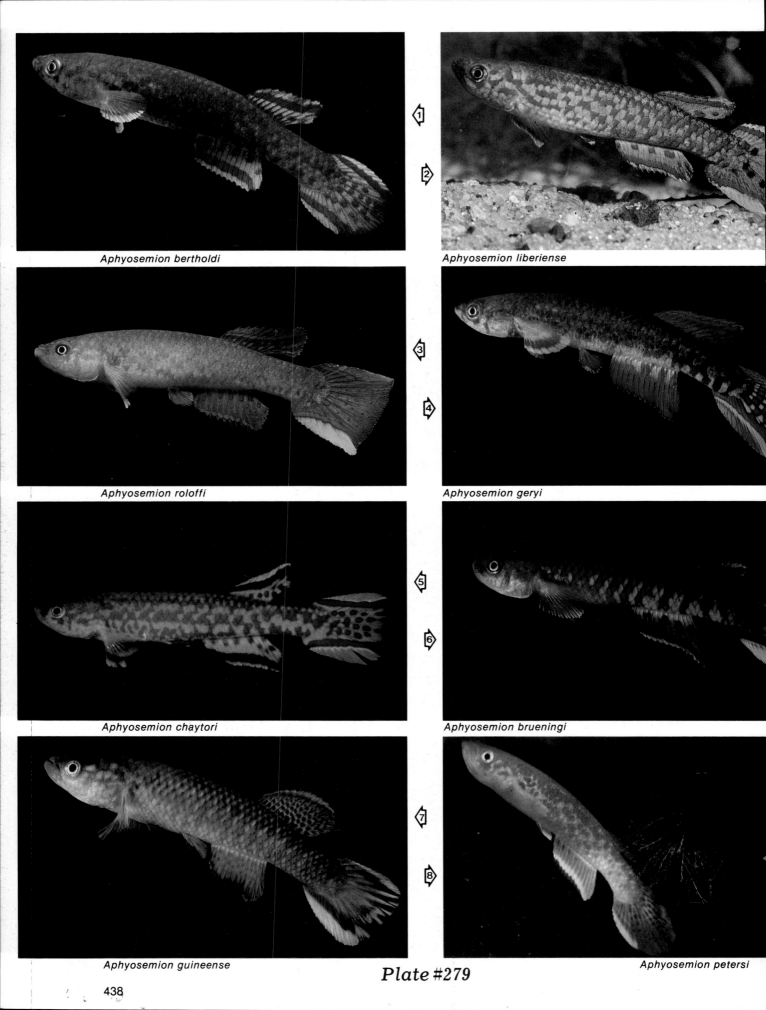

Aphyosemion bertholdi

Aphyosemion liberiense

Aphyosemion roloffi

Aphyosemion geryi

Aphyosemion chaytori

Aphyosemion brueningi

Aphyosemion guineense

Aphyosemion petersi

*Plate #279*

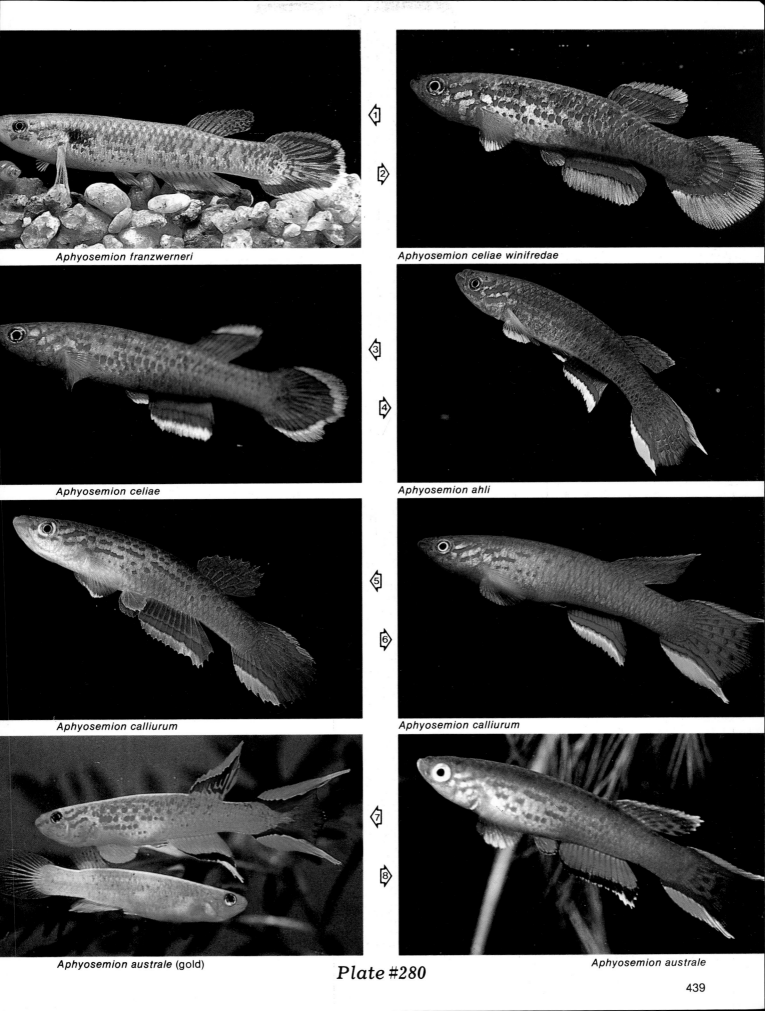

Aphyosemion franzwerneri

Aphyosemion celiae winifredae

Aphyosemion celiae

Aphyosemion ahli

Aphyosemion calliurum

Aphyosemion calliurum

Aphyosemion australe (gold)

Aphyosemion australe

*Plate #280*

439

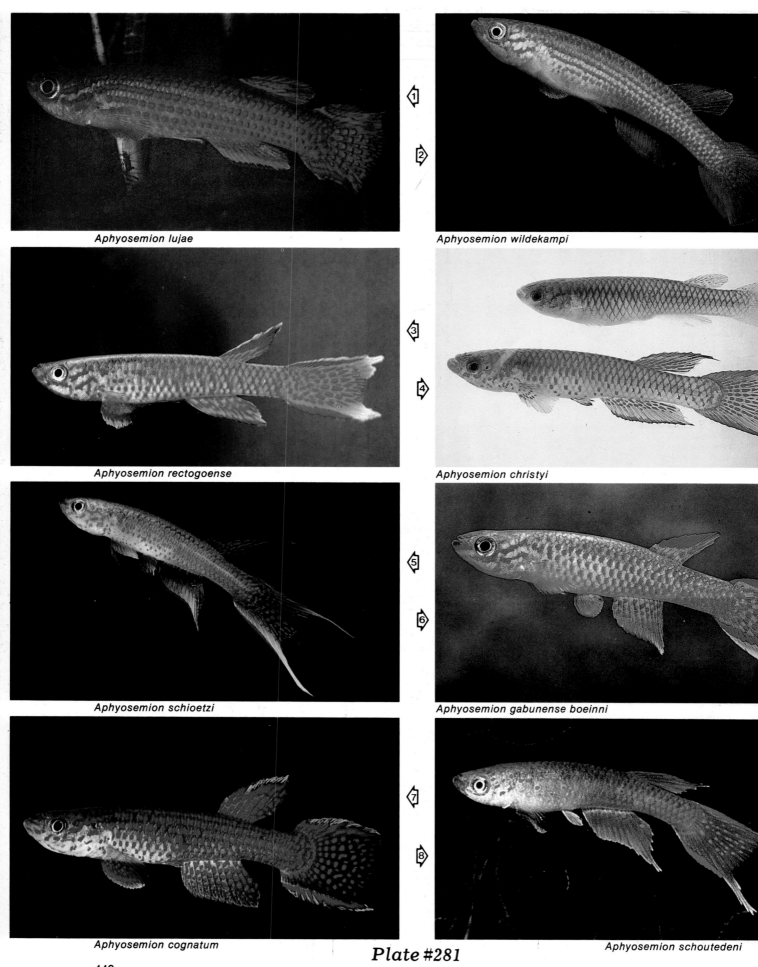

Aphyosemion lujae

Aphyosemion wildekampi

Aphyosemion rectogoense

Aphyosemion christyi

Aphyosemion schioetzi

Aphyosemion gabunense boeinni

Aphyosemion cognatum

Aphyosemion schoutedeni

*Plate #281*

440

Aphyosemion puerzli

Aphyosemion ndianum

Aphyosemion exiguum

Aphyosemion elegans X bualanum ??

Aphyosemion bualanum

Aphyosemion rubrifascium

Aphyosemion kiyawense male

Aphyosemion kiyawense female

*Plate #282*

441

Aphyosemion walkeri

Aphyosemion spurrelli

Aphyosemion arnoldi

Aphyosemion filamentosum X rubrilabiale

Aphyosemion rubrilabiale

Aphyosemion filamentosum-complex

Aphyosemion filamentosum

Aphyosemion filamentosum var.

*Plate #283*

442

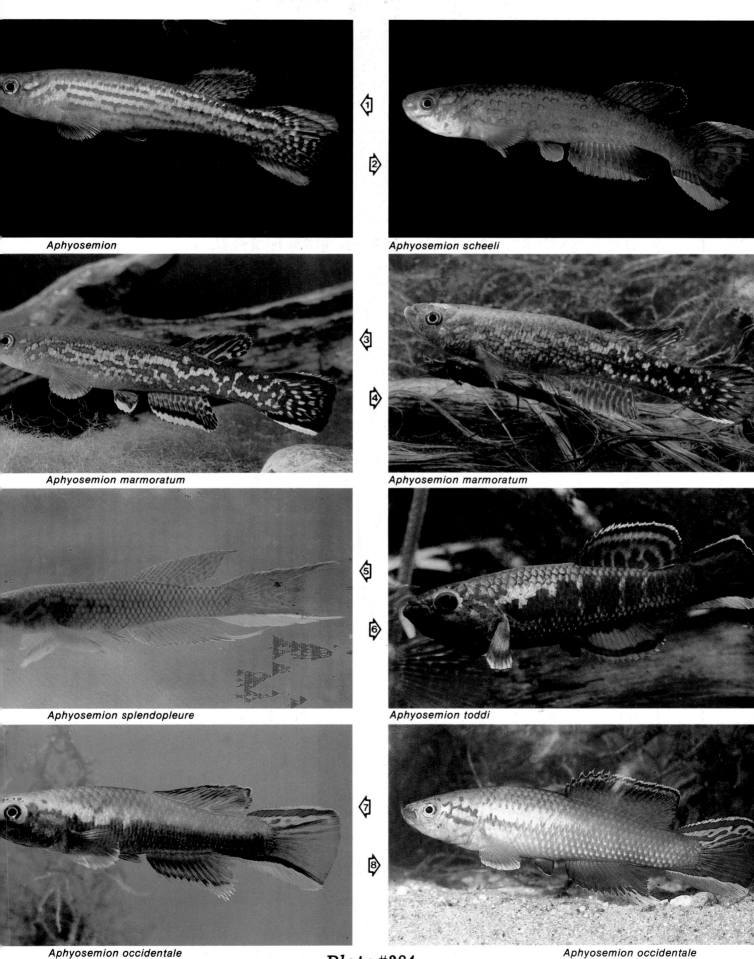

Aphyosemion

Aphyosemion scheeli

Aphyosemion marmoratum

Aphyosemion marmoratum

Aphyosemion splendopleure

Aphyosemion toddi

Aphyosemion occidentale

Aphyosemion occidentale

**Plate #284**

443

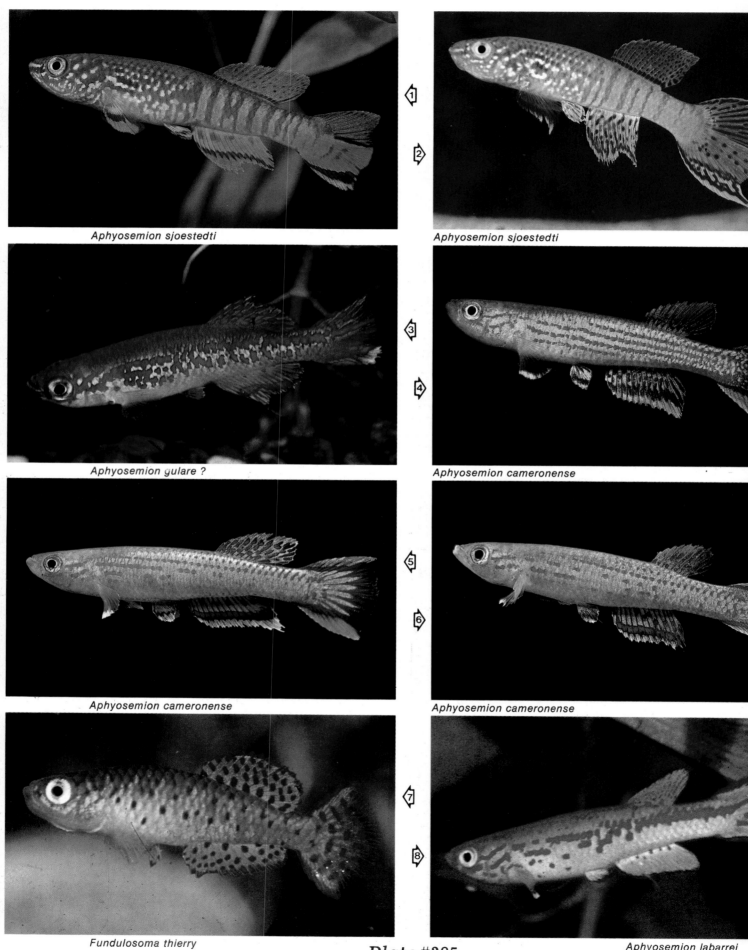

Aphyosemion sjoestedti

Aphyosemion sjoestedti

Aphyosemion gulare ?

Aphyosemion cameronense

Aphyosemion cameronense

Aphyosemion cameronense

Fundulosoma thierry

Aphyosemion labarrei

*Plate #285*

444

*Nothobranchius palmqvisti*

*Nothobranchius sp. (Dar es Salaam)*

*Nothobranchius lourensi*

*Nothobranchius janpapi*

*Nothobranchius sp. (Mbeya)*

*Nothobranchius sp. (Salima)*

*Nothobranchius kuhntae*

*Nothobranchius guentheri*

*Plate #286*

445

*Nothobranchius furzeri*

*Nothobranchius korthausae*

*Nothobranchius rachovii*

*Nothobranchius rachovii* var.

*Nothobranchius rachovii* var.

*Nothobranchius rachovii* blue var.

*Nothobranchius kirkii*

*Nothobranchius kirkii*

**Plate #287**

*Nothobranchius patrizii*

*Nothobranchius steinforti*

*Nothobranchius lourense*

*Nothobranchius orthonotus*

*Nothobranchius melanospilus*

*Nothobranchius jubbi jubbi*

*Nothobranchius palmqvisti*

*Nothobranchius palmqvisti*

**Plate #288**

447

*Pachypanchax playfairii*

*Pachypanchax playfairii*

*Pachypanchax homalonotus*

*Epiplatys huberi*

*Epiplatys chevalieri*

*Epiplatys chevalieri*

*Epiplatys annulatus*

*Epiplatys annulatus*

**Plate #289**

*Epiplatys sexfasciatus*

*Epiplatys sexfasciatus*

*Epiplatys sexfasciatus*

*Epiplatys dageti monroviae*

*Epiplatys dageti monroviae*

*Epiplatys dageti monroviae*

*Epiplatys duboisi*

*Epiplatys duboisi*

**Plate #290**

449

*Epiplatys njalaensis*

*Epiplatys roloffi*

*Epiplatys macrostigma*

*Epiplatys macrostigma*

*Epiplatys macrostigma*

*Epiplatys macrostigma*

*Epiplatys grahami*

*Epiplatys grahami*

*Plate #291*

*Epiplatys bifasciatus*

*Epiplatys bifasciatus*

*Epiplatys fasciolatus*

*Epiplatys fasciolatus*

*Epiplatys spilargyreius*

*Epiplatys spilargyreius*

*Epiplatys spilargyreius X fasciolatus*

*Epiplatys barmoiensis*

**Plate #292**

451

*Lamprichthys tanganicanus*

*Procatopus* (?) "Fire-tail"

*Procatopus gracilis*

*Procatopus similis*

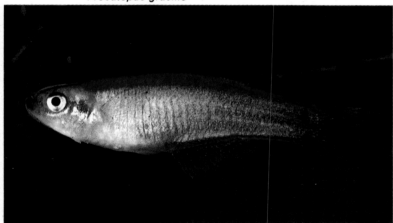
*Procatopus aberrans*

*Procatopus similis ?*

*Procatopus nototaenia*

*Procatopus nototaenia*

**Plate #293**

Aplocheilichthys katangae

Plataplochilus cabindae

Aplocheilichthys macrophthalmus

Aplocheilichthys "Micropanchax" (female)

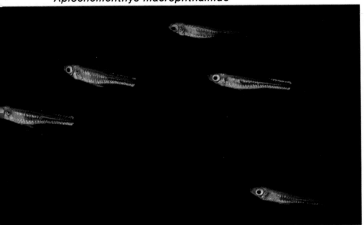

Aplocheilichthys myersi

Aplocheilichthys rancureli

Aplocheilichthys spilauchen

Aplocheilichthys spilauchen

*Plate #294*

453

## CICHLIDS OF LAKES MALAWI, TANGANYIKA, AND VICTORIA

The African Rift Valley contains a number of lakes that have become important to aquarists mainly as sources of fishes of the family Cichlidae. Two of these, Lake Malawi and Lake Tanganyika, have provided the bulk of the species imported, with Lake Victoria a distant third. Cichlids are the prime targets for the exporters as they constitute the major portion of the fish fauna of all three lakes. Lake Malawi, for example, has more than 250 described species (undoubtedly more to come) of cichlids as compared to fewer than 50 non-cichlid species. Lake Tanganyika is not too different, with about 175 described cichlid species and fewer than 75 non-cichlid species. More cichlids will undoubtedly be described from Lake Tanganyika as well. Lake Victoria follows a similar pattern, with more than 175 cichlid species and only 40 or so non-cichlids.

What also makes these lakes somewhat unique as far as aquarists are concerned is their chemistry, especially the strongly alkaline pH. Normal pH values for these lakes are: Malawi, 7.7-8.6; Tanganyika, 8.6-9.2; and Victoria, 7.1-9.0.

The cichlids of these lakes have undergone an explosive evolution that has become a major research topic among ichthyologists today. The term "species flock" has been applied to the cichlids of these lakes as well as other fishes. The result of the evolutionary trends gives the aquarist a wide variety of diverse species to choose from. In Lake Tanganyika is found the largest cichlid, *Boulengerochromis microlepis,* growing to a length of 90 cm or more. Lake Tanganyika also provides some of the smallest cichlid species that grow no larger than 3.5 cm and live in abandoned snail shells. These shell-dwellers have become very popular in the hobby and are the current rage. Also found in Lake Tanganyika are small cichlids that act much like marine gobies and have for that reason been dubbed the goby cichlids. These are members of the genera *Eretmodus, Tanganicodus,* and *Spathodus.* The most speciose genus in the lake is *Lamprologus,* its more than 40 species providing many aquarium favorites, among which are *L. brichardi, L. compressiceps, L. sexfasciatus,* and the shell-dwellers, all of which belong to this genus. One genus, *Julidochromis,* contains only a half dozen or so species, but all have been imported for the aquarium trade. One of the challenges of Lake Tanganyika is a still rather high-priced species called *Cyphotilapia frontosa.* It has been bred—but not very often—and there is still a demand for the progeny. Perhaps the leading species of Lake Tanganyika cichlid as far as aquarists are concerned is *Tropheus moorii.* This species has evolved a myriad of color patterns, and new color varieties are being imported as fast as they are discovered.

Lake Malawi is no laggard in the provision of aquarium favorites. The cichlid fauna is generally divided (for convenience) into the

*Haplochromis* species and the mbuna or rock-dwelling cichlids made up of a number of genera. Somewhere in between these are the peacocks of the genera *Aulonocara* and *Trematocranus*. Although more closely related to the *Haplochromis* species, they are found around the rocks and aquarists have given them honorary mbuna status. *Haplochromis moorii* is perhaps comparable to Lake Tanganyika's *Cyphotilapia frontosa* in desirability and providing a challenge to aquarists. The diversity of the *Haplochromis* species surpasses by far that of the *Lamprologus* species of Lake Tanganyika. Malawi boasts more than 100 species of *Haplochromis*, with more in the process of being discovered and described. It is from this genus that the more recent new imports come. They dazzle the aquarist mainly with blues with overtones of violet and green. One species is even referred to as "electric blue." Several species of mbuna have evolved color variations that rival those of *Tropheus moorii*. Of these, perhaps the best known is one of the earlier imports, *Pseudotropheus zebra*; not far behind are *Pseudotropheus tropheops* and the two species of *Labeotropheus*.

The lake cichlids are mostly easy to keep, hardy, and good spawners. As long as aquarists are able to accommodate their need for a very alkaline pH, lots of room, and plenty of rockwork caves (especially for the mbuna), they should have no problem. Food is no problem although it is often forgotten that many of the lake species feed mainly on plant material and should receive at least some vegetable matter in their diets. Tanks with good algal growth are strongly recommended, and rearing tanks with algae are almost a must. Of course there are all kinds of feeding adaptations in the lake cichlids (including scale-eaters, eye-biters, sand-sifters, leaf-scrapers, etc.), but none seems to pose too much of a problem for aquarists.

There are basically two different reproductive types in the lakes, mouthbrooders and substrate-spawners. Mouthbrooders are by far the most common, especially in Lakes Victoria and Malawi. Although Lake Tanganyika has its share of mouthbrooders, most of the species (including all known *Lamprologus* species) are substrate-spawners. The mouthbrooders all spawn in a more or less similar manner, although there are some variations on this theme. The female is courted by the male and a site is selected for egg deposition. All other fishes are generally evicted from the area, in some cases meaning driven from the tank itself or killed outright. The eggs are laid "cichlid fashion" on a flat surface or in a pit in the sand and are fertilized immediately by the male as the two fish circle each other. By the time the female comes back to the eggs she takes them up in her mouth. This continues until all eggs are shed by the female and ensconced in her buccal cavity. Some males will guard the female but others will ignore her once spawning is completed, depending on the species and sometimes even on the individual. Aquarists generally remove the brooding female to a brooding tank where she will be safe from the attacks of other fishes or the advances of the amorous male. In about three weeks the fry are released from the mother's mouth and are able to fend for themselves. The female is ready, at least for a week or so, to accept the fry back into her mouth in the presence of some suspected danger. Most females do not eat during the incubation period, so females should be kept away from the tank containing the males until they have had time to build up their strength again. Aquarists with a nervous disposition or who wish to spare the female the long incubation period will strip the eggs from her mouth and return her to her original tank right away. The eggs are hatched artificially next to gentle aeration. Most spawnings of mouthbrooders do not provide a great number of eggs—somewhere in the neighborhood of 50 or so is relatively common.

The substrate-spawners spawn in a manner typical for cichlids. After courtship and cleaning of a substrate, the female lays a string of eggs and the male follows, fertilizing them. Once the female has become depleted she or the male or both will stand guard over them until they hatch and become free-swimming. The choice of site depends a great deal upon the species involved. Some spawn in depressions or pits dug in the sand, some on a flat portion of a rock or leaf, and some hide their eggs on the roof or floor of caves, well protected from the prying eyes of other fishes.

Haplochromis tetrastigma

Haplochromis tetrastigma

Haplochromis "Electric Blue"

Haplochromis sp.

Haplochromis annectens

Haplochromis "Electric Blue"

Haplochromis fenestratus (female)

Haplochromis fenestratus (male)

**Plate #295**

*(Plates #295 through #325 are of Cichlids of Lake Malawi)*

457

*Haplochromis jacksoni*

*Haplochromis cf. chrysonotus*

*Haplochromis chrysonotus*

*Haplochromis cf. chrysonotus*

*Haplochromis sp.*

*Haplochromis sp.*

*Haplochromis nitidus*

*Haplochromis tetrastigma*

*Plate #296*

458

*Haplochromis stonemani*

*Haplochromis hennydaviesae*

*Haplochromis auromarginatus*

*Haplochromis longimanus*

*Haplochromis eucinostomus*

*Haplochromis decorus*

*Haplochromis argyrosoma*

*Haplochromis nkatae?*

**Plate #297**

*Haplochromis nototaenia* (female)

*Haplochromis nototaenia* (male)

*Haplochromis pholidophorus*

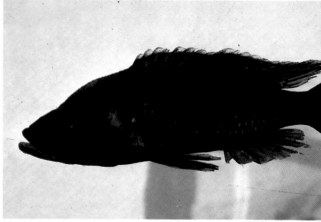

*Haplochromis woodi*

*Haplochromis woodi?*

*Haplochromis modestus*

*Haplochromis macrostoma* (juv.)

*Plate #298*

*Haplochromis macrostoma* (adult)

460

*Haplochromis plagiotaenia*

*Haplochromis* sp.

*Haplochromis* sp.

*Haplochromis mollis?*

*Haplochromis subocularis*

*Haplochromis lepturus*

*Haplochromis placodon* (female)

*Haplochromis placodon* (male)

*Plate #299*

*Haplochromis sphaerodon* (male)

*Haplochromis sphaerodon* (female)

*Haplochromis obtusus*

*Haplochromis anaphyrmus*

*Haplochromis sp.*

*Haplochromis lateristriga*

*Haplochromis melanotaenia*

*Haplochromis sp.*

**Plate #300**

462

*Haplochromis nigritaeniatus*

*Haplochromis similis* (male)

*Haplochromis cf fenestratus*

*Haplochromis cf fenestratus*

*Haplochromis spilonotus*

*Haplochromis strigatus*

*Haplochromis virginalis*

*Haplochromis labrosus*

**Plate #301**

463

*Haplochromis compressiceps*

*Haplochromis compressiceps*

*Haplochromis kiwinge*

*Haplochromis cf. labridens*

*Haplochromis labridens*

*Haplochromis cf. taeniolatus*

*Haplochromis taeniolatus* (female)

**Plate #302**

*Haplochromis taeniolatus*

*Haplochromis moorii*

*Haplochromis moorii*

Haplochromis electra

Haplochromis electra

Haplochromis johnstoni

Haplochromis callipterus

Haplochromis rostratus (juv.)

**Plate #303**

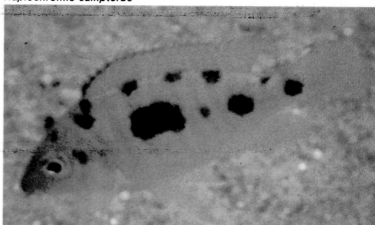

Haplochromis tetrastigma

465

*Haplochromis venustus*

*Haplochromis venustus*

*Haplochromis mloto*

*Haplochromis mloto*

*Haplochromis* cf. *euchilus* (juv.)

*Haplochromis* cf. *euchilus* (adult)

*Haplochromis euchilus* (juv.)

*Haplochromis euchilus* (adult)

*Plate #304*

*Haplochromis livingstoni*

*Haplochromis livingstoni*

*Haplochromis fuscotaeniatus (juv.)*

*Haplochromis fuscotaeniatus*

*Haplochromis polystigma*

*Haplochromis polystigma*

*Haplochromis linni + Haplochromis polystigma*

*Haplochromis linni*

**Plate #305**

467

All fishes on this page are of the *Labidochromis/Melanochromis textilis/exasperatus/joanjohnsonae* complex.

*Plate #306*

*Pseudotropheus tropheops*

*Pseudotropheus tropheops*

*Pseudotropheus tropheops (white form)*

*Pseudotropheus novemfasciatus*

*Pseudotropheus sp.*

*Iodotropheus sprengerae*

*Gephyrochromis lawsi*

*Gephyrochromis moorii*

**Plate #307**

469

All photos on this page are of morphs of *Pseudotropheops tropheops.*

*Plate #308*

470

*Pseudotropheus aurora*

*Pseudotropheus* sp.

*Pseudotropheus* sp.

*Pseudotropheus crabro*

*Pseudotropheus microstoma*

*Pseudotropheus tropheops*

*Pseudotropheus tropheops*

*Pseudotropheus tropheops*

**Plate #309**

471

*Pseudotropheus elongatus* (var.)

*Pseudotropheus elongatus* (var.)

*Pseudotropheus elongatus*

*Pseudotropheus* sp.

*Pseudotropheus brevis* (female)

*Pseudotropheus brevis* (male)

*Pseudotropheus elegans*

*Pseudotropheus elegans* (juv.)

**Plate #310**

*Pseudotropheus lanisticola*

*Pseudotropheus livingstonii*

*Pseudotropheus "eduardi"*

*Pseudotropheus "eduardi"*

*Pseudotropheus* sp.

*Pseudotropheus tropheops*

*Pseudotropheus* sp.

*Pseudotropheus* sp.

*Plate #311*

473

*Pseudotropheus zebra* (var.)

*Pseudotropheus zebra* (var.)

*Pseudotropheus zebra* (var.)

*Pseudotropheus zebra* (var.)

*Pseudotropheus livingstonii*

*Pseudotropheus livingstonii*

*Pseudotropheus lombardoi* (female)

*Pseudotropheus lombardoi* (male)

*Plate #312*

474

All photos on this page are of morphs of *Pseudotropheus zebra*

*Plate #313*

475

*Pseudotropheus zebra* (male)

*Pseudotropheus zebra* (male)

*Pseudotropheus zebra* (female)

*Pseudotropheus zebra* (female)

*Pseudotropheus zebra* (albino)

*Pseudotropheus zebra* (gold)

*Pseudotropheus zebra* (white)

*Pseudotropheus zebra* (pale yellow)

Plate #314

476

*Labeotropheus fuelleborni* (male)

*Labeotropheus fuelleborni* (female)

*Labeotropheus fuelleborni* (male)

*Labeotropheus fuelleborni* (male)

*Labeotropheus fuelleborni* (male)

*Labeotropheus fuelleborni* (female)

*Labeotropheus fuelleborni* (male)

*Labeotropheus fuelleborni* (female)

*Plate #315*

477

*Labeotropheus fuelleborni* (male)

*Labeotropheus fuelleborni* (male)

*Labeotropheus trewavasae*

*Labeotropheus trewavasae*

*Labeotropheus trewavasae* (female)

*Labeotropheus trewavasae* (female)

*Labeotropheus trewavasae* (male)

*Labeotropheus trewavasae* (male)

*Plate #316*

Labidochromis caeruleus

Labidochromis caeruleus

Labidochromis fryeri

Labidochromis "freibergi"

Labidochromis sp.

Labidochromis sp.

Labidochromis vellicans

Labidochromis mathothoi

*Plate #317*

479

*Cynotilapia afra*

*Cynotilapia afra*

*Cynotilapia sp.*

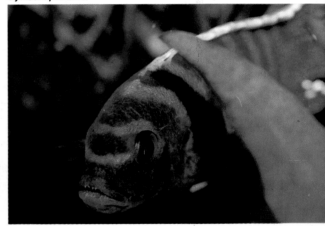

*Cynotilapia sp.*

*Cynotilapia sp.*

*Cynotilapia afra (var.)*

*Cynotilapia axelrodi (male)*

*Cynotulapia axelrodi (female)*

**Plate #318**

*Melanochromis simulans* (male)

*Melanochromis simulans* (female)

*Melanochromis vermivorus* (female)

*Melanochromis vermivorus* (male)

*Melanochromis vermivorus*

*Labidochromis* sp.

*Labidochromis* sp.

*Labidochromis* sp.

*Plate #319*

*Melanochromis auratus* (male)

*Melanochromis auratus* (female)

*Melanochromis auratus* (var.) (male)

*Melanochromis auratus*

*Melanochromis chipokee* (male)

*Melanochromis chipokee* (female)

*Melanochromis johanni* (var.)

*Melanochromis johanni* (var.) (female)

Plate #320

482

*Melanochromis johanni* (male)

*Melanochromis johanni* (female)

*Melanochromis johanni* (male)

*Melanochromis johanni* (male)

*Melanochromis melanopterus*

*Melanochromis parallelus*

*Melanochromis perspicax*

*Melanochromis perspicax*

*Plate #321*

483

*Chilotilapia rhoadesii*

*Chilotilapia rhoadesii*

*Cleithrochromis bowleyi*

*Hemitilapia oxyrhynchus*

*Petrotilapia tridentiger*

*Petrotilapia nigra*

*Genyochromis mento*

*Genyochromis mento*

**Plate #322**

484

*Lethrinops lethrinus*

*Lethrinops parvidens*

*Lethrinops polli*

*Lethrinops* sp.

*Rhamphochromis* sp.

*Rhamphochromis macrophthalmus*

*Diplotaxodon argenteus*

*Doplotaxodon ecclesi*

*Plate #323*

485

*Trematocranus* sp.

*Trematocranus peterdaviesi*

*Lethrinops aurita*

*Lethrinops christyi*

*Lethrinops furcicauda*

*Lethrinops furcicauda*

**Lethrinops gossei** (male)

**Lethrinops gossei** (female)

*Plate #324*

*Aulonocara nyassae* (orange shoulder)

*Aulonocara nyassae* (female)

*Aulonocara nyassae* (Peacock Blue)

*Aulonocara nyassae* (Maleri gold)

*Aulonocara* sp. (Night Aulonocara)

*Aulonocara* sp. (white dorsal edge)

*Trematocranus jacobfreibergi* (male)

*Trematocranus jacobfreibergi* (female)

*Plate #325*

487

*Astatotilapia bloyeti*

*Aulonocranus dewindti*

*Callochromis macrops macrops* (female)

*Callochromis macrops* (Tanzania)

*Chalinochromis brichardi*

*Chalinochromis brichardi*

*Chalinochromis n. sp.*

*Chalinochromis n. sp.* (juv.)

**Plate #326**
*( Plates #326 through #357 are of Cichlids of Lake Tanganyika)*

*Julidochromis regani*

*Julidochromis regani* (var.)

*Julidochromis regani* (melanistic)

*Julidochromis regani* "Kigoma"

*Chalinochromis brichardi*

*Chalinochromis brichardi*

*Chalinochromis brichardi* "bifrenatus"

*Chalinochromis brichardi* "Dhoboi"

**Plate #327**

*Julidochromis ornatus*

*Julidochromis ornatus*

*Julidochromis transcriptus*

*Julidochromis ornatus/transcriptus*

*Julidochromis dickfeldi*

*Julidochromis ornatus/transcriptus*

*Julidochromis marlieri*

*Julidochromis marlieri*

*Plate #328*

490

*Julidochromis dickfeldi*

*Julidochromis dickfeldi* (southern form)

*Julidochromis marlieri* (Zaire)

*Julidochromis marlieri*

*Julidochromis ornatus* (Uvira form)

*Julidochromis* n. sp. (southern coast)

*Julidochromis* sp. (southern coast)

*Julidochromis* sp. (southern coast)

*Plate #329*

*Cyphotilapis frontosa*

*Cyphotilapia frontosa* (juv.)

*Cyprichromis brieni*

*Cyprichromis brieni* (subadult)

*Eretmodus cyanostictus*

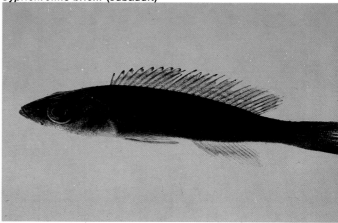

*Cyprichromis brieni* (juv.)

*Spathodus marlieri*

*Spathodus erythrodon*

**Plate #330**

*Petrochromis fasciolatus*

*Petrochromis polyodon*

*Perissodus paradoxus*

*Perissodus straeleni*

*Grammatotria lemairei*

*Perissodus microlepis*

*Ophthalmochromis ventralis*

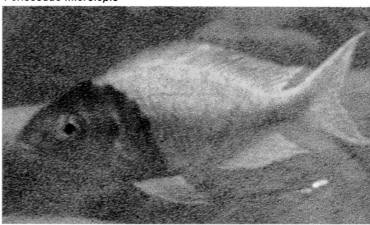

*Ophthalmus ventralis ventralis*

*Plate #331*

493

Petrochromis trewavasae (male)

Petrochromis trewavasae

Petrochromis n. sp. (Nyanza Lac var.)

Petrochromis n. sp.

Petrochromis orthognathus

Simochromis curvifrons

Simochromis curvifrons

Simochromis curvifrons

Simochromis babaulti (var.)

Simochromis babaulti

Simochromis curvifrons

Simochromis babaulti

Petrochromis sp.

Simochromis diagramma

Astatoreochromis straeleni

Simochromis dardennei

*Plate #333*

495

Simochromis diagramma (southern)

Simochromis diagramma (southern)

Simochromis n. sp.

Spathodus marlieri

Telmatochromis bifrenatus (adult)

Telmatochromis bifrenatus (subadult)

Telmatochromis temporalis (freak)

Telmatochromis vittatus

*Plate #334*

*Petrochromis fasciolatus*

*Petrochromis* sp.

*Telmatochromis vittatus*

*Reganochromis calliurus*

*Telmatochromis bifrenatus?*

*Telmatochromis caninus*

*Triglachromis otostigma*

*Telmatochromis temporalis*

**Plate #335**

497

*Tropheus brichardi*

*Tropheus brichardi "Blue-eyed Tropheus"*

*Tropheus duboisi (narrow white band)*

*Tropheus duboisi (juv.)*

*Tropheus duboisi (wide yellow band)*

*Tropheus duboisi (no band)*

*Tropheus polli*

*Tropheus polli*

*Plate #336*

*Tropheus duboisi* (broad band)

*Tropheus duboisi* (Bemba var.)

*Tropheus duboisi* (juv.)

*Tropheus* sp. (Mpulungu var.)

*Tropheus moorii* ("Moliro" dom. male)

*Tropheus moorii* ("Moliro" dom. male)

*Tropheus moorii kasabae* (Kalambo var.)

*Tropheus moorii kasabae* (Kala var.)

*Plate #337*

*Tropheus moorii* ("Kigongo-Makobola Bronze" var.)

*Tropheus duboisi?* ("Blue-faced" var.)

*Tropheus moorii* "Uvira-Kalunda"

*Tropheus moorii?* (Flat-nose var.)

*Tropheus moorii* "Chipimba Cape"

*Tropheus moorii* "Chipimba Cape"

*Tropheus brichardi*

*Tropheus moorii* "Nyanza-Lac" var.?

*Plate #338*

*Telmatochromis* n. sp. (Kalemie)

*Tropheus moorii*

*Tropheus moorii* (green w/orange dorsal)

*Tropheus moorii* (orange/black var.)

*Tropheus moorii* (orange/black)

*Tropheus moorii* (black/red)

*Tropheus moorii* (cherry-cheek)

*Tropheus moorii* (Cape Banza var.)

**Plate #339**

*Tropheus moorii* (Kiriza var.)

*Tropheus moorii* (Kiriza male)

*Tropheus moorii* (Kiriza or Kaiser II)

*Tropheus moorii* (Kiriza female)

*Tropheus moorii* (Bemba orange)

*Tropheus moorii* (fed on algal diet!)

*Tropheus moorii* "annectens" (juv.)

*Tropheus moorii* "annectens" (Kaniosha)

**Plate #340**

*Tropheus moorii* "annectens" (Kaniosha)

*Tropheus moorii* "annectens" (Kaniosha juv.)

*Tropheus moorii* "annectens" (Musimu)

*Tropheus moorii* "annectens"

*Tropheus moorii* "annectens" (canary cheek)

*Tropheus moorii* "annectens" (juv.)

*Tropheus moorii* "annectens" (Kaniosha)

*Tropheus moorii* "annectens" (Kitas a var.)

*Plate #341*

503

*Tropheus moorii* "Bemba Orange"

*Tropheus moorii* ("Red/Black" var.)

*Tropheus moorii* "Kamba Bay"

*Tropheus moorii* "Kamba Bay" (juv.)

*Tropheus moorii*

*Tropheus moorii* "Rainbow" or "Chaitika Cape"

*Tropheus moorii* (SW type)

504

*Tropheus moorii* "Kabeyeye"

**Plate #342**

*Tropheus moorii* ("Murago" var.)

*Tropheus moorii* (juv. 4 cm. long)

*Tropheus moorii* ("Murago" adult)

*Tropheus* sp. (green var.)

*Tropheus moorii* (lemon striped)

*Xenotilapia* sp.

*Xenotilapia flavipinnis*

*Xenotilapia melanogenys*

Plate #343

505

*Xenitilapia spilopterus*

*Aulonocranus dewindti*

*Xenotilapia flavipinnis*

*Xenotilapia sima*

*Xenotilapia ochrogenys*

*Xenotilapia sp. (flavipinnis?)*

Pierre Brichard and fish photo setup

*Plate #344*

506

Rocky point of land in one of the Rift Lakes

Haplochromis pfefferi

Tanganicodus irsacae

Haplochromis horei

Haplochromis benthicola

Limnochromis auritus

Cardiopharynx schoutedeni?

Lobochilotes labiatus

Lobochilotes labiatus

Plate #345

507

*Haplochromis burtoni*

*Aulonocranus dewindti*

*Boulengerochromis microlepis*

*Bathybates ferox*

*Callochromis macrops melanostigma*

*Callochromis pleurospilus*

*Cardiopharynx schoutedeni*

*Ophthalmochromis ventralis*

**Plate #346**

508

*Cyprichromis leptosoma* (southern)

*Cyprichromis nigripinnis*

*Cardiopharynx schoutedeni*

*Trematocara* n. sp.

*Haplochromis benthicola* (female)

*Haplochromis benthicola* (male)

*Haplotaxodon microlepis*

*Haplotaxodon microlepis* (male)

**Plate #347**

509

*Lamprologus brichardi*

*Lamprologus brichardi*

*Lamprologus sp. "Magarae"*

*Lamprologus brevis*

*Lamprologus callipterus*

*Lamprologus attenuatus (nuptial colors)*

*Lamprologus toae*

*Lamprologus caudopunctatus*

Plate #348

510

Lamprologus brichardi (var.)

Lamprologus brichardi (Ubwari)

Lamprologus buscheri

Lamprologus cunningtoni

Lamprologus n. sp.

Lamprologus n. sp.

Lamprologus calvus

Lamprologus compressiceps (Ubwari)

*Plate #349*

511

*Lamprologus compressiceps*

*Lamprologus calvus*

*Lamprologus compressiceps* (var.)

*Lamprologus falcicula*

*Lamprologus furcifer* (orange var.)

*Lamprologus leleupi melas*

**Lamprologus leleupi?**

**Lamprologus leleupi**

*Plate #350*

512

*Lamprologus elongatus*

*Lamprologus cunningtoni*

*Lamprologus furcifer*

*Lamprologus sp.*

*Lamprologus leleupi*

*Lamprologus leleupi*

*Lamprologus meeli*

*Lamprologus lemairei*

*Plate #351*

513

*Lamprologus niger*

*Lamprologus obscurus*

*Lamprologus moorii* (yellow form)

*Lamprologus moorii* (black form)

*Lamprologus niger?*

*Lamprologus mustax*

*Lamprologus falcicula*

*Lamprologus mondabu*

**Plate #352**

*Lamprologus lemairei* (juv.)

*Lamprologus mondabu*

*Lamprologus mustax* (female)

*Lamprologus mustax* (male)

*Lamprologus multifasciatus*

*Lamprologus niger*

*Lamprologus ocellatus*

*Lamprologus ocellatus* w/parasite

*Plate #353*

*Perissodus straeleni*

*Lamprologus tretocephalus*

*Lamprologus tretocephalus* (subadult)

*Cyphotilapia frontosa*

Cyphotilapia frontosa

Lamprologus tretocephalus

*Cyphotilapia frontosa* (juv.)

*Lamprologus fasciatus*

**Plate #354**

*Lamprologus tetracanthus*

*Lamprologus tetracanthus*

*Lamprologus savoryi*

*Lamprologus sexfasciatus*

*Lamprologus pleuromaculatus*

*Lamprologus prochilus*

*Lamprologus ocellatus*

*Lamprologus ornatipinnis*

**Plate #355**

517

This remarkable series of photographs shows spawning behavior of *Lamprologus brevis*, one of the shell-dwelling cichlids of Lake Tanganyika. The two upper photos at left show a sub-adult male posturing, and in the two photos above right a fully adult male is shown with his spawning partner immediately before (upper photo) and after the female has begun to enter the shell. Below left the male is shown before entering the shell himself, while below right he is shown during stages of his entrance.

*Plate #356*

Haplochromis benthicola

Lamprologus sexfasciatus (yellow race)

Lamprologus attenuatus

Lamprologus elongatus

Lamprologus profundicola

Lamprologus profundicola (juv.)

Ophthalmotilapia nasutus

Ophthalmotilapia nasutus

*Plate #357*

519

*Haplochromis macrognathus*

*Haplochromis sauvagei*

*Haplochromis dichrourus*

*Haplochromis cinereus*

*Haplochromis riponianus*

*Haplochromis brownae*

*Haplochromis lacrimosus*

*Haplochromis lacrymosus*

## Plate #358
*(All cichlids shown on this plate are from Lake Victoria)*

*Pseudocrenilabrus philander* male

*Pseudocrenilabrus philander* female

*Pseudocrenilabrus multicolor* male

*Pseudocrenilabrus multicolor* female

*Tylochromis lateralis*

*Tylochromis polylepis*

*Stomatepia mariae*

*Serranochromis robustus*

**Plate #359**

*Cyathopharynx furcifer*

*Cyathopharynx furcifer*

*Ophthalmotilapia ventralis*

*Ophthalmotilapia ventralis*

*Ophthalmotilapia nasutus*

*Ophthalmotilapia nasutus*

*Ophthalmotilapia ventralis*

Plate #359A

*Ophthalmotilapia nasutus*

*Sarotherodon leucostictus*

*Sarotherodon leucostictus*

*Sarotherodon mossambica*

*Sarotherodon mossambica*

*Sarotherodon mossambica*

*Sarotherodon mossambica*

*Sarotherodon sp.*

*Orthochromis cf. machodoi*

*Plate #359B*

*Tilapia kottae*

*Sarotherodon grahami*

*Tilapia shirana*

*Tilapia shirana*

*Tilapia pungo*

*Tilapia kumba*

*Tilapia aurea*

*Tilapia leucosticta*

**Plate #360**

524

Tilapia mariae

Tilapia mariae

Tilapia tholloni

Tilapia sp.

Tilapia rendalli

Tilapia nilotica

Tilapia sp.

Tilapia sp.

*Plate #361*

525

*Sarotherodon mossambicus*

*Sarotherodon mossambicus*

*Tilapia ovalis*

*Tilapia* sp.

*Tilapia* sp.

*Tilapia* sp.

*Tilapia* sp.

*Tilapia* sp.

*Plate #362*

526

*Steatocranus casuarius*

*Steatocranus casuarius*

*Steatocranus gibbiceps* juv.

*Steatocranus mpozoensis*

*Teleogramma brichardi*

*Teleogramma brichardi*

*Steatocranus tinanti*

*Steatocranus tinanti*

Plate #363

527

Pelvicachromis subocellatus

Pelvicachromis subocellatus

Pelvicachromis subocellatus

Pelvicachromis subocellatus

Pelvicachromis humilis (Kenema)

Pelvicachromis subocellatus

Pelvicachromis humilis (Kasewe)

Pelvicachromis humilis (Kasewe)

Plate #363A

Nanochromis dimidiatus

Nanochromis dimidiatus

Nanochromis dimidiatus

Nanochromis dimidiatus

Nanochromis splendens females?

Nanochromis splendens male

Nanochromis parilius

Nanochromis parilius

Plate #364

*Pelvicachromis pulcher*

*Pelvicachromis pulcher*

*Pelvicachromis aff. pulcher*

*Pelvicachromis aff. pulcher*

*Pelvicachromis pulcher*

*Pelvicachromis pulcher*

*Pelvicachromis pulcher*

*Pelvicachromis pulcher*

Plate #364A

*Pelvicachromis aff. pulcher*

*Pelvicachromis aff. pulcher*

*Pelvicachromis aff. pulcher*

*Pelvicachromis taeniatus* (Calabar)

*Pelvicachromis taeniatus* (Lobe)

*Pelvicachromis taeniatus* (Lobe)

*Pelvicachromis taeniatus* (Kienke)

*Pelvicachromis taeniatus* (Kienke)

Plate #364B

*Pelvicachromis roloffi*

*Pelvicachromis roloffi*

*Pelvicachromis taeniatus "klugei"*

*Pelvicachromis taeniatus "klugei"*

*Pelvicachromis taeniatus* striped anal

*Pelvicachromis subocellatus ?*

*Pelvicachromis taeniatus ?*

*Pelvicachromis taeniatus ?*

**Plate #365**

*Pelvicachromis pulcher* male yellow form

*Pelvicachromis pulcher* male red form

*Pelvicachromis pulcher* female yellow

*Pelvicachromis pulcher* female red

*Pelvicachromis* sp. aff. *pulcher*

*Pelvicachromis* sp. aff. *pulcher*

*Pelvicachromis pulcher* pink var.

*Pelvicachromis pulcher*

*Plate #366*

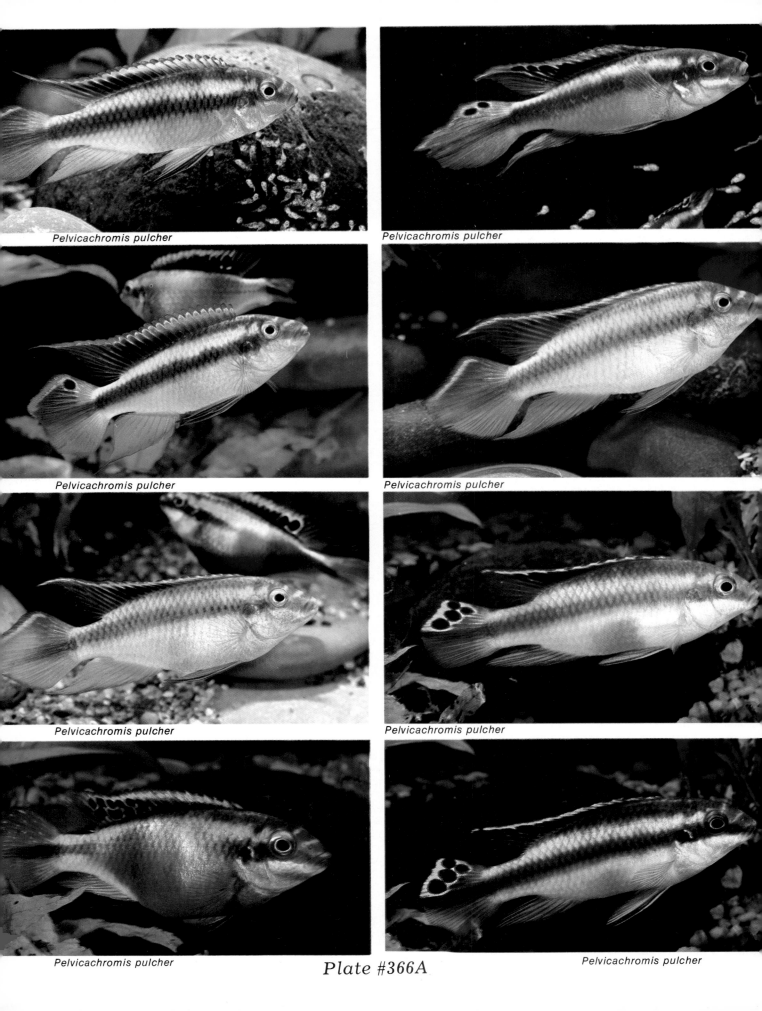

*Pelvicachromis pulcher*

*Pelvicachromis pulcher*

*Pelvicachromis pulcher*

*Pelvicachromis pulcher*

*Pelvicachromis pulcher*

*Pelvicachromis pulcher*

*Pelvicachromis pulcher*

Plate #366A

*Pelvicachromis pulcher*

*Pelvicachromis taeniatus* (Muyuka)

*Pelvicachromis taeniatus* (Muyuka)

*Pelvicachromis taeniatus* (Moliwe)

*Pelvicachromis taeniatus* (Moliwe)

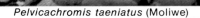
*Pelvicachromis taeniatus* (Nigeria)

*Pelvicachromis taeniatus* (Nigeria)

*Pelvicachromis* aff. *subocellatus*

*Pelvicachromis* aff. *subocellatus*

Plate #366B

Chromidotilapia batesii

Chromidotilapia batesii

Chromidotilapia guentheri

Chromidotilapia guentheri

Chromidotilapia guentheri var.

Chromidotilapia kingsleyi

Thysia ansorgii

Thysia ansorgii

*Plate #367*

536

*Hemichromis lifalili*

*Hemichromis lifalili*

*Hemichromis bimaculatus* (female)

*Hemichromis bimaculatus* (male)

*Hemichromis bimaculatus* var.

*Hemichromis bimaculatus* var.

*Hemichromis thomasi*

*Hemichromis thomasi*

*Plate #368*

537

*Hemichromis cristatus*                    *Hemichromis cristatus*

*Hemichromis cristatus*                    *Hemichromis cristatus*

*Hemichromis bimaculatus*                  *Hemichromis bimaculatus*

*Hemichromis paynei*                       *Hemichromis paynei*

*Plate #368A*

*Lamprologus leloupi*

*Lamprologus leleupi* (Lunangwa)

*Lamprologus gracilis*

*Lamprologus olivaceus*

*Lamprologus "Magarae"*

*Lamprologus compressiceps "Orange"*

*Julidochromis ornatus*

*Julidochromis* sp. (Kapampa)

*Plate #368B*

*Hemichromis fasciatus*

*Hemichromis fasciatus*

*Hemichromis elongatus*

*Hemichromis elongatus*

*Hemichromis elongatus? juvenile*

*Hemichromis elongatus*

*Lamprologus mocquardi*

*Lamprologus congolensis*

**Plate #369**

540

Ctenopoma acutirostre

Ctenopoma acutirostre

Ctenopoma ansorgii

Ctenopoma ansorgii

Ctenopoma congicum

Ctenopoma congicum

Ctenopoma multispinis

Ctenopoma kingsleyae

*Plate #370*

541

*Tropheus moorii kasabae* (Lupota)

*Tropheus* sp. (Moba)

*Tropheus* sp. (Mtoto)

*Petrochromis* "Golden"

*Cyprichromis* sp. (Zaire)

*Cyprichromis* cf. *leptosoma*

*Callochromis macrops melanostigma* (nest)

*Plate #370A*

*Cyprichromis* cf. *leptosoma*

*Ctenopoma* cf. *argentoventer*

*Ctenopoma* aff. *ocellatum*

*Ctenopoma* cf. *oxyrhynchus*

*Ctenopoma acutirostre*

*Ctenopoma maculata*

*Ctenopoma petheri*

*Ctenopoma ansorgii*

*Ctenopoma ansorgii*

Plate #370B

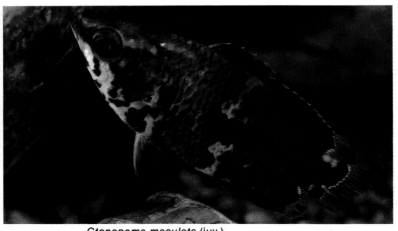

Ctenopoma maculata (juv.)

Ctenopoma maculata

Ctenopoma nanum

Ctenopoma nanum

Ctenopoma muriei

Ctenopoma nigropannosum

Ctenopoma oxyrhynchus

Ctenopoma ocellatum

*Plate #371*

*Channa obscurus*

*Glossogobius giuris*

*Periophthalmus papilio*

*Periophthalmus barbarus*

*Periophthalmus barbarus*

*Periophthalmus barbarus*

*Lates niloticus*

*Lates microlepis*

**Plate #372**

545

*Ctenopoma damasi*

*Ctenopoma kingsleyi* (bottom)

*Ctenopoma multispinis*

*Ctenopoma multispinis*

*Ctenopoma multispinis*

*Sandelia capensis*

*Sandelia bainsii*

*Sandelia bainsii*

Plate #372A

Pelvicachromis roloffi

Pelvicachromis roloffi

Nanochromis parilius

Nanochromis parilius

Nanochromis caudifasciatus

Nanochromis caudifasciatus

Nanochromis robertsi

Nanochromis sp. (Zaire)

*Plate #372B*

*Mastacembelus frenatus*

*Mastacembelus moorii*

*Mastacembelus reticulatus*

*Mastacembelus ophidium*

*Mastacembelus ellipsifer*

*Mastacembelus tanganicae*

*Enneacampus ansorgii*

*Enneacampus ansorgii*

**Plate #373**

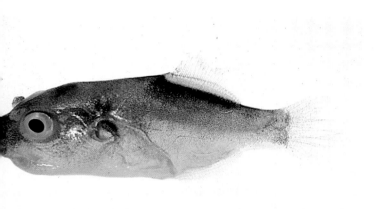

Chonerhinus naritus (juv.)

Chonerhinus naritus

Tetraodon mbu

Tetraodon miurus

Tetraodon schoutedeni

Tetraodon schoutedeni

Tetraodon duboisi

Bedotia geayi

Plate #374

549

Tetraodon miurus

Tetraodon miurus

Tetraodon fahaka

Tetraodon fahaka

Tetraodon mbu

Tetraodon fahaka

Tetraodon schoutedeni

Tetraodon schoutedeni

Plate #374A

# Southeast Asian Region

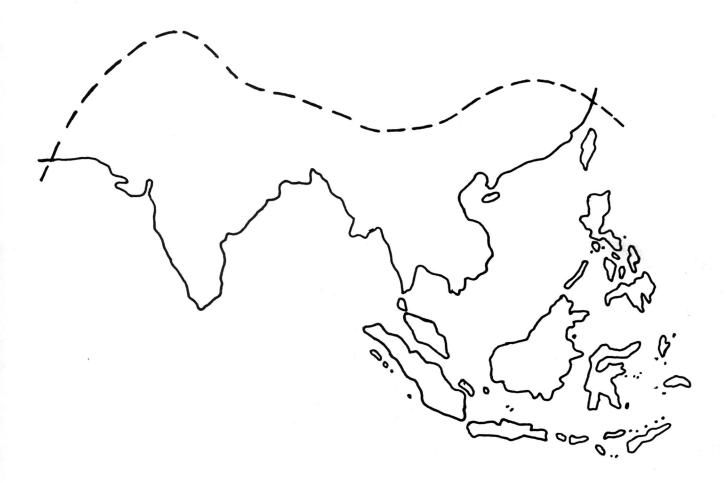

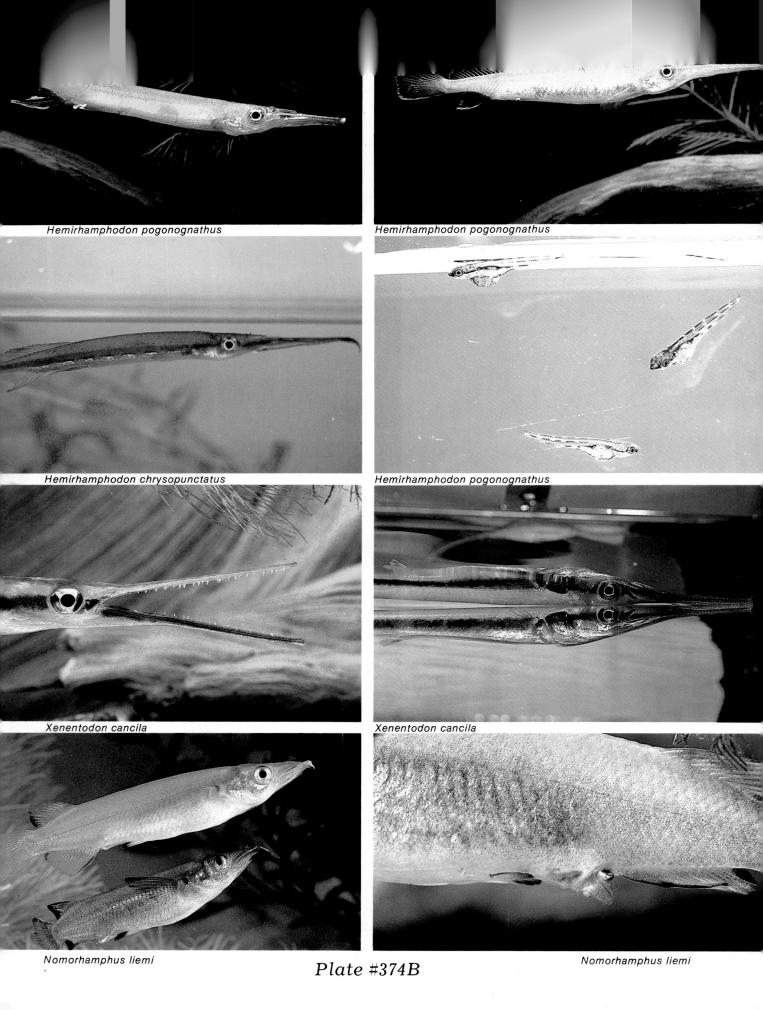

Hemirhamphodon pogonognathus

Hemirhamphodon pogonognathus

Hemirhamphodon chrysopunctatus

Hemirhamphodon pogonognathus

Xenentodon cancila

Xenentodon cancila

Nomorhamphus liemi

Nomorhamphus liemi

Plate #374B

*Scleropages formosus* (silver form)

*Scleropages formosus* (gold form)

*Scleropages formosus*

*Dermogenys pusillus?*

*Nomorhamphus liemi* (female)

*Nomorhamphus liemi* (male)

*Nomorhamphus liemi*

*Xenentodon cancila*

**Plate #375**

553

*Puntius conchonius*

*Puntius conchonius* var.

*Capoeta arulius*

*Puntius semifasciolatus*

*Puntius sachsi*

*Barbodes lateristriga*

*Capoeta tetrazona* (Albino)

*Capoeta tetrazona*

Plate #375A

Puntius nigrofasciatus

Puntius "Odessa"

Barbodes everetti

Capoeta oligolepis

Puntius filamentosus

Puntius lineatus

Barbodes pentazona

Plate #375B

*Acanthophthalmus javanicus*

*Acanthophthalmus anguillaris*

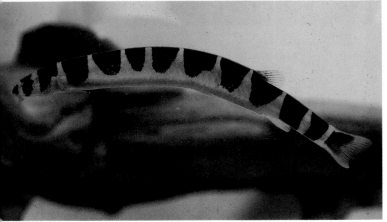

*Acanthophthalmus kuhlii*

*Acanthophthalmus myersi*

*Acanthophthalmus semicinctus*

*Acanthophthalmus shelfordi*

*Acanthophthalmus shelfordi*

*Acanthophthalmus myersi* var.

*Plate #376*

556

Botia beauforti

Botia berdmorei

Botia dario

Botia dario

Botia lohachata

Botia hymenophysa

Botia macracantha

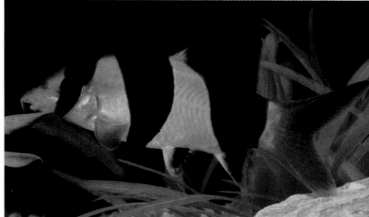
Botia macracantha

Plate #377

557

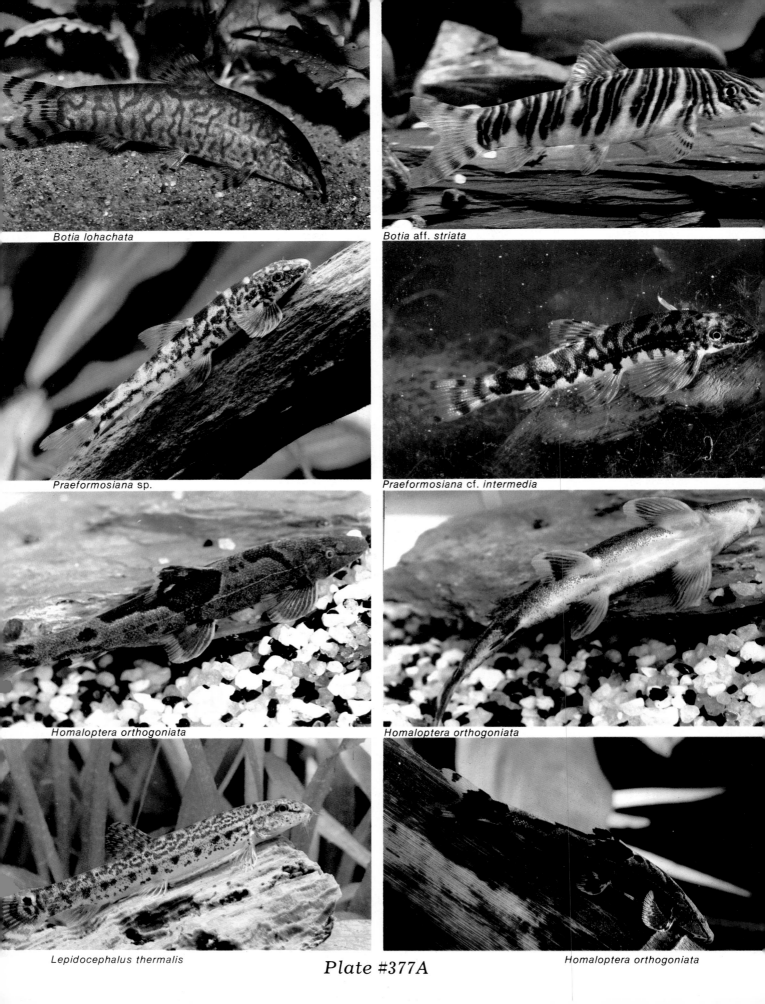

Botia lohachata

Botia aff. striata

Praeformosiana sp.

Praeformosiana cf. intermedia

Homaloptera orthogoniata

Homaloptera orthogoniata

Lepidocephalus thermalis

Plate #377A

Homaloptera orthogoniata

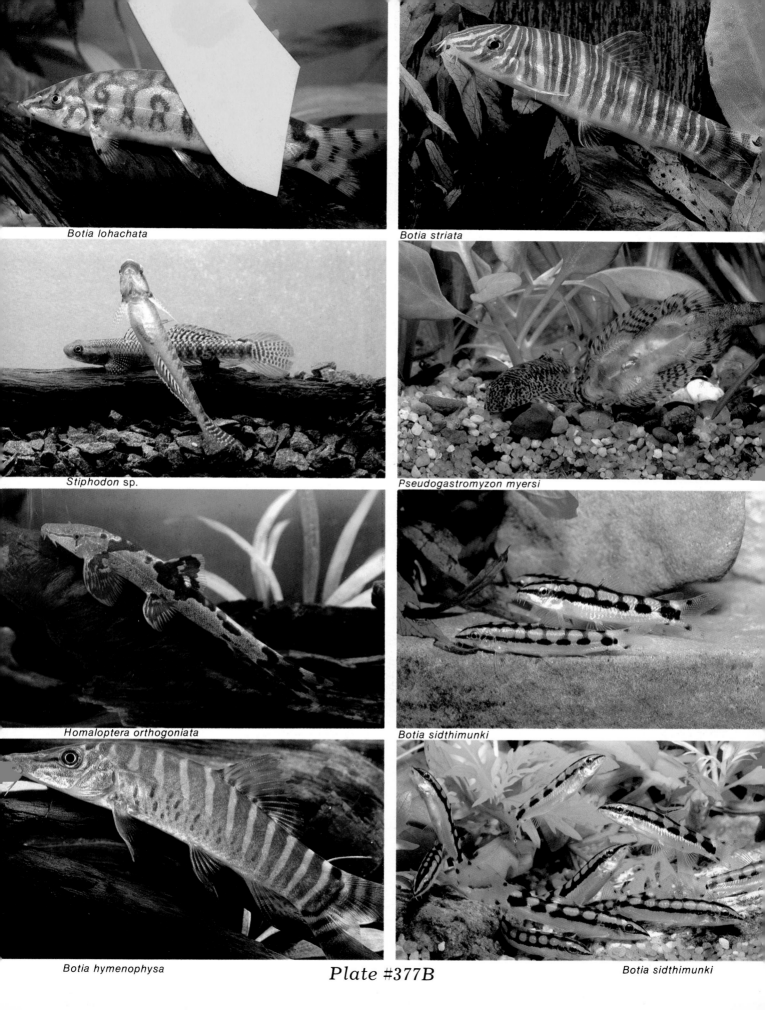

Botia lohachata

Botia striata

Stiphodon sp.

Pseudogastromyzon myersi

Homaloptera orthogoniata

Botia sidthimunki

Botia hymenophysa

Plate #377B

Botia sidthimunki

*Botia lecontei*

*Botia modesta*

*Botia morleti* (juvenile)

*Botia morleti*

*Botia sidthimunki*

*Botia sidthimunki*

*Botia sidthimunki* (var.)

*Botia sidthimunki* (var.)

**Plate #378**

Botia hymenophysa juv.

Botia morleti juv.

Botia hymenophysa? (var.)

Botia striata

Lepidocephalus thermalis

Lepidocephalus berdmorei

Lepidocephalus guntea

Lepidocephalus jonklaasi

**Plate #379**

561

*See plate #377*

*See plate #378*

*See plate #377*

### *Botia striata* Rao • Zebra Loach

RANGE: Southern India.
HABITS: Peaceful and lively; likes to be in a group of its own species.
WATER CONDITIONS: Soft, slightly acid water best, but does well in a variety of conditions. Temperature 20 to 25°C.
SIZE: Attains a length of about 6 cm in the aquarium; grows larger (10 cm) in nature.
FOOD REQUIREMENTS: Live foods, especially tubificid worms, are preferred, but it will accept normal aquarium substitutes.

### *Lepidocephalus thermalis* (Valenciennes) • Lesser Loach

RANGE: Over all of Sri Lanka below 1,600 feet and also southern India.
HABITS: Fond of still pools with an abundance of leaf debris in which it can burrow. Also found (? accidentally) in hot springs. One of the last fishes to die when a pool dries up.
WATER CONDITIONS: Not choosy. Should have clean, warm water but otherwise will tolerate most aquarium conditions.
SIZE: 40-50 mm.
FOOD REQUIREMENTS: Eats mostly small vegetable matter and debris, but will adjust to small insects and worms in the aquarium.

### *Lepidocephalus berdmorei* (Blyth) • Berdmore's Loach

RANGE: Apparently known only from Thailand and Burma.
HABITS: Likes to burrow into the bottom material and is not seen very often. A peaceful fish for a community aquarium.
WATER CONDITIONS: Slightly acid water of average hardness is acceptable. Water temperatures should be between 23 and 28°C. Water changes are recommended.
SIZE: Attains a length of at least 8 cm.
FOOD REQUIREMENTS: Mostly insect larvae (chironomids and mosquito larvae in aquaria) and worms are preferred.

### *Lepidocephalus guntea* (Hamilton-Buchanan) • Gunte

RANGE: India to the Near East.
HABITS: A shy fish that likes to burrow in the substrate. Peaceful and can be added to a community tank.
WATER CONDITIONS: Clean water that is slightly acid and medium hard is sufficient. Temperatures of 23-28°C are best. Water changes on a regular basis are beneficial.
SIZE: Attains a length of about 8-10 cm.
FOOD REQUIREMENTS: Feeds from the bottom, mainly on insects and their larvae (chironomids) and worms (tubificid worms).

### *Lepidocephalus jonklaasi* Deraniyagala • Jonklaas's Loach

RANGE: Endemic to Sri Lanka, where it is found in the Akuressa forest.
HABITS: Peaceful and suitable for a community tank. Likes to burrow and should have a suitable substrate. In nature it is found in shaded pools in hill streams where the bottoms have much leaf debris.
WATER CONDITIONS: Not critical. Slightly acid water at normal aquarium temperatures are sufficient. Regular water changes are recommended.
SIZE: Attains a length of about 7-9 cm.
FOOD REQUIREMENTS: A variety of foods that fall to the bottom are acceptable. Tubifex worms and chironomid larvae are preferred, and it should also have vegetable matter.

*Noemacheilus notostigma* Bleeker • Fighting Loach

RANGE: Sri Lanka.
HABITS: Best kept by themselves in pairs or several pairs in a large tank with a number of hiding places.
WATER CONDITIONS: Not critical, but the water should be clean. Temperature 24 to 27°C.
SIZE: To 8 cm.
FOOD REQUIREMENTS: Any kind of food accepted, but there should be live foods given at times.

*Nemacheilus botia* (Hamilton-Buchanan) •
Mottled Loach

RANGE: Upper India.
HABITS: Peaceful toward other fishes and will not harm plants. Are useful in cleaning up unwanted algae and food left by other fishes.
WATER CONDITIONS: Water should be slightly alkaline but not very hard. Temperature 75 to 80°.
SIZE: To 4½ inches.
FOOD REQUIREMENTS: Not at all fussy about foods. Should have some soft algae to pick at in addition to their regular diet.

*See Plate #379*

*Noemacheilus fasciatus* (Cuvier & Valenciennes) •
Barred Loach

RANGE: Sumatra, Java, Borneo.
HABITS: Best given a tank of their own; chooses and defends its own territories.
WATER CONDITIONS: Soft, slightly acid water. Temperature 24 to 26°C.
SIZE: To 9 cm.
FOOD REQUIREMENTS: Likes worms and other live foods, but not a fussy eater.

*Misgurnus mizolepis* Guenther • Chinese Fine-
scaled Loach

RANGE: Occurs over much of southern China south into northern Southeast Asia.
HABITS: A typical weatherfish, occurring in every type of waterbody from rivers to ditches. Survives drying well, as it can burrow into the bottom and also breathe atmospheric air.
WATER CONDITIONS: Although this species ranges south into tropical Asia, it is basically a cooler water fish and will survive well at 18°C and higher. Water conditions unimportant, but best kept clean.
SIZE: 10 to 21 cm. There are many described subspecies and varieties that differ greatly in adult size and color pattern.
FOOD REQUIREMENTS: Prefers small crustaceans, insect larvae, and worms, but will adjust to almost any type of diet. Some vegetable matter should be tried as well.

Noemacheilus notostigma (var.)

Noemacheilus notostigma

Noemacheilus cf. notostigma

Noemacheilus botia

Lepidocephalus thermalis

Lepidocephalus thermals (var.)

Noemacheilus fasciatus

*Plate #380*

Misgurnus mizolepis

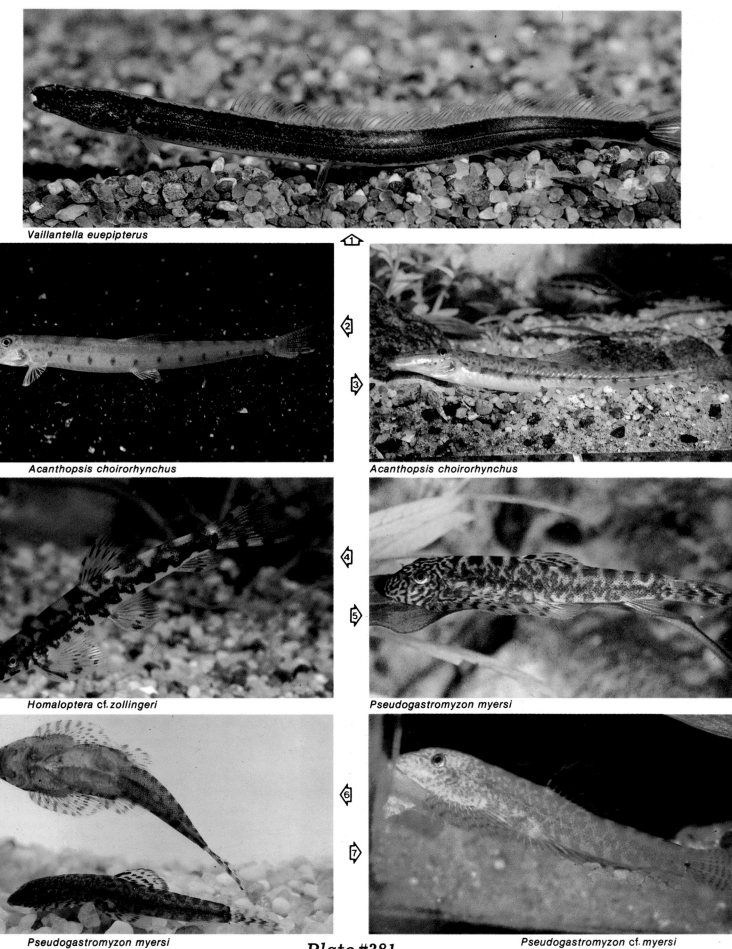

Vaillantella euepipterus

Acanthopsis choirorhynchus

Acanthopsis choirorhynchus

Homaloptera cf. zollingeri

Pseudogastromyzon myersi

Pseudogastromyzon myersi

Pseudogastromyzon cf. myersi

*Plate #381*

565

### *Vaillantella euepipterus* (Vaillant) • Chocolate Long-finned Loach

RANGE: Rivers of Borneo. A secretive fish that is seldom collected.

HABITS: In nature this odd species is a burrower in rapid streams, so it is not too easy to keep in the aquarium. The substrate must be of gravel smooth and soft enough to allow burrowing, yet there must be a current to provide heavily oxygenated water. Nocturnal, shy, and delicate; imported only by accident.

WATER CONDITIONS: Not choosy as long as it is clean and well-oxygenated. Can probably stand lower temperature than most loaches because of its stream habitat.

SIZE: 60-80 mm.

FOOD REQUIREMENTS: Feeds well on live tubifex worms and bloodworms of appropriate size.

### *Acanthopsis choirorhynchus* (Bleeker) • Long-nosed Loach

RANGE: Southeastern Asia, Sumatra, Borneo, Java; occurs in fresh water only.

HABITS: Mostly nocturnal; in the daylight hours it usually remains buried in the gravel with only its eyes showing.

WATER CONDITIONS: Neutral to slightly acid water. Temperature between 24 and 30°C.

SIZE: Wild specimens attain a length of 18 cm; in captivity they remain smaller.

FOOD REQUIREMENTS: Living foods only: tubifex worms, white worms, daphnia, etc.

### *Homaloptera* cf. *Zollingeri* Bleeker • Zollinger's Hillstream Loach

RANGE: Occurs at least in Java, Sumatra, and Thailand.

HABITS: Peaceful and suitable for a community tank of non-aggressive fishes. Clings to hard surfaces where it scraps algae from rocks in swift currents.

WATER CONDITIONS: Not critical, but there should be above-average aeration and filtration for this current-loving species. Normal aquarium temperatures are sufficient.

SIZE: Attains a length of about 10 cm.

FOOD REQUIREMENTS: An algae-eater that should be supplied with sufficient amounts of vegetable matter. The diet can be supplemented with various other aquarium foods.

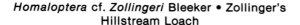

### *Pseudogastromyzon myersi* Herre • Myers' Hillstream Loach; Hong Kong Plecostomus

RANGE: Hong Kong Island.

HABITS: Peaceful and suitable for a community tank. Generally useful as an algae-eater.

WATER CONDITIONS: Not critical, but sufficient aeration and regular water changes are recommended.

SIZE: A rather small species attaining a length of only about 5 cm.

FOOD REQUIREMENTS: This is an algae-eater and should have sufficient quantities of vegetable matter.

## SOUTHEAST ASIAN CYPRINIDS

To the aquarist the countries of Southeast Asia are the true home of the cyprinids (family Cyprinidae), with hundreds of species of barbs, rasboras, sharks, and related fishes that are suitable for the home aquarium. In fact, the great majority of aquarium cyprinids come from Southeast Asia, as the African species are only sporadically imported and seldom bred, while the American and European species cannot take warm water temperatures. Many Southeast Asian barbs and danios are common bread-and-butter fishes of the hobby and can be found in every petshop regardless of its size.

The danios (*Danio* and *Brachydanio)* are perennial beginner's fishes because they spawn so easily under the most spartan aquarium conditions, are bred in huge numbers on fish farms, and are cheap. Additionally, their spotted and striped patterns and constant activity make them a center of attention in a small aquarium. Like virtually all the Asian cyprinids, the danios have an active chasing spawning ritual that results in hundreds or thousands of eggs flying around the tank to end up in the substrate or the plants. Also like most other cyprinids, danios have a reputation as egg-eaters, and often elaborate measures—such as special grills or layers of glass beads—must be taken to prevent the parents from eating their own eggs. The eggs develop in a day or two into small fry that are hardy and will feed on fine live or prepared foods. Strained egg yolk and sifted crushed flake foods are often successfully used to raise danio and other cyprinid fry, making these fishes especially satisfying when the aquarist has neither the experience nor the time to raise live foods.

The literally dozens of Southeast Asian barbs fall into the same three major genera as the African barbs—*Barbodes, Capoeta,* and *Puntius*—and are just as impossible to separate on the barbel characters. Additionally, there are numerous other genera that are barb-like in at least some ways and are occasionally imported, though these oddballs are seldom bred and usually disappear soon after each importation. Many species of barbs that have never become well-established in the hobby even though they seem suitable prove to be the young of larger species. Several Indian and tropical Asian barbs grow to over a meter in length and are important food fishes and may even be popular game species.

Also often reaching large sizes are the various species of sharks, *Labeo* and *Morulius* and a few other genera, which often are more common in village fish markets than aquaria. Fortunately, some of the most colorful species of Asian sharks are also relatively small, even the adults not reaching 25 cm, and these are among the most popular aquarium species. The name "shark" as applied to the cyprinids is of course misleading and probably never should have been used to begin with, but after 50 years it is hard to break an old

567

habit. In aquarium jargon, "shark" applies to any cyprinids with streamlined bodies, long heads, and high, erect dorsal fins. This would include not only such things as the red-tailed black shark and the black shark, but also the Apollo sharks (*Luciosoma*), which admittedly don't look much like a *Labeo* species. Although until recently it has proved almost impossible to spawn sharks in the aquarium (or even in ponds), the technique of induced spawning after injection of pituitary hormones may eventually change this and allow anyone willing to do the work to spawn the common sharks.

The rasboras are a complicated and large group that is poorly understood both scientifically and aquaristically. Only the harlequin rasbora (*Rasbora heteromorpha*) and its close relatives are truly common in the aquarium, and they are also the most distinctively shaped and patterned of the familiar species, with the deep body and black "pork chop" pattern setting them off from the other common species. Although about a dozen species of rasboras are imported on a sporadic basis, some of them attractive and simple to breed, only the harlequins persist in the hobby. Many rasboras are silvery fishes that lack any type of personality, which certainly accounts for their absence from the hobby. By the way, the genus *Rasbora* is now being split. The group of large silvery species related to *Rasbora daniconius* and *R. cephalotaenia* is now placed in the genus *Parluciosoma*, for instance.

Certainly one of the most neglected of the Southeast Asian cyprinids must be the White Cloud Mountain minnow, *Tanichthys albonubes*. One of the smallest yet most colorful of common aquarium fishes, many people consider it to be *the* beginner's fish. Sometimes it seems that the fish is almost impossible to kill unless you let the tank dry up or boil over. Actually, this little stream fish prefers water at lower temperatures than usually maintained in the aquarium.

A word about the Siamese algae-eater is necessary in any discussion of Southeast Asian cyprinids, although technically it belongs to a different family than the other fishes we've talked about. The genus *Gyrinocheilus* (there are several described species but they are all very much alike and probably impossible to distinguish in life) belongs to its own family, Gyrinocheilidae, because of modifications of the gills and operculum. While adhering to stones and wood at the bottom of rivers and streams in order to rasp algae, it takes water into its gills and then exhales it through special openings at the upper edge of the operculum where the gill covers connect to the side of the head. Although this may seem like a minor difference from the normal cyprinids, it is a drastic change in a very fundamental body process. Algae-eaters are of course staples of the aquarium trade, though they are usually seen only at small sizes (few get enough algae to reach maturity in the aquarium).

*Chela dadiburjuri*

*Chela caeruleostigmata*

*Chela "Pseudobarilius"*

*Chela laubuca* (Burma)

*Chela laubuca*

*Chela* sp.

*Esomus metallicus*

*Esomus danricus*

*Plate #382*

*Rasbora vaterifloris*

*Rasbora pauciperforata*

*Rasbora borapetensis*

*Rasbora agilis*

*Rasbora urophthalma*

*Rasbora maculata*

*Rasbora brittani* (male)

*Rasbora brittani* (female)

**Plate #383**

Rasbora heteromorpha espei

Rasbora heteromorpha espei

Rasbora heteromorpha

Rasbora heteromorpha

Rasbora meinkeni

Rasbora elegans

Rasbora sumatrana

Rasbora sumatrana var.

**Plate #384**

Rasbora trilineata

Rasbora trilineata

Rasbora caudimaculata

Rasbora dorsiocellata

Rasbora myersi

Rasbora somphongsi

? Rasbora

Rasbora einthoveni

**Plate #385**

572

*Parluciosoma cephalotaenia*

Rasbora "Pike Rasbora"

*Parluciosoma daniconius*

Rasbora sp.

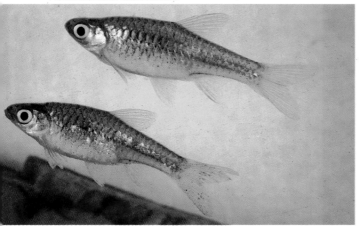

Rasbora "Nondescript"

Rasbora sp.

Rasbora kalochroma

*Rasborichthys altior*

*Plate #386*

*Danio aequipinnatus*

*Danio aequipinnatus* (pair)

*Danio malabaricus*

*Danio malabaricus* (pair)

*Brachydanio albolineatus*

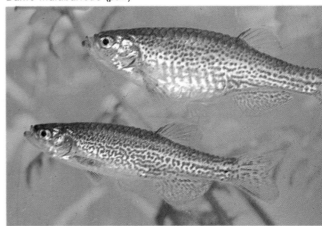

*Brachydanio frankei*

*Brachydanio kerri*

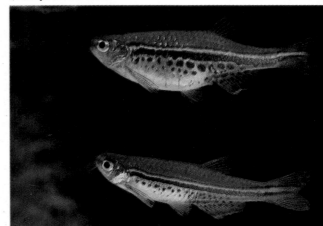

*Brachydanio nigrofasciatus*

Plate #387

574

*Brachydanio rerio* (var.)

*Brachydanio rerio*

*Luciosoma bleekeri*

*Luciosoma setigerum*

? *Luciosoma*

*Leptobarbus melanopterus*

*Leptobarbus hoeveni* (juv.)

**Plate #388**

*Leptobarbus hoeveni*

575

*Zacco macrolepis*

*Zacco macrolepis*

*Zacco platypus (juv.)*

*Barilius nanensis*

*Zacco platypus (male)*

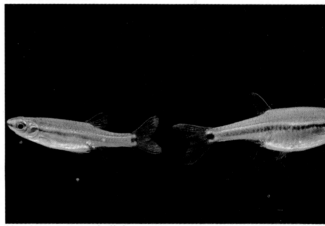

*Hemigrammocypris lini*

*Probarbus julienni*

*Leptobarbus hoeveni*

**Plate #389**

576

*Barbodes binotatus*

*Barbodes binotatus*

*Puntius* sp. "Odessa Barb"

*Puntius* sp. "Odessa Barb"

*Puntius filamentosus* (juv.)

*Puntius filamentosus*

*Puntius naryani*

*Puntius naryani*

**Plate #390**

577

*Puntius ticto*

*Puntius ticto*

*Puntius conchonius*

*Puntius conchonius*

*Puntius conchonius*

*Puntius conchonius*

*Puntius conchonius (longfin)*

*Puntius conchonius (veilfin)*

**Plate #391**

*Puntius nigrofasciatus*

*Puntius nigrofasciatus (male)*

*Puntius nigrofasciatus*

*Puntius nigrofasciatus (var.)*

*Capoeta semifasciolatus*

*Capoeta semifasciolatus*

*Puntius sachsi (albino)*

*Puntius sachsi*

**Plate #392**

579

*Capoeta*

*Capoeta*

*Capoeta chola*

*Puntius amphibius*

*Puntius pleurotaenia*

*Capoeta chola*

*Puntius dorsalis (bronze var.)*

*Puntius dorsalis (red var.)*

**Plate #393**

*Puntius somphongsi*

*Capoeta* cf *binotatus*

*Capoeta* cf *binotatus*

*Capoeta* "Bigscale"

*Capoeta* sp.

*Capoeta oligolepis*

*Capoeta oligolepis* (male)

*Capoeta oligolepis* (albino)

**Plate #394**

581

*Barbodes pinnauratus*

*Barbodes pinnauratus*

*Barbodes schwanenfeldii*

*Barbodes schwanenfeldii*

*Barbodes daruphani*

*Barbodes fasciatus*

**Barbodes everetti**

*Barbodes everetti*

**Plate #395**

*Capoeta tetrazona* varieties

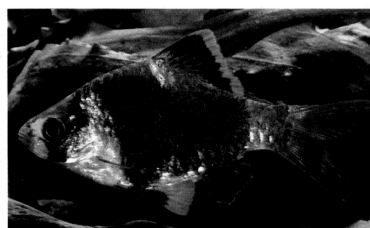

*Plate #396*

*Capoeta arulius* (juv.)

*Capoeta arulius*

*Capoeta titteya* (female)

*Capoeta titteya* (male)

**Barbodes lateristriga**

**Puntius lineatus**

**Barbodes binotatus**

**Barbodes binotatus**

**Plate #397**

Barbodes pentazona?

Barbodes pentazona hexazona

Barbodes pentazona rhomboocellatus

Barbodes pentazona pentazona

Tanichthys albonubes (Brown form)

Tanichthys albonubes

Tanichthys albonubes (longfin var.)

Tanichthys albonubes (Blue form)

*Plate #398*

585

*Cyclocheilichthys apogon* (juv.?)

*Cyclocheilichthys apogon*

*Cyclocheilichthys apogon*

*Osteocheilus* sp.

*Hampala macrolepidota*

*Rohtee alfrediana*

*Osteochilus hasseltii*

*Osteochilus vittatus*

*Plate #399*

*Balantiocheilos melanopterus* (var.)

*Balantiocheilos melanopterus*

*Barbichthys laevis*

*Barbichthys laevis*

*Labeo bicolor*

*Labeo bicolor*

*Labeo erythrurus*

*Labeo erythrurus*

Plate #400

587

Labeo frenatus

Labeo frenatus

? Barbichthys laevis

? Labeo

Labeo forskali.

Labeo frenatus ?

Morulius chrysophekadion

Morulius chrysophekadion

Plate #401

588

Epalzeorhynchus siamensis

Epalzeorhynchus kalopterus

Epalzeorhynchus siamensis?

Gyrinocheilos aymonieri

Gyrinocheilos aymonieri

Gyrinocheilos aymonieri

Paracrossocheilus vittatus

Crossocheilus oblongus

Plate #402

589

## SPAWNING IN SOUTHEAST ASIAN AQUARIUM CYPRINIDS

Most of the Southeast Asian cyprinids that have come onto the aquarium scene fall into the category of "egg-scatterers" as far as their spawning habits are concerned. They vary from species to species in such particulars as the degree of adhesiveness of the eggs (the eggs range from not sticky at all to very sticky), the degree to which the parent fish rely on the presence of plants to both set the spawning mood and to act as receivers of the eggs (some species will not normally spawn unless live plants or reasonable facsimiles of live plants are present in the tank, whereas others will spawn readily in completely bare tanks), the time of day at which spawning normally commences (some preferring the dawn and others the dusk) and other relatively small considerations. But in the main the term "egg-scatterer" is nicely apt: the main run of Southeast Asian aquarium cyprinid species scatter the eggs and let them lie where they fall, whether that means stuck in a clump of plants or strewn over the bottom stratum, and they give them no heed at all except perhaps to eat them.

A definite exception to the rule of who-cares-where-the-eggs-go is the popular *Rasbora heteromorpha* (and its closely allied species/races), a cyprinid that exhibits cichlid-like solicitude in the choosing of a spot upon which to deposit the eggs—even if, unlike the cichlids, it doesn't pay much attention to the eggs after they're laid. The spawning pattern of *Rasbora heteromorpha* is much less specialized than the spawning of cyprinids such as the bitterlings, but it is a departure from the norm nonetheless.

Above: views from the front and rear of a pair of *Capoeta tetrazona* as they go through their spawning gyrations prior to actual release of the eggs during this spawning; eggs, visible in the artificial spawning grass, have already been released during previous clinches.

Below: The male (in background in both photos) is more colorful than the female and has both a greater intensity of red in his fins and a greater area of red coloration during the spawning. The photos show the trembling of the fish and their side-to-side posture immediately before the eggs are expelled and fertilized.

*Plate #403*

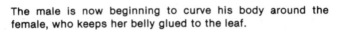

The male in this pair of *Rasbora* of the *R. heteromorpha/espei/ hengeli* complex is closely following the female, who has taken up her position near the leaf chosen as the site for the eggs.

The male is now beginning to curve his body around the female, who keeps her belly glued to the leaf.

The spawning partners have now slid under the leaf and positioned themselves upside down.

Fully in the embrace of the male, the female is attaching the eggs to the underside of the leaf.

*Plate #404*

*Bagrichthys hypselopterus*

*Bagrichthys sp.*

*Leiocassis siamensis*

*Leiocassis siamensis*

*Mystus vittatus*

*Mystus vittatus*

*Mystus micracanthus*

*Glyptothorax callopterus*

Plate #405

593

*Osteochilus* sp.

*Puntius bimaculatus*

*Epalzeorhynchus siamensis*

*Labiobarbus festiva*

*Capoeta* aff. *binotatus*

*Rasbora paucisquamis*

*Capoeta* "Bigscale"

*Rasbora* sp.

Plate #405A

*Rasbora kalochroma*

*Rasbora trilineata*

*Rasbora cf. trilineata*

*Brachydanio kerri*

*Rasbora borapetensis*

*Rasbora kalochroma*

*Rasbora einthoveni*

*Rasbora caudimaculata*

Plate #405B

Heteropneustes fossilis

Chaca bankanensis

Platytropius siamensis

Pangasius sutchi

Kryptopterus bicirrhis

Kryptopterus bicirrhis

Ompok bimaculatus ?

Plate #406

Ompok sabanus

*Aplocheilus blocki*

*Aplocheilus blocki*

*Aplocheilus dayi*

*Aplocheilus dayi*

*Aplocheilus lineatus*

*Aplocheilus lineatus*

*Aplocheilus panchax*

*Aplocheilus panchax*

**Plate #407**

597

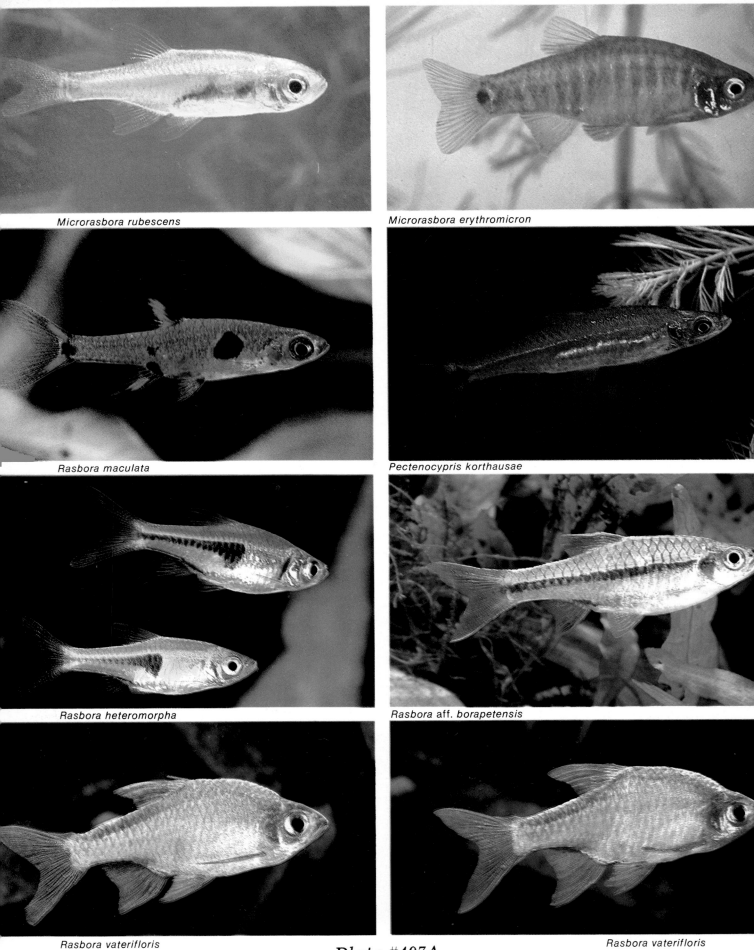

*Microrasbora rubescens*

*Microrasbora erythromicron*

*Rasbora maculata*

*Pectenocypris korthausae*

*Rasbora heteromorpha*

*Rasbora aff. borapetensis*

*Rasbora vaterifloris*

*Rasbora vaterifloris*

Plate #407A

*Aplocheilus lineatus*

*Aplocheilus lineatus*

*Aplocheilus panchax*

*Aplocheilus panchax*

*Oryzias celebensis*

*Oryzias celebensis*

*Doryichthys martensii*

*Doryichthys martensii*

Plate #407B

*Oryzias javanicus*

*Oryzias javanicus*

*Oryzias latipes*

*Oryzias latipes*

*Oostethus brachyurus*

*Doryichthys* "Red-belly"

*Oostethus brachyurus*

**Plate #408**

*Indostomus paradoxus*

Badis badis badis

Badis badis badis

Badis badis badis (female)

Badis badis burmanicus

Pristolepis fasciatus

Pristolepis fasciatus (juvenile)

Nandus nandus

Nandus nandus

*Plate #409*

Badis badis badis

Badis badis badis

Channa cf. striatus

Badis badis burmanicus

Nandus nandus

Nandus nandus

Scatophagus tetracanthus

Scatophagus argus

Plate #409A

## *Channa asiatica* (Linnaeus) • Northern Green Snakehead

RANGE: Found over a wide area of Asia, from the USSR and China to Japan and northern Southeast Asia.
HABITS: Found in all types of habitats from ponds and lakes to rivers, streams, and rice paddies. Like the other members of the genus, it builds and guards a nest for its eggs. Note the absence of the ventral fins.
WATER CONDITIONS: Not choosy. Will tolerate quite a bit of pollution, but of course prefers clean water.
SIZE: A rather small species seldom exceeding 250 mm in length. Juveniles under 100 mm have a more contrasting pattern.
FOOD REQUIREMENTS: Will take almost any living food, especially fishes, shrimp, insects, and even a bit of vegetable matter.

## *Channa micropeltes* (Cuvier & Valenciennes) • Red Snakehead

RANGE: Southeast Asia, into India.
HABITS: A voracious, greedy species, but not everything that it kills is destined to serve as food, as it often kills without eating the fishes it has destroyed.
WATER CONDITIONS: Not critical; this is a very hardy and adaptable fish.
SIZE: Up to 1 meter; usually offered for sale at 8 to 10 cm.
FOOD REQUIREMENTS: Eats most meaty (living and non-living) foods when young; in larger sizes prefers live fishes and amphibians but will take chunks of meat.

## *Channa striatus* (Bloch) • Chevron Snakehead

RANGE: Virtually all of tropical Asia, from India to southern China, Southeast Asia, and to the Indonesian area. Widely introduced because of its commercial importance as a food fish.
HABITS: Found in most sluggish or still waters and even buries itself deeply in the mud when the water dries. The parents build a nest in shallow water and lay floating eggs that hatch in just 3 days.
WATER CONDITIONS: A warm-water fish that thrives under virtually all conditions.
SIZE: The fish shown are juveniles under 10-15 cm long. As the species grows the color pattern virtually disappears and the fish becomes wholly dark brown. Adults reach at least a full meter in length.
FOOD REQUIREMENTS: Will eat anything that comes close enough to grab, including fishes, invertebrates, snakes, frogs, and small mammals.

## *Chanda baculis* Hamilton-Buchanan • Pla Kameo or Burmese Glassfish

RANGE: Burma, India and Thailand in the Sikuk River, in the headwaters of the Menam Chao Phya, in the lower Menam Nan and in the Bung Borapet.
HABITS: A dainty but beautiful small fish; peaceful.
WATER CONDITIONS: Strictly a freshwater species which prefers the higher temperatures in the upper 20's °C.
SIZE: The smallest of the large genus *Chanda*. Rarely larger than 5 cm.
FOOD REQUIREMENTS: Prefers live foods, but accepts frozen brine shrimp and some dry foods in pellet form. Requires copious amounts of live food such as microworms and daphnia.

## *Channa orientalis* Bloch & Schneider • Ceylonese Green Snakehead

RANGE: Sri Lanka.
HABITS: A rather delicate species that likes clean water and is often found in pools near mountain streams. Young fish are often found with their parents. Like *C. asiatica*, this species lacks ventral fins.
WATER CONDITIONS: Will take almost any water conditions in the aquarium, but because of its small size it is more sensitive to poor water.
SIZE: Probably the smallest member of the family, adults barely reaching 100 mm in length.
FOOD REQUIREMENTS: Will take almost any living food of reasonable size.

## *Channa argus* (Cantor) • Spotted Snakehead

RANGE: A mostly northern fish with several subspecies in Russia, China, Japan, and northern Southeast Asia. Likely to be found almost anywhere in subtropical Asia.
HABITS: One of the larger but more colorful snakeheads, this species is found in almost any type of water body, from ponds to rivers. Like the other snakeheads, the presence of air cavities above the gills (like the labyrinth organs of gouramis) allows it to survive in very oxygen-depleted waters and even to travel overland when a pond dries up.
WATER CONDITIONS: Not choosy. Perhaps should be kept a bit cooler than most other snakeheads because of the more northern distribution (22-25°C).
SIZE: Reaches at least 40 cm in length, but seldom exceeds 25 cm in much of its range.
FOOD REQUIREMENTS: Eats almost anything.

## *Chanda ranga* Hamilton-Buchanan • Glassfish, Glass Perch

RANGE: Northern India, Bengal to Burma.
HABITS: Very numerous in rice paddies and other shallow bodies of water in their habitat; peaceful in the aquarium.
WATER CONDITIONS: Requires somewhat hard water with a light salt content. Once established in an aquarium, they should be moved as little as possible. Temperature about 26°C.
SIZE: 5 cm; in nature they become slightly larger.
FOOD REQUIREMENTS: Some prepared foods are unwillingly accepted, but the bulk of foods given should be alive.
COLOR VARIATIONS: Body light amber with a glassy transparency. In the males, the soft dorsal fin and the anal fin have a bright blue edge.

Channa asiatica

Channa orientalis

Channa micropeltes

Channa argus

Channa striatus

Channa striatus

Chanda baculis

Chanda ranga

604

*Plate #410*

Datnioides quadrifasciatus

Datnioides microlepis

Datnioides microlepis

Monodactylus argenteus

Toxotes chatareus

Toxotes jaculator

Scatophagus argus

Scatophagus argus

*Plate #411*

605

### *Datnioides quadrifasciatus* (Sevastianov) • Many-Barred Tiger Fish

RANGE: Thailand, India, Burma and the Indo-Australian Archipelago.

HABITS: Peaceful; will not molest other fishes, but will swallow those which are small enough to be eaten.

WATER CONDITIONS: Neutral to slightly acid. Temperature 23 to 26°C.

SIZE: To 38 cm in their natural waters.

FOOD REQUIREMENTS: Larger live foods, chunks of shrimp or raw fish.

COLOR VARIATIONS: Yellowish to coppery in color with 8 to 10 dark brown bars, some of which unite as the fish grows older.

### *Datnioides microlepis* Bleeker • Siamese Tiger Fish

RANGE: Thailand, Sumatra and Borneo.

HABITS: Peaceful; will not harm any fish it cannot swallow.

WATER CONDITIONS: Neutral to slightly acid. Temperature 23 to 26°C.

SIZE: To 38 cm in its natural waters; much smaller in the aquarium.

FOOD REQUIREMENTS: Larger live foods or chunks of shrimp or raw lean beef.

COLOR VARIATIONS: Body yellow to cream or pinkish, with black vertical bars.

### *Toxotes chatareus* (Hamilton-Buchanan) • Seven-spotted Archer Fish

RANGE: India to the New Hebrides (including the Indo-Australian Archipelago, Thailand, Vietnam, Philippines, New Guinea and northern and northeastern Australia).

HABITS: Peaceful to slightly aggressive; best kept with other brackish water fishes.

WATER CONDITIONS: Although pure fresh or pure salt water can be tolerated, brackish water is best. Temperature 22 to 28°C.

SIZE: A maximum size of about 20 cm is attained; usually smaller in aquaria.

FOOD REQUIREMENTS: Live foods, especially insects, are best; other foods, even hamburger meat, are also accepted.

### *Scatophagus argus* (Gmelin) • Spotted Scat

RANGE: Tropical Indo-Pacific region along the coasts.

HABITS: Peaceful toward other fishes, but will graze on aquatic plants right down to the roots.

WATER CONDITIONS: Fairly hard, alkaline water with a teaspoon of salt per four liters of water added. Temperature 23 to 26°C.

SIZE: To 33 cm in their home waters; about half that in captivity.

FOOD REQUIREMENTS: Live foods of all kinds, with the addition of vegetable substances like lettuce or spinach leaves; will also eat frozen foods.

### *Monodactylus argenteus* (Linnaeus) • Mono

RANGE: Coastal waters from eastern Africa to Fiji.

HABITS: Shy and often gets panicky when frightened; best kept in a small group in a roomy tank.

WATER CONDITIONS: Slightly alkaline water with about a quarter teaspoon of salt to each liter is acceptable. Temperature 23 to 25°C.

SIZE: Wild specimens attain 23 cm; seldom exceed half that in captivity.

FOOD REQUIREMENTS: All sorts of live foods.

COLOR VARIATIONS: Body silvery, with a golden sheen above; two black vertical bars, one through the eye and the other through the pectoral base.

### *Toxotes jaculator* (Pallas) • Archer Fish

RANGE: India, Burma, Malaysia, Philippines, East Indies and Thailand.

HABITS: Usually peaceful, but individual specimens can be aggressive; not a good community fish unless kept with other fishes liking slightly brackish water.

WATER CONDITIONS: Water should be slightly salty; tank should be large. Temperature 23 to 29°C.

SIZE: Over 15 cm, but always sold at a much smaller size.

FOOD REQUIREMENTS: Best food is live insects which the fish captures for itself, but it will accept meaty substitutes; some hobbyists claim that it will accept dry food, but this depends on the individual fish.

*Etroplus suratensis* (Bloch) • Banded Chromide

RANGE: India and Sri Lanka; in the mouths of streams and
bays.
HABITS: Somewhat quarrelsome; should be trusted only with
fishes of its own size or bigger.
WATER CONDITIONS: Requires a generous addition of salt
to the water, a tablespoonful for every 4 liters, or 10% sea
water added.
SIZE: Wild specimens may measure up to 40 cm, but we seldom see them more than 8 cm in length.
FOOD REQUIREMENTS: Should be generously fed with a
variety of live foods or frozen full-grown brine shrimp.

*Etroplus maculatus* (Bloch) • Orange Chromide

RANGE: India and Sri Lanka.
HABITS: Fairly peaceful with fishes of its own size, but can-
not be trusted completely.
WATER CONDITIONS: Water should be fresh and clean, with
about a quarter teaspoon of salt added to each liter.
SIZE: About 8 cm.
FOOD REQUIREMENTS: Should be provided with living or
frozen foods; dried food taken only when very hungry.

*Gnatholepis knighti* Jordan & Everman • Pond Goby

RANGE: Pacific islands to Southeast Asia. As with most
gobies, the identification of this species is somewhat
doubtful.
HABITS: A brackish water species usually found in sea-side
ponds and the mouths of rivers. Can be adapted to freshwater aquaria.
WATER CONDITIONS: Warm, alkaline water with salt added
is necessary.
SIZE: 30-45 mm.
FOOD REQUIREMENTS: Like most small gobies, it will take
small live foods such as daphnia and cyclops, as well as
the standard brine shrimp. Some will adjust to taking
prepared foods as well.

*Ctenogobius schultzei* (Herre) • Redneck Goby

RANGE: Hong Kong to the Philippines.
HABITS: Found in clear, running water over sand bottoms as
well as in estuarine areas, so quite adaptable. Spawns
readily in the aquarium. Females are very plain and lack
the enlarged, brightly colored gill areas of the breeding
males.
WATER CONDITIONS: Temperature 25°C and higher. Some
salt should be added to the water, at least at first.
SIZE: 50-60 mm.
FOOD REQUIREMENTS: Likes cyclops, daphnia, brine shrimp
nauplii, and most other small live foods.

Etroplus suratensis

Etroplus suratensis

Etroplus maculatus

Etroplus maculatus

Etroplus maculatus (var.)

Etroplus maculatus (var.)

Gnatholepis knighti

Ctenogobius schultzei

**Plate #412**

608

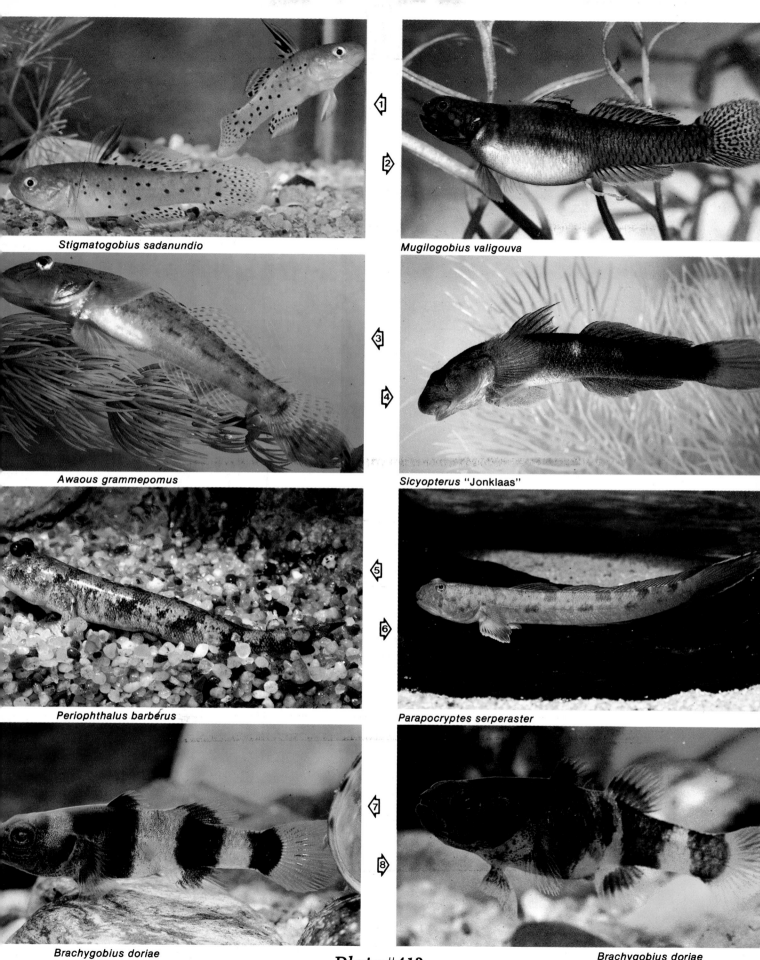

Stigmatogobius sadanundio

Mugilogobius valigouva

Awaous grammepomus

Sicyopterus "Jonklaas"

Periophthalus barberus

Parapocryptes serperaster

Brachygobius doriae

Brachygobius doriae

*Plate #413*

609

## *Stigmatogobius sadanundio* (Hamilton-Buchanan) • Knight Goby

RANGE: Indonesia, Burma, India and the Philippines.
HABITS: A bottom-dwelling fish which requires live food.
WATER CONDITIONS: Originally from brackish water areas, this fish is not at home in soft water conditions. Add salt to the water, at least one tablespoon for 8 liters.
SIZE: Up to about 9 cm.
FOOD REQUIREMENTS: Must have copious feedings of live foods, preferably worms; frozen brine shrimp is eagerly taken.

## *Awaous grammepomus* (Bleeker) • Stippled River Goby

RANGE: Tropical Indo-West Pacific from India and Sri Lanka to the Philippines and Java.
HABITS: Although sometimes found in estuarine areas, it is typically a goby of large, often fast-flowing rivers on tropical islands. Here it is found on sandy to rocky substrates and uses the large head and lips to look for food under rocks.
WATER CONDITIONS: Warm, hard water is preferred; salt may be added to ensure the right chemistry.
SIZE: One of the larger gobies, often reaching 100 mm in length and approaching 150 mm. In some areas it is large enough to use for food.
FOOD REQUIREMENTS: Will take anything small enough to swallow—the size of the mouth should indicate that it is not to be trusted with small fishes. Some vegetable matter is also taken.

## *Periophthalmus barbarus* (Linnaeus) • Mudskipper

RANGE: East Africa to Australia.
HABITS: Cannot be combined with any other group of fishes; shy at first, but later can be tamed effectively.
WATER CONDITIONS: Water must have salt, ½ teaspoon to the liter, added; there should be an area where the fish can climb out. Temperature 24 to 27°C.
SIZE: To 15 cm.
FOOD REQUIREMENTS: Worms and other living insects.

## *Brachygobius doriae* (Guenther) • Doria's Bumblebee Goby

RANGE: Borneo and the Malayan Archipelago.
HABITS: Should be kept by themselves in a small aquarium. Hiding places should be provided.
WATER CONDITIONS: Water should have an addition of one heaping teaspoonful of table salt per 4 liters. Temperature 24 to 26°C.
SIZE: Up to 2.5 cm.
FOOD REQUIREMENTS: Small live foods exclusively.

## *Mugilogobius valigouva* (Deraniyagala) • Mullet-headed Goby

RANGE: Sri Lanka.
HABITS: A small estuarine goby of unimpressive colors. It can be adapted to freshwater aquaria on occasion.
WATER CONDITIONS: Since this species is estuarine, it must have salt added to the water. Hard, alkaline water is necessary, as for most other brackish water species.
SIZE: Small, only 15-20 mm long.
FOOD REQUIREMENTS: The small adult size and small mouth mean that only the finest foods will be taken. Related species also will eat a bit of algae as part of their diet.

## *Sicyopterus* "Jonklaas" • Jonklaas's Mountain Goby

RANGE: Sri Lanka.
HABITS: Peaceful; clings to glass or rocks with sucker-like pelvic fins.
WATER CONDITIONS: Requires cool (21°C), well-aerated, clear water.
SIZE: Average 15 cm; females larger than males.
FOOD REQUIREMENTS: Prefers a lush growth of algae on rocks and aquarium glass; will also eat prepared foods containing a large amount of vegetable matter.

## *Parapocryptes serperaster* (Richardson) • Slim Mudskipper

RANGE: Southeast Asia from India to China, most numerous in Malayan Archipelago.
HABITS: Aggressive.
WATER CONDITIONS: Warm, brackish water required. Temperature 24 to 27°C.
SIZE: To about 25 cm.
FOOD REQUIREMENTS: Will accept only rich, meaty foods, in most cases only living foods; tubifex worms, earthworms and small live fishes are accepted, and will gladly take softbodied insects.

### *Anabas testudineus* (Bloch) • Climbing Perch

RANGE: India, Sri Lanka, Burma, Southeast Asia, southern
China, Philippine Islands and Malaysia.
HABITS: Aggressive; should be kept by themselves. Large
aquarium should be provided and kept covered.
WATER CONDITIONS: Not critical. Has a wide temperature
tolerance, 18 to 30°C.
SIZE: Up to 25 cm; becomes mature at 10 cm.
FOOD REQUIREMENTS: Eats almost anything; in the absence
of live foods, canned dog food with a high beef content is an
acceptable substitute.
COLOR VARIATIONS: Dirty gray to greenish, with a dark spot
at the caudal base and another just behind the gill plate.

### *Osphronemus goramy* Lacepede • Giant Gourami

RANGE: Great Sunda Islands; introduced in other places as
a food fish.
HABITS: Peaceful; because of their size they should be kept
only with large fishes.
WATER CONDITIONS: Not critical as long as the water is
clean. Temperature 23 to 28°C.
SIZE: Up to 60 cm in natural waters; about half that in the
aquarium.
FOOD REQUIREMENTS: Should get large amounts of shrimp,
clams, mussels, etc., to which is also added vegetable
matter such as boiled oatmeal.

### *Helostoma temmincki* Cuvier and Valenciennes •
### Kissing Gourami

RANGE: Thailand, Indonesia, Sumatra, Borneo, Java, Malay
Peninsula and Cambodia.
HABITS: Prefer a large aquarium. Plants are not necessary
though they do enjoy "chomping" on them to remove
whatever has fallen onto them or grown over them. They
are easily overcrowded and unless they are given plenty
of room their growth is stunted, they develop a "hollow
belly" and they die.
WATER CONDITIONS: The water conditions are not critical,
but they do much better in slightly hard water with a pH
of 7.0. Temperature 26°C.
SIZE: Up to 30 cm.
FOOD REQUIREMENTS: A greedy eater which never tires of
looking for food. Their major diet should consist of frozen
brine shrimp and worms now and then. They seem to get
along very well on salmon eggs (the dried prepared form
available as fish food) and shredded shrimp, though this
usually fouls the water.

### *Belontia signata* (Guenther) • Combtail

RANGE: Sri Lanka.
HABITS: Vicious toward smaller fishes; should be kept only
with those which are able to take care of themselves.
WATER CONDITIONS: Large tank is required. Water not
critical. Temperature should be at least 25°C.
SIZE: 12.5 cm.
FOOD REQUIREMENTS: Very greedy; will take coarse dried
foods, but prefers chunks such as pieces of earthworms
or lean raw beef.
COLOR VARIATIONS: Sides are a reddish brown, lighter in
the belly region; outer edge of the tail is fringed.

Anabas testudineus (xanthistic)

Anabas testudineus

Osphronemus goramy (juvenile)

Osphronemus goramy (adult)

Helostoma temmincki (green)

Helostoma temmincki (pink)

Belontia signata

Belontia signata

*Plate #414*

*Parosphromenus deissneri*

*Parosphromenus filamentosus*

*Trichopsis pumilus*

*Trichopsis schalleri*

*Betta bellica*

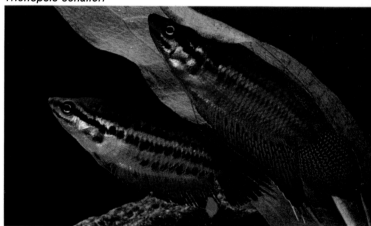

*Trichopsis vittatus*

*Betta imbellis*

*Betta brederi*

**Plate #415**

*Parosphromenus filamentosus*

*Parosphromenus filamentosus*

*Parosphromenus parvulus*

*Parosphromenus deissneri*

*Parosphromenus paludicola*

*Parosphromenus paludicola*

*Parosphromenus nagyi*

*Parosphromenus nagyi*

Plate #415A

Betta pugnax

Betta pugnax

Betta pugnax (Malaysia)

Betta pugnax (S. Thailand)

Betta pugnax (Sumatra)

Betta pugnax (female)

Betta imbellis

Betta imbellis

Plate #415B

*Betta macrostoma* (male)

*Betta macrostoma* (female)

*Betta akarensis*

*Betta macrostoma* (male) var.

*Betta taeniata*

*Betta pugnax*

*Betta unimaculata*

*Betta smaragdina*

*Plate #416*

All fish on this page are forms of *Betta splendens*.

*Plate #417*

*Betta splendens*

*Betta splendens*

*Betta splendens*

*Betta splendens*

*Betta splendens*

*Betta splendens*

*Betta smaragdina*

Plate #417A

*Betta splendens*

Betta anabatoides

Betta anabatoides

Betta picta

Betta picta

Betta picta

Betta bellica

Betta bellica

Plate #417B

Betta bellica

Macropodus concolor

Belontia hasselti

Macropodus opercularis (blue)

Macropodus opercularis

Pseudosphromenus cupanus

Macropodus opercularis (albino)

Malpulutta kretseri

Pseudosphromenus cupanus dayi

*Plate #418*

Colisa chuna (female)

Colisa chuna (male)

Colisa labiosa (pair)

Colisa fasciata (male)

Colisa lalia (female)

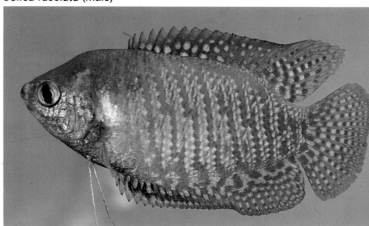
Colisa lalia (male)

Sphaerichthys osphromenoides

Colisa lalia (var. sunset)

*Plate #419*

621

Sphaerichthys osphromenoides

Sphaerichthys osphromenoides

Sphaerichthys acrostoma

Sphaerichthys osphromenoides selatanensis

Sphaerichthys acrostoma

Sphaerichthys acrostoma

Malpulutta kretseri

Sphaerichthys acrostoma

Plate #419A

*Helostoma temmincki*

*Osphronemus goramy*

*Anabas testudineus*

*Belontia signata*

*Trichopsis vittatus (Penang)*

*Trichopsis vittatus*

*Macropodus chinensis*

*Plate #419B*

*Macropodus opercularis*

*Trichogaster microlepis*

*Trichogaster leeri*

*Trichogaster trichopterus* (wild)

*Trichogaster pectoralis*

*Trichogaster trichopterus*

*Trichogaster trichopterus* (cosby)

*Trichogaster trichopterus* (gold)

Plate #420

*Trichogaster trichopterus* (white)

The female waits under the nest for the approach of the male. Her obviously egg-laden condition is a good sign that she is ready to spawn, and the white "pimple" at her vent is further proof.

The male (longer fins) sidles up to the female under the nest (which is seen to contain eggs from previous embraces during this same spawning) and will soon wrap his body around the female's.

Having expelled and fertilized the eggs (visible at the female's vent and right under the head of the male), the spawning partners separate. The male recovers more quickly than the female and will collect the eggs while the female remains semi-paralyzed for a few moments.

The *Betta* fry shown here have hatched and will soon attempt to leave the nest, but at this stage they're not quite ready to swim freely yet.

*Plate #421*

## BREEDING BEHAVIOR OF THE SIAMESE FIGHTING FISH

The Siamese Fighting Fish, *Betta splendens*, is one of the most popular of all tropical fish species kept by aquarists, and it's also one of the easiest species to induce to spawn. Assuming that the potential spawning partners are not physically deficient as the result of abuse or genetic deformity, *Betta splendens* usually will spawn if the sexes are separated before spawning and the temperature of the water in which the potential parents are kept is brought up to within a degree or two of 27°C.

The male's readiness to spawn is evidenced by his construction of the nest of bubbles into which the eggs will be placed during and immediately after the spawning itself; the female's readiness is indicated by her general plumpness in the belly area.

At the beginning of the spawning ritual, the male chases the female around the tank with much blustering and fin-slapping and gill-flaring, accompanied by occasional nips (and, unfortunately, an occasional beating to death in cases in which the male and female are simply incompatible or the female is unable to signify willingness to spawn). Once the parents come into agreement and settle down to spawn they position themselves under the nest, and the male wraps his body around the female, who turns belly-up during the nuptial embrace. The female then releases a group of eggs, which are fertilized by the clouds of sperm released by the male. The eggs slowly sink to the bottom of the tank, and the male follows to retrieve them; some he catches on the fly, before they've reached the bottom, and others he picks up after they've hit the bottom. After being retrieved, the eggs are ejected from the male's mouth into the bubblenest; the eggs generally stay put once they're in the nest, but sometimes eggs fall out and have to be placed back into the nest by the male. (The female, incidentally, sometimes helps in the egg-retrieval process.)

The spawning embrace/egg release/egg retrieval sequence is repeated until the female is depleted of eggs or the spawning breaks off for some other reason, but in any event the female should be removed after it has become plain that she is no longer welcome in the spawning tank. The male often will make that plain enough, but in some cases the parents can be left together in the spawning tank with no fighting at all. The male should be left in the tank at least for the first day or two after the spawning so that he can tend the nest and eggs; at the 27°C temperature suggested as proper for spawning it usually takes a little longer than a day for the eggs to hatch, and it takes about another day and a half before the fry become capable of wandering away from the nest area.

Other nest-building anabantoids have spawning patterns similar in the main to that exhibited by *Betta splendens*, although variations in the pattern are of course shown from species to species. The variations for the most part consist of differences regarding whether the eggs rise or sink, whether the male allows the female to play any part in retrieving the eggs or tending the nest, the extent and thickness of the nest and the degree to which it incorporates vegetation, how badly the male beats up on the female and things like that—but regardless of which species is involved and regardless of whether the aquarist will make any attempt at all to raise the fry, the spawning act itself is fascinating to watch.

**Macrognathus siamensis** (Guenther) • Spot-finned
Spiny Eel

RANGE: Thailand.
HABITS: Fairly peaceful with fishes its own size or not too much smaller, but it has been known to attack tiny species and half-grown individuals of large species.
WATER CONDITIONS: Soft, slightly acid water is best. Temperature 24 to 29°C.
SIZE: Up to 25 cm.
FOOD REQUIREMENTS: Usually reluctant to accept dry foods, although will sometimes pick these up from the bottom; tubifex worms are eagerly accepted.

**Mastacembelus armatus** (Lacepede) • White-spotted
Spiny Eel

RANGE: India, Sri Lanka, Thailand and Sumatra.
HABITS: Mostly nocturnal; should have places where it can hide.
WATER CONDITIONS: Not important as long as the water is clean. Temperature 24 to 27°C.
SIZE: To 76 cm in native waters.
FOOD REQUIREMENTS: Living or frozen foods, especially worms.

**Mastacembelus circumcinctus** Hora • Half-banded
Spiny Eel

RANGE: Thailand.
HABITS: Found in lakes and sluggish rivers. Although generally peaceful, it should not be trusted with small fishes.
WATER CONDITIONS: Not choosy as long as the water is relatively warm (to about 26 or 27°C) and clean.
SIZE: Probably reaches at least 200 mm, but most specimens under 150 mm.
FOOD REQUIREMENTS: Like other spiny eels, it prefers living foods of small to medium size, especially worms and crustaceans. Can be adapted to prepared foods.

**Mastacembelus** "Smith" • False Armatus Spiny Eel

RANGE: Southeast Asia.
HABITS: A small, peaceful eel that is not yet identified. The rows of spots along the middle of the back and at the base of the dorsal fin seem to resemble the variable *M. armatus,* but the rest of the pattern of the body and head is quite distinctive. Spiny eels are often hard to identify and their variability makes the situation even more complex.
WATER CONDITIONS: Likes warm, clean water, like other spiny eels.
SIZE: Seems to be a small species, under 150 mm in length.
FOOD REQUIREMENTS: Prefers live foods but will take some prepared foods.

**Mastacembelus zebrinus** Blyth • Zebra Spiny Eel

RANGE: Burma.
HABITS: A generally peaceful fish, but not above eating baby fishes.
WATER CONDITIONS: Not critical if extremes are avoided. Temperature 22 to 26°C.
SIZE: Up to 46 cm in the wild; usually seen at no more than 13 cm.
FOOD REQUIREMENTS: Small moving live foods are preferred, but prepared foods are readily accepted, provided pieces are not too large.

**Mastacembelus erythrotaenia** Bleeker • Spotted Fire Eel

RANGE: Java, Borneo and Sumatra.
HABITS: Mostly nocturnal and a bit shy at first; hiding places should be provided.
WATER CONDITIONS: Not important as long as the water is clean. Temperature 24 to 26°C.
SIZE: To 46 cm.
FOOD REQUIREMENTS: Very fond of worms and other live foods such as daphnia and brine shrimp.

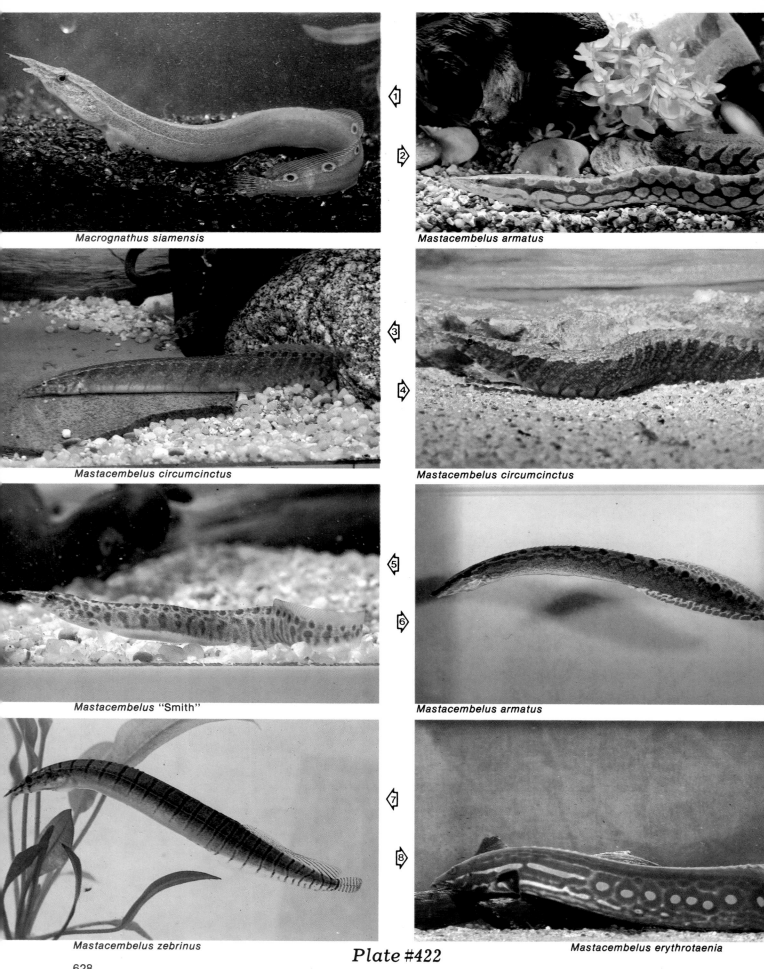

Macrognathus siamensis

Mastacembelus armatus

Mastacembelus circumcinctus

Mastacembelus circumcinctus

Mastacembelus "Smith"

Mastacembelus armatus

Mastacembelus zebrinus

Mastacembelus erythrotaenia

Plate #422

628

*Tetraodon cutcutia*

*Tetraodon cutcutia*

*Tetraodon palembangensis*

*Tetraodon palembangensis*

*Carinotetraodon somphongsi* (female)

*Carinotetraodon somphongsi* (male)

*Tetraodon fluviatilis*

*Carinotetraodon lorteti*

Plate #423

629

## Tetraodon cutcutia Hamilton-Buchanan • Malayan Puffer

RANGE: Malaysia and parts of India, in fresh and brackish waters.
HABITS: Quarrelsome toward other fishes and even among themselves.
WATER CONDITIONS: Hard, alkaline water with salt added, one teaspoonful per 4 liters. Temperature 24 to 27°C.
SIZE: To 15 cm.
FOOD REQUIREMENTS: Live foods in the larger sizes or chopped-up pieces of table shrimp; crushed snails are a delicacy.

## Tetraodon palembangensis Bleeker • Figure-eight Puffer

RANGE: Southeastern Asia and Malaysia Peninsula.
HABITS: A fin-nipper; tends to be pugnacious.
WATER CONDITIONS: Does best in water to which a teaspoon of salt per 4 liters has been added.
SIZE: Up to 18 cm.
FOOD REQUIREMENTS: Prefers larger live foods like fishes or shrimp.

## Carinotetraodon somphongsi (Klausewitz)• Somphongs' Puffer

RANGE: Tachin River system of Thailand.
HABITS: Peaceful toward fishes other than puffers.
WATER CONDITIONS: For best results the water should be neutral to slightly alkaline and moderately hard. The recommended temperature range is 23 to 26°C.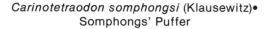
SIZE: Attains a length of at least 7 cm in aquaria, possibly larger in the wild.
FOOD REQUIREMENTS: Live foods, especially snails are preferred, but pieces of frozen foods are accepted.

## Tetraodon fluviatilis Hamilton-Buchanan • Round-spotted Puffer

RANGE: Widespread from India to the Philippines, including Southeast Asia and the East Indies.
HABITS: In nature this is a fish of the estuarine areas, sometimes ascending larger rivers. Although commonly found in pure fresh water, it is more typically a brackish water fish. Like all other puffers, it is a fin-nipper and can be dangerous to any other fishes in the aquarium.
WATER CONDITIONS: Warm water with a good bit of salt added (at least one teaspoon per 4 liters) is best, but the fish is actually quite adaptable.
SIZE: Reaches at least 150 mm in length, but usually smaller.
FOOD REQUIREMENTS: Takes most live foods and also prepared foods. Crustaceans and molluscs are sometimes preferred.

## Carinotetraodon lorteti (Tirant) • Red-bellied Puffer

RANGE: Thailand and adjacent areas.
HABITS: An estuarine to riverine fish that is almost strictly freshwater. Males are distinguished by the red fold of skin on the belly and the bright red markings at the bases of the fins. Peaceful.
WATER CONDITIONS: Moderately hard and warm water (25°C) is recommended.
SIZE: Seldom exceeds 50-60 mm in the aquarium.
FOOD REQUIREMENTS: Live foods are accepted over prepared foods, but the fish will eventually adapt to frozen or freeze-dried preparations.

# Australasian Region

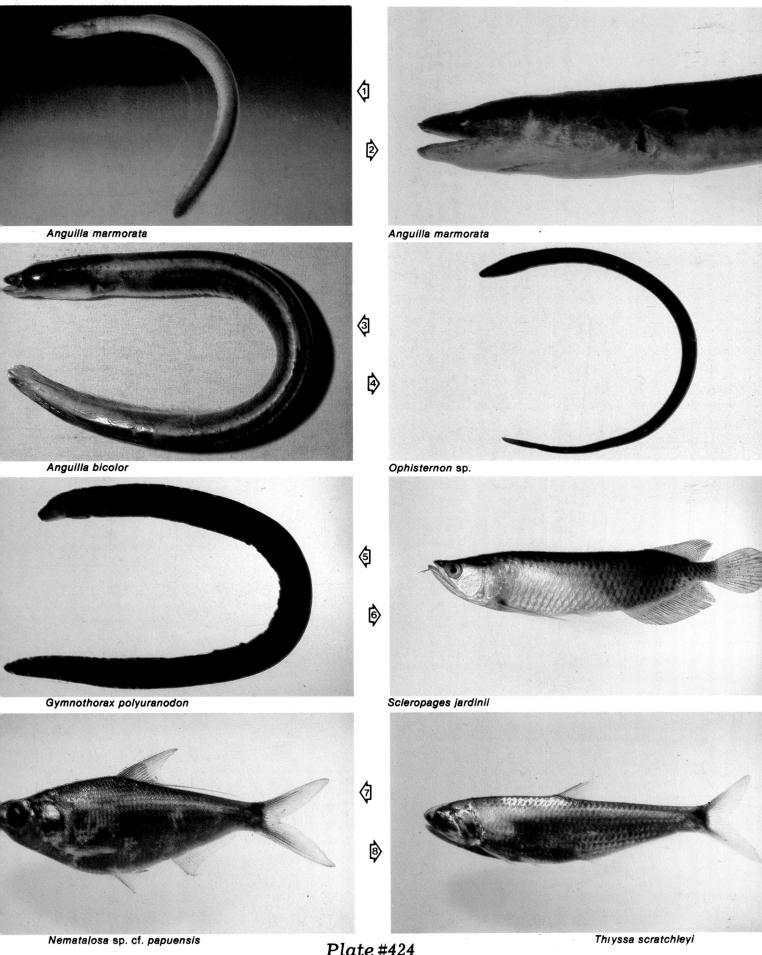

Anguilla marmorata

Anguilla marmorata

Anguilla bicolor

Ophisternon sp.

Gymnothorax polyuranodon

Scleropages jardinii

Nematalosa sp. cf. papuensis

Thryssa scratchleyi

*Plate #424*

*Anguilla marmorata* Quoy & Gaimard • Giant Long-finned Eel

RANGE: Widely distributed in the Indo-Pacific region.
HABITS: Occurs mostly in coastal freshwater streams. Although most of their life is spent in fresh water, they migrate to the sea to spawn. Small individuals can be kept in aquaria, but they are very adept at getting out of the tank and wandering across the floor. Therefore a good tank cover is needed.
WATER CONDITIONS: Not critical as long as extremes are avoided.
SIZE: Attains a length of up to 2 meters.
FOOD REQUIREMENTS: Eels accept a wide variety of meaty foods and pose no feeding problems in home aquaria.

*Anguilla bicolor* McClellend • Short-finned Freshwater Eel

RANGE: Philippines through the East Indies to New Guinea and the Bismarck Archipelago.
HABITS: Inhabits coastal freshwater streams. Migrates to the sea to spawn and die. Tanks must be well covered as these eels are masters at getting out. The anterior nostrils may be orange.
WATER CONDITIONS: Not critical. The surroundings must be relatively clean.
SIZE: Attains a length of about a meter.
FOOD REQUIREMENTS: Carnivorous (at least in adults) and will accept a variety of foods. Not to be trusted with smaller fishes.

*Gymnothorax polyuranodon* (Bleeker) • Freshwater Moray Eel

RANGE: East Indies to New Guinea and the Fiji Islands.
HABITS: Occurs in rivers near the mouths. Like other morays, this one has sharp teeth and must be handled with care.
WATER CONDITIONS: Not critical. Can withstand some salt in the water.
SIZE: Attains a length of about 70 cm.
FOOD REQUIREMENTS: Morays feed on small fishes and invertebrates. Squid normally is a favorite food.

*Nematalosa* cf. *Papuensis* (Munro) • Golden-cheek Herring, Fly River Threadback Herring

RANGE: Apparently endemic to New Guinea.
HABITS: A schooling fish that occurs at least in the Fly River of New Guinea. Probably not suitable for home aquaria.
WATER CONDITIONS: Should have plentiful aeration. Otherwise, not much is known about the keeping of this species.
SIZE: Attains a length of at least 22 cm.
FOOD REQUIREMENTS: This is a filter-feeder and should receive as food small filterable material that is floating in the water.

*Ophisternon* sp. • Dusky One-gilled Eel

RANGE: Not known, but inhabits at least New Guinea.
HABITS: An estuarine eel that enters fresh waters. Like other species in the family Synbranchidae, this eel has a single gill opening on the lower surface of the throat.
WATER CONDITIONS: Can be maintained in fresh, brackish, or salt water.
SIZE: Not known, but probably 50 cm or more.
FOOD REQUIREMENTS: Normally feeds on small fishes and invertebrates. Aquarium foods are usually accepted.

*Scleropages jardini* (Kent) • Northern Spotted Barramundi

RANGE: Northern Australia and New Guinea.
HABITS: Normally a surface-feeder that will eat smaller fishes as well. Must be kept in a relatively large tank. A buccal incubator.
WATER CONDITIONS: Not critical, although the species may be a bit sensitive to temperature changes. No salt should be added to the water.
SIZE: Attains a length of at least 50 cm.
FOOD REQUIREMENTS: Primarily small fishes and crustaceans. Larger individuals will even take frogs.

*Thryssa scratchleyi* (Ramsay & Ogilby) • Fly River Anchovy

RANGE: Known only from freshwater rivers of New Guinea.
HABITS: A fairly common species in the Upper, Middle, and Lower Fly River. They possibly are catadromous (migrating to the sea to spawn). The identification is somewhat doubtful.
WATER CONDITIONS: Anchovies are usually extremely delicate fishes that do not do well in aquaria. Many species die as soon as they are touched by a net. Normal aquarium conditions can be tried.
SIZE: One of the largest species of the family, with the maximum known length 37.1 cm.
FOOD REQUIREMENTS: Apparently feeds on fishes in nature. These can be easily supplied in aquaria along with other meaty fare.

## THE SEA CATFISHES, FAMILY ARIDAE

The sea catfishes, as their name implies, are predominantly marine or estuarine catfishes, although some of the species are restricted to fresh water. The species that are encountered in New Guinea are mostly freshwater catfishes, with some species found in brackish or fully marine environments.

Identification of the various species (or even genera) of sea catfishes is very difficult, leading to a lot of confusion among workers in the group and aquarists who wish to keep them. Fortunately, the differences between the various species as far as keeping them in captivity is concerned or their life histories are not great enough to be of any consequence. One of the main problems with these catfishes (and many other catfishes as well) that aquarists should be aware of is the potential of the dorsal and pectoral spines for inflicting nasty wounds. These spines are strong, sharp, and serrated, and with the fish thrashing about in the net or in one's hand with these spines extended there are bound to be accidents. That they could also become entangled in the aquarium net is obvious.

One of the most interesting aspects of the life history of the sea catfishes is their method of brooding eggs. The eggs are quite large, approximately 15 mm in diameter, and are retained in the mouth of the male parent for the duration of the incubation period. The male does not eat at all during this time, which may last for approximately two weeks. As usual for mouthbrooders with large, yolky eggs, the number of eggs per spawning is somewhat limited. An average seems to be in the neighborhood of some 200 to 300 eggs.

Some species are relatively small (15-20 cm) but others can grow quite large (to a meter). Only the smaller species or the young of the larger species can readily be kept in the size tanks normally maintained by aquarists. A 200-liter tank would not be overly large for any of these fishes. The water conditions are not critical, and these fishes can be kept in freshwater tanks quite easily. They can stand the addition of salt to the tank, but it must be remembered that the New Guinea species are mostly riverine in habitat.

Feeding ariid catfishes does not seem to be a problem. They will accept a variety of meaty aquarium foods, especially chopped shrimp and chopped fishes. They normally feed on the bottom in typical catfish fashion.

Hemipimelodus papillifer

Arius "leptaspis"

Arius n. sp. #1

Arius graeffei

Brustarius nox

Hemipimelodus velutinus

Arius solidus

636

**Plate #425**

Arius stirlingi

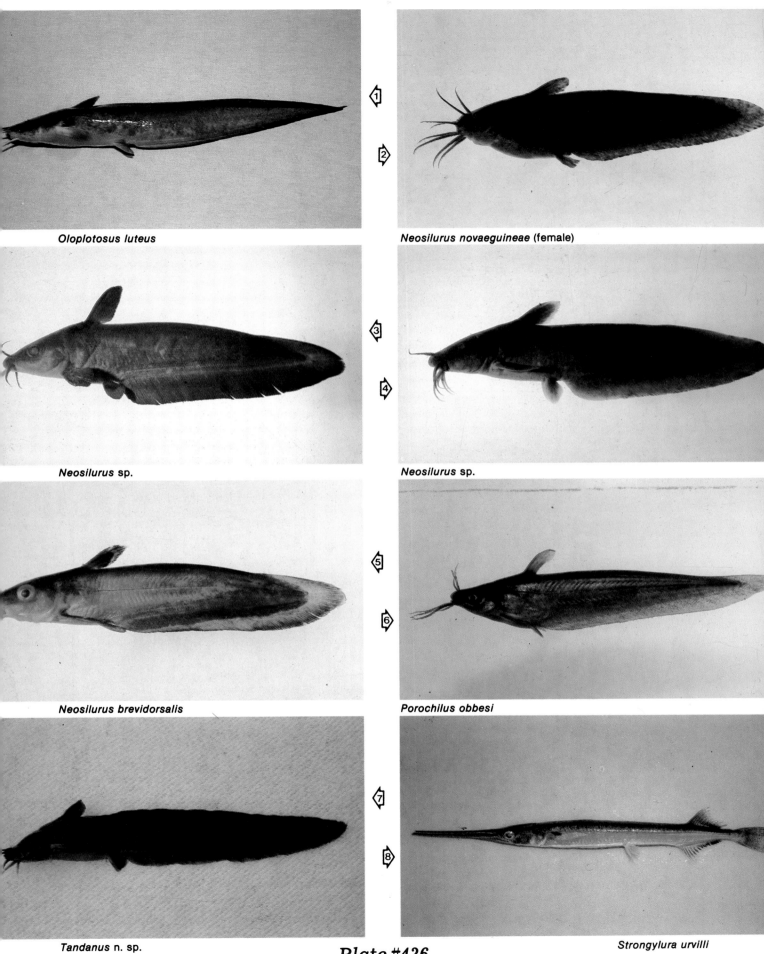

*Oloplotosus luteus*

*Neosilurus novaeguineae* (female)

*Neosilurus* sp.

*Neosilurus* sp.

*Neosilurus brevidorsalis*

*Porochilus obbesi*

*Tandanus* n. sp.

*Strongylura urvilli*

**Plate #426**

## Oloplotosus luteus Gomon & Roberts • Orange-whiskered Catfish

RANGE: Known only from the highlands of the Fly River, New Guinea.
HABITS: This is a catfish of moderate to swift waters where the bottom consists of variable-sized rocks and cobbles.
WATER CONDITIONS: Not critical. Being from swift-flowing currents means that the water should be clean, clear, and well aerated. Normal temperatures should prevail.
SIZE: Attains a length of about 14 cm.
FOOD REQUIREMENTS: Will accept a variety of aquarium foods such as chopped shrimp and fishes.

## Neosilurus sp. • Tandans (two species?)

RANGE: Papua New Guinea, one from the Bensbach River (# 3) and one from near Bewani (# 4).
HABITS: Like the other species of tandans, these two species are bottom-fishes that grub around searching for food. The dorsal fin spine is stiff and strong and may be poisonous. As possibly new species, nothing much is known about their habits.
WATER CONDITIONS: Not critical. Efficient filtration is necessary, and a relatively high level of aeration is recommended.
SIZE: Not known, but should be in the neighborhood of 7-10 cm.
FOOD REQUIREMENTS: Chopped fishes and shrimp suit the tandans quite well. They are able to search them out once they fall to the bottom by using their senses of smell and their barbels.

## Neosilurus brevidorsalis (Guenther) • Short-finned Catfish

RANGE: Southern rivers of New Guinea.
HABITS: Apparently restricted to freshwater rivers. A typically bottom-living catfish that grubs in the bottom material for food.
WATER CONDITIONS: Not critical. A good filtration system should be in use as this species tends to stir up the bottom mulm, causing turbid conditions.
SIZE: Attains a length of about 20 cm.
FOOD REQUIREMENTS: Carnivorous; will feed on meaty aquarium foods such as chopped fishes and chopped shrimp.

## Tandanus n. sp. • False-spine Tandan

RANGE: Australia.
HABITS: A typical catfish that grubs among the bottom material for good things to eat. Most likely prepares a hollow nest in which to deposit the eggs. Male tandans usually guard the eggs until hatching or even a short time thereafter.
WATER CONDITIONS: Not critical. Can thrive under most normal aquarium conditions.
SIZE: At least 10 cm.
FOOD REQUIREMENTS: Will accept a wide variety of aquarium foods. Make sure that they fall to the bottom where the catfish can most easily dispose of them.

## Neosilurus novaeguinea • New Guinea Tandan

RANGE: Western New Guinea (Irian Jaya).
HABITS: Like a typical catfish, it grubs about in the bottom with its barbels, seeking out bits of food.
WATER CONDITIONS: Not critical. Sufficient filtration is necessary. Temperatures for a normal community tank are sufficient.
SIZE: Attains a length of about 7 or 8 cm.
FOOD REQUIREMENTS: Meaty foods that fall to the bottom are best for this catfish.

## Porochilus obbesi Weber • Obbes's Catfish

RANGE: Northern Territory of Australia and part of New Guinea.
HABITS: A bottom-dwelling catfish that grubs in the bottom for bits of food. Cannot be trusted with very small fishes.
WATER CONDITIONS: Not critical. Sufficient filtration is required for keeping the tank clean with a fish that stirs up the bottom.
SIZE: Attains a length of at least 8 cm.
FOOD REQUIREMENTS: A carnivorous species that will accept aquarium foods that find their way to the bottom of the tank. Chopped fishes and shrimp are ideal.

## Strongylura urvilli (Valenciennes) • D'Urville's Long Tom

RANGE: East Indies and New Guinea.
HABITS: Usually seen in brackish or fresh waters. A surface fish with sharp teeth. This species is not to be trusted with smaller fishes. May aggregate with others of the same species. An excellent jumper. Needs plenty of room.
WATER CONDITIONS: Not critical. Does well in both fresh and brackish water at normal aquarium temperatures.
SIZE: Attains a length of over 40 cm.
FOOD REQUIREMENTS: Small fishes will soon disappear from their tank; will take other foods from or near the surface.

### *Zenarchopterus dunckeri* Mohr • Duncker's River Garfish

RANGE: Northern shores of New Guinea.
HABITS: Occurs mainly in salt water, but also enters harbors and rivers, where they swim at the surface. This species, like most other *Zenarchopterus*, has a midlateral silvery stripe. Sometimes there is a broad band of dark spots below it. A livebearer.
WATER CONDITIONS: Not critical. Normal temperatures are suitable.
SIZE: Attains a length of about 18 cm.

### *Zenarchopterus robertsi* Collette • Roberts's Garfish

RANGE: Eastern New Guinea (Kumasi River).
HABITS: A livebearer that spends most of its time at or near the surface. It is generally peaceful, but small fishes will be eaten if the opportunity arises.
WATER CONDITIONS: Seems to prefer slightly hard water with a pH a little above neutral. Temperatures can be in the normal range for tropical fishes. In nature the fish is found in clear, fairly swift-flowing streams around logs and debris.
SIZE: Attains a length of at least 13 cm.

## NEW GUINEA RAINBOWFISHES

Rainbowfishes were once known basically by a single species or even a mixed bag of species all under the single common name "Australian Rainbowfish," which probably was, or at least included, *Melanotaenia maccullochi*. Recently, however, due to the work of Dr. Gerald R. Allen rainbowfishes have taken on a new meaning and are gaining in popularity as new and different species are presented to the aquarist. Much of the recent popularity is due to the spectacular Red Rainbowfish, *Glossolepis incisus*, with *Melanotaenia herbertaxelrodi* and *M. boesemani* coming up fast in popularity.

Some of the popularity is due to the fact that these simply are nice, peaceful, hardy fishes that are easily spawned in captivity. A tank of about 80 liters capacity can easily house three or four breeding-size rainbowfishes comfortably. The water type is not critical, as rainbowfishes can tolerate a wide range of conditions but seem to do best at temperatures between 22 and 24°C and a pH of about 7. A water hardness around 100-150 ppm is recommended. *Iriatherina* species like the water a bit more on the acid side, as do some *Pseudomugil* species. The tank should be well planted. *Vallisneria, Ceratopsis,* and *Fontinalis* are recommended by Dr. Allen. The beauty of these fishes can best be seen when they receive an hour or two of direct sunlight each day. Artificial lighting can make up the difference to keep the plants growing well. The rainbowfishes will eat a variety of aquarium foods. Live foods should be offered on a regular basis (brine shrimp, mosquito larvae, *Drosophila,* and even ants).

The male usually initiates courtship, which consists of chasing, displaying, and intensification of coloration. When ready, the female will accept the male's advances by swimming into a dense plant thicket; the male follows. With the pair side by side the eggs are expelled into the plants, becoming attached there by thread-like filaments. Spawning continues sporadically for a two-week period, with only a few eggs deposited each day. Hatching occurs in about a week to 12 days. Parents can be removed after a week of spawning as they tend to eat the eggs or newly hatched fry. *Iriatherina, Pseudomugil,* and *Popondetta* are not prone to this fry-eating habit. Growth is rapid, and sexual maturity is reached before the end of the first year. Small species have a life span of about two to three years, the larger rainbows about four to eight.

Zenarchopterus dunckeri

Zenarchopterus robertsi (male)

Melanotaenia maylandi?

Melanotaenia sexlineata

Melanotaenia oktediensis

Plate #427

Melanotaenia monticola

*Melanotaenia macculiochi* (male upper)

*Melanotaenia goldiei*

*Melanotaenia goldiei* (male upper)

*Melanotaenia goldiei* (female)

*Melanotaenia herbertaxelrodi* (male)

*Melanotaenia herbertaxelrodi* (female)

*Plate #428*

641

Melanotaenia monticola (male upper)

Melanotaenia papuae

Habitat of *M. sexlineata* and *M. goldiei*

Habitat of *M. parkinsoni*

Melanotaenia parkinsoni

Melanotaenia parkinsoni

*Plate #429*

Melanotaenia parkinsoni (female)

Melanotaenia parkinsoni (male)

Melanotaenia pimaensis (female)

Melanotaenia splendida rubrostriata

Melanotaenia affinis (male upper)

*Plate #430*

Melanotaenia affinis (male)

Melanotaenia affinis (male)

Melanotaenia boesemani

Chilatherina bulolo

Chilatherina campsi (male)

Chilatherina campsi (male)

Chilatherina campsi (female)

Plate #431

644

Chilatherina crassispinosa (male upper fish)

Habitat of Chilatherina fasciata

Chilatherina fasciata (male upper)

Chilatherina fasciata (male)

Chilatherina axelrodi

Chilatherina lorentzi (female)

*Plate #432*

645

Glossolepis maculosus (male above)

Habitat of *Glossolepis multisquamatus*

① ②

*Glossolepis multisquamatus* (male)

*Glossolepis multisquamatus* (female)

③ ④

⑤ ⑥

Glossolepis wanamensis

**Plate #433**

*Glossolepis incisus*

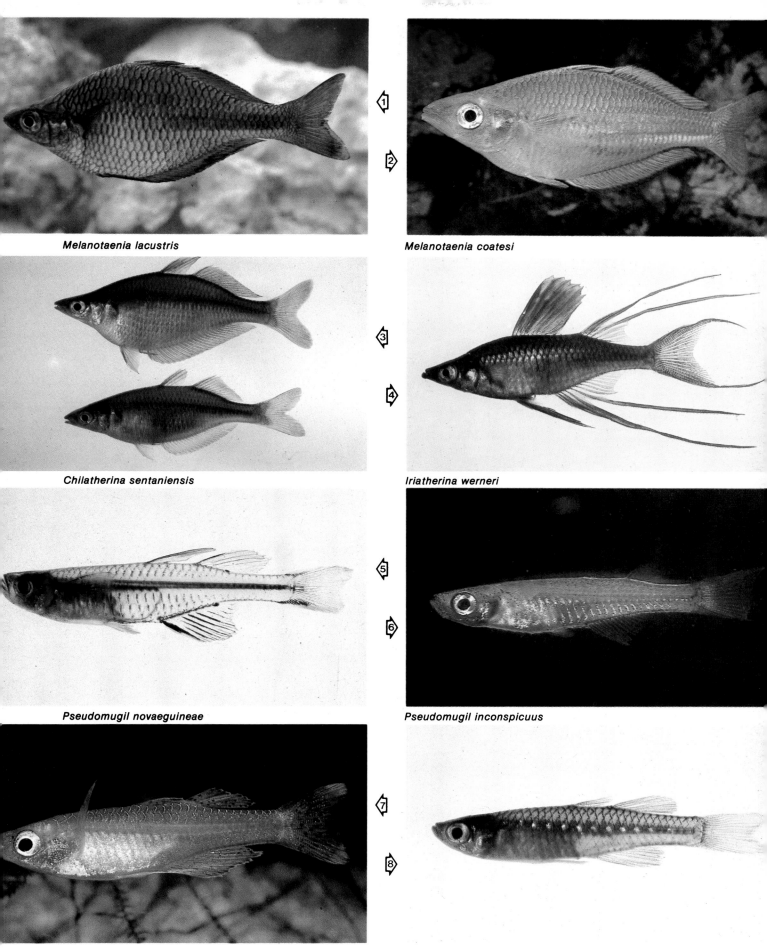

Melanotaenia lacustris

Melanotaenia coatesi

Chilatherina sentaniensis

Iriatherina werneri

Pseudomugil novaeguineae

Pseudomugil inconspicuus

Pseudomugil sp.

*Plate #434*

Pseudomugil tenellus

647

Pseudomugil paludicola

Iriatherina werneri

Popondetta connieae

Popondetta connieae

Popondetta furcata

Habitat of *Popondetta connieae*

*Plate #435*

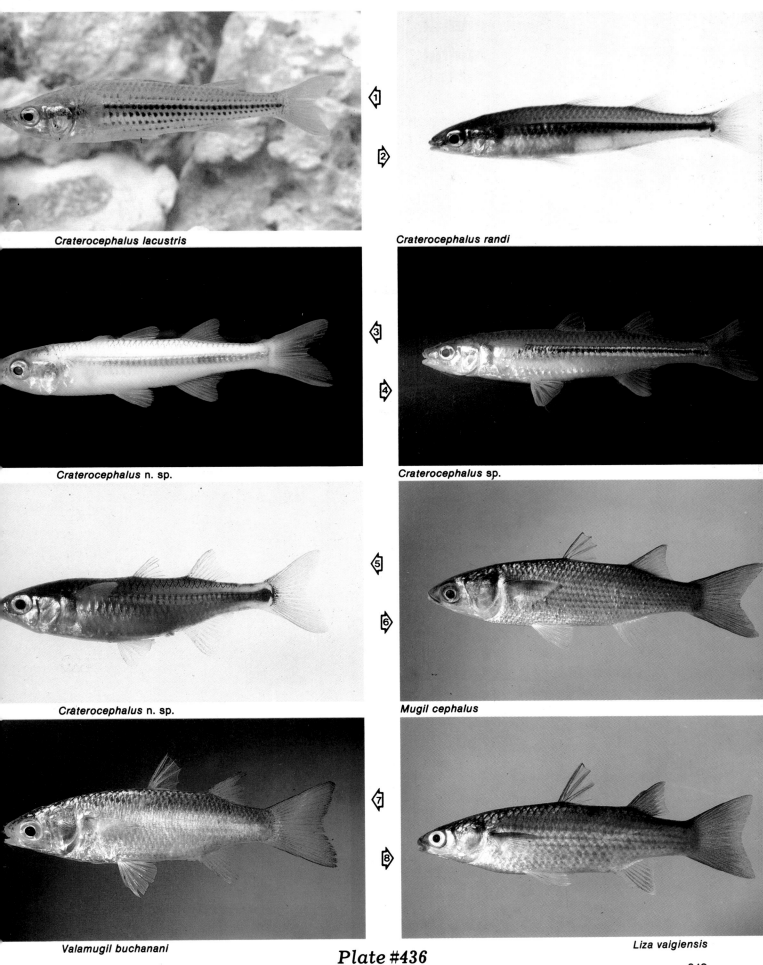

Craterocephalus lacustris

Craterocephalus randi

Craterocephalus n. sp.

Craterocephalus sp.

Craterocephalus n. sp.

Mugil cephalus

Valamugil buchanani

Liza vaigiensis

**Plate #436**

*Craterocephalus lacustris* Trewavas • Lake Kutubu
Hardyhead

RANGE: Apparently restricted to Lake Kutubu in New
Guinea.
HABITS: A strictly freshwater species that usually is found
along the perimeter of the lake near the surface. Sheds
small, slightly adhesive, demersal eggs. Colors of the
spawning pair may become stronger at that time.
WATER CONDITIONS: Not critical. Does best in pure fresh
water but is tolerant of salt. Temperatures of 23-28°C are
acceptable.
SIZE: Attains a length of about 13 or 14 cm.
FOOD REQUIREMENTS: Feeds mainly on insects and small
crustaceans. Small live foods are best, but it will accept
other aquarium foods in time.

*Craterocephalus randi* Nichols & Raven • Kubuna
River Hardyhead

RANGE: At least the Kubuna and Fly Rivers of New Guinea,
possibly also northern Australia.
HABITS: Occurs in swift-flowing riffles as well as deep pools.
Spawns by shedding tiny eggs that adhere to vegetation,
rocks, etc.
WATER CONDITIONS: Not critical. Normal temperatures for
aquaria are recommended.
SIZE: Attains a length of about 3 cm.
FOOD REQUIREMENTS: In nature feeds on aquatic insect
larvae, filamentous algae, and bits of higher aquatic
plants. A balanced diet including vegetable matter
should therefore be offered.

*Craterocephalus* spp. • Hardyheads

Several species of *Craterocephalus* have been collected in
New Guinea that have not as yet been identified. These may
actually turn out to be new species. They behave in much the
same manner as other species of the genus and are often
found in small, lively schools. Spawning consists of shedding
small adhesive eggs that adhere to objects on the bottom.
Food consists of insects (they are beneficial in that they
destroy a large number of mosquito larvae) and small
crustaceans. Most of the species are no more than 8 cm long.

*Mugil cephalus* Linnaeus • Striped Mullet

RANGE: Throughout the subtropical and tropical waters of
the world in fresh water, brackish water, and pure ocean
water.
HABITS: This fish is found in a very wide range of habitats
from very deep marine waters to shallow ponds, streams,
and rivers that are completely fresh but under tidal
influence.
WATER CONDITIONS: Warmer waters and lots of room. Does
well in large circular tropical aquaria with either fresh,
brackish or salt water. Thrives at temperatures over 20°C.
SIZE: May reach 60 cm, but usually found at half that size.
FOOD REQUIREMENTS: A plankton feeder. Eats brine
shrimp when small.

*Valamugil buchanani* (Bleeker) • Buchanan's Mullet

RANGE: Abundant and widespread in the warmer waters of
the Indo-West Pacific region.
HABITS: Inhabits shallow coastal waters, the young usually
entering estuaries or penetrating into pure fresh water.
WATER CONDITIONS: Does well in pure fresh to brackish and
even marine waters. Temperatures should be in the normal range for tropical species.
SIZE: Attains a length of about 40 cm.
FOOD REQUIREMENTS: Generally feed on fine algae and
slime on the bottom mud. Should receive vegetable matter in an aquarium along with other aquarium foods.

*Liza vaigiensis* (Quoy & Gaimard) • Diamond-scale
Mullet

RANGE: Widely distributed in the Indo-West Pacific.
HABITS: A coastal fish in which the young enter estuaries
and even move up into pure fresh water. The pectoral
fins are black in the juveniles but are yellow-margined in
adults.
WATER CONDITIONS: Does well in fresh or brackish water
aquaria. Normal aquarium temperatures for tropical
species are adequate.
SIZE: Reaches a length of about 45 cm.
FOOD REQUIREMENTS: Feeds on fine algae and bottom
slime in nature. In an aquarium it will take some
substitutes but should also receive algae or other
vegetable matter.

## *Doryichthys retzi* (Bleeker) • Ragged-tail Pipefish

RANGE: East Indies and Philippines to New Guinea, the Bismarck Archipelago, and New Caledonia.

HABITS: This is an estuarine species that commonly enters fresh water. Females deposit eggs in the male's brood pouch. After incubation the male will "give birth" to the young pipefishes. Some of the caudal rays are apparently extended, giving rise to the common name.

WATER CONDITIONS: Does well in brackish or fresh water at temperatures between 23 and 27°C.

SIZE: Attains a length of about 11.5 cm.

FOOD REQUIREMENTS: Should be offered small live foods such as baby brine shrimp or even baby guppies, depending upon the size of the pipefish.

## *Oostethus brachyurus* (Bleeker) • Red-line Pipefish

RANGE: Widespread in the Indo-Pacific.

HABITS: The female deposits eggs in the "brood pouch" of the male, who incubates them until they hatch. In this species the brood pouch is not developed but is reduced to a pair of lateral bony plates that serve to hold the eggs in place.

WATER CONDITIONS: An inhabitant of river mouths and estuaries, so it can tolerate fresh to brackish conditions. Normal aquarium temperatures are sufficient.

SIZE: Attains a length of up to 25 cm.

FOOD REQUIREMENTS: Live foods such as newly hatched brine shrimp are usually necessary to keep pipefishes for any length of time. Baby guppies may also be accepted.

## *Hippichthys spicifer* (Rueppell) • Black-barred Freshwater Pipefish

RANGE: Indo-Pacific.

HABITS: A peaceful fish that should not be kept with aggressive feeders. The female places her eggs in the male's brood pouch and he "gives birth" to the young.

WATER CONDITIONS: Usually found in brackish or fresh water and may be common in the lower reaches of rivers. Can tolerate salt in the water. Temperatures should be in the normal range for tropical species.

SIZE: Attains a length of 17 cm.

FOOD REQUIREMENTS: Usually a bit finicky about feeding. Best results are obtained with live foods, especially brine shrimp.

## *Toxotes jaculator* (Pallas) • Archer Fish

RANGE: India, Burma, Malaysia, Philippines, East Indies and Thailand.

HABITS: Usually peaceful, but individual specimens can be aggressive; not a good community fish unless kept with other fishes liking slightly brackish water.

WATER CONDITIONS: Water should be slightly salty; tank should be large. Temperature 23 to 29°C.

SIZE: Over 15 cm, but always sold at a much smaller size.

FOOD REQUIREMENTS: Best food is live insects which the fish captures for itself, but it will accept meaty substitutes; some hobbyists claim that it will accept dry food, but this depends on the individual fish.

## *Toxotes lorentzi* Weber • Primitive Archerfish

RANGE: Northern Territory of Australia and New Guinea.

HABITS: Like other archerfishes, this species will shoot insects out of the overhanging vegetation by using droplets of water propelled with deadly accuracy. The scales are smaller than in the other species.

WATER CONDITIONS: Fresh to slightly brackish water is acceptable. Normal water temperatures are proper.

SIZE: Attains a length of about 14 cm.

FOOD REQUIREMENTS: Will accept a variety of aquarium foods. Insects and insect larvae are, of course, preferred.

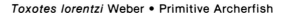

## *Toxotes chatareus* (Hamilton-Buchanan) • Seven-spotted Archer Fish

RANGE: India to the New Hebrides (including the Indo-Australian Archipelago, Thailand, Vietnam, Philippines, New Guinea and northern and northeastern Australia).

HABITS: Peaceful to slightly aggressive; best kept with other brackish water fishes.

WATER CONDITIONS: Although pure fresh or pure salt water can be tolerated, brackish water is best. Temperature 22 to 28°C.

SIZE: A maximum size of about 20 cm is attained; usually smaller in aquaria.

FOOD REQUIREMENTS: Live foods, especially insects, are best; other foods, even hamburger meat, are also accepted.

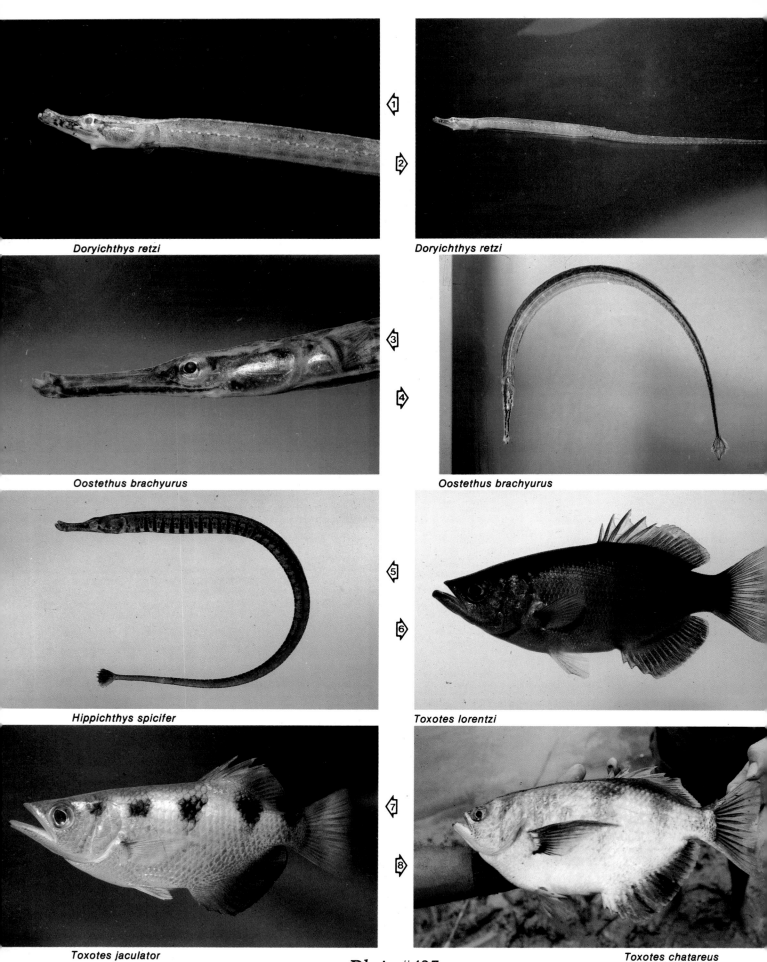

Doryichthys retzi

Doryichthys retzi

Oostethus brachyurus

Oostethus brachyurus

Hippichthys spicifer

Toxotes lorentzi

Toxotes jaculator

Toxotes chatareus

*Plate #437*

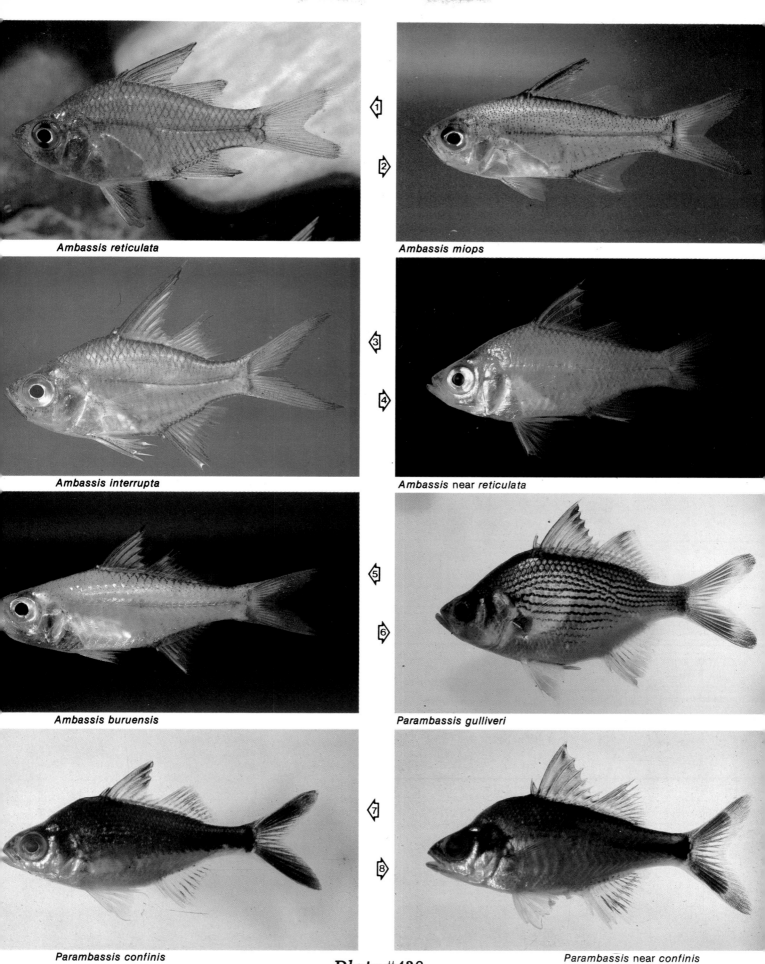

*Ambassis reticulata*

*Ambassis miops*

*Ambassis interrupta*

*Ambassis* near *reticulata*

*Ambassis buruensis*

*Parambassis gulliveri*

*Parambassis confinis*

*Parambassis* near *confinis*

*Plate #438*

653

## *Ambassis reticulata* Weber & De Beaufort • Reticulated Perchlet

RANGE: Southern Papua. If this is a synonym of *A. macleayi* as is suspected, it actually occurs from New Guinea to Australia.
HABITS: A freshwater glassfish.
WATER CONDITIONS: Not critical. Can take salt added to the water.
SIZE: About 8-9 cm.
FOOD REQUIREMENTS: Takes most small live foods.

## *Ambassis miops* Guenther • Flag-tailed Glassfish

RANGE: Much of the southern Pacific, including small islands.
HABITS: A bay and estuarine species that penetrates freshwater.
WATER CONDITIONS: Prefers brackish water or fresh water with sizable additions of salt.
SIZE: Reaches at least 10 cm in length.
FOOD REQUIREMENTS: Takes most small invertebrates and small fish fry.

## *Ambassis interruptus* Bleeker • Long-spined Glassfish

RANGE: Andaman Islands, East Indies, the Philippine Islands, New Guinea, and Australia.
HABITS: Seems to prefer brackish mangrove estuaries. Will enter freshwater streams, but ventures no more than about 20 kilometers from the sea.
WATER CONDITIONS: Should be kept in brackish water or water with at least some salt content. Normal aquarium temperatures are acceptable.
SIZE: Attains a length of over 10 cm.
FOOD REQUIREMENTS: Small invertebrates. Brine shrimp, daphnia, cyclops, and bloodworms (chironomid larvae) are best, but other foods are accepted.

## *Ambassis buruensis* Bleeker • Buru Glassfish

RANGE: Found over a very wide range from Southeast Asia to the Pacific Islands.
HABITS: A coastal and estuarine species that also occurs in pure fresh water.
WATER CONDITIONS: Not critical.
SIZE: About 8 cm long.
FOOD REQUIREMENTS: Although it will adapt to prepared foods, it prefers small living foods of all types.

## *Parambassis gulliveri* (Castelnau) • Giant Perchlet, Giant Glassfish

RANGE: Southern New Guinea and northern Australia.
HABITS: Usually occurs in relatively large freshwater rivers that have high turbidity levels. Probably spawns in the summer months. Largest of the glassfishes and probably will outgrow many smaller tanks quickly. Also called *Ambassis gulliveri*.
WATER CONDITIONS: Not critical. Does well under most aquarium conditions.
SIZE: Reaches a length of at least 28 cm.
FOOD REQUIREMENTS: Feeds on small invertebrates. Will accept the usual aquarium live foods and some of the prepared foods.

## *Parambassis confinis* Weber • Papuan Perchlet

RANGE: Irian Jaya and the Sepik River.
HABITS: A species of freshwater rivers and lakes.
WATER CONDITIONS: Warm water is about the only requirement.
SIZE: Over 10 cm long.
FOOD REQUIREMENTS: Like other glassfishes, it will take most small live foods.

## *Denariusa bandata* (Whitley) • Penny Fish

RANGE: Occurs in rivers along the coast of northern Australia.

HABITS: Commonly found in fairly large schools after the wet season, usually in areas where there is heavy weed growth or even in swampy areas. Often eaten by birds (herons, terns, cormorants).

WATER CONDITIONS: Tolerant of most conditions. Although a freshwater species, it can tolerate a good deal of salt in its water.

SIZE: Attains a length of 4.5 to 5 cm.

FOOD REQUIREMENTS: Will accept a variety of aquarium foods, especially live foods.

## *Tetracentrum apogonoides* Macleay • Four-spined Perchlet

RANGE: Southern Papua.

HABITS: A species of freshwater rivers that grows to a rather large size for a glassfish. Easily recognized by the presence of four stout anal spines (most glassfishes have only three).

WATER CONDITIONS: Found in freshwater rivers. Warm, oxygenated water the only requirement.

SIZE: To at least 18 cm.

FOOD REQUIREMENTS: Will take almost all live foods of suitable size.

## *Xenambassis honessi* Schultz • Honess's Perchlet

RANGE: Found near Buna, Papua.

HABITS: Poorly known, but a species of freshwater coastal streams.

WATER CONDITIONS: Uncertain, but can probably tolerate some salt.

SIZE: Only about 8 cm long.

FOOD REQUIREMENTS: Small invertebrates.

## *Xenambassis simoni* Schultz • Simon's Perchlet

RANGE: Known only from near Buna, Papua.

HABITS: An obscure species from freshwater coastal streams.

WATER CONDITIONS: Not known with certainty.

SIZE: About 11 cm long.

FOOD REQUIREMENTS: Takes most small invertebrates, especially insects.

## *Lates calcarifer* (Bloch) • Silver Barramundi; Giant Perch

RANGE: Found in the tropical coastal rivers of Australia and from China to the Persian Gulf.

HABITS: Live most of their early lives in fresh water but move downstream into estuarine waters during spring to late summer to spawn. Large numbers of floating eggs are spawned; the fry hatch out quickly and have absorbed their yolk sacs in about five days.

WATER CONDITIONS: The young do best in fresh water, although they can tolerate the addition of salt to the aquarium water. Temperatures of 27° to 28°C are recommended.

SIZE: Grows quite large, with individuals of close to 2 meters and almost 60 kilos known.

FOOD REQUIREMENTS: Young feed on aquatic insects, small crustaceans, small fishes, and plant material; older giant perch feed mostly on larger fishes and crustaceans.

## *Kurtus gulliveri* Castelnau • Nursery Fish

RANGE: Northern Australia and New Guinea.

HABITS: The male incubates the eggs on a hook that develops on his head.

WATER CONDITIONS: Lives equally well in fresh and brackish waters. Probably hard, alkaline water is preferred. Can survive low oxygen conditions.

SIZE: Attains a length of 63 cm.

FOOD REQUIREMENTS: Requires a well balanced diet, perhaps heavy on shrimp or other meaty foods such as live fishes.

## *Kuhlia rupestris* (Lacepede) • Jungle Perch; Rock Flagtail

RANGE: A fairly common species in torrential rivers of northern Queensland, Australia, but also found from East Africa to the Tuamotu Archipelago in pools and mountain torrents.

HABITS: Freely moves back and forth from marine to fresh water. Possibly spawns in brackish water.

WATER CONDITIONS: Not critical. Does equally well in fresh and salt water. Temperatures 21°C to 26°C suitable.

SIZE: Attains a length of over 50 cm.

FOOD REQUIREMENTS: Feeds mainly on crustaceans but will also take other items, including figs that fall into the water.

## *Kuhlia marginata* (Cuvier) • Spotted Flagtail

RANGE: Widely distributed in the central and western Pacific from Tahiti to the East Indies and Japan to New Guinea.

HABITS: Commonly found in brackish and freshwater environments. An active and hardy fish.

WATER CONDITIONS: Not critical. Does well under a variety of conditions. Normal temperatures should be acceptable.

SIZE: Attains a length of about 21 to 22 cm.

FOOD REQUIREMENTS: Not a fussy eater. Will accept a variety of aquarium foods.

Denariusa bandata

Tetracentrum apogonoides

Xenambassis honessi

Xenambassis simoni

Lates calcarifer

Kurtus gulliveri

Kuhlia rupestris

Kuhlia marginata

*Plate #439*

656

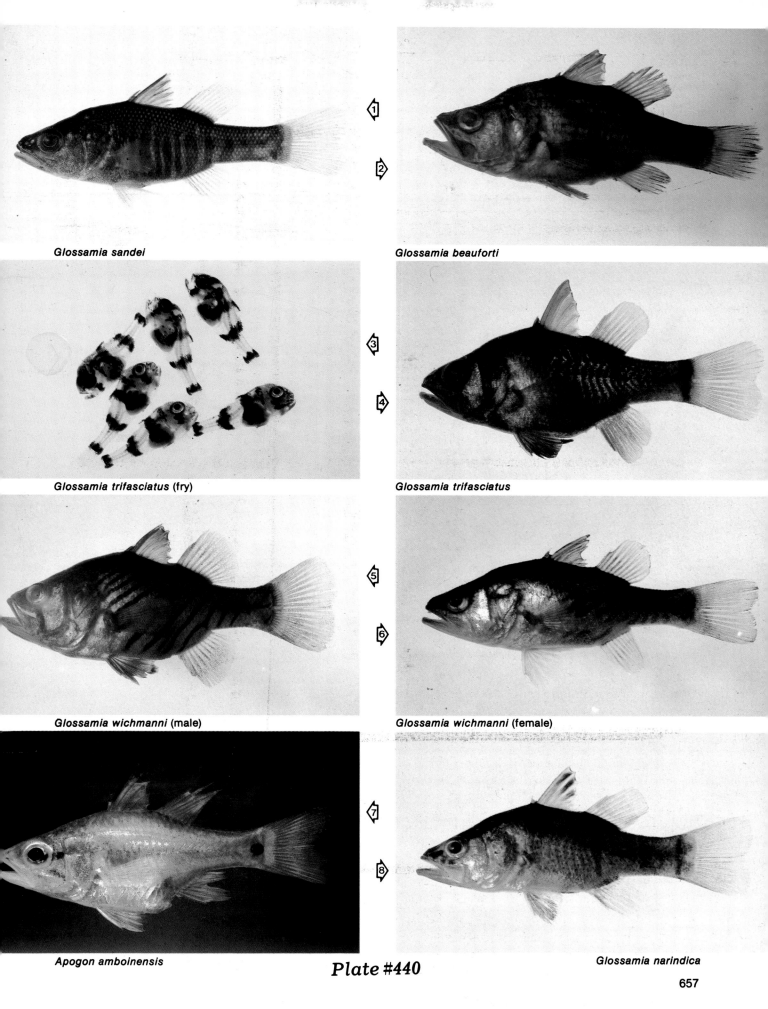

Glossamia sandei

Glossamia beauforti

Glossamia trifasciatus (fry)

Glossamia trifasciatus

Glossamia wichmanni (male)

Glossamia wichmanni (female)

Apogon amboinensis

Glossamia narindica

*Plate #440*

## *Glossamia sandei* (Weber) • Giant Cardinalfish

RANGE: Central and southern New Guinea.
HABITS: Most likely a mouthbrooder, as are many cardinal-fish species in both marine and fresh water. Not to be trusted with fishes that it can swallow.
WATER CONDITIONS: A freshwater cardinalfish of tropical rivers. The water chemistry is not critical and the temperatures should be in the normal range for tropical species.
SIZE: According to Weber, its describer, this species grows to more than 23 cm, making it the largest cardinalfish.
FOOD REQUIREMENTS: Will accept a variety of meaty foods and will dispatch any small fishes that are placed in the aquarium.

## *Glossamia trifasciata* (Weber) • Three-banded Cardinalfish

RANGE: Known only from the rivers of central-southern New Guinea.
HABITS: A freshwater species that is also a mouthbrooder. The three bands that are the basis of both the scientific and common names can readily be seen in the fry in our photo. In the adult they are more obscure.
WATER CONDITIONS: Not critical. A freshwater species that does well in temperatures between 23 and 28°C.
SIZE: Attains a length of about 13 or 14 cm.
FOOD REQUIREMENTS: Accepts chopped fish, chopped shrimp, and other meaty aquarium foods.

## *Glossamia wichmanni* (Weber) • Wichmann's Cardinalfish

RANGE: Northern New Guinea.
HABITS: A mouthbrooder that apparently will spawn year-around if conditions are right. This species has been divided into two subspecies (*A. w. wichmanni, A. w. gjellerupi*) on the basis of number of scales in a lateral series.
WATER CONDITIONS: A freshwater species that will do fairly well under normal aquarium conditions.
SIZE: Attains a length of between 18 and 22 cm.
FOOD REQUIREMENTS: Will accept normal aquarium foods, especially meaty types, along with live fishes.

## *Apogon amboinensis* Bleeker • Ambon Cardinalfish

RANGE: A wide-ranging species distributed in the tropical Indian Ocean and the western Pacific from southern Japan to New Guinea.
HABITS: This is more of a brackish water species in New Guinea, although it does enter fresh water. It is a mouthbrooder.
WATER CONDITIONS: Lives well in both fresh and brackish water. Temperatures between 23 and 28°C are suitable.
SIZE: Attains a length of about 10 cm.
FOOD REQUIREMENTS: Does well on chopped fish, chopped shrimp, frozen foods, and an occasional live fish.

## *Glossamia beauforti* (Weber) • Beaufort's Cardinalfish

RANGE: New Guinea and the Aru Islands.
HABITS: A striking fish with a number of horizontal lines crossing the body. However, it sometimes turns quite dark, obscuring these lines. A mouthbrooder that lives exclusively in fresh water.
WATER CONDITIONS: Not critical. Should be given temperatures in the normal range (about 23-28°C) for tropical species.
SIZE: Attains a length of about 19 cm.
FOOD REQUIREMENTS: Will accept a variety of meaty foods normally available for aquarium fishes. Small fishes are also taken.

## *Glossamia narindica* Roberts • Nose-spot Cardinalfish

RANGE: Known only from the Middle Fly River of New Guinea.
HABITS: A mouthbrooder that apparently spawns year-around with interruptions due only to temporarily unfavorable conditions. This species was described quite recently (1978). Not to be trusted with fishes that are small enough for it to swallow.
WATER CONDITIONS: Not critical. A freshwater tropical species.
SIZE: Attains a length of about 13 cm.
FOOD REQUIREMENTS: This is a piscivore in nature but will accept a variety of meaty foods in the aquarium. Small live fishes of course would be the most natural food.

## *Pingalla lorentzi* (Weber) • Lorentz River Grunter

RANGE: Central portion of southern New Guinea and possibly the Jardine River in Australia.

HABITS: A fairly hardy species that is not very aggressive. Like other species in this family, it makes grunting noises at times.

WATER CONDITIONS: Not critical. A tropical species, so temperatures should be between 23 and 28°C.

SIZE: Attains a length of at least 6-7 cm.

FOOD REQUIREMENTS: Will accept a variety of aquarium foods. Some vegetable matter should be included in its diet.

## *Hephaestus lineatus* • Lined Grunter

RANGE: Apparently known only from Irian Jaya in New Guinea.

HABITS: Generally carnivorous and should not be trusted with fishes much smaller than itself. Fairly active and nicely patterned.

WATER CONDITIONS: Not critical. Does well in standard aquarium setups at normal temperatures.

SIZE: Attains a length of at least 10 cm.

FOOD REQUIREMENTS: Not a fussy eater. Will accept a variety of aquarium foods.

## *Hephaestus adamsoni* (Trewavas) • Adamson's Grunter

RANGE: Known from Lake Kutubu in New Guinea, some 3,000 feet above sea level.

HABITS: Typical of the grunters. An active fish that does well under normal aquarium conditions. Known also as *Therapon adamsoni* and *Madigania adamsoni*.

WATER CONDITIONS: Not critical. Temperatures between 20 and 23°C are proper.

SIZE: Attains a length of about 21-22 cm.

FOOD REQUIREMENTS: Will dine on small fishes as well as any small pieces of shrimp or fish. Will accept frozen aquarium foods.

## *Terapon* sp. • Plain-tailed Flagtail

RANGE: New Guinea. This seemingly undescribed species is very similar superficially to *Hephaestus lineatus* but can be immediately separated by the much higher dorsal spines.

HABITS: Typically found in coastal streams.

WATER CONDITIONS: Unknown, but can probably survive well in most conditions.

SIZE: To about 10 cm.

FOOD REQUIREMENTS: Insects, insect larvae, small crustaceans, smaller fishes; vegetable matter should be offered.

## *Leiopotherapon affinis* (Mees & Kailola) • Fly River Grunter

RANGE: Known only from the Upper, Middle, and Lower Fly and Morehead Rivers, New Guinea. There is a possibility that it is the same species as *Amniataba percoides* of Australia.

HABITS: Somewhat aggressive and active. Not to be trusted with fishes much smaller than itself.

WATER CONDITIONS: Not critical. Normal aquarium temperatures will suffice.

SIZE: Attains a length of at least 10 cm.

FOOD REQUIREMENTS: Eats a number of aquarium foods. Beefheart is said to be a good conditioning food.

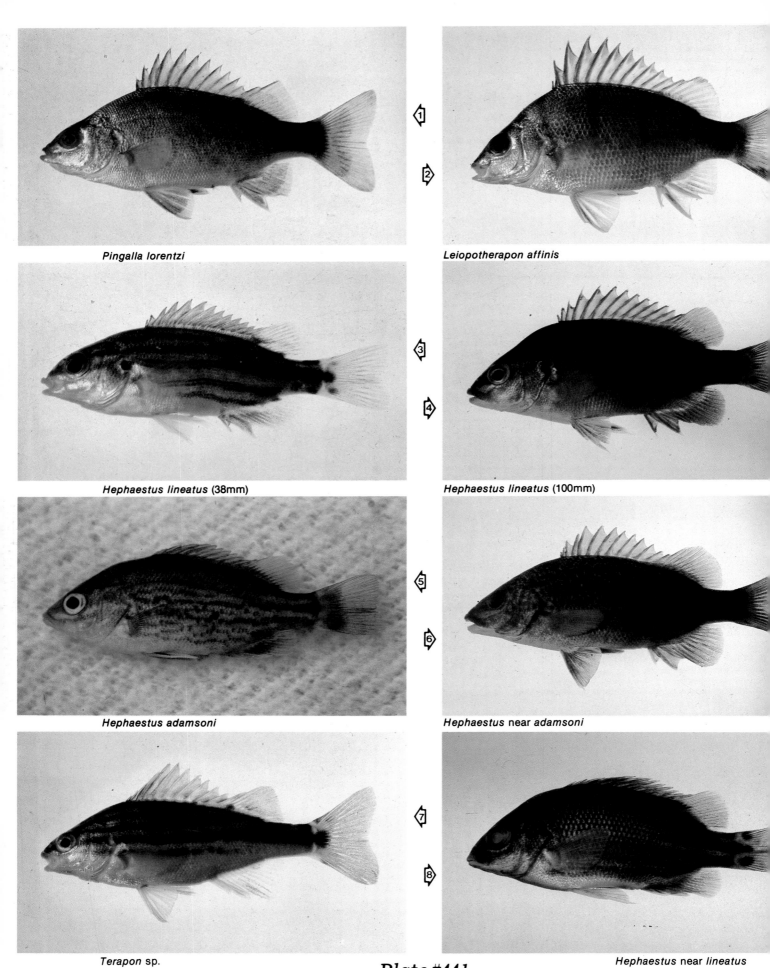

Pingalla lorentzi

Leiopotherapon affinis

Hephaestus lineatus (38mm)

Hephaestus lineatus (100mm)

Hephaestus adamsoni

Hephaestus near adamsoni

Terapon sp.

Hephaestus near lineatus

**Plate #441**

660

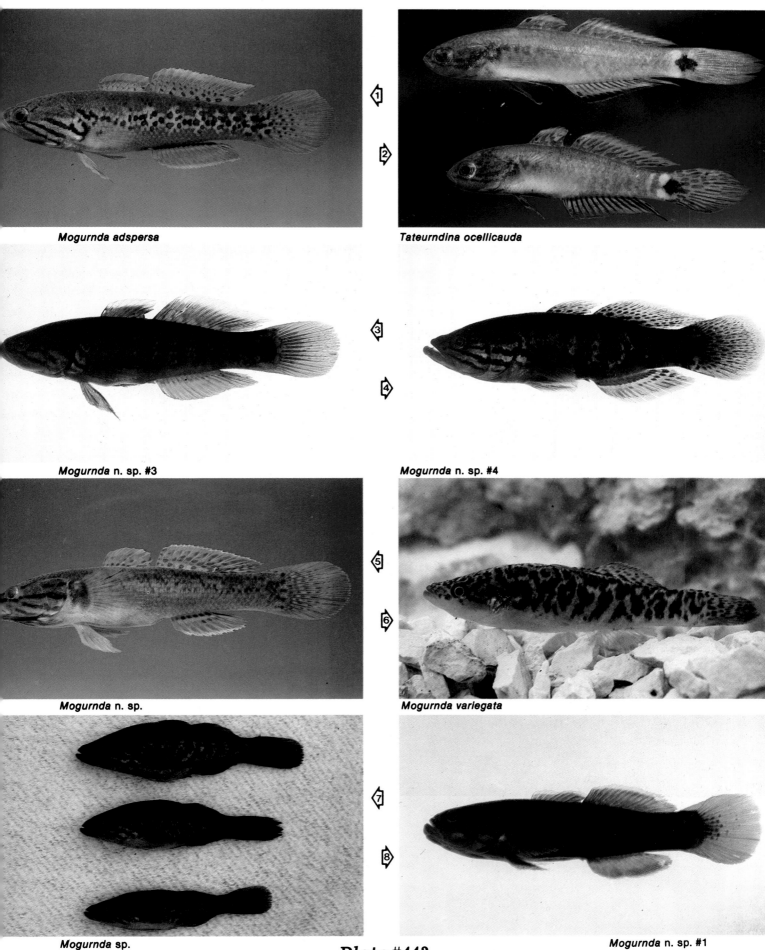

Mogurnda adspersa

Tateurndina ocellicauda

Mogurnda n. sp. #3

Mogurnda n. sp. #4

Mogurnda n. sp.

Mogurnda variegata

Mogurnda sp.

Mogurnda n. sp. #1

**Plate #442**

## NEW GUINEA GOBIES

Of the literally thousands of species of gobies, well over 75% are marine fishes found from shallow muddy estuaries to the white coral sands of tropical reefs. There are a great number of species that have penetrated into freshwater realms in the tropics, however, and freshwater gobies are not uncommon in Central and South America, Africa, and Southeast Asia. However, they probably reach their peak of variety in New Guinea and Australia. Here there are relatively few other freshwater fishes with which to compete for food and living space, and the broad ecological tolerances inherent in gobies have allowed many different types to find homes in the shallow streams and small rivers of these areas.

Unfortunately, few of the New Guinea gobies are imported on a regular basis, although two or three have found what seem to be permanent homes in the aquarium hobby. The numerous species of *Glossogobius* and *Oxyeleotris* are usually just brownish fishes, but they are common and easy to keep in the aquarium. The really exotic types of gobies such as the metallic *Stiphodon*, the high-finned *Sicyopterus*, and the big-mouthed *Butis* are rarities in the aquarium and often come from niches too specialized to allow duplication in the aquarium.

The species of *Mogurnda* and *Tateurndina* are exceptions to the usual rule of inavailability of New Guinea gobies. Because of their bright spawning colors and ease of spawning in the aquarium, they have caught on at least temporarily in the hobby, especially in Europe. *Tateurndina ocellicauda* is now spawned regularly and is seen fairly often in petshops. Its spawning habits were covered in detail in the April, 1983, issue of *Tropical Fish Hobbyist* and illustrated in numerous color photos. Although so far only the Australian *Mogurnda mogurnda* is common in the hobby, the several New Guinea species of *Mogurnda* are very much like it in general appearance and behavior and almost certainly spawn the same way; spawning of *Mogurnda mogurnda* was covered in the June, 1984, issue of *Tropical Fish Hobbyist*.

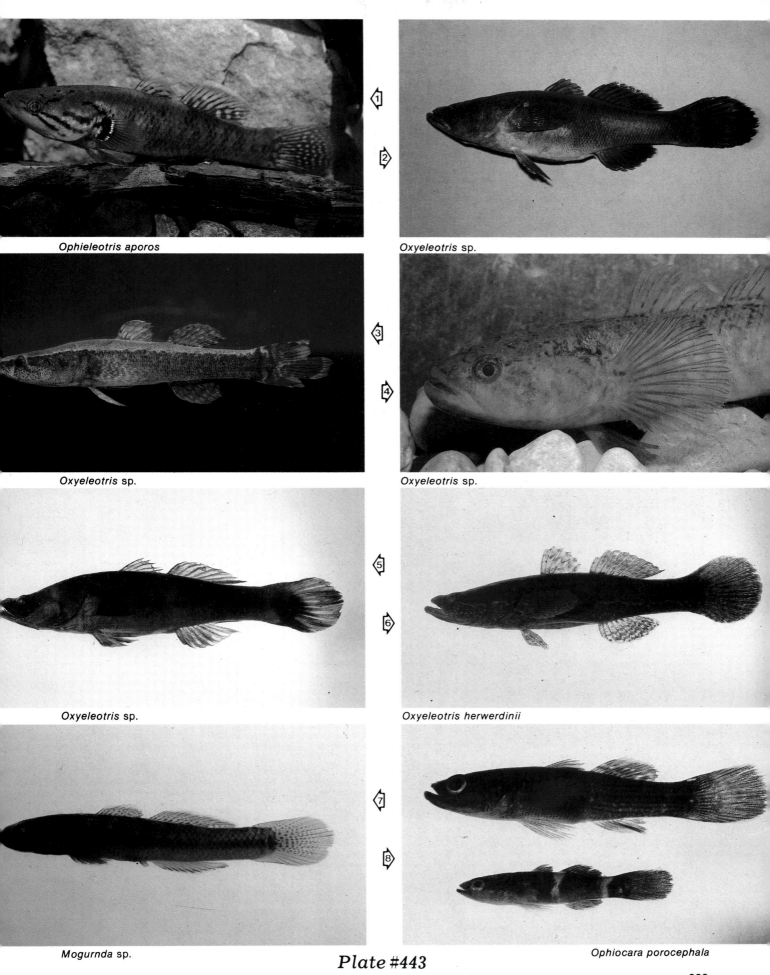

Ophieleotris aporos

Oxyeleotris sp.

Oxyeleotris sp.

Oxyeleotris sp.

Oxyeleotris sp.

Oxyeleotris herwerdinii

Mogurnda sp.

Ophiocara porocephala

*Plate #443*

663

**Butis amboinensis**

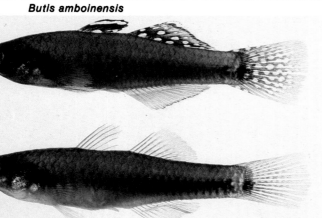

**Eleotris** sp.

**Hypseleotris cyprinoides**

**Gobiomorphus** n. sp.

**Glossogobius** n. sp. #13

**Glossogobius celebius**

**Glossogobius** sp.

**Plate #444**

**Glossogobius** n. sp. #16

Glossogobius biocellatus

Glossogobius sp.

Glossogobius sp. (concavifrons complex)

Glossogobius koragensis

Glossogobius brunnoides complex

Awaos crassilabrus

Periophthalmus vulgaris

Stenogobius genivittatus

*Plate #445*

665

*Belobranchus belobranchus*

*Stiphodon elegans*

*Sicyopterus cyanocephalus*

*Sicyopterus zosterophorus*

*Sicyopterus longifilis*

*Redigobius bikolanus*

*Plate #446*

1
2
3
4
5
6

666

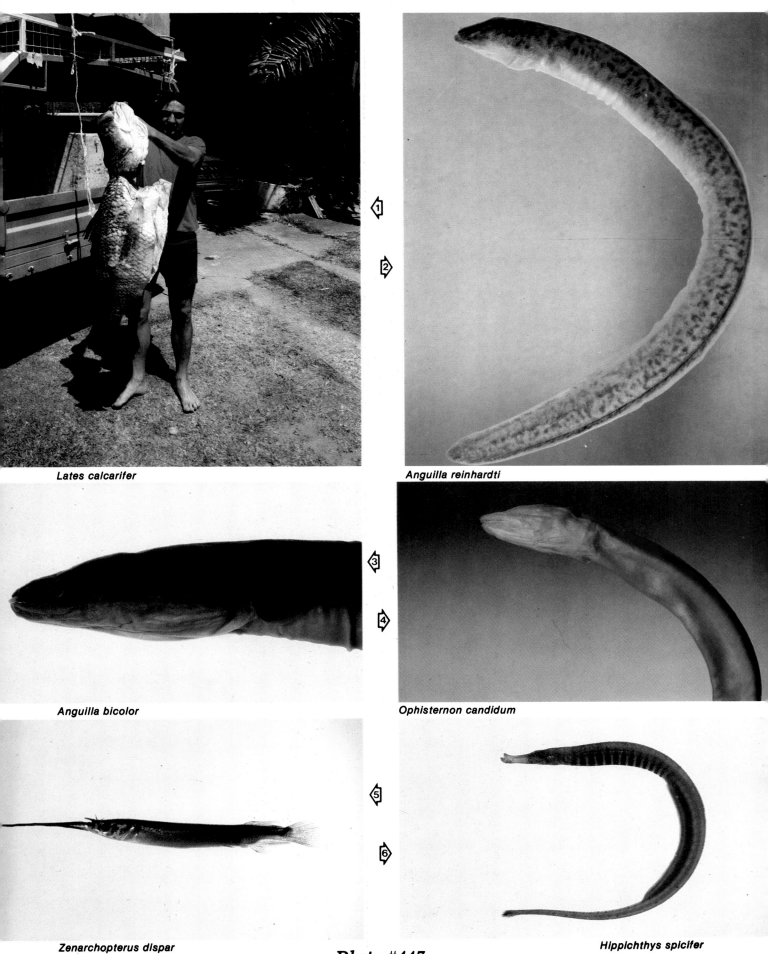

Lates calcarifer

Anguilla reinhardti

Anguilla bicolor

Ophisternon candidum

Zenarchopterus dispar

Hippichthys spicifer

*Plate #447*

667

*Lates calcarifer*
*See Plate #463*

*Anguilla bicolor*
*See Plate #424*

*Zenarchopterus dispar* (Cuvier & Valenciennes) •
Spoon-fin Garfish

RANGE: From Queensland in Australia to the East Indies.
HABITS: Occurs in marine environments as well as the still
waters of mangrove creeks and rivers. Often seen in
small shoals at the surface. A livebearer, the male with a
modified anal fin.
WATER CONDITIONS: Not critical. Normal aquarium conditions will suffice.
SIZE: Attains a length of about 15 cm.
FOOD REQUIREMENTS: Generally eats insects and small
crustaceans. Live foods are probably necessary in the
aquarium, at least at first.

*Anguilla reinhardti* Steindachner • Long-finned Eel

RANGE: Eastern coast of Australia as well as New Caledonia
and Lord Howe Island.
HABITS: Spawns in the ocean, producing pelagic eggs. The
young eels (elvers) return to fresh water and after
several years make their own spawning run to the sea.
WATER CONDITIONS: Elvers can be kept in fresh, brackish
or salt water. The tank must be carefully covered to prevent them from getting out.
SIZE: Large adults may grow to almost a meter in length
but usually are much smaller. Elvers of about 30 cm or so
are usually the ones kept in aquaria.
FOOD REQUIREMENTS: These are carnivorous fish and can
be fed small fishes, pieces of fish and shrimp, and other
meaty foods.

*Ophisternon candidum* (Mees) • Blind Freshwater Eel

RANGE: Found only in the dark, subterranean waters of
North West Cape, Western Australia.
HABITS: The most obvious character of this eel is that it is
eyeless. Its living color is white (the specimen seen here
is preserved) as in most cave-dwelling species. Despite
its lack of eyes, it gets around quite well and is able to
find its food without much ado.
WATER CONDITIONS: Probably would prefer water on the
alkaline side with temperatures in the range of 23-27°C.
The aquarium should be dimly lighted.
SIZE: Attains a length of about 37 cm.
FOOD REQUIREMENTS: Will accept a variety of meaty foods,
especially those that give off an odor for it to home in on.

*Hippichthys spicifer*
*See Plate #437*

### *Galaxias cleaveri* • Mud Galaxias, Tasmanian Mudfish

RANGE: Restricted to swampy environments of coastal Tasmania.

HABITS: Little is known about the habits of this species. It probably spawns in late winter. Captured when drains are being cleaned and may even be dug out of the mud or from under logs.

WATER CONDITIONS: Probably should be kept in slightly acid water at cool temperatures.

SIZE: Attains a length of about 12 cm.

FOOD REQUIREMENTS: Feeds on insects and material obtained from the detritus. Will accept some live and prepared aquarium foods.

### *Galaxias nigrostriata* Shipway • Striped Galaxias

RANGE: Found only in the southwestern section of Australia.

HABITS: Apparently spawns in peaty water. A pretty species with black stripes bordering an orange, yellow, or white ground color.

WATER CONDITIONS: Fairly hardy but does best in acid water. The use of peat is recommended. Should be placed only in unheated aquaria.

SIZE: A small species of 5-7 cm.

FOOD REQUIREMENTS: Feeds on invertebrates such as small crustaceans and insects and their larvae. Will accept a number of live aquarium foods and eventually some of the prepared foods as well.

### *Galaxias fuscus* • Jellybean Jollytail

RANGE: Known from at least Victoria, Australia.

HABITS: Found in freshwater streams in the colder regions of Australia. A colorful species as can be seen in the accompanying photo. Does well in captivity.

WATER CONDITIONS: Not critical. Water should be slightly acid and relatively cool (unheated tanks).

SIZE: Attains a length of about 6 cm.

FOOD REQUIREMENTS: Feeds on insects and small crustaceans. Aquarium foods are accepted.

*Scleropages jardini*
*See Plate #424*

*Tandanus* sp.
*See Plate #453*

Galaxias cleaveri

Galaxias fuscus

Galaxias nigrostriata

Galaxias nigrostriata

Scleropages jardini

Tandanus n. sp.

*Plate #448*

Galaxias auratus

Galaxias brevipinnis

Galaxias fontanis

Galaxias fontanis

Galaxias maculatus

Galaxias maculatus

Galaxias johnstoni

Galaxias olidus

*Plate #449*

671

## *Galaxias auratus* Johnston • Golden Galaxias

RANGE: Occurs only in Lakes Sorell and Crescent and associated rivers in Tasmania.
HABITS: Spawns in the southern winter or spring. A nice aquarium fish because of its golden color.
WATER CONDITIONS: Purely fresh water. A cool-water fish that is eaten by trout.
SIZE: Normally 14 cm, but could grow as large as 24 cm.
FOOD REQUIREMENTS: Feeds on small aquatic insects and crustaceans. Live aquarium foods are acceptable.

## *Galaxias fontanis* Fulton • Swan Galaxias

RANGE: Known only from the upper reaches of the Swan River in Tasmania.
HABITS: Occurs in shallow, rocky, spring-fed streams. Probably spawns during the warm mouths. The entire life is lived in fresh water.
WATER CONDITIONS: Not critical. A cool-water species and should not be placed in a heated aquarium.
SIZE: Usually about 7 cm, but can grow to 9 cm or more.
FOOD REQUIREMENTS: Probably feeds on aquatic insects and crustaceans in the wild. Will accept living aquarium foods and may be coaxed onto prepared foods as well.

## *Galaxias maculatus* (Jenyns) • Common Jollytail

RANGE: Coastal streams of southern and southeastern Australia, Tasmania, New Zealand, the Chatham Islands, Patagonian South America, and the Falkland Islands.
HABITS: Small schools occur in quiet or slowly flowing streams and rivers and at lake margins. Spawning occurs during a full or new moon in autumn after a downstream migration. Several thousand eggs scattered in vegetation are left high and dry until high spring tides cover them again (2 weeks) and they hatch. The larvae spend winter in the sea.
WATER CONDITIONS: A cool-water species that needs an unheated tank.
SIZE: Usually 10 cm, but may grow to almost twice that length.
FOOD REQUIREMENTS: Aquatic and terrestrial insects are its natural foods. Does well on chironomid larvae (bloodworms).

## *Galaxias johnstoni* Scott • Clarence Galaxias

RANGE: Occurs only in the Clarence Lagoon, its tributaries, and the upper Clarence River in Tasmania.
HABITS: An uncommon species that probably is solitary and secretive. Probably bottom-living in both still and moving waters.
WATER CONDITIONS: Strictly fresh water. A cool-water species requiring an unheated tank.
SIZE: Attains a length of up to 10 cm, but usually smaller.
FOOD REQUIREMENTS: Most likely feeds on aquatic insects and small crustaceans as well as other benthic invertebrates. Aquarium fare is accepted, especially live foods.

## *Galaxias brevipinnis* Guenther • Climbing Galaxias

RANGE: Inland lakes of Tasmania and coastal drainages of Australia from Sydney to Adelaide as well as New Zealand and the Chatham, Auckland, and Campbell Islands.
HABITS: Occurs in small rocky streams as well as lakes. A secretive solitary species commonly hiding among the rocks. Some larvae are thought to go to sea on hatching, returning when 4-5 cm long.
WATER CONDITIONS: A cool-water species to be kept in an unheated aquairum.
SIZE: Usually about 16 cm, but can get much larger.
FOOD REQUIREMENTS: Feeds on benthic invertebrates. Aquarium foods, especially live foods, are acceptable.

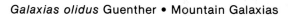

## *Galaxias olidus* Guenther • Mountain Galaxias

RANGE: Eastern Australia at moderate to high elevations.
HABITS: Occurs in small, loose schools in pools and runs as well as solitary individuals around the rocks of the stream margins. Spawning occurs in the spring (no migration to the sea).
WATER CONDITIONS: Prefers clean, clear, cool waters. Easy to keep.
SIZE: Commonly seen at 6 or 7 cm but can grow to twice that length.
FOOD REQUIREMENTS: Feeds on a variety of insects and other small invertebrates. Aquarium substitutes accepted.

Galaxias occidentalis

Galaxias occidentalis

Galaxias parvus

Galaxias pedderensis

Galaxias rostratus

Galaxias truttaceus

Galaxias tanycephalus

Galaxias tanycephalus

*Plate #450*

### *Galaxias occidentalis* • *Westralian Jollytail*

RANGE: Occurs only in the extreme southwestern corner of
   Australia.
HABITS: Not a very common species and very little is known
   about it. May be found only in some of the rivers north of
   Perth and south and west of that city.
WATER CONDITIONS: Not critical. Should be housed in an
   unheated aquarium.
SIZE: Attains a length of about 12-15 cm.
FOOD REQUIREMENTS: Small aquatic insects and crusta-
   ceans. Will accept live aquarium foods such as daphnia,
   cyclops, mosquito larvae, and chironomid larvae.

### *Galaxias parvus* Frankenberg • Dwarf Galaxias

RANGE: Endemic to southwestern Tasmania.
HABITS: Likes the quiet waters of swamps, backwaters,
   pools and lake margins where there are rocks and abundant vegetation. A spring spawner in which there is no
   migration to the sea.
WATER CONDITIONS: Not critical. A cool-water species that
   can only be housed in an unheated tank.
SIZE: A small species of about 7 cm (can grow to 9 cm).
FOOD REQUIREMENTS: Easy to keep and feed. Accepts a
   variety of aquarium fare, but live foods should be included.

### *Galaxias pedderensis* Frankenberg • Pedder Galaxias

RANGE: Occurs only in Lake Pedder and associated
   streams in Tasmania.
HABITS: Hides among the rocks along the shores of the lake
   and the streams. Apparently there is no seaward migration.
WATER CONDITIONS: Not critical, but should only be housed
   in an unheated tank.
SIZE: Attains a length of 11 cm.
FOOD REQUIREMENTS: Feeds on aquatic invertebrates,
   especially insects. Will accept aquarium foods,
   preferably live.

### *Galaxias rostratus* Klunzinger • Murray Jollytail

RANGE: Restricted to the Murray-Darling River system
   of Australia. Locally abundant.
HABITS: Prefers the quiet waters of lakes, lagoons, and backwaters. Usually seen in midwater schools. Several thousand demersal eggs are scattered randomly at
   temperatures between 9 and 14°C. They hatch in about 9
   days.
WATER CONDITIONS: A cool-water species (note spawning
   temperatures) that requires an unheated tank.
SIZE: Seldom exceeds about 10 cm.
FOOD REQUIREMENTS: Feeds on a variety of aquatic insects and crustaceans. Aquarium foods are acceptable.

### *Galaxias truttaceus* (Valenciennes) • Spotted Mountain Trout

RANGE: Coastal drainages of southern Victoria, Australia,
   islands of the Bass Strait, and Tasmania; also found in
   Western Australia.
HABITS: A fall or early winter spawner whose larvae make a
   seaward migration. Juveniles return during spring when
   they are about 5 cm long. Found along the margins of
   rivers and streams where there is abundant cover and
   little water movement. Also found under cover on the
   lake bottoms.
WATER CONDITIONS: A cool-water species requiring an
   unheated tank.
SIZE: Usually seen at a size of 12 to 14 cm but does get as
   large as 20 cm.
FOOD REQUIREMENTS: Feeds mostly on insects, both
   aquatic and terrestrial. Chironomid larvae are an excellent food along with mosquito larvae when available.

### *Galaxias tanycephalus* Fulton • Saddled Galaxias

RANGE: A rare species known only from Arthurs Lake and
   Woods Lake in Tasmania.
HABITS: Occurs around boulders of man-made groins and
   apparently shuns the weed beds near these groins. Ap-
   parently no migration to the sea.
WATER CONDITIONS: Must have a cool-water aquarium.
SIZE: About 7 cm, but can grow as large as 11 cm.
FOOD REQUIREMENTS: Small aquatic insects and crusta-
   ceans are acceptable.

*Galaxias maculatus*
*See Plate #449*

*Galaxias tanycephalus*
*See Plate #450*

*Galaxiella munda* • Swan Galaxias

RANGE: This species is known only from just north of Perth to about Albany in southwestern Australia.
HABITS: This is a relatively newly discovered species and little is known about its habits. It is expected to behave much like other species of the genus.
WATER CONDITIONS: Not critical, but should be housed in an unheated aquarium.
SIZE: Probably reaches a length of about 6 or 7 cm.
FOOD REQUIREMENTS: Feeds on small aquatic insects and crustaceans. Similar aquarium foods are accepted.

*Galaxias truttaceus*
*See Plate #450*

*Paragalaxias mesotes* McDowall & Fulton • Arthurs Paragalaxias

RANGE: Only in the central plateau of Tasmania in Arthurs Lake, Woods Lake, and the Lake River below Woods Lake.
HABITS: Seems to prefer to hide among rocks and boulders rather than among vegetation along the shores of the lakes. No seaward migration.
WATER CONDITIONS: A cool-water species that must be kept in an unheated aquarium.
SIZE: Attains a length of a little over 7 cm.
FOOD REQUIREMENTS: Feeds on crustaceans and insects. Aquarium foods, especially live brine shrimp, daphnia, and chironomid larvae, accepted.

*Lepidogalaxias salamandroides* Mees • Long-finned Galaxias

RANGE: Found only in extreme southwestern Australia.
HABITS: Mating involves internal fertilization after little or no courtship. A week after copulation the ovipositor appears and some 100-150 eggs are laid. The adults usually die shortly after reproducing. Young fish may burrow into the mud bottom for a period of estivation when their pools dry up. Easy prey to fungal infections.
WATER CONDITIONS: The pH should be very low, at least below 6 and possibly even to 4.5. A cool-water species for which the temperature should not exceed 20°C, preferably 12-15°C.
SIZE: Attains a maximum length of 6-7 cm, normally smaller, with females larger than the males.
FOOD REQUIREMENTS: Will accept only live foods.

675

Galaxias maculatus

Galaxias tanycephalus

Galaxias truttaceus

Galaxiella munda

Paragalaxias mesotes

Lepidogalaxias salamandroides

**Plate #451**

676

Galaxiella pusilla

Galaxiella pusilla

Paragalaxias dissimilis

Paragalaxias dissimilis

Paragalaxias eleotroides

Paragalaxias eleotroides

Paragalaxias julianus

Paragalaxias mesotes

Plate #452

677

*Galaxiella pusilla* (Mack) • Eastern Pygmy Galaxias,
Dwarf Galaxias

RANGE: Southeastern Australia and Tasmania.
HABITS: Spawns in late winter to early spring, the ripe females courted by 2 to 3 males. A pair will choose the surface of a rock or underside of a leaf, where eggs are laid
individually and then ignored. 150-200 eggs per female
are laid over a 2-3 week period.
WATER CONDITIONS: A thickly planted aquarium with a
slightly acid pH and gentle aeration is recommended.
Temperatures should be on the low side as this fish
spawns at 16-21°C.
SIZE: A tiny species with 3 cm males and 4 cm females.
FOOD REQUIREMENTS: Live foods are preferred, particularly mosquito larvae, brine shrimp, and small cladoceran
crustaceans.

*Paragalaxias dissimilis* (Regan) • Shannon Paragalaxias

RANGE: Known only from the Central Plateau of Tasmania.
HABITS: Possibly a nocturnal species hiding by day under
rocks, vegetation, or other debris and coming up into
midwater to feed at night. Will remain in midwater in
aquaria when not frightened. No seaward migration.
WATER CONDITIONS: A cool-water species that requires an
unheated tank.
SIZE: About 5 cm, but will grow to 7.5 cm.
FOOD REQUIREMENTS: Small midwater crustaceans and
aquatic insects. Prefers live foods in aquaria but may be
coaxed onto prepared foods.

*Paragalaxias eleotroides* McDowall & Fulton • Great
Lake Darter Galaxias

RANGE: Known only from Great Lake (where it is common)
and Shannon Lagoon on the Central Plateau of
Tasmania.
HABITS: Hides among the vegetation, rocks, and debris of
the lake floor. A bottom fish that will sit propped up on its
pectoral fins and scoot about like a goby or darter. No
seaward migration.
WATER CONDITIONS: A cool-water species requiring an unheated tank.
SIZE: Attains a length of 4-6 cm.
FOOD REQUIREMENTS: Feeds on aquatic insects and crustaceans. Will accept aquarium foods, especially if alive.

*Paragalaxias julianus* McDowall & Fulton •
Julian Paragalaxias

RANGE: Found only on the high altitude Central Plateau of
Tasmania.
HABITS: Common under the cover of rocks, vegetation, and
debris on lake bottoms. Little else is known, but there is
no apparent seaward migration.
WATER CONDITIONS: A cool-water species that requires
unheated tanks.
SIZE: Attains a length of over 9 cm (one of the largest species
of the genus).
FOOD REQUIREMENTS: Feeds on aquatic insects and crustaceans. Will accept aquarium fare.

*Paragalaxias mesotes*
*See Plate #451*

*Neosilurus ater* (Perugia) • Black Catfish, Narrow-fronted
Tandan, Butter Jew

RANGE: Northern Australia and New Guinea.
HABITS: Has been known under at least three generic names, *Tandanus, Neosilurus,* and *Lambertichthys.* Lives on the bottom where it grubs for bits of food. Probably builds a nest for spawning that is guarded by the male.
WATER CONDITIONS: Not critical. A tropical species, so temperatures should be in the normal range for other tropical fishes.
SIZE: May grow to as much as 50 cm.
FOOD REQUIREMENTS: Will accept a variety of foods including small live fishes.

*Neosilurus hyrtlii* Steindachner • Hyrtl's Tandan

RANGE: Occurs only in the river systems of Queensland, Australia.
HABITS: A bottom-living catfish that grubs along the bottom for food.
WATER CONDITIONS: Not critical. A good filtration system is usually necessary to accommodate the material stirred up by the catfish.
SIZE: Attains a length of at least 40 cm.
FOOD REQUIREMENTS: Carnivorous. Accepts meaty food and live fishes.

*Porochilus rendahli* • Rendahl's Tandan

RANGE: Australia.
HABITS: Not known for certain. Normally grubs in the bottom material for its food and should be fed accordingly. Some species of tandan are egg-scatterers over gravel in streams where the water is swift-flowing.
WATER CONDITIONS: Not critical. Normal pH and temperatures should apply.
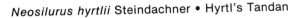
SIZE: Attains a length of about 15 to 20 cm.
FOOD REQUIREMENTS: Accepts a variety of foods that fall to the bottom of the aquarium. Not a fussy eater.

*Tandanus bostocki* Whitley • Cobbler

RANGE: Found only in rivers of southwestern Australia.
HABITS: A bottom-dwelling catfish that tends to stir up the bottom material. Good filtration is necessary. Said to build nests and that the male guards the eggs and young.
WATER CONDITIONS: Not critical. Temperatures should be on the low side (unheated tank).
SIZE: Attains a length of at least 40-50 cm.
FOOD REQUIREMENTS: Carnivorous. Frozen and fresh chopped fishes and shrimp can be offered along with small live fishes.

*Tandanus tandanus* Mitchell • Dewfish

RANGE: Endemic to eastern Australian rivers.
HABITS: Creates a saucer-shaped depression in which to lay the eggs. The eggs, about 3.2 mm in diameter, hatch in about a week. In another two weeks the young are 15 mm long and resemble their parents.
WATER CONDITIONS: Not critical.
SIZE: Reaches a length of almost a meter and a weight of about 7 kilos.
FOOD REQUIREMENTS: Feeds in the wild on shellfish and shrimp. In aquaria will accept most frozen foods including chopped meat and dead fishes. Feeds from the bottom as do most catfishes.

Neosilurus ater

Neosilurus ater

Neosilurus hyrtlii

Neosilurus hyrtlii

Neosilurus hyrtlii

Porochilus rendahli

Tandanus bostocki

Tandanus tandanus

*Plate #453*

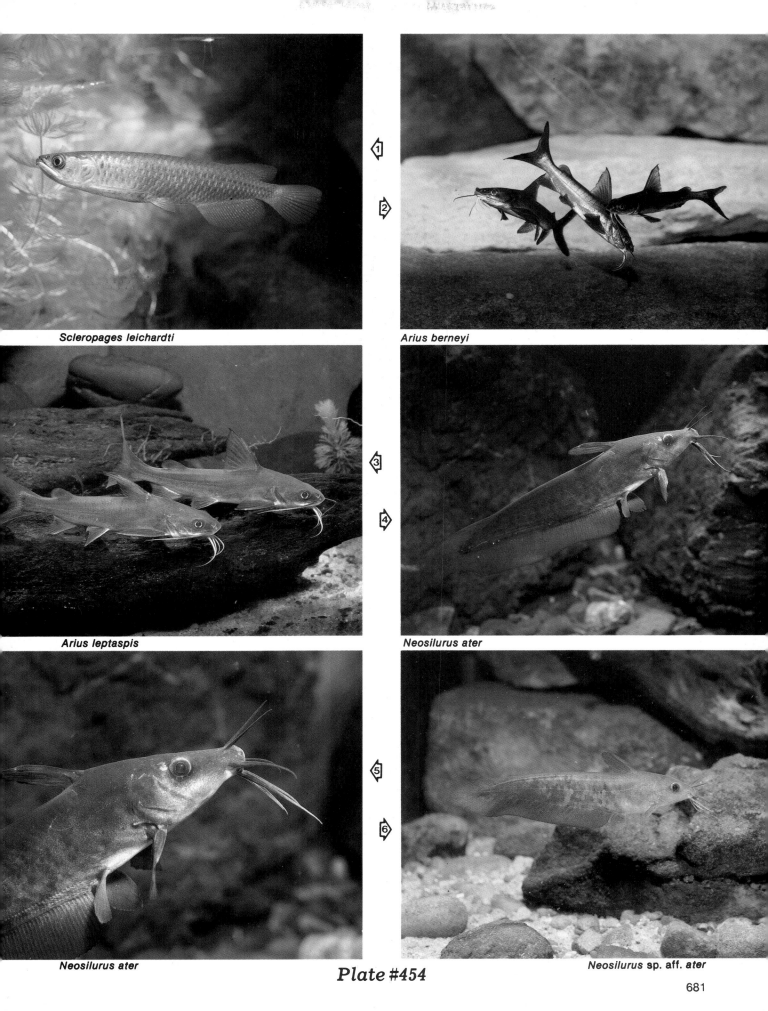

*Scleropages leichardti*

*Arius berneyi*

*Arius leptaspis*

*Neosilurus ater*

*Neosilurus ater*

*Neosilurus sp. aff. ater*

**Plate #454**

### *Scleropages leichardti* Guenther • Spotted Barramundi

RANGE: Fitzroy River system of Queensland, Australia. Has been introduced elsewhere in Queensland.

HABITS: A buccal incubator. Some 70-200 10-mm eggs are carried in the mouth at one time. Spawning may occur when water temperatures rise above 20°C.

WATER CONDITIONS: Not critical.

SIZE: Reaches a length of almost a meter.

FOOD REQUIREMENTS: Normally feeds at the surface on insects. Will also feed on small fishes, crayfishes, and even frogs. In an aquarium most meaty foods and small live fishes are accepted.

### *Arius berneyi* Whitley • Berney's Catfish

RANGE: Found only in northern and northeastern Australia.

HABITS: Paternal mouthbrooders; that is, males carry the eggs in their mouths during the incubation period of about two weeks. Also called *Hexanematichthys berneyi*. The species was named after the Australian naturalist F.L. Berney.

WATER CONDITIONS: Equally at home in fresh or marine water.

SIZE: Attains a length of up to 20 cm.

FOOD REQUIREMENTS: A carnivorous species that will accept meaty foods and live fishes.

### *Arius leptaspis* (Bleeker) • Salmon Catfish

RANGE: Rivers of coastal Australia and New Guinea.

HABITS: Males incubate some 100-300 eggs in the mouth. The eggs, about 14 mm in diameter, hatch in approximately two weeks, during which period the males do not feed. Also known as *Hexanematichthys leptaspis*.

WATER CONDITIONS: Occurs in pure fresh water to full marine water. Larger individuals are sensitive to colder waters.

SIZE: A mouthbrooding male weighed in at 1.6 kilos. Grows to at least 50 cm.

FOOD REQUIREMENTS: Will accept a wide variety of foods, including small fishes.

*Neosilurus ater*
*See Plate #453*

*Neosilurus hyrtlii*
See Plate #453

*Porochilus obbesi*
See Plate #426

*Pseudomugil mellis* Allen & Ivantsoff • Honey Blue-eye

RANGE: Found only in southern Queensland, Australia.
HABITS: Spawns easily in aquaria supplied with Java moss or a similar spawning medium. Eggs placed there in hatch in about 18 hours, the fry feeding on infusoria or fine powdered food. They attain sexual maturity at the end of one year.
WATER CONDITIONS: The water should be acid (pH 4.4 to 5.8) and the temperature on the high side (25°C to 32°C). Their natural water is tea-colored and there is dense vegetation.
SIZE: Reaches a maximum size of about 30 mm, most only 25 mm.
FOOD REQUIREMENTS: Feeds on insects and small crustaceans (newly hatched brine shrimp for example), as well as chopped liver and spinach.

*Tandanus tandanus*
See Plate #453

*Craterocephalus stercusmuscarum* (Guenther) • Fly-specked Hardyhead

RANGE: Common in northern and northeastern Australian river systems.
HABITS: An excellent and sought-after aquarium species. Swims near the surface and is effective in mosquito control. Said to "leap-frog" over objects floating in its path, so an aquarium cover is necessary.
WATER CONDITIONS: Not critical. Temperature should be about 23°-26°C.
SIZE: Reaches a length of 7.5 cm.
FOOD REQUIREMENTS: Will accept prepared or even dried foods that can be taken near the surface or that float. Of course would prefer small floating insects and larvae.

*Ambassis agrammus agrammus* Guenther • Sailfin Perchlet

RANGE: Northern Australia and New Guinea.
HABITS: Relatively peaceful, but males may squabble a bit. Most are schooling fishes, and it is best that several be kept together. A fairly efficient mosquito control fish.
WATER CONDITIONS: Not critical. Extremes should be avoided. Can stand a bit of salt in their water.
SIZE: Attains a length of 7 cm.
FOOD REQUIREMENTS: Mosquito larvae, daphnia, and other such live foods are best, but it eventually will accept prepared aquarium foods.

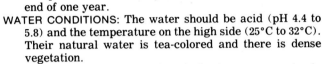

Neosilurus hyrtlii

Porochilus obbesi

Tandanus tandanus

Pseudomugil mellis

Croterocephalus stercusmuscarum

Ambassis agrammus

Plate #455

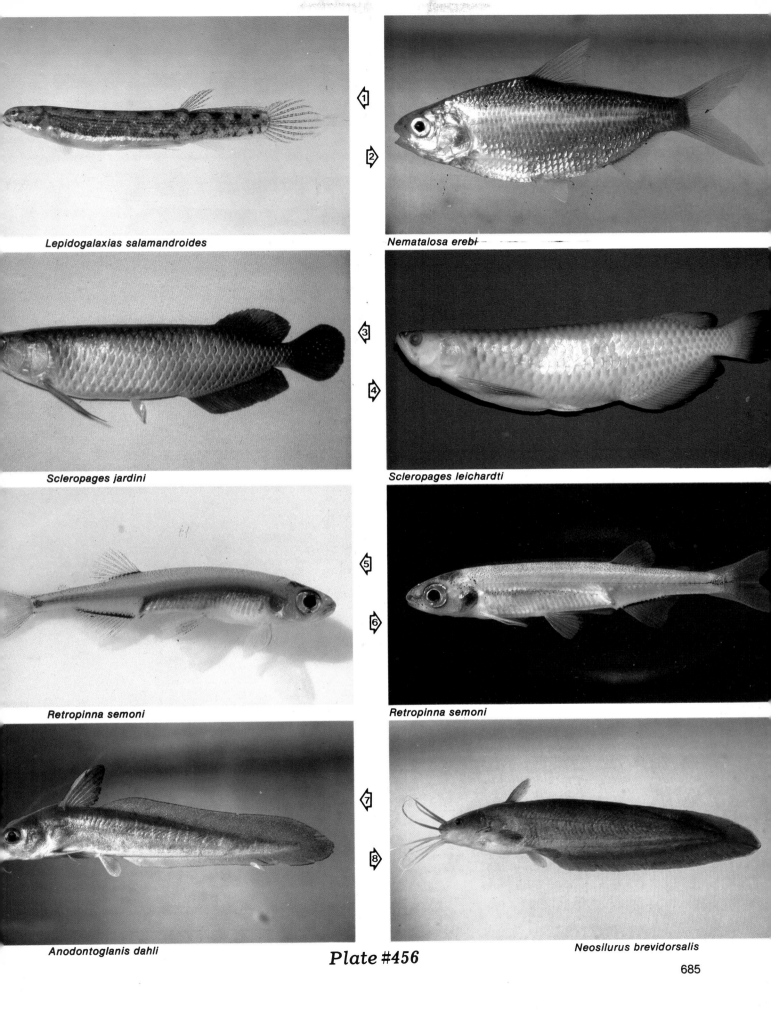

*Lepidogalaxias salamandroides*

*Nematalosa erebi*

*Scleropages jardini*

*Scleropages leichardti*

*Retropinna semoni*

*Retropinna semoni*

*Anodontoglanis dahli*

*Neosilurus brevidorsalis*

Plate #456

685

*Nematalosa erebi* (Guenther) • Bony Bream

RANGE: Rivers of Australia.
HABITS: Spawns in the Australian spring and summer months. A schooling fish.
WATER CONDITIONS: Not critical, but should have plentiful aeration.
SIZE: Attains a length of about 40 cm.
FOOD REQUIREMENTS: In the wild it feeds on vegetable matter (algae and aquatic plants), insects, and organic material filtered from the ingestion of mud. Aquarium foods should contain vegetable matter. Chironomid larvae and mosquito larvae are also very good.

*Lepidogalaxias salamandroides*
See Plate #451

*Scleropages jardini*
See Plate #424

*Scleropages leichardti*
See Plate #454

*Retropinna semoni* (Weber) • Australian Smelt

RANGE: Southeastern Australia.
HABITS: Active surface schooling fish that help eradicate mosquito larvae. The coloration is such that the fish are almost invisible against a sandy background.
WATER CONDITIONS: Lives in both fresh and salt water. Prefers cooler water temperatures than the northern Australian tropical species.
SIZE: Normally 5 to 6 cm, rarely to twice that size.
FOOD REQUIREMENTS: Mosquito larvae, various worms, and even dry food.

*Anodontoglanis dahli* (Rendahl) • Toothless Catfish
RANGE: Restricted to northern Australia. Relatively rare.
HABITS: Builds saucer-shaped nests in sand or gravel bottom. Will breed in small ponds. The flesh is orange-colored and considered excellent.
WATER CONDITIONS: Not critical.
SIZE: To at least 15 cm.
FOOD REQUIREMENTS: Bottom feeders that will eat almost anything that is available. Although the mouth is toothless, there are "teeth" in the gullet.

*Neosilurus brevidorsalis*
See Plate #426

*Neosilurus* sp.
*See Plate #453*

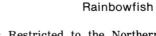

## *Melanotaenia splendida fluviatilis* (Castelnau) • Crimson-spotted Rainbowfish

RANGE: Coastal section of southern Queensland and northern New South Wales.

HABITS: Relatively peaceful and suitable for a community aquarium. This subspecies has been considered as a distinct species by some authors. It inhabits a variety of environments including streams, lakes, ponds, and reservoirs but seems to prefer clear water with minimal flow.

WATER CONDITIONS: Not critical. A hardy species that can live within a pH range of 5.3-7.5 and a temperature range of 18 to 28°C.

SIZE: Males grow to about 9 cm but are normally only 7 cm; females grow to about 6.5 cm.

FOOD REQUIREMENTS: Prefers live foods but will accept other aquarium foods as well.

## *Rhadinocentrus ornatus* Regan • Southern Soft-spined Rainbowfish

RANGE: Southern Queensland and northern New South Wales Australia.

HABITS: Active mid-water swimmers; peaceful.

WATER CONDITIONS: Neutral to slightly alkaline water to which a little bit of salt has been added. Temperature should range from about 22 to 26°C.

SIZE: Attains a length of about 8 cm.

FOOD REQUIREMENTS: Will readily accept most common aquarium foods, but for best conditioning should have some live foods.

*Pseudomugil mellis*
*See Plate #455*

## *Strongylura kreffti* (Guenther) • Long Tom

RANGE: Northern and northeastern Australia and New Guinea.

HABITS: These are surface fish capable of not only leaping from the water, but they engage in "tail-walking" along the surface. This is an efficient predator so it cannot be kept with smaller fishes. Sometimes seen in small schools or aggregations.

WATER CONDITIONS: Not critical. Can tolerate some salt in the water.

SIZE: Reaches a length of about 65 cm.

FOOD REQUIREMENTS: Does best on small fishes that swim near the surface. Will accept shrimp and other meaty food if it remains in the upper water levels.

## *Melanotaenia trifasciata* (Rendahl) • Banded Rainbowfish

RANGE: Restricted to the Northern Territory and Cape York Peninsula of Australia.

HABITS: This species spawns daily, releasing 30-50 eggs per spawning. The eggs hatch in about a week, yielding tiny fry that need the smallest of foods (infusoria or egg yolk infusion).

WATER CONDITIONS: Needs clean, fresh water with a pH of 7.5 and a hardness of 50-200 ppm. Trouble occurs if the pH drops below 6.8. The temperature should be on the high side, 24-30°C.

SIZE: Attains a maximum size of 9-10 cm.

FOOD REQUIREMENTS: An avid consumer of duckweed, green algae, and other vegetable matter. Mosquito larvae, daphnia, brine shrimp, and other live foods preferred, but will take frozen and prepared foods.

## *Pseudomugil signifer* Kner • Southern Blue-eye

RANGE: Australian states of Queensland and New South Wales.

HABITS: A peaceful, active fish.

WATER CONDITIONS: Prefers alkaline, slightly hard water but is adaptable to life in water of different composition. Best temperature range 22 to 26°C.

SIZE: To about 6 cm for males.

FOOD REQUIREMENTS: Accepts all standard aquarium foods except large, chunky prepared foods.

## *Pseudomugil gertrudae* Weber • Gertrude's Blue-eye

RANGE: New Guinea and Aru Islands to Queensland, Australia.

HABITS: A peaceful, active species.

WATER CONDITIONS: Not critical, but prefers hard alkaline water, perhaps with some salt added. The best temperature range is 20 to 26°C.

SIZE: A small species rarely exceeding 2.5 cm in length.

FOOD REQUIREMENTS: Does well on live foods such as mosquito larvae, tubificid worms, etc.

Neosilurus sp.

Strongylura kreffti

Melanotaenia splendida fluviatilis

Melanotaenia trifasciatus

Rhadinocentrus ornatus

Pseudomugil signifer

Pseudomugil mellis

Pseudomugil gertrudae

*Plate #457*

Cairnsichthys rhombosomoides

Rhadinocentrus ornatus

Iriatherina werneri

Pseudomugil tenellus

Pseudomugil signifer

Pseudomugil signifer

Plate #458

689

*Cairnsichthys rhombosomoides* (Nichols & Raven) •
Cairns Rainbowfish

RANGE: Inhabits only a small area in the vicinity of Cairns, Queensland, Australia.
HABITS: A relatively short-lived species (maximum about 3 years) that is somewhat delicate to handle. With sufficient water from their natural habitat they may make it to your aquarium safely and are relatively easy to care for from then on. Males have yellow margins on the dorsal and anal fins.
WATER CONDITIONS: Once acclimated to captivity, this species can be cared for in the same manner as the rainbowfishes. A pH that is neutral to slightly alkaline and a temperature of 22-24°C should suffice.
SIZE: Males grow to about 7 cm, females to 6.5 cm.
FOOD REQUIREMENTS: It is best to start with live foods such as brine shrimp, daphnia, and chironomid larvae. Other aquarium foods can be added in time.

*Iriatherina werneri* Meinken • Featherfin Rainbow

RANGE: West Irian (on island of New Guinea). Queensland
HABITS: Peaceful and active.
WATER CONDITIONS: pH and hardness are not critical, as long as extremes are avoided. Temperature 24 to 27°C.
SIZE: To about 4 cm.
FOOD REQUIREMENTS: Accepts most standard aquarium foods, but only in small sizes.

*Rhadinocentrus ornatus*
See Plate #457

*Pseudomugil tenellus* Taylor • Delicate Blue-eye

RANGE: This small species is known only from the East Alligator River system of the Northern Territory, Australia.
HABITS: A typical habitat would be a marshy pond or quiet backwater with mud or gravel bottoms and abundant vegetation. The water may be green with suspended algae, and water lilies float on the surface.
WATER CONDITIONS: The water can be neutral to slightly acid and the temperature a bit on the warm side (28-35°C in nature).
SIZE: Reaches a length of only about 2.6 cm.
FOOD REQUIREMENTS: Should be fed the finest of live foods (newly hatched brine shrimp is good).

*Pseudomugil signifer*
See Plate #457

### *Melanotaenia eachamensis* Allen & Cross • Lake Eacham Rainbowfish

RANGE: Known only from Lake Eacham on the Atherton Tableland in Queensland.
HABITS: A lake-dwelling species of rainbowfish that prefers the clear, shallow water along the shoreline. Relatively peaceful, making a suitable community tank fish. A well planted tank is recommended.
WATER CONDITIONS: Not critical. A pH of about neutral and a temperature between 23 and 27°C suits them very well. A 20-25% water change every month or so is recommended.
SIZE: Attains a length of about 5-6 cm.
FOOD REQUIREMENTS: Accepts a variety of aquarium foods but should receive some live foods regularly for best results.

### *Melanotaenia nigrans* (Richardson) • Dark Australian Rainbow

RANGE: Northeastern Australia as far south as Sydney.
HABITS: Peaceful and very hardy; prefers to be kept in small groups.
WATER CONDITIONS: Neutral to slightly alkaline water to which a small amount of salt has been added. Temperature 19 to 24°C.
SIZE: To 10 cm.
FOOD REQUIREMENTS: Easily fed; accepts prepared foods as readily as live or frozen foods.

### *Melanotaenia splendida*

This species has been broken up into a number of subspecies, some of which have been known as full species at one time or another. Five of the subspecies *(australis, inornata, tatei, fluviatilis,* and *splendida)* occur in Australia, with a sixth *(rubrostriata)* in southern New Guinea. They are most easily distinguished by their point of origin.

### *Melanotaenia gracilis* Allen • Slender Rainbowfish

RANGE: This species is restricted to the Drysdale and King Edward River systems in the extreme northern portion of Western Australia.
HABITS: Prefers large watercourses and isolated rocky pools. The water flow is usually minimal. A peaceful fish suitable for community tanks.
WATER CONDITIONS: A neutral pH with temperatures between 22 and 24°C is best. The tank should be heavily planted and regular water changes should be made. Some sunlight on the tank is beneficial.
SIZE: Males reach a length of about 7.5 cm, females 6.5 cm.
FOOD REQUIREMENTS: Small live foods are preferred, but it will accept a variety of other foods commonly used for aquarium fishes.

### *Melanotaenia splendida inornata* (Castelnau) • Checkered Rainbowfish

RANGE: Generally streams flowing into the Gulf of Carpentaria in Northern Territory, Australia, but also an island or two in the Torres Straits.
HABITS: A peaceful species suitable for a community tank. Easily spawned in a well planted tank. A couple of hours of sunlight on the tank are beneficial.
WATER CONDITIONS: A neutral pH with temperatures between 22 and 24°C is acceptable. Regular water changes are recommended.
SIZE: Males reach a length of about 10 cm, females 8.5-9.0 cm.
FOOD REQUIREMENTS: Eats a variety of aquarium foods. Live foods should be offered on a regular basis.

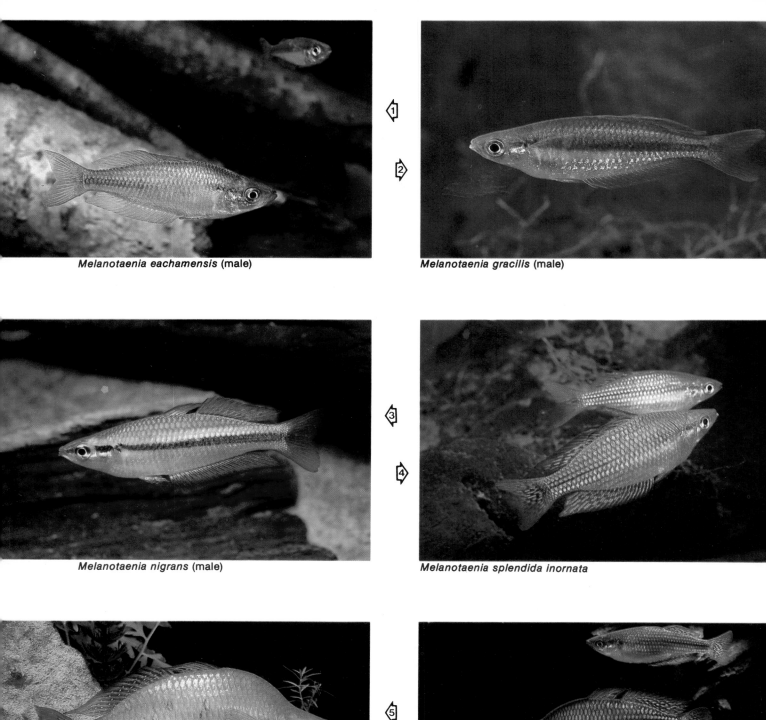

Melanotaenia eachamensis (male)

Melanotaenia gracilis (male)

Melanotaenia nigrans (male)

Melanotaenia splendida inornata

Melanotaenia splendida

Melanotaenia splendida inornata (female upper)

*Plate #459*

Melanotaenia nigrans (male upper)

Melanotaenia splendida australis (male)

Habitat of *M. splendida australis*

Habitat of *M. splendida fluviatilis* and *Pseudomugil signifer*

Habitat of *M. splendida inornata*

Habitat of *M. splendida inornata*

*Plate #460*

693

*Melanotaenia splendida australis* (Castelnau) •
Western Australian Rainbowfish

*Melanotaenia nigrans*
*See Plate #459*

RANGE: Found in northwestern Australia.

HABITS: Found in rivers, lakes, smaller streams, swamps and marshy lagoons where the water flow is minimal. They occur at or near the surface of deeper pools in stream habitats where there is vegetation or log debris. In lake habitats they are found around the shallow margins.

WATER CONDITIONS: Not critical. A pH range of 6.5-7.8 and a temperature range of 25-32°C occur in their natural habitat. Periodic water changes (20-25% every month or so) are recommended. Some sunlight is beneficial.

SIZE: Males reach 9 cm, females about 7.5-8.0 cm.

FOOD REQUIREMENTS: Normal aquarium foods are accepted, but there is a preference for live foods.

*Melanotaenia splendida splendida* (Peters) • Eastern
Australian Rainbowfish

RANGE: This species occurs in river systems east of the
Great Dividing Range of Queensland.
HABITS: A very variable species, each stream seeming to
have a different strain. Prefers small streams but also
occurs in lakes and reservoirs. The water in the habitat
varies from clear to turbid and there may or may not be
vegetative cover.
WATER CONDITIONS: Occurs in nature in water temperatures from 20-29°C and a pH range from 6.4-7.2. A 20-25%
water change should be made every month or so.
SIZE: Males grow to 11 cm, females to about 10 cm.
FOOD REQUIREMENTS: Small live foods are preferred, but
it will accept other frozen and prepared foods as well.

*Melanotaenia trifasciata*
*See Plate #457*

695

*Melanotaenia splendida splendida* (males)

*Melanotaenia splendida splendida* (male)

*Melanotaenia splendida splendida* (female upper)

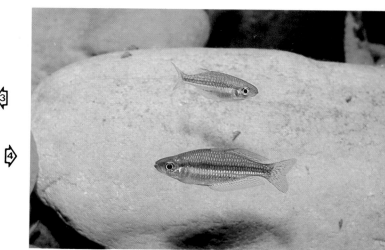

*Melanotaenia splendida splendida* (male lower fish)

*Melanotaenia trifasciata* (male)

*Melanotaenia trifasciata* (male)

*Plate #461*

*Craterocephalus cuneiceps*

*Craterocephalus marjoriae*

*Craterocephalus randi*

*Craterocephalus stercusmuscarum fulvus*

*Craterocephalus stercusmuscarum*

*Craterocephalus stercusmuscarum*

*Craterocephalus* sp.

*Craterocephalus* n. sp.

*Plate #462*

### *Craterocephalus cuneiceps* • Deep Hardyhead

RANGE: Found only in western Australia between 20°S and 30°S latitudes.
HABITS: A poorly known species that probably behaves like other species of the genus.
WATER CONDITIONS: Not critical. Will tolerate some salt in their water. The best temperatures are on the lower side of the normal range for aquaria.
SIZE: Attains a length of about 7 to 8 cm.
FOOD REQUIREMENTS: Does well on live aquarium foods. Known as a destroyer of mosquito larvae.

### *Craterocephalus marjoriae* Whitley • Marjorie's Freshwater Hardyhead

RANGE: Known only from the coastal streams of Queensland, New South Wales, Northern Territory, and northwestern Australia.
HABITS: A schooling species inhabiting shallow waters where there is a sandy substrate. During the breeding season the color changes to a bright canary yellow.
WATER CONDITIONS: Not critical. Easy to keep under normal aquarium conditions.
SIZE: Attains a length of up to 8 cm.
FOOD REQUIREMENTS: Accepts a variety of aquarium foods, even dried foods.

### *Craterocephalus* spp. • Hardyheads

Hardyheads of the genus *Craterocephalus* make relatively good aquarium fishes. They often like to school and are said to lay tiny adhesive eggs of pinhead size. None of them grow very large (between 8 and 10 cm maximum). They feed on small aquatic animals and are inveterate mosquito eaters. Several of the species are quite colorful, especially when in breeding colors.

*Quirichthys stramineus* Whitley • Strawman; Blackmast

RANGE: River systems of northern Australia.
HABITS: With external teeth on its lips the strawman is able to scrape the surface of plants and other submerged objects. It has even been reported to nibble on wader's legs. Peaceful and hardy and makes an excellent aquarium fish.
WATER CONDITIONS: Not critical. A neutral pH and water temperature around 23° to 26°C are recommended. Addition of salt to the water is possible.
SIZE: Attains a length of about 7 cm.
FOOD REQUIREMENTS: Will accept a variety of aquarium foods as long as they are small. Will also scrape plant leaves for food.

*Ophisternon* sp. • Single-gilled Eel

These eels make unusual aquarium inhabitants and are usually kept only by aquarists looking for something different. They are usually hardy but seem to be able to escape from aquaria quite easily through even the most minute space. A cover is therefore highly recommended.

*Priopidichthys* sp. • Plain-head Perchlet

RANGE: Coastal areas of New Guinea.
HABITS: The species of this genus are often found in fully marine situations and also commonly penetrate estuaries and tidal rivers. Relatives of this possibly undescribed species range from the Indian Ocean to the Pacific Islands.
WATER CONDITIONS: Hard water with salt added is preferable.
SIZE: Reaches at least 10 cm in length.
FOOD REQUIREMENTS: Predaceous on smaller crustaceans and fishes.

*Ambassis agrammus agassizi* Steindachner • Olive Glassfish, Olive Perch

RANGE: Northwestern, northern, and eastern Australia, with the exception of Northern Territory (range of *A. agrammus agrammus*).
HABITS: Will breed in aquaria. In nature this species is usually found among aquatic vegetation. Very abundant.
WATER CONDITIONS: Not critical. A freshwater fish that could tolerate some salt in its water if necessary. Normal aquarium temperatures should prevail.
SIZE: Attains a length of at least 7 cm.
FOOD REQUIREMENTS: Small invertebrates are eaten in nature. Live aquarium foods are acceptable (brine shrimp, daphnia, bloodworms, mosquito larvae, etc.).

*Ophisternon gutturale* (Richardson) • One-gilled Eel

RANGE: Northern Australia near river mouths.
HABITS: This estuarine eel commonly and regularly enters fresh waters. It has no paired fins, no scales, minute eyes, and a single gill opening located on the lower surface of the throat.
WATER CONDITIONS: Lives well in fresh, brackish or even full salt water.
SIZE: Grows to more than 60 cm.
FOOD REQUIREMENTS: Feeds on small invertebrates and fishes. Will accept a variety of prepared and frozen aquarium foods.

*Lates calcarifer*
*See Plate #439*

Quirichthys stramineus

Ophisternon gutturale

Ophisternon sp.

Lates calcarifer

Priopidichthys

Ambassis agrammus agassizi

Ambassis agrammus agassizi

*Plate #463*

Ambassis agrammus agassizi

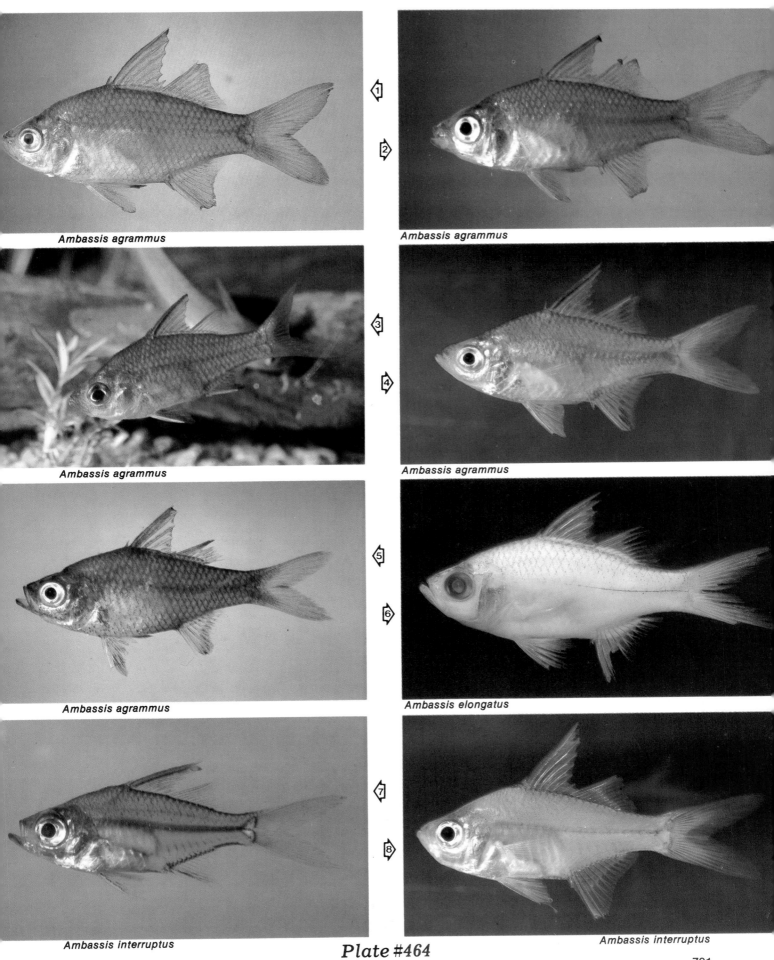

Ambassis agrammus

Ambassis agrammus

Ambassis agrammus

Ambassis agrammus

Ambassis agrammus

Ambassis elongatus

Ambassis interruptus

Ambassis interruptus

Plate #464

*Ambassis agrammus*
See Plate #455

*Ambassis elongatus*
See Plate #465

*Ambassis interruptus*
See Plate #438

*Ambassis elongatus* (Castelnau) • Yellowfin Glassfish

RANGE: Gulf of Carpentaria drainage of northern Queensland, Australia.
HABITS: Occurs in freshwater streams that frequently have moderate to high turbidity levels. Often occurs in schools.
WATER CONDITIONS: Not critical. Normal aquarium temperature ranges are sufficient.
SIZE: Attains a length of at least 4-5 cm.
FOOD REQUIREMENTS: Small invertebrates are eaten in the natural environment. Aquarium foods, especially live foods, are acceptable.

*Ambassis commersoni* Cuvier & Valenciennes •
Commerson's Glassfish

RANGE: A wide-ranging species that is found from the western Indian Ocean to the Fiji Islands. Its range includes the Philippines and Australia.
HABITS: This is an estuarine species that will ascend rivers into pure fresh water.
WATER CONDITIONS: Does well in pure fresh water as well as brackish water. Normal temperature ranges are acceptable.
SIZE: Attains a length of at least 10 cm.
FOOD REQUIREMENTS: Feeds on small invertebrates. Does well on live aquarium foods. Will accept prepared and frozen foods if coaxed.

*Ambassis macleayi* Castelnau • Reticulated Glassfish

RANGE: Northern Australia and south-central New Guinea.
HABITS: This species is most usually seen in the heavily vegetated peripheries of swamps and margins of rivers.
WATER CONDITIONS: Prefers pure fresh water in a well planted aquarium. Normal temperatures are sufficient.
SIZE: Grows to about 8 cm.
FOOD REQUIREMENTS: Feeds on small invertebrates. Live aquarium foods such as cyclops, daphnia, brine shrimp, etc. are accepted along with some prepared foods.

*Ambassis marianus* Guenther • Mary River Glassfish

RANGE: Eastern Australia (Queensland and New South Wales).
HABITS: Occurs in brackish mangrove estuaries, tidal creeks, and the lower reaches of freshwater streams.
WATER CONDITIONS: Occurs naturally in brackish water, so the water should have at least some salt content. Temperatures should be in the normal aquarium range.
SIZE: Attains a length of about 8 cm.
FOOD REQUIREMENTS: Prefers small invertebrates. Brine shrimp, cyclops, daphnia, bloodworms, and other small live foods are best.

*Parambassis gulliveri*
*See Plate #438*

Ambassis elongatus

Ambassis elongatus

Ambassis commersoni

Ambassis macleayi

Ambassis macleayi

Ambassis macleayi

Ambassis marianus

Ambassis gulliveri

**Plate #465**

Craterocephalus dalhousiensis

Ambassis macleayi

Parambassis gulliveri

Parambassis gulliveri

Nannoperca n. sp.

Nannatherina bostocki

Leiopotherapon macrolepis

Amphitherapon caudovittata

*Plate #466*

705

## Craterocephalus dalhousiensis • Dalhousie Hardyhead

RANGE: Known only from east-central Australia.
HABITS: Lays tiny eggs that adhere to submerged objects during the summer months. The sexes are distinguishable on the basis of external shape.
WATER CONDITIONS: Not critical. Can tolerate some salt in the water. A pH slightly on the alkaline side and temperatures between 23 and 27°C are recommended.
SIZE: May attain a length of about 8 cm.
FOOD REQUIREMENTS: Feeds on snails and plant material in nature. Will accept a variety of aquarium foods but should also receive some vegetable matter as well.

*Ambassis macleayi*
*See Plate #465*

*Parambassis gulliveri*
*See Plate #438*

## Nannoperca n. sp. • Golden Pygmy Perch

This new species of Pygmy Perch comes from Australia, probably along the eastern portion of the continent. The small fishes of this genus make excellent aquarium fishes and have been spawned in captivity. The eggs are shed while the parents are swimming and then sink to the bottom, where they adhere slightly. Hatching occurs in about 2-3 days.

## Nannatherina bostocki • Shy Mountain Perch

RANGE: Australia.
HABITS: A fish of rivers and cool lakes. Adapts well to aquaria and can probably be bred in captivity.
WATER CONDITIONS: Hard, alkaline water that is relatively cool (20°C) should be tried.
SIZE: Reaches at least 3 cm.
FOOD REQUIREMENTS: Small lives foods of all types are accepted.

## Leiopotherapon macrolepis • Kimberley Spangled Perch

RANGE: The northwestern Kimberley region of Western Australia.
HABITS: Maturity is reached at a small size (just over 11 cm). Probably spawns at night, releasing a large number of demersal non-adhesive eggs. Hatching occurs in about two days.
WATER CONDITIONS: Not critical. A hardy species that can adapt to most aquarium conditions.
SIZE: Probably does not grow to much more than 12 or so centimeters.
FOOD REQUIREMENTS: Will accept a variety of aquarium foods, but prefers live foods.

## Amphitherapon caudavittatas (Richardson) • Yellowtail Grunter, Flagtail Grunter

RANGE: Western Australia, Northern Territory, Queensland, and New Guinea.
HABITS: Lives equally well in marine and brackish water and enters freshwater estuaries. Not to be trusted with very small fishes.
WATER CONDITIONS: Not critical. Normal aquarium temperatures are adequate.
SIZE: Attains a length of about 25 to 26 cm.
FOOD REQUIREMENTS: Feeds on small invertebrates and fishes. Does well on most aquarium foods.

*Ambassis agrammus agassizi*
See Plate #463

*Denariusa bandata*
See Plate #439

*Bostockia porosa* (Castelnau) • Nightfish

RANGE: Southwestern Australia.
HABITS: This rather drab-looking fish has not become much of a favorite with aquarists. Not only is it not colorful, but it also is nocturnal and not seen very often.
WATER CONDITIONS: Not critical. Since this species is found in temperate Australia it should be placed only in a cool water tank.
SIZE: Attains a length of about 15 cm.
FOOD REQUIREMENTS: Will accept a variety of aquarium foods including small fishes. Remember to feed in dim light or at night.

*Macquaria ambiguus* (Richardson) • Golden Perch; Yellowbelly

RANGE: Eastern Australia in sluggish, sometimes turbid, inland rivers.
HABITS: Spawning occurs with a combined rise in water level and a rise in temperature to more than 23°C. Adults appear to move upstream to spawn up to a million eggs that are released into the currents. In about a day and a half hatching occurs, yielding 3.2 mm fry. Females are generally larger than males. May be golden, blackish, or dark above with a yellow belly.
WATER CONDITIONS: Not critical. Will survive under crowded conditions in nature, but this is not recommended in aquaria.
SIZE: Females about 29 cm, males closer to 20-23 cm.
FOOD REQUIREMENTS: Feeds on fishes, crustaceans, molluscs, and other small animals. Will lie in ambush in shady or weedy places waiting for prey animals to pass by. Will accept a wide variety of aquarium foods including feeder fishes.

*Bidyanus bidyanus* (Mitchell) • Silver Perch

RANGE: Eastern Australia.
HABITS: Spawning is induced by a rise in the water level in its natural habitat. It moves upstream when temperatures exceed 23°C to shed up to a half million semi-buoyant eggs. Hatching time is about 30 hours, and the yolk sac is absorbed in about five days. May spawn at 18 cm (2 years old). A schooling fish.
WATER CONDITIONS: Not critical. Can tolerate temperatures from 2° to 37°C (but only for short periods of time at either extreme).
SIZE: Reaches a length of over 60 cm.
FOOD REQUIREMENTS: Feeds on a wide variety of material including aquatic insects, crustaceans, molluscs, plant material, and even plankton. Will accept a variety of aquarium foods.

Ambassis agrammus agassizi

Denariusa bandata

Bostockia porosa

Bidyanus bidyanus

Bidyanus bidyanus

Macquaria ambigua

Plate #467

708

Macquaria australasica

Macquaria colonorum

Maccullochella macquariensis

Maccullochella macquariensis

Maccullochella peeli

Amniataba percoides

*Plate #468*

709

*Macquaria australasica* (Cuvier & Valenciennes) •
Macquarie Perch

RANGE: Southeastern Australia, mainly in the cool higher
altitude reaches of the Murray-Darling River systems.
HABITS: Spawning occurs at about three years of age (at
30 cm). Large numbers of eggs are shed in spring or
early summer in shallow, fast-flowing streams. The eggs
are adhesive and become attached to the gravel of the
bottom.
WATER CONDITIONS: Needs clean, clear, cool water that is
highly oxygenated.
SIZE: Attains a length of about 43 cm.
FOOD REQUIREMENTS: Most of the diet in nature consists of
insects or insect larvae. Will accept suitably sized
aquarium foods.

*Maccullochella macquariensis* (Cuvier & Valenciennes)
Trout Cod

RANGE: Apparently restricted to the Murray River drainage system in southeastern Australia.
HABITS: Spawns (like many of its relatives) with a rise in
water level due to storm runoff and a rise in water
temperature to about 21°C. Close to and possibly the
same species as *M. peeli*, the Murray cod. Said to mature
earlier than the Murray cod.
WATER CONDITIONS: Not critical.
SIZE: To more than 50 cm.
FOOD REQUIREMENTS: Feeds mainly on crustaceans but
also takes molluscs and fishes. Aquarium fare is generally accepted.

*Maccullochella peeli* Mitchell • Murray Cod

RANGE: Endemic to rivers of eastern Australia.
HABITS: Unlike its close relative the trout cod, the Murray
cod does not seem to need a rise in water level to spawn
(although it helps) but it does need a temperature rise to
20°C or more. More than 20,000 adhesive eggs can be produced. Hatching occurs in 1-2 weeks. The Murray cod has
a marbled pattern and projecting longer jaw; the trout
cod is spotted and has an overhanging upper jaw.
WATER CONDITIONS: Not critical.
SIZE: Attains a length of up to 2 meters. First spawns at
about 50 cm.
FOOD REQUIREMENTS: The greatest part of the diet is
crustaceans, but molluscs and small fishes are also included. Aquarium specimens will accept a variety of
foods. Reported to eat mice in nature if available.

*Macquaria colonorum* (Guenther) • Estuary Perch

RANGE: Formerly restricted to southern and eastern
Australia (including Tasmania) but may have been introduced into Western Australia and as far as Fiji.
HABITS: Spawns after a downstream migration to estuaries
in late winter or early spring. Small pelagic eggs are produced. The young estuarine perch have dark blotching at
the anterior of the dorsal, anal, and pelvic fins. A second
form, called *novemaculeatus*, is sometimes accepted.
WATER CONDITIONS: Not critical. Does best in the cooler
temperature ranges.
SIZE: Attains a length of about 50-60 cm.
FOOD REQUIREMENTS: A carnivorous species that will accept a variety of meaty aquarium foods.

*Amniataba percoides* (Guenther) • Black-striped Grunter

RANGE: Rivers of Australia.
HABITS: An aggressive and active fish that cannot be kept
with fishes much smaller than itself.
WATER CONDITIONS: Not critical.
SIZE: Attains a length of about 15 cm.
FOOD REQUIREMENTS: Will accept most live or frozen foods,
especially small feeder fishes.

*Maccullochella macquariensis*
*See Plate #468*

*Maccullochella peeli*
*See Plate #468*

*Hephaestus fuliginosus* (Macleay) • Sooty Grunter

RANGE: River drainages of north and northeastern Australia. Relatively common.
HABITS: Spawning occurs during the summer months (wet season), with tens of thousands of non-adhesive demersal eggs shed that apparently fall into the crevices of the gravel. The fry hatch out in about 42 hours and have absorbed their yolk sac in another 96 hours.
WATER CONDITIONS: Not critical, but the water temperature should not fall below 12°C.
SIZE: Attains a length of 38 cm.
FOOD REQUIREMENTS: Feeds on a variety of items in nature including insects, worms, crustaceans, frogs, plant roots, and palm berries that fall into the water.

*Amniataba percoides*
*See Plate #468*

*Hephaestus carbo* (Ogilby & McCulloch) • Coal Grunter

RANGE: Found only in northern Australia. Occurrence is very patchy and they are not abundant.
HABITS: Prefers clear, moving water with sandy bottoms. The Coal Grunter first spawns when about 13 cm long. Several thousand adhesive, demersal eggs are shed.
WATER CONDITIONS: Needs clean, clear, well-oxygenated water. The temperature should at least be above 15°C.
SIZE: Attains a length of 18-19 cm.
FOOD REQUIREMENTS: Shrimp and other crustaceans form most of the diet. In aquaria most frozen foods (including shrimp) can be fed.

*Hephaestus jenkinsi* (Whitley) • Jenkins's Grunter

RANGE: Northwestern Australia.
HABITS: Occupies a variety of waters from clear to turbid and sluggish to swiftly flowing. May also be found over different bottom types including sand, mud, and rocks. Some individuals develop thick fleshy lips such as seen in some fishes of the family Cichlidae.
WATER CONDITIONS: Not critical. Will fare well in most normal aquarium conditions.
SIZE: Attains a length of about 15 cm.
FOOD REQUIREMENTS: Will accept a variety of aquarium foods.

Maccullochella macquariensis

Maccullochella peeli

Amniataba percoides

Hephaestus fuliginosus

Hephaestus carbo

Hephaestus carbo

Hephaestus jenkinsi

Hephaestus jenkinsi

*Plate #469*

Hephaestus carbo

Hephaestus fuliginosus

Leiopotherapon unicolor

Pingalla midgleyi

Scortum barcoo

Syncomistes butleri

*Plate #470*

713

*Hephaestus carbo*
*See Plate #469*

*Hephaestus fuliginosus*
*See Plate #469*

*Leiopotherapon unicolor* (Guenther) • Jewel Perch; Spangled Grunter

RANGE: Widely distributed in Australian river systems. Also found in small pools, isolated billabongs, etc.
HABITS: The jewel perch matures at a small size, and even small fish can produce more than 20,000 eggs (older fish may produce up to 100,000 eggs). Spawning occurs at night once the temperature exceeds 20°C. Hatching occurs in about 50 hours. Also called *Madigania unicolor*.
WATER CONDITIONS: Not critical. Can withstand a wide temperature range (7° to 37°C), but fungal infections may occur at long exposure to temperatures below 10°C.
SIZE: Attains a length of 24 cm.
FOOD REQUIREMENTS: Feeds on small invertebrates such as crustaceans, molluscs, and aquatic insects, as well as plant material. Should be offered a balanced diet including plant material.

*Pingalla midgleyi* Allen & Merrick • Black-blotch Grunter

RANGE: Apparently restricted to the Katherine and Alligator River systems, Northern Territory, Australia.
WATER CONDITIONS: Not critical. In nature found over sand and rocky bottoms, pH 7-6.2. Fairly hardy and will do well under most normal aquarium conditions. Temperatures should be between 23 and 28°C.
SIZE: Attains a length of 6-15 cm.
FOOD REQUIREMENTS: Feeds primarily on benthic algae. Must be given a good portion of vegetable material in its diet.

*Scortum barcoo* (McCulloch & Waite) • Barcoo Grunter

RANGE: Occurs only in east-central Australia.
HABITS: Typical of species of *Scortum*, there will be black spots or blotches on the sides at times. These vary considerably in position, size, and number, even on the same fish. In dim aquarium light the Barcoo Grunter becomes silvery in color and the spots tend to disappear. Spawning assumedly occurs after the summer flooding.
WATER CONDITIONS: Not critical.
SIZE: Attains a length of over 30 cm; females mature at 25 cm.
FOOD REQUIREMENTS: Will accept a variety of prepared and frozen aquarium foods.

*Syncomistes butleri* Vari • Butler's Grunter

RANGE: Western Australia from the Bow to the South Alligator Rivers.
HABITS: Occurs in lagoons, streams and rivers in a variety of conditions. Water movement was slow to rapid and clarity was clear to turbid. Occurred over a variety of bottoms.
WATER CONDITIONS: Not critical. Normal aquarium conditions only are needed.
SIZE: Attains a length of at least 12 cm.
FOOD REQUIREMENTS: Apparently adapted to feeding on filamentous algae. Must give a diet of greens including filamentous algae if possible.

*Hephaestus welchi* (McCulloch & Waite) • Welch's Grunter

RANGE: Found only in east-central Australian rivers in sluggish, turbid areas where there are high salt concentrations.

HABITS: Females mature at about 28 cm and may produce up to 100,000 eggs per spawning. Eggs are semi-buoyant and non-adhesive, hatching after some 30 hours in the downstream currents. The yolk sac is absorbed after about five days.

WATER CONDITIONS: Not critical. Temperatures in the range of 21° to 25°C are adequate.

SIZE: Attains a length of 35 cm or more.

FOOD REQUIREMENTS: Small fishes and crustaceans are its basic diet, and these items can be fed in aquaria. Welch's Grunter will accept other aquarium fare, including various worms, as well.

*Leiopotherapon*
*See Plate #470*

*Leiopotherapon aheneus* Mees • Western Australian Grunter

RANGE: Known only from the Ashburton and Fortesque Rivers in Western Australia.

HABITS: The habitat of the Western Australian Grunter is permanently running water from springs. Juveniles are reported to have indistinct vertical bands on their sides.

WATER CONDITIONS: Not critical. Should have sufficient aeration. Temperatures can be on the cool side.

SIZE: Grows to a length of 12 cm, making it one of the smaller species of grunter and more suitable for aquaria.

FOOD REQUIREMENTS: Feeds on crustaceans and small fishes. Accepts a variety of aquarium foods, both love and prepared.

*Pingalla gilberti* Whitley • Gilbert's Grunter

RANGE: Found only in the Gilbert, Norman, and Flinders Rivers, Cape York Peninsula, northern Australia.

HABITS: Similar to that of other grunters. Named for John Gilbert, naturalist with Leichhardt's expedition, who was speared by the natives. The Gilbert River was also named after him.

WATER CONDITIONS: Not critical. Temperatures from 21°C to 27°C are suitable.

SIZE: Attains a length of about 9 or 10 cm.

FOOD REQUIREMENTS: Accepts a variety of aquarium foods both live and prepared, but a large vegetable content—especially filamentous algae—should be included.

*Pingalla lorentzi*
*See Plate #441*

*Pingalla midgleyi*
*See Plate #470*

*Syncommistes butleri*
*See Plate #470*

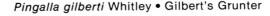

Hephaestus welchi

Leiopotherapon unicolor

Leiopotherapon aheneus

Leiopotherapon aheneus

Pingalla lorentzi

Pingalla gilberti

Pingalla  midgleyi

Syncomistes butleri

**Plate #471**

716

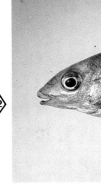

Syncomistes kimberleyensis

Syncomistes trigonicus

Edelia vittata

Edelia vittata (male)

Nannatherina balstoni

Nannatherina australis

Nannatherina obscura

Nannoperca oxleyana

**Plate #472**

## *Syncomistes kimberleyensis* Vari • Kimberley Grunter

RANGE: Known only from the Bow River in the Kimberley region of Australia.
HABITS: Little known. Found in an isolated pool over a sand and rock bottom where the water was green and murky.
WATER CONDITIONS: Probably will live well under normal aquarium conditions.
SIZE: Only juveniles of up to 36 mm known.
FOOD REQUIREMENTS: Feeds mainly on filamentous algae. Aquarium specimens should be offered a high vegetable content in their diet.

## *Syncomistes trigonicus* Vari • Triangle Grunter

RANGE: Northwestern Australia, principally the Roe, Prince Regent, and Drysdale River drainages.
HABITS: Occurs in fresh water where it is clear or slightly murky and over a variety of bottom types.
WATER CONDITIONS: Should live well under normal aquarium conditions.
SIZE: Attains a length of at least 13 cm.
FOOD REQUIREMENTS: Its normal diet is filamentous algae. As an herbivore it should receive the bulk of its diet as vegetable matter.

## *Edelia vittata* Castelnau • Westralian Pygmy Perch

RANGE: Endemic to the fresh waters of the southwestern corner of Australia.
HABITS: Has a lifespan of about five years. Some 40 to 50 eggs are laid separately by each female. The Westralian pygmy perch matures in its first year at about 3 cm.
WATER CONDITIONS: Not critical. Comes from a cool water area, so the tank should be kept no higher than room temperature.
SIZE: A small species growing to about 7 or 7.5 cm.
FOOD REQUIREMENTS: Most of its diet consists of insects and insect larvae. To these can be added small-sized aquarium foods both living and frozen.

## *Nannatherina balstoni* (Regan) • Balston's Perchlet

RANGE: Apparently endemic to rivers in the Albany area of southwestern Australia.
HABITS: Although first thought to be a kind of hardyhead (Atherinidae), this species was eventually placed in the Kuhliidae. Said to do well as an aquarium fish.
WATER CONDITIONS: Not critical. This species comes from the cooler latitudes of Australia and should be kept in an unheated tank.
SIZE: Attains a length of only about 7.5 cm.
FOOD REQUIREMENTS: Will accept a variety of aquarium foods.

## *Nannatherina australis* Guenther • Southern Australia Pygmy Perch

RANGE: Endemic to the southeastern portion of Australia including Tasmania.
HABITS: The fins of the male (excepting the pectorals) turn bright red before spawning. Scatters demersal eggs randomly while swimming. The eggs are slightly adhesive and hatch in about three days. Makes an excellent aquarium fish.
WATER CONDITIONS: Not critical. Will spawn at temperatures in the range of 16° to 21°C. Should be maintained at relatively cool temperatures.
SIZE: Attains a length of from 6 to 8 cm.
FOOD REQUIREMENTS: Feeds on insects and insect larvae, small crustaceans, and various prepared aquarium foods.

## *Nannatherina obscura* (Klunzinger) • Yarra Pygmy Perch

RANGE: Known only from Victoria in southern Australia.
HABITS: Similar to the Westralian Pygmy Perch. A very suitable aquarium fish that will breed in captivity. Scatters slightly adhesive (?) eggs randomly.
WATER CONDITIONS: Not critical. Can tolerate lower water temperatures as it comes from a cool temperate area.
SIZE: Length apparently does not exceed 7 cm.
FOOD REQUIREMENTS: Will accept small live foods and some frozen and prepared foods. Be sure to offer a balanced diet.

## *Nannoperca oxleyana* Whitley • Oxleyan Pygmy Perch

RANGE: Coastal waters of southern Queensland and northern New South Wales in Australia. Said to be common in many freshwater dune lakes.
HABITS: A peaceful aquarium fish that is readily spawned. Apparently an egg scatterer.
WATER CONDITIONS: Not critical. Normal temperature range of 21° to 26°C is sufficient.
SIZE: Attains a length of about 7 cm.
FOOD REQUIREMENTS: Will accept a wide variety of live and frozen foods suitable for aquarium fishes.

*Edelia vittata*
*See Plate #472*

*Nannatherina australis*
*See Plate #472*

*Nannoperca oxleyana*
*See Plate #472*

*Toxotes chatareus*
*See Plate #437*

*Toxotes oligolepis* Bleeker • Few-scaled Archerfish

RANGE: Molucca Islands, Irian Jaya, and Western Australia.
HABITS: Like other archerfishes, this species will spit drops of water at insects in order to knock them into the water so they can be eaten. This is a rare species looking like the banded pattern of *T. jaculator*. It differs by having 5 dorsal fin spines versus 4 for *jaculator*. Peaceful.
WATER CONDITIONS: Not critical. Will thrive in fresh, salt, or brackish water. Temperatures should be around 23-28°C.
SIZE: To 12-13 cm.
FOOD REQUIREMENTS: Small bits of chopped fish and shrimp and a variety of insects including small flies are taken.

*Toxotes lorentzi* Weber • Primitive Archerfish

RANGE: Northern Territory of Australia and New Guinea.
HABITS: Like other archerfishes, this species will shoot insects out of the overhanging vegetation by using droplets of water propelled with deadly accuracy. The scales are smaller than in the other species.
WATER CONDITIONS: Fresh to slightly brackish water is acceptable. Normal water temperatures are proper.
SIZE: Attains a length of about 14 cm.
FOOD REQUIREMENTS: Will accept a variety of aquarium foods. Insects and insect larvae are, of course, preferred.

Edelia vittata (female)

Nannatherina australis

Nannoperca oxleyana

Toxotes chatareus

Toxotes oligolepis

Toxotes lorentzi

**Plate #473**

Glossamia aprion

Glossamia aprion

Glossamia aprion

Toxotes chatareus

Toxotes oligolepis

Gadopsis marmoratus

Gadopsis marmoratus

Gadopsis marmoratus

**Plate #474**

721

*Glossamia aprion* (Richardson) • Queensland
Mouthbrooder; Mouth Almighty

RANGE: Occurs in river drainages of northern and eastern
Australia and Papua New Guinea.
HABITS: Spawning occurs when temperatures rise beyond
22°C. The eggs are laid in a ball that possibly is
enveloped in a thin membrane. The male picks up the
eggs in his mouth and broods them for about two weeks
(until hatching), apparently without feeding during this
time. May be subdivided into two subspecies: *G. a.
aprion* and *G. a. gilli.*
WATER CONDITIONS: Not critical. Water temperatures of
from 21° to 26°C are suitable.
SIZE: Attains a length of about 17 or 18 cm.
FOOD REQUIREMENTS: Feeds well on small feeder fishes (or
any other small fishes available to it in the aquarium)
and other live foods. Reported to shun dead or non-
moving food.

*Toxotes chatareus*
*See Plate #437*

*Toxotes oligolepis*
*See Plate #473*

*Gadopsis marmoratus* (Richardson) • River Blackfish;
Slippery

RANGE: Southeastern Australia, including Tasmania.
HABITS: This mostly nocturnal species lays a few (less than
500) large (about 4 mm diameter) eggs. Eggs were seen
attached to the inside of hollow logs. Adults have been
tamed enough to take food from a person's hand.
WATER CONDITIONS: Not critical. A cool-water species that
requires generally lower temperatures than the tropical
species.
SIZE: Usually seen less than 30 cm long, but attains lengths
of more than twice that.
FOOD REQUIREMENTS: Insects and insect larvae when
small, adding crustaceans, worms, molluscs, and small
fishes to their diet as they grow.

*Glossogobius aureus* Akihito & Meguro • Golden Goby

RANGE: Tropical western Pacific.
HABITS: A bottom-living species occurring mostly in brackish water.
WATER CONDITIONS: This species is best kept in a brackish water tank. Normal aquarium temperatures are acceptable.
SIZE: Attains a length of over 10 cm.
FOOD REQUIREMENTS: Will accept a variety of aquarium foods, preferably live.

*Glossogobius* near *celebius* (Valenciennes) •
Reticulated Goby

RANGE: At least in New Guinea (almost the entire island) and northern Australia. *G. celebius* also occurs in the Celebes and other islands near New Guinea. The Australia version of this fish is often called *G. concavifrons*, usually considered to be a synonym of *G. celebius*.
HABITS: Found in both highland and lowland rivers, streams, and lakes. Also in estuarine situations. Very adaptable.
WATER CONDITIONS: Not critical as long as warm and well-oxygenated. Will tolerate salt added to the water but does not need it.
SIZE: Reaches almost 10 cm in length.
FOOD REQUIREMENTS: Prefers insects in all forms, but will adapt to prepared foods.

*Mogurnda adspersa* (Castelnau) • Purple-spotted Gudgeon

RANGE: Queensland and New South Wales, Australia.
HABITS: Prefers slow-flowing waters with a good supply of weeds and where there are solid objects on which to spawn. They spawn in the warmer months (temperatures 20-34°C) after an elaborate courtship. About 280-1,300 transparent eggs that have an adhesive disc are produced. Males guard. Hatching is in 3 days to a week, and feeding commences in about another week. Males develop nuchal humps.
WATER CONDITIONS: Not critical. Fairly hardy and easy to keep. Will breed in aquaria.
SIZE: Attains a length of 12 cm (more commonly 7 cm).
FOOD REQUIREMENTS: A variety of invertebrates are eaten, particularly insect larvae and worms. Also feeds on small fishes. Aquarium fare is readily accepted.

*Mogurnda mogurnda* (Richardson) • Purple-striped Gudgeon

RANGE: Most of tropical Australia.
HABITS: Not well known. Most available information probably actually pertains to *M. adspersa*, from which this species differs primarily in scale counts. Occurs in rivers as well as muddy waters.
WATER CONDITIONS: Not critical. Does well under normal aquarium conditions.
SIZE: Normally about 10 cm long, but can grow to over 17 cm.
FOOD REQUIREMENTS: Feeds on small invertebrates. Will accept a variety of aquarium foods.

*Hypseleotris aureus* • Golden Gudgeon

RANGE: Discovered in the Murchison River, Western Australia.
HABITS: Males are more colorful than females. Small eggs are attached to objects on the bottom and guarded by the male.
WATER CONDITIONS: Not critical. A fairly hardy fish that can be kept under normal aquarium conditions.
SIZE: Attains a length of at least 6 cm.
FOOD REQUIREMENTS: Accepts a wide variety of aquarium foods including prepared foods.

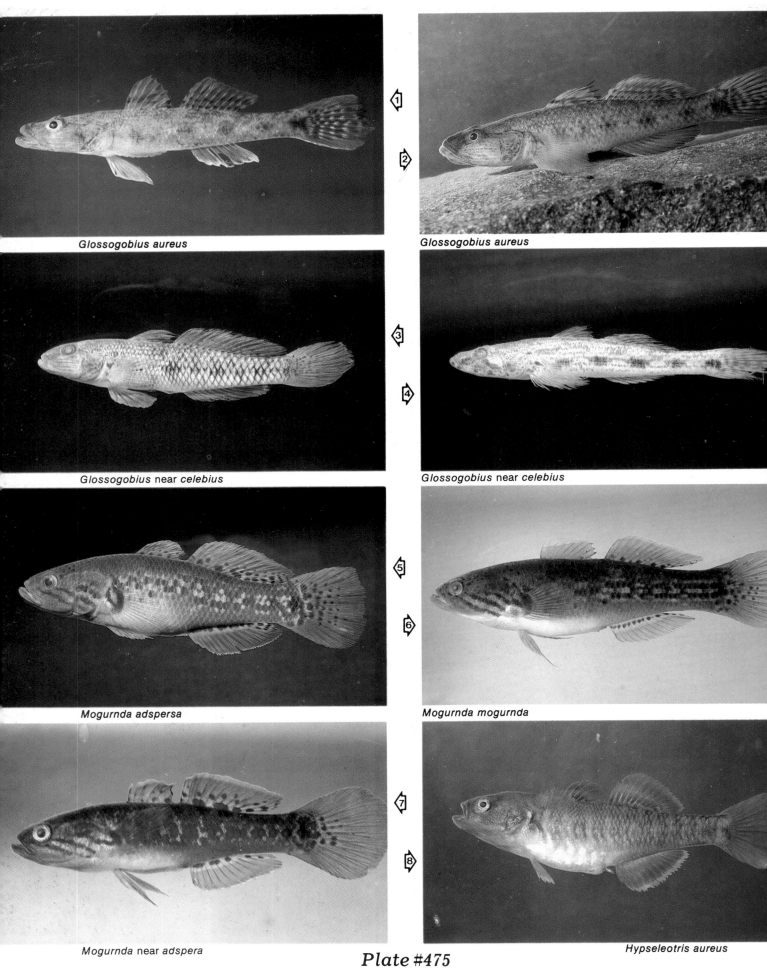

Glossogobius aureus

Glossogobius aureus

Glossogobius near celebius

Glossogobius near celebius

Mogurnda adspersa

Mogurnda mogurnda

Mogurnda near adspera

Hypseleotris aureus

**Plate #475**

724

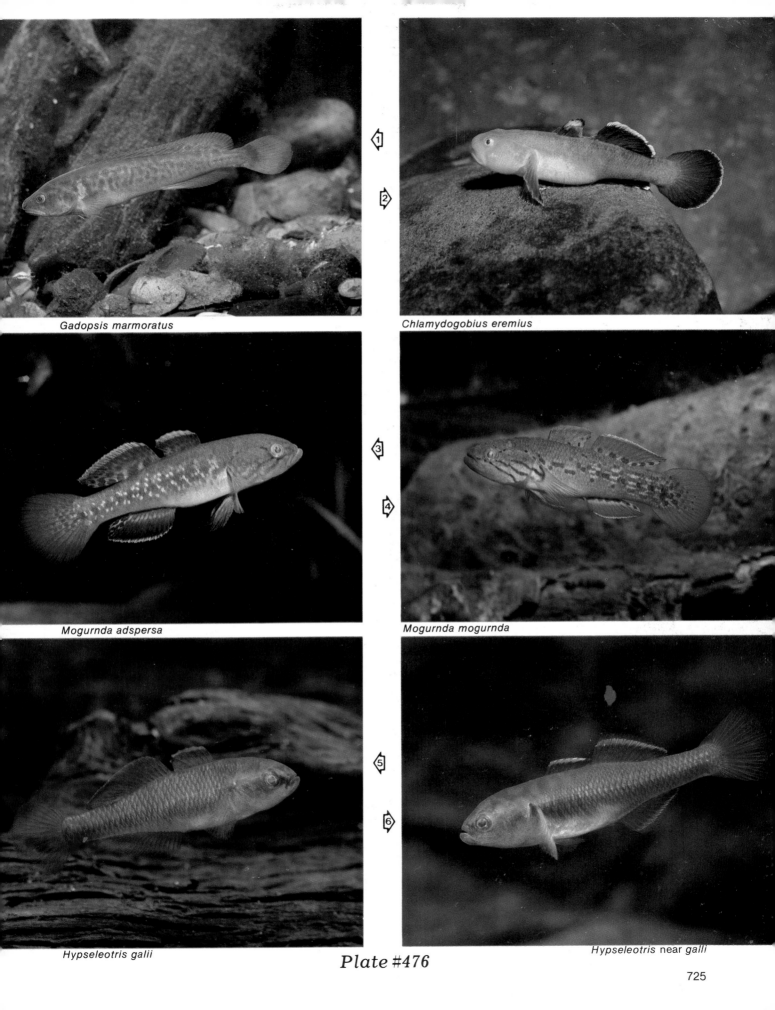

Gadopsis marmoratus

Chlamydogobius eremius

Mogurnda adspersa

Mogurnda mogurnda

Hypseleotris galli

Hypseleotris near galli

Plate #476

*Chlamydogobius eremius* (Zietz) • Desert Goby

*Gadopsis marmoratus*
*See Plate #474*

RANGE: Central part of Australia to southern part of North-ern Territory. Apparently restricted to the Lake Eyre drainage.

HABITS: Inhabits pools and streams associated with artesian springs and bores. Spawns from November to March (southern summer). About 150-250 eggs are produced by each female. The male has a broader head than the female and its genital papilla is long and slender; that of the female is short and stubby.

WATER CONDITIONS: Not critical. This goby exists under all sorts of adverse conditions including sudden changes in salinity and temperature. If the oxygen content drops it can utilize aerial respiration.

SIZE: Reaches a length of about 6 cm.

FOOD REQUIREMENTS: Omnivorous, feeding on filamentous algae, small insects and crustaceans, and detritus. Easy to feed in aquaria.

*Mogurnda adspersa*
*See Plate #475*

*Mogurnda mogurnda*
*See Plate #475*

*Hypseleotris galii* (Ogilby) • Fire-tailed Gudgeon

RANGE: Common in coastal streams of Queensland and New South Wales, Australia.

HABITS: Males fan and guard the eggs until they hatch some 4-5 days later. Males develop nuchal humps and have longer posterior dorsal and anal fin rays. Breeding males also turn dark, the reddish orange of the fins becoming stronger.

WATER CONDITIONS: Purely fresh water. Does well in aquaria that are well planted. Otherwise no particular conditions are necessary.

SIZE: Males grow to 5.5 cm, females to only 4 cm.

FOOD REQUIREMENTS: Feeds on small aquatic inverte-brates but accepts a variety of aquarium foods, preferably alive.

*Hypseleotris* near *galli*
*See Plate #476*

### Gobiomorphus coxi (Krefft) • Cox's Gudgeon

RANGE: Apparently restricted to rivers of New South Wales, especially the southern portion.

HABITS: Seems to prefer more swiftly flowing waters, even rapids. Apparently able to climb out of water over obstructions. A substrate spawner (on rocks) with the male guarding the nest and fanning the eggs. The eggs hatch in a few days.

WATER CONDITIONS: Does not tolerate salt in the water as well as do some of the other gobies. Prefers well oxygenated water. Does best in aquaria kept at room temperature.

SIZE: Normally attains a length of 15 cm, occasionally to 19 cm.

FOOD REQUIREMENTS: Feeds on small aquatic insects. In the aquarium mosquito larvae and chironomic larvae are best bets.

### Philypnodon n. sp. • Dwarf Flathead Gudgeon

RANGE: Southern Queensland, New South Wales, Victoria and South Australia.

HABITS: Found in quiet areas over rocks, muddy bottoms and weedy areas. Inhabits estuarine waters to pure fresh water. Males have larger mouths, more bulbous heads, and larger pelvic fins. They also turn very dark when spawning.

WATER CONDITIONS: Not critical. Will live in fresh and brackish waters.

SIZE: Usually 4 cm but may grow a little larger.

FOOD REQUIREMENTS: Accepts a variety of living and prepared aquarium foods.

### Megalops cyprinoides (Broussonet) • Oxeye Herring, Indo-Pacific Tarpon

RANGE: Widespread in the tropical Indo-Pacific from East Africa to Tahiti. Occurs in all Australian seas.

HABITS: A marine species in which young individuals (between 20 and 50 cm) are found in freshwater situations. Spawning takes place in the warm months in shallow waters or estuaries, producing a leptocephalus-like larva.

WATER CONDITIONS: Young specimens suitable for aquaria can be kept in fresh or brackish water.

SIZE: Grows to more than 150 cm.

FOOD REQUIREMENTS: Adults eat fishes and crustaceans; the young will also feed on insects and their larvae.

### Notesthes robusta (Guenther) • Bullrout

RANGE: Queensland and New South Wales, Australia.

HABITS: A bottom-dwelling species that should not be kept with fishes it can swallow.

WATER CONDITIONS: Tolerant of a wide range of water conditions. Will even live in brackish water.

SIZE: Attains a length of about 30 cm, but more commonly is 15 to 20 cm long.

FOOD REQUIREMENTS: Will accept many different foods, including small shrimp, worms and fishes.

Hypseleotris "midgleyi"

Gobiomorphus coxi

Gobiomorphus near coxi

Philypnodon n. sp.

Megalops cyprinoides

Notesthes robusta (juvenile)

*Plate #477*

728

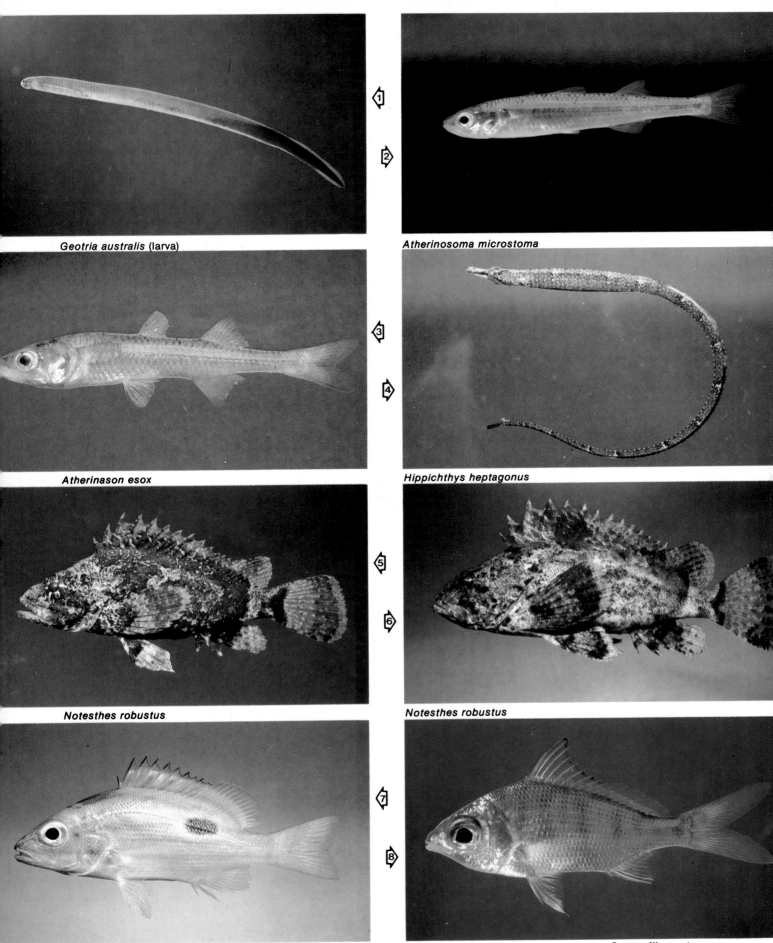

Geotria australis (larva)

Atherinosoma microstoma

Atherinason esox

Hippichthys heptagonus

Notesthes robustus

Notesthes robustus

Lutjanus russelli

Gerres filamentosus

*Plate #478*

729

## Geotria australis Gray • Pouched Lamprey

RANGE: Southeastern and Western Australia, Tasmania, New Zealand, and Patagonian South America.

HABITS: Undergoes a complicated life cycle from a larval *ammocoete* stage through a *macrophthalmis* stage, then the *velasia* stage, and finally to the adult. Ammocoetes are filter-feeders; adults die after spawning.

WATER CONDITIONS: Depending upon the stage, either saltwater or pure fresh. Not normally kept in home aquaria.

SIZE: Ammocoete 10 cm; macrophthalmia 8-10 cm; velasia 35-67 cm; adults may shrink a bit from the *velasia* stage.

FOOD REQUIREMENTS: Varies with stage.

## Atherinason esox • Tasmanian Hardyhead

RANGE: Tasmania, Australia.

HABITS: A small species found in cool Tasmanian coastal waters. Generally a surface fish, often traveling in small schools. Peaceful but not very colorful, being somewhat translucent with a silvery lateral band.

WATER CONDITIONS: Not critical. Probably does best with a small amount of salt added to the aquarium. A cool-water fish that should not be placed in a heated aquarium.

SIZE: Attains a length of about 7 or so cm.

FOOD REQUIREMENTS: Does best on small live foods, particularly crustaceans and small insects.

## Atherinosoma microstoma (Guenther) • Smallmouthed Hardyhead

RANGE: Abundant along the southeastern coast of Australia, including Tasmania.

HABITS: Not much is known. Possibly a continual breeder. Whether the lateral stripe becoming pinkish to red or the eye becoming the same color is sexual in nature is not known.

WATER CONDITIONS: Apparently a delicate fish that is hard to keep under any conditions.

SIZE: To 7 cm in New South Wales, but reaches 9 cm in Tasmania.

FOOD REQUIREMENTS: Feeds on small crustaceans and aquatic insects.

## Hippichthys heptagonus Bleeker • Heptagonal Pipefish

RANGE: East Indies to New Guinea and possibly west to Sri Lanka.

HABITS: Occurs in full sea water to brackish water of estuaries and fresh water of streams and brooks. The male incubates the eggs in a brood pouch until they hatch.

WATER CONDITIONS: Not critical. Will exist in most types of water from salt to fresh. Normal temperatures of 23-28°C are suitable.

SIZE: Attains a length of about 14 cm.

FOOD REQUIREMENTS: Needs small live foods such as newly hatched brine shrimp.

*Notesthes robustus*
*See Plate #477*

*Notesthes robustus*
*See Plate #477*

## Lutjanus russelli (Bleeker) • Moses Perch, Russell's Snapper

RANGE: Indo-West Pacific region including Japan and Australia.

HABITS: Primarily a marine fish, but enters estuaries where the water has very little salt content. Called "Moses perch" because of the black spots or "St. Peter's finger-marks," although the true fish of the legend is a species of *Tilapia*.

WATER CONDITIONS: This fish can be treated as a marine fish or can be kept in a lower salinity brackish situation.

SIZE: Attains a length of over 50 cm.

FOOD REQUIREMENTS: A carnivorous species that will eat small fishes and crustaceans. Frozen foods are also accepted.

## Gerres filamentosus Cuvier • Spotted Silverbelly

RANGE: Widely distributed in the western Pacific and Indian Oceans.

HABITS: Occurs in shallow coastal waters, bays, and river mouths, ascending to fresh water.

WATER CONDITIONS: Not critical. This species is probably best maintained in a brackish water aquarium or even in pure salt water. Normal aquarium temperatures are sufficient.

SIZE: Attains a length of at least 25 cm.

FOOD REQUIREMENTS: Feeds on small invertebrates that live in the sand. These are obtained with their very protrusible mouths. Aquarium foods are generally accepted, but some individuals may not take to them.

*Kuhlia rupestris*
*See Plate #439*

**Lutjanus argentimaculatus** (Bonnaterre) • Mangrove Jack; River Roman

RANGE: Widespread over the entire Indo-Pacific area including the Red Sea. In Australia it is found in the northern and eastern coastal areas.

HABITS: Commonly found around mangroves in tidal areas but does move well upstream into pure fresh water. Spawns in estuaries, where it scatters large numbers of pelagic eggs. Only small individuals are generally kept in aquaria.

WATER CONDITIONS: Does well in fresh, brackish, or marine aquaria. Temperatures should be between 21°C and 26°C.

SIZE: Can attain a length of up to a meter.

FOOD REQUIREMENTS: A carnivorous species feeding on fishes, crustaceans, etc. Will accept most meaty aquarium foods.

**Pseudophrites urvillii** (Cuvier & Valenciennes) • Congolli

RANGE: Freshwater streams and estuaries of southern and southeastern Australia and Tasmania.

HABITS: Does not seem to be concerned about whether it is living in fresh or salt water or what type of habitat it is in as it may be found in a wide variety of either. Nothing is known about the spawning habits.

WATER CONDITIONS: Primarily a marine species but lives as well in brackish or pure fresh water. A cool-water species.

SIZE: Normally 15 to 20 cm, but grows to 30 cm.

FOOD REQUIREMENTS: Eats a wide variety of foods including worms, crustaceans, and insects and their larvae. May also include some plant material as well.

**Butis butis** (Buchanan) • Bony-snouted Gudgeon

RANGE: Tropical western Pacific Ocean, including the tropical coasts of Australia.

HABITS: Commonly occurs in brackish estuaries but also extends up coastal rivers into pure fresh water. Prefers slow-moving waters. Can be sexed using genital papillae: female's is short and fat with a few small, fine flaps at tip; male's is thinner and flat and with fine scalloped flaps at tip.

WATER CONDITIONS: Not critical. Can be kept in fresh, brackish or pure marine water with ease.

SIZE: Normally less than 10 cm, but can reach as much as 15 cm in length.

FOOD REQUIREMENTS: Small fishes and crustaceans can be fed in aquaria. It will accept other foods as well.

**Ophieleotris aporos** (Bleeker) • Snakehead Gudgeon

RANGE: Northern Australia and New Guinea.

HABITS: Spends most of its time on the bottom. Tankmates must be large enough to take care of themselves as this fish will regard anything small enough to eat as potential food.

WATER CONDITIONS: Not critical. Clear, clean, well-aerated water is recommended. Temperatures between 21° and 26°C are suitable.

SIZE: Reaches a length of about 30 cm.

FOOD REQUIREMENTS: This carnivorous species will eat live fishes as well as most other meaty foods offered.

**Brachirus salinarum** Ogilby • Salt-pan Sole

RANGE: Occurs only in the area of Australia surrounding the Gulf of Carpentaria. Not widespread.

HABITS: Not well known. Probably similar to that of the other species of *Brachirus*. Typically fresh water.

WATER CONDITIONS: Not critical. Normal aquarium conditions should be acceptable.

SIZE: Attains a length of about 14 cm.

FOOD REQUIREMENTS: Will accept a variety of aquarium foods. These should sink to the bottom where the sole can get to them.

Kuhlia rupestris

Lutjanus argentimaculatus

Pseudophrites urvilli

Butis butis

Ophieleotris aporos

Brachirus salinarum

732

*Plate #479*

*Mugilogobius* n. sp.

*Periophthalmus regius*

*Arenigobius bifrenatus*

*Kurtus gulliveri*

*Caranx papuensis*

*Acanthopagrus australis*

*Chelonodon patoca*

*Chelonodon patoca*

*Plate #480*

### *Mugilogobius* n. sp. • Wanmorr Goby

RANGE: Eastern Australia.
HABITS: Most of the species of this genus of rather non-descript gobies are found in bays and estuaries, penetrating fresh water on occasion.
WATER CONDITIONS: Alkaline, warm water with salt added should be tried.
SIZE: 2-4 cm.
FOOD REQUIREMENTS: Will take both small live foods and vegetable matter as will most gobies.

### *Arenigobius bifrenatus* (Kner) • Bridled Goby

RANGE: From Western Australia along the southern coast of the continent to New South Wales and Tasmania.
HABITS: This is a relatively common species in the sea grass beds as well as in fresh water a couple of kilometers or so from river mouths. It is a bottom-living species and somewhat aggressive.
WATER CONDITIONS: Not critical, living equally well in fresh brackish, or pure salt water. Does best in cooler water aquaria.
SIZE: Attains a length of about 20 cm or more.
FOOD REQUIREMENTS: Will accept a variety of aquarium foods, especially live foods.

### *Caranx papuensis* Alleyne & Macleay • Papuan Trevally

RANGE: This species ranges from Papua New Guinea to northern Queensland.
HABITS: The Papuan trevally may be a synonym of *C. sansun* according to some authors. The young fish are the ones entering brackish waters of harbors and estuaries, the adults keeping to more open waters. This fish is not to be trusted with fishes small enough to swallow. It is very active.
WATER CONDITIONS: The addition of at least some salt to the water is advisable. Normal conditions for a brackish water aquarium are suitable.
SIZE: Attains a length of about 80 cm.
FOOD REQUIREMENTS: Small fishes plus a variety of meaty foods will be sufficient for the Papuan trevally.

### *Chelonodon patoca* (Hamilton-Buchanan) • Milk-spotted Puffer

RANGE: India to China and Southeast Asia, south to the East Indies and northern Australia.
HABITS: The color pattern is very good camouflage when seen against the bottom of a river. Normally taken in clear flowing water with no plants, but seems to like *Vallisneria* in the aquarium. Not a good community fish as it is an inveterate fin-nipper.
WATER CONDITIONS: A usually estuarine species, so salt may be provided in the aquarium water.
SIZE: To 30 cm.
FOOD REQUIREMENTS: Prefers fresh fish (will eat small live fishes in aquaria) or hermit crabs. Will accept dry and frozen foods.

### *Periophthalmus regius* (Whitley) • Royal Mudskipper

RANGE: This specimen was collected in the Daintree River in Queensland, Australia. This species may be a synonym of a wider ranging species.
HABITS: Mudskippers are known for their habit of skipping across mud flats, usually in estuarine situations. They can remain out of water for quite some time as long as they remain moist. Aquarists usually provide them with a "dry" resting place out of the water.
WATER CONDITIONS: Hardy fish that do well in fresh, brackish or full marine water. Temperatures should be in the range of 23-28°C.
SIZE: Attains a length of about 15-16 cm.
FOOD REQUIREMENTS: Prefers small invertebrates including insects. Will take a variety of aquarium foods as substitutes.

*Kurtus gulliveri*
*See Plate #439*

### *Acanthopagrus australis* (Guenther) • Australian Bream

RANGE: Creeks, rivers, estuaries, and coastal waters of central and southern Queensland.
HABITS: There is a spawning migration during midwinter toward waters in the vicinity of ocean beaches. Colors vary depending upon locality, with lighter individuals inhabiting the clear ocean waters and darker ones in the more muddy estuarine areas.
WATER CONDITIONS: Not critical. Does well in a variety of water conditions. Temperatures should be between 23 and 27°C.
SIZE: The average size seems to be about half a kilo, although fishing records have much larger individuals (even up to 4 kilos).
FOOD REQUIREMENTS: Feeds on a wide variety of crustaceans, fishes and even young oyster spat. It will accept similar foods in the aquarium.

### Scatophagus argus (Gmelin) • Spotted Scat

RANGE: Tropical Indo-Pacific region along the coasts.

HABITS: Peaceful toward other fishes, but will graze on aquatic plants right down to the roots.

WATER CONDITIONS: Fairly hard, alkaline water with a teaspoon of salt per four liters of water added. Temperature 23 to 26°C.

SIZE: To 33 cm in their home waters; about half that in captivity.

FOOD REQUIREMENTS: Live foods of all kinds, with the addition of vegetable substances like lettuce or spinach leaves; will also eat frozen foods.

### Neoceratodus forsteri (Krefft) • Australian Lungfish

RANGE: Endemic to eastern Australia. Found originally only in the Burnett and Mary Rivers, but may have been introduced into more southerly rivers of Queensland as well.

HABITS: A primitive lungfish whose fossil ancestors go back some 400 million years. It normally breathes by means of its gills, but it also has a functional lung and can utilize air from the surface. It can live for several days out of water if kept damp. Spawning occurs in spring during the night in shallow water. The eggs are adhesive and stick to aquatic plants.

WATER CONDITIONS: Very tolerant of water conditions. Does best at normal aquarium temperatures.

SIZE: Attains a length of over 150 cm.

FOOD REQUIREMENTS: Feeds on a variety of foods including tadpoles and adult frogs, earthworms, frozen and pellet foods, and even some vegetable material.

### Exyrias puntang (Bleeker) • Silver-spotted Goby

RANGE: Western Pacific Ocean from Japan to New Caledonia and westward to the Andaman Islands.

HABITS: Occurs in coastal and brackish waters. A bottom-living species.

WATER CONDITIONS: Not critical. Can tolerate some salt in the water. Normal aquarium temperatures should prevail.

SIZE: Attains a length of about 16 cm.

FOOD REQUIREMENTS: Feeds on small invertebrates. Will accept a variety of aquarium foods including prepared and frozen items.

*Awaous crassilabrus*
*See Plate #445*

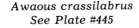

### Favonogobius suppositus (Sauvage) • Southwestern Australian Goby

RANGE: Western Australia.

HABITS: A not very active bottom-living species. Members of the genus are said to lay their eggs among rocks.

WATER CONDITIONS: Not critical. The aquarium should be maintained at room temperature.

SIZE: Attains a length of about 9 cm.

FOOD REQUIREMENTS: Feeds on small invertebrates. Will accept most aquarium foods that reach the bottom levels where it lives.

### Favonogobius tamarensis (Johnston) • Tamar River Goby

RANGE: Restricted to southern and southeastern Australia, including Tasmania.

HABITS: Seems to prefer the quiet waters of estuaries and coastal lakes where the bottom is usually covered with silt or mud. Breeds in the spring. Males have larger mouths, more bulbous cheeks, and the posterior dorsal and anal fin rays are more elongate than in females.

WATER CONDITIONS: Not critical. Equally at home in fresh, brackish, or salt water.

SIZE: Attains a length of about 11 cm.

FOOD REQUIREMENTS: Will accept a wide variety of aquarium foods.

Scatophagus argus

Neoceratodus forsteri

Neoceratodus forsteri

Awaous crassilabrus

Exyrias puntang

Favonogobius suppositus

Favonogobius tamarensis

*Plate #481*

736

# INDEX

"Odessa", *Puntius*, 555, 577
*odoe, Hepsetus*, 391, 397
*ogoense, Aphyosemion*, 436
Ohio Lamprey, 16
*okaloosae, Etheostoma*, 59
*oktediensis, Melanotaenia*, 640
*olidus, Galaxias*, 671, 672
*oligolepis, Capoeta*, 555, 581
*oligolepis, Moenkhausia*, 169, 170
*oligolepis, Toxotes*, 719, 720, 721, 722
*Oligosarcus argenteus*, 149, 150
*olivaceum, Etheostoma*, 66
*olivaceus, Lamprologus*, 539
Olive Glassfish, 699
Olive Perch, 699
Olivesilver Catfish, 426
*olmstedi, Etheostoma*, 53
*Oloplotosus luteus*, 637, 638
*ommata, Leptolucania*, 26, 27
*Ompok bimaculatus*, 596
*Ompok sabanus*, 596
*oncinus, Liosomadoras*, 214
*Oncorhynchus kisutch*, 19
Onegilled Eel, 699
Onelined African Tetra, 403
Onespot Astyanax, 163
Onespot Hemiodus, 128
*Oostethus brachyurus*, 600, 651, 652
*opercularis, Biotoecus*, 357
*opercularis, Macropodus*, 620, 623
*ophidium, Mastacembelus*, 548
*Ophieleotris aporos*, 663, 731, 732
*Ophiocara porocephala*, 663
*Ophisternon candidum*, 667, 668
*Ophisternon gutturale*, 699, 700
*Ophisternon* "species", 633, 634, 699, 700
*Ophthalmotilapia nasutus*, 519, 522
*Ophthalmotilapia ventralis*, 493, 508, 522
*Opsaridium*, 431
Orange Chromide, 607
"Orange Fin", *Apistogramma*, 358
Orangespotted Sunfish, 32
Orangewhiskered Catfish, 638
*orbicularis, Poptella*, 159, 160
*orbignyanus, Brycon*, 151, 152
*orientalis, Channa*, 603, 604
*ornata, Garra*, 433
*ornata, Poecilia*, 317
*ornatipinnis, Lamprologus*, 517
*ornatipinnis, Polypterus*, 389, 390, 394
*ornatipinnis, Synodontis*, 421
*ornatus, Chrysichthys*, 425, 426
*ornatus, Corydoras*, 245, 247
*ornatus, Julidochromis*, 490, 491, 539
*ornatus, Pimelodus*, 219
*ornatus, Rhadinocentrus*, 687, 688, 689, 690
*ornatus, Rivulus*, 271, 272
*ornatus, Synodontis*, 418

*orphnopterus, Corydoras*, 246
*Orthochromis machadoi*, 523
*orthognathus, Petrochromis*, 494
*orthogoniata, Homaloptera*, 558, 559
*orthonotus, Nothobranchius*, 447
*ortonianus, Prochilodus*, 132, 133
*Oryzias celebensis*, 599
*Oryzias javanicus*, 600
*Oryzias latipes*, 600
*osburni, Etheostoma*, 46
*osphromenoides, Sphaerichthys*, 621, 622
*Osphronemus goramy*, 611, 612, 623
*osseus, Lepisosteus*, 16, 17
*osteocarus, Corydoras*, 228, 241, 244
*Osteochilus hasselti*, 586
*Osteochilus* "species", 586, 594
*Osteochilus vittatus*, 586
*Osteoglossum bicirrhosum*, 106, 107
*Osteoglossum ferreirai*, 106, 107
*Otocinclus*, 240
*Otocinclus affinis*, 260
*Otocinclus* "species", 261
*otostigma, Triglachromis*, 497
*ouachitae, Percina*, 40
*ovalis, Tilapia*, 526
Oxeye Herring, 727
Oxleyan Pygmy Perch, 718
*oxleyana, Nannoperca*, 717, 718, 719, 720
*Oxyeleotris*, 662, 662
*Oxyeleotris herwerdinii*, 663
*Oxyeleotris* "species", 663
*oxyrhyncha, Percina*, 36
*oxyrhynchus, Ctenopoma*, 543, 544
*oxyrhynchus, Hemitilapia*, 484
*oxyrhynchus, Sternarchorhynchus*, 200

**P**

*Pachypanchax homalonotus*, 448
*Pachypanchax playfairii*, 448
*pacu, Myleus*, 140, 141
Paddlefish, 16
*paleatus, Corydoras*, 243
*palembangensis, Tetraodon*, 629, 630
*pallididorsum, Etheostoma*, 61
*palmaris, Percina*, 38
*palmas, Polypterus*, 389, 390, 394
*palmeri, Nematobrycon*, 161, 162
*palmqvisti, Nothobranchius*, 445, 447
*paludicola, Parosphromenus*, 614
*paludicola, Pseudomugil*, 648
Panama Pencil, 110
*panamense, Sturiosoma*, 240
*panamensis, Lebiasina*, 110, 111
*Panaque nigrolineatus*, 252, 259, 260
*Panaque suttoni*, 252, 259, 260
*panchax, Aplocheilus*, 597, 599
*panda, Corydoras*, 242
*Pangasius sutchi*, 596

rhoadesii, Chilotilapia, 484
Rhodesian Tetra, 402
rhodesiensis, Hemigrammopetersius, 401
Rhodeus ocellatus, 100, 101
Rhodeus sericeus, 90, 91, 92, 101
Rhodeus suigensis, 100
rhodostomus, Hemigrammus, 187, 188
rhombea, Acheilognathus, 99
rhombeus, Serrasalmus, 145, 146
rhomboides, Curimata, 130, 135
rhomboocellatus, Barbodes, 585
rhombosomoides, Cairnsichthys, 689, 690
rhynchophorus, Campylomormyrus, 396
Rhytiodus argenteofuscus, 123
Rhytiodus microlepis, 123
riggenbachi, Aphyosemion, 436
riisei, Pseudocorynopoma, 157, 158
Rineloricaria, 248
Rineloricaria castroi, 262, 263
Rineloricaria fallax, 262
Rineloricaria filamentosa, 251
Rineloricaria hasemani, 262
Rineloricaria lanceolata, 263
Rineloricaria "species", 262, 263
Rio Meta Black Tetra, 171
Rio Napo Rivulus, 271
riponianus, Haplochromis, 520
River Blackfish, 722
River Roman, 731
rivulatus, Aequidens, 342
Rivulichthys, 274
Rivulus, 435
Rivulus agilae, 271, 272
Rivulus amphoreus, 271, 272
Rivulus atratus, 271, 272
Rivulus beniensis, 271, 272
Rivulus cylindraceus, 277, 278, 280
Rivulus holmiae, 277, 278
Rivulus limoncochae, 271, 272
Rivulus magdalenae, 279, 280
Rivulus ornatus, 271, 272
Rivulus peruanus, 279, 280
Rivulus punctatus, 277, 278, 280
Rivulus strigatus, 279, 280
Rivulus urophthalmus, 279, 280
Rivulus xiphidius, 279, 280
roanoka, Percina, 38
robbianus, Synodontis, 414, 417
Roberts's Garfish, 639
robertsi, Barbodes, 428
robertsi, Moenkhausia, 169, 170
robertsi, Nanochromis, 547
robertsi, Synodontis, 416
robertsi, Zenarchopterus, 639, 640
robertsoni, Cichlasoma, 330
robineae, Corydoras, 244
robusta, Gila, 20, 21
robustus, Corydoras, 237

robustus, Notesthes, 727, 728, 729, 730
robustus, Serranochromis, 521
Rock Flagtail, 655
rodwayi, Hemigrammus, 183, 184
Roeboides caucae, 149, 150
Roeboides descalvadensis, 149, 150
Rohtee alfrediana, 586
roloffi, Aphyosemion, 438
roloffi, Epiplatys, 450
roloffi, Ladigesia, 390, 401
roloffi, Pelvicachromis, 532, 547
rondoni, Gymnorhamphichthys, 203, 204
Rope Fish, 387
rostratus, Galaxias, 673, 674
rostratus, Haplochromis, 465
rostratus, Rhamphichthys, 200
"Rosy", Bryconops, 195, 196
Rosy Bryconops, 195
Rosy Tetra, 179
rotundatus, Triportheus, 153, 154
Roughskinned Catfishes, 206
Roundspotted Puffer, 630
Roundtail Chub, 20
Royal Mudskipper, 734
rubescens, Microrasbora, 598
"Rubra", Megalamphodus, 191, 192
rubrifascium, Aphyosemion, 441
rubrilabiale, Aphyosemion, 442
rubripinnis, Myleus, 138, 140, 141
rubropunctatus, Labeo, 433
rubrum, Etheostoma, 57
Rudd, 90
rufilineatum, Etheostoma, 56
Rummynose Tetra, 187
rupestre, Etheostoma, 48
rupestris, Kuhlia, 655, 656, 731, 732
Russell's Snapper, 730
russelli, Lutjanus, 729, 730
Russian Bitterling, 90
ruthenus, Acipenser, 78, 79
Rutilus rutilus, 92

S
sabanus, Ompok, 596
Saberfin, 270
sachsi, Puntius, 554, 579
sadanundio, Stigmatogobius, 609, 610
Saddled Galaxias, 674
sagitta, Etheostoma, 44
Sailfin Perchlet, 683
Sailfin Shiner, 22
Sailfinned Prochilodus, 132
Saiz' Tetra, 175
saizi, Hyphessobrycon, 175, 176
sajica, Cichlasoma, 332, 334
salamandroides, Lepidogalaxias, 676, 678, 685, 686
"Salima", Nothobranchius, 445
salinarum, Brachirus, 731, 732

*Salmo gairdneri*, 18
*Salmo trutta*, 18, 19
*salmoides, Micropterus*, 31
Salmon Catfish, 426, 682
Saltpan Sole, 731
*saludae, Etheostoma*, 70
*Salvelinus fontinalis*, 18, 19
*Salvelinus namaycush*, 19
*salvinii, Cichlasoma*, 329
*sanchesi, Corydoras*, 241
*sanchezi, Serrasalmus*, 143
*sanctaefilomenae, Moenkhausia*, 169, 170
*sandei, Glossamia*, 657, 658
*Sandelia bainsii*, 546
*Sandelia capensis*, 546
*sapayensis, Aequidens*, 344
*Sarcocheilichthys sinensis*, 96
*Sarotherodon grahami*, 524
*Sarotherodon leucostictus*, 523
*Sarotherodon mossambicus*, 523, 526
*Sarotherodon* "species", 523
*Sartor respectus*, 127
*sauvagei, Haplochromis*, 520
*savoryi, Lamprologus*, 517
*saxatilis, Crenicichla*, 345
*sayanus, Aphredoderus*, 16, 17
*scalare altum, Pterophyllum*, 363
*scalare scalare, Pterophyllum*, 363, 367
*Scaphirhynchus platorynchus*, 16, 17
*Scardineus erythrophthalmus*, 90, 91, 92
*Scatophagus argus*, 602, 605, 606, 735, 736
*Scatophagus tetracanthus*, 602
*schalleri, Trichopsis*, 613
*scheeli, Aphyosemion*, 443
*Schilbe marmoratus*, 409, 410
*Schilbe mystus*, 409, 410
*Schilbe uranoscopus*, 409, 410
*schioetzi, Aphyosemion*, 440
*Schizodon fasciatum*, 119, 122
Schmard Tetra, 187
*schmardae, Hemigrammus*, 187, 188
*scholzei, Hyphessobrycon*, 175, 176
Schomburgk's Leaf Fish, 203
*schomburgki, Myleus*, 140, 141
*schomburgki, Polycentrus*, 203, 204
*schoutedeni, Aphyosemion*, 440
*schoutedeni, Cardiopharynx*, 507, 508, 509
*schoutedeni, Synodontis*, 420
*schoutedeni, Tetraodon*, 549, 550
"Schultz", *Astyanax*, 165
Schultz's Spotfinned Killie, 275
*schultzei, Ctenogobius*, 607, 608
*Schultzites axelrodi*, 171, 172
*schwanenfeldii, Barbodes*, 582
*schwartzi, Corydoras*, 247
*Sciades marmoratus*, 219
*Sciades pictus*, 219
*sciera, Percina*, 35

*Scleropages formosus*, 553
*Scleropages jardini*, 633, 634, 669, 670, 685
*Scleropages leichardti*, 681, 682, 685, 686
*scomberoides, Hydrolycus*, 147, 148
*Scortum barcoo*, 713, 714
*scratchleyi, Thryssa*, 633, 634
Sea Catfishes, 635
*securis, Thoracocharax*, 136, 137
*sellare, Etheostoma*, 50
*Semaprochilodus squamilentus*, 132, 133
*Semaprochilodus taeniurus*, 131
*Semaprochilodus theraponura*, 131
*semiaquilus, Corydoras*, 232
*semicinctus, Acanthophthalmus*, 556
*semifasciolatus, Puntius*, 554, 579
*semitaeniatus, Hemiodopsis*, 128, 129
*semoni, Retropinna*, 685, 686
*Semotilus atromaculatus*, 24, 25
*senegalus, Polypterus*, 389, 390
*sentaniensis, Chilatherina*, 647
*septemfasciatum, Cichlasoma*, 334
*septentrionalis, Corydoras*, 236
*sericeus, Rhodeus*, 90, 91, 92, 101
*serpae, Hyphessobrycon*, 178, 179, 180
Serpae Tetra, 178, 179
*serperaster, Parapocryptes*, 609, 610
*Serranochromis robustus*, 521
Serrasalmidae, 144
*Serrasalmus*, 144
*Serrasalmus antoni*, 143
*Serrasalmus denticulatus*, 143
*Serrasalmus eigenmanni*, 142
*Serrasalmus elongatus*, 142, 145, 146
*Serrasalmus gibbus*, 143
*Serrasalmus hollandi*, 138, 145, 146
*Serrasalmus* "Iridescent", 142
*Serrasalmus manueli*, 145, 146
*Serrasalmus nattereri*, 138, 145, 146
*Serrasalmus notatus*, 142
*Serrasalmus piraya*, 145, 146
*Serrasalmus rhombeus*, 145, 146
*Serrasalmus sanchezi*, 143
*Serrasalmus serrulatus*, 145, 146
*Serrasalmus spilopleura*, 143
*Serrasalmus striolatus*, 142, 143
Serrated Piranha, 146
*serriferum, Etheostoma*, 69
*serrulatus, Serrasalmus*, 145, 146
*setigerum, Luciosoma*, 575
Sevenspot Archer Fish, 606, 651
*severum, Cichlasoma*, 337
*sexfasciatus, Distichodus*, 395, 405, 406
*sexfasciatus, Epiplatys*, 449
*sexfasciatus, Lamprologus*, 454, 517, 519
*sexlineata, Melanotaenia*, 640
*sexradiata, Gambusia*, 318
Shannon Paragalaxias, 678
Sheephead Metynnis, 140